Microsoft®
Windows® 2000
Professional

Paul Cassel

SAMS

Unleashed

Microsoft Windows 2000 Professional Unleashed

Copyright ©2000 by Sams Publishing

International Standard Book Number: 0-672-31742-7

Library of Congress Catalog Card Number: 99-63532

Printed in the United States of America

First Printing: February 2000

02   01   00   4   3   2   1

Trademarks

Warning and Disclaimer

ACQUISITIONS EDITOR
Angela Kozlowski

DEVELOPMENT EDITOR
Jeff Durham

MANAGING EDITOR
Charlotte Clapp

PROJECT EDITOR
Karen A. Walsh

COPY EDITOR
Pat Kinyon

INDEXER
Greg Pearson

PROOFREADER
Juli Cook

TECHNICAL EDITORS
Bruce Handley
Scott Roberts
Rob Tidrow
Jason Wright

TEAM COORDINATOR
Pamalee Nelson

MEDIA DEVELOPER
Jason Haines

INTERIOR DESIGN
Gary Adair

COVER DESIGN
Aren Howell

COPYWRITER
Eric Borgert

PRODUCTION
Ayanna Lacey
Heather Hiatt Miller
Stacey Richwine-DeRome

Contents at a Glance

Bonus: Appendix C, "Updated Device List" can be found on the CD-ROM included in the back of this book!

Contents

Bonus: Appendix C, "Updated Device List" can be found on the CD-ROM included in the back of this book!

About the Authors

Paul Cassel has been working with computers since he built his first one when he was nine years old. He has experience working with mainframes, minicomputers, and all types of personal computers from the Altair to the most modern types. His experience with Windows 2000 dates back to the predecessor system, Windows NT, back in its first design phase in the very early 1990s. Cassel has written more than 20 books on computer topics, including eight on operating systems such as Windows NT and Windows 2000. He consults with government and private industry on operating systems, database application and theory, application design, and networking. He lives in New Mexico.

Glen Bergen began his computing career working with Unix and Microsoft operating systems. For the past three years, he has taught Microsoft courseware at PBSC in Canada. Although he has a tendency to move across Canada every couple of years, he plans on staying in Edmonton for a while. When he isn't pounding the keyboard or placing his nose in a book, he enjoys spending time walking with his wife. Glen plans on taking a little time to enjoy life.

David Berry has an extensive background in technical and IT skills, Web site design work, application development, and technical support, with more than 16 years of diverse experience with government and federal agencies as well as competitive business markets. Presently he works for the Internet Planning and Coordination Division for the State of Connecticut and has his own Web site design firm. David is a graduate of the University of Connecticut, a member of the Connecticut Army National Guard, with more than 16 years of military service, and is a Microsoft Certified Professional in FrontPage. He currently resides in Cromwell, CT with his wife Donna, daughter Alexandra, and son Anthony. He can be reached at dberry@connix.com.

Dave Bixler is the Manager of the Technology Services Department of one of the largest systems integrators in the United States. He has been working in the industry since the mid-1980s, working on paper tape readers, network designs, server implementations, and network management. Lately Dave has been focused on Internet technologies, including DNS and Web Servers, information security, firewalls, and a 6000-user Virtual Private Networking (VPN) implementation. Dave has also worked on a number of Macmillan USA books as an author, technical editor, and book reviewer. Dave's industry certifications include Microsoft's MCP and MCSE, as well as Novell's MCNE, and a number of others. Dave lives in Cincinnati, Ohio, with his very patient wife Sarah, sons Marty and Nicholas, and two Keeshonds, Zeus and Arcus.

Irfan Chaudhry has been working as a consultant for the past several years with various-sized clients, including Fortune 500 companies and nationally recognized legal firms. The projects he has worked on range from designing LAN/WAN environments to migration projects involving NT, Unix, and NetWare. He has been involved with several Internet-based projects including implementing E-commerce Web sites and designing environments to run Web-based applications. He has his MCSE and is currently working on his MCSD. Irfan has written and been published previously on the topics of Windows NT, NetWare, IIS, SQL Server, SQL Server Programming, and Windows 2000. He works as a Senior Network Engineer at Affiliated Distributors. He is always thankful for his loving wife Noreen and her consistent support.

Chris Farnsworth covers high tech for the Orange County Register in Orange County, Calif.

Edward Tetz graduated from Saint Lawrence College in Cornwall, Ontario with a diploma in Business Administration in 1990. He spent a short time in computer sales, which turned into a computer support position. He has spent the past eight years performing system and LAN support for small and large organizations. In 1994 he added training to his repertoire. He is both a Microsoft Certified Trainer and a Microsoft Certified Systems Engineer. He has experience with Apple Macintosh, IBM OS/2, and all Microsoft operating systems. He is currently an Information Technology Coordinator and an Instructor for PBSC Computer Training, delivering certified training in most Microsoft products.

Rick Tempestini lives in Chalfont, Pennsylvania with his wife and two sons. Rick earned his master's degree in Information Science from Penn State University and has extensive experience in SQL Server, Visual Basic, and Windows NT. In addition to this book, Rick co-authored *Microsoft SQL Server 7.0 Programming Unleashed*. Rick is a senior consultant for TriTech Solutions, Inc., working for clients in Pennsylvania, New Jersey, and Delaware. Rick can be reached at `rickt@TriTechSolutions.net`.

Dedication

This book is dedicated to my daughter Tirilee Cassel, who allowed Daddy enough time to get it written, and to Margie Morrison, a wonderful spirit who gave me the energy I needed to get it done.
-Paul Cassel

Glenn Berg, thanks for everything.
-Glen Bergen

To my wife Donna, daughter Alexandra, and son Anthony for their love and support, and to all my family and friends who continue to provide encouragement to me.
-David J. Berry

My loving wife Sarah, the only woman on the planet who could put up with me.
Thanks for your patience and support.
-David Bixler

This book is dedicated to my wife, Sharon, and children, Emily and Mackenzie. If not for their support and understanding, I would not have the time or ability to write.
-Ed Tetz

Acknowledgments

A casual glance at this book would imply that I'm the sole author of all the material here. That's not the case. Several co-authors who are specialists in their field contributed to this book to make the information in it the best available. These are Glen Bergen, Dave Berry, Dave Bixler, Irfan Chaudhry, Chris Farnsworth, Edward Tetz, and Rick Tempestini.

Any book is a collaboration, although most of the credit or blame falls on the author. This book, due to its technical level, required an extraordinary amount of effort on the parts of editors to make sure the material is correct and presented in a lucid, well-organized manner. These editors are Dave Bixler, Scott Roberts, Jason Genser, Bruce Handley, Rob Tidrow, Jason Wright, Pat Kinyon, Karen Walsh, and Juli Cook.

Finally I'd like to acknowledge Angela Kozlowski's contribution, which made this book possible. She was the one who had the overall vision to keep this project on track and on time.

-*Paul Cassel*

To my parents, Harvey and Shirley: Thank you for always being there. And to my wife, Jen: Thank you for just being you.

-*Glen Bergen*

A special thanks to my wife who continues to put up with the long hours and time I spend away from the family locked in my office working on my many projects. Without her support and understanding I'd never have been able to pursue my career goals and ambitions. To my daughter and son, for the time I've had to spend away from them while I'm busy working, and to my many friends and colleagues for their advice and assistance time and again.

-*David J. Berry*

Tell Us What You Think!

As the reader of this book, *you* are our most important critic and commentator. We value your opinion and want to know what we're doing right, what we could do better, what areas you'd like to see us publish in, and any other words of wisdom you're willing to pass our way.

You can fax, email, or write me directly to let me know what you did or didn't like about this book—as well as what we can do to make our books stronger.

Please note that I cannot help you with technical problems related to the topic of this book, and that due to the high volume of mail I receive, I might not be able to reply to every message.

When you write, please be sure to include this book's title and author as well as your name and phone or fax number. I will carefully review your comments and share them with the author and editors who worked on the book.

Fax: 317-581-4770

Email: michael.stephens@macmillanusa.com

Mail: Michael Stephens
        Associate Publisher
        Sams Publishing
        201 West 103rd Street
        Indianapolis, IN 46290 USA

Introduction

The First Unleashed Series

Sams Publishing, a division of Macmillan Computer Press, started the Unleashed series several years ago with the intermediate to advanced level reader in mind. The idea of this and other book lines had some similarity to the product placement strategy of modern marketing theory. That is, there would be a specific product for every market segment with the Unleashed series aimed at the most technically adept. This book returns to the original format.

The initial series was a success due to its adhesion to the promise of delivering value to this market at a time when most computer books aimed at the novice to intermediate reader. People who had some computer experience didn't need to hear once again how to use a mouse, what a *window* is, or how to use a menu. They were reluctant to buy books that may have had some content relevant to their needs but was mostly taken up by topics they had long ago mastered.

Along with a plethora of beginner books, there were advanced topics and concepts not being covered at all. These tended to fall into the categories of what a system Administrator needed to know to run a corporate network or what an advanced workstation user needed to know about tuning his computer for optimal performance for a specific use (like video production).

The Unleashed series addressed this need. It made it a point not to discuss topics at a level a reader could find in the great mass of beginner books but, instead, delved deeply into those topics and introduced concepts and discussions not even mentioned in lower-level books.

Changes to the Format

The original idea worked until we Unleashed authors grew greedy. We had a hit series on our hands with many loyal readers who would buy these books based on the strength of having read another in the series. So an Unleashed book on Microsoft Windows would be an easy sell to a system administrator who had benefited from a language Unleashed book. It would never sell (or be returned after the sale) to a novice user, which was all right because the beginners weren't the target market. However, there were many more novices than intermediate to advanced users, so we decided that we were leaving money on the table by starting the material at such a high level.

We began to sneak novice topics into our Unleashed books in hopes of snaring a few lower-level sales. Within a short while, the few sneaks turned into a flood. This had two ill effects. First, we had to bump some advanced material to fit in the novice material. Second, the meat of the book was lost in a sea of featherweight topics. We broke faith with the readers and we ended up losing sales because our books didn't meet the needs of either novices or the adepts.

You see, the novices were still better served by other books that really targeted their needs and weren't larded up (to the novice view) with incomprehensible material. The adepts were upset at the loss of some advanced topics so material they could have written got included.

The Making of a High Value Book

Macmillan is in the business of selling books. When books from hit series start to sell poorly, it will get the company's attention. The situation with the Unleashed series got a lot of attention starting in the beginning of 1999. The fix to indifferent sales was obvious—again include only intermediate to advanced material in the series to deliver a terrific amount of value to the upper-level reader.

To achieve this, Macmillan returned to the original formula adding some modern twists. *Windows 2000 Professional Unleashed* is the first wave of this trend. We spent a great deal of time deciding which topics would be of greatest value to the intended readership—the intermediate, advanced, and system-administrator level users. We then looked at each topic and decided what needed to be covered within it.

The next stage was getting it written. To that end, we recruited some of the best Windows NT and Windows 2000 authors to collaborate on this book. Nobody can be an expert on all aspects of any product. Rather than me, the lead author, doing the entire task (and leaving some areas covered in a mediocre fashion), it was decided that only top experts for each area could produce top material. Top material is what we wished for, and it's what we got.

The final stages are development, technical, and copy editing. The development cycle takes the author material and runs it by one or more experts to assure that nothing of value has been omitted. This cycle also makes sure the material is presented clearly for the intended readership (you, I hope). The technical edit is a very exacting cycle where editors who are intensely familiar with Windows 2000 Professional review the chapters making sure the material is technically correct. Finally, the copy editor polishes the writing presentation for word usage, grammar, style, and clarity.

The end product is a book, written by some of the best people in the field, that is reviewed and edited by more of the best people. This assures you that the material is not only what a intermediate to highly-advanced reader will find useful, but that it's presented in an accurate, well organized, and lucid manner.

What's Included, What's Excluded

Take a look at the Table of Contents. You'll find no chapters on the meaning of the Desktop in Windows, how to use a menu, or what it means to copy a file. These are valid topics for the novice market, but not for this book's intended readership.

In lieu of these novice topics, you'll find serious discussions on setting up Internet Information Services (IIS), setting up and interfacing with Linux, advanced information on how to set up and use security features in Windows 2000, a lot of material on optimizing the operating system for various purposes, and so on.

You'll notice that the vast majority of the topics in this book are of no interest to novices. In many cases, they won't even know what the topic means and, in almost all cases, they won't be able to understand the material even if they understand the topic. This book isn't for them.

It is for the serious computer user who, having mastered the basics, wants to extend his knowledge into advanced territory. It's for the system administrator who, instead of re-inventing the wheel, will learn from the experiences of top-system administrators who have contributed to this volume. It's for the advanced user who wants to polish up his skills in a particular area.

Do You Need This Book?

This book isn't cheap. You can buy books that purport to contain good, if not exactly equivalent, information for less money. However, time and success have value, actual monetary value too. Where this book stands out from the others is in the density and volume of information contained within it.

Just as no one author could have written this entire book, no single reader is likely to be familiar with, much less an expert on, all the material contained in this book. A highly capable and successful system administrator will find value in the material that's newly noted to be part of his or her job, such as Linux, IIS, or setting up an intranet. An expert video producer will find value in the chapters dealing with optimizing the operating system for maximum throughput. A newly-minted Microsoft systems engineer will find value in simply being able to look up the answers to his company's users' questions.

In short, there is something of value for every intermediate-and-up reader contained in this book, or we've failed our design goal. Is this book for you? Because you're holding it, why not take a look at the Table of Contents or Index now and turn to a section that you have an interest in? Did you find that the chapter covered the information you wanted? If so, this book is for you.

Defining Windows 2000

PART

I

What Is Windows 2000 Professional?

CHAPTER 1

Microsoft Windows 2000 is derived from Microsoft Windows NT. That earlier operating system was designed to be a standalone (optionally networked) operating system created from scratch without any serious architecture compromises. Unlike its Microsoft predecessors, MS-DOS, Windows 3.x, and Windows 9x, Windows 2000 has capabilities and security comparable to enterprise operating systems such as UNIX and VMS. In fact, the chief architect of Windows NT, Dave Cutler, was also the chief architect of VMS.

One of the philosophical differences between Windows 2000 and its enterprise competitors is 2000's stress on being much easier to use and administer than anything else in its class. This, as well as many popularly priced applications, makes Windows 2000 Professional a good, perhaps the best, choice not only for heavy-duty workstation type uses, but for general business computing as well.

Other equivalent operating systems, such as UNIX, lack Windows 2000's wide array of applications or are very difficult to administer or both. Easy-to-administer operating systems, such as Windows 95/98 and its successors, lack Windows 2000's robustness, multitasking abilities, and scalability.

What today has evolved into Windows 2000 Professional got off to a slow start in the market. Its hardware requirements, especially RAM, required a serious commitment in money, and the benefits, due mostly to a lack of native applications, were few. After its release, however, Microsoft began a developer relations campaign to create the applications that would make the use of Windows 2000 more attractive to both workstation types and to general business. With the introduction of Windows 95/98, this campaign intensified and developers responded. At roughly the same time, system component costs, especially RAM and hard drive costs, dropped dramatically.

The combination of low-cost Windows 2000 hardware and the burgeoning crop of interesting software for Windows NT and its successors sparked quite a bit of interest in the adoption of Windows 2000, not only for workstations but for an everyday operating system, to replace MS-DOS, Windows, or OS/2. The introduction of Windows NT 4 in 1996 saw that spark change to a conflagration.

Here at last was an operating system with an interface any user could love, an uncompromising architecture, and a huge selection of popularly priced applications. To top the cake, due to lower hardware prices, it ran on popularly priced computers. In many ways, Windows 2000 is the apogee of operating systems. It fulfills the technical promise unmet by lesser operating systems, such as MS-DOS, Windows, and OS/2, while also meeting user needs (and application availability) unmet by its technical equivalents, especially UNIX.

The Architecture of Windows 2000

The processors capable of running Windows 2000 Professional are also capable of running processes in various levels of privilege. A level of privilege gives certain power and also affords certain protection. For example, Intel processors use four privilege levels, or *Rings* in Intel terminology. Ring 0—the most privileged ring—pretty much allows any processes running there to do anything; Ring 3—the least privileged—affords the greatest protection while allowing little in the way of power.

Windows 2000 runs part of itself in Ring 0 and part of itself in Ring 3. Windows 2000's terminology for this split is *User mode* and *Kernel mode*. User mode is the part of the operating system running in Ring 3. It interacts with the user and user applications. Kernel mode runs in Ring 0 and communicates with the hardware. Figure 1.1 illustrates the two modes of Windows 2000. Note that there is no way for applications to communicate with the hardware except through Windows 2000.

FIGURE 1.1

The architecture of Windows 2000 blocks any direct interaction between the computer hardware and applications. NT itself runs in two modes, User and Kernel. In Intel processors, this is the equivalent of running in Ring 0 and Ring 3.

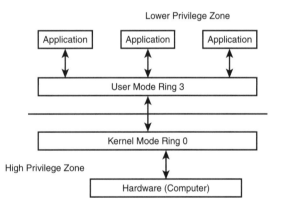

The reason for splitting the system this way is to prevent system anomalies, or, to put it bluntly, crashes. If an application can get to the most privileged areas of a computer, it can do anything it pleases. This way, an entire computer session is at the mercy of any application programmer's abilities and intentions.

The all-too-common lockups and crashes with MS-DOS and Windows are, for the most part, due to applications doing something wrong in an area of high privilege. Although Windows 2000 can't do anything about bad programming, it can protect itself and the session from the consequences.

Why the Split?

Windows 2000 could have had only one mode, Kernel, affording the same protection as it does now—if it ran only native applications. Microsoft made the decision that Windows 2000 would be as much a universal operating system as feasible. That decision led to the splitting of Windows 2000.

> **Note**
>
> Windows 2000 will run only OS/2 version 1 or text mode applications. It will not run the later OS/2 graphical mode applications.

The User mode part of Windows 2000 is multifaceted. It can run not only Windows 2000 and other Windows 16 programs (made for Windows previous to Windows 95), but some applications native to OS/2. This decision was and remains controversial. There's no doubt that some enterprises, especially the governmental ones, could more readily adopt Windows 2000 if it ran a great array of existing applications; but this ability loads up Windows 2000 with capabilities rarely needed by the general public.

Although the splitting of NT into two modes doesn't compromise its security in any way, it does increase (if marginally) the size of any Windows 2000 installation. Some hope that future versions of Windows 2000 will drop OS/2, but it's very unlikely that Windows 2000 will ever coalesce into a one-mode operating system. There's no functional reason for doing this; it would be a lot of work and quite disruptive to the Windows 2000 community.

With Windows NT 4, Microsoft moved the GDI, or Graphics Device Interface (the display part of NT), to the Kernel. Previous versions of Windows 2000 had these services in User mode. This means that NT 4 and its successor Windows 2000 are much faster in displaying graphics, but it also exposes the entire session to vagaries of display device drivers.

> **Note**
>
> Due to architectural changes, many drivers that worked fine under Windows NT 4 will not work at all under Windows 2000.

This was another controversial move on Microsoft's part. Many pundits said that the company had sacrificed Windows 2000's reliability on the altar of speed. However, in practice, Windows 2000 has been at least as reliable as previous versions that had the GDI in User mode, so these fears have been proved unfounded.

At least part of the reason the fears about the consequences of GDI's move to Kernel have been unrealized is Microsoft's testing and certification of drivers. Unlike just about any service or program running under Windows 2000, hardware and graphics drivers address the hardware directly, bypassing Kernel and even the Hardware Abstraction Layer or HAL. Thus, poorly made drivers of any type can destroy an NT session and even the entire installation.

Recognizing this, Microsoft has instituted a certification process for drivers that addresses the hardware. As each driver/hardware combination passes certification, Microsoft adds it to a Hardware Compatibility List (HCL). This is a constantly updated list available for downloading at various sites, including Microsoft at www.microsoft.com. If you use only those drivers appearing on the HCL, you can rest assured that your Windows 2000 installation will be as robust as possible.

The OS/2 subsystem will fully work only under Intel versions of Windows 2000.

> **Note**
>
> Starting with Windows NT version 4 the NT family, of which Windows 2000 is a part, will not support OS/2's HPFS (High Performance File System). This support was last supported under Windows NT version 3.51.

DOS and Older Windows Applications

The User mode handles two types of applications: Win32 (or native Windows 2000) and OS/2. In addition, Windows 2000's User side has the capacity to run DOS and Win16 applications. Together, these form the fourth facet of Windows 2000. Due to its origins as a one-application/one-machine-at-a-time operating system, Windows 2000 handles DOS applications differently from the others.

> **Note**
>
> The OS/2 facet of Windows 2000 communicates with the Kernel part through the Win32 subsystem for mouse, keyboard, and screen services. Windows 2000 directs all other services for these facets directly to the Kernel. The Win32 facet uses the Win32 subsystem for all services.

Each DOS application gets its own virtual machine, courtesy of the NT Virtual Device Machine (NTVDM), an aspect of User mode. To a DOS application, Windows 2000 seems like its own *x86* machine complete with I/O, a memory stack, and just about any other service it expects to find running under DOS. In this way, Windows 2000 runs DOS applications quite robustly. For many years, people hoped for a robust way to run multiple DOS applications on the same machine. OS/2 was first with this capacity, but Windows 2000 goes further with it.

The difference between running under Windows 2000 and DOS isn't apparent to most DOS applications. Windows 2000 "wraps" the DOS session in a protective layer, preventing the session from directly addressing the hardware, as is common with many DOS programs. When the DOS program makes a direct hardware call, Windows 2000 will trap that call, translate it into an acceptable set of instructions, and then reply to the call in a way that mimics the return from hardware the application expects. If Windows 2000 can't translate a call or a return, it politely shuts down the DOS application rather than risk corrupting the session.

Win16, or older Windows applications, have always been troublesome for the newer operating systems. These tend to be transition programs, not quite like DOS "cowboys," yet a far cry from modern Win32 applications. Windows 2000, through the NTVDM, has two ways to run these applications: in a shared virtual machine and in a separate virtual (or memory space) machine.

Take a look at Figure 1.2. This shows the Windows 2000 Professional Task Manager with a Win16 application launched.

FIGURE 1.2

Launching a Win16 program in Windows 2000 Professional starts the NTVDM. The Win16 program runs under this manager.

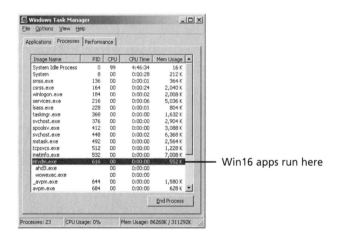

Win16 apps run here

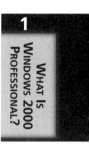

Note the three entries enclosed in the box. The first is the NTVDM, the second is the application itself (AHD3.EXE), and the third is the WOW executive. WOW stands for Windows On Windows, the service NT uses to run older Windows applications.

Launching a DOS program, in this case CAT.COM, launches its own NTVDM and runs in its own memory space, as you can see in Figure 1.3.

FIGURE 1.3

Launching a DOS program launches another instance of the NTVDM. This runs it in its own virtual machine, or own address space. The program itself (CAT.COM) isn't shown in Task Manager. Only the NTVDM service that wraps the program shows.

Additional
Win16
program

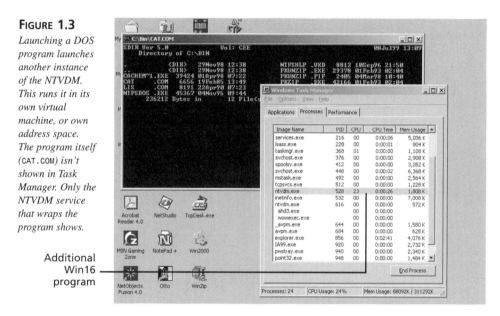

Closing the DOS program (for the sake of clarity) and opening another Win16 program, this time Oxford English Dictionary, shows that both Win16 programs, AHD3.EXE and CAT.COM, are running in the same virtual machine, as seen in Figure 1.4.

Windows 2000 Professional has "wrapped" both Win16 programs (American Heritage and Oxford Unabridged dictionaries) in the same virtual machine where they cooperatively multitask with each other just as they would under Windows 3.*x*. They also, like Windows 3.*x*, share the same address space and therefore can interfere with each other. The NTVDM, while running Win16 programs, is susceptible to similar problems that plagued us under Windows 3.*x*. One misbehaved program can bring down all other programs. Figure 1.5 is a simplified schematic of how Win32, the 16-bit emulation of NT, and WOW work together.

FIGURE **1.4**

Launching another Win16 program shows that, by default, Windows 2000 Professional will run all such pro- grams in the same address space.

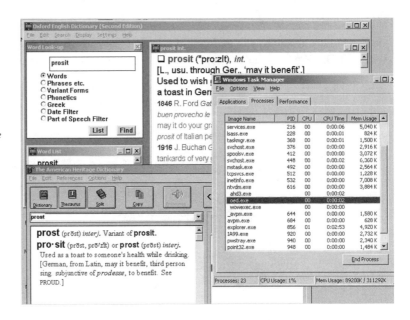

FIGURE **1.5**

A simplified schematic of the 16-bit subsystem of Windows 2000, WOW, and Win32 show their rela- tionship to each other. The entire structure is the Windows 2000 VDM for Win16 applications.

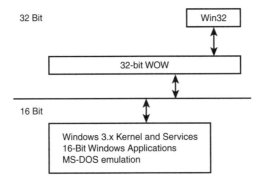

However, because Windows 2000 itself is controlling the NTVDM, Win16 programs can't bring down the entire computer session as they could under Windows 3.*x* and, to a lesser degree, under Windows 95/98.

You can optionally run Win16 programs in their own virtual machine. This topic, as well as other hints for tuning legacy programs are covered in Chapter 5, "Tuning Windows 2000 Performance."

Portability

Windows 2000's design includes a Hardware Abstraction Layer (HAL), a small executive that handles all communications with hardware. This allows Microsoft to port Windows 2000 to different hardware platforms by doing nothing more than rewriting the HAL.

Initially, Microsoft saw Windows 2000 as a universal operating system. The system would, for the most part, remain the same while each platform had its own HAL. This was a similar plan to Digital's with VMS.

The four processors supported during the early part of NT's history were three RISC ones: Digital's Alpha (now Compaq Alpha), the MIPS, and Motorola's PowerPC. The single CISC processor supported was the Intel *x*86 series, such as the 80386, the 80486, and the Pentium series.

However, success on a platform requires more than just a good running HAL. It also requires native applications. Although Windows 2000 for a RISC processor will run common Intel CISC applications, it will run them slowly. The lack of native applications and the prospect for native applications, along with the growing skepticism about RISC processors' advantages, has doomed two of these platforms—MIPS and the PowerPC—to NT history. Today, Microsoft supports only Intel CISC and Compaq's (Digital) Alpha RISC processors under Windows 2000.

Although this situation might change to include more current processors, it's unlikely. RISC's inroad into mainstream businesses hasn't occurred to any extent. Rather, Intel CISC processors now threaten traditional RISC territory, such as graphics workstations. Meanwhile, chip design teams from Intel and others are looking beyond both RISC and CISC architectures to new designs that will outperform both. In all likelihood, Windows 2000 will remain solely on the Alpha and Intel platforms until they're both succeeded by the newer designs, which will be supported by the then current versions of NT.

> **Note**
>
> Only a few years ago, RISC promoters were foretelling the imminent doom of Intel CISC processors, which were supposed to be replaced for common business use by the RISC. Ironically just the opposite has occurred. Today, former RISC-only platforms like Silicon Graphics (SGI) have moved not only to Intel processors, but also to Windows 2000 and away from RISC and UNIX.
>
> *continues*

This wasn't due to technical superiority, but to the dual forces of "good enough" and price. A top of the line graphics workstation might work slightly better using UNIX and a RISC processor, but at a cost that couldn't justify its marginal performance improvement over Intel and Windows (Wintel).

For most applications, even demanding ones, Wintel is better than good enough and quite inexpensive compared to what was available only a short time ago. For common business and home tasks, it is clearly superior to any-thing available—nothing's close.

Multiprocessor Support

Windows 2000 will run on systems sporting more than one CPU, or processor. Very roughly speaking, each doubling of processor count increases performance of processor-intensive operations 80 percent. Thus, a mainboard with two Pentium III processors will run *approximately* at 180 percent of the speed of a single processor mainboard, all other things being equal.

This speedup occurs only for computationally intensive operations (such as floating-point math) and not for the entire system. Also, the application must be multithreaded (most are) to take advantage of this multiprocessing. Some manufacturers are issuing propri-etary systems having as many as eight Pentium class processors for use with Windows 2000 and similar operating systems. Although aimed squarely at the server market, these systems will work with Windows 2000 Professional, making, if equipped with a strong graphics subsystem, a great graphics workstation.

DirectX

Games sell computers. The big gripe about Windows from gamers is that it's slower to display graphics than MS-DOS when programmers aiming games for MS-DOS write routines to directly manipulate hardware. In addition, Microsoft conceptualized Windows 2000 as a graphics workstation operating system. Both games and graphics require fast displays.

Although Microsoft initially decided on a non-game type of accelerated graphic routines (such as OpenGL), it has recently had a rethink and has added DirectX support to all current versions of Windows, including Windows 2000. DirectX is a series of routines to make Windows as responsive as MS-DOS in graphics displays. Although DirectX isn't really the equivalent in speed to hardware-optimized direct addressing under MS-DOS yet, it's much faster than standard Windows GDI. The video portion of DirectX is Direct Draw. In addition, DirectX adds services for sounds (Direct Sound) and inter-computer communications (Direct Play) for the purposes of multiple computer gaming.

The entire DirectX structure is quite complex. In short, Direct Draw resides between the application and the GDI. The Direct Sound resides between the application and the I/O manager in Kernel. Finally, Direct Play resides between the application and either TAPI (Telephony Application Programming Interface) and the TCP/IP socket, Winsock, or both.

Windows 2000 Professional Security

Computer security spans two issues: data integrity and access control. Windows 2000 exceeds any previous version of a Microsoft operating system in both aspects.

Windows 2000 Professional optionally requires a logon, and that logon governs most security issues. You can establish user accounts for yourself or others who might have access to your computer. There is no limit to the amount of accounts you establish. You can also group these accounts according to common permissions. That is, you can establish classes of users and assign rights to those classes; when you establish a person as part of a class, that person is given the class rights. Windows 2000 refers to these classes as *user groups*.

This has been a very short overview of Windows 2000 Professional security. Chapter 7 and Chapter 22, "Users and Groups," both delve into this topic in detail as it relates to access control. Chapter 9, "Working with the Windows 2000 File System," covers data integrity and some file-oriented aspects of data access.

Multitasking

Windows 2000 is a true 32-bit multitasking operating system. To again oversimplify, on a single-processor system, only one instruction can be completed at a time, which might strike you as nullifying any advantage multitasking might offer. However, given today's Pentium-based systems, which process upwards of 800 million instructions per second (MIPS), and RISC chips such as the Alpha, which have demonstrated speeds of beyond 1700 MIPS, this concern is no less relevant. Multitasking in Windows 2000 refers primarily to the method in which the operating system handles multiple processes running concurrently.

First, it is helpful to understand a little bit about how Windows applications work. Windows applications at the system level are not event-driven applications; they are message-driven. Windows applications generate messages and respond to messages. To facilitate this, the operating system maintains what is called a *message queue*. This is a stream of messages waiting for system resources and processing cycles, a response from another application, or the operating system. First, let's look at how Windows 3.*x* handled multitasking, and then at Windows 95/98, and finally at Windows 2000. This will help demonstrate the progress Windows has made and will show how Windows 2000 surpasses the others in this area.

Windows 3.X

Windows 3.*x* is absolutely not a multitasking environment, despite opinions to the contrary. Because Windows 3.*x* is really just a shell sitting on top of DOS, and DOS is a single-tasking (non–re-entrant) environment, it stands to reason that Windows cannot very well be multitasking. Although it is possible to have multiple applications open at once and even assign a priority to background applications, it is still a single-tasking environment. Anyone who has ever spooled a print job in the background has noticed significant performance degradation. The print job dominates the message queue while processing, rendering, spooling, and finally printing the job. Windows 3.*x* uses a single message queue and one shared memory pool. Because of this, if one application hangs or crashes, usually the rest of the system follows shortly thereafter. If the application is hung, it basically jams the message queue and no other applications can process their messages, usually resulting in the user having to destructively reboot the system with the three-fingered salute, Ctrl+Alt+Delete.

The other aspect is the shared memory pool. Because all applications share the same memory space, it is possible for one application to write to memory that is already allocated to another application or even the operating system, generally resulting in a general protection fault (GPF). Sometimes these are recoverable, but most often the system is unstable after this and needs to be rebooted.

Windows 3.X's Successors

The Windows 95/98 and so forth series has done a lot to alleviate the majority of these problems, but still suffers some of the same shortcomings. Windows 95/98 has mostly overcome the heap limits of Windows 3.*x*. Thus, it is uncommon to receive Out of Memory errors. Although it is still possible to receive these errors, it is usually due to a problem with the application and not Windows 95/98. Windows 95/98 falls between Windows 3.*x* and Windows 2000 in the way it multitasks. Although not a true 32-bit multitasking environment, Windows 95/98 is a move in the right direction.

Windows 95/98 handles Win32 and Win16 programs quite differently. It, too, has the ability to spawn VDMs similar to NT and 2000's. In it, each Win32 application has its own message queue, but Win16 applications still share a common message queue. This means that the Win32 applications preemptively multitask among themselves while the VDMs preemptively multitask with the Win32 applications. The Win16 applications cooperatively multitask among themselves, with all Win16 applications sharing a common queue.

> **Note**
>
> In cooperative multitasking, the application program must "willingly" yield to the operating system. A preemptive multitask means the operating system can demand an application yield and also can assign priorities to various processes.

Suppose there are three Win32 applications, two Win16 applications, and two VDMs running. In a conceptually clockwise fashion (see Figure 1.6), each Win32 application and VDM has the opportunity to process a message, and one Win16 application has the opportunity to process a message (whichever application is next in the queue).

FIGURE 1.6

An illustration of the Windows 2000 multitasking model.

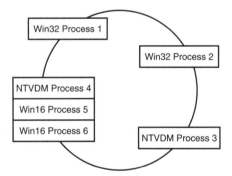

Referring to Figure 1.6, the message processing sequence would be as follows: 1, 2, 3, 4, 5, 1, 2, 3, 4, 6. This is how it works when everything is running smoothly and each process is running with the same priority. If needed, the system can increase or decrease a process's priority and allocate more processing time to another process, preempting the others (thus the name). In the event that a Win16 application will not release control of the Win16 queue, two scenarios are probable. Either that application will continue to process every time the Win16 queue has the opportunity for system resources, or the queue will hang, potentially crashing the Win16 applications. If a Win32 application hangs, the remaining applications continue to function properly, because each has its own queue, as do the VDMs. The benefit here is that if a single application hangs or misbehaves, it should not affect the rest of the system too drastically. Windows 95/98 also provides a feature of Windows 2000, the Task Manager. By pressing the Ctrl+Alt+Delete key sequence, a task list is brought up that enables you to terminate an application no longer responding to the system. However, this Task Manager is not as powerful as that offered by Windows 2000. The Windows 95/98 Task Manager only allows you to terminate running applications, whereas the Windows 2000 Task Manager allows you to terminate any process running on the system, even background processes.

> **Note**
>
> Each Win16 application has one thread, each VDM has two threads, and each Win32 application has at least one thread (and possibly more, depending on the application).

In Windows 95/98, as with NT, each process can address up to 4GB of virtual memory, thus alleviating the Out of Memory errors for the most part. Of this 4GB of virtual memory, 2GB is system-addressable memory and 2GB is application-addressable memory. Obviously, most systems do not have this much memory. This is the theoretical limit to which each process can map. The Virtual Memory Manager (VMM) in Windows 95/98 uses demand paging to page memory to and from disk as needed, optimizing system performance.

The Windows 2000 Family

As with Windows 95/98, Windows 2000 provides each application process with a 4GB virtual-memory address space and utilizes demand paging in the same fashion (demand paging was adopted from Windows NT into Windows 95/98). Being a true 32-bit environment, Windows 2000 uses a single Virtual Machine (VM) to run Win16 applications, just as it runs an emulator for OS/2 applications. If you recall, the Win32 subsystem is at the core of the User mode environment. The Win16 subsystem is coordinated and scheduled by the Win32 subsystem. As with Windows 95/98, Windows 2000 preemptively multitasks Win32 applications. The key difference is in how it handles Win16 applications.

Win16 applications are multitasked in the same fashion as in Windows 95/98, all being queued in a single VM and cooperatively multitasking among themselves. Remember, however, that Windows 2000 offers an option of running a Win16 application in a separate memory space. This allows Win16 applications to have their own virtual address space, eliminating the possibility of one application violating another application's address space and corrupting it. The primary reason for the limitation on Win16 applications and multitasking is to have backward compatibility. This will be less of an issue in the future, because most popular applications now have 32-bit versions available. As with Windows 95/98, applications can be forcibly terminated, if necessary, by using the task list. The task list in NT and 2000 is brought up either by right-clicking the Taskbar and choosing Task Manager or by using the Ctrl+Alt+Delete key sequence and selecting Task Manager. You can then select the application and choose End Task.

In theory, Windows 3.x will also allow shutting down of out-of-control tasks; but in practice, once a process or application runs wild, you usually cannot. Ironically, the reason is Windows 3.x's lack of true multitasking. Processes can grab the entire operating system and prevent the events (keyboard or mouse) from breaking its cycle.

Windows 95/98 usually will allow you to break in on a runaway process, but not always. Early on, Windows 95 users ruefully learned that endless loops could be as fatal as endless loops in older Windows. This is true in Win32 applications as well as Win16, although not as much of a problem as in Windows 3.x. Windows 98SE is better than Windows 95 in this aspect, but not nearly as robust as Windows 2000 Professional.

The serious problem remaining with Windows 95/98 is its lack of memory protection. Crashes in Windows 95/98 all too often wreak havoc with the operating system's stability, forcing a reboot. The good side is that these instabilities generally don't cause a system crash enabling an orderly shutdown/startup without data loss. Still, it's an inconvenience at the least. It can be a real time waster if the system that needs to be rebooted has shared resources, because the boot will disrupt any connected users.

Windows 2000 Professional's chief contributions to the desktop are its multitasking abilities and its memory protection.

> **Note**
>
> Windows 2000 cannot run Win16 applications that depend on VxDs. VxDs are virtual device drivers that control hardware directly. If your older programs require VxDs to run, you can't run them under Windows 2000.

Improvements and Changes from Previous Versions of Windows NT

Windows 98 and Windows 2000 share many common characteristics. Some of the concepts and technologies for Windows 95/98 were borrowed directly from Windows NT 3.5*x*; likewise, some of the aspects of Windows 95/98 have been incorporated into Windows 2000. The following section describes the similarities between the two—and, more importantly, what differentiates them.

The User Interface

At first glance, Windows 2000 looks identical to Windows 95/98. Looks can be deceiving. Beyond the interface and some navigational similarities, these two operating systems are worlds apart.

First, take a look at the similarities. The obvious likeness is the desktop itself. As you can see in Figure 1.7, Windows 2000 has taken on the Windows 95/98/NT 4 user interface. The initial layout is identical: My Documents, My Computer, My Network Places, Recycle Bin, and the optional Briefcase (not shown in Figure 1.7). The Taskbar and the familiar Start button are identical to other Microsoft operating systems. The area between the tray on the far right of the Taskbar and the applications area is the new Quick Launch Taskbar first introduced as a standard operating system feature in Windows 98. Prior to then, it was part of a version of Microsoft Internet Explorer.

Architecturally, there are many more similarities, due mostly to the fact that much of the Windows 95/98 core architecture was borrowed and adapted from Windows NT 3.5*x* and early parts of Windows 2000 (while it was under development). Windows 2000 Professional has also included some other useful features of Windows 95/98, namely Wordpad (an enhanced version of Write), Internet Explorer 5.01, Autorun (automatically plays autorun-enabled CD-ROMs when inserted into the drive), some games including an Internet site for online games, and the capability of dynamically changing screen resolution without restarting the system.

FIGURE 1.7

The user interface (UI) in Windows 2000 Professional bears more than a little similarity to Windows 95/98.

The User Interface of Windows 2000 Professional

As with the Windows 95/98 desktop, My Computer is the container of storage devices, printers, and access to the Control Panel.

My Network Places provides graphical browsing of your network and the capability of using shared resources located on the network. The optional Inbox is the Microsoft Exchange email client. This provides an inbox for various electronic mail systems, including MS Mail, MS Exchange, and Internet (SMTP) Mail. Third-party MAPI drivers can be added for other services, such as CompuServe, as they are made available.

> **Note**
>
> Mercifully you can rename Desktop items like My Network Places to something adult. Right click the icon you want to rename and choose Rename from the context menu.
>
> I'll continue to use Microsoft's names throughout the book for consistency's sake. Believe me, I will change things as soon as I no longer need to make these screen shots.

The Recycle Bin works identically to Windows NT 4 and 95/98. This can provide some degree of safety against accidentally deleted files. If you have ever mistakenly deleted important files, you will appreciate this.

> **Note**
>
> Many administrators choose to disable the use of the Recycle Bin due to disk space or security issues. You can change Windows 2000 Professional to delete files right off rather than putting them in the Recycle Bin by right clicking the bin, choosing Properties from the context menu, and then choosing the appropriately named check box from the Properties dialog box.

Another welcome feature of Windows 2000 is My Briefcase. This optional component affords a simple form of data replication between computers. Although most people use this facility to keep files current between their desktop and laptop computers, it has capabilities that can be exploited by the entire enterprise. This is an example of a well-received feature of Windows 95/98 that has made its way to Windows 2000.

The Start button on the Taskbar is just that—the place to start. This produces a pop-up menu identical to that found in Windows 95/98. The Shut Down option is used to initiate a system shutdown to allow the user to log off the system or to log on differently. The Run command allows a GUI way to start a program. Alternatively, a user can launch from the Explorer or from a command-line prompt. The Help option provides access to system help files using the standard Windows help engine. The Search option provides searching capabilities (locally and over the network) for files, folders, and computers. The Settings entry provides access to the Control Panel, printer settings, and the Taskbar configuration. The Taskbar option also enables customization of the Programs menu and the option of clearing the Documents list from the Start menu. The Documents folder provides quick access to the most recently used files for the logged-on user. These can be files such as Word documents, Excel files, or Internet locations, depending on which file types are registered with the system.

Selecting the Programs choice from the Start menu will bring up many familiar items. Here, by default, you find at least two more folders: Accessories and the Startup folder.

Choosing the Accessories option produces more subfolders and programs. There is the familiar productivity killer, the Games folder, which has the ever-present Solitaire and Minesweeper, a game called Freecell (a much more addicting variation of Solitaire), and Pinball. New to Windows 2000 is the Entertainment folder. This is another feature found in Windows 95/98 and brought over by popular demand. Here, you will find a built-in CD Player and Sound Recorder, as well as a Volume Control—certainly nothing critical or earth-shattering, but useful nonetheless. Down the list, you find many familiar items:

Address Book

Calculator

Command Prompt

Imaging

Notepad

Paint

Synchronize (synchs items you were working on offline)

Windows Explorer

WordPad (the upgraded Write)

Note

What is the Explorer? That is a good question if you are not familiar with Windows 95/98. The Explorer, in the most fundamental explanation, is a replacement for File Manager. This can get confusing, because you can still use the old File Manager. And, whereas in Windows 3.*x* your operating shell was Program Manager (progman.exe), in Windows 2000 and Windows 95/98 the default operating shell is Explorer (explorer.exe). However, both Windows 2000 Professional and Windows 95/98 include a version of progman.exe for their operating systems. That will give a Windows 3.*x* look to those who, for whatever reason, prefer it to the new Explorer desktop. Although many requested the option of running progman.exe instead of Explorer, the superiority of the Explorer UI makes its use quite rare.

Several items were excluded from the preceding list because they merit further explanation. In the Communications folder is HyperTerminal which is included from Windows 95/98. It is a long overdue and welcome inclusion for those suffering with the older Terminal. It adds support for the more popular transfer protocols (such as Zmodem).

There is also a Phone Dialer, one of the first telephony applications. This is basically a speed-dial program that enables you to dial out using your modem. It's not particularly useful or practical for most people unless combined with an application that can communicate with it.

> **Note**
>
> For reasons cloaked in dark mystery, Microsoft chose to eliminate the good old File Manager from Windows 2000 Professional, but to retain Program Manager. If you can find the file manager from Windows NT 4, it'll work fine under 2000.

Also, if your computer has TCP/IP installed, there is a Telnet item. This is a terminal emulation program for use over TCP/IP networks such as the Internet. It is a bare-bones version that is limited to the most basic functionality, but in the absence of another version it does the job. Telnet is not present in the Accessories\Communications folder by default. However, you can run Telnet from the Run menu by clicking the Start button, Run, and typing `telnet.exe`.

> **Note**
>
> Your configuration of Windows 2000 might vary considerably from the items in this section. Exactly what's in your operating system is dependent upon certain setup options. The examples here are representative of a typical system, but it's unlikely that they'll match your system exactly.

Other chapters cover various aspects of the Administrative Tools folder (inside of the Control Panel by default) and further discuss its applications. This folder contains the system maintenance and administration applications. Here, or in other areas of the Control Panel, you can do system backups, configure disk drives, manage users on the system, get specific information about the system, monitor performance, and view error logs. These applications are largely unchanged in power from previous versions but look and are accessed in completely new ways under Windows 2000. They are often underutilized and not exploited to their full potential. These can be invaluable utilities to systems administrators and should not be discounted.

The Startup folder is identical to the group by the same name in previous versions of Windows. Anything placed in this folder will be run when a user logs on. Note that due to 2000's security, items put in the Startup folder do not start when the system starts, but when a user logs on. If the user does not have sufficient rights to execute the application, it will fail to launch. If you would like a program to start when the system starts, you must install it as a service and configure it appropriately.

The Command Prompt entry in Start, Programs, Accessories launches an NTVDM (NT's Virtual DOS Machine), which provides access to a DOS-style command prompt. Make no mistake—unlike other previous Windows versions, DOS doesn't lie beneath the surface of Windows 2000. A NTVDM is a 32-bit emulation of the DOS environment, provided by the Win32 subsystem, which is user-configurable as desired. This can be extremely useful in many situations, specifically for troubleshooting network problems. Finally, there is the Windows 2000 Explorer, mentioned previously.

Personalized Menus

Another controversial feature of Windows 2000 Professional is personalized menus. This feature or annoyance limits the menu entries and submenus you see to those most recently used and also will order most recently used items to the top of the menu. You can see the entire menu (assuming the programmer hasn't intentionally limited the application) by moving your cursor to the chevron at the bottom of the truncated menu.

People either love or hate this feature. It works not only in Windows 2000 Professional's Start menu, but if active, in compliant applications such as Microsoft's own Office 2000.

You can deactivate personalized menus by right clicking the Taskbar choosing Properties from the context menu. Then, just deselect the personalized menus checkbox and you're set.

This will not deactivate personalized menus in compliant applications. To do that, you need to make a similar Options choice within those applications. Figure 1.8 shows a personalized Start menu. This installation of Windows 2000 Professional hasn't any history logged at this point, so only a few menu entries appear in Start, Programs. Figure 1.9 shows the same menu expanded to show all its entries by clicking the cursor on the chevron located at the bottom of the menu in Figure 1.8.

FIGURE 1.8

Windows 2000 uses personalized menus that are turned on by default. Note the ToolTip entry for compliant applications installed to Windows 2000 Professional.

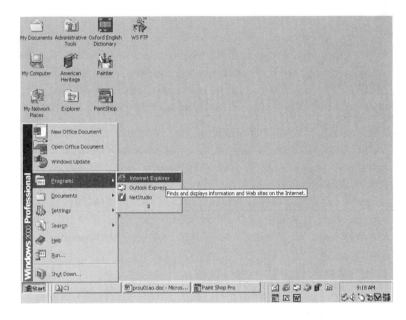

FIGURE 1.9

Here are the actual Programs menu entries for the computer shown in Figure 1.8. The most recently used entries, the ones that will show "above" the chevron are highlighted by Windows 2000 Professional.

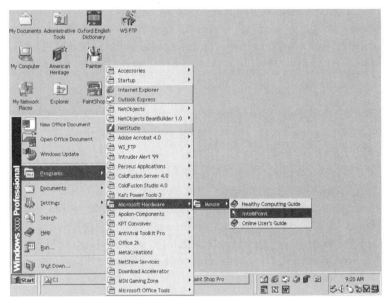

The Control Panel

The Windows 2000 Professional Control Panel is similar to that of Windows 95/98, as you can see in Figure 1.10. They do, in fact, share many common elements. Windows 2000, however, has some applets that are absent in Windows 95/98. The following is a listing of the various Control Panel applets, each with a brief description of function:

FIGURE 1.10

The Windows 2000 Control Panel bears a great deal of similarity to the Windows 95/98 one. The TweakUI entry isn't included in the standard Windows 2000 setup.

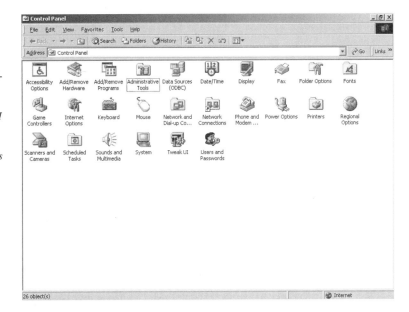

- *Accessibility Options* provides usability features and enhancements for people with disabilities. Support has greatly improved over NT. This entry is optional.

- *Add/Remove Hardware* is the hardware wizard—a way to detect and install new hardware or to fix hardware errors. You can use the hardware wizard to configure/install either Plug-and-Play (PnP) compliant or non-compliant hardware.

- *Add/Remove Programs* provides the ability to install, configure and uninstall applications cleanly and completely, provided the application vendor complied with installer specifications. This applet also provides access to Windows 2000 Setup (not the same as the setup to change mouse/keyboard as described previously). Here you can add, remove, and reconfigure components of Windows 2000.

- *Administrative Tools* launches the folder with administrator tools such as MMC, Internet Service Manager, and Performance Monitor. The exact components in this folder depend on system configuration.

- *Data Sources ODBC* manages (register) ODBC data sources. This isn't installed by default in all systems.

- *Date/Time* is the standard applet to set the system date and time. A notable feature of the NT family available since version 3.5*x* is the capability to have the system automatically adjust for daylight savings time, if applicable to your locale.

- *Display* configures your display adapter and monitor, including your screen saver. You can also access this applet by right clicking the Desktop and choosing Properties.

- *Fax* configures Microsoft Fax, the fax send and receive facility built into Windows 2000 Professional.

- *Folder Options* customizes the look of Explorer, My Computer, and open folders. You can choose the conventional look (customized to your heart's content) or the newer Web look, which makes your local folders resemble Web sites.

- *Fonts* enables you to view currently installed fonts and add or remove fonts.

- *Game Controllers* allows you to configure items like joysticks and such.

- *Internet Options* enables the system to be configured to access the Internet through a proxy server, configure Internet Explorer, configure mail and news (Usenet) clients, and set various options useful for Internet surfing and security.

- *Keyboard* enables configuration of repeat key delay and rate and cursor-blink rate. Additional locales can be added here also.

- *Mouse* enables configuration of double-click speed, swapping buttons, mouse speed, and animated cursors. If IntelliMouse has been installed, it allows further options, such as wheel activation, cursor scrolling, wheel click, and more.

- *Network and Dial Up Connections* enables network installation and configuration. This option is also available by right-clicking the My Network Places icon and selecting Properties.

- *Phone and Modem Options* provides a modem wizard to assist in the installation and configuration of modems plus entries for telephony.

- *Power Options* is an applet to configure Advanced Power Management issues. This is also available by right clicking the Desktop and choosing Properties.

- *Printers* is an applet that greatly simplifies the installation and configuration of printers. Included is an Add New Printer wizard to assist in the installation of both local and network printers.

- *Regional Options* enables localization of Windows 2000 Professional 4. This allows options of local time zone, currency, date format, and other international settings.

- *Scanners and Cameras* is a utility for configuring imaging hardware.

- *Scheduled Tasks* is a folder with a wizard for adding automatically launched tasks, usually administrative items such as Scandisk or backups. You can also use the command line utility AT for such tasks.

- *Sounds and Multimedia* is an applet for associating sounds with system and application events, as well as configuring audio and video hardware.

- *System* allows monitoring and configuration of system-wide options, such as performance tuning, startup options in BOOT.INI, environment, and hardware profiling.

- *Users and Passwords* is a way to administer user groups and individual users' rights and permissions.

Most of these applets are directly adopted from either Windows 3.*x* or 95/98 or NT 4. The majority act identically or very closely to their counterparts, but Windows 2000 has an ever-growing list of Control Panel applets that are specific to it. Note that some of these applets may not be installed on your system by default.

Quite a list, isn't it? This goes to show just how extensive and well thought out this operating system is. Microsoft has designed Windows 2000 to meet the most critical and demanding needs of computing today and leave room for future growth. This is the operating system for the next generation of computing.

Windows 2000 Networking

A major feature of Windows 2000 is its native networking support. Being one of the original design goals, network support is built into the operating system itself, providing a high degree of integration.

Natively, Windows 2000 Professional supports many protocols and services for seamless network integration, even in heterogeneous environments. The following are the standard supported protocols:

- AppleTalk
- NetBEUI
- NWLink IPX/SPX (Novell)
- TCP/IP

Additionally, Windows 2000 Professional provides a host of different network services:

- Client Service for NetWare (NDS aware)
- FTP server
- Microsoft TCP/IP printing support
- Network monitor agent
- Remote access service (RAS)—also called Dial-Up Networking or DUN
- SAP agent
- SNMP service
- PPTP client (point-to-point tunneling protocol)
- Peer Web Services

Clearly, Windows 2000 Professional is capable of being integrated into almost any existing network.

> **Note**
>
> The client service for NetWare provides file and print support for NetWare 3.*x* and later servers, and it allows for security authentication by NetWare servers and the execution of logon scripts. It does not, however, support NetAdmin or NWAdmin at the time of this writing.

The Network Monitor agent allows a remote server computer running Microsoft's Network Monitor to attach to the system running the agent and monitor another portion of the network. The RPC support has been improved to provide support for RPC on Banyan networks, in addition to TCP/IP-based networks. The SAP agent is for use with NetWare networks to broadcast available services and resources, and the SNMP service is for use on TCP/IP networks with monitoring applications that can respond to or monitor SNMP traps.

Windows 2000 Professional supports up to ten inbound network connections and unlimited outbound connections (up to the limitations of the physical hardware of the network). The Remote Access component in 2000 supports a single inbound dial-up connection, which can be useful for attaching to the network from a remote site. The RAS component can also be configured to dial out and serves very well as a dial-up PPP connector to an Internet service provider.

Windows 2000 Professional can operate in either a domain or workgroup environment. If it is on a network with Windows 2000 Server computers, it can be configured to participate in a domain to use centralized security accounts. It can also operate in a workgroup capacity for peer-to-peer networking, although this becomes fairly complicated if there are several computers—each will have its own set of user accounts and security database. Windows 2000 Professional can also use a NetWare server for centralized security and validation.

Fault Tolerance

Windows 2000 Professional supports the creation of volume sets, the combination of multiple partitions into a single logical volume, stripe sets without parity for improved disk access, and mirrored partitions.

Volume sets and stripe sets without parity must be formatted using NTFS. Existing volume sets can be extended as needed to include up to 32 separate partitions. Stripe sets can also include up to 32 partitions. Advanced disk features will be revisited in Chapter 10.

Windows 2000 Professional also provides features to support system backups and UPS subsystems that can perform a clean system shutdown in the event of a power failure.

Capacity

At this point, Windows 2000 will support up to four processors, but Microsoft's desire to market Windows 2000 to the graphic workstation market makes it a good bet that this will soon expand. Windows 2000 will recognize up to 2TB of storage memory and 4GB of physical RAM or VRAM.

File Systems

As implied earlier, Windows 2000 Professional natively recognizes FAT16, FAT32, and NT File System (NTFS) volumes. Performance and security depend on which file system NT is addressing. There's nothing NT can do to give the older FAT file systems added fault tolerance. Unless your volumes are quite small or need to be recognized by non-2000 Windows or DOS, NTFS is the way to go.

Sundry and Interesting Items New to Windows 2000 Professional

Windows 2000 Professional (and the entire Windows 2000 line) is based on Windows NT with compatibility features emulated from the Windows 98 side. The following are a few of the most interesting.

- *A new dialog box, Add/Remove Programs, in Control Panel for managing application program configuration, installation and removal*—This same dialog box controls many aspects of Windows 2000 Professional's configuration.

- *A new installer that allows remote installation and administration of programs to selected user*—This same facility can also be used by an administrator to repair broken or failed installations.

- *A component-based Microsoft Management Console (MMC) allowing snap-in components for added flexibility*—Windows 2000 comes complete with several components installed such as Event Viewer, Service Manager, and Disk Manager.

- *IntelliMirror*—This allows an administrator to configure any workstation to behave in a way customized to the user logged on to that workstation. This allows users to roam freely and enjoy the same user interface and program selection wherever they log on from.

- *A hardware wizard and Plug and Play (PnP) facility*—This is documented and fully-compliant with the state-of-the-art in hardware technology.

- *Support for mobile users both in mobile computers and docking devices*—Previous versions of Windows NT were deficient, at best, at this.

- *Microsoft Fax*—This is included for built-in Fax capacity.

- *Interactive troubleshooters*—There are now part of the Help system, making user level troubleshooting (error correction) much easier than in any previous version of Windows.

- *Significantly enhanced aid for users with disabilities*—These include alternative help systems.

- *Smart card (and other alternative) logons.*

- *Connect to the Internet wizard*—This simplifies user procedures when establishing an Internet account.

- *Windows Update*—This makes sure your users have the latest drivers and other Windows 2000 component parts. Windows Update is Web-based and transparent to users.

- *High security encryption for sensitive files stored on NTFS volumes*—Temporary files created by programs are likewise encrypted for added security if the user chooses to make it so.
- *Certificate management (through the MMC) for security and authentication of email communications*—Users can manage their own certificates while administrators can manage their own and users'.
- *Improved driver support for multimedia type hardware.*
- *Integration of the Euro symbol set.*
- *Improved Outlook Express email and news client with Identities feature and improved mail filtering*—This helps reduce or eliminate junk or other unwanted communications.
- *Improved Internet Explorer for easier and faster Web browsing and FTP transfers.*
- *Vastly increased support for non-English languages and international configurations.*
- *And the list goes on*—The adventure is just beginning.

Summary

Windows 2000 Professional is the clear choice of operating systems for demanding users and critical environments, and it has the capacity to meet computing needs today and tomorrow. With features such as integrated networking and dial-up support, an intuitive user interface, an advanced file system and architecture, and fault-tolerent options, this truly is the operating system for the next generation of computing.

Pre-Installation and System Analysis

Setting up Windows 2000 Professional, like so many things in life, can be made much simpler and easier by adequate planning. The last thing you need is to be making critical decisions—or worse, buying and installing hardware—during the setup process. Given proper planning, setting up Windows 2000 Professional on one computer or corporate-wide should go smoothly with very little, if any, interaction on the part of the Administrator (or user).

Speaking in the broadest terms, setup of Windows 2000 Professional has three phases:

- Inventory hardware to assure the setup team, or yourself, that your target computers have adequate resources to run and are compatible with Windows 2000 Professional
- Deciding on installation options
- Deciding on a setup strategy

That sounds simple, and in overview it is. However, the overview glosses over a lot of detail work that you need to get right to succeed in having a glitch-free setup experience. Take all the time you need to make sure your setup plan is complete, and save yourself a lot of frantic worry during the actual setup process.

Inventory

Depending on your point of view, Windows 2000 Professional has either a modest list of required hardware or a bloated one. The difference is whether you view the required list from a historical view or from a current technology view. For example, those who have been using small computers for more than a decade view RAM requirements of 64MB as huge, while those who are new to the game tend to take such things in stride. For most of the 1980s, the standard business computer sold in non-corrected dollar values just under $5,000—the cost of the original business PC the IBM XT. A heavy machine then had a 20 or 30MB disk and at best 640KB of RAM. Today, these values are off the scale on the tiny end. Also, one doesn't need to spend $5,000 for a serious machine. A good machine that will run Windows 2000 Professional today costs less than $2,500, complete with accessories. A bare machine is less than $2,000.

Sticking to the minimums or even staying close to them isn't a good idea. There is a vast difference in how well Windows 2000 will run on a minimum machine as opposed to a proper one. Table 2.1 shows the minimum requirements and comments about those minimums.

TABLE 2.1 Minimum Windows 2000 Requirements

Category	Minimum	Comment
RAM	64MB	Windows 2000 Professional runs abysmally with less than 64MB RAM. It really starts to fly at 128MB.
Disk space for host volume	650MB	Unlike some Windows, Windows 2000 Professional stores much data within its own directory. Like all Windows, its home directory expands as you install applications. The minimum practical disk requirements for Windows 2000 Professional is closer to four times the minimum recommended by Microsoft. Even that's not generous. Practically speaking, the host volume for Windows 2000 Professional should have at least 1.5GB of space. Microsoft recommends a 2GB disk overall.
Display	SVGA	Windows 2000 Professional and most of its applications don't look right in standard VGA resolution. The true minimum is a 15/16-bit display depth at 800×600 resolution. That will yield roughly 32,000 or 64,000 colors. Most people can't see a difference between 16-bit color depth and 24-bit depth capable of roughly 17,000,000 colors.
Mouse	Any compatible	The new wheel-equipped mice work with many Windows 2000 Professional services and applications.
Removable drive		Diskette, removable hard drive, CD CDR, CDR/W, or other.
		CD-ROM for any workstation that will host the setup process.
Network Interface		Optional in a way. Few people who need Windows 2000 Professional will make do without any kind of network. A network here includes dial-up network access, such as to the Internet. A 32-bit adapter will pay off in increased local area network speed while a ISDN, ADSL, cable modem, or other similar high speed access will make your online time vastly less tedious.

2

PRE-INSTALLATION
AND SYSTEM
ANALYSIS

Hardware Compatibility

Making sure you have the iron to run Windows 2000 Professional is only part of the battle. Windows 2000, based on Windows NT as it is, has historically been quite selective about what hardware it will support. In past versions of Windows NT, Microsoft attempted to placate users of older hardware by making it quite compatible with legacy components. This did not win Windows NT many converts, nor did it show the operating system in the best light.

Rather than trying to make Windows 2000 support even more existing hardware, Microsoft took the rather bold stance of tightening up 2000's hardware support scope. To put it in a nutshell, Windows 2000 Professional will run on today's and tomorrow's systems but, in many cases, not yesterday's. This will force some upgrading in many instances. Upgraders will have as a consolation the knowledge that they are getting a better system for their bother and expense.

Why the Lost Legacy?

Keep in mind that Windows 2000 follows Windows NT 4 in having the Graphics Device Interface (GDI) in User instead of Kernel as in previous Windows NT versions. This requires a new driver specific to Windows 2000 or a late version of NT for every display adapter. In many cases, manufacturers weren't interested in updating the drivers for their older products, resulting in an orphaning of those products under 2000. Microsoft will make homegrown drivers only for products it believes to be in wide use, not every product in exsistence.

> **Note**
>
> ASPI stands for Advanced SCSI Programmer's Interface. SCSI stands for Small Computer Peripheral Interface. ASPI is a software "layer" or translation component that manages communication between SCSI hardware and all other relevant parts of your computer.

As Windows NT 4 changed some basic architecture, so does Windows 2000 Professional make some changes when compared to NT 4. For example, there have been some fundamental changes in the manner SCSI devices work. Software that uses ASPI drivers usually need revision.

Microsoft maintains a list of all hardware that it has tested and found to work properly with Windows 2000. Getting a current version of this list to check on your equipment's 2000 compatibility is vital unless you are absolutely sure your hardware is 2000 ready.

This list is the Hardware Compatibility List (HCL). There's a copy on the Windows 2000 distribution CD-ROM in the form of a standard Windows help file. This file is named for the month and year of its creation plus HCL and has the `.hlp` extension. Look in the `root` directory for it.

However, due to production lag, the list on any CD-ROM is out of date. Microsoft maintains a current version of this list on its Web site at `http://www.microsoft.com/hwtest`. It is also available at other Web and FTP distribution points.

Note

If you have cause to call Microsoft technical support for Windows 2000 Professional, the staff will be very reluctant to troubleshoot problems that involve hardware not listed on the HCL. In fact, they'll be so reluctant, that you shouldn't bother to call.

Similarly, if you have an OEM (Original Equipment Manufacturer) version of Windows 2000 Professional, the OEM will be very reluctant to help you if you have added legacy equipment to the hardware sold with the copy of 2000. This is true even if the legacy hardware is from the same OEM.

Note

An OEM version is one branded from both Microsoft and another company, such as a computer manufacturer.

The architecture of Windows 2000 is the reason behind all of the fuss involved with hardware support. Unlike previous versions of DOS and non-NT Windows, Windows 2000 does not allow User mode processes direct access to the hardware components. The reason for this design is portability and modularity, which is consistent with the rest of the Windows 2000 philosophy.

By implementing a Hardware Abstraction Layer (HAL), the underlying hardware is masked to the operating system. This allows a single device driver to be portable across all hardware platforms.

All non-I/O hardware requests (accessing a network resource, for example) are passed from the appropriate subsystem to the Win32 subsystem, which then sends the request through security validation to the Executive Services and then to the Kernel, which passes the request to the HAL. The HAL "virtualizes" this request, interprets it, and makes the appropriate hardware call (sending a data stream over the network interface).

The internals of the HAL are somewhat involved; the preceding explanation is greatly simplified to illustrate the process involved. The end result is that the operating system is not restricted to a specific hardware architecture. This enables Microsoft to port

Windows 2000 to other hardware platforms much more easily than it could rewrite all the hardware system calls. This also enables developers to write a single device driver for a specific piece of hardware.

Due to this hardware abstraction architecture, many communications programs (such as fax and modem software) do not function properly under Windows 2000. These programs require direct access to the hardware components. Initially, this was a problem, but there are now a host of such applications for Windows 2000—and support is growing.

Keep in mind that time is money. That includes your time as well as support's time, either at Microsoft or an OEM. Most non-supported hardware problems can be resolved easily or shouldn't be attempted at all. After all, what gain is there in spending a full day getting a display adapter to work when you can buy a compatible one for under $100? I never did get my old reliable 33.6 modem to work under Windows 2000 Professional. After fiddling for about an hour, I realized I had things to do and people to see. I ended up donating the modem to the same charity that recycles clothes when my daughter outgrows them and buying a new 56 one for $47. I consider that cheaper than even spending another half hour fussing with the old one. I can say the same thing about standard video cards and network interface cards (NICs).

The safest path is to attempt an installation only on machines that have all their components on the HCL. It's not the only safe path, though. Microsoft can't test everything instantly, and there might be perfectly good hardware that for some reason or another hasn't made it to the HCL yet—or might never at all. If you have a trusted vendor who says his hardware is Windows 2000-compatible, you should feel safe with that hardware, even if it doesn't appear on the HCL. If you have a problem, you'll have to call the vendor, because Microsoft will, in all likelihood, say something like, "We told you so."

The Case for Windows 98SE

It's just fine to say that all hardware should appear on the HCL, and if it doesn't, go out and buy some that does before setting up. In reality, corporate policies often make such buying impossible, even if it doesn't mean much expense.

Windows 98 and the latest Windows in the same line (as well as their progenitor Windows 95) is as supportive of out-of-date and weird hardware as Microsoft could make it. It's a good fallback position for client machines containing seriously incompatible hardware until they can be replaced or brought up to date. The workers using those client machines might not be thrilled at being passed over for Windows 2000 Professional, but its better than starting a battle against legacy hardware that you can't win.

The Checklist

Any enterprise-wide upgrade to Windows 2000 Professional for network client machines should have a checklist to organize the operation. The following is a sample checklist— yours will no doubt vary because no two installations are identical in all particulars:

- Is the upgrade team assembled and identified? Have they received the proper training for the upgrade operation? Have they been selected not only for technical expertise, but for their "people abilities" as well?

- Will you do a pilot rollout or try to install the upgrade over the entire enterprise at one time? Will you install by user class or by department? If you choose to do a department-by-department rollout, have you notified all affected departments of the rollout schedule to eliminate "2000 envy?"

  If you choose a pilot program of one department or a group of users, have they received the needed training in advance of the program?

- Have you tested all existing software with Windows 2000 Professional for the target installation group? Windows 2000 Professional has been exhaustively tested with standard out-of-the-box programs and does a very good job of running all of them. It does much better here than with hardware. The problems usually arise when a company uses customized programs written specifically for it rather than off-the-shelf software. Don't expect any problems with major programs (but test anyway), but do test very carefully customized or specialized programs, especially those from companies now out of business.

- Is all the hardware for the target group on the HCL? If not, are you sure you have the necessary drivers and have tested the unapproved hardware with Windows 2000 Professional? Check with vendors to see if they've tested their older hardware under Windows 2000. Unless your hardware is mostly on the HCL or you have the very latest, you should expect to upgrade at least some items like modems, display adapters, and network interface cards (NICs).

- Have you decided whether to do a clean installation of Windows 2000 Professional or install as a true upgrade over an existing operating system? Clean installations have a much greater chance of perfect-appearing setups, but require the users or the upgrade group to re-setup their applications software. In some cases, you might decide to use centralized clean upgrade on both Windows 2000 Professional and applications. This is particularly attractive if your upgrade to Windows 2000 Professional is scheduled to occur at roughly the same time as your applications upgrade. In any case, a clean install of Windows 2000 Professional will require a restoration of local (client-based) data files.

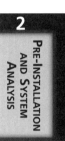

2

PRE-INSTALLATION AND SYSTEM ANALYSIS

- Have you assigned new passwords (if necessary) to the target group? Security leaks are inevitable. This is a good time to ensure, as much as reasonably possible, that your new system starts out safe without inheriting the leaks (stolen passwords) from your old system.

- Have you performed the pre-setup steps of virus checking, disk defragmenting, and redundant backups? Be sure to turn off virus checking in hardware (BIOS) for Windows 2000 Professional setup and then turn it back on again (if this is your policy) after you're up and running.

- Will you install locally or through a server using a tool such as Systems Management Server (SMS)? If the latter, have you tried a pilot push installation prior to attempting installations on production machines? A good place to get an overview of Microsoft's management software is `http://www.microsoft.com/Windows/server/Eval/strategic/ValueIM.asp`.

- When will you perform the upgrade to Windows 2000 Professional? Will you try during normal work times to enlist the help of users or during off-hours to avoid disrupting the normal workflow?

- Have you notified department managers of target upgrade groups what to expect during the upgrade process?

- Have you told all users and managers what you expect of them and when you expect it (such as backups)?

Although there's no technical reason to schedule a pilot upgrade program to a group that's similar in all but size to your enterprise, there's no better way to uncover faults in your assumptions and your checklist than doing this.

When choosing a pilot group for the upgrade test, make sure it includes a fair profile of your enterprise. Choosing a department full of power users with the latest equipment isn't a fair test if your enterprise includes many users with less motivation, older equipment, or both. You don't want to see surprises during the full installation effort that you've avoided during the pilot due to careful selection of a pilot group. Give it and your team a fair test.

Note

Ideally, your Windows 2000 Professional test should include your most naïve person using the most obsolete equipment. You might as well find out all that can happen on the front end.

Possible Trouble Spots

Some hardware means heartbreak for the Administrator installing Windows 2000 Professional. The following are some problematic items and areas.

- *Oddball Hardware*—The computer industry is quite creative. Over the years, people and companies have brought out some interesting pieces of hardware. Unfortunately for the inventors and adopters, many of those items now reside in the bit bucket of the computer industry. In some cases, the hardware is quite useful, but also quite rare. Some examples of this hardware are robotic vision interfaces (video), robotic control hardware, and interfaces for controlling a security system.

  If the manufacturer is still in business and interested in writing drivers for its older hardware (fat chance on this one), you might have a shot at getting some of this stuff to run under Windows 2000. However, in too many cases, the manufacturer is gone or uninterested in putting the effort in to support older equipment. Sometimes the manufacturer will have new and improved stuff intended for use with Windows 2000. If so, you can solve your problem by throwing money at it. If not, you're likely out of luck.

  Rarely you can make some modern driver work with older hardware that doesn't have a dedicated driver. This usually isn't worth the Administrator's time tracking this stuff down unless the number of affected computers is huge.

- *Older Disk Controllers*—Computer history has seen the wreck of many disk controller interface schemes that are little known today. Just a few years ago, SCSI was rare and unreliable in PCs, and IDE and EIDE was unknown. Disk interfaces were MFM, RLL, ESDI, and even the (then) hot ARLL.

  It's unlikely that you'll encounter those controllers today in a potential 2000 installation because the capacities of those disks were tiny compared to today's disk. However, you might. If you do, and even if they work with Windows 2000 Professional, consider ditching them in favor of U/EIDE or SCSI.

  Windows 2000 depends on virtual RAM—RAM emulated in a paging, or swap, file. The speed of this VRAM, and thus of Windows 2000 itself, depends on the speed of this VRAM, which means that a potential bottleneck with 2000 is disk speed.

  ESDI, ARLL, MFM and RLL disk/controller combinations operate at speeds that seem glacial today. In many cases, they'll fail to work under 2000. In all cases, they should be replaced by their more modern counterparts.

- *Video Cards*—If there's a single place that's the heartbreak hill of 2000 setup, the lost world of orphaned video cards is it. Some cards even give Windows 98 a hassle.

The world of video cards is one that changes faster than any other aspect of computer peripherals. There is constant intense competition between manufacturers to have the latest cards sporting the best speed, the newest interface, or the most features. The prize for have such a card is a top rating for that card in a national magazine that will lead to millions of dollars in sales and a dominant position in the market. After a manufacturer achieves dominion, it can set its own standards, thus cementing its position for quite a while.

Manufacturers do all they can to bring out new models intended to trump other manufacturers who are trying to do the same to them. They have little (if any) interest and no motive to support already sold cards with newer drivers.

- *Stealthy Peripherals*—These are hardware items that fool setup. In some cases, manufactures intentionally make their hardware seem like something else for compatibility. Some (quite old today) IBM-brand hardware was "wired" to run only in IBM-brand computers. These approved computers had trademark *IBM* in firmware (BIOS). Some cloners got around this move by putting a phrase like *not IBM* or *IBM-compatible* in their firmware. A search routine for the string *IBM* would find *IBM* without violating Blue's trademark. These strategies fool proprietary hardware and software. They can also fool setup programs. This situation is quite rare today.

In other cases, manufacturers modify their hardware during a model run. Most video cards and modems undergo firmware modifications during their model runs. These modifications can foil setup by seeming to run with a particular driver when they can't.

Unless your hardware is incredibly uniform, you are incredibly lucky, or your installation target is quite small, you will hit one or more hardware problems during setup. Careful inventory taking will eliminate or anticipate these trouble spots, but it very rarely can eliminate them entirely.

The Inventory Process

If you're installing on a single machine or only a few, your inventory chores are rather easy. You can just make a list of what's in them and do an eyeball comparison to the HCL.

However, in a corporate setting, having hundreds or even thousands of computers, you can't do an eyeball inventory. You should have a complete inventory already, but few do. Even those who try to maintain running inventories find that they are out of date. Users add stuff to their machines, swap parts around, departments go out and buy equipment to meet their particular needs, and other events conspire to make even the most well-kept list inaccurate.

Although you can walk around your organization taking a manual inventory similar to a retail item count, if you have more than a few computers, you should look into software that helps you manage networks including the inventory. One such program is Microsoft's Systems Management Server (SMS). Such a program has more uses than just inventory. For example, you can arrange for a hands-off "push" setup of Windows 2000 using SMS.

You must inventory the following things, but this list isn't exhaustive. You will probably want to add more items.

- Computer identifying number (inventory number), department, location, and the user assigned to it.
- CPU type and speed.
- Amount of RAM.
- Hard disk type (viz. SCSI, IDE, and so on) and capacity.
- BIOS date, brand, and version.
- Peripheral types, versions and brands. Be sure to include multimedia boards and removable drives like CDRW (CD Read/Write) and ZIP.
- NIC type and version.
- Video card type.

Remember this list is minimal.

2

PRE-INSTALLATION
AND SYSTEM
ANALYSIS

> **Note**
>
> You can simplify your system management chores and upgrade projects quite a bit by placing the inventory information into a database management system, such as Microsoft Access. Once it's there, you can write simple queries to determine which (if any) machines need upgrading before installing any particular software. For example, let's say that your company has some Super Vision display cards that you've learned are incompatible with a particular upgrade. If you have your inventory in Access, you can query it and within seconds learn of all machines with such display adapters. From there, it's simple to decide if you want to spend the money to upgrade these machines or if it's more cost effective to just drop the entire idea.
>
> Microsoft Access isn't a trivial program to learn, especially if you have little database experience. A good place to start is *SAMS Teach Yourself Microsoft Access 2000 in 21 Days*, published by SAMS.

Deciding on Setup Options

For the most part, Windows 2000 Professional will configure itself according to the client machine on which it finds itself. There's not that much you can do, or should even want to do, to change this.

However, there are several installation options over which you do have control. You'll find the setup process in the next chapter, but before you actually run setup, or if you're planning a centralized setup, you need to make certain choices.

These choices come down to two broad categories: 2000 applet options and network protocols.

2000 Applet Options

Windows 2000, like Windows 98SE, Windows NT, and its various other antecedents, has many installation options. Microsoft chooses those options if you select the Typical installation on a bare system. You have little choices on an upgrade. If you decide to do a "push" setup using a tool such as SMS, or if you decide to do a Custom setup at each console, you will face a wide choice of applet combinations.

> **Note**
>
> The term *applets* applies both to the little programs in Control Panel and to minor applications, such as the Calculator, distributed with Windows 2000 Professional.

In some cases, the applets you choose will depend on company policy, but you should also, if possible, give weight to the following:

- User satisfaction
- User requirements
- Disk space

For a great many users, the more custom their workstation (client machine), the happier they are. This is the reason for the hearty sales of such non-productivity programs as the After Dark screen saver. Similarly, users like to install and play games, both those that come with Windows and those available *a la carte*.

Although it's true that many users will spend company time using applets (especially games), in some ways, this time isn't wasted if it increases employee morale and therefore increases productivity. Employees figured out how to really waste company time and assets well before the invention of the personal computer. Many users have gotten much better with their keyboards and mice by playing these games.

> **Note**
>
> The Internet age was upon us before Windows 2000 Professional came about. Many companies sponsor employee Internet accounts where those employees clearly spend time doing non-business related activities.
>
> You need to set policy about computer use on and off the Internet including game play, Web surfing, customization of workstations, and other related areas. This is a good place to coordinate with Human Resources, but even if you choose to go it alone, you need to set policy, not capriciously choose what activities to limit after you see them. From such behavior great suits stem.

In very rare instances is disk space a consideration when it comes to installing applets. At worst, these will eat up a few megabytes of disk space. When disks were 20MB total, this was a serious consideration. With today's typical business computer's disk space ranging above 25GB, it isn't.

Although the final decision as to what applets and games (if any) become part of an installation usually isn't part of a user's decision matrix, it's prudent to give users' feelings consideration when deciding these things.

> **Note**
>
> People are touchy about printing because, for many, it's the end product of their work. Be sure all users are set up so that all the printers they need to do their work easily are available to them.

Network Options

Windows 2000 has been designed to work with a wide variety of standard networking protocols and services. The most common ones come standard with the distribution disk. In some rare cases, you'll need to contact the vendor for client drivers. The following is a list of the commonly-used standard network protocols bundled with Windows 2000 Professional:

- *NetBEUI*—This is an extension of the older NetBIOS. It's a fast, small, limited protocol useful for small-to-medium-sized LANs of up to about 150 clients and servers.

  NetBEUI's great advantage is its simplicity. It self-configures at installation time, both as to addresses and binding to the client NIC (Network Interface Card). Its chief drawback is its inability to work with routers, therefore limiting its network size.

- *IPX/SPX or NWLink*—IPX/SPX is the protocol of the older Novell NetWare connectivity solution. Many enterprises have installed NetWare as a legacy protocol. Some of these companies choose to upgrade to Windows 2000 piecemeal rather than all at once. This leaves islands of the older NetWare in an otherwise modern Windows 2000 networking installation.

  For those companies, Microsoft has included a NetWare client for Windows 2000 Professional. This is NWLink, an enhanced version of Novell's NetBIOS. Both Microsoft's and Novell's protocols can simultaneously exist bound to the same NIC.

- *TCP/IP*—This is the standard networking of the Internet and UNIX. Due to its flexibility, it's finding wide support outside of its traditional bastions.

TCP/IP probably provides the best interoperability of all protocols. It has evolved into the *lingua franca* of computers. The *stack,* or TCP/IP layer, included with Windows 2000 Professional is 32 bits and includes both SLIP and PPP services.

You can't go wrong by choosing this protocol and, in many cases, you'll have to opt for it either exclusively or in addition to another choice, such as NetBEUI. Many networks run NetBEUI over TCP/IP.

If you choose this as your networking protocol, you'll need to assign IP numbers to each client on your network. If you choose Windows 2000 Server as your server operating system, you can assign a block of numbers to DHCP (Dynamic Host Control Protocol) for easier (after it's set up) client management. DHCP dynamically assigns an IP to a client upon log on.

> **Note**
>
> Chapter 17, "Setting Up TCP/IP Protocol Access," and Chapter 21, "Windows 2000 Networking Protocols," deal with TCP/IP and networking protocols, respectively.

If you run NetBEUI, you should also consider configuring a Windows Internet Naming Service (WINS) server. This handles name resolution between the TCP/IP and NetBEUI protocols.

After you've set up a TCP/IP layer and configured all the needed services, you can connect to any other TCP/IP network or device.

Appletalk

Appletalk is a limited, but common in the Macintosh world, protocol originally designed as a very simple connectivity solution for Apple-brand computers.

This requires a server on the network to have installed Windows 2000 Services for the Macintosh. When all the pieces are in place, it allows Windows 2000 computers to talk to dialed-up Macintosh machines.

Remote Access Service

Remote Access Service (RAS) is a highly flexible service allowing client connection to a remote (not on the LAN or WAN) server. For the most part, people use RAS for the following:

- To access the company server or LAN from mobile (laptop) computers
- To allow telecommuting employees to participate, through dial-up lines, in a workgroup
- To allow connectivity to the Internet via dial-up for individual computers or those on a LAN/WAN without a gateway

Windows 2000 includes support for both the older SLIP and PPP standards. If your server supports both, use PPP, which has stronger authorization.

Peer-to-Peer Sharing

Peer-to-Peer sharing is an optional service for Windows 2000 Professional installations allowing resource sharing of any or all resources "owned" by the computer. These resources are usually drives (or volumes), directory structures, or printers. How and what is shared depends on your company's security work policies. You can turn this capacity on or off using the User Rights Policy Editor.

The security for peer sharing is user-level based on the accounts established on the server. If you don't have server-based account validation, you can use share-level security for each resource. This works identically in Windows 2000 as it did in Windows 95, 98, CE (and successors), and Windows 3.11.

Virtual Private Network

A virtual private network (VPN) is a private link between two or more nodes using the Internet infrastructure. A VPN is much more private (secure) than a standard Internet connection.

The advantage of using the Internet's structure is price. A standard landline or satellite connection can be prohibitive for many enterprises. After you're connected to the Internet, there is very little marginal cost to using a VPN, and that cost is all in the setup.

A node for a VPN can be an individual computer or a LAN (local area network).

After the Installation

The time to plan for what to do after the Windows 2000 Professional upgrade is finished is before it's started. If your standard enterprise application suite is straightforward, such as a current version of Microsoft Office with a few Access or Excel custom applications, you shouldn't have any compatibility issues.

That's a dream situation. Most individuals and virtually all enterprises have at least a few oddball applications that departments either can't or choose not to upgrade to current technology. In addition, some users not familiar with the new user interface (UI) will be confused upon encountering it. To address these problems, you need to develop two programs prior to any pilot programs. The pilot installations will, if you choose to perform them, let you fine-tune your programs.

Supporting Users

If you have an existing support desk or system, you'll need to train its staff for anticipated problems users might hit when first using Windows 2000 Professional. This is a catch-22 because you can't know what problems your help desk people should anticipate until you do the rollout. This is an excellent reason to try a pilot program first.

Microsoft maintains a list of what's new and improved for all their operating system upgrades. Distribute this information to your help desk folks because, reasonably speaking, most users will run into difficulties in the new or changed areas.

If you're not upgrading in the same line, but doing a cross, such as from NetWare to Windows 2000 or from Windows 95 to Windows 2000, ask yourself what benefits this will bring your people. Then plan, no matter your good intentions, that these same people will have trouble using these benefits. Plan accordingly.

Because you'll have to expand your support staff at least temporarily for the Windows 2000 Professional rollout, you can afford to post a few of them at a time within the department or with users selected to be the pilot group. Rotate this close support staff regularly to give all your support people real experience with new 2000 users.

As your close support staff gains experience with the pilot users, enter their encountered problems and proven solutions in your support database. This will give all your support staff individuals the benefit of the entire support group's experiences. If you don't have a support desk database, consider creating one. Even a simple database—one that an experienced Access developer can put together in a day or so—will be very worthwhile in preventing your staff from solving already-solved situations.

Training Users

It's simple. The way to reduce support costs is training. The way to increase user satisfaction with Windows 2000 Professional is training. The way to increase enterprise productivity is training. The way to increase employee satisfaction on the job is training. The way to make users feel appreciated is to have your company spend some training money on them.

Few folks, and nobody in Human Resources (Personnel), will dispute those claims, yet only some enterprises take the steps to adequately train their users. Even those that plan to often fail to follow through on those plans. Here's an opportunity for you to be different and, in being so, be better: Train your users. This will make your life simpler and more peaceful.

> **Note**
>
> If your users have some Web experience and you're itching to try your hand at being a Webmaster, consider an intranet as a substitute for classroom training. It's a heck of a lot cheaper than a wetware teacher (live person) in a class. It also reflects well on your flexibility as an Administrator.
>
> Another interesting and simple alternative to the classroom with wetware is to distribute a homemade CD-ROM with Windows 2000 Professional lessons on it. All you need is a CD-ROM with a "home page" linking local files also on the CD-ROM for a computer-based tutorial (CBT) system. Again, this is bone simple to do using modern word processors such as Word or WordPerfect. It should make you look aces to management too.
>
> Chapter 24, "Setting Up an Intranet," covers this topic in great detail. It will take you step-by-step through this entire process. You can burn an intranet onto a CD-ROM if you prefer this manner of distribution.

The training specifics for your users depend on three things:

- Their level of expertise
- What you expect from a user
- Their previous experience

Users coming from MS-DOS or a text-based UNIX will need training in a GUI, while those used to the venerable X-Windows won't. Users coming from Windows 95, 98, or NT 4 will require much less training, if any. What training these users require will depend on what you expect at the user level. The following are some topics to cover for a typical group of users migrating from Windows 3.*x*, the Macintosh, or a later version of OS/2.

- The Windows 2000 Professional desktop
- The organization and use of the Start button
- Using the Explorer on the local machine
- The meaning of shortcuts, creating shortcuts
- Sharing resources
- Locating shared resources through the Network Neighborhood, connecting to those resources
- Setting up a local printer, sharing that printer
- Getting help for Windows 2000 Professional
- Using the context-sensitive right mouse button (vital to UNIX and Macintosh folks who tend to be lost when it comes to the right button conventions)
- Mouse basics (for those coming from a command-line background)
- Installing local applications, saving data locally and to shared resources
- Using OLE in applications
- Creating and using scraps on the desktop
- Locating files, directories, and computers using the Find resource in Explorer and in Start
- Customizing settings, such as display colors, screen resolution, and color depth
- Assigning sounds to events
- A tour of the Control Panel
- The Command Line Interface (CLI)

In all likelihood, that entire list will have items you don't want to teach your users, and it makes some assumptions about your users' abilities that may not be true.

Any training program is better than no training program. A formal training program, even a very abbreviated one, is vastly superior to on-the-fly, trial-and-error experimenting. If your organization doesn't have the facilities for such training, consider leasing a facility that does.

Training Methods

Try to have the same people responsible for user support do the training if you go classroom/wetware. Outside trainers will surely have their own agendas, their own curricula, and their own slants. Also, they have no concern about what happens after the training session, because they'll have moved on.

Classroom Method

If you create and execute your own training program, you also can train your people using your company's specific applications and weighted to your company's needs. For example, if your company has to do a lot of bidding, you can train using the example of integrating an Excel spreadsheet in a Word document for your OLE section. Training is specific. The closer you train to your company's (or you, the system Administrator's) needs, the better trained will your people be.

Consider running a pilot program with pilot training done by your support staff or beta testing the intranet or Computer Based Training (CBT). Then have the same people support the users participating in the pilot program. They will gain experience with real users in real situations in your real enterprise. This experience will point out not only checklist deficiencies, but also holes in the pilot training program. Your user feedback will be vital to making a good program. If you have a good relationship with your users, they might also request specific additions (beyond Windows 2000 Professional) to the training program. This can be an opportunity for you to empire build.

Then have the now-experienced support staff train the rest of the staff because by this iteration they have evolved into trainers who know what training your users need. They also have a great deal of self-interest in seeing the users get good training. Otherwise, the users might end up overwhelming the support staff, thereby making them and you look bad. There's nothing like self-interest to motivate a teacher.

The Video Option

You can do a decent video production today for a little bit of money compared to a few years ago. This might be a viable training option in a few companies with the video broadcast either through a network or distributed by tape.

In its early days, TV was thought by many to be a great potential teacher. Educators in that bygone era thought the new medium was a great way to broadcast great teachers and great lectures to eager students throughout the land. Well, this didn't happen mostly because people prefer entertainment to education.

Video teaching falls into the same situation. If you just show yourself lecturing about Windows 2000 Professional, you'll anaesthetize your students. You'll have to add some sizzle to your production to keep their attention.

Also, unless you'll be beaming a broadcast to a classroom with students and workstations, they won't be able to play as they learn, reducing the stickiness of the lesson.

There might be a few places where video works, but most places will do better with live folks (the wetware circuit) or a CBT over the network or on a CD-ROM. A CD-ROM is easier to produce too.

Review Chapter 24 for some good coverage on how to create content. After you have the content, the software that comes with your CD burner will have instructions on how to transfer the content from your disk to a CD-ROM.

Upgrading from an Existing Operating System or Going Clean

Unless you have to, don't do this. While Windows 2000 Professional has been designed to upgrade Windows NT, Windows 98, and Windows 95, doing so can cause any problems in those installations to migrate to the new system. You are much better off doing the five step:

> **Note**
>
> Before installing Windows 2000 Professional in any configuration, stop anti-virus checking software in BIOS (firmware). If you run 2000's setup from an existing Windows, also turn off virus checking software. While most virus checking software won't interfere with Windows 2000's setup, you might just get unlucky and find one that does.

1. Backup the system redundantly.
2. Format your disk or, if you prefer, partition the disk and then format.
3. Install Windows 2000 Professional.

4. Install applications.

5. Restore data and customization options (if applicable).

If you must upgrade or you choose to try this method, the following sections discuss some considerations.

File Systems

Before moving on, the following is a mini-tutorial on the various file systems in use by Microsoft operating systems.

- *FAT (FAT16)*—This is the standard file system (FAT stands for File Allocation Table) used on all hard and floppy disks since PCs were in their infancy. Actually, there was a FAT12 that preceded FAT16, but that's never seen today outside of museums. FAT is the standard file format readable by all Microsoft operating systems including Windows 2000.

- *FAT32*—This is an improved FAT introduced right after Windows 95 in 1994. It allows for more file entries, greater efficiency, and larger volumes than FAT16. Windows 95 OSR2 and successor operating systems, such as Windows 98, can read FAT32 volumes. Windows 2000 can also read FAT32 volumes, but predecessor systems such as Windows NT cannot.

- *NTFS*—NTFS stands for NT File System, a vastly improved file system for use with NT and successor operating systems, such as Windows 2000. NTFS allows for more efficient file storage and (at last!) decent security. This is the system you should use unless some consideration (such as a dual boot scenario) overrides. Windows 2000 uses the original NTFS and an enhanced NTFS. It will use the original NTFS if it senses dual or triple booting with Windows NT. Windows NT can access old NTFS, but only Windows 2000 (and successor systems) can read the newer variation of NTFS.

Windows 9x

Windows 9x includes Windows 95, 95 OSR2, 98, and 98SE and their successors. To install on a machine that boots only Windows 2000 (in contrast to a dual boot machine that boots both Windows 2000 and something else), do the following:

1. Backup redundantly.

2. Decompress any drives compressed with DriveSpace or DoubleSpace. Windows 2000 Professional won't use these types of drives. If you want to use FAT32 partitions in Windows 2000, create them now because there is no utility in the new operating system to do this. There is little if any reason to use FAT32 with

Windows 2000, however. Windows 2000 can read and write to FAT32 for compatibility with dual boot systems (those running both Windows 98 and Windows 2000).

3. Check the HCL for hardware compatibility. Make sure the hardware will host the new operating system and not hose it.

4. Run Windows 2000 Professional setup from the CD-ROM or other distribution media.

5. You will be given an opportunity to format non-NTFS volumes to NTFS. If you will only be running Windows 2000 on this system, convert to NTFS.

6. Follow the prompts.

7. Re-install applications.

6. Restore data.

If you currently dual boot Windows NT 4 and Windows 98, you can triple boot into those two plus Windows 2000 Professional by following these instructions and leaving the old operating systems in place.

1. Backup redundantly.

2. Decompress any drives compressed with DriveSpace or DoubleSpace to which you want Windows 2000 to have access. Keeping a drive compressed will make it inaccessible to Windows 2000 Professional. If you want to use FAT32 partitions in Windows 2000, create them now because there is no utility in the newer operating system to do this.

3. Check the HCL for hardware compatibility. Make sure the hardware will host the new operating system and not hose it.

4. Run Windows 2000 Professional setup from the CD-ROM or other distribution media onto its own folder (directory) preferably on its own NTFS volume (see step 5). Because Windows 98 can't read NTFS volumes, this will keep Windows 2000 Professional "safe" from Windows 98. Generally, people use C: for Windows 98SE and any other drive for Windows 2000. You can place Windows 2000 on a volume with Windows NT if you have the disk space.

5. You will be given an opportunity to format non-NTFS volumes to NTFS. You don't need to do this, but it's a good idea to make Windows 2000 invisible to Windows 98SE, especially if you have a security issue. Windows 98 isn't a secure operating system, while Windows 2000 is. Having data and Windows 98 on a Windows 2000 system using the FAT (or FAT32) file system removes almost all security features from Windows 2000 Professional.

6. Follow the prompts. You'll notice that on boot up you'll have a choice to boot into Windows 2000 or Windows 98.

7. Install applications to Windows 2000.

8. Restore data.

> **Note**
>
> Windows 2000 uses a new NTFS structure unreadable by Windows NT 4 without a special service pack. If you install Windows 2000 on a NTFS volume where Windows NT 4 exists, it will use the slightly less capable, but compatible NTFS, making all FAT16 and NTFS volumes available to both Windows 2000 and Windows NT 4.

Windows NT 4 and 3.51

The following steps are appropriate to take when upgrading from these earlier versions of Windows NT to Windows 2000.

1. Backup redundantly.

2. Run Disk Manager (optional) to re-allocate disk usage.

3. Check the HCL for hardware compatibility. Make sure the hardware will host the new operating system and not hose it.

4. Run Windows 2000 Professional setup from the CD-ROM or other distribution media. You can run directly from Windows NT or boot using the diskettes.

5. You will be given an opportunity to format non-NTFS volumes to NTFS. If you will only be running Windows 2000 on this system, convert to NTFS.

6. Follow the prompts.

7. Re-install applications.

6. Restore data.

Summary

Windows 2000 has many hardware restrictions that most DOS and Windows users will be unaccustomed to and probably consider unnecessarily cumbersome. It is not without cause. This provides easy portability to other hardware platforms.

Just think. If there was some major technological breakthrough and suddenly systems were 2,500 percent faster for the price of today's desktop system, it wouldn't be too difficult or take too long for Windows 2000 to be ported to that platform.

Whenever possible, use hardware that is on the HCL. Remember that if it is not on the HCL, it might not work; or you might have to wait for driver support and, most likely, Microsoft technical support will not provide support for it.

Before buying any hardware not listed on the HCL, find out whether there are drivers available for Windows 2000. Although this is a new concept, it does serve a good purpose. Save yourself headaches and buy supported hardware.

As with so many things, success with any Windows 2000 setup depends on careful planning. Part of planning should include pilot setup testing, anticipation of after-installation user support needs, and user training. The more effort you put in planning the installation, the less effort you'll spend putting out fires.

Installing Windows 2000 Professional

CHAPTER 3

This chapter will prepare you for the installation of Windows 2000. The first step in the whole process will be to obtain the media. Chapter 2, "Pre-Installation and System Analysis," should have had you check your intended hardware, so you should know if it can accept Windows 2000. This chapter will pick up from that point and guide you through the installation process. You will go through the setup, step by step, and see what options are available through the installation. You will also take a look at upgrading from previous operating systems, like Windows 9x, Windows NT 3.51, and Windows NT 4.0.

To aid you in setting up multiple or remote workstations, you will learn about disk imaging with the SYSPREP utility and remote installations. The chapter will finish with the completion of the installation process. Chapter 4, "Troubleshooting the Setup," will deal with troubleshooting of setup problems.

Step-by-Step Setup

The installation of Windows 2000 is not all that different from the installation of other Microsoft operating systems, such as Windows 98 or Windows NT 4.0. Because Windows 2000 is based on NT technology, if you are familiar with the Windows NT installation process, you will have fewer questions than if you have only installed Windows 98. This section will examine the following areas:

- Starting the installation
- Setup switches
- Character Mode Install
- GUI Mode Install

Starting the Installation

Every process has a starting point. In the case of the Windows 2000 installation, you have three options from which to choose:

- From floppy disk
- From source files without floppy disks
- From bootable CD-ROM

Because each of these start types are a little different, each will be examined.

> **Note**
>
> If you do not have the installation disks for Windows 2000, you will be able to make a set. You will need four disks for Windows 2000 Professional or other version of Windows 2000. Each version has its own disks, so the Professional disks cannot be used to set up Server or Advanced Server. To create the boot disks, you can use one of the two executable files found in the \BOOTDISK directory of the Windows 2000 CD-ROM. Also in this directory, there will be four image files that contain the disk images of the four boot disks. If you are running MS-DOS, you should run the MAKEBOOT.EXE file; if you are using Windows NT, you can run MAKEBT32.EXE. This creates a set of boot disks you can use for the rest of the Windows 2000 installation. The four disks are called Windows 2000 Setup Boot Disk, and Windows 2000 Setup Disk #2, #3, and #4.
>
> Unlike Windows NT 4, if these disks are not blank, they will be overwritten with the boot disk images, but you should try to ensure the disks do not have any bad sectors. This can be done easily by performing a full format of the floppy disks. This should not be necessary with new, preformatted disks.

Starting Setup from Floppy Disk

To start the installation using the setup floppy disks. Place the first disk, Windows 2000 Setup Boot Disk, in your computer and reboot. You will prompted to insert disk two, three, and four. During this process, the Windows 2000 kernel will be loaded from the floppy disks. Starting from floppy disks, you will immediately start the Character Mode Installation, which is discussed in the "Character Mode" section later in this chapter.

Starting Setup from Source Files Without Floppy Disks

If you have Windows 9x or Windows NT Workstation installed on your computer, you can perform the installation without the boot floppy disks. When you place the CD-ROM into your computer, Autorun will launch SETUP.EXE, which will display a navigation screen as well as a dialog box. The dialog box will ask you, "Would you like to upgrade to Windows 2000?" You can also open the \I386 directory on the Windows 2000 Professional CD-ROM and launch WINNT32.EXE. Winnt32 will allow you to use setup switches to automate the installation. Either of these methods will launch a wizard to prepare your installation.

The Windows 2000 Setup Wizard will allow you to choose between a clean installation and an upgrade installation. The Wizard will always recommend an upgrade (see Figure 3.1), but you may choose not to if you plan to leave your computer in a dual boot configuration. If you choose to go with a dual boot configuration, you will have to reload any applications that you want to use within Windows 2000 Professional.

FIGURE 3.1

You have a choice between upgrading and migrating your applications, or maintaining a dual boot configuration.

If you choose to upgrade your installation, you will be walked through the following three stages (see Figure 3.2):

- Software and hardware upgrade files
- Search for system incompatibilities
- Create an upgrade report

FIGURE 3.2

The upgrading process has been streamlined to make the whole procedure as painless as possible.

If your computer is currently on a network, Setup will gather information about your domain, based on your computer name and logon domain. You will also be able to create a new computer account in a Windows NT domain if you know the name and password of an account that has sufficient privileges (see Figure 3.3). If you do not know if you currently have a computer account or the name of your domain, consult your administrator.

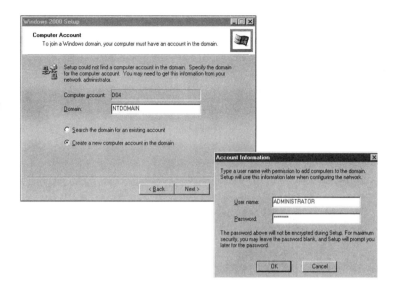

FIGURE 3.3

If you want to participate in a Windows NT domain, you will need to have a computer account in the domain.

As of the writing of this book, none of the shipping applications had upgrade packs, but Microsoft has provided this as a method of upgrading applications to be compatible with Windows 2000 during the OS installation. If you do have upgrade packs, Windows 2000 will prompt you for their location so they can be installed (see Figure 3.4). Hopefully this will become the preferred method of distributing updates. Upgrade packs should be distributed by the application manufacturers.

FIGURE 3.4

Upgrade packs can provide an easy method of installing updates to applications.

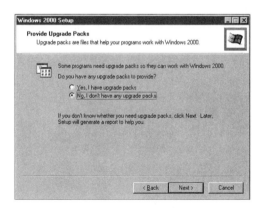

3

INSTALLING WINDOWS 2000 PROFESSIONAL

Rather than automatically converting your hard drive files systems over to NTFS (NT File System), Setup prompts you for a choice (see Figure 3.5). If you plan to dual boot your computer at any time in the future, you should not upgrade your drives to NTFS. If you upgrade to NTFS, the only operating system that will be capable of reading data directly from the hard drive is Windows 2000, because NTFS has been upgraded to Version 5 with Windows 2000. If you are not sure, you should not upgrade your drive because it can be upgraded after you complete your installation. If you choose to upgrade your drive to NTFS, you will not have to worry about others who have access your drive across the network through a shared folder because it is still your computer that reads the data from the hard drive.

FIGURE 3.5

You should always think twice before converting your hard drive to NTFS because it rules out all chances of dual booting your computer.

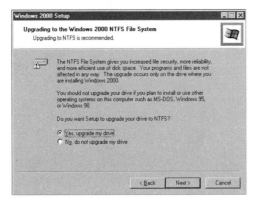

The upgrade report will let you see what you should expect after the upgrade is completed (see Figure 3.6). You still have an opportunity to back out of the installation at this point. The upgrade report lists any applications for which known problems exist, if there are hardware components that will not work with Windows 2000, or if there are any other issues with the upgrade.

FIGURE 3.6

The upgrade report is designed to flag potential problems and let you decide if you want to continue.

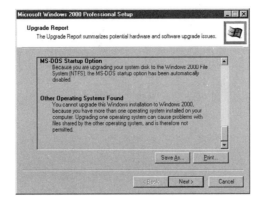

The last screen that appears before the reboot or file copy is started is the Special Setup Options (see Figure 3.7). This screen allows you to set language options for your installation, advanced setup options, as well as the ability to load some of the accessibility options. Language Options allows you to specify the code page support and keyboard layouts. Advanced Options allows you to set the location of the source files, the installation directory, to copy all files to the hard drive prior to rebooting—in the event that your CD-ROM is not supported by Windows 2000—and to choose the installation partition if you are not upgrading. There are only two Accessibility options that can be enabled from this screen, they are the Microsoft Magnifier, to enlarge screen images, and the Narrator, to read all of the dialog boxes.

FIGURE 3.7

Special setup options allow for customization and loading of accessibility options during the installation.

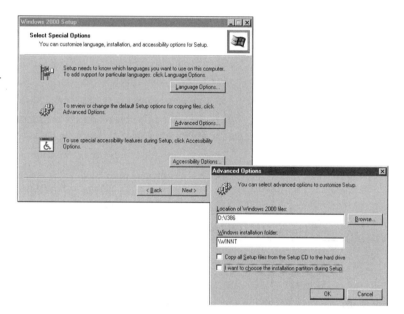

After the upgrade screens have been completed, the boot sector on your computer will be upgraded and a number of files will be copied to your hard drive to support the reboot into Windows 2000. The rest of the upgrade process should continue without much user input while the computer reboots and goes through both the Character Mode and GUI Mode installation.

Starting Setup from a Bootable CD-ROM

If you have a computer that supports booting from the CD-ROM, you will be able to put the Windows 2000 CD-ROM into your drive and reboot the computer. This will launch into the Character Mode portion of the setup. This process will be described in the "Character Mode" section later in this chapter. After installation, you should set the CD-ROM to boot after the hard drive, or not at all.

Setup Switches

The 16-bit Windows 2000 installation application, WINNT, has several switches that have been detailed in Table 3.1. This executable can be called from MS-DOS or 16-bit operating systems.

TABLE 3.1 WINNT Installation Switches

Switch	Description
/S[:sourcepath]	This specifies the location of the source fields for Windows 2000. This is required for unattended installations.
/T[:tempdrive]	Windows 2000 places copied files on a drive. When performing unattended installations, this is used to specify the drive onto which to install Windows 2000.
/I[:inffile]	Allows you to specify a different DOSNET.INF file. This controls the Character Mode installation.
/U[:answer_file]	Performs setup using the settings found in the specified file.
/UDF:id[,UDF_file]	Performs setup using the settings found in the UDF file to override settings found in the answer file based on the ID.
/R[x]:folder	Copies the specified folder to the drive during the installation.
/E:command	Specifies a command to be executed at the end of GUI setup. This runs without a user logged on, so CMDLINES.TXT is a better method of post installation application launching.
/A	Enables Accessibility Options during setup.

If you have a 32-bit Windows operating system installed on your computer, you will have to run WINNT32 from the \I386 directory. Winnt32 supports some of the same switches, but also has many unique switches. Table 3.2 summarizes the options that are available.

TABLE 3.2 WINNT32 Installation Switches

Switch	Description
/tempdrive:*drive_letter*	Performs the same function as /T in Table 3.1
/unattend[*num*][:*answer_file*]	Performs the same function as /U in Table 3.1, except that *num* can be used to specify how long a Windows 2000 computer should wait before rebooting after the file copy.
/copydir:*folder_name*	Creates the specified folder within the WINNT directory.

Switch	Description
/copysource:*folder_name*	Same as Copydir, but the folder is deleted after setup. This is useful for files that are to be installed during the installation.
/cmd:*command_line*	Executes a command after the completion of final setup phase. This is after the second reboot and user configuration, but before the user's shell is loaded.
/debug[*level*][:*filename*]	Sets the log name and log level. The log levels are: 0, log sever errors; 1, log errors; 2, log warnings; 3, log informational alerts; and 4, log detailed information.
/syspart:*drive_letter*	Copies all of the setup startup files to a specified drive and marks the partition as active. This drive can then be taken to another computer and setup will continue with the hardware detection phase.

Character Mode

After you have finished copying files and restarted your computer, or you have begun setup from floppy disk or bootable CD-ROM, you are in the beginning phase of the Character Mode portion of Windows 2000 setup.

At this point, setup consists of a character-based blue screen similar to the old MS-DOS setup. In the bottom border of the screen is any pertinent information related to the current setup procedure—the current file being copied or loaded, for example, or various options that might be available at a given time.

The Character Mode blue screen with Windows 2000 Setup in the top-left corner appears and initial system files are loaded, as shown in the status filed in the bottom border of the screen. This will stay static throughout the Character Mode installation. At this time, Windows 2000 setup will load the system kernel. The first option that you will see is to press F6 to load a third-party SCSI or RAID driver. If you do not do this at this time, you will be given a chance later if there are no conflicts.

When the kernel loads, it will provide support for basic I/O devices like the keyboard and basic video (VGA) if it cannot detect your video card. Other devices that are supported during setup include the following:

- ACPI and ISA Plug and Play buses
- IEEE 1394(Firewire) SBP2 Storage

- PCMCIA
- USB Hub Driver
- USB Keyboard Driver

At any point in Setup, you can press F1 for help on the current item, or you can press F3 to exit the setup program. If you exit Setup, you will need to rerun Setup later to install Windows 2000 Professional. Typically, you do not want to end Setup after it has begun unless there is a problem. If you do end Setup, you probably can still boot to your previous OS, depending on how far the setup process went and how you chose to configure Setup. Unless you reached the point of specifying where to install Windows 2000 and elected to upgrade your previous OS, you will be able to boot to your previous system when you restart the computer. If you chose to upgrade your current OS, the results will be unpredictable, and you will probably have to successfully complete the installation of Windows 2000 or reinstall your previous OS.

One of the first steps in the installation of Windows 2000 is to rewrite your boot sector. This allows Windows 2000 to be the default boot OS in a dual boot situation. If you cancel your installation after this has happened, you will have to modify the BOOT.INI on the root of your C drive, or SYS your hard drive with a system disk from your previous OS. If you choose to edit your BOOT.INI file, you will have to remove the Hidden and Read-Only attributes from it in the properties of the file or by typing the following line at a command prompt:

```
ATTRIB -R -H C:\BOOT.INI
```

Then you will want to change to default entry in the file to read:

```
DEFAULT=C:\
```

This will cause the boot menu to be displayed during each reboot, but it will then proceed to boot to either MS-DOS, Windows 95 or Windows 98. If your other OS is Windows NT, the default entry would reference the Windows NT installation and could also be set using the System control panel.

If you choose to SYS your hard drive, you will have to boot from a Startup Disk for your OS and then at the command prompt type:

```
SYS C:
```

This will read the system files from your current drive and place them on the C drive. It will also rewrite the boot sector to allow your previous OS to boot.

Mass Storage Device Detection

After the initial process of loading the device drivers and files needed for setup and making selections about your system type, Windows 2000 setup runs a mass storage device detection process to locate hard drives, CD-ROM drives, and SCSI or RAID controllers in your system. If you are using a controller or CD-ROM that is not on the Hardware Compatibility List (HCL), you will need to have a driver disk for it at this time. If you do not have the necessary drivers for your storage devices, Windows 2000 might not be able to find an appropriate location to which to install.

Windows 2000 Setup will then attempt to locate your SCSI, RAID, or other disk controller driver. This is done by attempting to load all shipping drivers. These drivers are

- Compaq Drive Array
- IDE CDROM (Atapi 1.2)/PCI IDE Controller
- NRC 53C710 SCSI Host Adapter
- Adaptec AHA154x/AHA-164x SCSI Host Adapter
- Adaptec AHA 151x/AHA 152x/AIC 6x60 SCSI Adapter
- Adaptec AHA 2920/2905/Future Domain 16xx/PCI/SCSI2 go
- Symbios Logic C1800 PCI SCSI Adapter
- Buslogic SCSI Host Adapter
- Adaptec AHA 294x/AHA 394x/AIC 78xx SCSI Controller
- Mylex DAC960/Digital SWXCR-ExRaid Controller
- Qlogic PCI SCSI Host Adapter
- AMD PCI SCSI Controller/Ethernet Adapter
- Buslogic Flashpoint
- Compaq 32-bit Fast-Wide SCSI-2/E
- Emulex LP6000 Fiber Channel Host Adapters
- Qlogic QLA2100, 64 bit PCI-Fiber Channel Adapter
- Adansys SCSI Host Adapter
- Adansys 3550 Ultra Wide SCSI Host Adapter
- AMI MegaRaid Controller
- Compaq Fiber Channel Host Controller
- Diamond Multi Media Systems SCSI Host Adapter
- Initio ultra SCSI Host Adapter

3

INSTALLING
WINDOWS 2000
PROFESSIONAL

- Qlogic ISP 1240 SCSI Host Adapter
- JNI Fiber Channel Adapter
- Adaptec AHA-294x42/AIC-7890 SCSI Controller
- IBM Server RAID Adapter
- Symbios Logic C8xx PCI SCSI Host Adapter
- Symbios Logic C896 PCI SCSI Host Adapter

Additional device controllers and storage devices can be explicitly specified here, as well as hardware for which you have an OEM-supplied driver disk. To specify additional drives, adapters, or controllers, press S when given the opportunity to do so. You will be presented with a list of possible devices and given an option of Other (requires disk provided by a hardware manufacturer).

If you have installed a device that is supported but is not detected, you can try to manually specify it, but you probably have a configuration problem that prevented Windows 2000 Setup from detecting it in the first place.

To install support for a device for which you have a driver disk, select the Other option and provide the OEM-supplied disk when prompted. When a dialog box is presented with the various devices supported by the supplied driver, select the appropriate device and press Enter. Windows 2000 Setup will need to copy a few files from the disk at a later point in Setup, so keep the disk available. It is also a good idea to keep all such device disks with your Windows 2000 setup boot disks and an emergency repair disk (discussed later in this chapter) in the event that you must reinstall Windows 2000 sometime later.

When you have finished specifying mass storage devices or all mass storage devices have been detected, press Enter to continue Setup.

If this is the first time you have run Windows 2000 Professional Setup on this machine, press Enter to continue Setup. If you have another version of Windows 2000, Windows NT, or have had a failed installation attempt, you will see an option to repair a damaged Windows 2000 installation; this is discussed in Chapter 4.

You will then have to agree with the Licensing Agreement. To read the agreement in full press Page Down or press F8 to accept it.

System Settings and Installation Location

Windows 2000 Setup now examines all hard drives that have been found for content and available space, and then determines which file system is installed on the drive. If another version of Windows 2000 is found on any drive, you are prompted to decide whether to upgrade the existing installation or install a fresh copy of Windows 2000 Professional. To upgrade the existing installation, press Enter; to install a fresh copy, press N. If Setup detects an incomplete installation, it will also allow you to complete or repair that installation.

Setup displays a list of hardware and software components of the current system as detected. This lists the computer type, display, keyboard and keyboard layout, and the pointing device. If you want to change any items on the list, use the arrow keys to select the appropriate item, press Enter, and select the correct setting. When the settings are correct, press Enter.

You are now presented with a list of detected hard drives and partitions. Select the partition to which you want to install Windows 2000 Professional and press Enter. To create a partition on a drive with free space, use the arrow keys to select the partition, press C, specify the partition size, and press Enter.

To delete an existing partition, use the arrow keys to select the partition and press D. You are presented with a screen asking you to confirm that you want to delete the selected partition and warning you that all information contained will be lost. To delete the partition, press L. To go back and not delete the partition, press Esc.

When you are satisfied with the partition configuration and have selected a partition to which to install Windows 2000 Professional, press Enter.

> **Note**
>
> If you install Windows 2000 Professional to C:\WINNT, you may avoid some boot problems if you develop errors in BOOT.INI. See "BOOT.INI Problems" in Chapter 4, "Troubleshooting the Setup."

Windows 2000 Setup lists the partition to which you have chosen to install Windows 2000 Professional, its file system type, partition size, and space free, and disk ID. Select the file system that you want to use for this partition—NTFS or FAT—and press Enter. If the current partition is formatted with the FAT file system, your choices will be

- Format the partition using NTFS file system.
- Format the partition using FAT file system.
- Convert the partition to NTFS file system.
- Leave the current file system intact (no change).

> **Tip**
>
> If security is an issue or you intend to use drives larger than 2GB, I recommend NTFS as the file system for its advanced security capabilities and its capability to efficiently manage large drive volumes. In a dual boot system, FAT would be the appropriate choice for the C drive, and possibly other drives, but NTFS drives will not be accessible from the other operating systems.

You are now asked whether you want Windows 2000 Setup to perform an exhaustive secondary examination of your hard drives. To allow the examination, press Enter. To skip the exhaustive examination, press Esc. Basically, the exhaustive secondary examination is similar to a directory scan by the old Scandisk program in DOS. It checks your drive for errors, but it is time-consuming if there are a lot of files on the drive. If this is a new drive or you believe it might be deteriorating in performance, you might want to use this option.

Windows 2000 Setup now builds a list of files that need to be copied and begins the copy process. The current file being copied is displayed in the bottom-right corner of the screen with a progress indicator in the center of the screen. This can take a long time, you may want to take a break while this is happening.

When the file copying is complete, Windows 2000 provides a message telling you to remove disks from the Floppy drive and CD-ROM because it will attempt to reboot your computer in 10 seconds. Press Enter to restart your computer immediately.

GUI Mode

When your computer restarts, you are presented with the Windows 2000 boot menu. The installation reinitializes itself by default; do not choose another selection or the boot menu items will no longer list the setup of Windows 2000 Professional (this can be confusing if it happens).

Setup now reinitializes and continues copying the files needed to complete Setup. The rest of the setup process takes place using a setup wizard similar to that found in Windows 95. The initial screen advises you that the Wizard will guide you through the rest of the setup process. The next steps in the setup process are as follows:

- Detecting and Installing Devices
- Regional Settings
- Your Name and Company Name

- Computer Name and Administrator Password
- Date and Time
- Installing Windows 2000 Networking
- Starting File Operations
- Finishing setup

Detecting and Installing Devices

Windows 2000 Professional will use several hardware detection methods to locate the devices that are in your computer. This process can be lengthy. Windows 2000 has been optimized to locate Plug and Play devices, and can have trouble locating non-Plug and Play devices. If this happens, these devices can be loaded after Windows 2000 is installed. As the dialog box on your screen will suggest, this process will take several minutes. "Several minutes" in Microsoft time means several, so plan to take some time out and do something else. The process actually seems to take longer if PNP devices are present. While your video card and monitor are being detected, your monitor will probably flicker as the refresh frequency is identified. There is a status bar in this window that will let you know how things are going, or if they are going. When the detection process is complete, you will move onto the Regional settings.

Regional Settings

Regional Settings allow you to setup the default regional settings for both the operating system defaults and the currently logged on user. These regional settings include the display formats for Numbers, Date, Time and Currency. In addition to these numeric formats, you are also able to choose a keyboard layout.

If you set the System Locals, these will be used by the OS and can only be changed at installation. User Locals will set the default local for the users, but this can be modified through the Regional Settings control panel.

Your Name and Company Name

Windows 2000 Professional will prompt you for both your name and your company name. You can leave the company blank, but you must fill in your name. This information is used to record the registered user for the PC and create a local user account if the PC is not in a domain. The next window will prompt you for the computer name.

Computer Name and Administrator Password

Setup will automatically choose a name for your computer. This name will be made up of the first word or eight letters from your company name and a randomly generated number. If you have left your company name blank, it will use the first word or eight letters of your name. If you do not like the name provided, or if you are required to use a different name to integrate into your Windows 2000 or Windows NT Domain, you will be able to change it. You will also have to choose a password for the local Administrator account. This account can be used to perform any local maintenance of the PC that may be required.

> **Note**
>
> Be sure to use a password you will not forget or record and store it in a safe place, because you might need this in the future if you encounter problems or need to reconfigure your system. If you forget the administrator password and have no other administrator accounts, you need to reinstall Windows 2000 Professional to re-create the administrator account and specify a new password.
>
> Also note that passwords in Windows 2000 are case-sensitive. This means that *Password, password,* and *PASSWORD* are not the same. You must enter your password exactly as you entered it when you created the account.

Date and Time

The Date and Time screen enables you to set the current date and time on your computer. The current system setting will be displayed and can be changed from here if necessary.

Unless you live in the Pacific U.S., you will want to change your time zone to match your local area. In addition to setting your time zone location, you can also specify if your locality uses Daylight Savings Time. When Daylight Savings Time is enabled, your system will adjust the time by one hour twice a year.

Installing Windows 2000 Networking

Setup will attempt to detect the type of networking devices you have installed in your computer. It will then load default services for you. If you have a network card, you will be prompted to continue with default networking settings or custom. The default networking settings will load Client for Microsoft Networks, File and Printer Sharing for Microsoft Networks, and TCP/IP.

Starting File Operations

You are now almost finished with the setup. Windows 2000 Professional will copy the required files to your drive and complete the setup. After the file copy is completed, your computer will perform final tasks.

Finishing Setup

The last phase of Setup is the performing of Final Tasks. Setup will complete by performing the following tasks:

- Install Start Menu Items
- Register Components
- Save Settings
- Remove Temporary Files

After these tasks are completed, your computer must be rebooted.

Upon rebooting, the Network Identification Wizard will automatically start. This Wizard's job is to decide how to handle logins. The default will create a new user with the same name as the registered user from earlier in the installation. If you do not like that name, you can change it, assign a password, and confirm the new password. The other option is to require that all users must enter a username and password to use this computer. After this last set of questions, your shell will load and you will be able to start using Windows 2000.

Upgrading from WINDOWS 2000

If you have a previous version of Windows 2000 installed on your computer, you will be able to upgrade it to the current release by running WINNT32 as discussed in "Starting Setup from Source Files Without Floppy Disks." This process will update your OS to the newer version of Windows 2000. You may want to do this if you have a beta evaluation copy of Windows 2000 installed on your computer.

Boot Partition Versus System Partition

With Windows 2000, there are special limitations that are placed on both the System and Boot partitions. These limitations are often mentioned, and it will help you to know which partitions are being referred to. This section will look at the differences between these two partitions and which files you should expect to see on each.

The System partition is the partition on which the PC locates the Master Boot Record (MBR). This is the active primary partition on the hard drive. When Windows 2000 is installed, the MBR is modified to look for NTLDR as the boot loader. There are several files that will be located on the System partition, which include:

- NTLDR
- BOOT.INI
- NTDETECT.COM
- NTBOOTDD.SYS (only if booting from a SCSI controller that has the board BIOS disabled)
- BOOTSECT.DOS (only if previous boot sector existed on the drive)

These files are required to initialize the load of Windows 2000. The role of each file will be discussed in Chapter 4, "Troubleshooting the Setup."

Windows 2000 loads the Kernel from the Boot partition. This partition contains the Kernel, which is stored in the System32 directory as the file NTOSKRNL.EXE. Other directories that will exist on the Boot partition include the following:

- WINNT
- Program Files
- Documents and Settings
- Temp

These directories make up the Boot partition, in addition to a hidden file on the root of the boot partition, PAGEFILE.SYS. This file should be approximately the same size as the amount of RAM on your computer and is used as additional virtual memory for your computer.

Neither the Boot or System partitions are allowed to part of either a volume set or a stripe set.

The PnP Process

Windows NT 4.0 did not support Plug and Play (PnP) out of box, but Windows 2000 is there in a big way. Windows 2000 is fully Plug-and-Play aware, and initially has support for thousands of drivers. This is demonstrated during the installation process of Windows 2000 while you are not able to manually load a network card driver, if one is not detected. The basic Plug and Play process is broken up in the following way:

- Enumeration
- Configuration
- Conflicts and resolution

The frontline components in the Plug and Play process are the Bus Enumerators. Bus Enumerators exist for every major system bus that could be in your Windows 2000 computer; this includes ISA, PCI, USB, and other motherboard buses. It is the job of the Enumerators to contact all of the devices on the various buses and find out what they are. Each Plug and Play device is provided with a Plug and Play ID that it reports back to the Enumerator along with various resource requirements—even Plug and Play devices are limited in their scope of resources. After this has been accomplished on each bus, the results are handed over to the PnP Configuration Manager.

It is the job of the Configuration Manager to inventory all the items that have been discovered, and to decide if all the items can remain at their current configuration. If there are problems or conflicts with the current settings, the Configuration Manager will call on the Resource Arbitrators to solve problems. The Resource Arbitrators will look at all of the possible configurations and decide which combination of resources will work best. Because the OS cannot reconfigure legacy devices, they will always be allowed to stay at their current resources. Once a valid configuration has been achieved, the Resource Arbitrators let the Configuration Manager know the new configuration. The Configuration Mmanager then passes reconfiguration requests out to each of the Bus Enumerators to carry out the job of reconfiguring the destination cards or devices.

Configuring Networking

This section will briefly cover networking (it is covered in depth in Part V, "Networking Windows 2000 Professional." If you have a network card that is located during the installation of Windows 2000, you should have some knowledge of what services and protocols may be installed. Basic networking is made up of three components:

- Adapters
- Protocols
- Clients and services

Adapters are your network interface cards (NICs). They are responsible for communicating with other computers on your network. To communicate with other computers, you must be able to deliver data to other computers—this delivery mechanism utilizes a network *protocol*. Once the data arrives, you hope there is somebody at the other end who is capable of reading what you sent—this is the job of the *clients and services*.

If you do not make any changes to the default installation, you will have the TCP/IP protocol loaded, with both the Client for Microsoft Networks and File and Printer Sharing for Microsoft Networks. This will enable you to both publish and reach files on a network of Microsoft clients. You also have the ability to load the client services for NetWare.

Sysprep

Sysprep can be used to prepare a master computer for disk imaging. In the past, imaging a Windows 2000 hard drive would leave you with a computer that had a duplicate Security Identifier (SID), and that led to problems joining Windows NT domains. In addition to the SID problem, there was also a problem with loading the image onto a different model of computer. Sysprep fixes these problems.

Sysprep is an executable that can be run to remove settings from an installation of Windows 2000. You should run this utility on a freshly installed copy of Windows 2000. Sysprep supports four switches that are listed in Table 3.3.

TABLE 3.3   Sysprep Switches

Switch	Description
Quiet	Requires no user interaction.
PNP	Will require the computer to perform full Plug and Play detection on reboot.
Reboot	Forces the computer to restart rather than shutdown.
Nosidgen	Does not regenerate a new SID on restarting Setup. This should only be used if the computers are not going to be incorporated into Active Directory Services or a domain.

After running Sysprep, the computer will shutdown and can then be imaged with your choice of disk imaging software. The new computer will start a mini setup on reboot.

Automated Installations

There are many ways to automate the installation of Windows 2000. Some of these methods are complex, while others are relatively easy. This section will look at the major methods you could implement to perform your Windows 2000 installation. These methods include the following:

- Remote Installation Services (RIS)
- Setup switches for Automation
- Unattend.txt
- Uniqueness Definition Files (UDF)
- Setup Manager
- Syspart

You will now take a look at each of these methods in detail.

Remote Installation Services (RIS)

Remote Installation Services require that you have an Active Directory Service (ADS) structure already implemented on your network. RIS is a service that is loaded onto a Windows 2000 Server. It intercepts BOOTP network packets that are requesting the loading of an OS from the network. These packets are generated through a PXE (Preboot Execution) compliant network card. For this service to work, the RIS server is registered with ADS to accept these types of packets.

Once the service has been enabled, your workstation computer must be set to boot from its network card, or you must get a special boot disk from your Administrator. After this is done, you will be prompted for a username and password by the network setup application when booting. This will fetch setup options from ADS and perform the required setup. The setup options created for ADS through the Setup Manager will be discussed later in this section.

This would be a good method of installing a large number of workstations during a rollout of new workstations. But, due to its complexity in setup and execution, it is not a good solution for a small number of installations.

For information about setting up Remote Installation Services, see "Planning for Windows 2000 Deployment" in the Microsoft Windows 2000 Server Resource Kit.

Setup Switches for Automation

To perform an automated installation, you must have created some additional support files, most notably the UNATTEND.TXT and UDF files. These files can be created in a text editor and are described in the two following sections. To have Windows 2000 Setup use these files, you will have to specify them on the setup command line. The following is a sample of a command line necessary to call the Windows 2000 setup using these files.

```
Winnt /S:Z:\I386 /U:Z:\UNATTEND.TXT /UDF:COMP1,Z:\COMPUTER.UDF /T:d
```

The actual command could be either WINNT.EXE or WINNT32.EXE because they will both support these switches. /S is used to specify the source directory for the Windows 2000 Professional files. /U denotes that this is to be an unattended installation with the name of the answer files following the switch. /UDF is used to reference both the unique identifier and the file in which it will be found. The UDF allows you to override settings that may be found in the UNATTEND.TXT file. This is useful for specifying computer names and IP addresses. If the filename for the UDF is left out, you will be prompted for a floppy disk containing the $UNIQUE$.UDF file during the installation. This author has found this procedure to be hit and miss, so I recommend that you specify the filename you want to use. /T specifies the location of the temporary files. When creating the UNATTEND.TXT file, you are able to specify the directory name for your Windows directory, but not the drive on which you want it to reside; the Windows directory will be created on whichever drive you specify as your temporary files drive.

UNATTEND.TXT

The UNATTEND.TXT file is an answer file for the installation of Windows 2000. Its purpose is to answer the questions that the Setup Wizard wants to ask. This file has a specific structure, and information about its structure can be obtained by reading the Windows 2000 Resource Kit. An easier way to create this file is to use the Setup Manager application that is also found on the resource kit, as well as Microsoft's Evaluation and Deployment Kit.

The structure of the UNATTEND.TXT file is similar to that of an INI file. There are several sections, each with items and values. The basic sections are

- [Unattended]
- [GuiUnattended]
- [UserData]
- [Display]
- [LicenseFilePrintData]
- [GuiRunOnce]
- [TapiLocation]
- [RegionalSettings]
- [MassStorageDrivers]
- [OEMBootFiles]
- [OEM_Ads]
- [SetupMgr]
- [Identification]
- [Networking]
- [NetAdapters]
- [NetClients]
- [NetServices]
- [NetProtocols]
- [params.MS_TCPIP]

Microsoft usually orders the sections in this order, but the order is not important in most cases.

To give you a feel for the structure of the file, the following is an excerpt of the first three sections in a basic UNATTEND.TXT file:

```
[Unattended]
    UnattendMode=ProvideDefault
    OemPreinstall=No
    TargetPath=WINNT
    Filesystem=LeaveAlone

[GuiUnattended]
    AdminPassword=password
    TimeZone="004"
    AutoLogon=Yes
    AutoLogonCount=1


[UserData]
    ProductID=502931-270111-203418-317296-502720
    FullName=Staff
    OrgName="Acme Inc."
    ComputerName=*
```

With a properly designed file, you can avoid all user interaction. This file can be used alone or in conjunction with the UDF file described in the next section.

Uniqueness Definition Files (UDF)

UDF files are used to custom tailor UNATTEND.TXT files for specific installations. This file has entries for unique identifiers, either user names, computer names, or something else. Each entry denotes which sections should be processed. The following is an example of a UDF file.

```
[UniqueIds]
Comp1 = UserData,GuiUnattended,Network
Comp2 = UserData,GuiUnattended,Network
Comp3 = UserData,GuiUnattended,Network
Comp4 = UserData,GuiUnattended,Network
Comp5 = UserData,GuiUnattended,Network

[COMP1:Network]
DoNotInstallInternetServer = 1

[COMP1:GuiUnattended]
AdvServerType = LANMANNT

[COMP1:UserData]
```

```
FullName="Bob Smith"
OrgName="Acme Inc."
ComputerName="WORKSTATION42"

[COMP2:Network]
Workgroup = ACME_FINACE

[COMP2:GuiUnattended]
AdvServerType = LANMANNT

[COMP2:UserData]
FullName="Mary Wills"
OrgName="Acme Inc."
ComputerName="Laptop23"
```

This file would accept /UDF:COMP2 as a parameter to call the installation of Mary Wills computer named Laptop23. To make installations easier to configure, UNATTEND.TXT files and UDF can be used in conjunction. UNATTEND.TXT files can be created for each hardware type you may have in your organization; these files will contain all networking defaults such as protocols, DNS, and gateways. The UDF files can contain all computer specific data, such as computer name, IP address, and workgroup names.

Setup Manager

Setup Manager is an application designed to take the work out of creating UNATTEND.TXT and UDF files. You will find a copy of it on the Windows 2000 Professional Resource Kit; the executable is SETUPMGR.EXE. When the application opens, it will welcome you to the Windows 2000 Setup Manager Wizard. You will be able to use this program to create or edit answer files. Setup Manager can set up various types of installations for you including Professional, Server, or Sysprep (see Figure 3.8). The installation choice you make here will change some of the dialog boxes with which you are presented; for example, if you do a server installation, you will be asked about your licensing model.

FIGURE 3.8

Setup Manager can create files for any type of Windows 2000 installation.

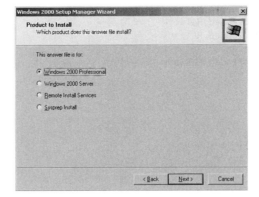

After making your choice about the product you want to install, you also have an option to choose the level of user interaction (see Figure 3.9); this can range from only setting defaults and letting the user confirm or override settings to fully automated with no user input at all.

FIGURE 3.9

Setup Manager lets you choose the level of user interaction.

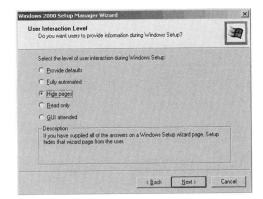

You can also set the computer name for the installation script (see Figure 3.10). If you assign multiple computer names, then Setup Manager will actually create a UDF for you, with unique ID's matching each of the computer names you provide.

FIGURE 3.10

Setup Manager can be used to create a UDF.

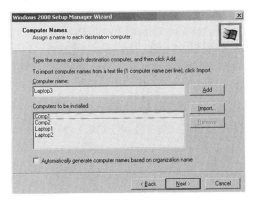

Next you will be prompted for the password for the default administrator account. There is a check box that can be used to automatically log on the administrator to complete the setup. If you choose this option, the Administrator password must be left blank.

Setup Manager then moves onto the network settings (see Figure 3.11). If you choose to go with the typical settings (which seem to be more typical every day); you will have the

Client for Microsoft Networks installed, along with TCP/IP using DHCP for configuration. For more information about configuring TCP/IP, see Chapter 17, "Setting Up TCP/IP Protocol Access," and Chapter 21, "Windows 2000 Networking Protocols."

FIGURE 3.11

Even networking can be configured through the Setup Manager.

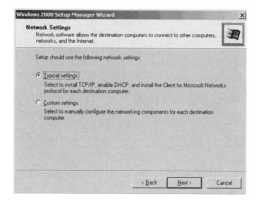

As part of networking, you will also be able to assign either a workgroup name for the computer or a domain name if it will be integrating into a Windows NT domain (see Figure 3.12). To have full access to resources, you may have to belong to a domain. If this is necessary, you will either have to have a computer account already created, or you will need to know the identity of somebody who is able to add computers to the domain.

FIGURE 3.12

To allow for full resource access, Setup Manager allows you to join a Windows NT domain.

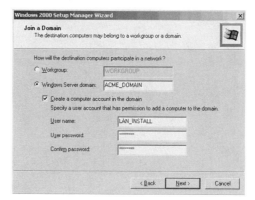

The last of the required settings is the Time Zone. This actually has as a choice, to not make a choice; but choosing not to choose, is still a choice. The default time zone is Pacific Time (U.S. and Canada)—GMT -8:00.

After choosing a time zone, you will be asked if you would like to make Additional Settings. If you choose to, you will be asked for the following:

- Telephony settings
- Regional settings
- Installation Folder
- Install Printers
- Run Once
- Distribution Folder
- Provide Additional Mass Storage Drivers
- Alternate Hardware Abstraction Layer
- Commands to Run at the End of Setup (CMDLINES.TXT)
- OEM Branding
- Copy Additional Files and Folders

At the end of all of this, you will be asked to provide the name and location that you would like to give to this UNATTEND.TXT filc. If necessary, Setup Manager will create a <UNATTEND).UDF as well, and it will always create a <UNATTEND>.BAT file that contains the setup command line.

Syspart

The Syspart switch prepares another drive to be placed in a computer and booted to complete the installation of Windows 2000. A sample command line to call Syspart would be:

```
winnt32 /unattend:UNATTEND.TXT /s:install_source /syspart:second_drive
➥/tempdrive:second_drive
```

Where *install_source* is the location of the Windows 2000 Professional source files, and *second_drive* is the drive letter associated with the first primary partition of drive that is to be removed.

After this command has finished executing, you will be able to remove the second drive from your computer and place it in the target computer. When the computer reboots, it will continue with the GUI-mode install of Windows 2000 Professional.

Finishing Touches

After completing the installation of Windows 2000 Professional, you will likely want to change some of the installed components. To do this, you will want to use the Add/Remove Programs control panel. The control panel will initially open on Change or

Remove Programs, which can be used to remove unwanted applications. If you want to add Windows Components, choose this option; this will allow you to add several optional networking components.

Summary

This chapter took you through a typical installation of Windows 2000 Professional. You were given a step-by-step breakdown of the process, as well as presented the different options for starting the installations. Additionally, you looked into upgrading from an existing copy of Windows 2000. You also saw several live methods of automating the installation of Windows 2000.

Troubleshooting the Setup

IN THIS CHAPTER

Even with the best-laid plans, things can and will go wrong; it is the nature of computers. This chapter will take a look at the best place to be prior to starting setup, how to deal with problems, and some common problems with the Windows 2000 Setup.

Ideal Setup Scenarios

The ideal setup is a setup that requires little or no troubleshooting. Whenever possible, it is good to be in the best possible situation prior to starting any installation. In the case of Windows 2000, the following are some advantageous setup situations:

- Many identical workstations
- All hardware is less than one year old from major manufacturers
- Clean installation, rather than upgrade

Because you cannot be guaranteed a trouble-free setup, if you are given any suggestions to help you, you should take that information under advisement and consider it.

Many Identical Workstations

One of the more favorable situations for a major rollout of Windows 2000 is to have several identical workstations to set up. This can sometimes be a major chore, even if you are choosing specifications and purchasing all the same model PCs from a major manufacturer.

Most manufacturers have learned, with Windows 95 and Windows 98, over the last few years, that identical should actually mean identical. It has not been uncommon to find computers that are sold as the same, having different sound or video chips integrated onto the motherboard; this gets even worse with components that are not integrated. But as I said, most major manufacturers have learned their lesson and try not to make too many component substitutions behind the scenes. If there have been changes to the components, Windows 98 or Windows 2000 will let you know by not initializing the drivers for these devices, so these changes will not be hidden for long.

If you manage to get a block of PCs that are close representations of each other, you will be able to implement some of the mass rollout features of Windows 2000. The rollout methods include:

- Disk imaging with software like Drive Copy or Ghost
- SYSPREP
- RIS (Remote Installation Service)
- Installation scripts with Setup Manager

Disk imaging, SYSPREP, and RIS each allow you to create a standard PC configuration that can then be duplicated for each workstation. This allows you to take time with the basic or initial configuration and then perform a mass duplication.

Installation scripts, on the other hand, create an installation that will take a little longer to install and also can be configured to perform application installs. The application installations will have to be scripted or repackaged to have them complete an unattended installation of the workstation.

Because all of these installation methods require completion of the full installation of at least one computer, you should be able to have all of the bugs worked out of the installation—well at least most of the bugs—prior to your rollout. Bugs would refer to updated drives or hardware configuration settings that are required to allow all of the components and applications on your system to function properly. It could also refer to items with problems that you cannot resolve, but with which you are willing to live.

All Hardware Is Less Than One Year Old from Major Manufacturers

Over the years, there have been many hardware standards that have come and gone. Some products have had a lot of staying power, while others have been discarded in short order. Some hardware that has demonstrated power include SCSI, Serial, and PCMCIA buses; while EISA, CGA, and EGA have all but disappeared. One of the new standards that is challenging to have widespread adoption is Plug and Play. While Plug and Play is not required to use a device with Windows 2000, it can make your installation run much smoother. When Plug and Play was first emerging in the market as a standard, Windows 95 adopted it as an integral part of the OS. While Windows 95 had many problems working with Plug and Play devices, it did provide a training ground for both Microsoft and device manufactures. Many of the bugs have been worked out now, and Windows 2000 appears to have Plug and Play well in hand. This is not to say that Windows 2000 does not work with older hardware.

Windows 2000 ships with a large database of drivers and is able to detect and load generic (or specific) drivers for many pieces of older hardware. Because many PCs that ship today are including many of the newer hardware components (USB, APCI, and AGP), Microsoft has taken the time to make sure that it will be able to communicate with these newer devices. This is a fine line to have to walk, follow cutting-edge technology, but not be forced into loading custom drivers for every device in your computer. By choosing newer hardware from the major vendors, you should be able to avoid this problem and many others.

Windows 2000's drivers follow a new model where the drivers are signed, tested, and certified by Microsoft. The goal of the this process is to raise the quality level in the driver code and to give the consumer the peace of mind of knowing that this driver has been tested and should not bring down your server. Not all manufacturer-supplied drivers will necessarily be signed by Microsoft, but many companies will be choosing to rollout only their Windows 2000 Professional computers with signed drivers to reduce the risk of problematic computers.

> **Note**
>
> If you want to know when you are using unsigned drivers, or prevent the use of them, you can change the setting in the System Control Panel. By choosing Driver Signing on the Hardware tab, you will be able to ignore signed driver checking, be warned before they are installed, or block the use of them all together (see Figure 4.1). The system default is to ignore checking for signed drivers. If you are a member of the Administrator's group, you are also able to make your choice of the default for the computer. If you do not make your choice of a system default, all other users will be able to make the choice for themselves.

FIGURE 4.1

Driver signing options allow you to know when you are using drivers that are not signed.

Microsoft and the larger hardware vendors have all been working together to make sure that this new OS can be rolled out on their current hardware. They have all been spending a lot of money on research and development to ensure this, making them and Microsoft look good.

Clean Installation, Rather Than Upgrade

While it is often suggested that upgrading a previous version of Windows provides the quickest and most painless type of installation, this method also can cause erratic operations and software-based failures. That would mean that the ideal setup situation may be an upgrade, unless you are planning for the future; then the ideal setup situation would be the clean installation.

The problems of an upgrade setup come from the pre-Windows 2000 installation. Most Windows installations contain remnants from installed and then removed applications, utilities, drivers, and parts of Windows itself. The most troublesome aspect of these remnants are those obsolete drivers that come from removed or upgraded hardware, as well as newer versions of the drivers themselves.

Windows 2000 Professional is a remarkably stable system when it is properly installed. However, if you install this OS over a previous system, you have a series of minuses that are applied to your system's stability. If these minuses are numerous enough, you can expect to have an unstable system.

While these scenarios are nice, you will probably find that you end up working with a mixture of systems in the real world—some the same, some different, some with new hardware, some with old hardware, some clean installations (with freshly formatted hard drives), and some upgrade installations. Hopefully this section has got you thinking about how to best approach this mish-mash of systems with which you may have to work.

Re-running Setup with Optional Switches

After installing Windows 2000, you may find yourself in a position of having to re-run Setup to upgrade to a newer version of Windows 2000 or to repair your current installation. When you do this, it is possible to use additional switches at the end of your setup command line. The WINNT32 executable supports several switches that can be used to make your installations work with less difficulty. These switches include:

- CHECKUPGRADEONLY
- CMDCONS
- DEBUG [*LEVEL*] [:*FILENAME*]
- M:*FOLDERNAME*
- MAKELOCALSOURCE
- NOREBOOT

Each of these switches have a specific purpose, and they can all be used to help automate an installation that currently requires additional interaction, to see if there should be problems, or to fix problems that you are having.

CHECKUPGRADEONLY

CHECKUPGRADEONLY performs an extensive check of your computer system, examining both OS and hardware, for potential problems that could be encountered if you chose to upgrade your system. If this switch is used, it will create a file in your Windows directory named UPGRADE.TXT (for Windows 9x), or WINNT32.LOG (for NT 3.51 or 4.0). This file contains a copy of what may not be compatible with Windows 2000. The following is an example of an UPGRADE.TXT:

```
Upgrade Report
--------------
This report describes known problems you might encounter after you
upgrade to Windows 2000. Read this report to determine the hardware
files and upgrade packs you need, then visit Microsoft on the
Internet at http://www.microsoft.com/windows/professional/, or
contact your hardware or software manufacturer.

Contents:
        Software to Reinstall
        Program Notes
        General Information

Software to Reinstall
---------------------
The following programs need to be reinstalled after the upgrade,
because they use different files and settings in Windows 2000.

    Send to Mail Recipient
    Windows Messaging (in the Start Menu)

You should remove the program before upgrading. (Many programs can be
removed using Add/Remove Programs in the Control Panel). After
upgrading to Windows 2000, you can then reinstall the program.

Program Notes
-------------
This section describes issues that might affect some of the programs
you use. Be sure to read this section before you begin the upgrade to
Windows 2000.

MGA QuickDesk</B> (in the Start Menu)

    The MGA PowerDesk utilities do not support Windows 2000. You must
    uninstall them before upgrading, because the MGA PowerDesk
```

```
        uninstaller does not work with Windows 2000.
...


General Information
------------------
This section provides important information that you need to be aware
of before you upgrade.

Network Drives

Setup will not look for programs on the following network drives:

    h:\
    i:\

Disk Space

    Your computer does not have enough free disk space to install
    Windows 2000. You need at least 905 MB free on drive C:\.


DOS Configuration

    ...


Recycle Bin

    Setup found 3 files in your Recycle Bin. If you continue
    upgrading to Windows 2000, these files will be deleted.


Windows Messaging Services

    Setup has detected a version of messaging (MAPI) that does not
    function on Windows 2000.  Obtain an upgrade pack for your e-mail
    program, or reinstall it after upgrading to Windows 2000.
```

This file's sections will let you know what you should watch for. During the running of the executable, you will see the report and will be able to view it within the application or save the report to a location other than the default.

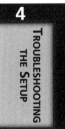

CMDCONS

CMDCONS allows you to install the Recovery Console. This tool lets you do some rudimentary repairs of your Windows 2000 system. The Recovery Console will be discussed in the "Recovery Command Console" section later in this chapter.

DEBUG [*LEVEL*] [:*FILENAME*]

The DEBUG switch allows you to change the level of recording that WINNT32 does. By specifying the level, you are able to get Setup to perform the following logging: 0—severe errors, 1—errors, 2—warnings, 3—information, and 4—detailed information for debugging. Each level will also record information that is more critical than the logging level. For example, warnings will log warnings, errors, and severe errors.

The default log filename is C:\WINNT32.LOG, but with the optional filename parameter. This file can be created anywhere.

M:*FOLDERNAME*

The M switch tells Setup to retrieve some installation files from an alternate location. The alternate location is passed as a parameter, and is checked first before reading files from their default location. Alternate installation files may be required to get some custom hardware components to work with Windows 2000. Although most hardware that is used in systems is standard, larger manufacturers, such as IBM and Compaq, sometimes customize components. This procedure will allow you to bypass applying post installation patches that are provided by some hardware manufacturers.

MAKELOCALSOURCE

MAKELOCALSOURCE will copy all of the source files that are required to install Windows 2000 to your hard drive during the start of the installation of Windows 2000. This means that you will require more hard drive space to perform the installation, but you will also not need the Windows 2000 CD-ROM after the first reboot. This can be useful if Windows 2000 is having a difficult time reading from your CD-ROM after the reboot. The source files should take close to 300 MB when copied to your hard drive.

NOREBOOT

The NOREBOOT switch tells WINNT32 just that, do not reboot when you are finished copying the setup files to hard drive. This is useful if you want to issue additional commands prior to the completion of the installation of Windows 2000. Some things you may want to accomplish with this switch include:

- Early starting of Setup on a computer that is still performing a production purpose. Starting the installation of Windows 2000 on a computer that is currently being used for business purposes may not be an appropriate thing to do.

- Preparing a disk to be duplicated to complete the actual installation of the OS when the image is installed onto another computer

These are some of the installation switches that you may want to re-run a setup with, to have it complete successfully.

The Clean Install Fall Back

If you finish the installation of Windows 2000 and find that the installation does not work properly, Microsoft has given you an easy fix. When you run WINNT32 on a computer that already has Windows 2000 installed on it, it gives you a choice to perform an upgrade on a clean installation (see Figure 4.2). The clean installation will allow you to replace the current Windows directory with a new one. One drawback of the clean installation is that you must reinstall all of your applications because any of their files in the Windows directory and entries in the Registry will be gone. This may not be a bad thing, if you are actually going to have a computer that will be able to run your applications. This is often something you will do if you have problems after performing an upgrade.

FIGURE 4.2
Clean installations will allow you to get rid of unused files in your Windows directory.

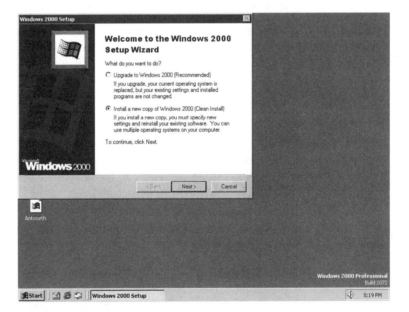

Facing Setup Failure

It is too much to hope for that all your installations will work the first time you attempt them. It is unfortunate, but it is likely that you will have several occasions when it seems like nothing you try will work. With the complexity of computers, the possible configurations, and the OSs, it is really amazing that any of it actually works. This section will take a look at some of the things that can go wrong and what you can do to attempt to get Windows 2000 Professional installed. The topics that will be covered include the following:

- Drivers.
- ACPI (Advanced Configuration and Power Interface).
- Motherboard and BIOS.
- OverClocked motherboards.
- Preference on installation method.
- Extraneous items in boot menu.
- Not sure of hardware, or you suspect a conflict.
- There are hangs or blue screens.

This by far is not a complete list of things that can go wrong with your installation, but it is definitely a list of some things that will help you with your installations. To make a list of everything that could go wrong would be like creating a list of the names of everybody in the world; it is too big and constantly growing.

Drivers

One of the things that this author has experienced is getting devices to work. These devices range from audio devices to video cards, and everything in between. Many devices will either expect you to have the drivers included with your OS or will include a set of drivers for the device. The drivers that they have decided to include are fairly recent, usually less than a year old, but this will not help much if the copy of the device you received has been sitting in your retailer's inventory for the last year because that makes the drivers two years old.

It is often best to let the OS try to pick a driver. If it is not able to choose an appropriate driver, you should go straight to the vendor's Web site and see if it has a version of the driver for you. Poorly chosen drivers can cause a wide variety of problems, ranging from a device that just does not work, to a computer that now has STOP events at bootup (Blue screens).

Many people will try to be cutting edge and only get the latest and greatest, but you should exercise some restraint when locating your drivers. Many companies are now allowing you to receive and use beta (pre-release) versions of their drivers. This may be useful for fixing a new problem with the device, but often the problem you are having is only new to you. If there is an option to download a beta version of the drivers you need and you cannot resist the urge, also pick up a copy of the driver—just in case you need to go back a step.

When you are having problems with a device, you can check the driver provider, date, and version in the Device Manager. To get to the Device Manager, open the System control panel and choose its button on the Hardware tab. After locating the device in question, right click it and get its properties.

ACPI (Advanced Configuration and Power Interface)

ACPI is supposed to make everyone's life so much easier than it was before. The purpose of ACPI is to take the responsibility of power management away from the system BIOS and give it to the OS. The benefit you derive from this is greater control over the whole power management environment because the BIOS is only really able to turn devices on or off. The problem arises when Windows 2000 Setup has a problem dealing with these devices. A typical symptom is that the computer hangs while Setup is starting, to which there are two solutions: Tell the computer you just have an ordinary PC, or disable ACPI altogether during the Setup.

If you choose to attempt to tell Windows 2000 Setup that you have an ordinary computer, you will have to wait for the initial Setup screen that prompts you to press the F6 key to load a third-party SCSI controller. When you see this prompt, you should quickly press the F5 key. This will cause Setup to continue and attempt to load a couple more components. Setup will then tell you that it was unable to determine that type of computer you have. This screen will give you the following choices:

- MPS Multiprocessor PC
- Standard PC
- Standard PC with C-Step i486
- Other

This allows you to choose a specific Hardware Abstraction Layer (HAL) for your Windows 2000 installation. Unless you are using a multi-processor computer or one that contains a C-Step designed motherboard (see hardware documentation for details), you should choose Standard PC to continue. If you have a specific type of computer that does include a Windows 2000 PC Configuration disk, you could also choose Other and then provide the disk when prompted.

To disable ACPI, you will have a little more work to do. First you should go into your system BIOS and tell it to disable ACPI—this is not required, but sometimes it does help. Then you can attempt the first portion of the setup. After running WINNT or WINNT32 from the Windows 2000 Professional CD-ROM, you will be prompted to reboot. You must then break into the reboot process; this can be done with a bootable floppy disk. It's also a good idea to put a copy of the Windows 9x EDIT.COM on this disk. When you reboot, locate the WIN_NT.~BT directory that contains the text file TXTSETUP.SIF. You will have to edit this file and change the ACPI section that should appear as follows:

```
[ACPIOptions]
ACPIEnable = 2
ACPIBiosDate = 01,01,1999
```

You will have to change the ACPIEnable entry to 0. The values represent: 0, ACPI will be disabled during the install; 1, ACPI will be enabled if there is an ACPI BIOS detected; and 2, ACPI will be enabled if the ACPI BIOS matches a version and date that is on the GoodACPIBios list. In most cases, it will default to 2. If you are starting your setup from the setup boot disks, TXTSETUP.SIF will be located on your first boot disk.

Motherboard and BIOS

Like always checking for new drivers, it seems that every device now comes with an upgradeable flash BIOS. There was a time—not so long ago—that this was only done with motherboards, and even that is kind of new. Now I can flash upgrade my motherboard, modem, NIC, and probably even my video card—although I have not had to yet. Most BIOS upgrades attempt to fix problems or improve performance, and, while this is admirable, some actually create new problems. This means that the latest BIOS revision is not always the best. Many manufacturers allow you download BIOS upgrades from their Web sites—usually buried deep in the product support section—and have now started including the second most recent BIOS for just that reason.

This means that if you are having a problem with the Windows 2000 installation, or if something is not working correctly, another avenue you have open to you is the BIOS. You can upgrade or downgrade your BIOS to see if the problem is fixed. I would check the manufacturer's Web site to see what the supposed fixes implemented in the BIOS are, and then decide if you want to upgrade. This can be a dangerous thing to do. If the process is interrupted or you use the wrong BIOS, you can be left with a motherboard that is useless.

> **Tip**
>
> If you are having a problem identifying your motherboard, you can try the http://www.motherboards.org Web site. This site can do a search of its database on a portion of the BIOS ID string. The ID string shows up when you reboot your computer during or just after the system post.

OverClocked Motherboards

If you want to get more bang for your buck, you can overclock your motherboard. Your CPU comes with a supported clock speed and expects you to install the chip in a computer running at fraction of the CPU speed. You motherboard has a clock speed and a processor bus multiplier. These settings allow you to take a 150MHz processor and place it on a motherboard that is running at 60MHz with a multiplier of 2.5. To overclock this computer, you could increase the motherboard speed—thus overclocking all the chipsets—to 66MHz and get a 165MHz computer; or you could increase the multiplier to 3.0 and get a 180MHz computer. Because the manufacturers of these computers want to make sure they at least meet their standards, they usually attempt to exceed them.

This process sounds attractive, but you should remember that not all CPUs are created equal, and some will not respond well to overclocking. Problems that can occur range from flaky, random errors to a CPU that will never boot again.

When dealing with an overclocked CPU, you may find that Setup will often hang. If you return your CPU to its regular speed, you should be able to complete the Windows 2000 installation. Some people have found that they are able to return their computers to the overclocked state afterwards. But once again, overclocking is not recommended or supported by most manufacturers.

> **Note**
>
> Your operating system will not be able to tell you if your computer has been overclocked. To find out, you will have to examine both your processor and your motherboard. Many new motherboards will allow you to see and change clocking speeds in the system BIOS, while others will require you to check and move jumpers. This will require your motherboard documentation. Rated clock speeds for your processor are usually written on the top or the bottom of your processor. To read these, you will have to open your PC and either remove the processor fan or the processor itself. Do not attempt this if you are not familiar with the process because it can result in damage to your computer or personal injury.

4

TROUBLESHOOTING THE SETUP

Preference of Installation Method

"Should I install Windows 2000 by booting from floppies, another OS, or the CD-ROM?" The answer is, you should use what your computer will allow to be used. I have been in situations where some of these methods will not work, even with my patience. Oftentimes, the installation will hang at different locations or fail at one of the system reboots.

It is hard to say whether the problems are related to hardware or software, but they seem to be hardware related in many cases. If you are installing from another OS, perhaps Windows 2000 does not like how the boot sector looks on that particular model of hard drive. If this is the case, make the boot sector look different. You can make the boot sector look different by deleting your partitions and creating them during the Windows 2000 setup that you started from floppy or bootable CD-ROM. I have seen entire groups of the same model computer that either had to be started from floppy or started without floppy; there seems to be no fixed pattern. I have also seen computers that appear to hang for up to 15 minutes before continuing with the installation.

The best rule to follow is to not be fixed on one installation method. Be prepared to change your installation method if it appears not to work.

After an Interrupted Setup, The New Setup Has Multiple Identical Options During Bootup

This is a problem caused by having spurious entries in `BOOT.INI`. To solve it, you should

1. Boot using an OS that is capable of reading the C drive. If the drive is still FAT, you could use a DOS floppy disk. After you have booted the computer, you can bring up a command prompt or MS-DOS prompt.

2. Enter the following command

   ```
   attrib -r -s -h c:\BOOT.INI
   ```

   to allow you to edit the file. To be safe, copy this file to another name, such as `Boot.bak`. This will allow you to restore your setup in the case of an editing error.

3. Launch an editor, such as DOS's EDIT. Figure 4.3 shows a `BOOT.INI` file with some spurious entries loaded into Notepad.

4. Edit out the spurious entries.

5. Save the file.

When you reboot, you'll be rid of those extra entries.

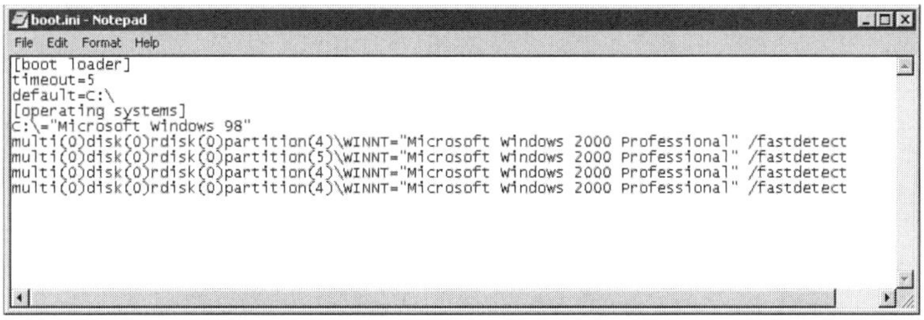

FIGURE 4.3

An interrupted Windows 2000 Professional setup can result in double vision.

```
boot.ini - Notepad
File  Edit  Format  Help
[boot loader]
timeout=5
default=C:\
[operating systems]
C:\="Microsoft Windows 98"
multi(0)disk(0)rdisk(0)partition(4)\WINNT="Microsoft Windows 2000 Professional" /fastdetect
multi(0)disk(0)rdisk(0)partition(5)\WINNT="Microsoft Windows 2000 Professional" /fastdetect
multi(0)disk(0)rdisk(0)partition(4)\WINNT="Microsoft Windows 2000 Professional" /fastdetect
multi(0)disk(0)rdisk(0)partition(4)\WINNT="Microsoft Windows 2000 Professional" /fastdetect
```

Setup or Windows 2000 Professional Runs Erratically or Freezes with a Blue Screen on Startup

These symptoms stem from a huge array of issues, but you can eradicate many of them by taking the following steps:

1. Run the Computer Management administration utility, either from the Administrative Tools control panel or from Programs in the Start menu, and open \SYSTEM TOOLS\SYSTEM INFORMATION\HARDWARE RESOURCES (see Figure 4.4). You will then be able to choose CONFLICTS\SHARING to see any listed conflicts or any of the resource areas like IRQs, MEMORY, or DMA. Check very carefully to make sure no devices are trying to use the same base addresses, address ranges, IRQ, or other system resources.

FIGURE 4.4

The System Information tool is now the replacement for WinMSD.

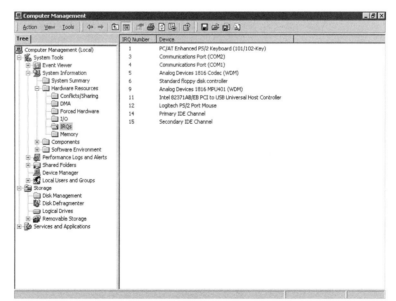

4

TROUBLESHOOTING
THE SETUP

2. Disable L2 cache in BIOS setup.

3. Disable any BIOS or video shadowing in BIOS setup.

4. Make sure there aren't any startup errors unrelated to the Windows 2000 installation. Can you boot into MS-DOS using a floppy?

5. If all else fails, remove all optional hardware from your computer. If Windows 2000 runs normally after this removal, add the hardware back one piece at a time until Windows 2000 returns to its unstable state. This should identify your culprit.

6. Run the Computer Management administration utility and open \SYSTEM TOOLS\DEVICE MANAGER and examine each device for possible conflicts (see Figure 4.5).

FIGURE 4.5

The properties for each device will tell you if there are any conflicts.

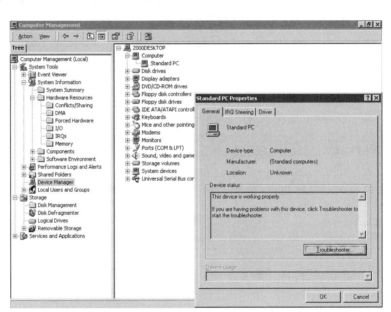

7. Open one of the troubleshooters. From the Start menu, choose Help, switch to the Index tab, and type the word **TROUBLESHOOTERS**. This will give you a list of all the troubleshooters that are available (see Figure 4.6). Choose the troubleshooter that matches the problems you are having. After answering a series of questions, you may be presented with the suggestion that fixes your problem.

FIGURE 4.6

There are many troubleshooters to help you solve your problem.

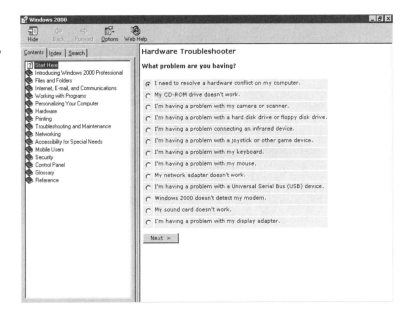

Because Windows 2000 is a complex set of programs that join together to form an operating system, sometimes the smallest thing can cause problems. Of the items mentioned in this section, most should not cause problems with your operating system, but apparently do.

Failure after Successful Setup

After Windows 2000 is installed, you may find that it continues to boot without any problems until one day when you power on your computer and find that it will not successfully boot up. This section will describe some common problems and their solutions.

The Computer Fails to Boot after a Successful POST (Positive On Self Test)

These problems stem from major system errors. The following are some of the reasons:

- Corrupted Master Boot Record (MBR)
- Lost or incorrect CMOS information
- Corrupt partition information
- The boot loader, NTLDR, is corrupt
- A peripheral card has lost contact with the mainboard
- A peripheral, such as a tape drive, has been left in an uncertain state

4

TROUBLESHOOTING
THE SETUP

To isolate the problem, see if you can boot into DOS using a floppy disk. If so, you may need to rerun Setup and perform a repair of the installation. If not, you'll need to diagnose your system to clear up the hardware error. In cases where hardware has entered an uncertain state, Windows 2000 Professional will not soft-boot but will boot all right after a complete power-down and startup. This resets most hardware, thus clearing most uncertain states.

If you think the problem is related to either the partition table or the MBR, you can use either FDISK—with some data loss—or the Recovery Console—covered later in this chapter in the "Recovery Command Console" section. Some third-party utilities claim to be able to restore lost partition tables or MBRs. The Resource Kit for Windows 2000 Professional has a utility, DSKPROBE.EXE, that will allow you to examine and, to a limited extent, fix both the table and the MBR.

Most errors of this type result in your having to run FDISK—to restore the partition—and then setup Windows 2000 Professional.

> **Note**
>
> Each fixed or hard drive in a computer has its own MBR. Windows 2000 Professional uses the MBR only on the first disk during startup.

Windows 2000 Startup Fails after the Boot Loader Initiates

Ifyour Windows 2000 install hangs during the blue screen, you probably have developed a hardware, driver, or hardware detection problem.

To get your computer to a bootable state, reboot and press the F8 key when the boot menu appears onscreen. (If the boot menu does not appear, read the "Boot Errors" section later in this chapter.) The boot menu gives you the following additional options:

```
Windows 2000 Advanced Options Menu
Please select an option:

        Safe Mode
        Safe Mode with Networking
        Safe Mode with Command Prompt

        Enable Boot Logging
        Enable VGA Mode
        Last Known Good Configuration
        Directory Services Restore Mode (Windows 2000 domain controllers only)
        Debugging Mode
```

```
Use [arrowup] and [arrowdown] to move the highlight to your choice.
Press Enter to choose.

Press ESCAPE to disable safeboot and boot normally
```

This menu allows you to boot into Safe Mode, which will load a limited number of drivers during the boot process, or Last Known Good Configuration, which will ignore the last set of configuration changes you made. By using Safe Mode, you keep your changes and can attempt to fix the problem yourself. If Safe Mode does not work, you will still have the option to use the Last Known Good Configuration.

If you suspect the problem is related to your RAM, you can use the MAXMEM switch in BOOT.INI. This switch can be added to the end of the boot-loaded item in BOOT.INI to limit the amount of physical memory that is used. Windows 2000 will use the RAM in its physical order in your computer. Because 32MB is the minimum amount of memory recommended for Windows 2000, you should not limit the RAM below that. A sample boot item from BOOT.INI would be

```
multi(0)disk(0)rdisk(0)partition(4)\WINNT="Microsoft Windows 2000 Professional"
➥/fastdetect /MAXMEM:32
```

This line would limit the memory to 32MB.

You get a Stop 0x0000007B Error

This error comes from an inaccessible or corrupt Partition Boot Sector. To solve this problem you can try the following:

1. *You have a virus*—Boot into DOS and run a virus scan/cleaner or use the software provided on the Windows 2000 Professional CD-ROM in SUPPORT\CA_ANTIV. This is a copy of InoculateIT AntiVirus AVBoot V1.1 that can be used to scan for and disinfect boot sector viruses.

2. *You have activated LBA after partitioning the disk*—Deactivate it. If you want to run LBA, you need to repartition the disk with LBA active and then re-setup Windows 2000 Professional.

3. *You have a mechanical problem that has corrupted your Partition Boot Sector*— You need to fix or replace the bad hardware, and then see whether there is anything you can salvage from the existing setup. Usually there isn't much, if anything, salvageable, and you need to run Setup again.

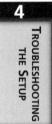

4

TROUBLESHOOTING
THE SETUP

Booting Up

This section will take a look at the boot process in detail and let you see what is happening during the entire process. It will also identify possible errors that can occur. These topics will be covered in the following order:

- The process
- The function of `BOOT.INI`
- Boot reference
- Boot errors

The Process

The entire boot process starts with the application of power to your computer. When the power makes its way to the BIOS ROMs on your computer, the BIOS ROMs start a process known as POST (Power On Self Test). During this test phase, POST will examine the memory on your computer and identify possible bad memory, check to see what types of drives are present, examine the presence of serial and parallel ports, look for a bus mouse, and locate a Master Boot Record (MBR) on a bootable drive.

Once a bootable device is found, your computer will read the Master Boot Record to find out what program is supposed to be loaded. Due to the space limits in the MBR, Windows 2000 will redirect it to the program called `NTLDR`.

`NTLDR` will switch the memory model to a flat memory model—ignoring the 640KB memory limit—treating memory as a continuous block. `NTLDR` will also read the `BOOT.INI` file and display the boot menu to you. After choosing to boot some version of Windows 2000, `NTLDR` will call on `NTDETECT.COM`.

`NTDETECT.COM` will perform a complete system test—similar to the POST. This test will examine your hard drives, serial ports, parallel ports, memory, keyboard bus, mouse bus, and processor type. After determining what hardware is present, `NTDETECT.COM` returns the hardware list tree to `NTLDR`, which then attempts to load the version of Windows 2000 that you selected. The hardware tree will eventually be loaded into the registry in `HKEY_LOCAL_MACHINE\HARDWARE`.

`NTLDR` then locates `NTOSKRNL` in the `SYSTEM32` folder of your Windows 2000 directory. When `NTOSKRNL` is loaded with `HAL.DLL`, control will be passed over to it. At this time, the rest of the OS will be loaded, and devices and services will be started up.

The Function of BOOT.INI

The BOOT.INI file is responsible for keeping track of different boot sectors that exist on your computer. It really does not do much in the way of detecting them because it is only a text file containing the locations of the boot sectors. Windows 2000 will create this file for you during the initial installation of Windows 2000, but you can create or modify this file yourself.

The BOOT.INI file has two basic sections: Boot Loader and Operating Systems. The Boot Loader section contains the boot menu time as well as the default OS that is supposed to be loaded. The Operating Systems section contains a list of the operating systems of which BOOT.INI is aware.

When Windows 2000 creates this file, it makes it Hidden, System, and Read-Only. If you want to change these attributes, you can get the properties of the BOOT.INI file—if you can see it—or you can use the following command:

```
ATTRIB -S -H -R C:\BOOT.INI
```

This command can be issued from a command prompt or from the Run command. Unlike some OS files, Windows 2000 does not care what attributes are on the BOOT.INI file, but you may want to re-apply the correct attributes to the file to prevent it from be modified by accident.

Because BOOT.INI is a text file, you can open it and edit it with your favorite text editor, such as Notepad. This allows you to add switches to the load items in the BOOT.INI file. Your BOOT.INI file should look something like the following:

```
[boot loader]
timeout=5
default=C:\
[operating systems]
C:\="Microsoft Windows 98"
multi(0)disk(0)rdisk(0)partition(4)\WINNT="Microsoft Windows 2000 Professional"
➥/fastdetect
multi(0)disk(0)rdisk(0)partition(5)\WINNT="Microsoft Windows 2000 Professional -
➥Regular" /fastdetect
multi(0)disk(0)rdisk(0)partition(4)\WINNT="Microsoft Windows 2000 Professional -
➥Test" /fastdetect
```

Boot Reference

If you think the contents of the BOOT.INI looks odd, you are correct. Rather than using terms with which you are more familiar, like C:\ or D:\, Microsoft has gone with multi(0)disk(0)rdisk(0)partition(1)\ and multi(0)disk(1)rdisk(0) partition(1)\. This strange formatting for the partitions is referred to as an *ARC*

4

TROUBLESHOOTING
THE SETUP

pathname. ARC stands for Advanced RISC Computing. The individual components that make up the ARC name are as follows:

- `multi` or `SCSI` refers to which bus—whether it is an AT-bus or a SCSI-bus—the system uses to access the Windows 2000 partition. This is confusing because SCSI is only used if the `WINNT` directory is located on a controller that has its SCSI BIOS disabled. If the BIOS is enabled, both SCSI and IDE devices are referred to using `multi`. For example, the first controller in IDE is `multi(0)`, the second, `multi(1)`, and so on.

- `disk` is the SCSI ID of the target device and is always `0` for multi devices.

- `rdisk` specifies the disk device on the multi controller that is to be accessed. The first drive on the controller's bus would be device `0`, the second would be device `1`, and so on. It is usually a number between 0 and 3. This number is also used to specify the SCSI Logical Unit Number (LUN) and is usually `0` for SCSI.

- `partition` specifies the partition that is to be accessed. This is the only case in ARC names that the first device is actually numbered `1`. Unlike the drive letters, partition numbers only apply to the specified drive. But, like drive letters, primary partitions are always numbered first. If you had a drive that already had Windows 98 installed on drive C—the first primary partition—and chose to install Windows 2000 on drive D, the first logical drive of the extended partition, Windows 2000 would be booting from partition(2). If, at a later date, you choose to create another new primary partition on your drive, Windows 2000 would boot from partition(3), even though Windows 2000 may still refer to the logical drive as D. Partition(2) would now be the newly created primary partition. Only the used spaces on your drive are assigned partition numbers.

If you can't boot Windows 2000 Professional after installing it, check to see that all the entries in the `BOOT.INI` have been set to the correct values, based on the previous description of the entries. If you have installed Windows 2000 onto a FAT partition, you will only have to boot with a DOS-bootable diskette to modify the `BOOT.INI` file. If the partition has been formatted with NTFS, you will have to create a Windows 2000 boot disk to access the system. To create this disk, you will need access to a Windows 2000 computer and then follow these steps:

1. Format a floppy disk using Windows 2000.
2. Copy these hidden files from the root of the C drive to the floppy: `NTLDR`, `NTDETECT.COM`, `BOOT.INI`, and `NTBOOTDD.SYS`, if it exists.

> **Note**
>
> The NTBOOTDD.SYS file should only exist if you installed Windows 2000 onto a disk that was using a SCSI controller with the BIOS disabled. The file is actually the SCSI driver for that adapter. While NTLDR and NTDETECT.COM are generic between systems, NTBOOTDD.SYS and BOOT.INI are specific to each computer. BOOT.INI can be edited with a text editor to have it function on other computers.

3. Modify the Read-Only file BOOT.INI to match the boot requirements of your computer.

4. Boot your computer with this disk.

If you have made the correct changes, your system will boot. You can then make the equivalent changes to the BOOT.INI file on your hard drive.

Boot Errors

You have now seen the basics of a system boot, examined the BOOT.INI file in some detail, and seen which files are required for booting your system into Windows 2000. This section will now examine some common errors that can occur due to missing or corrupt files. These files are

- NTLDR
- NTDECT.COM
- NTOSKRNL
- BOOT.INI

As with releases of Microsoft Windows NT Workstation, the boot process is often the area where the majority of troubleshooting occurs. Whether you are repairing corrupted boot files, such as the BOOT.INI or NTLDR, or tracking down conflicting IRQs, getting your hardware and Windows 2000 to cooperate can sometimes be a time-consuming process. Ultimately, though, understanding Windows 2000's boot process helps increase your fundamental knowledge of the operating system and provides a good building block toward understanding its more complex functions and capabilities.

Boot NTLDR Not Found

When you attempt to reboot your computer, you may receive the following message:

```
NTLDR is missing
Press any key to restart
```

4

TROUBLESHOOTING THE SETUP

When you receive this message, the first thing you should check is if you have left a floppy disk in your drive. When a disk is formatted using Windows NT or Windows 2000, the command in the boot sector launches NTLDR. If the file is not present, you will see the previous message. If you do not have a floppy disk in the drive, you should check to make sure the active partition on your hard drive is correct. If both of these items check out, you likely have a corrupt or missing NTLDR file. This file is found on the root of system partition.

> **Note**
>
> Microsoft defines the boot partition as the partition from which the Windows 2000 operating system boots. This is the partition that contains the <Windows 2000 folder>\SYSTEM32\NTOSKRNL.EXE. The system partition is the partition that contains the drive with the boot sector, NTLDR, NTDETECT.COM, NTBOOTDD.SYS (if present), and BOOT.INI.

To fix a corrupt or missing NTLDR, you will have to replace it with a good copy. If you have created a boot disk (as mentioned in the "Boot Reference" section earlier in this chapter), you will be able to boot the computer with that disk and copy the file from the floppy. If you have not created a boot disk, you can create it on another computer that is currently running Windows 2000. If that doesn't work, you will have to use the original four setup disks and the CD-ROM to perform an emergency repair. This will be discussed in Chapter 26, "Disaster Recovery."

NTDETECT Failed

If NTLDR works and performs its job, you may still encounter the following message:

```
NTDETECT failed
```

NTDETECT.COM is responsible for building a hardware tree for Intel-based computers. It scans for all basic hardware present on your computer. If you receive this error, you can restore NTDETECT.COM by using the same methods that were used to restore NTLDR.

Missing NTOSKRNL

There is a small chance—less if your System and Boot partitions are one in the same—that <Windows 2000 folder>\SYSTEM32\NTOSKRNL.EXE is actually missing. If this is the case, you will receive the following message:

```
Windows 2000 could not start because the following file is missing or corrupt:
<windows 2000 root>\system32\ntoskrnl.exe.
Please re-install a copy of the above file.
```

This message is usually due to a problem with the `BOOT.INI` file, rather than with the `NTOSKRNL.EXE` file. When troubleshooting, you should first examine the `BOOT.INI` file—problems with the `BOOT.INI` file will be discussed next. If there are no problems with the `BOOT.INI` file, you can assume that the problem is with the `NTOSKRNL.EXE` file.

If `NTOSKRNL.EXE` is actually missing, you will have to perform an emergency repair to replace this file and all other changed or missing files.

`BOOT.INI` Problems

Problems with the `BOOT.INI` file can actually cause a variety of error messages. The three most common will be discussed here.

If your `BOOT.INI` file is missing, but Windows 2000 is installed in the default location (`C:\WINNT`), you will see the following message:

```
Please select the operating system to start:

Windows 2000 (default)
```

This will not create a new `BOOT.INI` file for you, but it will display the boot menu to allow you to use the Advanced Options during the boot. This message will only show up if Windows 2000 has been installed to the default location. It is for this reason that you should attempt to install Windows 2000 to the default location whenever possible. This is excluded when another OS is already installed to drive C, either Windows 9x or Windows NT.

If you have an invalid device from which you are attempting to boot Windows 2000, you may get the following message:

```
Windows 2000 could not start because of a computer disk hardware
configuration problem.
Could not read from the selected boot disk. Check boot path
and disk hardware.
Please check the Windows 2000(TM) documentation about hardware
disk configuration and your hardware reference manuals for
additional information.
```

This message will occur if you are referencing either a disk controller or a disk with which `NTLDR` cannot communicate. This is likely a error in your `BOOT.INI` when referring to the disk or controller number, but it could also occur if you have prepped a disk for install in another computer and it is not configured correctly in your new computer.

If you have referred to your controllers and disks correctly but have directed `NTLDR` to a controller, disk, or directory that does not contain a copy of Windows 2000, you will receive the following message:

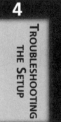

```
Windows 2000 could not start because the following file is missing or corrupt:
<windows 2000 root>\system32\ntoskrnl.exe.
Please re-install a copy of the above file.
```

As mentioned earlier, this could be caused by a corrupt NTOSKRNL.EXE file, but it is more likely that it's an error in the BOOT.INI. It could mean that you have directed NTLDR to a valid controller, disk, partition, or directory, but it was not a correct path. If there was a problem communicating with the controller, you would have received the earlier message about a hardware or configuration problem. This message is telling you that the hardware is fine, NTLDR just cannot find the NTOSKRNL.EXE file.

Unlike the other files that are required to successfully boot Windows 2000, the BOOT.INI file can cause a variety of errors, even misleading ones—like the missing NTOSKRNL.EXE file. While all of these files are required to boot your computer, it is useful to know what errors you can expect when you are having problems with your computer because it can greatly reduce the amount of time it takes to troubleshoot your errors.

Recovery Command Console

The Recovery Console is designed to give you one more chance before having to reinstall Windows 2000. It gives you command-line access to your system and boot partitions so you will be able to perform rudimentary error correction and troubleshooting. There are two ways to get to the Recovery Console: by installing it or by using the emergency repair processes.

If you choose to access the Recovery Console through the emergency repair process, you will have to initially boot your computer from the first setup disk and follow the instructions to insert all four disks in succession. When you complete this process, you will be given the choice of repairing a Windows 2000 installation or starting a new installation. If you choose to repair the installation, you will then be asked if you want to repair the installation using the emergency repair process or the Recovery Console. If you choose the Recovery Console, it will be launched from the Windows 2000 Professional CD-ROM.

If you choose to install the Recovery Console to your hard drive, you will have to run the following command from within Windows 2000:

```
WINNT32.EXE /CMDCONS
```

This command will install the Recovery Console onto your hard drive in a CMDCONS directory off the root of your System partition. When you install the Recovery Console, your BOOT.INI file will be modified to include booting to the Recovery Console. The following is an example of a BOOT.INI file:

```
[boot loader]
timeout=10
default=multi(0)disk(0)rdisk(0)partition(1)\WINNT
[operating systems]
multi(0)disk(0)rdisk(0)partition(1)\WINNT="Microsoft Windows 2000 Professional"
➡/fastdetect
C:\CMDCONS\BOOTSECT.DAT="Microsoft Windows 2000 Recovery Console" /cmdcons
```

After booting to Recovery Console, you will be asked to which Windows 2000 installation you would like to connect. If you only have one, the correct choice is 1. You will also be asked to provide the Administrator's password for that installation prior to being given access to the installation. The Recovery Console has several commands that are included with it; these range from normal DOS commands to Windows 2000-specific commands.

The basic DOS type file management commands are listed in Table 4.1.

TABLE 4.1 Basic File Management Commands

Command	Description
ATTRIB	Sets or changes the file attributes for a file.
	Syntax:
	ATTRIB -R¦+R¦-S¦+S¦-H¦+H *filename*
	+ Sets an attribute
	- Clears an attribute
	R Read-only file attribute
	S System file attribute
	H Hidden file attribute
	This version of ATTRIB only lets you change one attribute at a time.
CD or CHDIR	Shows the name of the current directory, or changes the current directory.
	Syntax:
	CHDIR [*path*]
	CHDIR [..]
	CHDIR [*drive:*]
	CD [*path*]
	CD [..]
	CD [*drive:*]
	.. Represents the parent directory
	CD drive: Displays the name of the current directory for that drive

continues

4

TABLE 4.1 continued

Command	Description
	Quotations should be used if the path being specified contains spaces.
	You will only be able to change to directories in the current Windows installation, the root of the disk, and local source files.
CLS	Clears the screen.
COPY	This command copies a file to another location.
	Syntax:
	`COPY source [destination]`
	Where *source* is the path and name of the file that is being copied, and *destination* is the path to the directory or filename to which the file is being copied.
	The *source* and *destination* directories must be the current Windows installation, source files, the root directory of the drive, or the CMDCONS directory.
	For security, only the *source* is able to be removable media.
	This version of the COPY command does not support wildcards, but will automatically expand files that are copied from the Windows installation CD-ROM.
DEL or DELETE	This command deletes a file.
	Syntax:
	`DEL [drive:][path]filename`
	`DELETE [drive:][path]filename`
	The delete commands have the same directory limitations as the COPY command.
DIR	DIR will display the contents of a directory.
	Syntax:
	`DIR [drive:][path][filename]`
	DIR is capable of displaying all files in a directory, including hidden and system files.
	The following is a list of attributes that can be applied to a file:
	D Directory
	R Read-only
	H Hidden file
	A Files ready for archiving

Command	Description
	s System file
	c Compressed
	E Encrypted
	P Reparse Point
	DIR has the same limit of directories as the COPY command.
FORMAT	Prepares a partition for use with Windows 2000.
	Syntax:
	FORMAT [*drive:*] [/Q] [/FS:*filesystem*]
	Where Q is used to perform a quick format, and FS specifies the type of file system to be used (FAT, FAT32, or NTFS).
HELP	Find correct syntax for a command.
	Syntax:
	command_name /?
	HELP *command_name*
MD or MKDIR	MD is used to create a directory.
	Syntax:
	MKDIR [*drive:*]*path*
	MD [*drive:*]*path*
	MD has the same limitation of directories as the COPY command.
RD or RMDIR	RD is used to remove or delete a directory.
	Syntax:
	RMDIR [*drive:*]*path*
	RD [*drive:*]*path*
	RMDIR has the same limitation of directories as the COPY command.
REN	REN is used to rename a file.
	Syntax:
	RENAME [*drive:*][*path*]*filename1 filename2*
	REN [*drive:*][*path*]*filename1 filename2*
	You cannot specify a destination drive or directory for the new file. For those actions, you would use COPY.
	RENAME has the same limitation of directories as the COPY command.

Table 4.1 reviewed what may seem like basic commands, but many of these commands now have a new twist when used under the Recovery Console.

The rest of the commands are Windows 2000 based. They can be broken into four basic categories; Disk Repair, Services and Devices, Text Viewing, and Other. The Disk Repair commands are covered in Table 4.2. These commands can be used to perform disk maintenance.

TABLE 4.2   Disk Repair Commands

Command	Description
CHKDSK	Examines a disk for errors.
	Syntax:
	CHKDSK [*drive:*] [/P] [/R]
	The P switch can be used to force check disk to run, even if the drive is not considered to be dirty.
	The R switch can be used to repair the disk and recover any data that is still readable. If this switch is not used, errors will only be reported.
	If you do not use any parameters, only the current drive will checked for errors.
	For CHKDSK to run, AUTOCHK.EXE must be present. By default, there will be a copy of it in the CMDCONS directory.
DISKPART	Used to repartition your drive.
	Syntax:
	DISKPART [/ADD¦/DELETE] [*device_name¦drive_name¦partition_name*] [*size*]
	Where ADD will create a new partition and DELETE will delete an existing partition.
	device_name refers to the system device, such as \Device\HardDisk0. If you do not know the device names, use the MAP command to get a listing of used devices.
	drive_name is the drive letter (D:) used when deleting a partition if the partition name (\Device\HardDisk0\Partition1)is not used.
	If you do not pass DISKPART any parameters, a user interface will open. This interface is similar to the interface that would be used during the Windows 2000 Setup.
FIXBOOT	Will write a new bootsector onto the System partition.
	Syntax:
	FIXBOOT [*drive:*]
	Where *drive* allows you to override the default System partition.
FIXMBR	Repairs the master boot record of the boot partition.
	Syntax:
	FIXMBR [*device name*]

Command	Description
	`device name` allows you to specify which device will receive the new MBR if you do not want to use the default boot device.

Some boot problems arise when a service or device has been improperly enabled or disabled. In the past, this would mean that you would have to replace the registry with a previous version or use the Last Known Good Configuration. Either of these choices would mean that some changes would be lost. The Recovery Console allows you to go into these components and surgically correct the problem. The service- and device-related commands are described in Table 4.3.

TABLE 4.3   Services and Devices Commands

Command	Description
DISABLE	Allows you to disable a service or device driver.
	Syntax:
	`DISABLE servicename`
	You can get a list of service names with the LISTSVC command.
	Before disabling the service, you will see its current start type. You should remember the start type in case you need to enable service later.
	For a list of start types, see the ENABLE command.
ENABLE	Allows you to enable a service or device driver.
	Syntax:
	`ENABLE servicename [start_type]`
	You can get a list of service names with the LISTSVC command.
	The different values that can be used for *start_types* are the following:
	`SERVICE_DISABLED`
	`SERVICE_BOOT_START`
	`SERVICE_SYSTEM_START`
	`SERVICE_AUTO_START`
	`SERVICE_DEMAND_START`
	You would more likely use the DISABLE command to disable a service or device.
	The ENABLE command will show you the old *start_types* before resetting it to the new value. You should make note of the current value in case you need to reset it.
	If you do not specify a new *start_types*, you will see what the current *start_types* is.
LISTSVC	The LISTSVC command lists all available services and drivers on the computer.

4

TROUBLESHOOTING
THE SETUP

The commands for viewing text files, such as your INI files, could have been included in the DOS command section, but these two commands behave very differently than their predecessors (see Table 4.4).

TABLE 4.4 Text Viewing Commands

Command	Description
MORE	This command displays a text file onscreen one page at a time. It also allows you to page up or down through the document.
	Syntax:
	MORE [*filename*]
TYPE	This command displays a text file onscreen one page at a time. It also allows you to page up or down through the document.
	Syntax:
	TYPE [*filename*]

While it is always nice to classify items, some items defy classification. These commands have been included in Table 4.5.

TABLE 4.5 Other Recovery Console Commands

Command	Description
BATCH	The BATCH command allows you to execute the contents of a text file as single commands per file line.
	Syntax:
	BATCH *Inputfile* [*Outputfile*]
	The *Inputfile* is the file that contains the commands you want to process, and *Outputfile* is where you want the results of those commands to be sent. If no output file is specified, the results go to the screen.
EXPAND	The EXPAND command expands a compressed file.
	Syntax:
	EXPAND *source* [/F:*filespec*] [*destination*] [/Y]
	EXPAND *source* [/F:*filespec*] /D
	The default directory for the destination file is the current directory.
	The Y switch can be used to suppress the overwrite messages.
	The F switch is used when the source contains more than one file. *filespec* is used to specify the file you want expanded. *filespec* can include wildcards.

Command	Description
	The D switch is used to display the contents of a compressed file.
	The possible destinations are the same as the destinations of the COPY command.
	If the file already exists, you will be prompted to overwrite the file.
LOGON	Enables you to log on to a Windows 2000 installation.
	Syntax:
	LOGON
	When you issue the LOGON command, you will be given a list of the available Windows 2000 installations. To log on, you will require the administrator password for that installation. This is the same process you would go through when starting up the Recovery Console. This command allows you to switch to a different installation on the same computer.
MAP	This command will display a mapping of your hard drives to their drive letters.
	Syntax:
	MAP [arc]
	MAP will display a listing of which physical devices match which drive letters. By specifying *arc*, you can have the device names written out using the *arc* device reference.
SYSTEMROOT	Sets the current directory to SYSTEMROOT.
	Syntax:
	SYSTEMROOT

When you are done with the Recovery Console and want to return to your—now fixed—version of Windows 2000, type **exit**. This command also reboots your computer.

The Recovery Console allows you to perform some basic troubleshooting and repair. It provides additional troubleshooting tools that have been needed in Windows NT for some time.

Help for Other Issues

No assemblage of setup errors and their solutions can possibly be complete, because new problems arise every day. By far the best resource for setup and other Windows 2000 Professional problems is Microsoft's Knowledge Base. This is a database Microsoft maintains for all its products. It contains the collective experience of users, Solution Providers, field representatives, and support staff.

You can search it from the Microsoft Web site at `http://support.microsoft.com/support`.

Some private sites have their own versions of a knowledge base. *Windows NT Magazine* maintains such a Web site at `http://www.winntmag.com`.

These private sites often contain information different than Microsoft's, but none of them are as large or comprehensive overall.

The USENET (Internet newsgroups) is a hotbed of Windows 2000 interaction. Microsoft maintains their own public news server at `news://msnews.microsoft.com`. They have several groups devoted to Windows 2000, from setup and deployment issues, to hardware issues, to games.

Online services, especially CompuServe, maintain forums dedicated to Windows products. In many cases, these forums are manned by users for peer-type support only, but the quality of the information is often as high as anywhere.

Finally, Microsoft maintains a support staff for non-OEM versions of Windows 2000 Professional. There is a fee for this support, but is often worth it. If you got your version of Windows 2000 from a vendor such as Compaq, your first line of support is that vendor. The quality of this support varies enormously, as you might suspect. If you're unhappy with your vendor's support of Windows 2000, you can always purchase the good stuff directly from Microsoft.

Summary

This chapter has covered topics that may be involved in setups that have gone awry. Although some products will not work initially with Windows 2000, that should not prevent you from looking at Windows 2000 as a stable secure operating system. It may be easier to setup Windows 98, but the setup routine for Windows 2000 is now just about as easy. It does often leave out devices that it does not know how to deal with, and these have to be handled after the installation.

Many corporations held off upgrades for a period of time while Windows 2000 was being developed, keeping Windows 3.1 or Windows 95 on the desktops, and not upgrading to Windows NT technology, until Windows 2000 was released. Because this is considered to be a major upgrade, it will be planned for, with full deployments schedules and tests conducted prior to being released to desktops in a slow and orderly fashion.

Fine-Tuning Windows 2000 Professional

PART

II

IN THIS PART

Tuning Windows 2000 Performance

CHAPTER 5

Everybody wants a fast computer. In fact, just about the only hard-and-fast rule that exists among all users is that they can never get enough speed. Most out-of-the-box Windows 2000 Professional setups will show decent, if not optimum, performance. However, after a while, especially after a few months or years of driver installs and deinstalls (also called *uninstalls*) and application installs and deinstalls, performance of that setup will deteriorate. This chapter will help you identify the areas of slowdown (bottlenecks) and what you can do to speed up those areas.

> **Note**
>
> This chapter, and Chapter 28, "Performance Monitor," cover different topics but are intertwined in the sense that you use the material in a coordinated fashion. I strongly suggest that you at least glance at Chapter 28 before proceeding with this chapter to have an idea of what material is covered.

Underlying Factors

The speed of a machine depends on several underlying factors. These factors determine the maximum performance level after tuning. Think of these factors using a car analogy. A perfectly tuned Mazda Miata won't be as fast as a slightly out of tune Porsche 996 due to the underlying factor of power to weight ratio and other related factors. If you want to go fast, the way to go is to spend the money and get the Porsche, not tune your Miata. This section covers the major factors that separate the Miatas from the Porsches in the world of Windows 2000 Professional.

Hard Disk Speed

There is nothing other than lack of RAM that will slow down a Windows 2000 Professional setup like a pokey hard disk. Windows 2000 uses a sophisticated algorithm to start hard disk virtual memory (VRAM or the paging file) well before physical RAM is exhausted. The reason is so that the step to VRAM isn't sudden, as it would be if 2000 waited until all physical RAM was used and then suddenly switched to a large unit of disk RAM. Because of this, the paging file comes into use even on very heavy workstations with greater than 1GIG RAM. Actually, you'd be surprised how fast today's applications eat RAM. Figure 5.1 shows the Performance Monitor with the Page File Use counter opened. This shows a 128MB computer running Microsoft Word 2000, Excel 2000, Access 2000, and Paint Shop Pro. Each program has a small document loaded. Note that the system is using a small percentage of the created paging file, instead relying mostly on the physical RAM in this machine.

FIGURE 5.1

Windows 2000 Professional creates and uses a paging file (VRAM), even with no applications loaded, but it doesn't use much of the file unless called on to do so by the applications.

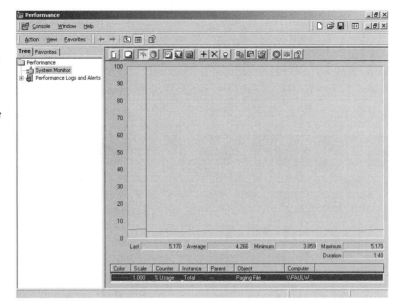

Figure 5.2 shows the Performance tab of the Windows Task Manager. This figure was captured at the same time as Figure 5.1. You can see that about 15MB of memory is still available even after the applications have been loaded, yet the system uses the paging file.

FIGURE 5.2

Although quite a bit of physical RAM is in use, Windows 2000 remains parsimonious with its storage in the paging file. At this point, as RAM demands increase, more and more percentage will go to paging.

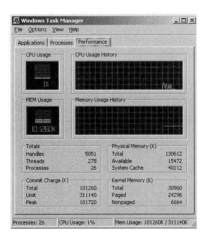

The paging file use is only part of the reason for getting a fast hard disk. Windows 2000 Professional applications are large, as are their data files. Applications include dynamic libraries, which are loaded as your use demands. Opening, closing, and accessing data is dependent on your hard disk speed. Windows 2000 Professional uses a disk cache to speed up apparent operations and repeat accesses, but your entire computer speed is largely governed by its hard disk throughput.

> **Note**
>
> Some people with very RAM-heavy computers get distressed that Windows 2000 uses virtual memory well before it runs out of physical RAM. The reason that 2000 uses virtual RAM from the start is to create a smooth transition from physical RAM to virtual RAM when the need becomes critical.

If you have even the slightest doubt remaining about the size of today's current application data files, take a look at Figure 5.3. This is a Microsoft Word 2000 file containing one byte (the letter *k*) of data. It's 19KB.

FIGURE 5.3

Today's applications require file sizes of rather large granularity due to the non-data information they store.

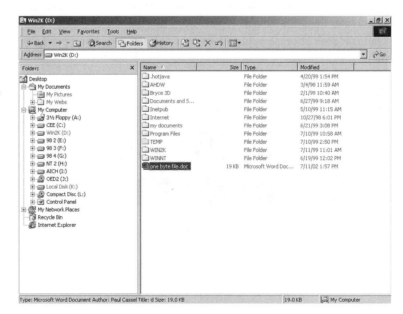

Processor Speed

Processor speed is a rather overrated element in total system performance. Surely, in otherwise identical systems, the one with the fastest clock will be the fastest computer; however, for most uses, the processor speed isn't the single greatest bottleneck.

If all things are otherwise equal and you can afford the freight, by all means get a faster clock speed processor. But put the budget for this behind other more important items, such as a speedy hard disk, the right processor type, RAM, and L2 cache.

Processor Type

As initially conceived, the Windows NT family was to be one operating system for many CPU types. One by one, Microsoft dropped support for non-Intel processors with the last one, the Compaq (DEC) Alpha, falling just before Windows 2000 Professional's release. Today the only processor family supported is Intel and its clones.

The world of Intel is the world of the marketer, and it seethes with confusion and traps. Each processor in Intel and Intel-clone land has its advantages and disadvantages. Choosing the optimum processor for your budget is more of a fine balancing act than a rational decision. The following is a short overview of the decision matrix for a few of the currently available processors.

When Windows 2000 Professional was released, most workstation buyers' choice was a Pentium II, III, Celeron, Cyrix, and AMD in various clock speeds (from about 333MHz to 600MHz). They also had L2 (level 2, or fast cache running at system speed) from 0 to 512KB.

> **Note**
>
> Generally speaking, you should match your L2 cache to the total system RAM with nobody using 0 L2, those with 64MB RAM or less (running Windows 2000 Professional?) with 256KB, and those with more than 64MB, 512KB. These recommendations are for workstations, not server applications. The latter require more cache.

Today there is quite a bit of competition between Intel and AMD for chip mindshare. The Pentium III rules some sort of roost as far as performance is concerned (in Wintel) where many consider the AMD line a better value, or for some games, even the better performer. Recently AMD, determined to be the performance (not just value) leader, has successfully challenged Intel for the speed champion.

5

TUNING WINDOWS 2000 PERFORMANCE

This is one of those areas where I can go on exhaustively about various comparisons between the chips offered today, but the realities of production mean that my comments will be dated by the time this book is printed.

So I'll close this short section with a recommendation that's time tested to be true. The best value in chips and mainboards (also called *motherboards*) is one or two steps behind the cutting edge. This means that if, at a certain point, the top speed Intel processor runs at 1GB MHz, seek the chip that's either one or two speeds below this for the best combination of price, performance, and longevity (in the sense of obsolescence).

This is a good policy on equal chips, but might not be during the chip thresholds—or model changes. If Intel or AMD brings out a much improved chip or one with features you think you'll want, buying below this chip will keep you in the value range for the present, but will mean faster obsolescence—in the sense that you'll grow dissatisfied with your purchase. The upshot is that such a bargain might be not such bargain in the long run.

Keep in mind that while the fastest, newest chips always cost more; they also will remain in service longer. There is also the pride of ownership. Few will openly admit to desiring the fastest and are willing to pay for it, but if not, how does Ferrari stay in business?

Perhaps I should close this section by reminding you that the best practice is to make sure you can upgrade your processor or at worst your mainboard. That will prevent you from being too heavily invested into any purchase.

Physical RAM

This is simple: the more the better. If you have too little, you're wasting your time and money running Windows 2000 Professional. Microsoft has the laughable minimum requirement of 32MB for Windows 2000 Professional. This puts you heavily into paging before the system is even loaded. You should only run a 32MB RAM system if you are in training to be a saint. By the time you spend a few days with your system, nothing will ever be able to try your patience.

Realistically, the system RAM for Windows 2000 Professional picks up where Windows 98SE and its successors stop. Windows 98SE systems perk up as you feed them RAM to about 64MB. That's also the realistic minimum level of physical RAM for Windows 2000 Professional. Actually, 128MB is closer to the truth with 256MB or even 512MB being a comfortable level if you run many processes or manipulate large files.

Figure 5.4 shows NetObjects Fusion (a Web site creation tool) with a substantial site loaded. The same screen shows the Performance tab of the Task Manager. Note that the use of memory is up to about 153MB on this 128MB system. Take a careful look at the other memory-eating statistics, such as threads, handles, and processes.

FIGURE 5.4

Even efficient applications need to use a lot of RAM if you load them with large data files.

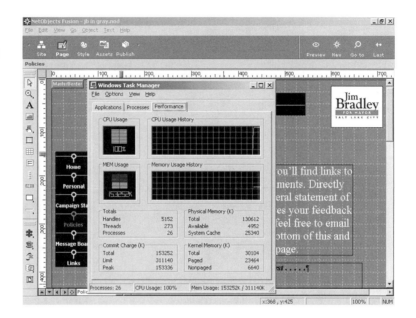

Figure 5.5 shows the same session as Figure 5.4, but the large site has been closed and a smaller one opened in its stead. Note that the physical RAM released by Windows 2000 Professional for this one change is roughly 30MB. Also note that the figures for threads, handles, and processes are way down. This shows that the only difference in whether the system uses roughly 153MB or 126MB RAM is the loaded file.

The moral of this example is that you should know what you're doing. If you're sure you'll use, say, only Word or WordPerfect for simple documents, you don't need much RAM. As soon as you start running many applications concurrently or loading large files, you need to up your RAM.

This applies to any data. The example used a site creation editor, but it could have just as easily shown the same phenomenon using a database, such as Microsoft Access and a large file of that type.

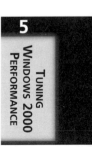

FIGURE 5.5

Change the loaded file and this system uses a full 30MB less of RAM.

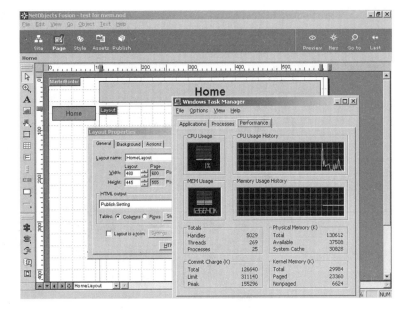

The Buss

The system buss, often misspelled as *bus,* can drastically affect system speed. Luckily for most, the adverse choices once available aren't being marketed much anymore.

Although it has had some criticism from electrical engineers (EEs), the now almost universal PCI buss, works decently enough for most uses. People will argue that the older Microchannel and EISA busses were superior, and maybe they were. However, the Microchannel buss died because it was proprietary to IBM brand systems (or requiring brutal licensing fees), and the EISA buss today exists only on mainboards directed to the specialized server market (and then it's rare). The somewhat fragmented VESA (or VL) buss has gone the way of the dodo replaced for video use by the much superior AGP.

You should make sure your critical system peripherals use the PCI buss instead of the ISA ones that usually accompany these systems (but are going away fast). There's no harm in plugging a modem or sound card in an ISA slot other than the slightly less reliable PnP, but an ISA video card has a distinct disadvantage compared to a PCI one, and both are inferior to AGP.

Similarly, a 32-bit PCI NIC (Network Interface Card) is the way to go for speedy Internet connections rather than the slightly cheaper ISA ones. Although technically the NIC isn't a part of the local system, if you need much in the way of Internet resources, a slow NIC can drag down the entire show.

Video Card

The speed of a system's video adapter greatly affects how fast a system seems to be. There's nothing like snappy screen refreshes to give the feeling of a snappy system.

Today, few video adapters run so slowly that they actually decrease the real-time use of a system. This implies that scrimping here won't make much, if any, difference in overall system performance. This is partly right and wholly wrong.

The two interfaces between users and the computer are the keyboard and the screen. Some would add the sound and video systems, but these are outside the scope of a performance discussion. Just as a lousy keyboard will slow down even the most adept typist, a slow screen will give the user an impression of a slow system.

Perceptions count as much as reality does here. A barely adequate adapter will save $150 over an excellent general-purpose one. This savings can ruin the entire user interface, so in the end it's poor economy.

If you're exploring the high end of the graphical world, such as 3D rendering, and have applications that support them, you should consider the specialized graphics adapters formerly available only for heavy workstations, such as those manufactured by Silicon Graphics (SGI).

Similarly, today's buyer should consider not only traditional video adapters, but newer initiatives such as Intel's AGP, the accompanying technology to some new chipsets and the next generation of Intel standards after the PCI.

A very fast video card can't make a slow system fast, but a mediocre card can make a fast system seem slow.

General Tuning by Option

Many people run a well-tuned system slower than its optimum speed because they unintentionally lard it up with baggage. This isn't necessarily the fault of users; it often occurs as installation programs add undetected services set to start up with the system.

There's nothing wrong with these services and programs, but they do rob your system of its speed because they eat RAM and launch processes.

Processes and Threads

Windows 2000 gains a process upon the launch of an application. A *process* is an executable program with at least one thread (naturally) and some memory addresses.

A *thread* is a part of a process running the program's instruction set. A program can launch many threads (multithreading), thereby concurrently executing several instruction sets at the same time.

For example, when Windows 2000 Professional runs both Microsoft Word and Excel, it's running two processes. However, each process can launch more than one thread. If Word paginates at the same time that it is running a spell check, it's multithreading.

The following are some tips to reduce system load:

- Reduce color depth. A 24/32-bit display takes more processing power than a 15/16-bit one. Very few people can tell the difference between a color depth of 16 or 24 bits. There is no advantage in the higher depth for business applications, such as Lotus 1-2-3 or Microsoft Word.

- Dump your wallpaper. The wallpaper eats some system resources all the time, not just when you have the desktop (or a folder) on display. Because most people use their computers with all the desktop occupied by applications, wallpaper doesn't even provide a lot of amusement value.

- Be aware of the resource cost of your add-ins. Many programs install themselves on your machine and then on your desktop and Start menu. They also launch a part of themselves automatically at each startup. Figure 5.6 shows the Processes tab for a simple system.

- In Figure 5.6, the entries IA99.EXE and AVPM.EXE are security processes (services). IA99 is Intruder Alert, a utility to block intruders coming "up the wire" in TCP/IP connections. It functions similarly to a firewall on a network. AVPM is an anti-virus monitoring program. These processes automatically launch themselves with each startup, even when the programs from the menus aren't started. There is nothing in the setup or the release notes for this program to indicate that this is the case.

  Note that in aggregate these processes take up as much system resources as a small program. They can also use at least as many processor cycles as some individual programs. In each of these cases, whether you run them automatically on startup is a user choice.

FIGURE 5.6

Programs often stealthily add themselves to your startup process. The Processes tab of the Task Manager is a good tool to detect such skullduggery.

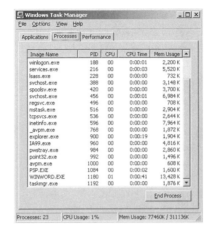

- If you add the preceding utilities to a marginal system, say one with 64MB of RAM, the system effectively loses enough physical RAM to become a sub-marginal system.

- Even the `point32.exe` process takes up 1.3MB RAM. This is the IntelliPoint software that comes with the Microsoft IntelliPoint Mouse (the wheel one). It wasn't that long ago that a heavy system came with one-half the total RAM this system uses to run the optional part of the mouse driver.

Note

The point isn't to eliminate these processes, but to be aware of them and the price that they exact on your system. Most people don't begrudge their systems the RAM for a virus checker or a firewall, because they figure the added safety worth the cost. Similarly, most people like the added features of the IntelliPoint mouse and gladly pay the cost in resources. However, if your system is marginal, the place to start investigating why it's fallen to sub-marginal is here.

- Detect and eliminate, if possible, defective programs having the Pac Man syndrome. Some programs won't release RAM as they close threads. The more you run these programs, the more resources they eat until a modest program, running for days or doing a lot of opening and shutting of files, can grow to overwhelm your system.

  In a perfect world, programmers would test their programs using readily available tools from vendors such as Nu-Mega, but they don't. The only way to detect these

5

TUNING WINDOWS 2000 PERFORMANCE

programs with limitless appetites is to check their memory load using the
Processes tab of the Task Manager or the Performance Monitor. Figure 5.7 shows
the Performance Monitor tracking a few counters for processes.

FIGURE 5.7

*Defective
processes can eat
your system up
like Pac Man run
wild. Here, the
Performance
Monitor is
tracking process
counters that
show how busy
the CPU is.*

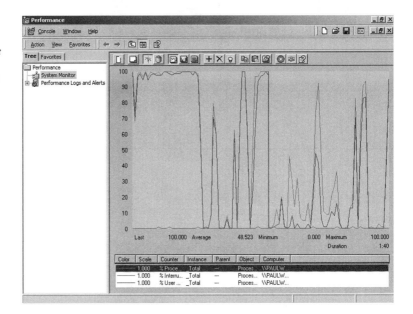

- Rid your system of orphaned shared resources. Windows 2000 Professional does a
  good job of tracking shared resources and eliminating them when they come to the
  end of their usefulness. This happens when their entry in SharedDlls decrements
  itself to its final decrement (becomes zero). Figure 5.8 shows a typical SharedDlls
  section. However, no system is perfect, and older installs of Windows 2000 have a
  few old drivers or shared resources loading when they shouldn't. This is more
  prevalent if you use many older 16-bit applications. Windows 2000 stores shared
  DLL information in HKEY_LOCAL_MACHINE\SOFTWARE\Microsoft\Windows\
  CurrentVersion\SharedDlls.

- To clean your Registry of spurious entries, use the REGCLEAN utility available for
  free from Microsoft (www.Microsoft.com). Also, manually inspect your
  System.ini and Win.ini files for unneeded entries put there by now unused or
  even removed Win16 programs. Finally, if you have a particular suspicion about an
  errant program, search through your Registry for it. Naturally, you should eliminate those keys only after taking the appropriate backup precautions.

FIGURE 5.8

The entries for shared DLLs appear under the SharedDlls *key in the Registry.*

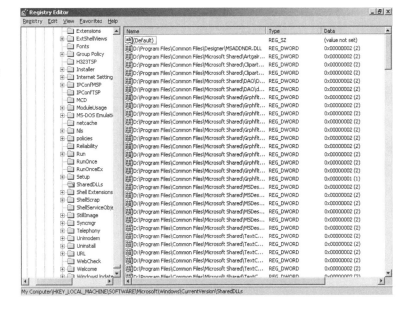

- Eschew icon madness. Every icon you see eats some resources. This is a big problem under Windows 3.11, but much less so under Windows 2000 or Windows 98 and its successors. However, this is a factor to keep in mind.

- Use NT File System (NTFS) if at all possible. NTFS is much more efficient and safer than FAT or VFAT, and has features never dreamed of in any FAT or VFAT system. Unless you need your volumes accessible to non-NTFS systems, use this better system.

- Locate your page file on a fast drive. If you have several disks in your system, use the fastest for the paging file. Remember, your system constantly accesses your paging file while you access even the most-used applications only occasionally. Figure 5.9 shows the dialog boxes where you can change the location and size of paging files. The best combination is to have the paging file on a different physical drive than the system or applications. To see the display in Figure 5.9, open the Control Panel, choose System, and then select the Advanced tab. Click the Performance button and then choose to Change the paging file. This will bring up the Virtual Memory dialog box you see in the front of Figure 5.9.

FIGURE 5.9

Windows 2000 Professional allows you to change the size of a paging (also called swap) file and its location. You can have your paging file over more than one disk, too. The important thing to keep in mind is to keep the file on your fastest disk.

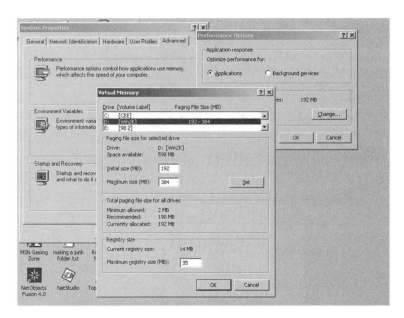

Optimizing and the Paging File

To get the best performance possible from your paging file, it needs to be optimized. The best way to do this is to relocate your paging file from your fastest disk/volume combination to any other place temporarily. Run a disk optimizer, such as Diskeeper or the optimizer that comes with Windows 2000 (a light version of Diskeeper), on the volume that is the permanent home of the paging file. Then set your paging file back to this now-optimized volume. This effectively defrags your paging file. You will need to reboot between paging file location changes to have this take effect.

- Optimize your disk regularly. There is a persistent myth that NTFS volumes never fragment. This is false. Just as optimizing (squeezing or defragmenting) is important on FAT volumes, it's equally important on NTFS ones.

- Get an optimizer and run it often. Most come with schedulers, so this operation doesn't, and shouldn't, affect your interaction with the computer. Both Diskeeper and the light version bundled with Windows 2000 can run in the background, but this will slow the system down. Also, file accessing can slow a system down to the point where background running, especially on a badly fragmented disk, isn't such a hot idea.

Diagnosing Bottlenecks

Once you've got your system running efficiently by choosing the right hardware and eliminating unneeded resource eaters, it's time to roll up your sleeves and start tuning in earnest. The Performance Monitor is the primary tool for detecting performance problems. Chapter 28, "Performance Monitor," tells you how to use and understand this tool.

Memory

The simplest measure of how much your system is slowed by memory issues is to see how much memory is in use at any one time. The Performance tab of the Task Manager gives a summary of memory uses, whereas the Processes and Applications tabs give some detail information. Obviously, if you're running many applications or running applications that eat a lot of RAM, you're going to be seeing more of your memory accesses from the paging file. This is dramatically slower than from physical RAM. Therefore, if you see your used memory rising close to your total available memory, your system is suffering from lack of physical RAM. Figure 5.10 shows the Performance tab of the Task Manager for a system where the committed memory is just about equal to the total physical memory. In this figure, the Commit Charge figure for memory use is the total RAM both physical and virtual "committed" to use. In this case, there is still physical RAM available, but the system is well into using the disk for RAM, thereby slowing performance slightly.

FIGURE 5.10

This system has memory use just about at the limit of physical RAM.

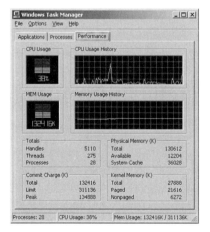

The more important performance statistic is the Page Faults counter from the Performance Monitor. This measures when the system must access memory other than the physical memory allocated to it. The word Fault in Hard Page Faults doesn't indicate a defect, but rather a less than ideal condition.

There are two kinds of page faults: hard and soft. A *fault* means that the system can't locate requested data from the working set or the memory currently available to an application. Hard faults mean the system must go to disk to resolve the information request. Soft faults mean the system can access the data from RAM. Naturally, a soft fault won't affect your system in any way you can detect, whereas a hard fault will.

Run the Performance Monitor and open the Page Faults counter from the Memory object. Figure 5.11 shows this counter running on the system shown in Figure 5.10.

FIGURE 5.11

The Page Fault counter of the Memory object is a good indicator of memory performance problems.

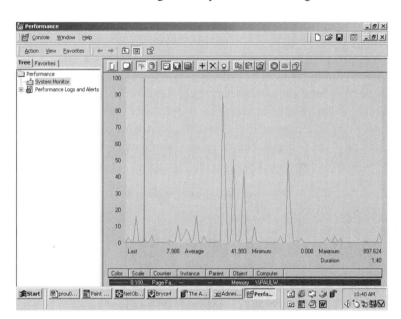

The following shows how to interpret this counter:

< 4 faults/second average	This indicates no memory problems.
=4 < 7 faults/second average	This indicates a problem that bears monitoring. A system in this range isn't performing at top levels.
>7 faults/second average	This is a system seriously suffering from RAM starvation.

To get an idea of where your system's performance lies, log the Page Faults counter a second time for the Memory and Process objects. You'd also do well to monitor other counters, such as the Page File Bytes from the Process object and Available Bytes from Memory. Run the log for several days of normal operation, logging at an interval of, at the most, a minute and, at the least, five minutes.

You need to study the log carefully to see events in combination that might degrade performance. A combination of page faults and disk accesses is a big tip-off that your system is dragging.

A useful tool available with the purchase of the Windows 2000 Professional Resource Kit is the Page Fault Monitor (pfmon), which generates a continually updated list of page faults and their generating applications. Figure 5.12 shows the end of a short run for this resource against itself.

FIGURE 5.12

The pfmon *utility is a relentless tracker of page faults, hard and soft.*

```
C:\WIN2K\System32\cmd.exe                                              _|□|×|
SOFT: LdrAccessResource+0x102 : 0x0344600c
SOFT: VirtualBufferExceptionHandler+0x47 : VirtualBufferExceptionHandler+0x47
SOFT: aullrem+0xd7 : 0x00820000
SOFT: RtlSizeHeap+0x3e0 : 0x00411004
SOFT: RtlFillMemoryUlong+0x10 : 0x00412000
SOFT: LdrAccessResource+0x102 : 0x77edf00c
SOFT: LdrAccessResource+0x102 : 0x77ee16e4
SOFT: LdrAccessResource+0x350 : 0x77ee2a28
SOFT: ZwPrivilegeCheck+0x1f : 0x77ee3694
SOFT: aullrem+0xd7 : 0x00820000
SOFT: DbgSsInitialize+0x2a6 : DbgSsInitialize+0x2a6
SOFT: RtlValidateProcessHeaps : RtlValidateProcessHeaps
SOFT: RtlpNtEnumerateSubKey+0x4d4f : 0x77fce2a8


        pfmon.exe Caused      30 faults had      15 Soft    3 Hard faulted VA's
        ntdll.dll Caused     341 faults had      45 Soft    2 Hard faulted VA's
      kernel32.dll Caused     40 faults had      32 Soft    2 Hard faulted VA's
        psapi.dll Caused       1 faults had       2 Soft    1 Hard faulted VA's
      imagehlp.dll Caused       3 faults had       3 Soft    1 Hard faulted VA's
                Caused      12 faults had      10 Soft    2 Hard faulted VA's

PFMON: Total Faults 427  (KM 6 UM 427 Soft 415, Hard 12, Code 67, Data 360)

K:\URK2K>
```

In this run, you can see that the application generated about 430 faults, of which 12 where hard ones. You can also direct pfmon to create a log file using different formats.

Figure 5.13 shows the output of pfmon, pfmon.log, opened in Notepad. The .log file is readable by Notepad+ (a freeware program available from the usual sources, such as www.shareware.com or www.tucows.com) and can be translated into programs such as Microsoft Access and Microsoft Excel for analysis. Usually, you'd be interested in the hard faults only when analyzing performance. Viewing the file in Notepad+ allows the leisurely examination of a pfmon run.

Although the Performance Monitor counter Page Faults/sec will report all page faults, the more important counter is hard page faults. Although there is no specific entry bearing that name as a Performance Monitor counter, the Page Reads/sec counter effectively reports this information. The standard counter combines both hard and soft faults. Most computers can recover without problems from soft faults. A *page fault* is when a mem-

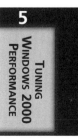

5

TUNING WINDOWS 2000 PERFORMANCE

ory page isn't in memory where the processor "expects" it to be. A soft fault means the page is located elsewhere in memory. A hard fault is where the processor must go to disk to find the requested page (data or code).

FIGURE 5.13

The log file from pfmon *allows careful examination of a run's results. This log captured both User and Kernel mode page faults for Paint Shop Pro (*psp.exe*).*

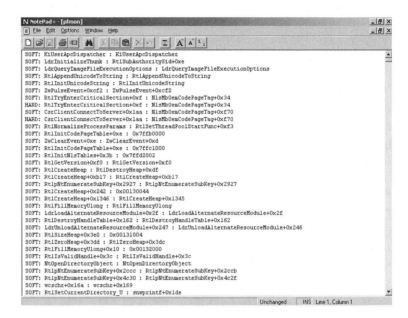

When a hard page fault occurs, the system must read from disk rather than from either the working set or cached memory. These reads are page reads, and there is a counter called Page Reads/sec. Therefore, you'll see a page read for each hard page fault. As a result, the page read, although not the same as a page fault, indirectly reports those hard faults.

The accompanying counter, Pages Output/sec, records how many pages need to be written to disk to clear the working set. Because either reading or writing to the disk eats up performance, monitor both.

In summary, to detect or monitor performance attributable to memory, log the counters for Page Faults/sec, Page Output/sec, and Page Reads/sec, at the very least. Log them at an interval of roughly 60 to 300 seconds for several days of typical use. Generally speaking, you don't need to do much analysis of the log. If either of the disk activity counters exceeds six or seven occurrences per second, you need more RAM, or you need to load fewer processes on the computer.

Figure 5.14 shows the charting of the one set of counters you might choose for memory analysis. This machine has 128MB RAM and only a few programs loaded. As you'd expect, there are few page faults or disk reads/writes. The spike of disk reads toward the middle of the chart was caused by opening a program triggered by the AT command.

FIGURE 5.14

The chart in Performance Monitor tracking memory performance limiters plus a Working Set counter.

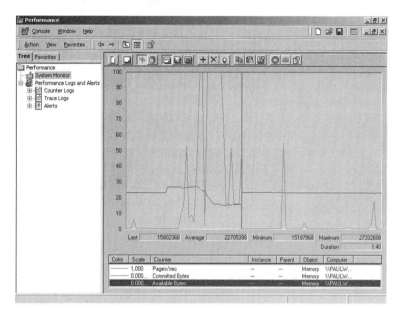

The other indication of a computer choking on too little RAM is the size of the paging file. Remember that this file is used by Windows 2000 Professional starting well before the committed and reserved physical RAM grows to its end to make for an easy transition onto VRAM. The greater the percentage of total memory that is disk-based, the lesser the performance. To put it another way, disk RAM percentage is inversely proportional to total computer performance.

The object Process has a counter Page File Bytes:_Total and a counter for individual processes (applications). The total counter is of the most interest in determining the performance hit from the paging file. Figure 5.15 shows the chart with the total page file counter and some process counters added. These processes are

- Intruder Alert 99 (IA99.EXE)
- Word for Windows (WINWORD.EXE)
- AVP Monitor for Windows (_avpm.exe)

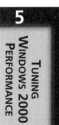

The chart shows how much each process is using the paging file (by bytes) as well as the entire system's paging file size.

> **Note**
>
> You might have a difficult time seeing the four lines representing the three processes and the entire system in Figure 5.15. The highest line (toward the middle of the chart vertically) is the system. The line just below the 10 on the scale is Winword. The other two processes demand little page file room, so they are crowded at the very bottom of the display area and are quite difficult to see in this format.

FIGURE 5.15

The Total instance of the Page File Bytes counter of the Process object in Performance Monitor is a good indicator of how much your system is depending on the paging file.

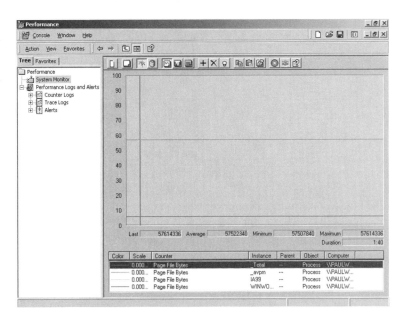

This system has a paging file of about 60MB, even with a total RAM of 128MB. This graphically shows how early Windows 2000 Professional goes to the paging file, even in the presence of a good deal of physical RAM.

Although you can also track an individual process's performance, there's little you can do about it other than refusing to use piggy applications. Keep in mind the characteristics of individual applications while monitoring them. For example, Microsoft Access will go to disk while transaction processing more often than Microsoft Word will while writing.

That doesn't mean Access is a piggy application, but rather that it is inherently different by design. Processor time counter of the Process object, as shown in Figure 5.16, is useful when evaluating how much memory or other resource an application eats, but there's little you can do other than not use the application if you don't like what you find. Figure 5.16 shows how much CPU time a process uses. The little bump toward the left of the display area shows the start of a spell check in Word. Note the two processes shown here, Word and Access, don't take up much processor time at all at idle.

FIGURE 5.16

You can monitor individual processes, but you must take into account inherent differences between processes when interpreting the results.

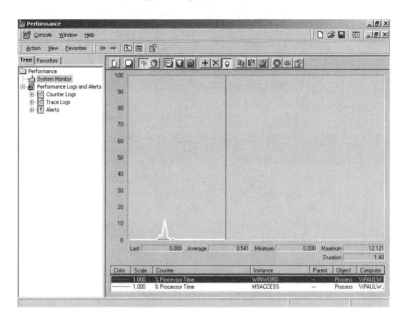

Disk Problems

You can use the Performance Monitor to determine various disk activity statistics using such counters as %Disk Time and Avg. Disk sec/Transfer. If the Performance Monitor for disk activity refuses to start, you'll have to activate the utility `Diskperf`. To activate `Diskperf` from the command line, start a CLI session (Start, Run, CMD) and then enter **Diskperf -y** or **Diskperf -ye** if the `Ftdisk` (fault-tolerant) service is running. The `-y` switch says to start monitoring at next startup. The `-ye` (all case-insensitive) switch says to start monitoring at the next startup on machines with disk striping.

Check the Services area of MMC if you are unsure about `Ftdisk`. Next, reboot and launch Performance Monitor. You can start `diskperf` for a remote computer by specifying its name on the command line, as shown in the following:

```
Diskperf -y \\Tirilee
```

This command will start the diskperf utility on the computer \\Tirilee the next time that computer is booted. Figure 5.17 shows the initialization of disk monitoring.

FIGURE 5.17

You need to start the diskperf utility. This is a command line program that's part of the standard Windows 2000 Professional distribution. You shouldn't have to use this utility.

Uncertainty

Remember your Physics 101. When monitoring or logging any disk performance objects, be sure to write your log to a disk other than the one being monitored. If you don't, the act of logging will affect your statistics.

If your Performance Monitor shows all zeros for disk counters, you need to start diskperf. Figure 5.18 shows the chart for a computer with diskperf running. As you can see, the counters provide a wealth of information.

As colorful as the chart in Performance Monitor is, it's a little tough to interpret the display. To make some sense of the Performance Monitor's output, either log or view the output in the report form. Figure 5.19 shows the Report view of Performance Monitor during the same period as the chart shown in Figure 5.17.

The following are some disk object counters to keep an eye on:

- *Disk Time*—The more disk thrashing, the less the performance. Make sure you're doing an apples-to-apples comparison here before coming to a conclusion.
- *Avg. Disk Queue Length3*—This is the backlog of disk read/write requests. A long queue indicates the disk can't keep up with system requests.
- *Disk Bytes/sec*—How fast is throughput? This is a good measure for comparisons between physical disks and even different computers.

FIGURE 5.18

The chart in Performance Monitor can track various counters for the instances of logical and physical disks.

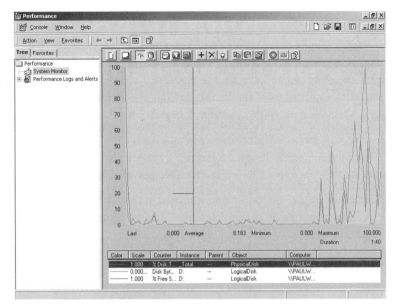

FIGURE 5.19

The Report view of the Performance Monitor is easier to interpret than the Chart view for some objects and their counters.

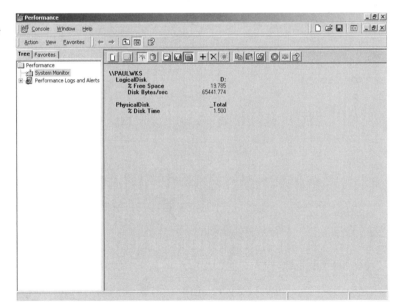

Processor

It's rare to find a computer that's severely bound by a processor, but they're out there. The System object is the way to detect such performance eaters. In fact, if you had to pick one object from which to infer the performance of a machine, the System object is the best. However, there's no reason to limit yourself to one object because Performance Monitor allows you to mix and match objects, instances, and their counters.

Figure 5.20 shows a Performance Monitor chart showing processor counters. Applying a Blur filter in Fractal Design Painter to a large bitmap caused the spikes in processor time that start on the right of the chart and also appear to the left.

The following are some of the most relevant objects and their counters. Keep in mind that momentary readings of a chart aren't indicative of your system. To get a better idea of performance, log your computer over several days under a load you think is typical.

FIGURE 5.20

Most processors that are part of business-oriented computers loaf along, but they have their jobs cut out for them when doing chores such as blurs.

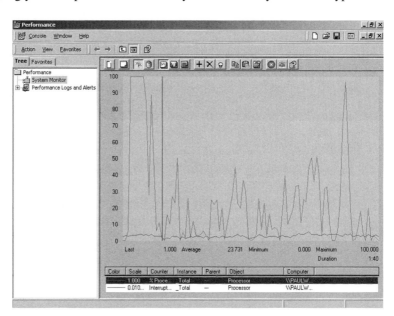

Processor Object:

- *%User Time and %Privileged Time*—The time the processor spends executing user mode and privileged operations.

- *%Processor Time*—How much of total time was the processor doing something? An idle processor is one with excess work capacity. Conversely, a processor that's busy chugging away constantly is working hard for its money.

Process Object:

- *%Processor Time*—Use the _Total instance to measure the total of all tasks that take up processor power. You can also use each processes' instance, but the _Total instance is the most critical measure for system information. This counter should remain about 100 percent because it's the total minus interrupts.

- *%User Time and %Privileged Time*—The time the processor spends executing user mode and privileged operations.

System Object:

- *Processor Queue Length*—How many threads are stacked up awaiting attention by the processor? This is the processor backlog.

- *%Total Processor Time*—Shows percentage of clock time for a given interval that saw the processor(s) busy.

Thread Object:

- *Thread State*—The processor status of a particular thread. This will vary from state 1 (ready) to state 5 (waiting).

- *Priority Current*—The priority of a particular thread (instance).

Unless you're doing processor-intensive chores, the least likely place you'll find your performance improvement possibilities is in the objects of this section. If, however, you do a lot of computational-intensive operations, such as raster graphics, matrix math, or similar operations, you should take a close look at CPU usage to speed up your computer. The Performance area of the MMC can track not only total processor time, but time-per-processor if you have more than one (a good idea if you are CPU-intensive).

Surprisingly, many applications, even those that you might think of as processor intensive, such as Microsoft Excel, generally don't exact too much of a toll on the processor as they do incremental calculations. If you want to see your processor-related instances soar, load a large spreadsheet and then force a recalculation. Other than rather artificial examples like that, most modern systems seem to be able to keep up with their processor requests.

Fixing Performance Problems

Once you've found your performance problem areas, you can do two things: live with them or fix them. Fixing disk and memory problems is fairly straightforward. You replace pokey disks with fast ones. Similarly, you just add physical RAM. The latter is more important because it affects the former. Adding RAM can effectively speed up a disk by increasing the room for a process' working set, thereby reducing the occurrence of page faults. More physical RAM also means more disk cache (dynamically created by Windows 2000 Professional), which also effectively (if not actually) increases the disk speed. There is no such thing as a disk fast enough (other than RAM disks) to make up for the lack of physical memory.

The moral of this performance tale is to add RAM whenever in doubt. The only instance where more general RAM won't increase performance at least somewhat is when your computer is utterly processor-bound. Even then, an increase of L2 cache (an unusually fast type of RAM) can give a goose to a computer slowed by its processor.

If that doesn't help, or if it's impossible, the only solution is a processor upgrade. This usually entails a mainboard (motherboard) switch, although the new Intel package found on the Pentium II and later Intel processors (SEC or Single Edge Connector) is supposed to offer processor upgrades with a current mainboard. This idea isn't new. In the past it hasn't worked, because when you want to change the processor, you usually want to change other mainboard items such as a support chipset.

The new Intel scheme of putting the CPU and related circuitry on a daughter board is supposed to solve all these problems. The world now wonders if it will.

Some Performance Red Flags

There are some red flag situations you should watch for using the Performance Monitor section of the MMC. If you see any of these, and find they tend to be the rule rather than the exception, you should address the problem by upgrading your hardware or by taking the software steps at the end of this section.

- Physical memory (RAM) below 4MB
- Disk activity (reads and writes both) above 90 percent
- Disk queue length in excess of twice the number of physical disks (usually no more than 2 in a Professional workstation)
- Processor time (total) or Paging File (total) use in excess of 90 percent

If you see any of these or other indices you think are adversely affecting your performance, here are a few things you can do.

- Make sure you're not monitoring so heavily that the actual examination of the system is bogging it down. Remember the Uncertainty Principle.

- Review your use of Services, making sure you run automatically only those absolutely necessary. For example, if you run a standalone computer or one where the network monitors for virus, you can usually shut off constant virus monitoring and instead run a virus check from time to time. If you go online outside of your network (dial up) to public places, you should then turn on monitoring for the time online.

- Increase the minimum size of the paging file to at least what your physical RAM is. Microsoft at one point recommended making your paging file twice physical RAM and then revised that recommendation to 100MB larger than physical RAM. Using the latest recommendation I have, that would mean a paging file set to be minimally about 230MB on a 128MB physical RAM system or about 600MB on a 512MB physical RAM system (this stuff need not be precise). Your paging file needs and general RAM needs will vary with your applications. Huge graphics or databases require huge RAM needs either from vRAM or pRAM.

- If you're on a network and are concerned that your logging/monitoring might be affecting your results significantly, monitor remotely.

- Carefully review what counters you're using. For example, the best counter for processor bottlenecks is queue length, not processor time usage. The latter is how busy the processor is, the former how long a "line" has formed for processing requests. A processor running at 80 percent always, but with no queue, isn't slowing the system down at all. As soon as a queue forms, however, the system is slowed.

Windows 16 Considerations

Chapter 2, "Pre-Installation and System Analysis," mentioned how Windows 16 (Win16 or Windows 3.X) applications run in a common address space created by the NTVDM. This can cause serious problems with ill-behaving programs all too common in this older format. Also, many of the Win16 programs still in use are in use because they've been created (programmed) specifically for a company rather than for general distribution. Because these programs haven't been through the rigorous testing common to general distribution programs, they malfunction all too often.

When one Win16 program misbehaves, it can take out other Win16 programs in its address space. Windows 2000 Professional can solve this problem by running each in its own address space. To do this, create a shortcut to the program (executable). Right-click the shortcut and choose Properties. Locate the Shortcut tab and click it. Note the check box Run in Separate Memory Space. Check that box and Windows 2000 Professional will launch a new NTVDM for this Win16 application. Figure 5.21 shows this dialog box with the check box checked.

FIGURE 5.21

You can instruct Windows 2000 Professional to launch a new NTVDM for each Win16 process if you're concerned with their interactions.

Summary

The best way to eliminate the need to tune performance is to create a system that comes tuned for the task at hand. A system should be designed for the applications it will run. This isn't usually the case at large shops, where all is sacrificed on the altar of uniformity.

The large shop's slouch toward mediocrity means those using common applications usually are all right. Grab any computer system off the shelf and it will run Microsoft Office 2000 or WordPerfect just ducky. The ones that suffer under the uniformity lash from generic systems are those running out-of-the-ordinary applications, such as Metacreations Bryce, Micrografx Picture Publisher, video editors, CD creation, and other multimedia or 3D applications.

Traditionally, those oddball application people required oddball machines, such as the moribund Apple Macintosh. However, a little forethought, combined with the type of system analysis possible when using the Performance Monitor, can create and then tune a standard Intel to rival most specialized iron.

Advanced Control Panel Tools

CHAPTER 6

One of the first things you may notice when you start Windows 2000 Professional for the first time is a much cleaner looking desktop and less cluttered Programs menu. With the release of Windows 2000, Microsoft has made a special effort to clean up any clutter on the desktop to provide you with a simpler Windows interface. To improve efficiency, the Control Panel has become the central place for you to go to manage and maintain your system.

The new Windows 2000 Professional Control Panel has been significantly reorganized to make it easier for you to perform regular maintenance tasks, make changes to system settings, and troubleshoot problems. In addition, there are other changes in the Control Panel that will help protect you from accidentally making any changes that will cause your system to not work properly.

New Features of the Control Panel

In this chapter, we will explore some of the new features included in the Windows 2000 Professional Control Panel such as Accessibility, Display, Printers, Scheduled Tasks, Users and Passwords, Network and Dial-Up Connections, Administrative Tools, the Add/Remove Hardware Wizard, Add/Remove Programs, Power Options, and System Icons.

We will not be covering some of the other Control Panel applets, such as Date/Time, Game Controllers, Keyboard, Mouse, and Sounds and Multimedia, because their functions haven't changed much since Windows NT Workstation 4.0 or Windows 98.

As I mentioned, the improved Control Panel is now the primary location for you to update and maintain your system. Printers, Scheduled Tasks, Network Connections, and Administrative Tools have all been moved to the Control Panel (see Figure 6.1).

FIGURE 6.1

The Windows 2000 Professional Control Panel has been reorganized to make it easier to change system settings, perform regular maintenance tasks, and troubleshoot problems.

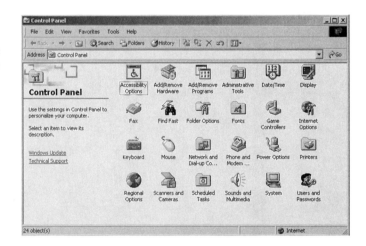

Advanced Control Panel Tools

CHAPTER 6

155

6

ADVANCED
CONTROL PANEL
TOOLS

Some of the new enhanced features in the Control Panel include the following:

- *More logical organization*—For example, if you are having problems with your modem, you can go directly to the Modem settings, select the Hardware tab, and choose Troubleshoot.

- *System*—Combines several applets to make it easier to configure settings (Network Identification, Hardware, User Profiles, and Advanced).

- *Users and Passwords*—This applet is used to add users and groups. If a non-Administrative user wants to change this information, the applet allows the user to change this information without having to log off and then log on.

- *Folder Options*—You can use this function to change the appearance of your computer's desktop and folder content. For example, you can select whether you want a single window to open (instead of cascading windows) when you open your folders. You can also choose whether you want folders to open with a single click or double click.

- *Add/Remove Hardware*—This centralized Wizard enables you to add, remove, unplug, and troubleshoot hardware. When Windows 2000 Professional detects new hardware, it checks the current settings for the device and installs the correct driver. The Wizard also shows a list of installed hardware and helps you check to be sure that each device is working properly.

- *Administrative tools*—In the enhanced Control Panel, advanced tools are in the same dialog box. Generally speaking, these are tools that a help desk person or IT professional needs to access; typical users don't need these tools to use their computers.

Some of the new Administrative tools include the following:

- *Component Services*—System Administrators use this tool to deploy and administer COM+ programs from a graphical user interface or to automate administrative tasks using a scripting or programming language.

- *Computer Management*—Administrators use this tool to manage local or remote computers from a single, consolidated desktop utility. Computer Management combines several Windows 2000 administrative tools (System Tools, Storage, Server Applications, and Services) into a single console tree, providing easy access to a specific computer's administrative properties.

- *Data Source (ODBC)*—This now includes connection Pooling to allow an application to reuse open connection handles, which saves round trips to the server.

- *Event Viewer*—This tool can allow you to view event logs to troubleshoot problems and export the event list log to a text file.

> **Note**
>
> Not all the options discussed in this chapter are installed by default. You can install the additional applets using the Add/Remove Windows Components Wizard, which I'll be discussing later in the "Easier to Manage" section of this chapter.

Using the Control Panel

The Control Panel is a convenient way to customize your computer. In the Control Panel, you can add and remove programs, fonts, and hardware; control how hardware, such as your mouse and modem, behaves; and select folder, display, sound, and other options. Programs in the Control Panel are referred to as *applets*.

To open a Control Panel feature, click Start, point to Settings, and click Control Panel. After the Control Panel is open, double-click the icon or folder of the feature you want to open.

The Control Panel Applets

The Control Panel consists of many handy applets that let you customize the way you work, change settings, and maintain your system. The Control Panel applets can be categorized into two major groups:

- *Easier Setup and Configuration*—These are the functions that most users generally perform, or would like to enable, once they've finished installing Windows 2000.
- *Easier Maintenance*—Windows 2000 has consolidated various functions into the new Control Panel that make it easier to manage your programs and your network settings. There are also applets to give you more power to administer, maintain, and troubleshoot problems on your system.

In this section, I will be discussing the details of each of the new improved features.

Easier Setup and Configuration

After buying a new computer, installing or upgrading an operating system, or just logging on to a new machine at the office, most people like to make some type of configuration changes immediately after installation to set up their machine with their preferred settings.

These changes generally include changing screen resolution, background colors, wallpaper, screen savers, setting up network configurations, setting up Internet connections, configuring your PC for the way you work, installing printers, other devices and software, adjusting regional settings, and scheduling tasks.

This section will discuss some of the new features of Windows 2000 that make it easier you to do this.

Display

One of the first things I like to do after installing a new operating system is to set up my screen resolution, color depth, background colors, and other display features.

Although Windows 2000 Professional's display configurations are different from the way you configured your display in Windows NT Workstation 4.0, Windows 98 users will recognize a similar look.

In the Display Properties dialog box, you can set the following options (see Figure 6.2):

- Background
- Screen Savers
- Appearance
- Web
- Effects
- Settings

FIGURE 6.2

The Display Properties dialog box.

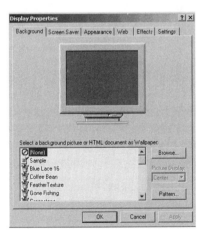

On the Settings Tab, you can set your screen resolution and color depth. There are also to other buttons to help you better configure your settings—Troubleshoot and Advanced. Most Windows 2000 applets come with a Troubleshoot option that allows you to launch the built-in troubleshooting wizard. This feature is handy if you're having a hard time identifying a problem.

You can click the Advanced button to open the dialog box shown in Figure 6.3. This is where you can configure your display adapter, your monitor, color management settings, font sizes, and other features.

FIGURE 6.3

The Advanced Display properties dialog box.

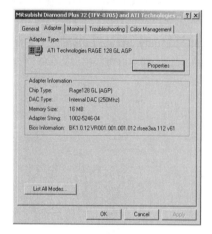

Tip

You can also access the Display properties by right-clicking your desktop and choosing Properties.

In addition to the normal display options that you're used to, Windows 2000 has a new multiple-monitor feature that increases your work productivity by expanding the size of your desktop. You can use this feature to connect up to ten individual monitors to create a desktop large enough to hold numerous programs or windows.

You can easily work on more than one task at a time by moving items from one monitor to another or stretching them across multiple monitors. For example, you can edit images or text on one monitor while viewing Web pages on another. Or you can open multiple pages of a single, long document and drag them across several monitors to easily view the layout of text and graphics. You could also stretch an Excel spreadsheet across two monitors so you can view numerous columns without scrolling. As you can see, this feature has many uses. You can use the Display Properties dialog box in Control Panel to configure the settings for multiple monitors.

Note

Not all video cards support the multiple-monitor feature that was first introduced in Windows 98. Check the capabilities of your video cards before trying this feature.

Accessibility Options

The accessibility options are used to help you meet your individual needs and are broken up into three major categories:

- Hearing-impaired tools
- Mobility-impaired tools
- Vision-impaired tools

Tip

Control Panel Accessibility options can also be used in conjunction with other Accessibility programs included with Windows 2000, such as the Magnifier, which enlarges a portion of the screen for easier viewing; the Narrator, which uses text-to-speech technology to read the contents of the screen; the Onscreen Keyboard, which provides users with limited mobility the ability to type onscreen using a pointing device; and the Utility Manager, which enables users to check an Accessibility program's status, start or stop an Accessibility program, and have programs start when Windows 2000 starts.

In addition to the settings in the Control panel, you can also use the Accessibility Wizard to help you set up the options and programs required to meet your individual needs. To access the Wizard, click Start, Programs, Accessories, Accessibility, and choose the Accessibility Wizard (see Figure 6.4).

FIGURE 6.4

The Accessibility Wizard helps you configure Windows 2000 for your vision, hearing, and mobility needs.

> **Note**
>
> The Accessibility tools that ship with Windows 2000 are intended to provide a minimum level of functionality for users with special needs. Most users with disabilities will need utility programs with higher functionality for daily use. For a list of Windows-based accessibility utilities, visit Microsoft's Accessibility Web site at `http://www.microsoft.com/enable/`.

Hearing-Impaired Tools

People who are deaf or hard-of-hearing can configure Windows 2000 to use visual cues in place of sounds or increase the volume level of program and system sounds. These features are

- *SoundSentry*—This feature provides visual warnings for system sounds.
- *ShowSounds*—This can be used to instruct programs to display captions for program speech and sounds.

> **Adding Sound Schemes**
>
> Sound Schemes are used to assign custom sounds to events. People who have difficulty hearing sounds within a certain frequency range can use sound schemes to adjust system and program sounds to make them more audible.
>
> To create a sound scheme
>
> 1. Open the Sounds and Multimedia Properties in Control Panel.
> 2. On the Sounds tab, under Sound Events, assign a sound for each event you want in a sound scheme.
> 3. Click Save As, and type a name for the new sound scheme.

The new scheme will appear in the Scheme list, so you can easily use these settings later.

To delete a sound scheme, select it in Scheme, and then click Delete.

Mobility-Impaired Tools

People who have motion-related disabilities can use Windows 2000 to configure their system to provide a more comfortable computing environment and help minimize the impact of mobility impairments on their work. These applets include the following:

- *StickyKeys*—Enables simultaneous keystrokes while pressing one key at a time
- *FilterKeys*—Adjusts the response of your keyboard
- *MouseKeys*—Enablesthe keyboard to perform mouse functions
- *SerialKeys*—Allows the use of alternative input devices instead of a keyboard and mouse

In addition to the accessibility applets in the Control Panel, you can also configure an Onscreen Keyboard under Programs, Accessories, Accessibility. The Onscreen Keyboard allows users to type using a pointing device.

Note

You can also use the Keyboard and Mouse applets in the Control Panel to add other accessibility features. The Keyboard applet provides keyboard layouts for users of alternative keyboards. This is especially useful for those who type with one hand. You can also use the Mouse applet in the Control Panel to configure the mouse for right- or left-handed users, adjust double-click speed, pointer speed and acceleration, and cause the mouse pointer to go directly to default buttons in dialog boxes.

Vision-Impaired Tools

Using the Display applet in the Control Panel, people who are visually impaired or have low vision can select larger fonts and icons, increase the size of screen elements by using a lower screen resolution, or change the size of windows and window borders. You can also adjust mouse properties by double-clicking Mouse in Control Panel to display larger or more visible mouse pointers and control the speed and animation of the mouse pointer.

> **Tip**
>
> While using Windows-based programs, you can change font sizes and colors, background color, and window size. In some programs, you can magnify what is displayed in the program's window.
>
> Using the Properties or Default dialog boxes in MS-DOS programs, you can change font types, sizes and colors, background color, and the size of the cursor and program window.

Vision-impaired tools include the following:

- *ToggleKeys*—With this feature, you can configure your PC to emit sounds when certain locking keys are pressed.
- *High Contrast*—Improves screen contrast with alternative colors and font sizes.

In addition to these applets, under Programs, Accessories, Accessibility, there are two other features you can configure: the Narrator, which uses text-to-speech technology to read the contents of the screen, and the Magnifier, which enlarges a portion of the screen for easier viewing.

Add/Remove Hardware

Windows 2000 supports plug-and-play hardware detection during the setup process. In most cases, it will detect and install drivers for all of your hardware. If Windows 2000 fails to recognize a piece of hardware, or you install new hardware later, you can use the Add/Remove Hardware Wizard applet in the Control Panel to configure the device.

> **Note**
>
> To add or remove hardware, you must be logged in to the system as an Administrator or as a user who is part of the Administrator group.

Although the Wizard looks different from the Add/Remove Hardware Wizard in Windows 98, it has some similar features. In this section, I'll discuss some of those features as well as the new enhanced features in Windows 2000. The Add/Remove Hardware Wizard (see Figure 6.5) includes the following features:

- Install/Uninstall Hardware devices
- Update Device drivers

Advanced Control Panel Tools

CHAPTER 6

163

6

ADVANCED
CONTROL PANEL
TOOLS

- Troubleshoot Hardware problems
- Unplug or Eject hardware

FIGURE 6.5

The Add/Remove Hardware Wizard.

After you start the Wizard, you're given the option of which hardware tasks you'd like to perform (see Figure 6.6). The first is to Add/Troubleshoot a device, and the second is to Uninstall/Unplug a device.

When you choose Add/Troubleshoot a device, Windows 2000 first checks to see if it detects any new Plug and Play devices. If it doesn't find any, it displays a dialog box (see Figure 6.7) that shows you all of the Hardware currently recognized by your system and the option to install new hardware.

FIGURE 6.6

The Add/Remove Hardware Wizard gives you two options from which to choose.

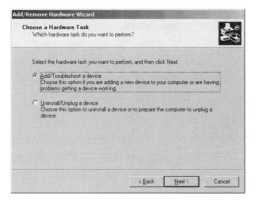

FIGURE 6.7

This dialog box allows you to add a new device or troubleshoot existing hardware.

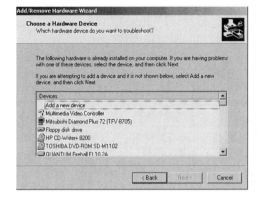

To add a new device, you have the option of letting Windows 2000 search for new hardware or selecting it from a list. If you want to troubleshoot a device, select it from the list and the Wizard displays the status of the device, whether it's configured properly, and then launches the Hardware Troubleshooter to help you repair it.

The second option when starting the Add/Remove Hardware Wizard, Uninstall/unplug a Device, allows you to permanently uninstall a device or temporarily Unplug or Eject a device.

The ability to Unplug/Eject a device is a new feature designed for Windows 2000. This feature enables you to stop a device so you can safely unplug it or eject it from your computer without shutting down the computer. An example of this would be a docked laptop or a USB device.

Windows 2000 warns you about any unsafe attempts to remove a device when you run the Wizard (see Figure 6.8).

FIGURE 6.8

This dialog box warns you of any unsafe attempts to remove or unplug a hardware device.

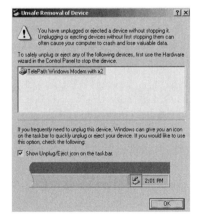

Configuring Network Options

The new Network and Dial-up Connections folder in the Control Panel now incorporates the previous Network applet and the Dial-up Connection Wizard that was formerly in My Computer.

Network and Dial-up Connections provides connectivity between your computer and the Internet, a network, or another computer. With Network and Dial-up Connections, you can gain access to network resources and functionality, whether you are physically located at the network's location or in a remote location. Connections are created, configured, stored, and monitored from within the Network and Dial-up Connections folder in the Control Panel.

If you're connected to a LAN, Windows 2000 allows you to create and set up your Network settings during installation. If the typical installation doesn't work properly or you skipped this option during set up, you can use the Network and Dial-up Connections applet in the Control Panel and adjust or create your settings.

When you open the Network and Dial-up Connections (see Figure 6.9), you can choose to make a new connection, view and change the properties of your existing connections, or check the status of your Local Area connection.

FIGURE 6.9

The Network and Dial-up Connections folder.

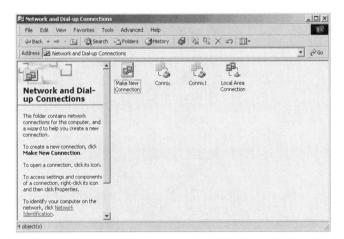

The Network and Dial-up Connections folder also provides you with additional feedback about your current connections. By clicking a connection, you can find out its type, device name, owner, and status. You can also double-click a connection to open its status dialog box (see Figure 6.10), which displays information about the connection, speed, and activity.

FIGURE 6.10

The Local Area Connection Status dialog box.

Choosing Make a New Connection activates the Network Connection Wizard, which provides a much easier way to set up a Network Connection than previous versions of Windows 9x and Windows NT. As shown in Figure 6.11, the user can select from the following types of connection choices:

- Dial-up to a Private Network
- Dial-up to the Internet
- Connect to a Private Network through the Internet
- Accept Incoming Connections
- Connect Directly to Another Computer

FIGURE 6.11

The Network Connection Wizard.

If you're like me, one of the first things you'll want to do after installing Windows 2000 is set up a Dial-up connection to the Internet. The new Network Connection Wizard is a vast improvement over the old Windows NT 4.0 Workstation Dial-up Networking. The only thing you need to know to set up a quick connection is a phone number, your username, and password. The Wizard does the rest. If you need to configure your connection

more later, you can right-click the connection, choose Properties, and you'll see the Connection Properties dialog box shown in Figure 6.12.

FIGURE 6.12

The Dial-up Connection Properties dialog box enables you to customize your connection settings.

The five main tabs of the dialog box consist are

- *General*—This tab is for changing modem settings, phone numbers, and dialing rules.
- *Options*—This tab is used for setting your dialing options, such as number of attempts, redialing, and prompts.
- *Security*—The Security tab contains advanced password security, dialing scripts, and authentication methods.
- *Networking*—Enables you to set the type of server you are calling and the installed network components.
- *Shared Access*—This allows other computers on your network to access external resources through this connection.

In addition, Windows 2000 allows you to set three different types of incoming connections—Virtual Private Networks (VPN), Dial-up, and Direct connections. This enables you to configure your computer to act as a remote server.

Power Options

By setting your Power Options, you can reduce the power consumption of any number of your computer devices or of your entire system. You do this by choosing a power scheme, which is a collection of settings that manages the power usage by your computer. You can create your own power schemes or use the ones provided with Windows 2000. The new Power Options applet enables you to

- *Choose a power scheme*—A power scheme is a predefined collection of power options. Choose a power scheme to apply settings that fit the way you use your computer, or use one as a starting point for creating your own personalized power scheme.

- *Put your computer on standby*—Standby is a state in which your monitor and hard disks turn off, so your computer uses less power. When you want to use the computer again, it comes out of standby quickly, and your desktop is restored exactly as you left it. Use Standby to save power when you will be away from the computer for a short time while working. Because Standby does not save your desktop state to disk, a power failure while on Standby can cause you to lose unsaved information.

- *Put your computer in hibernation*—Hibernation is a state in which your computer shuts down to save power but first saves everything in memory on your hard disk. When you restart the computer, your desktop is restored exactly as you left it. Use hibernation to save power when you will be away from the computer for an extended time while working.

- *Set a warning alarm when your battery is low*—You can set Power Options to set off a warning alarm when the level of battery reserve power falls below the levels you have defined as low or critical. You can easily change the battery level at which the alarm or message is activated.

- *Test your UPS configuration*—If you have an Uninterruptible Power Supply (UPS) unit attached to your system, you should make sure it will work when you need it to. After disconnecting the power to the UPS device, the computer and peripherals connected to the UPS device should continue operating, and a warning message should appear on the screen.

Infrared Support

Windows 2000 adds Infrared support, which enables you to transfer data over infrared connections. During the setup, Windows 2000 installs the Wireless Link program that transfers files to or from another computer running the Windows 2000 or Windows 98 operating system.

The following tasks are frequently performed with infrared and Wireless Link operations:

- *Establish an infrared link*—Before you can use Wireless Link operations, you must set up an infrared link on your computer.

- *Set up the computer for infrared*—The computer must be configured for infrared operations.

- *Send files with Wireless Link*—After an infrared link is established on your computer, files can be sent using Wireless Link.

- *Print to an infrared printer*—After a wireless connection is established with your printer, printing can be done as usual.

- *Make an infrared network connection*—Infrared connection to a network is possible with an infrared port.

Easier to Manage

Now that you've set up your new computer, you can start exploring the new features of the Control Panel that make administering your system easier to manage, such as your programs, system settings, and scheduled tasks.

This section will discuss some of the new features of Windows 2000 that make it easier you to do this.

Add/Remove Programs Wizard

The improved Add/Remove Programs Wizard helps you better manage programs on your system. The Wizard prompts you through the steps necessary to add a new program or to change or remove an existing program.

As you can see in Figure 6.13, you can use Add/Remove Programs to change or remove programs, add Windows 2000 components you chose not to include in the original installation (such as networking options or Indexing Service files), other operating systems (such as Windows 98 on a separate partition), or install new programs (such as Microsoft Office 2000).

FIGURE 6.13

The Add/Remove Programs dialog box.

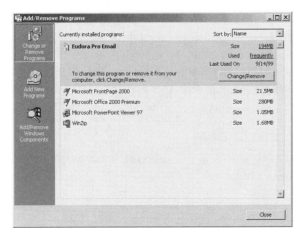

Two of the dialog box's additional capabilities are

- *Sorting*—This allows you to sort the list of programs by size, frequency of use, and time of last use.

- *More Information*—This new dialog box gives you more information about the programs on your system. This feature allows you to see the last time a program was used and the frequency of its use to enable you to determine if out-dated programs are left on your system. You can also see how much disk space it's using.

You can also choose to add programs from a CD-ROM or floppy drive, as well as install new Windows features, system updates, and device drivers over the Internet from Microsoft Windows Update (see Figure 6.14).

FIGURE 6.14

The new Wizard allows you to add programs from several locations.

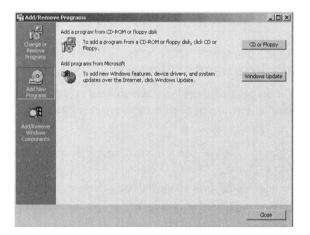

If your computer is connected to a network, your Network Administrator can make programs available for you to install or assign them as mandatory to install. When you run the Wizard, the programs you are authorized to add are displayed at the bottom of the screen. If your network Administrator has organized programs into categories, you may need to select a different option in Category to see the program you want to add. To install a network program, select the program you want to add, and then click Add.

Administration Tools

The following administrative tools appear in both Windows 2000 Professional and Windows 2000 Server:

- *Component Services Explorer*—Used by system Administrators to deploy and administer COM+ programs from a graphical user interface or to automate administrative tasks using a scripting or programming language. Software

developers can use Component Services Explorer to visually configure routine component and program behavior, such as security and participation in transactions, and to integrate components into COM+ programs.

- *Computer Management*—Used to manage local or remote computers from a single, consolidated desktop utility. Computer Management combines several Windows 2000 administrative tools into a single console tree, providing easy access to a specific computer's administrative properties.
- *Data Sources (ODBC)*—Open Database Connectivity (ODBC) is a programming interface that enables programs to access data in database management systems that use Structured Query Language (SQL) as a data access standard.
- *Event Viewer*—Used to view and manage logs of system, program, and security events on your computer. Event Viewer gathers information about hardware and software problems and monitors Windows 2000 security events.
- *Performance*—Used to collect and view real-time data about memory, disk, processor, network, and other activity in a graph, histogram, or report form.

The Microsoft Management Console

As the Windows operating system becomes more and more powerful, and as users begin to expand the services they are providing to include Internet services, managing all these resources can be a real hassle. UNIX systems have been struggling for years to develop tools that enable Administrators to easily manage all the different services that can be hosted on a single machine.

Of course, there are many different offerings for managing services, and Windows 2000 includes the Microsoft Management Console (MMC) to handle this. The MMC is designed to offer a common management interface for the myriad of services that can be provided, from different Active X controls to the Internet Information Server (IIS). The MMC includes a variety of features for managing your system, network, and Web sites, and allows you to organize your tools by task, schedule, or any number of other methods.

How the Microsoft Management Console Functions

The first thing you should know is that the MMC itself is not an application that actually manages anything. Instead, it provides a framework for other management tools. It provides a standardized interface and architecture for adding snap-ins, which are the modules that actually perform the administrative tasks.

Snap-ins are provided by Microsoft or other software vendors. A *snap-in* is a COM object that provides the actual management functions. For example, if you're using Microsoft FrontPage 2000, you'll notice that all features for managing your Webs, server extensions, and other functions are now done through the MMC FrontPage Server Extensions snap-in.

The MMC is a powerful tool because it provides a flexible interface for administering all types of services. Because of this flexibility, the interface is very simple and straightforward. The MMC is designed around the concept of consoles, and all management is performed through a console. The main window, shown in Figure 6.15, is divided into planes, which contain different types of information for managing services.

FIGURE 6.15

The MMC provides a consistent interface for managing different types of snap-ins.

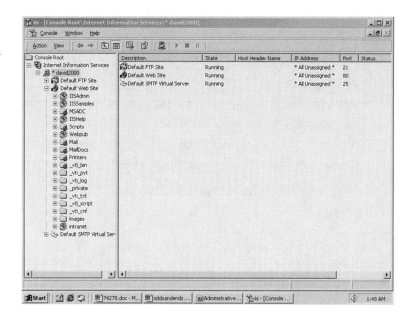

MMC Consoles

In the MMC, a *console* is simply a collection of different snap-ins or components designed to facilitate the management of a particular service. If you were administering a news server, for example, you might have a number of tasks to perform, such as expiring old articles or rebuilding the news database. These tasks could be listed in the MMC Console, enabling you to perform them quickly and easily with the click of a button.

Each console can have as many services as you want to add, although it might make sense to group similar administrative tasks or tasks for a specific service into one console. The beauty of the MMC design is that you can have as many consoles as you want on your system. In the Windows 2000 Control Panel, you can have the Internet Service Manager, the Computer Management, the Component Management, and the Server Extensions Administrator consoles all listed under the Administrative Services folder, depending on which features you installed.

The Console Tree (Scope Plane) and Details Plane (Results Plane)

The main MMC window is divided into two sections. The section on the left side of the window is called the *Console Tree* (in previous versions it was called the *Scope Plane*). The section of the right is called the *Details Plane* (in previous versions it was called the *Results Plane*).

Each of these two sections has a specific purpose. The Console Tree shows each of the administrative options that are available in a console. These can include snap-ins (management modules), various controls, and URLs, depending on the configuration of the service you are administering.

As an example, suppose you are administering an intranet site (see Chapter 24, "Setting up an Intranet"). Your tree might contain three items: a snap-in for your mail service, one for your news server, and one for your Web server. Each item that appears is called a *node*, which you can select by clicking it. All items in the Console Tree are contained within the *Console Root*, which simply groups all your nodes together.

MMC User Modes

The MMC is designed to be a flexible administration tool, so different users in your organization might need to use the MMC to manage various resources. Anytime you are sharing access to a resource, such as server management tools, you will want to provide for different levels of administration.

The MMC supports four modes: Author mode and three variants of User mode. These modes are designed to accommodate as many administrative needs as possible. The following is a brief description of these modes:

- *Author Mode*—In Author mode, you have full access to all of the MMC's features. You can add or remove nodes from the Console Tree, add/remove snap-ins, create and manage windows, and alter any of the applications options. This is the default mode for the MMC, and it's similar to having administrative rights on a server.

- *User Mode—Full Access*—In full Access User Mode, users have full access to all of the MMC's functionality but cannot add or remove nodes from the Console Tree or change the options for the MMC Console.

- *User Mode—Delegated Access, Multiple Window*—The same restrictions that apply to Full Access apply to Delegated Access as well. In addition, the user can view only areas of the console that were visible when the author saved the .msc (the MMC default extension) file for the console. The Delegated Access mode provides a mechanism for limiting access to certain administrative tasks in the MMC.

- *User Mode—Delegated Access, Single Window*—The same restrictions that apply to Delegated Access—Multiple Windows apply to Single Windows as well. The major difference is that, in this node, the user cannot open multiple windows.

With these User Mode options, you can configure the MMC to be used by a variety of administrators, depending on individual roles.

Snap-Ins

At the heart of the MMC are the modules that control individual aspects of system management—the *snap-ins*. These snap-ins are part of the architecture of the MMC and enable you to easily add management functionality to your individual consoles.

Snap-ins are not loaded automatically into the MMC. When you install a component that can be managed using the MMC, the appropriate snap-ins also are installed on your system. From there, you can add those snap-ins to any MMC Console that you are building for administration. To add a snap-in

1. Open your MMC by double-clicking an icon or choosing Start, Run, and typing `mmc /a` in the Open field.

2. Choose Console, Add/Remove Snap-ins. The Add/Remove Snap-in dialog box appears, as shown in Figure 6.16.

FIGURE 6.16

Adding and removing snap-ins from the MMC to create a console.

3. There are two tabs in this dialog box, one for standalone snap-ins and one for extensions. If you were going to extend an existing snap-in, you would select the Extensions tab.

4. Next, you need to choose where you want to add the snap-in. In this case, you will add it to the Console Root.

5. Click Add and the Add Standalone Snap-in dialog box appears to allow you to select the snap-in you want to add.

You can also use this feature to remove a snap-in.

Now that you have built a console, you will want to set the console options to control the level of access. To set the Console options, choose Console, Options in the MMC.

As you have seen, the MMC is a very powerful feature that is available to you in Windows 2000.

One of the most powerful of these is the Computer Management console, shown in Figure 6.17. Computer Management helps you manage local or remote computers using a single, consolidated desktop tool. It combines several Windows 2000 administration utilities into a single console tree, providing easy access to a specific computer's administrative properties and tools.

FIGURE 6.17
The Computer Management Console.

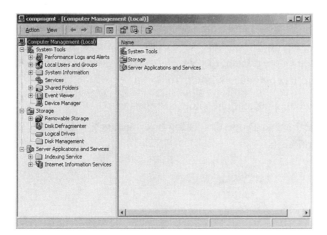

Scheduled Tasks

By using the Task Scheduler, you can schedule any script, program, or document to run at a time that is most convenient for you. Task Scheduler starts each time you start Windows 2000 and runs in the background. With the Task Scheduler, you can

- Schedule a task to run daily, weekly, monthly, or at certain times (such as system startup).
- Change the schedule for a task.
- Stop a scheduled task.
- Customize how a task runs at a scheduled time.

Scheduling different tasks is now easier than ever using the new Windows 2000 Scheduled Task Wizard (see Figure 6.18).

FIGURE 6.18

The Scheduled Tasks Wizard dialog box.

Customizing the Start Menu

Now that we've discussed all of the new features in the Control Panel, let's talk briefly about personalizing our Start Menu. One of the nice features in Windows 2000 is the ability to add the Control Panel to your Start Menu, giving you the convenience of having access to its components faster. To do this

1. Right-click the Taskbar and choose Properties.

2. When the Taskbar Properties dialog box appears (see Figure 6.19), click the Start Menu Options tab.

FIGURE 6.19

The Taskbar Properties dialog box.

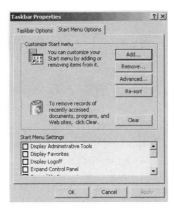

3. In the Start Menu Settings box, you can specify which folders you'd like to add to the Start Menu.

4. Check each box for the items that you'd like to enable.

There are several features you can enable. These include the following:

- *Display Administrative Tools*—Checking this box enables the Administrative Tools submenu, which consists of the following items: Component Services, Computer Management, Data Sources, Event Viewer, and Performance.

- *Expand Control Panel*—Checking this changes the Control Panel from a dialog box to fly-out menus you can use to quickly select a feature.

- *Expand Network and Dialup Connections*—Adds a quick fly-out menu for adding a new Network Connection or opening an existing connection.

- *Expand Printers*—Adds a fly-out menu for adding a new printer or accessing the properties of your existing printers.

As you can see from Figure 6.20, using this new feature can save you several steps.

FIGURE 6.20

You can change the Taskbar settings to put the Control panel right at your finger tips.

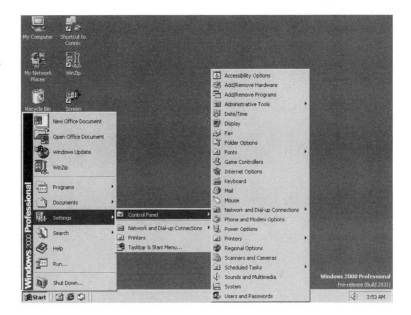

Tip

You can also display your Control Panel as a toolbar on your desktop, much like the familiar Microsoft Office or other shortcut toolbars. Simply right-click the Taskbar and choose Toolbars, New Toolbar, select Control Panel (under My Computer), and choose OK. The New toolbar will appear in your Taskbar and you can drag it onto the desktop as a dialog box or to the top or sides of your screen so it's always visible.

Summary

In this chapter, you have seen that the improved Control Panel is now the primary location for you to update and maintain your system. Printers, Scheduled Tasks, Network Connections, and Administrative Tools have all been moved to Control Panel.

The new Control Panel applets in Windows 2000 are a vast improvement over the features that were available in Windows NT 4.0 Workstation and also include more advanced features than the Windows 98 Control Panel. All of these add up to making your life easier when it comes to configuring and maintaining your system.

Fine-Tuning Windows 2000 Security

CHAPTER

7

Windows 2000 Security Overview

When we talk security on any operating system, we talk about locking down information so that no unauthorized user can access it. Security is a big concern for both corporate and home users. Microsoft has built security into Windows 2000 Professional that will allow administrators to control information and activities on the machine. This chapter is an overview of some of the advanced security options in Windows 2000 that will allow you to control access to your machine. This also includes the ability to grant specific privileges to users or groups that will allow them to administer the workstation or simply log on and perform a specific task. Lock up your information and applications, but be careful not to lock yourself out.

Users and Password

One of the first steps to controlling security is to create specific user accounts to be used by individuals who need access to a particular computer resource. By providing individual accounts and passwords, administers are able to control specific access and audit system use (if necessary). Windows 2000 Professional provides a way to require that all users log in to the system prior to using it.

> **Note**
>
> It is just as important to require users to log out of the system when they have finished using it. This makes the environment secure and prevents unauthorized users from walking up and using a computer that is already logged in. In this case, the unauthorized user can now have all the permissions of the logged in user without the proper security clearances.

By default, Windows 2000 Professional does not require a password to be entered when the machine is booted up. I recommend changing this setting immediately following the installation of the operating system. The default logged in user is the administrator who can perform any function on the computer. Don't wait; take care of this issue immediately.

This section explains how to change the default log on settings of Windows 2000, as well as providing an overview of the security environment in Windows 2000 Professional.

Built-In Accounts

Windows 2000, by default, adds two accounts to the machine during the installation. The first is the Administrator. This Administrator account is the default logged in account and

has the power to perform any task on the system. These tasks include simple tasks from shutting down the computer to the more complex tasks of creating and managing user accounts and groups. The second account created during the installation is the Guest account. This account is a catchall account with minimum security that is used if a user does not have an account or password. By default, the Guest account is disabled by the installation procedure. This account should only be enabled for specific purposes because it can pose a security threat by allowing too many people to gain access to the machine. Perform the following steps to see how these accounts are defined:

1. Click Start, Settings.

2. Click Control Panel.

3. Double-click the Users and Passwords icon and the screen shown in Figure 7.1 appears.

FIGURE 7.1

Default Users and Passwords settings after Windows 2000 installation.

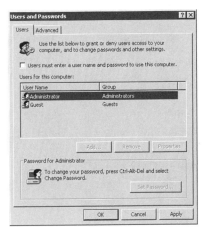

This dialog box represents the default security environment for a new installation of Windows 2000 Professional. By default, users are not required to log in to the system. Following the installation of Windows 2000, the operating system will automatically log you in as the Administrator of the machine. To change this default and enable user-based logins to the machine, place a check next to Users Must Enter a User Name and Password to Use This Computer. After this is checked, you will be able to add and remove accounts as well as alter their properties. In addition, with the Administrator account selected, there is additional information on how to change the password on that account. The Administrator account password must be changed by pressing the Ctrl+Alt+Del keys and selecting the Change Password button.

It is a good practice to add a new account for each individual user who will be accessing your workstation. This way, specific permissions can be used that will help control and protect the files and resources you choose. In addition, by creating specific accounts for each user, Windows 2000 will allow you to do user-level auditing for potential audit access to files and so on.

Creating New Users

This section covers creating new users on the local Windows 2000 Professional machine. If you are currently logged in to a Windows NT/2000 domain, it will be necessary to log out and log in to your local workstation to proceed.

Perform the following steps to create new users:

1. Click the Start button on the bottom-left portion of the screen, choose Settings, and then choose Control Panel.

2. Double-click the Users and Passwords icon and then select the Users tab.

3. Check the box at the top labeled Users Must Enter a User Name and Password to Use This Computer. If this box is not checked, you will be unable to click the Add, Remove, and Properties buttons and, therefore, will be unable to add new users.

4. Click the Add button to bring up the Add New User dialog box. The key fields are User Name, Full Name, and Description as shown in Figure 7.2.

FIGURE 7.2

Adding a new user to the local account database.

In this example, I added a user named SmithJ. The Full Name and the Description columns are only there for documentation purposes. Windows 2000 does not use this information in any way. Upon log on to the system, the user name will be SmithJ. Before creating user accounts, check with your network administrator for any naming standards. In a corporate environment, it is important to follow standards wherever possible.

5. Click the Next button. A new dialog box will appear prompting you for a password for the new user. Key in the password exactly the same in both boxes provided.

6. Click the Next button. There is now a choice to be made regarding the access level of this new account. Refer to the "Groups" section later in this chapter for more information on which level to choose. Select the level of access and then click Finish. Figure 7.3 displays group references.

FIGURE 7.3

Selecting the access level to grant to the user.

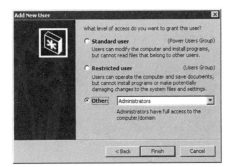

The new user has been created, as shown in Figure 7.4.

FIGURE 7.4

The new user account has been created.

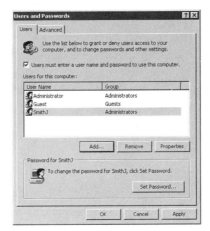

This dialog box can also be used to change the password for the user account selected in the list. It is a good idea to have users change their password periodically to prevent unauthorized access.

It is now possible to log in with the new account SmithJ as an Administrator of the system.

Additional Account Properties

Each account created in the system contains additional properties and settings to further customize the behavior and privileges of the account. To view these additional settings, perform the following steps:

1. Click Start, Settings.

2. Select Control Panel, and then choose Users and Passwords.

3. Click the Advanced tab, and then click the Advanced button.

4. In the left pane, double-click the Console Root, and then expand the Local Users and Groups (Local) selection.

5. Click Users. A list of all the local user accounts will be displayed in the right pane, as shown in Figure 7.5.

FIGURE 7.5

Locating the accounts in the Local User Manager dialog box.

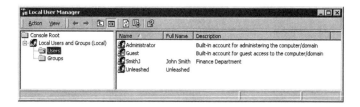

6. Double-click the newly created SmithJ account. A SmithJ Properties window appears, as shown in Figure 7.6.

FIGURE 7.6

Advanced user properties dialog box.

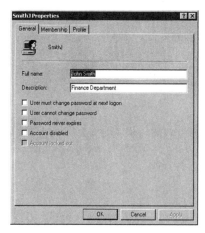

7. SmithJ's full name and description are shown onscreen. These entries are the same entries that I added in the previous section when I created this account. However, there are other settings that appear, as described in the following:

- *User Must Change Password at Next Logon*—This is a very useful setting. You can create an account with a default password (such as "password"). You can then force the user to change the password to something different when he or she logs on the next time. Many password hacking programs will try the word "password" for an account's password because it is so commonly used.

- *User Cannot Change Password*—This setting restricts a user from making changes to their password. This can be helpful if the Administrators issue unique passwords and want to control them for various uses.

- *Password Never Expires*—To maximize security on your machine, it is a good idea not use this setting. When checked, Windows 2000 will never force the user to change his or her password. I would recommend periodic password changes to help prevent unauthorized access of your machine.

- *Account Disabled*—Disabling accounts restricts the user from logging in to the machine. This may be necessary if a user goes on a sabbatical for two months and you don't want to delete the account and have to recreate it when he or she returns. You can simply disable the account when the user leaves and re-enable it when he or she returns.

- *Account Locked Out*—Windows 2000 can be configured to lockout accounts after a configured amount of failed login attempts. If a password-cracking program knew an account name and attempted to crack the password, it may lockout the account based on the system account settings. This way, the account will be locked out automatically after three attempts and cannot be unlocked without the help of an administrator.

8. Click the Member Of tab. The information on this tab pertains to the group membership of this account. This topic will be discussed in detail in the "Groups" section of this chapter.

9. Click the Profile tab. The following properties can be set on this tab:

- *Profile Path*—Path of the profile for this user account.

- *Logon Script*—Full path and name of the logon script for this account. A logon script is run after the user is validated and can connect the user to other network file sharing drives and printers.

- *Home Folder*—Choose a setting to connect the user to a local share for a home folder. A home folder on the network can be used for personal space just for this account. Environment variables can be used here to ease administration and prevent hard-coding account names.

Groups

Groups are used to help make complex security issues a little more bearable. Imagine that if every time you added a user to the machine, you had to specifically identify every place that user needed to access. Instead, the administrator can assign permissions to groups of users. When a new user requests access to a file or resource, the Administrator only has to add the new user to a group. By becoming part of a group, the new user will inherit all the permissions of the group. Therefore, if the group has permission to write to the \\Corporate\Sales directory, the new user will be able to write information to that group after that user becomes a member of the group.

> **Note**
>
> These groups are local groups that are created and stored on your workstation. All rights and permissions created with these groups are for your workstation only and do not affect the account databases on the network servers.

There are six default groups that will be created during the Windows 2000 Professional installation. User accounts can be placed in these groups to control specific tasks that each user is allowed to perform:

- *Administrators*—Users that have full access to the computer.
- Backup Operators—These users only have permissions to back up files via a backup program.
- *Guests*—Guests are restricted from installing programs and making other system changes. These users can access the computer and save files.
- *Power Users*—Users that are allowed to install programs and modify the system configuration. However, these users are restricted from accessing other users' files.
- *Replicator*—Group to support file replication.
- *Users*—Similar to Guests, having minimum security and no authority to modify the system configuration.

These groups do cover specific tasks that members are permitted to and restricted from performing. These built-in groups, however, do not provide specific permissions for files and directories on the file system.

> **Note**
>
> You must have the NTFS file system installed to grant and revoke specific file and directory permission. With the FAT and FAT32 file systems, you will be able to control only the share level permission.

To create a new group, perform the following steps:

1. Click Start, Settings.

2. Choose the Control Panel, and then double-click the Administrative Tools icon.

3. Locate the System Tools item under the Computer Management (Local) folder. Within this folder, locate the Local Users and Groups item.

4. The Groups folder is located under the Local Users and Groups folder. Right-click the Groups folder, and then choose Create New Group.

5. A new dialog box appears prompting you for the Name and Description of the group. To create a Finance group to hold all the users from the Finance Department, type `Finance` for the name and **Users from the Finance Department** in the description box.

6. To add users to the new group, click the Add button.

7. Scroll down in the box listing the users and groups on the workstation and then choose the SmithJ account created previously in this chapter.

8. Click Add to add the user SmithJ to the group. The new group will now have one user (SmithJ), as shown in Figure 7.7.

FIGURE 7.7

Adding a user to a new group.

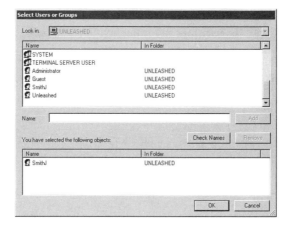

9. Click OK. The Finance group will appear displaying the all the members of the group, as shown in Figure 7.8.

FIGURE 7.8

Finalizing the new group creation.

10. Click Create to finalize the creation of the group, and then click Close to close the window. You will now be back at the Local User Manager screen. As you can see, the new group Finance is now listed among the groups in the list. This new group can now be used for any file or folder permissions. This group could now, based on your discretion, act as a model for all new users in the Finance Department. Therefore, adding a new user to the Finance group will provide complete access to all resources granted to the group—not the individual.

User Profiles

User profiles are created so that Administrators can have control over how users interact with the desktop environment on the workstation they log in to. Default user profiles are not created for a user until the user logs in for the first time. Once logged in, the default profile is created and the user obtains the default settings.

Perform the following steps to create a user profile:

1. Log in to the workstation as an Administrator or a member of the Administrator's group.
2. Open Windows Explorer and create a directory on your C: drive named **profiles**. This directory will be used to store the default profile you want users to access when using the system.
3. Click Start, Settings.
4. Click the Control Panel, and then double-click the System icon.

5. Choose the User Profile tab. Notice there are already a few default profiles saved on my local workstation, as shown in Figure 7.9.

FIGURE 7.9

User profiles.

On this screen, you can see that there are three profiles currently created. SmithJ has a local profile. Because it is local, this user can save and make changes to the desktop, Favorites, cookies, My Documents, and the Start menu. As an Administrator of the system, however, you can control this and not allow the user to delete a folder on the desktop, for example. Let's say you want the SmithJ account to always have the Finance folder on his desktop.

6. Click the SmithJ user profile and click the Copy To button.

7. A dialog box will now appear. In the Copy Profile To text box, type in `c:\profiles\finance.`

8. Click OK to save the profile.

9. To verify your work, open Windows Explorer and look in the `c:\profiles\finance` directory. What you will see here are the cookies, desktop, Favorites, My Documents, and Start menu folders. The next time a user logs in with this profile set in his or her account properties, he or she will automatically use these settings. Upon log off, any modification made will be updated in the profile if the user has the correct permissions.

10. In the `c:\profiles\Finance` folder, open the desktop directory and click the File menu at the top of the screen.

11. Click the New selection, and then choose Folder.

12. Type in **Finance** for the name, and then press the Enter key.

13. While still logged in as Administrator, right-click the new `Finance` directory just created and click Properties.

14. Choose the Security tab, and then click Add.

15. From the list of users provided, click SmithJ and then click the Add button (see Figure 7.10).

FIGURE 7.10

Adding file permissions to the profile directory.

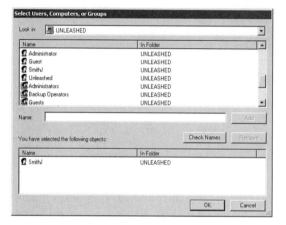

16. Click OK to continue.

17. Click the name John Smith to specify specific permissions, and choose Read & Execute, List Folder Contents, and Read, as shown in Figure 7.11.

FIGURE 7.11

Successfully added read-only file permissions.

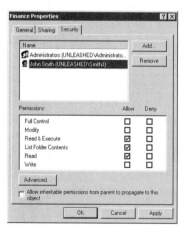

18. Click OK to continue.

19. The final step will be to alter the SmithJ logon properties and configure them to use the new profile. To do this, click the Start menu and then choose Settings.

20. Click the Control Panel item, and then double-click Administrative tools.

21. Double-click the Computer Management icon, and then drill down into Computer Management (Local) and then into System Tools.

22. Click Local Users and Groups, and then select Users.

23. Double-click SmithJ and then click the Profile tab.

24. In the Profile Path text box, type in the path to the directory where you saved the profile: `c:\profiles\finance`.

25. Log off as the Administrator and log back in as SmithJ. The Finance folder will now appear on the desktop. This directory can be deleted, but an error will occur stating that the roaming profile cannot be updated. Because the user is now accessing a profile, the Finance directory will appear the next time the user logs in.

As you can see, profiles in Windows 2000 Professional enable the Administrator to have additional control over the end user's desktop. These controls allow companies to standardize a desktop and control some of the user configuration options. This feature is very useful and can help reduce support calls.

Auditing

Auditing is an important part of Windows 2000 Professional administration. Windows 2000 Professional makes it possible to audit a variety of different user activities. Windows 2000 provides a way to look at virtually anything the user is doing. Each audited event is then inserted into the Event log for review.

Before any auditing can take affect in Windows 2000, it is necessary to enable auditing via the Microsoft Management Console. By default, the auditing options are not enabled. To enable auditing, it is first necessary to add the Group Policy Object to your Microsoft Management Console environment (MMC). This is accomplished by performing the following steps:

1. Click Start, Run.

2. Type in `mmc /a`, and then press Enter. This will start the MMC and allow you to configure it for additional management objects or snap-ins.

3. Click Console, and choose Add/Remove Snap-in, as shown in Figure 7.12.

FIGURE 7.12

*Adding a snap-in
to the Microsoft
Management
Console (MMC).*

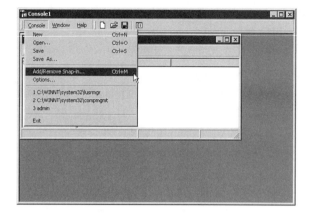

4. Click Add on the Add/Remove Snap-in dialog box.

5. Scroll down and select Group Policy.

6. Click Add, and then click Finish to save the setting.

7. Click Close to close the dialog box.

8. Click Console, Save. Assign a name for this console configuration and then click OK.

Scenario: You suspect that someone is logging on to your machine at night. You would like to find out who that is by enabling auditing. To do this, perform the following steps:

1. Launch the Microsoft Management Console application and open the file you created in the previous steps.

2. Double-click Console Root to expand, and then drill down to the Audit Policy folder located under the following directory structure: Local Computer Policy, Computer Configuration, Windows Settings, Security Settings, Local Policies, Audit Policy.

3. To enable auditing on logon events, double-click Audit Account Logon Events in the right pane.

4. When the Local Security Policy Setting dialog box appears, click Audit Success and Failure Attempts. Click OK to continue.

5. Exit the MMC, and click the Start button.

6. Choose Shutdown, and then choose Log off Administrator from the drop-down list box.

7. Click OK and then log back in. At this point, there will be a logon event in the security portion of the Event Viewer.

8. To view the Event Viewer, click Start, Settings.

9. Click the Control Panel, Administrative Tools.

10. Double-click Computer Management, and then drill down to System Tools, Event Viewer.

11. Click the Security Log and an entry should appear under the category of Account Logon. The Account Logon is now date and time stamped and secured.

Auditing is a very comprehensive feature in Windows 2000 Professional. In addition to auditing events, administrators have the ability to audit file and folder access.

Policies

Account policies are customizable in the Windows 2000 Professional environment. There are a variety of ways to control the security descriptors of all logins. To view the Account Policies, open the Microsoft Management Console Local Computer Policy module, as previously described in the "Auditing" section.

The settings for account password and lockout policies are located under Local Computer Policy, Computer Configuration, Windows Settings, Security Settings, and the Account Policies.

These settings control the following parameters:

Password Policy

- *Store Password Using Reversible Encryption For All Users In The Domain*

- *Enforce Password History*—This setting is useful to prohibit users from changing their passwords to the same passwords that just expired. If they are able to do this, they are effectively not updating their passwords—they are simply buying themselves more time until the next required password change. I recommend setting this to at least 5.

- *Maximum Password Age*—The default setting for this is 42. Therefore, the user will be forced to change his or her password after 42 days. This setting can be within a range of 1–999 or set to Forever. I recommend setting this to 30 to force a new password for all users every 30 days.

- *Minimum Password Age*—Password days to expire before the next password change. This setting is useful to keep users from changing their passwords to different passwords (when forced to) and then immediately changing them back to their original. I recommend setting this to 2.

- *Minimum Password Length*—The default setting here is 0. I recommend setting this to at least 6. The longer the password, the more difficult it becomes to crack using password cracking software.

- *Password Must Meet Complexity Requirements of Installed Password Filter*—This setting is disabled by default but can be enabled, provided you have an installed password filter. Common uses here are to require both alpha and numeric data in your password. Again, using both letters and numbers provides more potential password combinations and, therefore, makes it more difficult for password cracking programs to be successful.

- *User Must Log On to Change Password*—This will prevent an unauthorized user from changing the password without logging in.

Account Lockout Policy

- *Account Lockout Count*—The default value for this setting is 0 Invalid Logon attempts. I would set this setting to 5. Therefore, if 5 invalid password attempts are made to a specific logon account, the account will be locked out and the potential hacker will not be allowed into the system. Again, this is another setting that protects against password cracking software.

- *Lockout Account For*—This can force a lock out for a specific time if the Account Lockout count has been exceeded. I recommend setting this to Forever to force the Administrator of the system to have to manually unlock the account. This forces the Administrator to be made aware of this event. If a time is set, the Administrator may not be aware of a potential hack into the system.

- *Reset Account Lockout Count After*—This is a setting set in minutes on when to reset the lockout count. For instance, if my account lockout count is set to 5, and I've forgotten my password and mistype it four times, I can have the count reset to 0 after a period of minutes. I recommend setting this to at least 30. This way, if you do mistype your password four times, you can wait half an hour and try again.

Dial-In Security

Windows 2000 Professional includes software for communication over a standard phone line. Windows 2000 Professional contains services for users to dial out and communicate with other computers and contains software that allows users to configure the workstation to accept incoming calls from other computers. By allowing incoming calls, your machine can become a Remote Access Server and allow sharing of files and print services on your machine. This type of connection is useful to dial in to your machine at the office, for instance. If your company does not have a dial-in network set up, your machine can act as the hub to entering the network.

> **Caution**
>
> Be careful when installing this feature. It could pose a potential security risk by making the entire network available to outside callers. It is important to check with your network administrator to make sure that installing this feature doesn't breech your LAN security.

To enable this feature, do the following:

1. Click Start, Settings.
2. Click Network and Dial-up Connections, and then double-click Make New Connection. Click Next.
3. Choose Accept Incoming Connections, and then click Next.
4. A dialog box will appear with a list of valid devices that can be used for incoming connections. Place a check in the Modem check box and then click Next.
5. A new dialog box will appear querying for information regarding Incoming Virtual Private Connections. Choose Allow Virtual Private Connections or Do Not Allow Virtual Private Connections. If you are unsure which to choose, always choose the option with the least security impact. It is important to grant only minimum access during setup. The more restrictive you are, the less chance someone will have to hack into your system.
6. Click Next.
7. At this point, you will be prompted to select which users will be allowed access to your machine over the modem. To minimize the security risk, select only the individuals that need to be log in. At this point, you are also given the opportunity to Add and Delete users if necessary.

> **Tip**
>
> Another very important security setting you can use here is Callback. For each user, you can specify a phone number to call back to after the user connects. For example, Fred will only call into the corporate headquarters from his home office. When granting Fred access to call a Windows 2000 machine, the setting can be made to have a mandatory callback. So, Fred dials the corporate network and has his username and password authenticated. Then, the host computer disconnects the call and immediately calls Fred back with the number specified in his user settings. Once Fred's computer is disconnected, it immediately waits for a call from the corporate headquarters. These settings prevent hackers from dialing in to the network or Windows 2000 computer, even if they have Fred's ID and password. The Callback settings are displayed when the Properties button is clicked.

Select the users that should be granted access, configure their callback settings, and then click Next to continue.

8. You will now be able to choose the network components that can be used when users log in. To increase security, for instance, you can choose to allow only connections using the NetBEUI protocol. You can tell everyone that will connect to install NetBEUI and use it as his or her dial-up protocol into your network. Now, anyone trying to hack into the system with TCP/IP will not be able to see anything on the network. This is a form of filtering.

   This is another area where extreme caution should be exercised. Only enable the components that your dial-in users will absolutely need. If they will not be using TCP/IP, I recommend not enabling it. The same is true for File and Printer Sharing and Client for Microsoft Networks.

   In addition, under the properties of both TCP/IP and NetBEUI there is a check box to Allow Callers to Access My Local Area Network. Only use this setting if absolutely necessary. By enabling this setting, users who dial in will be able to browse your entire network looking for trouble.

9. Click Next to continue. At the next dialog box, give the incoming connection a name and then click Finish. The machine is now ready for incoming connections.

Registry

The Registry in Windows 2000 Professional is a database that contains configuration information for both the hardware and software on the computer. The Registry is another area on the computer that can potentially contain sensitive data or configuration information that you do not want any other user to change.

> **Note**
>
> Extreme care must be taken when making changes to the Registry. Make a complete system backup prior to making any changes. If incorrect changes are made, the system could become unusable.

The Registry is organized similar to the directory structure of the file system. In file system terms, a Registry hive is any directory and all of its subdirectories. It may become important to change the permissions on certain Registry hives on your computer to prevent end user tampering. To change settings on a particular Registry hive, do the following:

1. Click Start, Run.
2. The tool used to set the Registry security is called REGEDT32.EXE. There is no default icon for this application. Type in **REGEDT32.EXE** and click OK.
3. Select the Registry hive where the security will be changed.
4. Click the Security menu, and then choose Permissions.
5. By default, the Administrators groups has full control of most Registry hives, and the Users group has Read permissions. If, for instance, you want to revoke access to the Users group for a particular hive, select the Users group in the box provided.
6. Click Remove.
7. Click OK to complete. The Users group no longer has permission to the Registry hive specified.

File System Security

File system security in Windows 2000 Professional includes specifying specific permission for both files and folders. To use file system security, however, the volume must be formatted with the NT File System (NTFS). If the file system is formatted with the File Allocation Table (FAT) file system, you will not be able to specify specific permissions for file and folders. File system security gives the Administrator of the system a way to protect files and folders from unwanted viewing, updating, or deleting.

Windows 2000 Professional has more sophisticated permission settings than previous versions. When specifying file or folder permissions, the Administrator is now able to view inherited permissions from parent directories. In addition, directories can be omitted from the inheritable permissions of parent objects. In previous versions, permissions were set on a folder. If the Administrator specified to apply the permissions to all subfolders, every directory under the current directory received the new permissions. This was dangerous. The new version will help you avoid costly mistakes. You will still have to be very organized under complex directory structures, but this new way should make your life easier.

Removing Everyone's Permissions

The default permissions on an NTFS formatted volume in Windows 2000 is that the Everyone group has all permissions granted. Every user with a login will be able to read, write, execute, and modify files and folders. If you have sensitive material on your machine, it will be very important to immediately change these permissions where appropriate.

To alter the permissions on a folder, do the following:

1. Open Windows Explorer and right-click the icon of the folder where the permissions will be altered.
2. Choose Properties, and then click the Security tab.

> **Note**
>
> If the Security tab is not available, the volume is not formatted for NTFS. To verify the file system type, click the General tab and look for the file system label. If the file system is FAT, the drive will have to be converted to NTFS to enable file and folder permissions. Before doing this, however, consult the Windows 2000 Professional documentation on converting volumes. After a volume is converted from FAT to NTFS, it cannot be converted back.

3. If available, click the Security tab to view all the security for the drive selected.
4. Click the Everyone group, as shown in Figure 7.13.

FIGURE 7.13

Default permissions for the Everyone group.

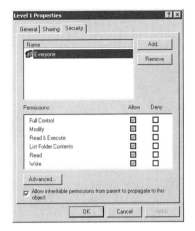

As you can see, the Everyone group is allowed Full Control. The rest of the Allow check boxes are grayed out because the permissions Full Control, Modify, Read & Execute, List Folder Contents, Read, and Write on this directory have been inherited from the parent (D:).

Be careful. If you deny any rights to the Everyone group here, no user (including the Owner and Administrator) will be able to write to this folder or any of the subfolders.

5. Click the Add button to add a permission entry to apply to this folder and all of its subfolders. Click a group desired and then click the Add button. The new group will now be listed in the permission box, along with the Everyone group.

> **Note**
>
> If the Administrator is allowed to view all files and folders on the machine, add the Administrators group to the permissions also. By default, the Administrators are the owners of all files and folders and, because of that fact, they have the ability to alter permissions on files and folders, even if they do not currently have any permissions to these objects.
>
> The Everyone permission settings cannot be altered here unless the Allow Inheritable Permissions from Parent to Propagate to the Object setting is unchecked.

6. Uncheck the Allow Inheritable Permissions from Parent to Propagate to Object box. The dialog box shown in Figure 7.14 appears.

FIGURE 7.14

The warning message displayed when disabling inheritable permissions.

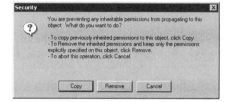

This is a warning that the permissions on your directory are about to be severely altered. You can abort this operation by clicking Cancel, copy previous permissions by clicking Copy, or remove inherited permissions by clicking Remove. In this case, we would like to remove inherited permissions and keep the permissions explicitly specified on this object. This way, the new group we added will have Full Control only, and the Everyone group will not be able to make changes.

Click Remove to Continue.

7. Click the group you added to the permissions and select Allow—Full Control.

8. Click OK to complete the security changes.

> **Note**
>
> By default, the files and folders of a volume structure are owned by the Administrators group. If, for some reason, you make a mistake with the permissions, a member of the Administrators group will be able to log on to the system and repair the permissions. If this is not secure enough, the ownership of a file or folder can be changed.

There are many more advanced ways to administer and customize the files and folders permissions on your workstation. Careful planning and organization in the beginning will save many headaches down the road if many users will be using a workstation with sensitive data. Read the Windows 2000 help files and check Microsoft's Web site (www.microsoft.com) for additional information.

Remote Access Service (RAS)

Windows 2000 Professional can be easily configured to gain access to another computer via a modem or ISDN line. Say, for example, that you would like to dial in to your computer at work. You can configure your workstation to dial the modem and log on to that system. After your account name and password are validated, you will be able to access resources on the machine and potentially the entire network (based on the configuration of the remote host).

To create a dial-in connection, do the following:

1. Click Start, Settings.
2. Click Network and Dial-Up Connections, and then double-click Make New Connection.
3. A Welcome screen to the Network Connection Wizard appears. Click Next to continue.
4. Select the Dial-up to Private Network radio button, and then click Next.
5. Select the Use Dialing Rules check box. This will allow you to enter an area code.
6. Type in the area code and phone number of the workstation that you are trying to dial, and then click Next.
7. You will now be prompted for the Connection Availability. If you want to make this connection available to any user logged in to your workstation, keep the default value of For All Users. If, however, you would prefer to have this available only for your login account, choose Only for Myself, and then click Next.
8. Type in a name for the connection at the next prompt, and then select whether you want the Wizard to add a shortcut to your desktop. Click Finish to continue.
9. The Connect Dial-up Connection dialog box appears. Type in the username of the account you will use to access the remote machine given to you by the Administrator of the remote machine. Once logged in, your machine will use this account and password to validate your security on all resources you request on the remote network.
10. Type in the username, password, and logon name, and then click the Dial button to dial the remote machine.

Note

For maximum security, do not select the Save Password option on this screen. By selecting the Save Password option, any user will be able to dial this connection if you leave your machine logged on and walk away from your desk. By not logging off, anyone can have access to both your machine and the remote machine. It is best to simply get into the habit of typing your password each time you use the remote connection.

Certificates

As Internet and e-commerce sites and services continue to grow at staggering rates, security becomes an issue. Whether you are placing an order at your favorite online bookstore or trading shares of stock, the security must be there for you to trust that the transaction is valid. Certificate services can be Windows 2000 servers or they can be third-party servers, such as Verisign. By requesting a certificate from a third party, your security can be enhanced beyond the typical username and password.

In the past, Windows NT supported older versions of the certificate server and really only enabled them through the Internet browser. Windows 2000 Professional supports the X.509 Version 3 certificate and now comes bundled with tools to manage and administer all the public certificates on your system. These new tools are closely integrated with the operating system and can be managed via a snap-in inside the Microsoft Management Console or via the Certificate Manager in the Control Panel.

To Open the Certificate Manager on your machine, do the following:

1. Click Start, Settings.
2. Choose Control Panel, and then double-click the Users and Passwords icon.
3. Select the Advanced tab, and then click Certificates. Tabs are shown at the top of the screen that group the authorities. Several default certificates are loaded with the installation of Windows 2000 to be used for various purposes.

To view the details of a certificate, perform the following steps:

1. Open the Certificate Manager, as described earlier, and then select the certificate from which you want to obtain the details.
2. Click View to browse the details of this certificate.

To add a new certificate

1. Open the Certificate Manager, and then click Import.
2. The Certificate Manager Import Wizard will start. Click Next to continue.
3. Locate the full directory and filename of the key file.
4. Click Next to continue.

Because billions of dollars are now transferred between parties on the Internet today, any additional security measures you can take will definitely help you sleep better at night. Contact Verisign (`http://www.verisign.com/`) or ask your system Administrators about the certificate securities that exist on your network.

Summary

Windows 2000 Professional has a very solid security mechanism to protect your computer and the data stored on it. Take your time and explore the various security aspects to learn how to protect it from a potential hacker attack.

The Windows 2000 Registry

The Registry has often been regarded with awe and reservation by most users. Its cryptic structure and lack of documentation has kept most users out of it. It was designed as a replacement for the multiple .INI files that often litter users' hard drives. The major purpose of the Registry is to hold configuration information about your computer, the operating system, and its applications.

This chapter should shed some light on the Registry, and remove some of the mystery behind it.

Understanding the Purpose of the Registry

Since the beginning of Microsoft's Disk Operating System (MS-DOS), there has always been a need for the storage of configuration information. This information was required initially by the OS, and was stored in a text file named CONFIG.SYS. To augment this file, another text file was able to automate some of the start-up procedures, AUTOEXEC.BAT. This made life easier for several users and lead programmers to the idea that certain configuration information could be left in external files, rather than having everything hard coded into their applications.

As Windows arrived on the scene, a standard format for these configuration text files was created; these were Initialization files (.INI). The INI files were used to store startup settings for both applications as well as the Windows operating system. Windows settings were stored in WIN.INI and SYSTEM.INI, with other settings stored in files like CON-TROL.INI, PROGMAN.INI, and PROTOCOL.INI. Other applications had the option of creating their own INI files that should have been stored in the Windows directory. Some programmers decided to store their INI files in their own directories, which would sometimes lead to having multiple copies of the same file with conflicting settings.

Eventually the multitude of INI files lead to problems finding the settings you wanted to change—enter the Registry. The Registry existed in Windows 3.0, but was only used to store the registration information for applications, or rather their file associations. Windows NT enhanced this registration, allowing applications to store any information desired in the Registry. Windows NT did not stop with letting other applications use the Registry, it also chose to store a majority of its own configuration in the Registry.

The number of components within the operating system that use the Registry are boundless. NTDETECT.COM performs a hardware detection that is stored in the Registry. NTOSKRNL.EXE uses that information and other settings to load the majority of the OS into memory. Services and devices get driver locations and settings from the Registry.

Setup programs retrieve and store information for their programs in the Registry. User preferences and user-related settings are stored in the Registry. Control panels and other applications (like Microsoft Management Console) provide an intuitive graphical interface to read and modify the Registry.

Microsoft is now promoting the idea of a network registry, which will be able to store and retrieve settings for a user who is anywhere on the network. This network registry is called Active Directory Service (ADS). In addition to all of the other information ADS will be able to store, it will also be able to store application settings for users.

Unless you happen to be an operating system component, like `NTDETECT.COM`, you will have to use one of the Registry editing tools. Microsoft has provided a few from which you can choose.

Editing Tools

Microsoft supplies three basic tools for editing the Windows 2000 Registry. These tools are

- REGEDT32
- REGEDIT
- Local Computer Policy (Microsoft Management Console)

Each of these tools have their specific strengths and weaknesses. While REGEDT32 and REGEDIT are general purpose tools, the Local Computer Policy is designed to setup an initial environment and to enforce security settings. REGEDT32 is the Windows NT Registry editor, and it is fully compatible with Windows 2000. REGEDIT has some improved features that were introduced with Windows 95, but lacks some functionality. Both of these editors can be launched through the RUN command in the Start menu.

REGEDT32

REGEDT32 was designed to edit the Windows NT Registry. It is now used to edit the Windows 2000 Registry. Its user interface has multiple Windows, one for each registry tree (see Figure 8.1). The main advantages of this registry editor are

- It is aware of all the registry data types.
- It supports Read Only mode.
- You are able to set permissions for registry access.

FIGURE 8.1

Although this is the most advanced Registry editor, its design is still based on the Windows 3.0 user interface.

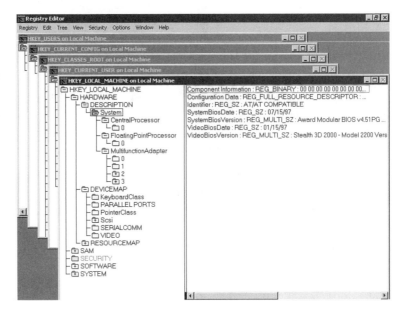

These advantages will be covered in more detail later in this chapter. They should be reason enough to use REGEDT32, although there are some drawbacks to this editor, which will be discussed when talking about REGEDIT in the next section.

REGEDIT

REGEDIT has been available since Windows 3.0, but served a different purpose with Windows 3.0. Its original purpose was mainly to handle the registration of applications with the operating system. This meant that it was responsible for taking care of remembering file associations and object classes for Object Linking and Embedding (OLE). With the release of Windows 95, the purpose of the registry was expanded to handle the storage of several settings (almost all) for the operating system, and allowed for the storage of all settings for applications. This is the same principle that is followed with Windows 2000. The other major change that was made with REGEDIT is the updating of the user interface, which is Explorer based (see Figure 8.2).

Some of the benefits of using this registry editor include:

- It supports a more advanced Find feature.
- It has a much easier to use Export and Import feature.
- You are able to store a list favorites for Registry keys.
- You are able to copy the key name for pasting into other applications.

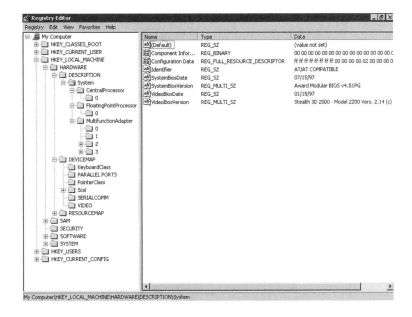

FIGURE **8.2**

REGEDIT uses the Windows 95 Explorer interface.

Exporting and importing Registry entries will be covered later in this chapter in the "Key Backup and Restore," "Using REGEDIT," and "Using REGEDT32" sections.

Local Computer Policy

The features supplied by the Local Computer Policy are the same as those received from Group Policies. The primary is that Group Policies are applied through Active Directory Services (ADS) and are applied to users and computers based on their membership in sites, domains, or organizational units (SDOUs). The Local Computer Policy management snap-in can be added to MMC by opening it in Author Mode. This can be done by typing **MMC** at the RUN command.

To add the Policy Editor, choose Add/Remove Snap-in from the Console menu. Select the Add button. The snap-in that will be added is Group Policy, which will become Local Computer Policy on the snap-in screen (see Figure 8.3).

After you have the Local Computer Policy snap-in added, you will be able to expand the tree to see Computer Configuration and User Configuration.

The changes you make in these settings affect your local computer and all users. If you decide that you will disable the RUN command (\User Configuration\Administrative Templates\Start Menu & Taskbar\Remove Run menu from Start Menu) for the current user, you will soon find that it is missing for all users. Most of the options that are available deal with either security restrictions (disabling features) or environment changes (modifying the user profile).

FIGURE 8.3

To modify the Local Computer Policy you will have to add the MMC snap-in.

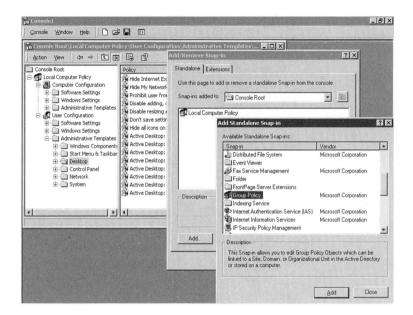

The Registry entries that the Policy Editor is aware of is based on the loaded templates. Templates can be used to allow the restriction and configuration of other registry settings. The template files are `*.AMD` files that are found in the `%systemroot%\INF` directory. The ADM files are text files, so they can be edited with any text editor. Many applications ship with their own ADM files that can be used with Windows 95/98/NT/2000.

The ADM files that are included with Windows 2000 include the default `SYSTEM.ADM`, which has all of the initial values in it. But Microsoft also included the following template files:

- Desktop Shell Settings and Restrictions (`SHELL.ADM`)
- Microsoft Comic Chat Settings and Restrictions (`CHAT.ADM`)
- Internet Settings for Internet Explorer (`INETSET.ADM`)
- Internet Restrictions for Internet Explorer (`INETRES.ADM`)
- Microsoft NetMeeting Settings and Restrictions (`CONF.ADM`)
- Active Channel and Offline Browsing folders Settings (`SUBS.ADM`)
- Outlook Express Settings and Restrictions (`OE.ADM`)

These additional templates can be added by right-clicking the Administrative templates under either User Configuration or Computer Configuration.

Safety When Editing

Microsoft has tried to make it perfectly clear to all users that they will not gladly support you if they find out you have made changes to your Registry. This is entirely due to the size and complexity of the Registry. I totally agree with this point of view, as it would be impossible to track down a problem to a specific poorly-changed Registry value.

> **Warning**
>
> Always use caution and common sense when working with any Registry editing tools. Some changes can result in having to reinstall the Windows 2000 Operating System.

When you plan to change anything in the Registry, you should first back up or record the current settings of the items you are adding, modifying, or deleting from the Registry. You should also be aware that when you type a change and commit it, the change has been made. The only way to back out of the change is to manually reverse it. This section will now look at the following items in Registry safety:

- Atomic changes
- Read Only Mode
- Key backup and restore

Safety should always be your first concern when entering the Registry.

8

THE WINDOWS 2000 REGISTRY

Atomic Changes

Atomic changes refer to the way changes are recorded in the Registry. It does not matter which Registry editing tools you use, they all have the same behavior. When you open a Registry editing tool, you create an active session with the Registry Database. Because this is a database, you read in the current values and see them on your screen. When you modify a field and move to the next one, any changes are immediately written to the Registry.

Read Only Mode

REGEDT32 supports additional safety by allowing you to put the editor into Read Only Mode. Choosing this option from the Options menu enables this. This feature will prevent accidental changes being made when you only plan to read the Registry.

Key Backup and Restore

Backing up and restoring Registry keys is the best way to migrate settings as well as recover from incorrect changes made to your Registry. The process and options differ depending on the editor you are using. The Local Computer Policy (MMC) does not allow for backing up Registry keys. You will only be able to back up keys with REGEDIT, REGEDT32, or some of the Registry tools included in the Windows 2000 Resource Kit. Because most changes will be made with either REGEDIT or REGEDT32, this section will be limited to those two products.

REGEDIT

If I were given a choice between applications to use for this process, I would choose REGEDIT. Its process is more foolproof than that of REGEDT32. Perform the following steps to backup a key or group of keys:

1. Select the key you want to backup in the navigation pane of REGEDIT.
2. Select Export Registry File from the Registry menu.
3. Choose a location to which to save the file, and leave the option to just export the Selected Branch. The default extension that is applied to this file will be .REG, but you may want to make it a .TXT. The reason for this change has to do with the file association. If you double-click a REG file, the settings stored in the file will be imported into your Registry. This often leads to accidental Registry imports.

To restore the key from the file that was backed up, you can locate the REG file and double-click it. This will import the setting from the REG into your Registry. It will overwrite current values, create values and keys that are not there, but will not delete keys. If you need a value deleted, you can set the data for the value to a null.

Other ways to import REG and TXT files into your registry include:

- Choose Import Registry File from the Registry menu, and select the file.
- Use a command prompt or the RUN command to type **REGEDIT C:\RegistryFiles\Importfile.TXT**, specifying the path to your Registry file.
- To make the importing silent, you can use **REGEDIT /S C:\RegistryFiles\Importfile.TXT**, specifying the path to your Registry file.

Since the REG file is a text file, you will be able to edit the file, and have the changed file imported into your Registry. If you use a tool other than EDIT.COM, you may find that the file becomes corrupt. If it is corrupt, you will see a misleading error message (see Figure 8.4) which states that the import was successful. You will know the file is corrupt because the values you expected to see in the Registry will not be there. Opening it with EDIT.COM, saving it, and closing the file can repair this file.

FIGURE 8.4

REGEDIT provides misleading error messages when import files are corrupt. Although the message states success, no changes have been made to the Registry.

The process is somewhat different with REGEDT32.

REGEDT32

If you choose to perform the backup and restore process with REGEDT32, the process follows this order:

1. Select the key you want to backup in the navigation pane of REGEDT32.

2. Select Save Key from the Registry menu.

3. Choose a location to which to save the file. REGEDT32 will not add an extension to this file. Choose an extension you want to use. The file that is saved is a binary file, so you will not be able to edit it, only import it back into the registry.

To restore this backed up key, you will have to first locate where it belongs and select the key in the navigation pane of REGEDT32. Then choose Restore from the Registry menu. It is important that you have the correct key (the one you backed up) selected during this import phase because the selected key is deleted when it is over written. See Figure 8.5.

FIGURE 8.5

The existing key is destroyed when a key is restored with REGEDT32.

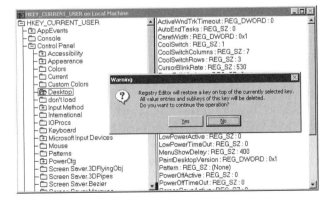

Either of these programs will get the job done, but, depending on your situation, you may opt to perform your backups and restores with one over the other. The real goal is to get the structure and contents of the registry backed up.

Elements of the Registry

The Registry has a well-defined structure and is permanently stored on your hard drive. The hierarchical structure of the Registry has several layers. The topmost layer is the subtrees. These subtrees will be discussed later in this chapter in the "The Windows 2000 Trees" section. The structure that is below the subtrees is detailed in Table 8.1.

TABLE 8.1   Registry Components

Registry	*Description Component*
Hive	Microsoft's official definition of a *hive* is a file on your hard drive that makes up a section of a registry subtree. If this is the case, the files mentioned earlier are the only hives (DEFAULT, USERDIFF, SAM, SECURITY, SOFTWARE, and SYSTEM). Many people will still refer to the first level of folders under the sub-tree as a hive.
Key	A key is the level of folders under a hive.
Sub-key	Sub-keys are all other folders under the key level. Many people are not really hung up on these two specific terms.
Value	Values are actually the names of the Registry entries.
Data type	Each value has an assigned data type. Data types are dealt with in more detail following this table.
Data	The actual item that is stored in the Registry.

Every Registry entry will be denoted by a path and a value. The path is composed of a subtree, hive, key, and sub-keys. The value is composed of a value name, data type, and data.

As each developer at Microsoft creates a new entry, he or she is able to choose the data type for the value. You may notice that many items in the Registry are enabled or disabled by setting a value to 0 (disabled) or 1 (enabled). The thing that tends to cause confusion is that sometimes the data type for this value is a string (REG_SZ), and other times it is a DWord (REG_DWORD). The data type that would best lend itself to this type of entry would actually be a Boolean value, but that data type does not exist in the Registry. The possible data types are listed in Table 8.2.

TABLE 8.2   Registry Data Types

Data Type	Description
REG_BINARY	Stores a 16-bit binary value or a 2-byte value.
REG_DWORD	Stores a word-length hexadecimal value, 8 hex digits. The size of this value is 32 bits or 4 bytes.
REG_EXPAND_SZ	String value with support for variables in the data (%systemroot%\SYSTEM32\CALC.EXE, for example).
REG_MULTI_SZ	String value with support for multiple values. This is used to store lists, such as the service group load order.
REG_SZ	String value. Out of the listed data types, this allows for the least memory-intensive value to be stored in the Registry; one character or one byte.

All the Registry entries have been placed into a hierarchical structure, whose top level consists of subtrees.

Although the Registry is usually thought of as a single entity, it is actually made of several files on your hard drive and has a maximum size limit (which is actually stored in the Registry).

The files on your hard drive that make up the Registry are found in %systemroot%\ SYSTEM32\CONFIG directory. These files are

- DEFAULT
- SAM
- SECURITY
- SOFTWARE
- SYSTEM
- USERDIFF

The Registry files also have other associated files whose filenames are made up of the filename plus the following file extensions:

- .ALT   This file extension is associated only with the HKEY_LOCAL_MACHINE\System hive and is its backup copy.
- .LOG   These files log the changes to keys and values of a hive.
- .SAV   These files contain a copy of the hives.

8

THE WINDOWS 2000 REGISTRY

Figure 8.6 shows the Registry files through Explorer. Notice, also, the .LOG, .ALT, and .SAV files.

FIGURE 8.6

The Registry configuration files.

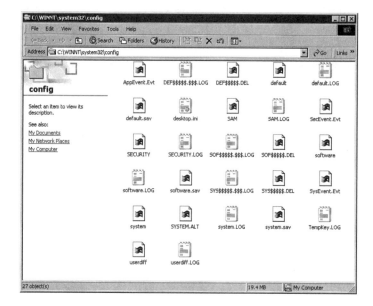

Although the Registry is located in fixed locations on the hard drive, it resides in an area of memory when in use. Because the size of the Registry can grow, it is necessary to limit the area of memory the Registry can hold. This limit is dictated by a value set within the Registry, itself. The RegistrySizeLimit value limits the area of memory that the Registry can consume. This value is located under HKEY_LOCAL_MACHINE\System\CurrentControlSet\Control and has a type of REG_DWORD. By default, the Registry size is set to about 25 percent of the available area of memory. The system tries to ensure that the RegistrySizeLimit remains within a minimum value of 4MB and a maximum value of 80 percent of the allocated area of memory.

You now know the location of the files that compose the Registry and the format that is used to store the data. The next items to examine are the actual Registry trees and the types of information that you can expect to find in each one.

The Windows 2000 Trees

The top-level unit of the Registry is the subtrees. These subtrees represent the initial classification of all Registry entries. Each subtree has a specific purpose. The five subtrees you will see in the Windows 2000 Professional registry are

- HKEY_LOCAL_MACHINE

- HKEY_CURRENT_USER

- HKEY_USERS

- HKEY_CURRENT_CONFIG

- HKEY_CLASSES_ROOT

To provide you with a better understanding of each subtree, you will now take a brief look at each.

HKEY_LOCAL_MACHINE

The HKEY_LOCAL_MACHINE part of the Registry contains configuration information relevant to the local computer. For example, the hardware configuration information collected by Windows 2000 during boot time is stored here. HKEY_LOCAL_MACHINE also contains installed drivers, their settings and configuration data, and the security accounts database. The information from HKEY_LOCAL_MACHINE is used by the system regardless of the currently logged in user.

HKEY_LOCAL_MACHINE is divided into five sections. These are HARDWARE, SAM, SECURITY, SOFTWARE, and SYSTEM. The following is an explanation of each of the subkeys:

- The HKEY_LOCAL_MACHINE\HARDWARE subkey stores the physical configuration of the computer. The information in this subtree is created at boot time by NTDE-TECT.COM. It contains hardware-specific information such as descriptions of processor architecture and system buses, driver mappings for both physical devices like keyboards, and other system resources (see Figure 8.7) The information in this subkey is also used by the Windows NT diagnostic program System Information Tool (use the Computer Management Admin Tool, and choose System Tools), through which it is presented in a far more readable format.

> **Note**
>
> If you type **WINMSD** at the RUN command, Windows 2000 Professional will open the MMC with the System Information Tool loaded.

- The HKEY_LOCAL_MACHINE\SAM subkey contains the Security Account Manager (SAM). On Windows 2000 Professional, SAM contains information on user and group accounts. Administrators use Local Users and Groups (System Tools in Computer Management) to access and maintain SAM information.

8

THE WINDOWS
2000 REGISTRY

- The HKEY_LOCAL_MACHINE\SECURITY subkey contains even more security information pertaining to policies and user rights. This information, however, is used locally by the security subsystem only.

> **Note**
>
> The SAM and SECURITY subkeys only allow the operating system to have permissions, thus denying you direct access to them through the Registry. You will have to use Local Users and Groups to access these subkeys. Editing them directly is very dangerous.

- The HKEY_LOCAL_MACHINE\SOFTWARE contains system-wide software configuration data. For example, a vendor might choose to supply a default configuration that is used each time a new user starts an application. Also, a vendor might store path information about installed products on a system that doesn't change when a new user logs on. This kind of information is also stored in the SOFTWARE section.

- The SYSTEM section contains information about the way Windows 2000 is configured to boot. It also contains information on Windows 2000 services, required device drivers, location of driver files, and other behavioral aspects of Windows 2000.

Figure 8.7 illustrates the HKEY_LOCAL_MACHINE subtree.

FIGURE 8.7

HKEY_LOCAL_
MACHINE *is very
machine oriented.*

HKEY_CLASSES_ROOT

The `HKEY_CLASSES_ROOT` part of the Registry is available only for compatibility reasons. It provides the same information as did the `REG.DAT` file in 16-bit Windows 3.*x*.

`HKEY_CLASSES_ROOT` contains the OLE file associations on the local computer. That is, when the File Types dialog box from Explorer's options is used to associate a file extension with an application, or when an association is made during an application installation, the association information is stored here.

`HKEY_CLASSES_ROOT` also contains definitions of every object that exists within Windows 2000. Objects range from files and applications, to modems and My Computer. Each object is registered with a class ID, which can be located under `HKEY_CLASSES_ROOT\CLSID`. These keys contain information about OLE components and shell interfaces. It is here that additional right-click functionality can be defined for an object.

Windows applications that are 32-bit do not use `HKEY_CLASSES_ROOT`, but rather an identical copy of this section that can be found under `HKEY_LOCAL_MACHINE\Software\Classes` (see Figure 8.8). These are not really copies, but rather two views of the same Registry file. Microsoft currently prefers the information stored under Software\Classes, but leaves the other copy for backward compatibility issues. If you manually change an entry in either of these subkeys, you will see that it has been updated in both locations.

8

**THE WINDOWS
2000 REGISTRY**

FIGURE 8.8

The
`HKEY_CLASSES_ROOT`
subtree.

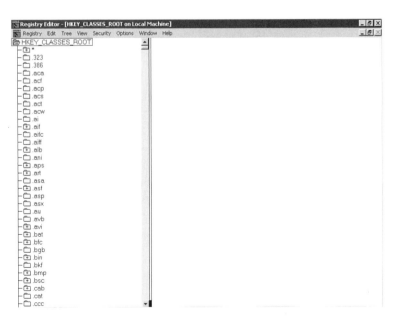

There are two distinct types of subkeys within the HKEY_CLASSES_ROOT:

- *Filename extensions*—Figure 8.8 illustrates the HKEY_CLASSES_ROOT. As you can see, there are a number of subkeys beginning with a dot plus a three-letter extension. These are definitions of filename extensions that allow applications to be associated with file types. These file type associations are defined during application installations and also manually through the use of the Open With command or the File Types tab of the Tools, Folder Options in Explorer. In many cases, they simply redirect you to another item in the classes key that may be more generic (for example, .log and .txt both point to an object called txtfile).

  Figure 8.9 shows an example of the definition of the .doc file type.

FIGURE 8.9

The .doc file type within the HKEY_CLASSES_ROOT *subtree.*

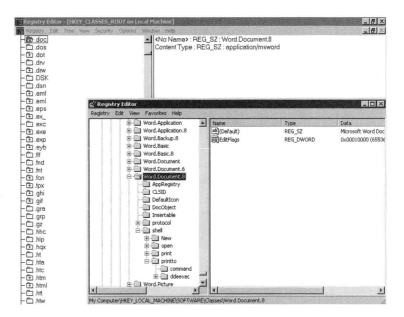

Apart from application installations or manual entries to the Registry, you can use the File Types tab within Explorer to map applications to file types. The File Types tab is accessed from the Folder Options entry of the Tools menu within Explorer. Figure 8.10 shows the Options dialog box and the File Types tab with the .doc file type selected. The application presently associated with .doc file types is Microsoft Word. This association allows you to double-click a .doc file and view it by invoking Microsoft Word.

FIGURE 8.10

Options available from the File Types tab of Folder Options.

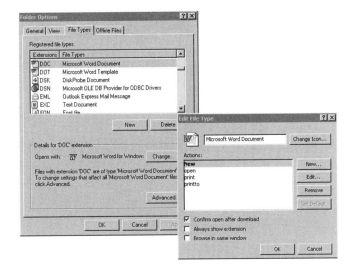

If you choose the Advanced button, you can then define an icon with a file type. This icon association determines what icon Explorer will display with a file type. You can also define additional actions to be preformed, such as Print and Print to; these two actions allow for printing to be initiated from Windows Explorer. You also have the option of always showing the file extension, even when all others are hidden.

- *Class definition*—Class-definition subkeys contain information on Component Object Model (COM) objects. Subkeys define specific COM properties, such as Dynamic Data Exchange (DDE). You should also note that Word Documents contain a CLSID key that contains a link to additional object definitions for this object. Figure 8.11 shows the subkey for Microsoft Word 8 (97) and the subkeys defining the DDE commands of Open and Print. This figure also shows the CLSID for that Word Document.

HKEY_CURRENT_USER

HKEY_CURRENT_USER holds the currently logged-in user's profile. A profile contains system settings as well as application-specific information. For example, the desktop's layout, available network resources, mapped drives, the contents of the Start menu, and screen colors are stored here. This information is stored in a NTUSER.DAT file for the current user.

8

THE WINDOWS
2000 REGISTRY

FIGURE 8.11

The Class definition and Class ID for Microsoft Word 8 (97).

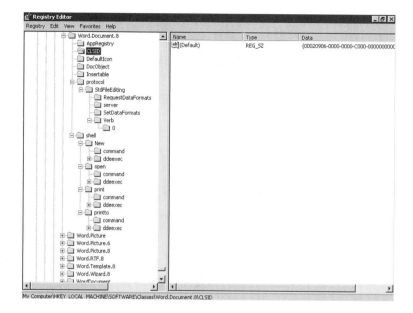

Most of the entries in HKEY_CURRENT_USER are created by installed applications and, thus, differ from system-to-system and from logged-in user–to–logged-in user.

However, there are some default subkeys created by Windows 2000 that are always available (see Figure 8.12). These are AppEvents, Console, Control Panel, Environment, EUDC, Identities, Keyboard Layout, Network, Printers, RemoteAccess, Software, SYSTEM, UNICODE Program Groups, Volatile Environment, and Windows 3.1 Migration Status. The following list describes these default subkeys:

- AppEvents defines application events. Application events are user-defined events that occur for particular events. For example, each time the machine boots up, you can configure a particular sound bite to play.

- Console defines the look-and-feel of character-mode applications, such as the Windows NT command prompt. Console can also define the size and position of program group windows.

- Control Panel contains user-specific settings from the Control Panel. This corresponds to information that was stored in the WIN.INI and CONTROL.INI files under Windows.

- Environment holds the user's environment variables that have been set via the System applet in the Control Panel. These settings correspond to user settings that were held within the AUTOEXEC.BAT file in DOS.

- EUDC stores the default End User Defined Characters (EUDC) typeface if the current typeface does not support these character types. This is used by Japanese and Chinese fonts, but can be use of in other languages.

- Identities stores the default and last user ID, as well as the last username.

- Keyboard Layout defines the language of the current keyboard layout. To change this setting, you must use the Keyboard applet within Control panel.

- Network is a subkey that is no longer in use.

- Printers contains a description of all printers available to the user. To change these values, you must first click Start and then select Settings, Printers.

- RemoteAccess stores remote access settings, such as your Internet Profile name.

- Software is the most interesting subkey because it holds all application settings for the current user. This includes system applications and Windows NT settings (for example, Task Manager preferences). This subkey has the same structure as HKEY_LOCAL_MACHINE\Software. Again, this information corresponded to application-specific information from the WIN.INI file under earlier versions of Windows.

- SYSTEM contains user-defined settings for items under HKEY_LOCAL_MACHINE\ SYSTEM. Currently, the only item that exists is a list of files that are not to be backed up.

- The UNICODE Program Groups subkey is not used unless the installation of Windows 2000 was an upgrade.

- Volatile Environment variables are listed in this section. It includes variables that are set during the login process, such as LOGONSERVER.

- The Windows 3.1 Migration Status is not used unless you are upgrading from Windows 3.x or Windows for Workgroups 3.x.

These keys store the entire Windows 2000 user configuration for the user.

8

THE WINDOWS
2000 REGISTRY

> **Note**
>
> Depending on the type of installation (upgrade or new install) and the components that are installed, you may find some differences in the keys that are listed in your HKEY_CURRENT_USER subtree.

FIGURE 8.12

The Registry
HKEY_CURRENT_USER
subtree.

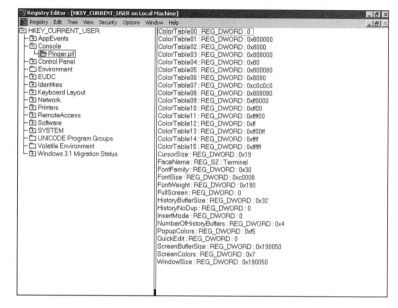

HKEY_USERS

HKEY_USERS contains the user profile for both the default user and the currently logged on user. The reason the current user is listed here as well is that when you make a remote connection with REGEDT32, you are only able to edit HKEY_LOCAL_MACHINE and HKEY_CURRENT_USER. This gives you the ability to edit settings for the current user when in a remote location. In a fashion similar to classes being found both in HKEY_CLASSES_ROOT and HKEY_LOCAL_MACHINE\SOFTWARE\CLASSES, the same user information can be edited in either location because it is the same data.

When users log in, their personal configurations, which are stored in NTUSER.DAT, are copied to their SID in HKEY_USERS. This data is also displayed as HKEY_CURRENT_USER. During logout, information from HKEY_CURRENT_USER or HKEY_USERS is copied back to the user's personal NTUSER.DAT.

There are always two subkeys in HKEY_USERS (see Figure 8.13):

- .Default   Prior to a user logging in, the user profile data that is used is stored here in default. If you set a wallpaper or screen saver here in default, it will be in effect when no users are logged on. When a user logs on to Windows 2000, then their settings will be in effect. The .Default subkey has a structure similar to HKEY_CURRENT_USER. This profile is stored in the %Systemroot%\system32\ config\Default file.

If you want to configure a custom profile for all new users, you should login to create a new `NTUSER.DAT`. This file can then be copied into the `%Systemroot%\system32\config` directory. This can be used by the workstation's administrator to preconfigure settings for all new users. For example, a company logo could be used as the default background image for all new users.

- `SID_#` Other subkeys, apart from `.Default`, are Security ID (SID) strings of the user to whom they apply. That is, the user's settings are not identified by username, but rather by a string supplied by NT security. However, it is possible to resolve a username from this security ID string by looking into `HKEY_LOCAL_MACHINE\Software\Microsoft\WindowsNT\CurrentVersion\ProfileList`, where the usernames are listed below the security ID strings.

FIGURE 8.13

The Registry `HKEY_USERS` *subtree.*

HKEY_CURRENT_CONFIG

`HKEY_CURRENT_CONFIG` is not really a separate Registry section, but rather a shortcut to the currently used hardware configuration from `HKEY_LOCAL_MACHINE\SYSTEM\CurrentControlSet\Hardware Profiles\Current`. (Hardware configurations, also known as *hardware profiles*, are created with the Hardware tab of the System Control Panel.) The `HKEY_CURRENT_CONFIG` subtree was introduced with the Windows NT 4.0 Registry and was added for compatibility reasons. The `HKEY_CURRENT_CONFIG` subtree stores differences that exist between multiple hardware profiles (see Figure 8.14). Hardware profiles are sets of configurations governing which devices and services will be executed by NT when loading.

8

THE WINDOWS
2000 REGISTRY

FIGURE 8.14

The HKEY_
CURRENT_CONFIG
subtree.

Hardware profiles are most useful for laptop computers. For example, one configuration is used while the laptop is docked to a docking station, and the other configuration is used while the machine is undocked. When you do have several hardware configurations on your computer, you can select the one to use when the machine boots. If your computer cannot detect which configuration it should use, it will wait for you to choose one or will load the default.

All hardware profiles are stored within the HKEY_LOCAL_MACHINE\System subtree. Even the current hardware profile is stored here under CurrentControlSet\Hardware Profiles\Current.

Using REGEDIT

Regedit is accessed by typing REGEDIT from the RUN command of the Start menu. The Regedit screen is split into two vertical panes:

- The left pane displays the Registry root, denoted by My Computer, with five subtrees below it. Each of these subtrees was explained previously in detail.

- The right pane is divided into two columns under which the Value Name and Value Data are displayed for the selected key in the left pane. Figure 8.15 shows the HKEY_CURRENT_USER\Console key selected on the left pane and its associated Value Names and Value Data displayed on the right.

FIGURE 8.15

The Registry through Regedit.

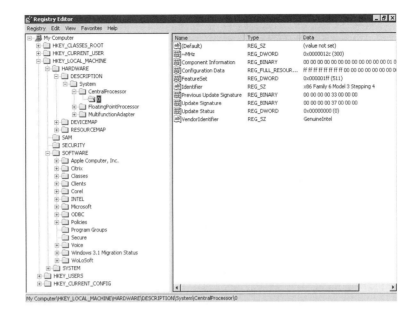

Regedit will always display both panes, but you can adjust the split between them either by clicking it with the mouse or by selecting Split from the View menu. Once you have highlighted the split (denoted by a change in the cursor), hold the left mouse button down and drag the split left or right to suit your needs. The View menu also has an entry to refresh the display. This can be executed by pressing the F5 key on your keyboard.

Traversing the Registry

Traversing through the Registry is the same as traversing through the file system using Explorer. You can use either the tab and arrow keys on the keyboard or the mouse to get around the Registry. Within the View menu is an option to display a status bar at the base of the window. This status bar is helpful because it displays your current position within the Registry. You can enable the status bar by selecting Status Bar from the View menu. To expand a subtree, you must select it using the mouse or the arrow keys. Once the subtree is selected, you can expand it by double-clicking it with the mouse or by pressing the Enter key on the keyboard. To collapse a subtree, you again select the subtree and press the Enter key or double-click a subtree with the mouse. Regedit also supports the right-click features for editing keys and value entries.

Adding a Key

To add a key to the Registry, you must do the following:

1. Position your cursor at the point in the Registry where you want to add the key.
2. From the Edit menu, select Add, Key.
3. A new subkey is immediately added under your current position. This key is called New Key #1 and is highlighted and ready for editing. Type the correct name for the new key and press Enter.
4. Now you must add a value entry for the key. Again, make sure you are positioned on the key to which you want to add the value entry. From the Edit Menu select New, and then select String Value, Binary Value, or DWORD Value, depending on the value entry you want to add.
5. The new value entry now appears on the right pane and is highlighted and ready for editing.
6. Edit the value entry to reflect the value you want. Press Enter to save the change.
7. To edit the value entry, select Modify from the edit menu. Ensure that the correct value entry is highlighted before you do so.
8. You are now presented with the Edit dialog box. Enter the value into the Value Data text box.

You can also rename keys and modify data values by highlighting the key or data value and selecting Rename or Modify from the Edit menu. If you choose Copy Key Name from the Edit menu, you will copy the full key path to the clipboard to paste into another document later.

Deleting a Key

To delete a key from the Registry you must highlight the key you want to remove and then select Delete from the Edit menu. The same procedure applies for the removal of value entries, as well.

> **Note**
>
> You cannot remove the predefined subkeys from the Registry.

Finding a Key

It can be difficult to locate keys and value entries within the Registry by hand. To ease your search efforts, select Find from the Edit menu. Figure 8.16 shows the Find dialog box. The Find operation will commence only from your current position within the Registry to the end of the Registry.

FIGURE 8.16

The Find dialog box.

The Find dialog box is made up of the following items:

- The Find What text box, where you enter the string you want to find.
- The Look At frame includes a check box for Keys, Values, and Data. When these boxes are checked, the Find operation will look in these associated areas.
- The Match Whole String Only option will determine whether the Find operation is to look for an exact or partial string match.

Saving the Registry

With Regedit, you have the ability to save the Registry keys and their subkeys to a text file with a .reg extension. This can be a useful option, because it allows you to store a copy of the Registry elsewhere, and you can use it to rebuild a Registry key or subkey later, or you can search it using your favorite word processor. To do so, you must perform the following steps:

1. Select the Registry key you want to save.
2. Select Export Registry File from the Registry menu.

   You are now presented with the Registry Export File dialog box, (see Figure 8.17).

FIGURE 8.17

Saving Registry keys.

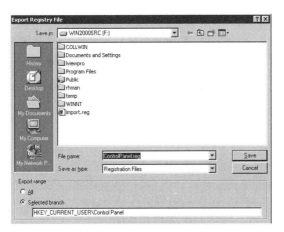

3. The top half of the dialog box enables you to name the text file and also to determine where it will be saved. In the Export Range frame, select the All radio button to save the entire Registry. To save the selected key or subkeys, select the Selected Branch radio button. Choosing a filename with a .txt extension can prevent you from accidentally merging these entries into your Registry. The default double-click action for .reg files is for merging into the Registry.

Restoring Registry Keys

As well as exporting the Registry to a text file, you can import that same text file back into the Registry. The following is a description of how to restore a Registry key:

1. Select Import Registry File from the Registry menu.
2. From the Import Registry File dialog box, locate the file you want to restore.
3. Select the file and click Open.

> **Warning**
>
> Care should be taken when importing Registry files because the import will merge with your existing Registry. Any duplicate entries will be overwritten with the values found in the file. If you corrupt the Registry this way, you may have to perform an Emergency Repair or reload the operating system.

Connecting to a Remote Registry

In Windows 2000, you have the ability to remotely administer a Registry. Provided you have permission to connect remotely to a remote Registry, you can see the remote Registry as if it were local. This is an invaluable option that can help an administrator to troubleshoot problems remotely. To connect to a remote Registry, select Connect Network Registry from the Registry menu and type in the name of the remote computer whose Registry you want to administer. You will now see a second computer in the left pane. It will have the sub-trees of HKEY_CLASSES_ROOT, HKEY_CURRENT_USER, HKEY_LOCAL_MACHINE, and HKEY_USERS (see Figure 8.18).

Using REGEDT32

Regedt32 is accessed by typing REGEDT32 from the RUN command in the Start menu. You can see that the Regedt32 screen is quite different from that of Regedit (refer to Figure 8.15). Figure 8.19 shows a sample Registry through Regedt32.

FIGURE 8.18

Remote Registry editing with REGEDIT.EXE.

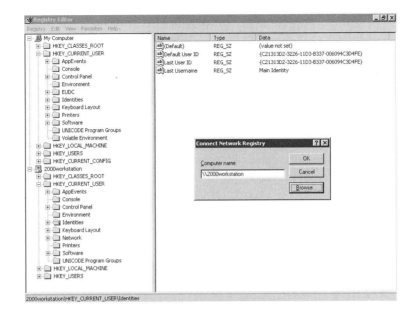

FIGURE 8.19

The Registry through Regedt32.

As you can see, Regedt32 displays the HKEY subtrees in separate windows. The Windows menu allows to you tile, cascade, arrange, and switch windows. You can also minimize and maximize each of them for ease of use. Because Regedt32 presents each of the subtrees in separate windows, any customization changes you make to one window will not be reflected in the others. Auto Refresh will allow the updates to be shown in all windows, but it slows down operations. Unlike Regedit, Regedt32 allows you to decide between views of the tree only (corresponding to the left pane in Regedit), the data only (corresponding to the right pane in Regedit), or a combination of both. These options are set under the View menu and only correspond to the currently selected window. Again, as with Regedit, you can define the split between the tree and data panes by either clicking it with the mouse or by selecting Split from the View menu. Once you have highlighted the split (denoted by a change in the cursor), hold the left mouse button down and drag the split left or right to suit your needs.

Traversing the Registry

Traversing under Regedt32 is the same as traversing under Regedit. First of all, select the window through which you want to traverse. You can use either the arrow keys or the mouse to move up and down the tree. Under the Tree menu, there are options for expanding the tree or current branch or for collapsing the current branch. Remember again that this is on a per-window basis. Alternatively, you can use either the mouse or the arrow keys. Once selected, a branch or tree can be expanded by double-clicking it with the mouse or by pressing the Enter key from the keyboard. To collapse a tree or branch, you press the Enter key with the tree or branch selected or double-click it with the mouse. To switch between the left and the right panes, you will be able to use the Tab key. Regedt32 does not support the right-click features for editing keys and value entries.

Adding a Key

To add a key to the Registry under Regedt32, you must perform the following steps:

1. Select the key under which you want to add the new key.
2. From the Edit menu, select the Add Key entry.
3. The Add Key dialog box appears. Type the name of the new key into the Key Name text box.
4. Leave the Class box blank until later.

Deleting a Key

To delete a key from the Registry under Regedt32, you must highlight the key you want to remove and then select Delete from the Edit menu. The same procedure applies for the removal of value entries, as well.

Note

You cannot remove the predefined keys from the Registry.

Finding a Key

The Find Key option in the View menu allows for the searching of keys only. Figure 8.20 shows the Find dialog box. The Find operation will commence from your current position within the Registry and will go to the end of that branch.

FIGURE 8.20

The Find dialog box.

Unlike the Find operation in Regedit, Find Key does not search value names or value data. It does, however, allow you to search in a particular direction, either up or down, and can search on case also.

Saving Registry Keys

This is the same Save operation as described previously for Regedit. In Regedt32, you can save Registry keys to a different location and restore them at a later date. To save a Registry key, you must perform the following steps:

1. Select the Registry key you want to save.
2. Select Save Key from the Registry menu.

   You are now presented with the Save Key dialog box, as shown in Figure 8.21.

FIGURE 8.21

Saving a Registry key with Regedt32.

3. Enter the name of the file and select its destination. Once completed, click Save. Since there is no registered extension for this type of file, you can choose one.

> **Note**
>
> If you are editing a remote Registry and want to save a key, remember to enter the UNC path (for example, *servername**sharename**filename*) rather than the network drive K:*filename* or a local drive. This is because the remote computer may try to use its own drive letter rather than yours.

Restoring the Registry Keys

Once saved to a safe location, the Registry key can be restored at a later date. The following is a description of how to restore a Registry key:

1. Select the key you want to restore.
2. Select Restore from the Registry menu.
3. Enter the filename and location of the stored hive in the Restore Key dialog box and then click Open.

> **Note**
>
> Remember to select the same key that was backed up. If the wrong key is selected, it will be erased when the saved key is loaded.

Connecting to a Remote Registry

To connect to a remote Registry in Regedt32, choose Select Computer from the Registry menu. You are presented with the Select Computer dialog box. You can enter the name of the remote computer into the Computer text box, or you can browse your way to it via the Select Computer list (see Figure 8.22). The remote computer will only display the HKEY_LOCAL_MACHINE and HKEY_USERS sub-trees.

Using Hives Remotely

There is an alternative to connecting to a Registry remotely with Regedt32. Regedt32 allows you to load entire hives that were saved from a remote Registry. This is ideal if you cannot connect to a remote Registry over the network, because now you can save a hive from the troublesome machine onto a floppy and transfer it anywhere.

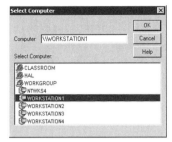

FIGURE 8.22

Connecting to a remote Registry opens additional windows holding the destination Registry.

To load a remote hive, you must perform the following steps:

1. First of all, you must save the hive by using Save key from the Registry menu (see the previous section, "Saving Registry Keys").

2. Once you have saved the file, you can load the hive into another Registry. To load a hive, you must first select either the HKEY_LOCAL_MACHINE or HKEY_USERS subtree.

3. When one of these is selected, choose Load Hive from the Registry menu.

4. Through the Load Hive dialog box, you can point to the location of the saved hive and load it. Again, if this is over the network, you'll have to use a UNC pathname.

Once you have finished with the hive, you can unload it as follows:

1. Select the top of the hive.

2. Choose Unload Hive from the Registry menu.

8

THE WINDOWS 2000 REGISTRY

Customizing Your System Through the Registry

There are several spots in the Windows 2000 interface that I would like to be able to change or add functions to the right click menu. One of these spots is with Registry files. These files will occasionally get corrupted if you edit them with Notepad. I prefer to edit them directly with EDIT.COM. I would also like to be able to leave the original association in place and still be able to right click the files to get them open. If I wanted to change the file association, this is far from Microsoft's recommended procedure. Microsoft would recommend either choosing Folder Options from the Tools menu in Explorer and then accessing the File Types tab, or selecting a REG file, and then Shift—right-clicking it and choosing Open With.

Open Regedit and locate the extension for **.reg** within HKEY_CLASSES_ROOT. This will tell you that the object class you want to edit is a regfile. Locate regfile and open the key. In the `regfile` key you will see two subkeys; `default icon` and `shell`. `shell` is the key you are interested in. `shell` has Edit, Open, and Print, and each of these has a command subkey. The default action for `edit\command` is `%SystemRoot%\system32\NOTEPAD.EXE %1`, where `%1` is the name of the file on which you are right-clicking.

Now that you have the structure, you can add your own key. Right-click on `shell` and choose New, Key. Name the new key **DosEdit**, and assign it a default value of **MS Dos Ed&itor**. Then right-click the `DosEdit` key and select New, Key again. Name this new key **command**. Make the default action for this new key, `EDIT.COM %1`. If you want to use `%SystemRoot%\system32\EDIT.COM %1`, you will have to make the default entry of type `REG_EXPAND_SZ`. Now locate a `.reg` file on your drive and right-click, you should have a new option and it should open the Dos Editor.

This same technique can be applied to any Registry class to add additional commands to your right-click menus. Some classes that may interest you in the CLSID key are `{208D2C60-3AEA-1069-A2D7-08002B30309D}` (My Network Places), and `{20D04FE0-3AEA-1069-A2D8-08002B30309D}` (My Computer). You will find InfoTip values under each of these keys that can be changed. These tips appear like Tool Tips when the user mouses over the icons on the desktop.

This gives you a small taste of the power of the Registry as a tool to modify your Windows 2000 operating system. The biggest things to remember are to backup the Registry and record the original values that existed in the keys when you started.

Summary

The Windows 2000 registry, like its predecessors, is a labyrinth of entries that can be overwhelming and confusing. Because it is a central location of all configuration information, the Registry is also extremely valuable for your computer's continued operation. It is due to these two factors that many users avoid the Registry in favor of other configuration tools, but will then miss out on the configuration changes that can only be accomplished through the Registry.

Microsoft does not officially support Registry editing, but they require you to edit your Registry to implement several fixes. The documentation for these fixes usually comes in the form of Knowledge Base articles. So it is strange that this non-supported tool is so widely relied upon. Many fixes or tweaks can be made to your Windows 2000 system through the Registry, and they are documented by Microsoft, other books, periodicals, and Web sites.

Some of the topics that were covered in this chapter include the editing tools for the Registry, safety tips while editing, the structure of the Registry, and editing the Registry. You also saw the differences between Regedit and Regedt32. This should allow you to make a choice between which editor you want to use in different situations.

This chapter should have prepared you to start delving into the Registry and exploring settings that exist there. You should also be prepared to make any changes needed to optimize your system.

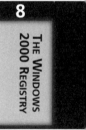

Working with Windows 2000 Professional

PART

III

IN THIS PART

Working with the Windows 2000 File System

IN THIS CHAPTER

A hard disk is logically divided into concentric rings, called *tracks*. Each track is divided into logical sections called *sectors*. Each sector contains either stored data or is vacant, awaiting data. The sector is the smallest unit of disk storage space. A sector can technically be any size, but it's almost always 512 bytes.

Aside from Multiple Zone Recording (MZR) type disks (becoming more prevalent), the number of sectors in each track remains the same because sector density increases as the tracks approach the center of the disk. As the tracks vary in size, depending on their location on the disk itself, the sector density rises in relation to a track's nearness to the center of the disk. Figure 9.1 shows a simplified schematic of the logical structure of a hard disk.

FIGURE 9.1

A hard disk is divided into sectors, usually of 512 bytes each.

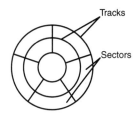

A computer's file system distributes and tracks data according to clusters made up of one or more sectors. A cluster can contain only one file. It can't have parts of various files in it. In other words, there's only one cluster for each file or part of a file. For example, if your computer has a cluster size of two sectors each having 512 bytes, it can store a file of up to 1,024 bytes in a single cluster. As soon as the file size exceeds the size of a single cluster, it gets a whole new cluster, even if the file doesn't fully populate the cluster.

Take a computer with the cluster size of 1,024 bytes. A file of 1,000 bytes will take up just about a whole single cluster. If the file grows to 1,100 bytes, it takes up all of one cluster plus a second one for the bytes above 1,024. Most of the second cluster doesn't contain any data, but it's lost for further data storage because the file system can't assign data storage to part of a cluster. The amount of cluster area unavailable for data storage is the disk's *overhang*, or *overhead*.

The file system assigns contiguous clusters when you store a file. This works until a file grows from its original size or you start erasing files. Here's what happens in those cases. Suppose you create and save a file to disk. The file system assigns clusters 20 and 30 to this file. Next, you create and save another file. This gets assigned clusters 31 and 45. If you open and increase the size of the original file, the file system needs more clusters, but the next in the series are occupied by file number 2. Therefore, it goes to the next free space starting with cluster 46. This causes file number 1 to be split between two noncontiguous clusters.

Similarly, if you erase file number 1 and then write another larger file to its clusters, the file system will use up its original clusters and then go searching for more wherever it can find them. This splitting of files across noncontiguous clusters is called *file fragmentation*.

The makers of a file system have to decide on some tradeoffs. A large cluster size will work against fragmentation, but it will be inefficient due to a large amount of overhead. In addition, all file systems are limited to the amount of clusters they can address. If a disk capacity is such that the cluster numbers threaten to climb beyond the addressable number, the cluster size must grow.

The FAT System

FAT stands for File Allocation Table, the central feature of this system. It was originally designed for early hard disks that were quite small compared to today's disks. The designers of the FAT system were looking at disks typically between 5 and 20MB. In all likelihood, they didn't consider today's storage needs, where even a moderately powerful computer will have a disk exceeding 20GB in capacity.

Figure 9.2 shows the structure of a FAT system for a particular partition. There are two copies of the actual file allocation table, an early attempt at ensuring data integrity. This FAT system was introduced with the IBM XT in the early 1980s. Today, it survives in the forms of FAT16 and the new and improved FAT32.

FIGURE 9.2

The FAT system is the original system for hard disk organization.

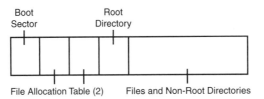

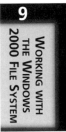

The File Allocation Table contains the following information about cluster usage:

- Cluster numbers
- Clusters available for files
- The files assigned to clusters and whether this is the last cluster for the file or a pointer to the next cluster containing a file
- Whether the cluster is marked as unusable

The FAT system can address a partition size of up to 4GB. As the partition grows, so does the cluster size. The format program assesses the partition size and creates the FAT structure shown in Figure 9.2. In the process of creating this structure, it decides how many sectors to assign per cluster. Table 9.1 shows how the format program assigns sectors.

TABLE 9.1 FAT's Cluster Sizes

Partition Size	Cluster Size in Bytes	Sectors in a Cluster
To 32MB	512	1
33–64MB	1024	2
65–128MB	2048	4
129–255MB	4096	8
256–511MB	8192	16
512–1,023MB	16384	32
1,024–2,047MB	32768	64
2,048–4,096MB	65536	128

As you can see, larger partitions yield cluster sizes that quickly grow inefficient. A partition of 1,500MB, hardly unusual today, will use up a full 32,768 bytes of disk space to store a file of only a few bytes. A quick bit of division will show you that each partition can contain roughly 64,000 clusters or a maximum of 64,000 files, assuming the unlikely situation of one file per cluster. The rule of thumb for disk overhead is number of files/.5 cluster size. Therefore, a partition theoretically can have an overhead of 50 percent of its entire size. In practice, the overhead is a good deal less, but in some extreme cases you'll encounter overheads approaching 40 percent.

People disagree on how large a partition having a FAT file system should be, but most agree that 511MB is about it. The newer FAT32 system is more efficient when it comes to overhead, but its use isn't as widespread as FAT16.

Rarely, you will hear the term VFAT. This is a FAT system with the capacity for long filenames (LFN).

You access FAT partitions under Windows 2000 Professional just as you do under MS-DOS, Windows, and Windows 98 and its successors.

Overview of the NT File System (NTFS)

The Windows 2000 File System (NTFS) is the successor system to the FAT, VFAT, and High Performance File System (HPFS) systems. The latter system was developed for IBM OS/2 and is supported by versions of Windows NT (2000's predecessor) prior to Windows NT 4.

NTFS meets the needs for a secure file system with the performance needed for the much larger volumes seen today, as compared with the time that inspired the FAT system. Similar to the UNIX file system, NTFS allows access privileges down to the file level.

NTFS uses the cluster scheme seen in FAT for data allocation, but at any given volume size it has less overhead. Table 9.2 shows NTFS's cluster sizes.

TABLE 9.2 NTFS's Cluster Sizes

Partition Size	Cluster Size in Bytes	Sectors in a Cluster
To 512MB	512	1
513–1024MB	1024	2
1025–2048MB	2048	4
2049–4096MB	4096	8
4097–8192MB	8192	16
8193–16,384MB	16384	32
16,385–32,768MB	32768	64
to 16 exabytes	65536	128

The structure of an NTFS volume is similar in look to FAT, but the details vary significantly, as you can see in Figure 9.3.

FIGURE 9.3

The NTFS structure superficially resembles the FAT system; however, the information kept and its format are significantly different in the two systems.

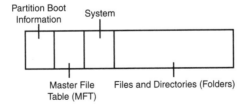

9

WORKING WITH THE WINDOWS 2000 FILE SYSTEM

The Master File Table (MFT) is somewhat analogous to the FAT, but it contains much more information than the earlier system. Figure 9.4 shows the structure of a typical entry in the MFT.

FIGURE 9.4

The MFT contains information well beyond what's found in the file allocation tables of a FAT system.

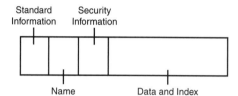

From a user's view, the single greatest addition to the MFT over the FAT is the security section. This contains information about a file's ownership and who has permissions to perform file procedures. FAT has nothing even slightly analogous to NTFS's security.

In addition, the MFT has a log file that keeps a record of disk activity. In the event of a system crash, Windows 2000 can restore its integrity using this log file. The log file's size depends on the volume size—it can grow to 4MB on very large volumes.

NTFS uses a new-for-PC structure called *streams*. A similar scheme, *dual forks*, has been in use in the Macintosh since that machine's inception. A stream identifies some data attribute. This allows a program to track different modifications to a file using a different stream for each. Within the MFT, a colon separates the file from the stream. For this reason, the colon is an illegal character in a filename.

> **Note**
>
> Windows 2000 is, as you can see from the splash screen, built on "NT Technology." NT stands for "new technology" as in newer technology than the previous Windows (3.x).
>
> NTFS stands for New Technology File System. Because 2000 is based on NT, the file system name persists, although some would no doubt like to see the modified NTFS that 2000 uses called something like 2KFS.

NTFS supports file-by-file compression but doesn't support, nor can it read, volume compression schemes such as DoubleSpace, DriveSpace, (from Windows 9x), or now rarely seen Stacker.

The only system that can read NTFS volumes is Windows 2000. You can't "see" or access files on an NTFS volume from Windows 98, previous Windows versions, or any version of MS-DOS. There is at least one utility available, NTFSDOS, that allows limited read-only file access on an NTFS volume from either MS-DOS or Windows 95.

> **Tip**
>
> You can increase NTFS performance by telling it not to create short (8.3) MS-DOS format filenames. Do this only if all your applications can see LFN. To do this, change the Registry value of NtfsDisable8dot3NameCreation in HKEY_LOCAL_MACHINE\System\CurrentControlSet\Control\FileSystem from its default of 0 to 1. Or just search for NtfsDisable8dot3NameCreation using Regedit and make the change when you find it.

FAT Versus NTFS

FAT is surely the *lingua franca* of file systems. Most personal computer operating systems from UNIX to Windows NT to DOS and Windows 2000 can read and even write to it. NTFS in its newest form is exclusive to Windows 2000, but it is more efficient in larger volumes and has safety and security features FAT has never heard of. Table 9.3 is a summary chart for these two systems.

TABLE 9.3   The Pros and Cons of File Systems

Application	*NTFS*	*FAT*
Volumes < 200MB	Poor	Good
Volumes 200–500MB	Fair	Good
Volumes 500–4000MB	Good	Poor
Volumes > 4,000MB	Good	N/A
Security	Good	N/A
Recoverability	Good	N/A
Undelete erased files	N/A	Good
Full access on dual boot machines	N/A	Good
Long filenames	Good	Good
Compatibility for Macintosh files	Good	N/A
File compression	Good	N/A in 2000
Volume compression	N/A	Good
Maximum partition size under Windows 2000	4EB	4GB

Windows NT had several third-party utilities that made undeleting files possible, such as the one from Executive Software. As of this writing, no such utilities exist for Windows 2000 Professional, but they're sure to come. Windows 2000 will, of course, undelete files from the Recycle bin, but that's not a true unerase operation because it is only a move to and from a folder.

A true unerase facility will search out remnants of a file and reconstruct them into a new file. Also files deleted from the command line interface (CLI) in Windows 2000 are deleted and can't be recovered using Windows 2000's Recycle Bin (because they're not moved into there).

Converting FAT to NTFS

The easiest way to install Windows 2000 Professional to a new installation is to use FDISK to create the volume structure you want, format the volumes to FAT, and then run SETUP. Windows 2000 setup will ask you whether you want to convert any of the existing volumes from FAT to NTFS prior to installing Windows 2000 Professional.

If you failed to do the conversion during setup, don't worry: You can convert existing FAT volumes to NTFS at any time, although the process can take several hours on volumes with a lot of data. You can't convert a full FAT volume to NTFS, because the conversion process requires up to 110MB free for temporary storage.

> **Note**
>
> Convert for Windows 2000 works on either FAT or FAT32 volumes.

The Command Line Interface (CLI) has, among its utilities, CONVERT, which is the program that does the conversion from FAT to NTFS. Once converted to NTFS, you can't return to FAT without reformatting the partition. This process erases data on the volume, so a full backup is required beforehand. Although the conversion of FAT to NTFS has a good deal of redundancy built in, it's a good idea to have a full backup before proceeding anyway.

To convert a volume from FAT to NTFS, start a CLI session by choosing Command Prompt from the Start, Programs menu. Enter convert [volume] /FS:NTFS [/v], substituting the drive letter you want to convert to NTFS for the [volume] parameter. The [/v] parameter is optional. It produces a verbose output for the conversion process. Verbose output echoes the stages of the conversion process to the screen.

If your system is on the volume you want to convert, or for any other reason CONVERT can't get exclusive access to the volume (a common situation), the program will tell you that it can't proceed until next bootup. If you agree to let it, the program will run the next time you boot up.

Figure 9.5 shows the CONVERT program, offering the option to do a conversion at next startup.

FIGURE 9.5

If the conversion program can't gain exclusive access to the target volume, it will offer to schedule the conversion at next startup.

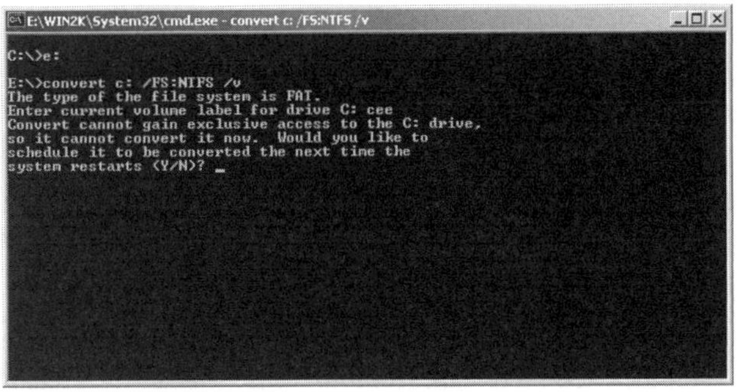

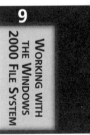

Keep in mind that NTFS volumes require a certain amount of "wasted" space for security features. This space grows as the volume grows, but it isn't proportional to volume size. This makes small volumes in NTFS very inefficient compared to FAT for two reasons:

- FAT doesn't have a serious overhead problem until volumes exceed 511MB.
- NTFS uses up a proportionally large part of small volumes for its security feature.

Although NTFS volumes can and do grow fragmented, this file system generally handles fragmentation better than FAT. Also, the physical layout of directories (folders) in NTFS enables faster file access than FAT, especially in larger volumes. However, file creation is slightly faster in FAT because NTFS has the added job of setting security attributes—something lacking in FAT.

Windows 2000 comes with a light version of DisKeeper—a defragmenter utility. You can upgrade to the full version which has added features such as the ability to schedule defragmenting sessions.

Lazy and Careful Disk Writes

Previous to NTFS, there were two general types of file systems. The low-performance, *careful write* types and the gung-ho, *lazy write* types. The original versions of MS-DOS use careful write technology. This performs disk write requests in a serial fashion, as they're requested. This soaks up computer time because the machine essentially halts while the disk is being written to. Although this type of scheme works all right for a single-process operating system such as MS-DOS, it tends to slow down excessively a system with many processes running, or a system with a virtual memory store, or both. However, this system is safe. If a system crashes, only the disk write in progress will be affected. Although this can cause some disk integrity loss, the loss will be fairly small in most cases.

The second type of file system is the lazy write system. This system saves write information to a RAM cache and, during processor idle time, commits the cached information to the disk. Microsoft added a lazy write cache (also called a *write-behind cache*) to MS-DOS 6.0. It caused havoc with users not familiar with this new and improved feature. Although the disk performance of the new cache speeded up not only MS-DOS but, more importantly, Windows 3.1, users assuming their systems still had a careful write scheme turned off their systems before the write from cache to disk. This caused serious data loss and disk corruption in many cases.

Microsoft changed the caching default from lazy write to careful write in subsequent versions of MS-DOS 6.*x*, leaving lazy write as an option for knowledgeable users. Although this made MS-DOS and Windows 3.1 to some extent safer, it did exact a performance hit.

With NTFS, Microsoft has combined the safety of careful write with the speed of lazy write systems. The trick is NTFS's recoverability. This system uses transaction processing to ensure the volume's integrity, because the system can always roll back transactions to a previously good state in the case of a system crash. Although some user data might still be lost, the volume should be accessible, except in the instance of corruption to the system areas of a volume.

In transaction processing, a write request remains in cache like a lazy write system, but a record of the request gets logged to a log file. It's this log file that allows rolling back of partially completed disk writes. This is similar to lazy write, but, in that scheme, a partial disk write is possible, thus corrupting an entire volume. If the NTFS system senses a partial write upon startup after a crash, it will go to the log file and roll back the disk transactions to the point of having no partial or bad writes. Microsoft calls this system *lazy commit* to distinguish it from the older and less reliable lazy write systems. The lazy commit system in NTFS is virtually as fast as lazy write and as safe as a careful write. Although nothing can prevent user data loss in the case of an unplanned shutdown, as occurs in a power loss scenario, NTFS comes as close as any file system in use today.

Rollback of transactions upon startup after a crash is completely automatic. It requires no user input.

NTFS also has a facility called *cluster remapping*, which moves data from a cluster reported as bad to NTFS to a good one. The file system then marks the cluster as bad in a bad cluster file, preventing its use again. This facility is similar to the third-party utilities that do the same thing for FAT.

The Disk Management Utility

Disk Management is a graphical utility useful for various disk management tasks. It's part of Administrative Tools, Computer Management folder under Control Panel—that is it's a component of the Microsoft Management Console (MMC). Using it, you can do the following tasks:

- Create partitions
- Delete partitions
- Monitor and display volume information
- Format volumes
- Scan and repair volumes for disk errors
- Extend volumes by adding regions of free space

Figure 9.6 shows Disk Management launched on a computer with a FAT, FAT32, and NTFS volumes along with two CD-ROM readers.

FIGURE 9.6

Disk Management combines many of the features of FDISK, format, *and* chkdsk, *along with some unique capabilities of its own.*

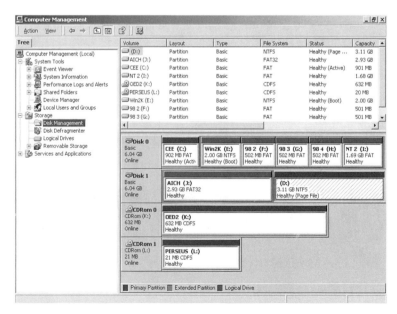

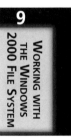

You need to be logged on with Administrator rights to use the Disk Management utility. When Disk Management starts, it flashes a message saying it's connecting with disk management (on the status bar).

Creating and Preparing Partitions

To create a new partition, follow these steps:

1. Choose the free space you want to convert. This, by default, shows up as a cross-hatch bar in the graphical display.

2. Right-click the space you want to use and then choose Create Partition. Disk Management will respond with a dialog box. You will have to choose which type of partition you want to create—primary, extended, or a logical drive within an established extended partition.

3. Follow the simple wizard steps.

You've just created a new partition where none was before.

Adding a New Disk

You can also extend a single partition to include free space from a newly added disk drive as long as the partition you want to extend doesn't hold Windows 2000 itself. Proceed as before, but select more than one area by pressing the Ctrl key as you click the existing partition and the new area. This enables the Extend Volume Set command on the Partition menu. Choose this and you'll extend the current volume to include the newly added disk space.

Caution

Windows 2000 will blithely allow you to span a volume across two physical disks. Doing so doubles your risk of losing that volume because failure of either disk will result in the loss of the volume.

Note

Right clicking any existing volume brings up a context menu with a Properties entry. This, in turn, will bring up the same dialog box as if you right-clicked a volume in Explorer and chose Properties.

Deleting Partitions

To delete a partition, click the partition you want to rid yourself of and then choose Delete from the Partition menu. You can't delete the boot partition or Windows 2000 system partitions. Remember that deleting partitions is permanent. Once they're gone, so is the data once stored there (except for separate backup sets).

Viewing and Monitoring

Disk Management is capable of three views of your disk in each the top and bottom section of the Administrator. The default view is called Volume List. You can also choose any view for either the top or bottom of the display from the View menu. Figure 9.7 shows the disk view on top with the graphical view persisting on the bottom.

FIGURE 9.7

The disk view of Disk Management shows disk information in a numerical format rather than the graphs in the graphical view. The disk view shows information about the disks themselves rather than the volumes contained on the disks.

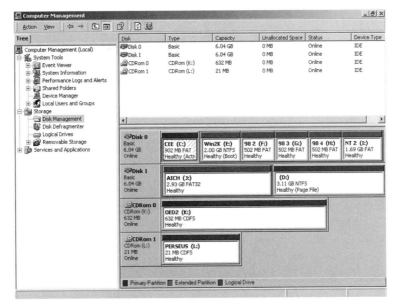

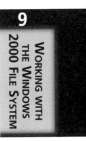

One advantage of the Volumes or Disk view is the ability to sort on any column by clicking the volume heading. Figure 9.8 is the same display as in Figure 9.7, but it is sorted by free space. Clicking again on the column head will sort the display in the reverse order.

Note

I enlarged the Views area of Disk Management to show more columns in Figure 9.8.

FIGURE 9.8

The Volumes view allows easy sorting of any disk characteristic by clicking the appropriate column head.

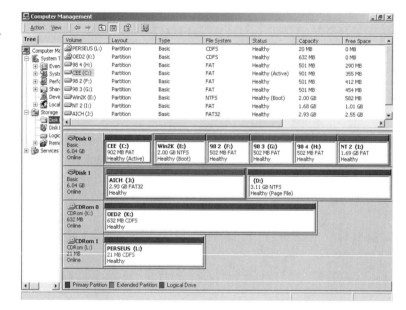

There is a compromise in the graphical Disk Configuration view: You can choose how Disk Management shows the regions. To make this choice, select the Settings entry in the View menu. Disk Management will pop up a dialog box, shown in Figure 9.9.

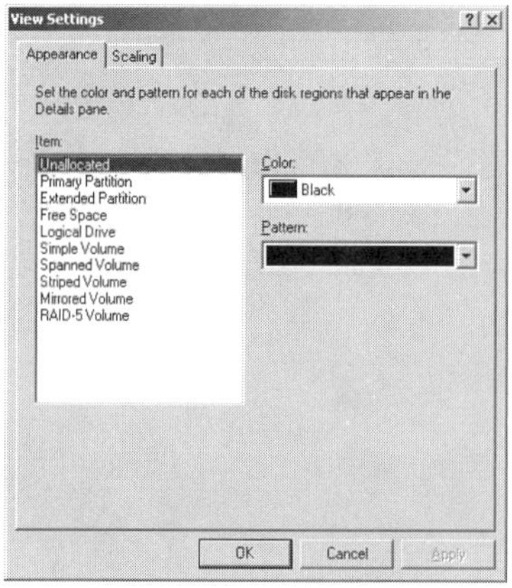

FIGURE 9.9

The View Settings dialog box allows user choices for the graphical disk configuration display.

In a similar way, you can vary the way Disk Management displays itself by choosing
Customize from Views (see Figure 9.10).

FIGURE 9.10

*The Customize
dialog box permits
configuration of
the display.*

The Logical Drives section of the console allows you to

- View drive properties
- Alter drive labels
- View and alter security settings for those drives

Figure 9.11 shows the Logical Drives view of the MMC.

FIGURE 9.11

*The Logical
Drives section of
the MMC is
another way to
alter volume char-
acteristics.*

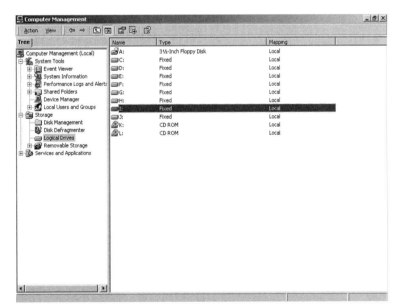

Changing Drive Letters

You can change the assigned drive letters for a volume by right-clicking the volume in either view and choosing Change Drive Letter and Path. Be careful when changing drive letters for volumes with installed programs. Altering this option won't change the settings in Windows 2000 Professional's Registry or any initialization (.ini) files needed by installed programs.

If you change a volume letter, Windows 2000 will try to find a moved program and is quite effective in doing so. Altering the mapping or assignment of drive letters in Windows 2000 will not affect the mapping of those volumes in the same computer booted in another operating system, such as Windows 98.

By assigning a drive letter rather than letting 2000 assign it using MS-DOS conventions, you make the drive letter "sticky." That is, it won't change as you add or remove volumes. This prevents applications from getting lost as you add or remove volumes. For example, if you assign a letter L: to a particular volume, that volume will remain L: until you intentionally change it. Windows 2000 will not move the drive up or down the alphabet as you add or remove other volumes.

> **Note**
>
> If you add a new physical disk with a primary volume assigned, Windows 2000 Professional will reshuffle drive letters orphaning applications on the previously mapped extended partitions. A fast way to return these applications to use is to use Disk Management to re-letter the drive back to what it was before the new disk was installed.

This eliminates the havoc wrought by automatic drive letter reassignment, which began with MS-DOS and still exists in non-NT Windows.

Indexing

Buried within Service and Applications exists a way to start, stop, and customize the indexing services for your computer. Indexing extracts keywords from documents making it a lot easier for Windows 2000 Professional's Search to find them. Search works either through Start or the Explorer.

Boots and Systems

The boot partition of a Windows 2000 Professional installation is the primary partition containing the boot files such as NTLDR, NTDETECT, and the boot.ini configuration file. The system partition is the partition containing the Windows 2000 system, itself. This is, by default, in the WINNT directory.

Many installations, especially dual boot ones, boot from a FAT primary volume, but they have Windows 2000, itself, on an NTFS partition other than the boot one.

The computer shown in the figures for this chapter uses a FAT volume C: as the primary and boot partition. It contains the boot loaders for MS-DOS and Windows 2000. The same FAT volume also contains the system files for Windows 95. The large volume D: is an NTFS volume containing the Windows 2000 Professional system under the WINNT directory.

To start indexing, locate the Indexing Service entry under the Service and Applications folder of the same MMC area where Disk Management exists. You can customize how lazy or careful the indexing works by choosing the Indexing Service entry and then choosing Action (menu), All Tasks, Tune Performance. You can choose from one of the pre-defined schemes or click the Customize button to make one of your own. Figure 9.12 shows the Customize dialog box.

FIGURE 9.12

You can customize how intrusive indexing is on your volumes.

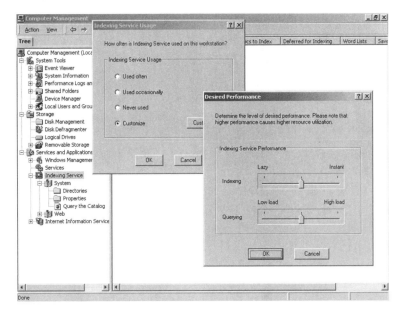

9

WORKING WITH
THE WINDOWS
2000 FILE SYSTEM

You can also right-click the Indexing Service and choose All Tasks, Tune performance to bring up the dialog box shown in Figure 9.12.

Standard Disk Management Tasks

As mentioned earlier, right-clicking a volume or disk in Disk Management (either top or bottom) View will bring up a context menu with a Properties entry. You can use this entry to do standard administrator-type tasks, just as you can from Explorer. Figure 9.13 shows the General tab of Properties while Figure 9.14 shows the Tools tab.

FIGURE 9.13

The General tab is mostly informational, but does contain a button to do a disk cleanup or to remove of files you determine are unneeded.

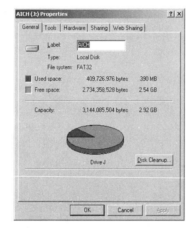

FIGURE 9.14

The Tools tab has buttons triggering backup, disk checker (diagnostic), and, if installed, a third-party defragmentation routine.

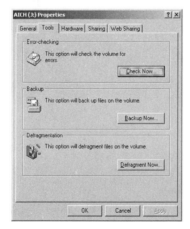

The computer shown in Figure 9.14 does not have a third-party defragmentation program, such as the full version of Diskkeeper for Windows 2000.

The Hardware tab of the Properties dialog box will show information for all the hardware (physical disks plus other drives) for the entire computer, not just the highlighted volume.

The Sharing tab is arguably the most complex. From there you can assign not only shares, but alter Permissions for various volumes and set caching options for programs or documents. Figure 9.15 shows the Sharing Tab of the Properties dialog box.

FIGURE 9.15

The Sharing tab is for accessing the sharing, caching (offline), and permissions of a particular volume.

You can customize the caching option for files on this volume to optimize for what you believe its intended use. Do this by clicking the Caching button shown in Figure 9.15. Figure 9.16 shows the Caching Settings dialog box.

FIGURE 9.16

The Caching Settings dialog box optimizes the cache for offline use.

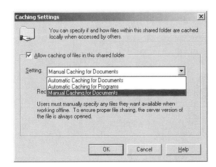

9

WORKING WITH
THE WINDOWS
2000 FILE SYSTEM

You can also create a new share and then edit permissions for it. To do this, click the New Share button. This brings up a dialog box that allows you to create a new share and edit the permissions. Figure 9.17 shows these dialog boxes.

FIGURE 9.17

You can create a new share and edit its permissions in two consecutive dialog boxes.

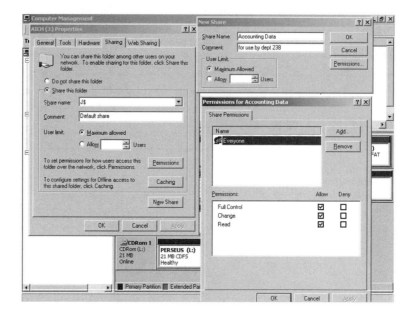

To add a group for auditing, click the Add button, which displays the Select Users, Computers, or Groups dialog box, shown in Figure 9.18.

FIGURE 9.18

To add a group to audit, click the Add button in the Permissions For Accounting Data dialog box shown in Figure 9.17.

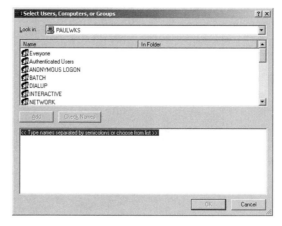

The Add button in the Permissions dialog box features an optional display of users in all groups. This is a handy reminder feature that has the actual capability of doing some User Manager chores, such as organizing your user groups.

The Web Sharing tab is only active when Microsoft Internet Information Service (IIS) is installed and active. Figure 9.19 shows this tab along with a subsidiary dialog box for creating an alias.

FIGURE 9.19

The Web Sharing tab is only active when IIS is installed and running.

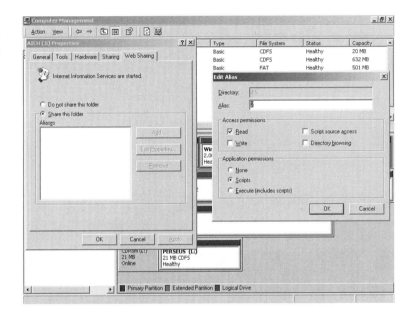

The Windows 2000 Explorer

Explorer for Windows 2000 resembles Explorer for Windows 98SE, but it has security and management extensions similar to Disk Management. In fact, Explorer for Windows 2000 includes the features of Disk Management's security, except at the folder (directory) and file levels instead of the volume level. Windows Explorer is, by default, located in Start, Programs, Accessories. Most people drag an entry to the Desktop or use the My Computer icon on the Desktop to launch Explorer.

Figure 9.20 shows Explorer opened to an NTFS volume containing the Windows 2000 Professional system files.

9

WORKING WITH THE WINDOWS 2000 FILE SYSTEM

FIGURE 9.20

The primary tool for working with files and folders in Windows 2000 is Explorer.

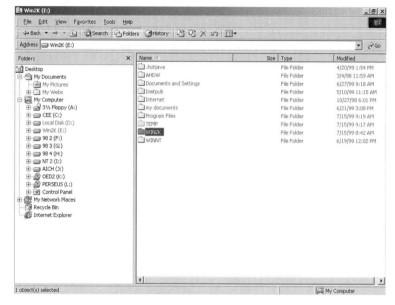

Explorer has two panes. The left pane shows folders, drives, and other computer resources (such as Control Panel), whereas the right shows the details for left side selections.

Fast Explorer

Shift+Double-Click My Computer will launch My Computer in Explorer view.

File Associations

By default, Explorer adheres to the document-centric approach to computing introduced in Windows 95. This approach is aimed at making novices comfortable by eliminating some display complexity. So, for the sake of simplicity, Explorer suppresses the display of file extensions for which there is an association in the Registry and system files such as .dll, .sys, and .vxd.

This might make a few novices more comfortable, but it seems to upset just as many. It doesn't do anything for intermediate-and-up users. To change the default display of files, open Explorer and click Folder Options in the Tools menu. Figure 9.21 shows the Folder Options dialog box.

FIGURE 9.21

The Folder Options dialog box can control the display of certain system files, file extensions, and other options.

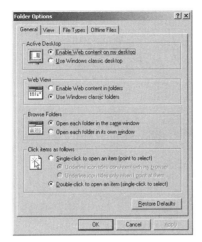

The File Types tab in the Folder Options dialog box controls file associations. Windows 2000, like previous versions of Windows, associates files with applications according to the file extension. Traditional file extensions were limited to three legal DOS (almost always letters only) characters. Windows 2000 can handle longer extensions, but tradition holds that most applications still use the shorter file extensions. This has a practical reason. If you set Windows 2000 Professional to keep an MS-DOS (8.3) filename along with the standard long filename (LFN), it will truncate the filename to the left of the dot, but not the extension to the right of the dot.

Therefore, the file

`My letter to you.doc`

has the short filename

`mylett~1.doc`

assigned to it by Windows 2000 Professional (unless you've edited the Registry to remove 8.3 filenames). If moved to a non-LFN computer, it will still be associated with the program linked to the .doc extension. However, if the file has the name

`My letter to you.longdoc`

the short filename is

`mylett~1.lon`

and so it loses its association.

To associate a file with an application, click the File Types tab on the Folder Options dialog box. Like previous Windows versions, Windows 2000 uses the file extension to associate files with applications. Figure 9.22 shows this tab.

FIGURE 9.22

The File Types tab of the Folder Options dialog box is where you can add, delete, and change file associations.

The list box in the middle of the tab has a list of the file types and their associations. You can scroll through this list to see the file type you want to edit or delete. Once you've found the entry you want to alter or delete, highlight it and click the Delete or Change button. Removing or deleting an association means that when you double-click the file having that extension in the Explorer, you won't have the associated application swing into action.

For the most part, you'll delete associations only for those applications that no longer exist on your computer. However, you'll have many reasons to edit an entry.

Windows 2000 setup programs can, in the course of setting themselves up, associate file extensions to their applications. You rarely have control over this process. So, for example, say you have the file extension .pcx associated with the application Picture Publisher and you install a new program also able to open the .pcx file type. That new application might, as part of its setup, disassociate the .pcx extension from Picture Publisher and grab the extension as its own.

This might not be your intention. The Change button on the File Types tab is the place to re-associate Picture Publisher with the .pcx extension.

The following example takes the files having the .pcx extension currently associated with the WANGIMG program and changes that association to the PaintShop Pro program.

Note

You can't literally follow along with this example unless you have exactly the same setup as the demonstration computer, however the procedure is the same no matter what the extensions or applications.

The first thing to do is find the .pcx extension in the list box shown in Figure 9.22. Once located, click the Change button. This brings up the Open With dialog box shown in Figure 9.23.

FIGURE 9.23

The Change File Type dialog box is the starting point for adding, deleting, and editing actions associated between a certain file type and an application. It leads to the Open With dialog box shown here.

The Change button on the File Types tab of the Folder Options dialog box (refer to Figure 9.22) can change the association but will keep the action as Open. Clicking Change displays the dialog box shown in Figure 9.24.

FIGURE 9.24

The Open With for Type dialog box is similar to the New dialog box, but it only allows editing for the application, not an addition of actions for the application.

To change the application, you can enter the path to the application or browse for it. Figure 9.25 shows browsing the file structure to locate the PaintShop application.

FIGURE 9.25

Browsing for an application is similar to browsing for anything in the Windows 2000 Explorer.

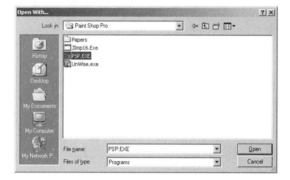

Once you've found the application to associate, double-click it. This will associate the application with the Open action for the file type specified. You can also use the Shift+Right-click in Explorer to open a file with a different application by using the Open With entry on the Context menu. Figure 9.26 shows a right-click on a `.gif` file and the Open With selection.

FIGURE 9.26

Shift+Right-click Open With and you'll get dialog box identical to the one you see in Figure 9.24.

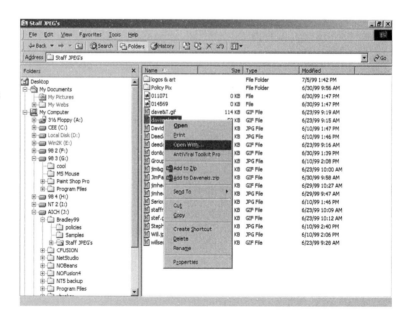

Adding a new action is similar to editing a current one, but you start by clicking the New button from the File Types tab in the Folder Options dialog box shown in Figure 9.22 and then adding an action or file type, such as Print, and then browsing to the associated action. The actions affect the context (right-click) menu in Explorer. For example, if you have two actions, Open and Print, associated with a file extension, those two actions will appear on the context menu when you right-click that file type. Adding more actions adds more entries to the context menu.

File Manipulation

You can open a Command Line Interface (CLI) session in Windows 2000 Professional and use the old MS-DOS commands for moving, copying, and deleting files. However, most people prefer the graphical method using the Windows 2000 Explorer. You can do all these operations in a variety of ways.

To copy a file from one drive to another, locate the drive in Explorer, click it, and then drag it to its new location. To move the file from one drive to another (not leaving a copy in two places), press the Shift key as you drag the file.

If you drag a file from one directory to another on the same drive, Explorer will, by default, move the file rather than copy it. To copy the file (end up with two copies), press the Ctrl key while dragging. When copying a file, Explorer will show a small plus sign next to it. When moving a file, Explorer will not show this plus sign. You can also use the standard editing keys of Ctrl+X (cut), Ctrl+C (copy), and Ctrl+V (paste). Figure 9.27 shows pasting to a folder with an existing file of the same name. Windows 2000 Professional adds a "Copy of" prefix to the file to differentiate it from the pre-existing file.

FIGURE 9.27

Explorer can copy, delete, or move files via Copy and Paste.

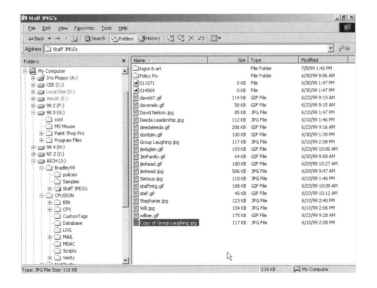

To delete a file, drag it to the Recycle Bin. This will move a file from its location to the Recycle Bin (a folder itself). To delete a file without moving it to the Recycle Bin, press Shift while dragging to the bin. You can also press Delete to delete a file or set of files.

Note

Files deleted from the CLI using the Erase and Delete commands aren't moved to the Recycle Bin; they are gone for good unless you have a third-party unerase utility installed.

If you don't like dragging, Explorer will let you move, copy, or delete a file in other ways. You can right-click a file and then cut it, delete it, or copy it. If you copy or cut it, you can right-click in another drive or directory to paste it. When cutting or copying in a Windows application such as Word or Excel, Windows actually copies an item to the clipboard. The actual file isn't copied in Explorer, but the effect remains the same.

The Edit menu has the Cut and Copy options as part of it. It also has an Undo command for the last undoable action. This is handy if you've accidentally dropped a dragged file to an unknown directory. Just click Edit, Undo Move, and your file pops back to its former location.

Explorer offers two ways to rename files. You can click, wait a few seconds, and then click a file in Explorer, which sends the graphic display into Edit mode. This is a bit tricky. Some people never seem to get the hang of this click, pause, click, and they end up double-clicking the file. The second way to rename a file is to right-click it and then choose Rename from the context menu. This will instantly take you into Edit mode. Figure 9.28 shows Explorer in Edit mode.

As in all noun-verb style GUIs, highlighting the items you want to take action on is an important part of Explorer file manipulation. Highlighting individual files is as simple as clicking them. Highlighting all files in a directory is simple, too. Just get to the target directory and select Edit, Select All from the Explorer menu. You can also press Ctrl+A to choose all files.

If you want to select a bunch of contiguous files (contiguous in the Explorer, not necessarily in the MFT or FAT or volume), select a file at one end of the block and then press Shift while clicking the file at the other end of the block. If you want to select a series of noncontiguous files, press Ctrl while clicking the files.

Figure 9.29 shows a block of files selected by the Shift+Click method.

FIGURE 9.28

If the click, pause, click routine ends up frustrating you, you can enter Edit mode for a file- name by high- lighting the file and then choosing Rename from the context menu in Explorer. Note the box around the filename.

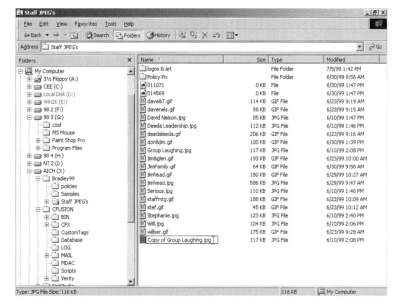

FIGURE 9.29

The Shift+Click method results in highlighting a block of contigu- ous files in the Explorer. Use the Ctrl+Click method for non- contiguous files.

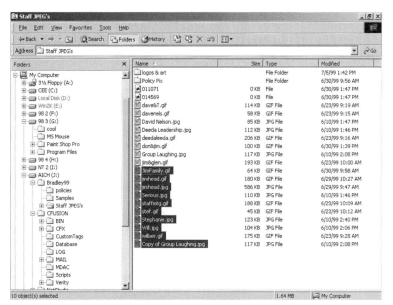

9

WORKING WITH THE WINDOWS 2000 FILE SYSTEM

You can combine your use of Shift and Ctrl to select two or more noncontiguous blocks. The selection in Figure 9.30 came about by using the usual Shift+Click method to high- light the first block, and then using Ctrl+Click to highlight one file of the next selection, and finally using Shift+Ctrl+Click on the last file of the second selection.

FIGURE **9.30**

You can choose noncontiguous file blocks within Explorer.

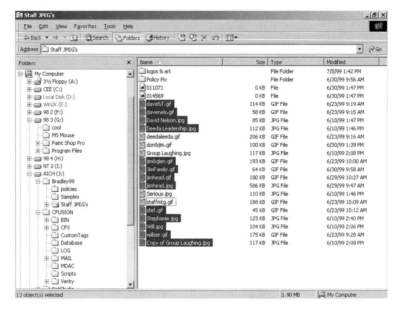

The Edit menu of Explorer has a very handy option called Invert Selection. This selects whatever is currently unselected. Figure 9.31 shows the selection from Figure 9.30 inverted.

FIGURE **9.31**

You can select the files you don't want to take action on and then choose the Invert Selection option from the Edit menu to select your target files.

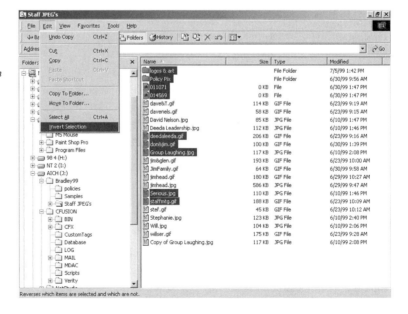

Viewing

Explorer has four possible views. The easiest way to choose different views is to make the toolbar visible by selecting Toolbars from the View menu (if it's not visible). The pull-down button on the far right changes the way Explorer shows files. The selections are, from top down

- *Large Icons*—Each file has a large icon with its name underneath. This is similar to the display in the Control Panel.

- *Small Icons*—Each file has its applications icon (if known) to the left of the file-name. Files are displayed in a wide format.

- *List*—Similar to small icons, but files are listed vertically.

- *Details*—Shows details such as type of file (or a guess), file time, date, and size.

- *Thumbnails*—Small view of the file contents (if available).

Figure 9.32 shows the directory from Figure 9.31 in the Thumbnails view.

FIGURE 9.32

The Thumbnails view of Explorer. Not all files have Thumbnail view, in which cases Explorer uses an icon placeholder.

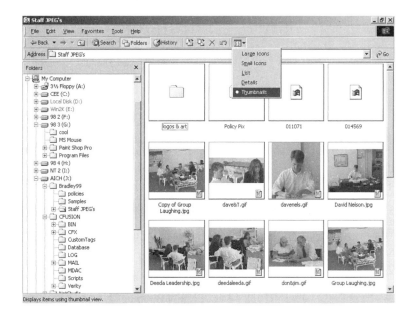

9

WORKING WITH
THE WINDOWS
2000 FILE SYSTEM

You can select and manipulate files in an identical fashion within any of the five views.

Shortcuts

During the early stages of the Windows 2000 Professional GUI, shortcuts were called *links* because they provided a link or a pointer to an actual file. The name *link* survives today in the extension of a link file L:1nk. A link or shortcut is a way to access a file from a location that's different from the file's actual whereabouts.

Figure 9.33 shows the location of the executable file to launch Microsoft Access.

FIGURE 9.33

Files under the new Windows 2000 Professional interface physically and logically reside in the same location.

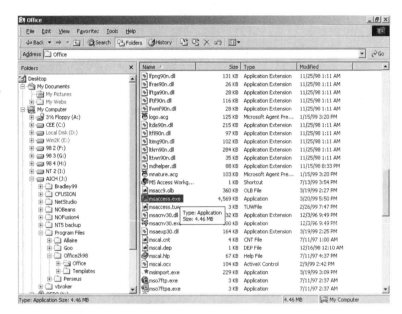

This file, MSACCESS.EXE, is in the location

```
\\Program Files\Office2k98\Office\MSACCESS.EXE
```

However, you will likely want to launch it from another location, such as the Desktop, Start menu, or both. This is what a shortcut does—it provides a link to the executable (or document) that you can locate anywhere.

To make a shortcut, right-click the file, drag it to a new location, and then drop it. Choose Create Shortcut (Here) from the pop-up menu. You can also make a shortcut by choosing New, Shortcut from a context menu, such as the context menu of the Desktop.

Figure 9.34 shows a shortcut to Access on the Desktop. By right-clicking the shortcut and choosing Properties, you can view the tabbed dialog box, also shown in Figure 9.34.

FIGURE 9.34

Note the target for this shortcut is the MSACCESS.EXE file shown in Figure 9.33.

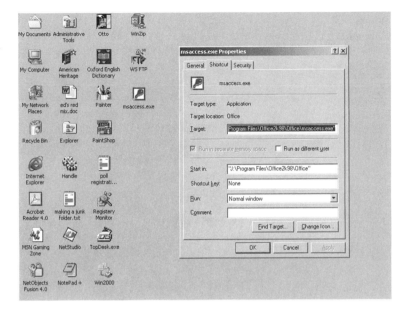

You can open a Properties dialog box for a shortcut by right-clicking the shortcut and then choosing Properties from the context menu. The shortcut Properties dialog box allows you to do many manipulations on a shortcut, such as setting its permissions (Security tab), locating its target, changing its attributes, or altering its icon. Figure 9.35 shows a change of icon for the shortcut shown in Figure 9.34.

Note

Setting permissions and other security items for a shortcut does not set or alter them for the target file.

Note

Icons are resources and can be located in various files such as .dll's or .exe's. In the example shown in Figure 9.35, the icons to choose from were resources located within the MSACCESS.EXE file itself. If you don't want to use one of these, you can browse for other icons in other files. Not all .dll's or .exe's have icon resources.

FIGURE 9.35

The properties you can alter for a shortcut vary from the serious, such as permissions and ownership, to the trivial, such as displayed icon.

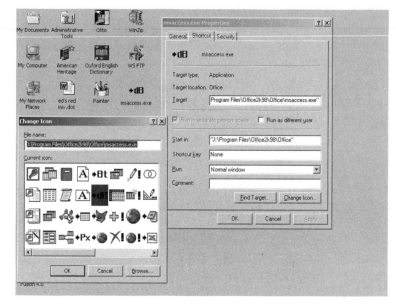

Security

Just as Disk Management allows anyone with Administrator rights to take ownership, set auditing, and set permissions for a volume, Explorer allows the same, but at the directory and file levels.

> **Note**
>
> FAT and FAT32 volumes have no security features. You will only be able to set security to files and folders on NTFS volumes. You won't even see a Security tab for files or folders on any FAT volume.

To change any security-related item for a file or directory from the Explorer, select the item or items you want to operate on and then right-click and choose Properties from the context menu. The Security tab has a basic dialog box, for fundamental access settings, and an Advanced button. The Advanced button has settings for

- *Permissions*—Allows anyone with the necessary security level to set access control for selected items
- *Auditing*—Allows adding or removing auditing (and type of auditing) for groups
- *Ownership*—Allows taking, but not giving, of ownership of selected items

For example, to eliminate access to a file for a group of users, first select the file you want to restrict. Right-click and then choose Properties from the context menu. Choose the Security tab and then click the Permissions button. Figure 9.36 shows the resulting dialog box.

Note

The owner of an file or folder controls permissions for it.

FIGURE 9.36

Setting permissions for a file starts with this dialog box accessed by the Advanced button on the Security tab of the Properties dialog box.

If the group you want to restrict doesn't appear in the list box, click the Add button. This button adds a group, not a set of permissions. Figure 9.37 shows the adding of the group. You can see the filename in the title bar of the Properties dialog box at the top-left of the figure.

FIGURE 9.37

You can add a group with a type of access from the Add dialog box. This dialog box shows the addition groups from the computer \\PAULWKS.

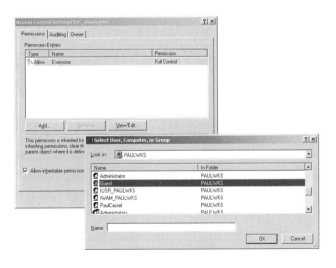

9

WORKING WITH
THE WINDOWS
2000 FILE SYSTEM

You can set the permissions for the added group from a checklist that will appear after you select a user group (or user) and click OK.

From this point on, any person logging on from the added group on \\PAULWKS will be able to access the specified resource in the way you set.

Using identical techniques, you can set permissions for volumes, file groups, and directories. Similarly, you can set auditing for these files or take ownership for your group by selecting the appropriate tab in the Advanced section of the Properties, Security dialog box.

Sharing and Mapping Files

Sharing a file, a directory, or a volume means you allow others on a network to gain access to those resources. It does not mean sharing resources with others logged on to the workstation. This latter capability is handled through security.

Mapping a file, directory, or volume means you map, or alias, another's shared resource to a volume letter on your workstation. As with many other Windows 2000 operations, you set security options when sharing, whereas you must have the requisite permissions to map.

Sharing Files

Sharing a file in Explorer is the same as sharing in Disk Management MMC shown previously in the section Standard Disk Management Tasks. Many people prefer using Explorer for sharing chores because it's faster to launch Explorer than the Disk Management component of the MMC.

To share a file, directory, or volume from Explorer, right-click the target object and then choose Sharing from the context menu.

> **Note**
>
> You can only share an object when the controlling object is already shared. For example, to share a file, you must have its folder shared. Similarly to share a folder, its host volume must be shared.

Alternatively, you can highlight the object, choose Properties from the File menu, and then choose the Sharing tab from the Properties dialog box. The context menu option is a direct jump to the Sharing tab of the Properties dialog box (see Figure 9.38).

FIGURE 9.38

You can jump directly to the Sharing tab of the Properties dialog box through the context menu, or navigate there from the Explorer menu choices File, Properties.

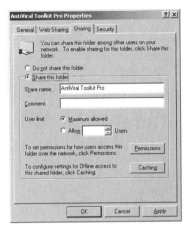

The Sharing tab has information about the shared status of Explorer objects. To share an object, choose the Share this Folder option button; then, if you choose, fill in a name or label to share the object as (see Figure 9.39). You can also set caching and permissions from this dialog box by choosing the appropriate buttons. Finally you can choose the maximum number of simultaneous connections or let an infinite number of users connect (default). Figure 9.39 shows the connections limited to 10.

FIGURE 9.39

Clicking the Shared As option button will give you a default name or label to share an object as. You can also fill in your own choice and set several other options while you're at it.

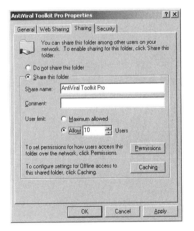

Setting permissions for a shared object has as many options, and it has a familiar look, as do most other Windows 2000 Professional security dialog boxes. In Figure 9.40, the default permission of full control for Everyone (effectively no security) has been deleted. In its place, the Users group has been granted Read (only) permission. Figure 9.40 still shows Everyone with full permission, but that will soon be removed in favor of adding a new group with full permissions and keeping Users with limited access.

9

WORKING WITH
THE WINDOWS
2000 FILE SYSTEM

FIGURE 9.40

The Permissions button from the Sharing tab has the usual dialog boxes for adding, deleting, and editing the permissions of users and user groups.

Note

The Shared As name, Wild Sounds, isn't valid from workstations without LFN enabled. If you use LFN in shared resources, make sure all the potential users of those resources have LFN enabled. If not, or if you're unsure, stick to the MS-DOS naming conventions. Workstations using older versions of Windows such as 3.11 can't have LFN. That's a feature introduced in Windows 95.

When you click OK through the various dialog boxes to accept the sharing you've just done, Explorer will visually indicate the shared resource by changing its icon to one with an extended hand. Figure 9.41 shows the folder just shared.

FIGURE 9.41

Explorer has a visual clue to shared resources—the extended hand.

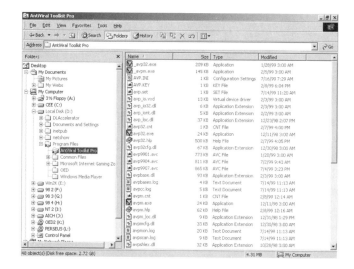

Mapping Files

Mapping a shared resource means assigning a drive letter to the network path to that resource. For example, it's just simpler to specify drive R: in a Save As dialog box than the actual path, which might be something like

```
\\Tirilee\Programs\Saves\Invoices
```

To map a shared resource, you first locate it (under My Network Places in Explorer) and then assign it a drive letter as an alias. You don't need to map a resource to use it, but if you regularly use a directory on a network, mapping and then connecting to that resource upon startup will save you some time. It's also easier to access a mapped resource than to browse for it.

Figure 9.42 shows mapping a shared resource, a directory called `pauls backup` on the `Tirilee-ex0wgpt` computer. After locating the shared resource (on Windows 2000 Server in this case), right click it and choose Map Network Drive from the context menu.

FIGURE 9.42

You don't need to map a shared resource to use it. In this case, the user found the shared resource, pauls backup, *on the* Tirilee-ex0wgpt *server through My Network Neighborhood/Computers Near Me.*

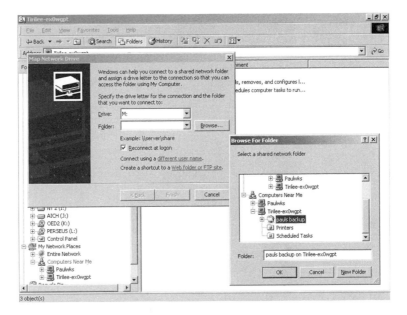

Figure 9.42 shows both the path to the shared resource and the two mapping dialog boxes if you choose to browse for (or directly enter) the shared resource you want to map through the Tools, Map Network Drive entry in Explorer's menu system. Figure 9.43 shows the dialog box with the path filled in—the result of locating the resource in My Network Places, right-clicking it, and then choosing Map Network Drive from the context menu.

FIGURE 9.43

Some people find browsing through Explorer and then choosing to map through the context menu faster than using Explorer's menus.

Change the file letter designation if you want and then click OK to make your choice of mapping stick. After you do, the new drive alias will appear in the left pane of your Explorer. Figure 9.44 shows the newly mapped drive alias and the file it contains.

FIGURE 9.44

After mapping a resource, you can see it in the left pane of Explorer and in the pull-down drive list. At this point, you can use a mapped resource just like any local drive to the extent of your permissions.

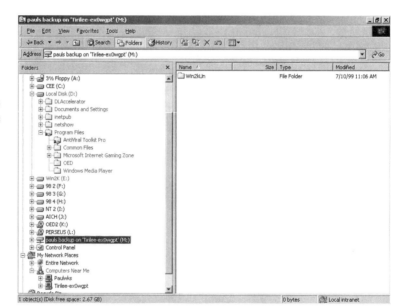

Other Context Menu Tricks

The context menu in Explorer contains quite a few options to make your computing experience easier or more convenient. Microsoft has allowed hooks into this menu for developers, so the screens shown here might not agree with the ones on other computers. Notably, the WinZip utility has been installed on the demo computer, so options to zip or unzip files appear on all the file or directory context menus.

Figure 9.45 shows a context menu with two additions—a virus checker (AVP) and the WinZip utility.

FIGURE 9.45

The context menu in Explorer will vary from computer to computer, depending on the Windows 2000 setup and installed applications.

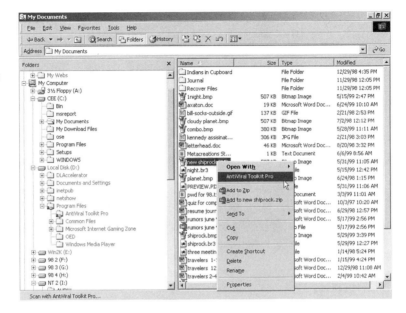

Viewing and Editing

By switching to Thumbnails view in Explorer, you can view small versions of the files so enabled within Windows 2000 Professional.

Choosing Open from the context menu will bring up the application associated with the file with that file loaded. You can also choose Open With to open a file with a non-associated application. Figure 9.46 shows the Open command issues to the file highlighted in Figure 9.45. In this example, the associated application is PaintShop Pro, but the file was opened using the Open With command and selecting Microsoft Paint as the target application.

Printing

You can use the Print choice from the context menu to send a file to the default printer. There is no real trick here. To print the file, Windows 2000 Professional calls up the application and then asks the application to print the document. A document printed this way will not appear on the MRU (Most Recently Used) file list of an application, so it's a sort of stealth way to print something. It will appear on the Documents menu of Start, however.

9

WORKING WITH
THE WINDOWS
2000 FILE SYSTEM

FIGURE 9.46

You can use Open With in the context menu to choose any appropriate (or not so appropriate) application with which to open a file.

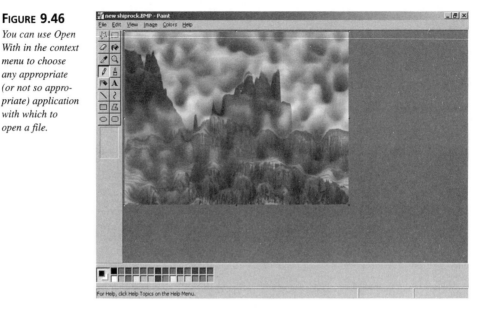

Sending To

You can send files or other Explorer objects to various devices or services though the Send To option of the context menu. The devices and services in the Send To entry of the context menu are those that are there by default, plus those that appear in the SendTo directory. Figure 9.47 shows a SendTo directory. This is a directory subordinate to the Documents and Settings folder for the logged on user.

FIGURE 9.47

The SendTo folder contains entries that will allow you to direct files from the context menu. This folder varies with each logged on user.

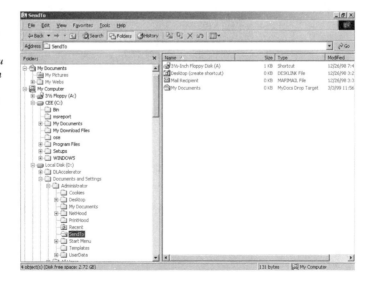

If you want to add an object to `SendTo`, add it to the directory or add a shortcut. Figure 9.48 shows a shortcut to the mapped drive M:, which is on `Tirilee` (see Figure 9.43).

FIGURE 9.48

The mapped drive M: will now appear on the Send To menu.

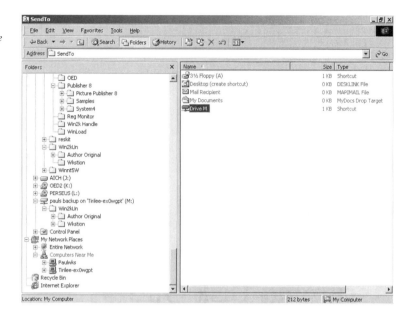

The shortcut was created by right-dragging the entry for drive M from the left pane of Explorer to the current user (`PaulCassel`) `SendTo` folder and then dropping it and choosing Create Shortcut (Here) from the pop-up menu. The name of the shortcut was then changed to drive M.

Figure 9.49 shows the Send To context menu entry after the addition to the `SendTo` folder show in Figure 9.48.

In a similar way, you can add applications or devices to this directory and then see them appear in the Send To entry of your context menu.

FIGURE 9.49

You can add many devices and services to your Send To context menu entry by adding them or their shortcuts to the SendTo *directory.*

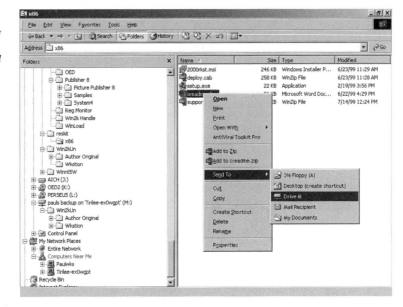

Assigning Disk Quotas

Faced with overwhelming demand, Microsoft finally added the ability to assign disk space quotas to users and groups for specific volumes. Using this facility, you can limit the amount of space users or user groups can "grab" on volumes. To set a quota

1. Double-click My Computer on the Desktop.

2. Locate the object (volume or folder) for which you want to assign a quota. Right-click it. Choose Properties from the context menu.

3. Click the Quota tab (see Figure 9.50).

4. Check the check box, Enable Quotas.

Note

You can only assign disk quotas in NTFS volumes.

FIGURE **9.50**

You must enable quota management before setting quotas for disk space. You can also choose to deny access to users who exceed their quota allotment.

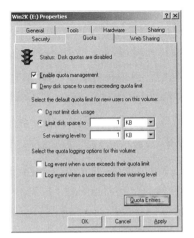

5. Click the Quota Entries button. Here is where you set the actual quotas. Click New Quota Entry to add a quota.

6. Select users or user groups to add. Click OK.

7. In the resulting dialog box, specify the options you choose for this user or group and then select OK.

Figure 9.51 shows the Guest account set for quotas with a limit of 10KB of space and a warning level of 8KB. When a user of the Guest group logs on, he or she will get 10KB of space on this volume and will get a warning that the quota is about to run out when he or she hits 8KB of storage for files he or she owns.

FIGURE **9.51**

Disk quotas are assigned by ownership. Here the Guest user group gets limited storage on a volume.

Summary

The FAT file system has the advantage of being as close to a universal file system as exists in computers today. However, it lacks modern capabilities, such as ensuring disk integrity and security. Also, it's not efficient in volumes greater than about 500MB and is limited to comparatively small volumes. The NT File System (NTFS) fills the need for a modern, secure file system created by the shortcomings of FAT.

The chief graphic tool for administering the file system is Disk Management. By using it, you can create, delete, view, and manipulate volumes and partitions. Disk Management also allows you to add or edit security for volumes as well as take ownership of them.

The Explorer is the chief graphic tool for manipulating files and directories. Using it, you can share, map, set security, copy, rename, delete, move, view, as well as other such options available in the Send To entry of your Context menu.

Installing Applications on Windows 2000

CHAPTER

10

Operating Systems and Application Programs

Windows 2000 Professional, like other Windows versions, uses the open architecture concept for itself and its applications. In a nutshell, this means the operating system and its native applications are made up of many components in a manner similar to a brick wall being made up of individual bricks.

The advantage of the open architecture is that many applications can share common parts, and the parts of either Windows 2000 Professional or its applications (or both) can be updated rather easily. The downside of all this openness is extremely complex installation and de-installation routines. Applications often replace parts of Windows, itself, with newer components. When running, they are actually, in a way, part of Windows, not just running under it.

If this weren't enough potential confusion, most applications require multiple entries in the Registry to run properly or at all. See Chapter 8, "The Windows 2000 Registry," for details about Windows 2000's registry. When removed, these programs need to have their registration entries removed also or Windows will malfunction or, at best, flash numerous warning messages at hapless users.

Vendors working in conjunction with Microsoft have come up with fairly standardized installation and de-installation (or *uninstallation,* as some prefer) programs, but they aren't foolproof. They can't be. Here's just one scenario of why that's the case.

Suppose a program, FastWord, uses a component, Fancy.dll, as part of its component package. Upon installation, FastWord's Setup copies Fancy.dll to the [%windows32%]\system32 directory and registers itself, along with Fancy.dll, in the Registry. In a perfect world, de-installation would remove Fancy.dll from [%windows32%]\system32 and from the Registry. However, what if another program, GreatCalc, also needs to use Fancy.dll and has installed it into [%windows32%]\system32? There aren't two copies of this file, because FastWord's version overwrote GreatCalc's during its setup.

If the de-installation of FastWord removes Fancy.dll from [%windows32%]\system32, it would cause GreatCalc to malfunction. On the other hand, if FastWord is the only application that uses Fancy.dll and de-installation fails to remove it from the machine, FastWord leaves an orphaned piece of itself behind.

> **Note**
>
> See the "Registry Entries," section later in this chapter for important information about how Windows 2000 handles component files that affect more than one application.

If that weren't enough, Windows components suffer from version madness. A component will retain the same name through many version changes. Each change should be a superset of the component and usually is, but that doesn't prevent another setup program from overwriting a newer version of the component with an older one. This results in a subset of the component's total abilities replacing the whole set of the original component. Usually this causes some sort of malfunction with the application needing all the component's features. Windows 2000 does have some mechanism for detecting an attempted overwrite of system files (with the option to restore), but its function depends on cooperation with the application program's setup process.

Until the application calls on the component to supply the (now) missing functions, this malfunction won't appear. So the installation of Application20 might ruin the existing installation of Application12, but in such a way that it doesn't show up for weeks or months. Worse, Application12 won't flash a message saying, "Application20's install of `Fancy.dll` has ruined my spell checker." It won't even flash a message hinting at the problem. Instead, it will just start acting in a bizarre manner.

RegClean

Microsoft has a utility called RegClean, which will go through your Registry trying to locate orphaned entries. It then offers to clear your Registry of these entries. After running, it creates a `.reg` file with the entries it deleted. Double-clicking this file in Explorer will restore the deleted entries, so in the vast majority of cases, running RegClean can't land you in worse shape than not running it.

You can find RegClean at Microsoft's Web and FTP sites as well as the usual places that contain Microsoft utilities. Figure 10.1 shows two `.reg` files from running RegClean. The first file, listed at 203KB, was run on a machine that hadn't had this utility run in a few months. The second file is the result of running an additional RegClean after only two weeks. This machine is a test bed, installing and uninstalling applications quite heavily.

The output of running RegClean on a well-functioning machine should result in `.reg` files of under 20KB. To run RegClean, double-click the file in Explorer or run it from the command line.

FIGURE **10.1**

To restore Registry entries deleted by RegClean, double-click the file the utility creates.

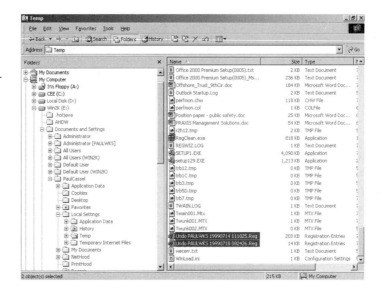

RegClean will run and not make any changes to the Registry if you tell it not to. This doesn't make much sense, because there's no reason to run it just for the sake of running, but the utility does offer you a way to back out, as you can see in Figure 10.2.

FIGURE **10.2**

RegClean will diagnose your Registry and then give you an option to apply its diagnosis as a fix.

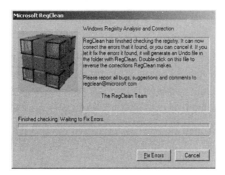

Safe Installs

There isn't a sure way around all setup problems. The only real solution, and it's a poor one, is to practice defensive installation, just as you would practice defensive driving. Defensive driving assumes that the other person will make errors. You take the responsibility of avoiding the potential resulting collision. Defensive installation assumes a problem with a setup routine, but it also means that you can restore your system to a pre-installation state in these cases.

The following are the steps to take in a defensive installation:

1. Make a new Emergency Repair Disk (ERD) to save the current configuration. See Chapter 26, "Disaster Recovery," for this procedure if you're unsure of it.

2. Back up the system and installation target volumes, including the local Registry. This backup should include any `.ini` files.

3. Make sure you have a boot disk, although having a setup go so bad that you need this is a rare occurrence.

4. Install the new application.

This will allow you to return to your previous state in case the setup of a new application goes awry. This routine isn't too effective in the case of an installation's problems showing up weeks after running setup, but it will allow you to return exactly to the pre-setup state. And that's better than nothing.

> **Note**
>
> There are a slew of third-party utilities that purport to be able to restore any system no matter how badly mangled by a setup program. These usually work by creating a snapshot of your system from which you can restore your machine to its pre-setup condition. They are, in short, automatic variations of the procedures described in this section.

If you want to take the trouble, you can create a before and after listing of directories to see what files have been added, written over with changed versions, or—in odd cases—deleted. To do this, start a command session (CLI) by choosing Start, Run, CMD.

To create a simple text file consisting of a sorted directory listing, navigate to that directory and enter

```
dir /on > filename.txt
```

If you want to suppress directory listings, enter

```
dir /a-d /on > filename.txt
```

Do this list for at least the [%windows32%] home system directory and the \system and \system32 subdirectories. If you want, you can create a huge listing of the home system directory and all its subdirectories by including the /s switch in the DIR command, but doing so creates an unwieldy file due to its size.

After running Setup, you can compare the before and after status of the directories using the FC (File Compare) command-line utility. The FC command takes the following parameters:

/a	Displays the start and ending lines for each difference
/b	Does a binary comparison

10

`/c`	Case-insensitive compare
`/l`	ASCII compare
`/LB`*n*	Stops the compare after finding *n* hits
`/n`	Line number display of mismatches
`/t`	Ignores tab expansion
`/w`	Removes whitespace (20H) characters
`/u`	Compares files as Unicode

To use `FC`, enter the following at the command prompt:

```
FC [parameters] Filename1 Filename2
```

Figure 10.3 shows a `\system32` directory listing made with the following command in Notepad:

```
dir /a-d /on > before.txt
```

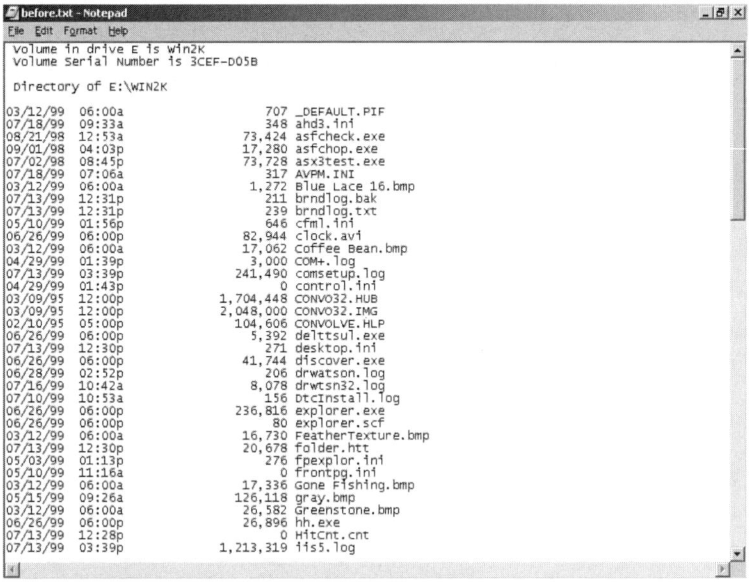

```
 Volume in drive E is Win2K
 Volume Serial Number is 3CEF-D05B

 Directory of E:\WIN2K

03/12/99  06:00a                   707 _DEFAULT.PIF
07/18/99  09:33a                   348 ahd3.ini
08/21/98  12:53a                73,424 asfcheck.exe
09/01/98  04:03p                17,280 asfchop.exe
07/02/98  08:45p                73,728 asx3test.exe
07/18/99  07:06a                   317 AVPM.INI
03/12/99  06:00a                 1,272 Blue Lace 16.bmp
07/13/99  12:31p                   211 brndlog.bak
07/13/99  12:31p                   239 brndlog.txt
05/10/99  01:56p                   646 cfml.ini
06/26/99  06:00p                82,944 clock.avi
03/12/99  06:00a                17,062 Coffee Bean.bmp
04/29/99  01:39p                 3,000 COM+.log
07/13/99  03:39p               241,490 comsetup.log
04/29/99  01:43p                     0 control.ini
03/09/95  12:00p             1,704,448 CONVO32.HUB
03/09/95  12:00p             2,048,000 CONVO32.IMG
02/10/95  05:00p               104,606 CONVOLVE.HLP
06/26/99  06:00p                 5,392 delttsul.exe
07/13/99  12:30p                   271 desktop.ini
06/26/99  06:00p                41,744 discover.exe
06/28/99  02:52p                   206 drwatson.log
07/16/99  10:42a                 8,078 drwtsn32.log
07/10/99  10:53a                   156 DtcInstall.log
06/26/99  06:00p               236,816 explorer.exe
06/26/99  06:00p                    80 explorer.scf
03/12/99  06:00a                16,730 FeatherTexture.bmp
07/13/99  12:30p                20,678 folder.htt
05/03/99  01:13p                   276 fpexplor.ini
05/10/99  11:16a                     0 frontpg.ini
03/12/99  06:00a                17,336 Gone Fishing.bmp
05/15/99  09:26a               126,118 gray.bmp
03/12/99  06:00a                26,582 Greenstone.bmp
06/26/99  06:00p                26,896 hh.exe
07/13/99  12:28p                     0 HitCnt.cnt
07/13/99  03:39p             1,213,319 iis5.log
```

FIGURE 10.3
This is a listing of the before setup status of the `\system32` *directory. To see what's changed after setup, you can run the* `FC` *utility on this and the* `after` *directory listing.*

After the listing shown in Figure 10.3 was run, an electronic camera was installed and then uninstalled on this Windows 2000 Professional system. After the uninstall program has run, enter the following command:

```
Dir /a-d /on > after.txt
```

This creates a text file showing an after install/uninstall listing of \system32. To see if the uninstall left any detritus, enter the following command:

```
FC before.txt after.txt > compare.txt
```

This command compares the two directory listings and enters the results in a file called compare.txt. Making a file is an easier way to view the output of FC than the console display. Figure 10.4 shows the file compare.txt in Notepad. After eliminating the false hits caused by the after.txt file itself, you can see that two entries remain different from before and after the installation of the electronic camera's software. These files are twaindrv.dll and pwrshot.cnt.

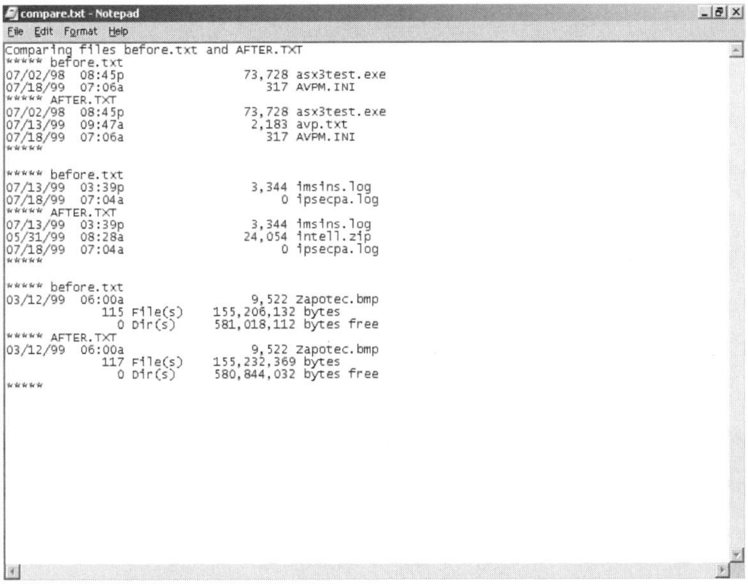

FIGURE 10.4

The output of FC redirected from the console and into a text file shown here in Notepad.

The output from FC takes a little getting used to. It not only shows mismatches but also surrounding text. There is usually one false hit caused by the existence of the redirected .txt file itself, but ignoring that shows the clear problem of having two additional files after listing that weren't there before listing. The reason the following command worked all right is because the FC utility defaults to an ASCII compare of the output suitable for this task:

```
FC before.txt after.txt
```

Therefore, it required no optional parameters.

At this point, you can delete these files, or more safely, use Explorer to move them to the Recycle Bin. If you're fairly sure they're benign or are serving some useful purpose, leave them in. Remember, files deleted from the command line (CLI) are permanently deleted unless protected by a third-party undelete utility.

> **Note**
>
> The DIR/FC method used here must be used with consideration due to the prevalence of false hits. For example, Figure 10.4 shows some changes in the AVP files. This is the virus checker for this system (www.avp.com), and it is appropriate that these files change from FC's view. Be very careful removing files so identified using the DIR/FC method. Be sure to boot again to make sure your system functions properly after their removal.

Altering Windows 2000 Professional

You can add or remove Windows 2000 Professional components using the Add/Remove Program Wizard. This works similarly to the Custom installation option you might have opted for during Windows 2000 Professional setup.

> **Note**
>
> Only during a clean install is the Custom option available during setup. If you are upgrading an application, you won't see the Custom option.

Figure 10.5 shows the Control Panel for a machine having the Accessibility Options applet. This suite of tools (and its specific contents) are part of Windows 2000 Setup/Configuration options. The following demonstration will install FrontPage Server extensions on a machine.

To add these options, or to add or remove any optional Windows 2000 Professional components, click Add/Remove Programs in the Control Panel. This brings up the Add/Remove option bar dialog box with a listing of currently installed applications, as shown in Figure 10.6.

FIGURE **10.5**

*This machine has
the Accessibility
Options applet.
You can add it if
missing or remove
it if present by
using Add/Remove
Programs.*

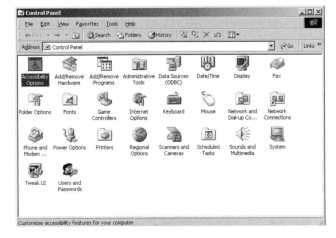

FIGURE **10.6**

*The Add/Remove
dialog box
launches with a
list box showing
all the currently
installed applica-
tions.*

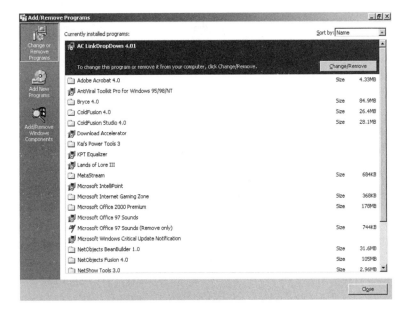

The Add/Remove Windows Components button (on the left side of the Add/Remove
Programs dialog box) shows all the currently installed optional portions of Windows
2000 Professional, as shown in Figure 10.7.

FIGURE 10.7

The gray check box next to Internet Information Services indicates that it's partly installed.

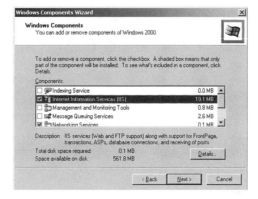

> **Note**
>
> The Add/Remove dialog box and installation routines in general have been vastly improved in Windows 2000 over previous Windows versions including 98SE and NT4. Not only does the new Add/Remove utility track program usage frequency, but new compliant programs, such as Microsoft Office 2000, can auto-detect and install components on demand.

This system has Internet Information Services (IIS) partly installed missing only a few parts, including FrontPage Server extensions. To add this facility, locate the Internet Information Services line in the Components dialog box.

Note the check box for IIS is gray, indicating that this option is partly installed. Double-click this entry to bring up a detailed view of this option. This displays another dialog box showing details for IIS. Locate FrontPage 2000 Server Extensions, click to add a check in the check box to the left of the entry and then click OK to exit the dialog boxes. Figure 10.8 shows the dialog box with IIS. Figure 10.9 shows its component details.

FIGURE 10.8

Many options in Windows 2000 can be partly installed, such as the IIS component.

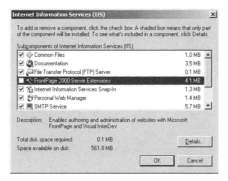

FIGURE 10.9

Windows 2000 Setup needs its distribution files to complete the requested component change.

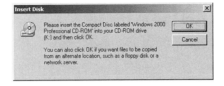

After clicking OK and then clicking Next when prompted to do so, Setup will need your distribution CD-ROM or other location for setup files. If you haven't done so already, you'll need to place your distribution CD-ROM in the drive or point to where on the network Windows 2000 Professional can find the distribution files.

After Setup accesses and installs the files, it closes down its File Copy dialog box, leaving you at the Install/Remove applet where you can install or remove other applications or components. In this case, the next time Control Panel was launched, it had the Accessibility Options applet as part of the panel. Figure 10.9 shows the distribution file location request dialog box.

You can also run Windows Setup from the distribution CD-ROM. Insert the CD-ROM in the drive and it should start up, giving you the screen shown in Figure 10.10. If it doesn't autostart, locate it in Explorer and double click Setup.

FIGURE 10.10

The Autostart feature of the distribution CD-ROM will launch this screen when you insert the CD-ROM into the drive during a Windows 2000 Professional session.

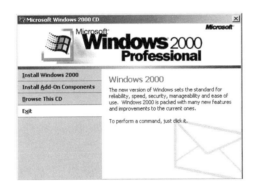

To run the Add/Remove routine, choose the second option from the splash screen, Install Add-On Components. This adds or removes portions of Windows 2000 Professional, not application programs.

To remove optional portions of Windows 2000 Professional, use the same technique but clear the check boxes for those components you want to remove.

10

INSTALLING APPLICATIONS ON WINDOWS 2000

Adding Applications

Only 32-bit applications are fully compliant with Windows 2000 Professional's installation specifications, but the operating system is designed to accommodate older programs as far as feasible. Each application classification, 32-bit, 16-bit (Win16) and MS-DOS applications have their own special considerations when installing or removing.

True 32-Bit Applications

Adding 32-bit applications is similar (or can be) to adding Windows 2000 Professional components. The vast majority of the applications you'll encounter will have one of a few standardized installation programs. To run them, you can use the Add/Remove Applications applet in Control Panel. If you prefer, you can use the Explorer to locate their `Setup.exe` programs on the distribution CD-ROM or disks. Double-click `Setup.exe` and then follow the instructions, which usually consist of some or all of the following choices:

- Into which directory to install the application
- The program group (if any) to create for convenient program launching
- The parts (components) of the program to install

In many cases, application distribution CD-ROMs will have an Autorun routine. As soon as you insert the CD-ROM, you'll launch into the Setup program.

The actual screens for program installation will differ, depending upon the particular install program used to create the installation routine and the needs of the application.

Figure 10.11 shows the start of the Setup program for Microsoft Office 2000 on a machine with an existing version of Office. Because there is an existing version of Office, this screen offers choices appropriate to the situation. These choices give information to the user, allowing intelligent addition or deletion of Office components.

The screen in Figure 10.11 has a similar function to the screen shown in Figure 10.7. The difference is that here the component options are for Office 2000; in Figure 10.7, the options are for Windows 2000 Professional.

FIGURE **10.11**

Office 2000, like many applications, allows the adding or removing of components from existing installations.

Adding or Removing 16-Bit Windows Applications

The method used to add or remove 16-bit applications depends upon the applications themselves. Few, if any, of these applications, even Windows native ones, use a Setup or Install routine compatible to Windows 2000 Professional's native expectations. Instead, Windows 2000 Professional tries to conform to the expectations of these older-style programs.

Many of these programs use .ini files or modify the two application-usable .ini files, system.ini and win.ini, which are the precursors of the Windows 2000 Professional Registry.

Windows 2000 Professional has a directory of the system folder called \system that serves as an analog to \system32 for shared 16-bit components. It is also able to use the system.ini and win.ini files. Some 32-bit applications use these files also. Figure 10.12 shows both these files for a Windows 2000 Professional setup.

> **Note**
>
> Figure 10.12 shows the use of the system editor (sysedit), supplied as part of Windows 2000 Professional but a holdover from older Windows. This editor will, when run, load for editing all the configuration files used by Win16 applications. To see it in action, enter Start, Run and then enter **sysedit** in the dialog box.

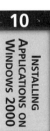

10

INSTALLING APPLICATIONS ON WINDOWS 2000

FIGURE **10.12**

In theory, the Registry should hold configuration information for all 32-bit applications, leaving win.ini *and* system.ini *for 16-bit applications only. However, theory and practice often diverge. Some 32-bit programs use either or both of the older* .ini *files.*

To add a 16-bit Windows program, take the following steps if you want to play it very safe:

1. Back up everything.
2. Create a "before" directory listing using any technique you prefer. Earlier on, you saw the use of the dir /a-d /on > before.txt routine. You'll need to do this for the [%windows32%]\system directory and the Windows directory.
3. Create backup copies of win.ini and system.ini.
4. Setup the application.
5. Create an "after" directory listing using any technique you prefer.

To remove a Windows 16-bit application that doesn't have an automated uninstall program (few do), perform the following steps:

1. Remove the application directories and contained files.
2. Remove any application-added entries to win.ini and system.ini. Do this by either editing the two files or restoring the files from their backups. Don't restore from backups if you've installed subsequent applications, because restoring might adversely affect these applications.
3. Run FC or in another way determine any added files to the [windows] and \system directories. Remove them if you're sure they aren't shared by another application.

4. Remove any `.ini` files related to the application. These almost always exist in the `\windows` directory.

5. Remove any shortcuts from Start, Programs, the Desktop, or any other location (such as the Startup folder) you or the Setup program might have created for them.

The good thing about 16-bit Windows applications is that rarely, if ever, will their partly installed components (or partly uninstalled bits and pieces of these applications) adversely affect Windows 2000 Professional or 32-bit applications. Additionally, most Win16 applications that add items to the `.ini` files also add headers identifying their entries. This isn't a rule, but it's fairly common.

Installing MS-DOS Applications

Few, if any, DOS applications you run will be aware of Windows 2000 Professional's existence. To install these older style applications, run their Install programs (if they exist). Many DOS programs are installed by copying the contents of their distribution disks to a directory.

Some DOS programs, especially games, will run under Windows 2000 Professional, but will change screen modes possibly distressing the look of your Desktop after they exit. The cost-to-benefit ratio of these programs is for you to decide. When Windows first became dominant in the early 1990s, there were many functional reasons to run older MS-DOS programs. Now, ten years later, almost all functions from those older programs have been duplicated in modern programs, or these functions have been rendered redundant, meaning that there is less reason to run them now than when Windows was new. Chapter 5, "Tuning Windows 2000 Performance," discusses some aspects of getting recalcitrant MS-DOS programs to run under Windows 2000 Professional.

What Setup Programs Do

Setup programs for 32-bit applications perform three broad services:

- Creating an application directory structure and installing the needed files in that structure.

- Adding shared, or potentially shared, components to the appropriate folder. This is usually `\system32`.

- Making the appropriate Registry entries.

The Setup program also often creates a file containing information about the installed components. If so, the uninstall program uses this information as a checklist. Often, if an uninstall routine fails mysteriously, the uninstall file is missing or corrupt.

There's nothing unusual or different about the first two chores of setup programs: creating a directory structure and installing files. Adding Registry entries is the real kicker. It's somewhat analogous to making `.ini` entries in the old `system.ini` and `win.ini` files or making an application's own `.ini` files. However, due to the complexities of Windows 2000 Professional (and Windows 98, too), the Registry entries are likewise complex.

CLSID or GUID

You'll see a long 16-digit (16 bytes or 128 bits) hexadecimal (BASE16) number as part of many Registry entries. This is the GUID, or CLSID. GUID stands for Globally Unique Identifier, whereas CLSID stands for Class ID. Although the numbers are the same, whether they're referred to as a GUID or a CLSID depends on the context.

A GUID is a unique identifier for a Registry entry. Unique in this context means the application entry has that number for itself. The number remains the same in all registries, and no other application, or application part, can use the same GUID for itself.

Microsoft distributes a "random" number generator, `GUIDGEN.EXE`, as part of its Software Development Kits (SDKs) for making GUIDs. Developers use the generated numbers to uniquely identify their applications. The uniqueness is supposed to be guaranteed by the impossibility of generating two identical numbers of that length. However, Microsoft maintains a database of assigned GUIDs that developers can check and register their GUIDs with just in case.

The Registry Entries

The type of entries made in the Registry by a setup program depends on the capacity of the program and what interactions it expects to have with other installed programs and Windows itself. Microsoft Excel is a good example of a program with many Registry entries. Following are three (of many) of them with their explanations.

Figure 10.13 shows one entry for Excel 2000 (version 9). The program, along with the other parts of Microsoft Office 2000, are versioned as 9, but are marketed as 2000. This entry is under `HKEY_CLASSES_ROOT\Excel.Application\CurVer`.

Similarly, the Setup program enters information about the file extensions associated with that program. The Registry area, `HKEY_LOCAL_MACHINE\SOFTWARE\Classes\`, shown in Figure 10.14, is this area.

FIGURE 10.13

The Registry entry for Excel telling Windows 2000 Professional and any other interested parties the official version for this application.

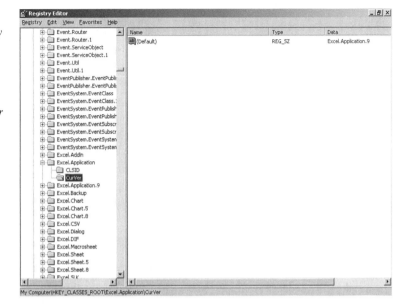

FIGURE 10.14

Here is the file extension area of the Registry. Users can add, modify or delete entries found here through the View-Options menu entry in Explorer on the File Types tab.

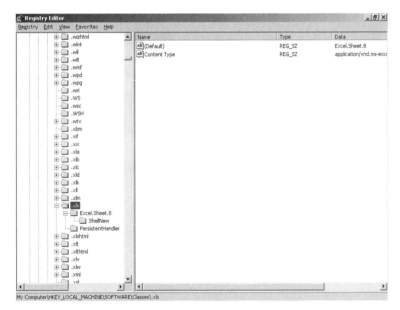

A very important part of the Registry is the SharedDLLs section. Windows 2000 Professional is, like all Windows versions, a component operating system. That is, the exact variant of Windows 2000 Professional you run is a core set of routines with added services depending on your hardware and installed or running options/services.

> **Note**
>
> The version given for Excel 2000 files is 8, not 9 (see Figures 10.13 and 10.14). This indicates that the file types between Excel 2000 and Excel 97 didn't change. It is also likely an oversight on Microsoft's part, and it is, at worst, cosmetic.

In the same way, applications running under Windows 2000 Professional are component applications. They, too, are a core set of routines with extensions often shared among other applications. The advantage of this system is that only one of each shared extension (file) needs to be present on a machine (or network, in some cases) or loaded into memory.

For example, the routines to access databases for some of Microsoft's products start with the letters DAO. These files might be used by more than one application.

The first application to need a DAO file installs it. Subsequent applications don't need to install this file, because it already exists. Doing another installation of an identical file will, at best, just overwrite an existing file or, at worst, install itself at a new location, thus wasting disk space.

Rather than having this scenario, the first application to install the DAO file enters it in the SharedDLLs section of the Registry with a value of 1. Each time an application needing this file is installed, it increments this number. Each time an application that uses this DAO file uninstalls, it decrements the entry's value. If an uninstall that includes the DAO file finds a value of 1 in the SharedDLLs section, it notifies the user that it's about to remove a shared component. This dialog box gives the user an option to continue or to retain the component.

Figure 10.15 shows the SharedDLLs section of the Windows 2000 Professional Registry HKEY_LOCAL_MACHINE\SOFTWARE\Microsoft\Windows\CurrentVersion\SharedDLLs.

The idea of the SharedDLLs section of the Registry is a good one, but it doesn't always work out. Uninstall routines fail, people uninstall programs manually without decrementing the SharedDLLs section, and other things go bump in the night to conspire against this facility. It's better than nothing, however.

FIGURE **10.15**

Here is the
SharedDLLs *sec-*
tion of the
Registry. This
workstation has
two registered
applications that
use the DAO file
for data access.
You can see these
two entries
directly above the
Edit dialog box.

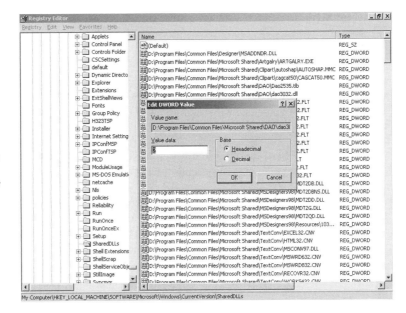

Troubleshooting Application Setups and Uninstalls

The following are some commonly encountered problems with suggested solutions.

Problem: After uninstalling a 16-bit application, you get the message that Windows 2000 Professional can't locate a part of that application.

Solution: Search system.ini and win.ini for orphaned entries related to the uninstalled application. Also, search for any other .ini file that might have been created at the time the program was installed. Take special care to look in the Run and Load sections of win.ini.

Problem: An error message for a 32-bit uninstalled program pops up upon startup. This message can be that Windows 2000 Professional can't find the application or a service failed during startup.

Solution: Look in the Startup groups for orphaned shortcuts. Similarly, examine the Run and Load lines of win.ini (there should be none, but look anyway). In the case of a service, search the Registry for the entries and delete them. Also examine the MMC in the Services folder. Make sure you've backed up your Registry before deleting any keys or altering values unless you are very sure you understand what you are about to do. There is also a Run key to the Registry that works similarly to the Startup folder. Check in there too.

10

INSTALLING
APPLICATIONS ON
WINDOWS 2000

Problem: Setup leaves a mysterious directory, such as ~Mssetup.t.

Solution: These are temporary directories that Setup should have deleted before ending. Some problem prevented Setup from doing so. You can delete these directories if you're sure Setup has finished running. You're on solid ground to assume any file or folder with a tilde (~) in its name is temporary, but to be sure, move the suspicious files or folders to another area where you can easily return them if your machine malfunctions subsequent to the move.

Problem: You try to uninstall a 32-bit application. You get an error message saying uninstall can't continue. The application exists on your machine.

Solution: You've probably lost a pointer file, such as DelsL1.isu, that uninstall needs to proceed. You'll need to uninstall the application yourself manually. Delete the installation's directory structure with the accompanying files. Back up the Registry. Remove unique entries in the Registry by searching for them and then deleting them. If you feel ambitious, decrement the application's entries in SharedDLLs. If you feel very ambitious, remove any unneeded .dll files and other shared components from \system32. You can also use Explorer (or Start, Search) to search for folders with the name uninstall in them. The folders might give you some leads as to what's up. Figure 10.16 shows the results of one search on a typical machine.

Problem: An application uninstalled and inactive on your computer still exists in the Install/Uninstall dialog box.

Solution: Remove the entry from the Registry from HKEY_LOCAL_MACHINE\SOFTWARE\ Microsoft\Windows\CurrentVersion\Uninstall.

Windows 2000 should, when requested to remove an inactive application (or one missing uninstall information), offer to remove it from the Currently Installed Programs list box. If it fails to do this, you can do some surgery on the Registry, but try Windows 2000's Add/Remove Programs Wizard first.

Figure 10.17 shows the Installed Applications list for the computer shown in Figure 10.16. In addition, most, if not all, of these applications have Registry entries specifying where their uninstall information lies. To see these entries, search on the application name within the Registry.

### CHAPTER 10

FIGURE 10.16
Searching for uninstall objects (folders) on this machine returned 65 hits.

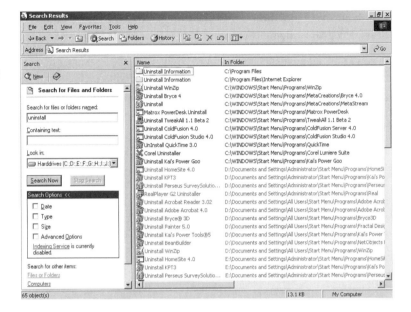

FIGURE 10.17
The installed applications section of the Add/Remove applet reflects Registry entries.

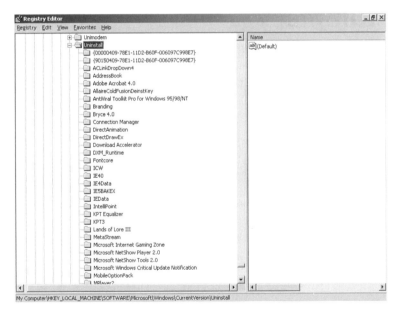

Problem: An application uninstalled or inactive on your computer still exists in the Start, Programs menu system.

If you know all elements are removed, right-click the Taskbar, choose Properties, and then select the Advanced tab. Locate the Remove button, click that and then you'll be presented with entries on the Start, Programs menu. Highlight the entry you want to remove and click OK. Figure 10.18 shows the dialog boxes for this procedure.

FIGURE 10.18

Orphaned Start, Programs menu entries can be removed easily and quickly by using the Remove facility in the Advanced tab of Properties for the Taskbar.

Summary

Installing applications in Windows 2000 Professional is similar to other versions of Windows, especially Windows 95 and 98. The chief tool for doing installations is the Add/Remove applet in the Control Panel. This applet has two tabs in its dialog box. The Install/Uninstall tab controls applications, whereas the Windows 2000 Professional Setup tab controls Windows 2000 Professional's optional components.

Installations usually go well, but things do go awry. The only way to assure yourself that you can return to a preinstallation profile is to back up your system so you can restore it if necessary.

Setup programs perform three broad functions. They create and populate a directory (folder) structure for the application, add common components to another folder (usually \system32), and make needed Registry modifications.

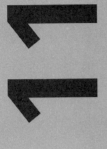

CHAPTER 11

Exploring the Command-Line Interface (CLI)

Windows 2000 Professional was designed from the outset to have a graphical user interface (GUI). Many people think of it as only having such an interface, but it also has integrated into the Command Line Interface (CLI).

The CLI for Windows 2000 Professional is similar to late versions of MS-DOS, minus those commands that aren't appropriate. Additionally, Windows 2000 has many CLI commands exclusive to it and never found in previous non-NT–based Microsoft operating systems.

Although the CLI of Windows 2000 has less variety than other competing operating systems, such as various shells of UNIX, the most important commands are all there. Also, many of the operations required from the command line in UNIX are possible through the GUI of Windows 2000. Even so, some UNIX fans who enjoy playing "stupid" shell tricks find the subset of commands in 2000 to be restrictive. There are third-party add-ons mimicking some of the common UNIX shells for those people. Also, some releases from Microsoft, such as the Resource Kit, add some interesting utilities.

What's In and Out of the CLI

The following is a list of the commands found in later versions of MS-DOS but deleted in Windows 2000 Professional, with an explanation and alternative, if known and existing, respectively:

- `Assign`   Obsolete command for re-assigning floppy disk drive letters. Not relevant in a Windows 2000 environment.

- `Choice`   A mysterious deletion. The reason for its deletion is a good topic for debate over Jolt colas.

- `CTTY`   You must issue commands from the console only.

- `Dblspace`   This compression scheme is unrecognized by Windows 2000 Professional due to data integrity concerns. Use the file compression routine native to Windows 2000 instead.

- `Defrag`   Use third-party defraggers such as Disk Keeper or Norton Utilities.

- `Dosshell`   Windows 2000 Professional uses `explorer.exe` as a shell. `Dosshell` was a slightly graphical user interface for Microsoft operating system users who didn't use Windows.

- `Drvspace`   See `Dblspace`.

- `EMM386`   Purposeless, given Windows 2000 Professional's architecture.

- `Fdisk`   Use the Disk Management part of MMC.

- `Include`   You have one DOS and only one DOS configuration.

- `Interlnk/Intersrv`   Purposeless with Windows 2000 Professional inherently providing a superset of these services. MS-DOS clients can connect to Windows 2000 using a net start disk or RAS.

- `Join`   NTFS and DOS capacity to handle larger volumes makes this command obsolete.

- `Memmaker` and supporting files   Facilities automatically done in NTVDMs.

- `Menu[color][default][item]`   See `Include`.

- `Mirror`   Make and use an ERD.

- `Msav`   Use third-party utilities. DOS and similar virus checkers aren't effective under Windows 2000 for many reasons.

- `MSBackup`   Use the surviving and still unreliable `backup` and `restore` if you're masochistic and don't really care about your data anyway. Use the real `Backup` facility included in 2000 if you're normal, or if the loss of your data will be troubling.

- `Mscdex`   Windows 2000 Professional virtualizes the CD-ROM drive, eliminating the need for real-mode drivers it can't use anyway.

- `Msd`   Use Windows 2000 Professional's diagnostics utilities.

- `Numlock`   You need to press the key yourself if you don't like the way things have turned out when turned on. Windows 2000 Professional will preserve the state of your Numlock at next bootup. That is, if you had the Numlock on when you shutdown, it will be on again when you startup under the same logon. This is part of the personalized settings for Windows 2000 Professional.

- `Power`   Windows 2000 Professional doesn't support this utility. This is now part of power management, which itself is part of Settings. Windows 2000 Professional is now, unlike previous versions of NT type operating systems, fully power-management enabled.

- `Scandisk`   NTFS volumes tend to be self-healing. You can use `Scandisk` from Windows 95 or MS-DOS for FAT volumes by booting to DOS. `Scandisk` might be dead from a CLI view, but it lives on in a much improved form run from the GUI. Right click a volume in Explorer and then choose Properties. The Tools tab has a Check Now button that will do a good diagnostic of the selected volume.

- `Smartdrv`   Windows 2000 Professional automatically and dynamically manages the disk cache. A `Smartdrv` for Windows 2000 would impinge on this hard won sovereignty.

- `Submenu`   See `Menu`.

- `Sys`   Windows 2000 is too big to `Sys` from or to a floppy disk.

- `Undelete`   Files deleted from Explorer are generally undeletable. Files deleted from the CLI aren't, unless a third-party utility protects your computer.

- `Unformat`   Don't format anything you don't want to stay formatted.

- `Vsafe`   See `MSAV`.

Most, if not all are included in Windows 2000's CLI. The reason I can't be specific about what's in and out to a certainty is that it depends on the version of MS-DOS you use as a reference.

In addition to MS-DOS commands, Windows 2000 adds TCP/IP commands (also in Windows 98 and its' successor's CLI) plus the whole series of `NET` commands exclusive to Windows 2000 (and NT before it). Pay special attention to the `NET` commands. Of all the ones in and out of Windows 2000 (compared to other Microsoft operating systems), these are the most useful. Also, don't overlook commands that you might assume are obsolete in Windows 2000 but aren't. Two such survivors are `MEM` and `EDLIN`. `MEM` remains as useful as ever, while `EDLIN` as mysterious. Perhaps it is in to give UNIX migrants who miss `SED` a good feeling.

Refer to Appendix B, "Windows 2000 Command Reference," for a list of the commands in Windows 2000 and usage examples. The Windows 2000 Help system also has a reference section on these commands.

Starting and Configuring the CLI

If you've used any recent Windows operating system, you're familiar with entering the Command Line Interface (CLI). The environment is similar to MS-DOS, many UNIX's, and previous command line Windows.

Starting the CLI

To start a CLI session, choose Start, Programs, Accessories, Command Prompt entry or you can use Start, Run, and then enter **cmd** in the dialog box. Either brings up a screen similar to Figure 11.1.

The title bar tells you that you're at the command prompt, and the command you executed is `cmd`. `cmd` is the command interpreter (shell) for Windows 2000. Windows 2000 Professional also contains a shell for DOS called, not surprisingly, `Command`. In most cases, it doesn't make any difference which shell you launch, but keep in mind that some DOS programs can become severely confused if launched under `cmd`. Also remember that `Command` is DOS-like, not 2000-like.

FIGURE **11.1**

The CLI should be familiar to anybody having seen MS-DOS, SCO UNIX, OS/2, or similar command line operating systems.

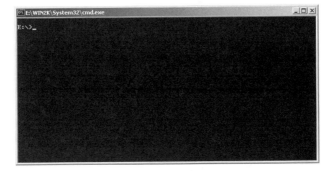

You can configure the window for your CLI using the same tools as under later DOS versions with some interesting additions. To see a menu for configuring the CLI, click the CLI prompt icon in the upper-left corner of the CLI window or press Alt+Spacebar. This will drop down a menu, as shown in Figure 11.2.

FIGURE **11.2**

Configuring the CLI isn't as much fun as a holiday on ice, but you can't fall through and get wet either.

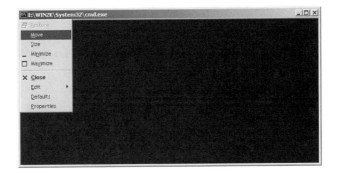

The Move and Size options on this menu are real head-scratching bafflers. You can move the window by clicking its title bar and dragging it just like any window. You can size it by clicking a border and dragging with the mouse.

The Maximize command will not really maximize the window but rather will only maximize it to its full size as a window. The window size is limited in the default view to the size of the font you choose. To make the window a real full-screen CLI, press Alt+Enter. This is a toggle. To get back to a window again, press Alt+Enter. This only works on Intel boxes because Alpha systems lack a full-screen mode.

The real action from this menu comes from the last entry, Properties. Click that and you'll bring up the tabbed dialog box shown in Figure 11.3.

FIGURE 11.3

No shocks here. The Properties entry brings up a tabbed dialog box.

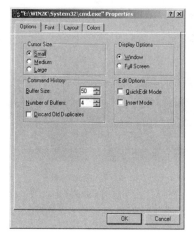

The following are the choices for the first and most useful tab, the Options tab:

- *Cursor Size*—This is how big that flashing part of the prompt is, not how large the command prompt appears to be. Choose large and the cursor becomes a block just about as big as a character box. If you change this option, the Properties dialog box will allow you to make the modifications for all instances of this shortcut or only this session.

- *Display Options*—Start in window or full screen? This is whether you need to hammer the session down to a window with Alt+Enter or you need to blow it up with the same key sequence. This option is only for Intel boxes.

- *Command History*—Windows 2000 Professional has the equivalent of DOSKEY built into its command shell for recalling commands. This property controls how many commands it keeps in its buffer and how big that buffer is. The larger the buffer, the less room available for programs, but not by much.

- *Quick Edit Mode*—Enables use of the mouse to highlight, copy, and paste. If unselected, you need to use the Edit subcommands from the pull-down menu. To use the Quick Edit, highlight the area you want to copy using the mouse and then press Ctrl+C. Ctrl+V pastes at the cursor.

- *Insert Mode*—The default for the line editor in the shell is overtype. Check this box if you prefer to be in Insert mode. The Insert key (INS) toggles this option in the editor.

The Font tab allows setting of the font type and size in either this session or all sessions. Figure 11.4 shows the Font tab that displays the setting of the font for this session to a larger true type rather than the default raster.

Figure 11.4

Changing the font size and type for a CLI session or shortcut will affect the size of the window the CLI occupies. Changes in this tab won't affect the full-screen mode (if available) of the CLI.

The Font tab will change the size and appearance of the prompt and any text displayed in the CLI window. Try some different fonts and note how the preview window alters its size and aspect ratio.

The command prompts aren't as flexible as the old DOS prompt with ANSI.SYS locked and loaded, but you can still rock out. As in times of yore, you can alter the prompt by entering the **prompt** command (at the CLI, not the Properties dialog box) followed by a parameter. The following are some possible parameters:

- $A & (Shift+7)
- $B ¦ (vertical line used for piping)
- $C (
- $D System date
- $E The Esc character
- $F)
- $G >
- $H Backspace
- $L <
- $N Drive
- $P Path
- $Q =
- $S Space or ASCII 32 (20h)
- $T System time

- $V Windows 2000 version

- $_ CRLF

- $$ $

- [Any Text] Any text

So, if you want to create a prompt that says

My Computer
Leave Alone

and show the time, you would enter

Prompt My Computer$_Leave Alone$_$t

at the prompt and press Enter or Return. You can see the command and the results in Figure 11.5.

FIGURE 11.5

You can get just about as silly with CMD *as you can with* ANSI.SYS. *To return to the default prompt, enter the command* **prompt** *with no parameters and then press Enter or Return.*

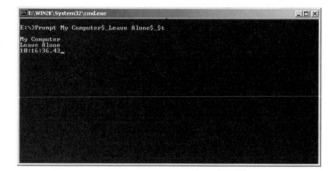

Windows 2000 has two prompt commands with no analogs in DOS:

- $+[more +'s]   Reflects pushed directories in the stack.

- $M   Displays the remote name associated with a network drive letter. This is null in a local drive.

The Layout tab lets you configure how wide and how deep (in characters) your screen will be (see Figure 11.6). It also allows you to set a default position for the CLI window.

FIGURE 11.6

*The Layout tab
allows the setting
of screen width,
depth, and place-
ment.*

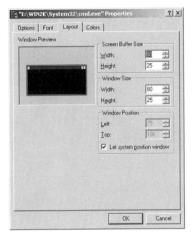

Figure 11.7 shows the results of setting the Screen Buffer and Window Size to 128 characters. Because the Windows 2000 display is only 80 characters wide, the CLI session
responds by placing scrollbars in the window.

FIGURE 11.7

*You can set the
Layout of the CLI
window to be
larger than 80
characters. Doing
so has somewhat
doubtful utility.*

The Colors tab in the Properties dialog box allows you to set the colors of the CLI (see
Figure 11.8). This is where newbies tend to set the foreground and background colors to
the same color, thereby making the session's commands invisible. You can set colors
both for the regular screen and pop-up text.

Note

When you click OK to change the look of the CLI, Windows 2000 Professional
will ask if you want to change for all CLI sessions or only this one. If you choose
All Sessions and then want to return to the Default, the menu for the CLI contains an entry for returning to this state.

FIGURE 11.8

The Colors tab not only allows selection of colors but also shows a preview of what you'll get when you click OK.

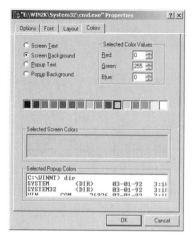

You can choose from the basic color bar in this dialog box or mix up your own colors using the RGB mixer in the Selected Color Values frame in the upper-right corner.

You can also change the title in the title bar by entering the command **title** with some following text. Figure 11.9 shows this command in action.

FIGURE 11.9

The title *command allows you to title your CLI window to a text of your choosing.*

Configuring the Shortcut or Program

The same options and more that are available to you from the CLI menu are available through the Properties tabbed dialog box of the program or shortcut itself. Figure 11.10 shows this dialog box for a shortcut to the Windows 2000 CLI, CMD.EXE.

FIGURE 11.10

The Command Prompt Properties tabbed dialog box for a shortcut to the CLI has a superset of the options available from the menu within the CLI.

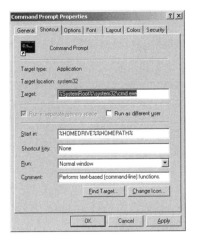

The following are the three major differences between setting options at the shortcut level and the menu level:

- The shortcut options will affect all instances of the CLI unless explicitly canceled or countermanded by a menu configuration.
- The shortcut dialog box has options for the shortcut itself, just like other shortcuts.
- The shortcut Properties dialog box contains a Security tab with buttons for Permissions, Auditing, and Ownership.

To get to the Properties tabbed dialog box, right-click the shortcut and choose Properties from the context menu.

Operating the CLI

If you've spent any time with MS-DOS, including the command line interface of Windows (that's DOS, too) or with a text-based UNIX system, such as SCO UNIX or other systems such as AmigaDOS, you should be quite comfortable with the CLI of Windows 2000 Professional. The basics of using a CLI are that you enter a command with parameters (sometimes) and then press the Return or Enter key to tell the system to execute (or try to execute) the command. The subtleties of a CLI are enormous, however.

MS-DOS is a bone-simple operating system that's been around in one form or another for about 20 years. Even so, there are people still discovering new twists or tricks with commands, batch files, or both. This is partly due to newer versions of DOS and DOS successors (such as Windows 98SE) being slightly different in implementation, giving rise to a lore of DOS-dom similar to the nitpickers of *Star Trek*.

Throw in a more complex command set, such as the one found in most UNIX shells (all today), plus a language or two to interact with that shell (such as AWK or Rexx), and you end up with one of those almost infinite fields of study. If you want to delve into these complex but rewarding areas, you can use the native Windows 2000 shell or buy a shell extending the 2000 command set. Two such shells are the 4DOS-type shell from J.P. Software and the Korn-like shell from MKS System. The latter especially is a real-time sink, but it's a lot of fun, too.

However, most people have all they can handle with the native Windows 2000 command set. Oddly enough, Microsoft has, for some reason, documented the command set fairly well.

Getting Information on the CLI

Appendix B is an expanded reference with examples for the more commonly used commands of the native Windows 2000 CLI.

The Help command from the Start menu is the main entry to the GUI Help system for Windows 2000 Professional. Searching this system on the keyword **command** will bring up an alphabetical listing of most of the CLI commands. Though generally okay, this listing isn't perfect, nor is it right all the time. Figure 11.11 is the GUI listing for the dir command.

FIGURE 11.11

The online Help system for the CLI in Windows 2000 is a good idea and well implemented, but it's incomplete in some areas.

Exploring the Command-Line Interface (CLI)

CHAPTER 11

321

11

EXPLORING THE
COMMAND-LINE
INTERFACE (CLI)

Figure 11.12 shows the command line Help system for the `dir` command. This gives the proper and complete information for this command. You can see the information is fairly complete.

FIGURE 11.12

The command-line Help for the `dir` *command gives the same information in a text format.*

To see the command-line Help text for any listed command, enter

`[command] / ?`

where `[command]` is any listed command, and press Return or Enter.

Slashes and Dashes

Commands need some way to know what you mean by the entries following them on the command line. For example, consider the following simple Directory (`dir`) command:

`dir d`

This will return a display to the console of any files named d in the current directory. Figure 11.13 shows the outcome of running this command.

FIGURE 11.13

Without any symbols, the `dir` *command takes the* d *in this command line to be a request to display any files named* d.

Change this command line to

`dir /d`

and the results will be the display shown in Figure 13.14.

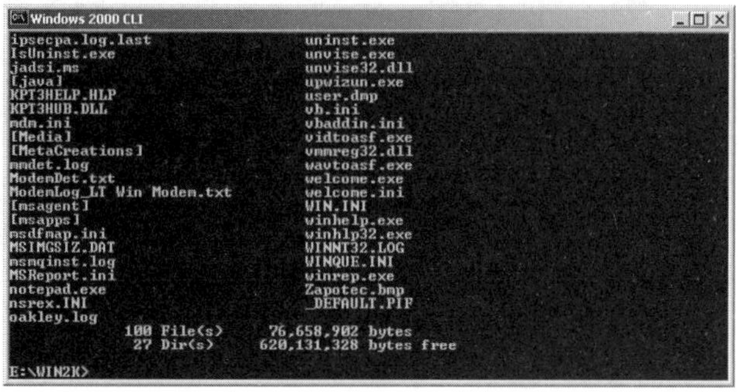

FIGURE 11.14

Add a slash (/) to the d *and the* dir *command understands that you mean a command line switch rather than a file specification.*

The difference between the two command lines is a simple slash. This tells the command interpreter (`CMD.EXE`, in this case) that the following character or characters form a switch rather than a variable.

The vast majority of commands in the CLI take switches. However, different commands require different switch symbols. As a general rule, the DOS-derived commands, such as `dir`, `FORMAT`, and `FIND`, want forward slashes as a switch symbol. The TCP/IP commands need dashes and will often try to interpret the slash as a variable.

For example, if you enter

`help ping`

on the command line, Windows 2000 Professional will respond as shown in Figure 11.15.

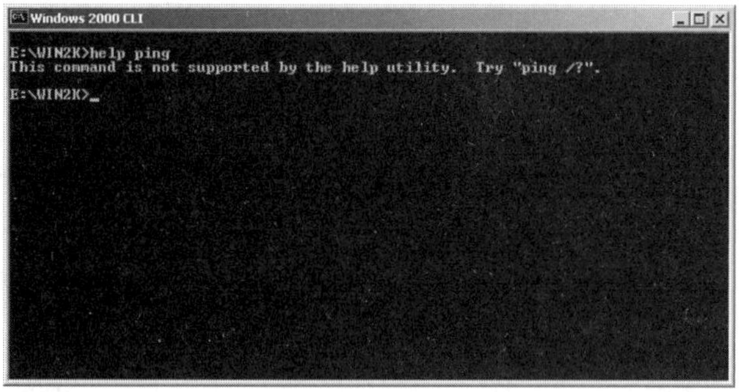

FIGURE 11.15

Seeking help on the ping *command will elicit a suggestion that you try the standard method to get help on an individual command.*

In previous versions of NT-based operating systems, such as Windows NT 4—the predecessor to Windows 2000, you had to know ahead of time whether to seek help using the slash or dash delimiter. Windows 2000 Professional will respond with help for all commands (all that I've tried anyway) using either the slash or the dash. Some command-line help requests (like for NTBACKUP) will launch the GUI help system.

Online Help is a real saver here because it always gives the switches correctly within the specific Help for a command.

Piping, Redirection, and Conditional Symbols

MS-DOS allows some piping and redirection of input and output. Piping means to direct input or output through a filter or utility. Redirection means to change the input or output from the default.

For example, the dir command echoes a list of files and folders to the screen (console). You can redirect the output to a file. You can also pipe the output through the SORT command to reorder the output from the command line switches (if any).

Windows 2000 takes this a bit further moving into the UNIX world somewhat. Adding the following symbols to your commands or batch files can add considerable power and flexibility to them. The following is a list of the command symbols you can use on your command line or in batch files:

- \> Redirection, usually from the console to a device or file. This works the same as DOS. For example, the following line:

  ```
  w.bat > myfile.txt
  ```

  redirects the output of the batch file w to a file myfile.txt rather than the console.

- \>\> Same as > but will append output if the named file exists. This works the same as DOS. For example, the following:

  ```
  v.bat >> myfile.txt
  ```

  will create myfile.txt and direct the output into that file. If myfile.txt exists, it will append the output of v.bat to the file.

- 2> Redirects only error output. This works the same as DOS. For example, the following:

  ```
  w.bat 2> error.fil
  ```

  will direct any errors stemming from running w.bat to the file error.fil.

> **Note**
>
> 2> is one of those very handy (in certain situations) but also almost unknown facilities in late DOS and Windows. Even seasoned Microsoft operating system hands seem to not know this one.

- < Places input from a source (usually a file) to a command capable of accepting the input. This works the same as DOS. For example, the following:

```
[command] < myfile.txt
```

runs the file `myfile.txt` through the `[command]` program. Thus, to sort a file and dump the output to a new file, you would enter

```
sort < myfile.txt > sorted.txt
```

- ¦ Pipes the output of one command to another command. This works the same as DOS. For example, the following:

```
dir ¦ sort
```

will run the output of the `dir` command through the `sort` command.

- ¦¦ Executes the command to the right of the symbol if the command to the left failed. For example, the following:

```
Type myfile ¦¦ echo no type radio
```

echoes `no type radio` if the `Type` command fails (for instance, if it can't find the file).

- 2>> Same as 2> but will append output if the file exists.

- ^ Interprets the next character as a literal, not a command. This allows you to use command symbols in filenames or parameters. For example, the following:

```
Dir ^&file.txt
```

allows the use of the `Dir` command with the file named `&file.txt`.

- ; or , Separates parameters, feeding them individually to a command. For example,

```
Dir myfile.txt;yourfile.txt
```

will execute `Dir` against the parameters `myfile.txt` and `yourfile.txt`, sequentially.

- () Groups multiple commands.

- & The AND of the CLI. Executes a series of commands sequentially from left to right. For example, the following:

Exploring the Command-Line Interface (CLI)

CHAPTER 11

325

11

EXPLORING THE
COMMAND-LINE
INTERFACE (CLI)

```
dir A:&dir B:
```

will run `dir` twice, once with the `A:` parameter and once with the `B:` parameter.

- `&&` Executes the command to the right if the command to the left is successful. (The inverse of the ¦¦ symbol.) For example, the following:

```
dir A:&& dir B:
```

will run `dir B:` only if `dir A:` worked.

Figure 11.11 shows the use of the ampersand (&) on a command line. Here, the command line

```
dir *.log & dir *.jpg
```

executed the `dir` command first with the parameter `*.log` and then with the parameter `*.jpg`. The output is the console display, showing files with both extensions.

The command

```
dir *.jpg & *.log
```

will not yield the same output. Instead, it will err on the `*.log` parameter.

The Batch Files

A batch file is a text file containing one or more commands that are executed upon the execution of the batch file, itself. For example, the batch file containing the text

```
dir d
dir d*
```

will first execute the `dir` command with the variable d and then with the variable d*. Batch files do have rudimentary flow control using primarily the `FOR` and `GOTO` commands. Virtually any command available on the command line can be run in a batch file. However, the `FOR` and `GOTO` commands have no existence outside of these specialized files. Batch files require either the `.bat` or the `.cmd` extension for Windows 2000 Professional to recognize them as batch files.

Although you can use batch files for any purpose you can think of, under Windows 2000 Professional, most people use them for backups.

For example, the `mybackup.cmd` file containing

```
ntbackup d:\winnt /a /b
ntbackup d:\my documents /a
```

will, when executed, first back up the winnt directory along with the local Registry, appending the backup to the existing tape, and then back up the my documents directory and append that to the tape as well.

Many users combine the AT command with a backup command set in batch files to start unattended backups after hours.

CMD, Command, and Environments

You can launch a CLI by starting either the CMD.EXE or the Command.com applications supplied with Windows 2000 Professional. CMD.EXE is a native Windows 2000 application, just like any other Windows 2000 applet. Running Command.com will launch an ntVDM (Windows 2000 Virtual Device Machine).

CMD.EXE will allow you to run native DOS programs under it, but when you do so, you "convert" it from a native 2000 application to an ntVDM.

There are two files, Autoexec.nt and Config.nt (in [%systemroot%]\system32), that will let you automatically configure the CLI or DOS programs upon their launch. These files act just like the autoexec.bat and config.sys files from DOS and Windows days, except for the limitations and extensions of running them under Windows 2000.

Optimizing DOS

The simplest way to optimize a DOS program for use in Windows 2000 Professional is to use the Properties dialog box. If you're a masochist or just hate to let go of any once-useful knowledge set, you can also manually create those crazy old .pif files from Windows and Windows 98 heritage. Windows 2000 doesn't care.

Don't overlook the wealth of options Windows 2000 gives you when running these older-style programs. Most problems with business-oriented DOS programs under Windows 2000 stem from people not configuring them correctly (or even not knowing that they can be configured). Figure 11.16 shows the tabbed (surprise!) dialog box for a DOS program.

The Memory tab in Properties of the program PKZIP 2.04g has had the XMS option being altered from None to Auto. As you can see from Figure 11.16, the memory options for a DOS program are many and varied. They include the normally problematic DPMI type of memory.

Windows 2000 is pretty good about accommodating the often bizarre needs of DOS programs, but it can't do it all automatically. Properties is the place to show that you're smarter than 2000.

FIGURE 11.16

The tabbed Properties dialog box for DOS programs under Windows 2000 has a blizzard of useful options. Somewhere in there exists the combination to make just about anything run well.

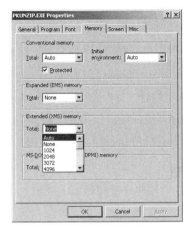

One greatly overlooked place to configure a DOS program is the Windows NT button on the Program tab. This will allow you to specify two configuration files for this program. These files take the place of the DOS `config.sys` and `autoexec.bat` files. By default, Windows 2000 will configure the NTVDM using `[%systemroot%]\system32\config.nt` and `[%systemroot%]\system32\Autoexec.nt`.

Click the Windows 2000 button to change this default. You can specify different configuration files for every DOS program on your system. Figure 11.17 shows the dialog box revealed when you click the Windows 2000 button on the Program tab of the Properties dialog box for an NTVDM. Within the world of Windows 2000, you have the freedom to make your NTVDMs any way you want them. How you use that freedom depends on you.

FIGURE 11.17

You can specify as many NTVDM configuration programs as you want.

Remember that you can get help with all these often mysterious MS-DOS settings by selecting an area and then pressing Shift+F1. Figure 11.18 shows such context help brought up for the rather obscure check box Compatible Timer Hardware Emulation.

FIGURE 11.18

Don't forget context help. It can be of enormous value with these often mysterious and rarely used commands.

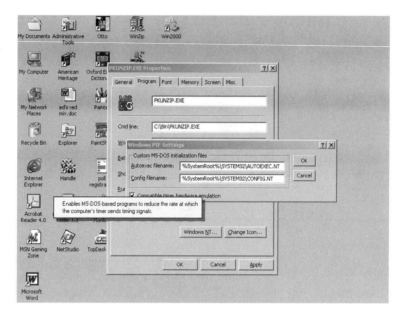

If you experience trouble with a DOS program under Windows 2000 and can't get the configuration right, try the following:

- Under the Screen tab, try running in a full screen rather than a window.

- Under the Screen tab, uncheck the Fast ROM Emulation and the Dynamic Memory Allocation options.

- Check your documentation to see whether your program requires DPMI or XMS memory. If so, locate and select the appropriate settings under the Memory tab.

- Under the Memory tab, specify the amount of memory to assign to the program rather than leaving this to the Auto daemon-like routine.

- Under the Misc tab, deselect the Always Suspend and Screen Saver options one at a time.

- Under Misc, try selecting the Mouse, Exclusive mode option.

- Study the documentation for your program and configure files to replace the recommended `config.sys` and `autoexec.bat` files; then use the Windows 2000 button on the Program tab to point at those files.

- If all else fails, run the program in a DOS boot session. You will need a DOS boot disk and a FAT volume for this.

Summary

The Command Line Interface (CLI) for Windows 2000 Professional is both a subset and a superset of the CLI for previous versions of Windows and for MS-DOS itself. To start a CLI session, run `CMD.EXE`, `Command.com`, or a shortcut to either from the GUI.

Although the variety of shell commands native to Windows 2000 isn't as rich as those found in most UNIX shells, it is richer than previous operating systems from Microsoft. You can increase the CLI environment by using third-party add-ons from vendors such as J.P. Software or MKS. With or without those add-ons, you can pipe, redirect, and use some conditional symbols on the command line.

`CMD.EXE` is a native Windows 2000 applet, whereas the DOS work-alike `command.com` runs always as an NTVDM. You can optimize the way DOS or OS/2 programs work under Windows 2000 by making a `.pif` file for them or by exercising options under their Properties dialog boxes. Each program can have its own configuration programs. Windows 2000 will, by default, use `Autoexec.2000` and `Config.2000` for CLI configuration files.

Printing and Faxing with Windows 2000

CHAPTER

12

Installing and configuring printers in Windows 2000 follows other Windows versions closely. However, the underlying principles of printing varies significantly due to 2000's architecture. If all you want to do is configure a printer and know how to do so under Windows, all you need to do is get the right driver and install. If you want to understand the way Windows 2000 handles printers, this chapter provides a short introduction.

Printers

Printing in Windows 2000 has always been a mixture of good news and bad news. The bad news is that the internal architecture is rather complex, but the good news is that printing works. Almost all the problems you'll find in printing are simple to fix. For example, the hardware isn't plugged in, connected, or turned on, or you have the wrong drivers. Remember that Windows 2000 needs its own drivers for printers. Previous drivers for other operating systems such as Windows 98 or even previous versions of Windows NT sometimes don't work or don't work well with Windows 2000.

Printing Basics

You need to understand the basics of printing on 2000 and the following 2000-specific definitions:

- The *printer device* is the output hardware. It might be a physical printer or a virtual printer, such as a fax adapter. Another form of virtual printer results in printing to a file.

- The *printer* is the software interface between the application and the printing device. That is, the application prints to a printer, and 2000 handles the transition to the printing device.

- The *printer spooler* is the list of jobs waiting to print at a printer. The actual list of jobs is the print queue. The spooler is a service that can be stopped or started like any service. Technically, it is a set of dynamic link libraries (DLLs) that receives, schedules, and distributes the printing chores.

- The *print monitor* is the software component that routes the final output from the printer to the printing device.

- The *print server* is the 2000 system on which the printer is defined and on which the print monitor runs.

- The *port* is the place where the print monitor sends the output. Usually, it is your system's parallel or serial port with an increasing number of USB ports coming online. It can also be a network port, for example, a Hewlett-Packard (HP) printer with a Jet Direct card.

These definitions might be different from other systems you've used, such as UNIX, but they are the definitions used with 2000, so you would be well served to learn them. Also, the way a print job moves from an application to an output device is 2000's own and differs in at least a few ways from other systems.

The following is an overview of how a job moves from an application to a printer:

1. The user of an application (such as Word or WordPerfect) chooses the print option for a document.

2. The application processes the document for printing and passes it on to the spooler. The spooler stores the print job to disk.

3. The local print provider analyzes the print job, altering as necessary for proper printing.

4. The provider passes control to the page processor, which can add a cover page to the job.

5. The disk feeds the job to the print monitor.

6. The hardware device receives the job for physical output formatted properly by the device driver for the printer.

12

PRINTING AND
FAXING WITH
WINDOWS 2000

Creating a Printer for Windows 2000

Before your application can do any printing, you first have to define a printer on your system, either by creating a printer on your machine or connecting to a printer somewhere on your network. After you create or connect to the printer, your applications can then use the printer, although you might want to modify the printer's configuration.

The printer folder in Windows 2000 Workstation is the place where all printing-related configuration and management is carried out. You can access the printer folder in one of the following ways:

- Open the My Computer folder. Open Control Panel (or open Control Panel from Start, Settings, or go right to Printers using Start, Settings, Printers).
- Select the Printers applet from the Control Panel.

The Printers folder is the same, no matter which method you choose to invoke it. The printer folder on my system is shown in Figure 12.1.

FIGURE 12.1

The Printers folder is the starting place to define (install and set up) a new printer or modify the settings of an existing printer.

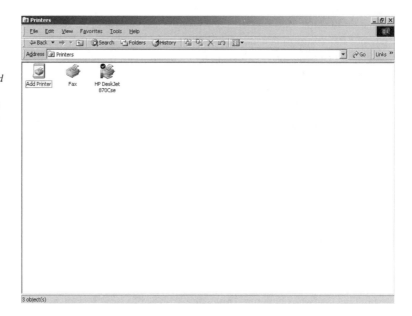

To set up a new printer on your system or connect to a printer on the network, you should use the Add Printer Wizard. Using this Wizard is a quick, easy, and almost fool-proof way to define the printer. To start this Wizard, double-click the Add Printer applet in the Printers group shown in Figure 12.1.

Only a member of the Administrators local group can create a new local printer. The process of setting up a new local printer is illustrated in Figures 12.2 through 12.11 and involves the following steps:

1. Specify whether the printing device is managed locally or is connected via the network, as shown in Figure 12.2. Unless you have a very old printer or one you know Windows 2000 can't detect, leave the Automatically Detect check box checked. This allows Windows 2000 to try Plug-and-Play technology for setting up the printer. You must have the printer physically connected and turned on for Plug-and-Play to work.

2. Start the Wizard's auto detect routine. Figure 12.3 shows that the Wizard detected an HP 870C printer. This will launch another wizard.

FIGURE 12.2

Telling the Wizard whether the new printer will be a local one or one you will access through a network.

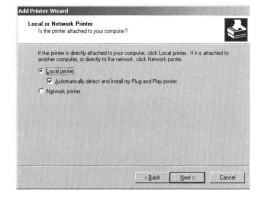

FIGURE 12.3

Plug-and-Play (PnP) worked here.

3. Click Next to start the Found New Hardware Wizard branched to when PnP found and correctly identified the local printer. In all likelihood, any detected printer will have a standard driver. Figure 12.4 shows your driver selection search choice. In the case that your printer isn't listed as part of the supplied drivers, or you have an updated driver CD-ROM or disk, you'll get a chance to choose the Have Disk button and point Windows 2000 to that location. In fact, you'll get that option next screen anyway. Choose Next to move on.

FIGURE 12.4

You need to tell the Wizard whether to use standard drivers or ones you supply.

4. You'll need to tell the Wizard where likely sources of drivers are. Here, the driver is part of the standard Windows 2000 Professional distribution CD-ROM, so I checked the CD-ROM Drives option as shown in Figure 12.5.

FIGURE **12.5**

Time to tell the Wizard where to look for its driver supply.

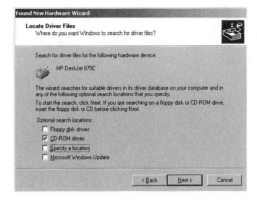

5. Click Next. Windows will hunt around some for the driver and, unless the driver location you specified lacks an appropriate driver, you'll get a success message. Click Next to move on to actually copying the driver. Figure 12.6 shows the success message box when the driver is finished successfully copying and you're ready to try a test page. By all means, try the test page as this gives you full assurance that things are working correctly.

FIGURE **12.6**

You're successful, and Windows will offer to print a test page.

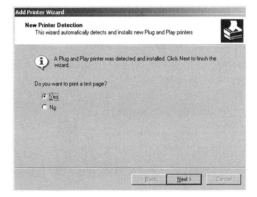

6. Figure 12.7 shows the start of the Add Printer Wizard, which is the manual way to add a printer through a wizard. This is the wizard that Windows leads you down (starting from Figure 12.2) if it can't detect a PnP printer or you tell it not to try.

FIGURE 12.7

You can also use the Wizard in manual mode. You'll have to if you don't have a PnP ready printer.

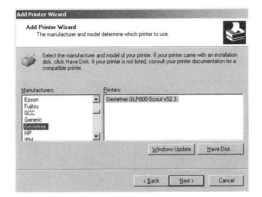

7. If your printer isn't on the list, that only means there is no printer driver for it supplied with Windows 2000. This is quite common. You should have a disk or CD-ROM from the printer manufacturer and here is where to use it. Click the Have Disk button, shown in Figure 12.7. That will bring up a dialog box asking you where the driver is located. If your printer is part of this list and sublist, choose it and click Next. If your printer requires a disk or CD-ROM, click Have Disk, point Windows to the source (doesn't have to be an actual local disk), and then click OK. Microsoft offers the ability to search the Windows Update site also. You must be connected to the Internet to use this facility. Figure 13.8 shows the dialog box to locate a driver.

FIGURE 12.8

If Windows 2000 can't find the needed drivers on the hard drive, it asks you for their location.

8. Manual printer setup requires that you choose a name for the new printer or leave Windows to make a good guess. Figure 12.9 shows the naming dialog box. Here is where you choose to use this printer as the default printer if there is already another printer defined. You can later change the default printer for any workstation.

FIGURE **12.9**

In non-PnP setup, you get a chance to name your printer in a specific dialog box.

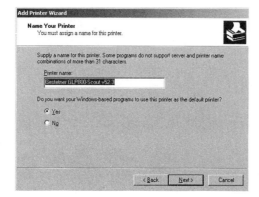

Figure 12.10 shows the stage in the Wizard where you elect to share your printer with other users on your network. If you choose to print a test page, Windows will output one page and then ask you if it printed correctly. If it didn't, or you lie and say it didn't, Windows will launch the Print Troubleshooter, a special part of the Help system. The Troubleshooter will help you diagnose some printer problems. Figure 12.11 shows the start of this Troubleshooter.

FIGURE **12.10**

You'll also have an opportunity to share the printer at this time. You can later choose to stop or start sharing any device.

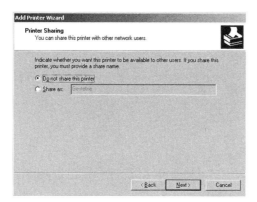

You can access the Print Troubleshooter by choosing the Troubleshooting entry under Printers in the standard Help system. The entry point is a little different than from the Printer Setup Wizard, but the effect is the same.

Besides choosing the wrong drivers, printer errors are mundane: the printer isn't turned on, the parallel or serial cable is not connected, the printer is out of paper, and so on. For the most part, troubleshooting these problems is very simple.

FIGURE **12.11**

The final step of a troubled setup is the Print Troubleshooter.

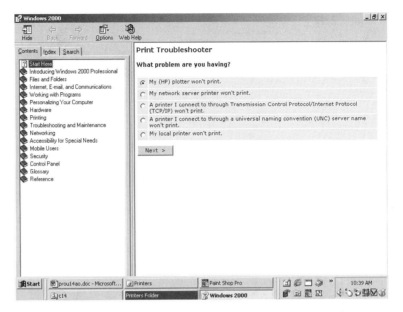

Tip

If you are responsible for Windows 2000 support and users phone you with printer problems, tell them to try the Print Troubleshooter first and call you back only if it fails to resolve the problem. Most printing problems can be resolved by using the Troubleshooter, but of course, your mileage on this situation may vary.

Network Printing

Setting up network printing is almost as easy as setting up local printing. If you're going to share your printer on the network, the previous instructions are all you need. If you want to connect to an existing printer on the network, you also use the New Printer Wizard. If you want to connect to a new printer on the network, you must define this printer first using the steps outlined previously. This process is really the same as setting up a local printer but you need to locate the printer on the network, using the familiar network browsing dialog boxes, or specify a printer using its network name.

Here are the steps.

1. Start the Add Printer Wizard from the Printers folder. Click the Network Printer check box to tell the Wizard that you'll be setting up a printer on the network. Figure 12.12 shows this option.

FIGURE **12.12**

Adding a printer from the network starts by telling the Wizard this is your intent.

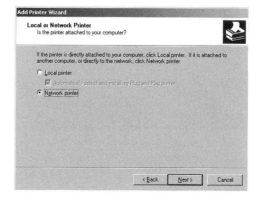

2. Specify the machine and the printer you want to add to your printers or choose Next to browse. You can see this step in Figure 12.13.

FIGURE **12.13**

Specify the printer and the machine to which it's locally connected by using the usual naming conventions. You can also use an Intranet printer by checking the lower option button.

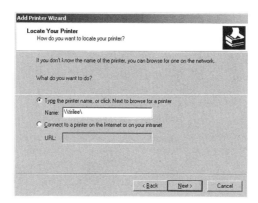

3. Once you've located or named the printer, the rest of setup is the same as for a local printer. If you have any questions about defining a local printer (or naming) see the previous section, "Creating a Printer for Windows 2000."

Note

If your company is using Directory Naming Services, the dialog displayed in Figure 12.13 will contain a radio button that enables you to find a printer in the directory. If you select that radio button and click Next, a dialog will be displayed that enables you to search the directory for a printer.

The network printer setup is much simpler than the local printer setup routine because the only task you're performing is attaching to a printer. All the tough work, such as making sure the printer works and the drivers are correct, has been done during local setup at the server.

Networked Printer Drivers

Setting up any printer is quick and easy, although you need to get the drivers somehow. These drivers are typically on your Windows 2000 Workstation CD-ROM. Alternatively, you might get them on a disk with new printers or you can download them from the Internet, especially from the manufacturer's Web or FTP site.

When you create a local printer, Windows 2000 loads the printer drivers for local printing. For network printing, 2000 gets clever; when you connect to a network printer, Windows 2000 simply downloads the printer driver for you from the machine on which the printer was initially created. That's it!

Windows 2000 achieves this by sharing the [%SYSTEMROOT%]\System32\Spool\Drivers folder as PRINT$. When a remote system wants to get print drivers from your system, it merely connects to \\*YOURSYSTEM*\PRINT$ (where *YOURSYSTEM* is the NetBios machine name, defined in the Network applet). Directly below, Windows 2000 creates one extra folder for each hardware platform for which drivers are held.

The only real issue to resolve is which printer drivers you should have located locally. A printer driver is a specialized form of an executable program, typically a DLL, designed to run on a particular version of Windows and hardware. If you define a printer for use by other users on the network, you need to hold all the printer drivers for all the various combinations of systems that are likely to access it. If Windows 2000 fails to find the correct drivers on the remote machine, it simply prompts for a location to find them, and, when fed the appropriate disk, CD-ROM, or network share point, it can then load the drivers for this alternative location.

With Windows 2000, you can automatically load printer drivers for other 2000 systems as well as for Windows 95/98.

If you access the printer via Windows for Workgroups, Windows 3.*x*, or DOS, you have to load the printer manually on each of the client systems. Also, if you connect from your system to a printer defined on a non-Windows 2000 system (for example, Windows 98), you also must load printer drivers manually.

Printer Ports

Most printing is done via a system's USB, FireWire, parallel, or serial port, and these ports are usually specified for local printing. Windows 2000 also supports other ports, including the Digital Network port, HP Network port, Lexmark DLC Printer port, Lexmark TCP/IP port, and the LPD port (for printing to UNIX printers).

These ports enable you to connect a printer to the network for your Windows 2000 system to print directly to the printer. This setup requires a different print monitor, which is loaded automatically when you define the appropriate network. To print to a UNIX printer, you must load the TCP/IP printing services. Details of TCP/IP protocol are covered in Chapter 17, "Setting Up TCP/IP Protocol Access."

Printing from DOS Applications

If you're using DOS applications, printing becomes slightly more difficult. Each DOS application requires its own printer driver. One of the greatest advancements Windows brought was the idea of defining one printer for all applications. DOS printer drivers are always application-specific. They must be obtained from the application manufacturer in almost all cases. In some rare instances, user groups maintain and create drivers for the programs that define their existence. However, finding drivers for current production printers can be impossible for older programs. Most vendors in the DOS business are either long gone or have stopped supporting their DOS applications because they have moved all their resources to their new Windows programs.

DOS applications also have a weak—if any—concept of sharing. They tend to "sit on" a configured LPT or COM port and dump their output, which is not much help when the printer is remote. To enable DOS applications to print successfully, you need to use the NET command from the CLI on the client system. Go to the command line and use the following syntax:

```
NET USE LPT2: \\server\remoteprinter
```

LPT2: is the port your DOS application uses, and *server* is the machine on which the printer shared as *remoteprinter* is located. To discontinue this connection, issue the following command:

```
NET DELETE LPT2: \\server\remoteprinter
```

After you use this command, you must tell your DOS application to use the port (LPT2:) you just set up by the USE command. Printing across the network should now work.

You can view the printers you're currently using by typing net use at the command line. Figure 12.14 shows this command used to specify the Agfa printer as printer port 2 on the server tirilee-ex0wgpt.

FIGURE 12.14

The CLI net command with the use parameter can spoof DOS applications. To spoof a program means to return a false message such as version number.

Managing and Reconfiguring Printers

After you define the printer, you might want to update the printer properties or manage the printing process. You can carry out both of these operations from the Printers folder.

To modify a printer's parameters, right-click the printer and choose Properties from the context menu. You then see a dialog box that is specific to the printer being managed so you can review and amend the printer's properties. The Properties dialog box for my installed DeskJet 870C printer is shown in Figure 12.15.

FIGURE 12.15

Choosing Properties from the context menu brings up a dialog box with a combination of the usual tabs, such as Security, as well as specialized tabs, such as Ports and Scheduling.

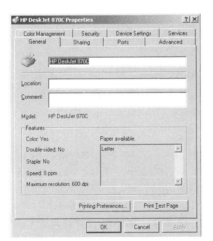

Advanced Configuration Options

Windows 2000 has a number of additional advanced printing features you might want to use. These features, which are set from the printer's Properties dialog box on the Advanced tab, are as follows:

- *Separator Page (button)*—Whenever Windows 2000 sends a job to be printed, you can print an optional separator, or cover page, at the head of the print job.

- *Available from①to*—Because a printer (from a software point of view) is the interface between the system and the printing device, you can make a printer available only during certain times of the day. Also, you can actually define two printers to print to a single print device and give one printer a higher priority. You do so by using the printer's scheduling area at the top of the dialog box shown in Figure 12.16.

FIGURE 12.16

On the Advanced tab, you can restrict the time a printer is available for use and its priority level.

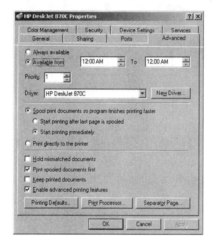

- *Print Processor*—The data type or default print processor. Leave this alone unless your application calls for special treatment and says so in its documentation.

- *Printing Defaults*—A way to view and set the default printer specifications for various users and groups.

Printer separator pages are useful for heavily used printers shared by many users where jobs might pile up in the output tray, although the feature is rather wasteful of paper and toner. At least three separator pages are installed by default. They are: PCL.SEP, PSCRIPT.SEP, and SYSPRINT.SEP. PCL.SEP is used for HP LaserJet Printers and switches the printer into PCL mode. PSCRIPT.SEP switches the printer into PostScript mode but does not actually print a separator page. SYSPRINT.SEP simply prints a page before each document. If you have an HP printer, use PCL.SEP.

Printer Security

In Chapter 7, "Tuning Windows 2000 Security," you learned about the general security model for Windows 2000. In summary, all Windows 2000 resources are owned, and the owner of the resource can enable other people to use that resource at his or her discretion. Additionally, any resource can be audited so that the use of the resource is logged to

Windows 2000's Event Log. Printers are just another resource, like directories and files, that you can secure. All security settings are configured from the printer's Security menu, part of the printer's properties, as shown in Figure 12.17.

FIGURE 12.17

The Security tab of the Properties dialog box contains the familiar security setup options.

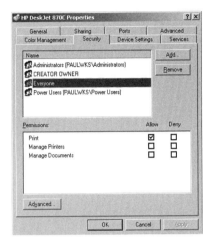

The first security issue to address is who can create a printer. Only members of the Administrators or Power Users groups can create a local printer unless you define another group with this permission. Any user has the right to connect to a remote printer, subject to the printer's access controls.

The person who creates a printer owns it. The owner has full control of the printer and can set the rights for every other user from full rights to denying access.

A user who has sufficient privileges can take printer ownership, as in files and directories. This person is typically a member of Administrators. Any user with the full control permission on that printer can likewise change ownership.

The owner of a printer can give any other group or user defined on the system access to the group by using the printer's Permissions dialog box, shown in Figure 12.18. To get to the dialog box you see in Figure 12.18, choose the Security tab in Properties, click the Advanced button (at the bottom), and then choose a user or group and click the View/Edit button.

You can give three different permissions to a printer: Print, Manage Printers, and Manage Documents. When applied to a group or user, these permissions define what the user can or cannot do with the printer.

FIGURE 12.18

The Permission Entry dialog box is well buried in the Security tab.

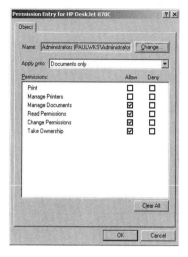

- *Print*—Send documents to a printer
- *Manage Printers*—Start and stop print jobs, change settings, change ownership (if available), adjust all printer properties
- *Manage Documents*—Start, stop, pause print jobs

As you can see from the list, although you can print to a printer, you can't do much else unless you have the full control permission.

Printer Auditing

As with any other secure object, Windows 2000 allows you to audit a printer, which means you can tell who did what to the printer and when. You set up printer auditing by clicking the Security tab, clicking the Advanced button, and then choosing the Auditing tab in the resulting dialog box. The Printer Auditing dialog box is shown in Figure 12.19.

With auditing, you first have to decide who to audit and then what to audit. You can audit any or all users or groups defined on your system by choosing the Add button. You can also remove users or groups by using the Remove button.

After you decide who to audit, you have to decide which events to audit. When Windows 2000 audits a printer, it is, in effect, recording the use of the acts shown in Figure 12.19.

FIGURE 12.19

The Auditing area on the Security tab allows you to log printer events to the Event Log. Here the Administrator is setting up what to audit with the Guest account.

Faxing

Microsoft has had an on and off relationship with fax as to whether it should be part of its operating systems. Although users and focus groups have almost universally wanted this a part of the systems Microsoft sells, it hasn't always been the case. Nobody at Microsoft who I spoke to could or would tell me why. I suspect that Microsoft, sensitive to monopoly accusations lately, has feared that it could be charged with displacing the vendors of faxing software if it incorporated this service into its systems.

The fax facility of Windows 2000 Professional is similar to the disk defragmentation facility. It's there, but it is bone simple and really doesn't threaten vendors who sell specialized faxing software.

Fax should install itself by default during setup. If you installed using a networked or customized script, it may not be so. In such cases, you'll have to contact your system administrator or whomever made the script or set the policy.

Fax acts like any other printer, but, of course, requires an output device—almost always a fax modem. To send a document using a fax output, choose File, Print from its menu, and then pull down the Name combo box and choose Fax from the list of printers. Figure 12.20 shows this common dialog box—this is the one in Word 2000.

FIGURE 12.20

On the Print common dialog box, you can choose to Fax as a printer output using the Name combo box.

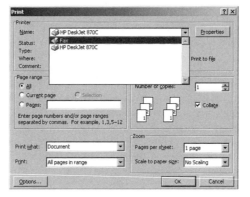

There are several settings you can adjust to fine tune your faxing. To see these options, open the Printers folder either through Explorer, Control Panel, or by using Start, Settings, Printers. Right click on Fax and choose Properties. Figure 12.21 shows the tabbed dialog box that results. Many of these properties are directly available on the context menu without going through the Properties selection. You can also access fax properties by choosing the Properties button in the Print common dialog box by selecting the Fax printer and then clicking the Properties button (to the right).

FIGURE 12.21

The Fax device has properties too, many of which are adjustable for fine-tuning your faxing experiences.

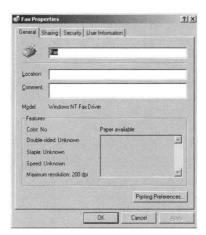

The two areas you'll surely want to customize are the User Information where you can enter your fax back number, name, and other fax-important information. The Printing Preferences button on the General tab has options to send faxes right off or hold them for cheap rate times.

When you choose Fax as a printer and click OK, you'll launch the Fax Send Wizard. The heart of the Wizard is where you enter the recipient either manually or from an address book. Figure 12.22 shows this dialog box.

FIGURE 12.22

You can enter recipient information either manually or from an address book.

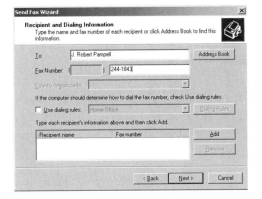

You'll also get a chance to send a cover sheet from a small selection Microsoft supplied with Windows 2000 Professional and then choose to send now or when cheaper rates apply, thus overriding the default you set up in Properties.

Once you've finished with the Wizard, it'll either send the fax right off or wait until a time you've specified. Figure 12.23 shows the Fax Monitor message box as it appears during the sending of a fax.

FIGURE 12.23

The Fax Monitor dialog box tells you of your faxing progress.

Once you've sent a fax and during transmission, you'll see a little printer icon in the Taskbar Tray. This is the Fax Service icon. Right click it, choose Fax Monitor Properties, and you'll open up a whole new array of faxing options including easy access to the faxing service in the MMC. Figure 12.24 shows this dialog box. The context menu also allows easy access to the fax queue and the My Faxes folder (for stored sent faxes).

FIGURE 12.24.

The Fax Service Properties dialog box.

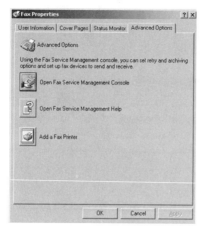

Here is where you enter defaults for the Fax Monitor, including whether it shows up on the Taskbar ever.

You can enter the Fax Services section of the MMC either through the dialog box in Figure 12.24 (click the top button in the Advanced Options tab) or through the regular Administrative Tools folder. Either route leads to the same place, Figure 12.25.

FIGURE 12.25

The MMC has a section for Fax Service.

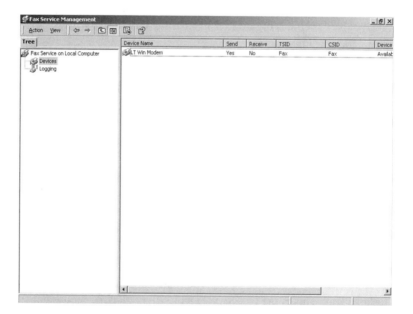

To change any setting available through Services, right click the appropriate device and choose Properties or any other option on the context menu. For example, to enable fax receive, right click the modem device and locate the appropriate check box. Figure 12.26 shows this dialog box. You can also turn on fax receive through the context menu.

FIGURE 12.26

The Fax Service will disable fax receive by default. Here is where you can turn it on.

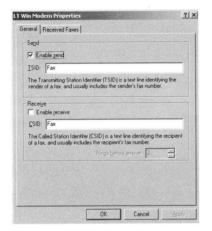

To change where Fax Services stores files, security, and various minor details like retry times, right click Fax Service on Local Computer entry in MMC and choose Properties.

Summary

You can easily set up printing and get working. Properly securing the printer takes a bit more work, but all the permissions are consistent with 2000's overall security model.

The fax service in Windows 2000 Professional is simple compared to fully-featured specialized faxing programs, but it gets the job done if your needs are simple too.

Windows 2000 Fonts

IN THIS CHAPTER

The Apple Macintosh wasn't the first personal-type computer capable of doing page layout chores, but it popularized the notion of Everyman as a typographer. For many years, Windows and DOS were poor also-rans in the personal typesetting race.

In recent years, however, the tools once exclusive to the Macintosh for performing the common document layout chores have either moved to Windows or have their equivalents in native Windows programs. Windows 2000, with its capability of harnessing powerful computer systems, is a natural for doing layout-type work on a PC. Even people who aren't interested in true layout work want their documents to look good. A familiarity with how Windows 2000 handles fonts is part of the knowledge set most people need to accomplish this or the more ambitious goal of actual typesetting.

What's a Font?

A font is a single typeface. A typeface is a family of characters, numbers, letters, punctuation marks, and so forth that share certain characteristics such as width of stroke, presence of a serif (explained next), and general shape. The word *font* usually means a family of characters apart from certain attributes, such as bold or italics. Figure 13.1 shows a few fonts or typefaces in Microsoft Word.

FIGURE 13.1

Different fonts have different looks. Most computer systems have a choice of over 40 fonts.

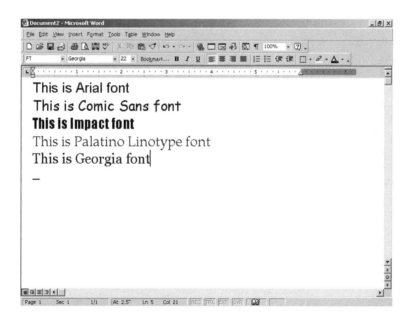

Although too many fonts can impede performance and consume disk space, many people have as many as 100 fonts available to them.

A font family is a group of similar typefaces. Windows 2000 recognizes the following five font families. These families aren't official, and the classification is somewhat arbitrary:

- *Decorative*—Such as Zapf Calligraphic
- *Modern*—Such as Bodini
- *Swiss*—Based on the Helvetica family
- *Roman*—Times Roman being the most common
- *Script*—Any font using a cursive style

A font in Windows 2000 Professional has the following three possible appearances:

- *Font style*—Examples are italic or bold
- *Font size*—The point size of a font
- *Font effects*—Effects include underlining

Figure 13.2 shows these appearance characteristics.

FIGURE 13.2

A font's appearance depends on its style, size, and effects.

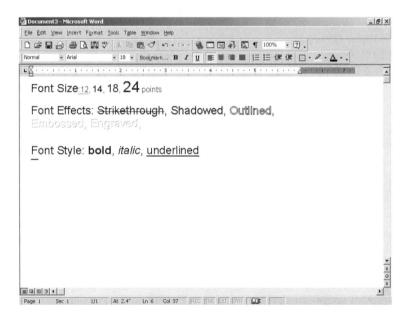

You can mix appearance attributes with fonts. For example, nothing prevents you from combining bold with strikethrough if you have a need for that type of display.

Windows 2000 uses the following additional terms to describe the final appearance of a typeface:

- *Weight*—Indicates how heavy the stroke is. The weight goes from light to extra bold.

- *Serif or non-serif*—Indicates whether the characters have a "tail" or projections that lead the eye from one character to another. Courier is a serif font and is generally easy to read. Arial is a non-serif or sans serif font. This type of font appears to most people as classier or neater in page layout schemes.

- *Pitch*—Indicates how much horizontal space is taken up by a character. This metric applies to fixed-pitched fonts such as Courier.

- *Spacing*—Indicates whether the characters all take up the same horizontal room per font size or whether they're proportional based on the layout of the face. Figure 13.3 shows a fixed and proportional font.

Figure 13.3

The serif in Courier New extends naturally thinner letters so that the letter I will be as wide as letters such as R. In Arial, the fonts take up space proportional to their spacing needs.

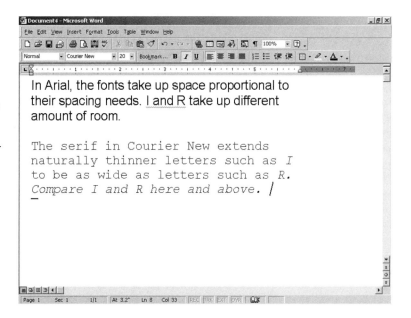

- *Slant*—Indicates how far from the vertical the characters are. Italics have some slant. Roman, or standard, fonts have none.

- *Width*—Indicates whether the font has been stretched or compressed.

- *X-height*—Indicates the height of half-line characters such as *e* and of the lower part of lowercase characters such as *h*.

Printer Fonts and Screen Fonts

In a perfect world, a font would just be a font, but this isn't yet a perfect world. Therefore, you can choose from two broad categories of fonts: printer and screen.

Printer fonts are created in the printer. Often, you can install these fonts to your Windows 2000 Professional system using distribution disks from the printer manufacturer. These fonts come in the following three flavors:

- *Downloadable soft fonts*—Usually reside on your hard disk and are installed with your printer. This way, Windows 2000 Professional can display fonts specific to the printer.
- *Device fonts*—Built in to the hardware (firmware, really) of the printer.
- *Printable screen fonts*—Fonts that Windows 2000 uses for screen displays, and they can also be interpreted by the printer to look the same.

Screen fonts are fonts Windows 2000 uses to display information on the screen or monitor. They don't necessarily have to be the same (although they might be named the same) as the fonts your printer can produce.

The symbol for each font is its *glyph*. Glyphs are either raster or vector. Two types of vector glyphs are of special interest to Windows 2000 users.

- *Raster fonts*—Bitmaps. Each pixel or screen dot is stored in memory for display or printing. Bitmaps resist scaling and rotation. Figure 13.4 shows a bitmap of three letters.

FIGURE 13.4

Bitmaps don't scale or rotate well. Here you can see the jagged look (jaggies) caused by scaling a small ABC to a larger size and then rotating it.

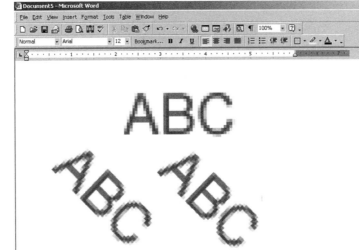

- *Vector* or *outline fonts*—Objects described by mathematical expressions. The computer doesn't remember each dot's or each pixel's placement, but it obeys a command like "draw a line from point A to point B of 1 point thickness," where the points are previously agreed-upon coordinates. Figure 13.5 shows an example of a vector font. This image is of lesser quality than it would be if printed because of technical limitations in the production of images and the reproductive process used in book publishing.

FIGURE 13.5

Vector fonts scale and rotate well because, in doing so, the computer need only change the mathematical expression. This is Arial font.

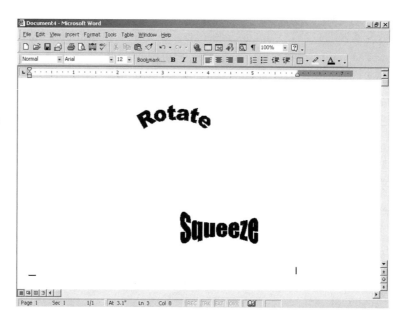

- *Open fonts*—Outline fonts with hinting. *Hinting* is information designed to skew the fonts, thus making them look better scaled and rotated than without the intelligent skewing. In the "Open Technology" section, later in this chapter, you learn more details about this important topic.

- *Adobe Type 1 PostScript fonts*—Hinted outline font types. Windows 2000 can handle this type of font. Originally, Adobe Type 1 PostScript fonts were the only quality font type, but a licensing dispute between Adobe and the rest of the world led to the need for TrueType and then Open fonts, which now technically equal Type 1 fonts. However, the true quality of the font depends on the font vendor. Open fonts vary more in quality than genuine Adobe-vended Type 1 fonts.

Generally speaking, raster fonts are developed for one size and orientation. They are also generally used for one device, printer, or screen. Windows 2000 can scale raster fonts, but they don't look very good if scaled too far from their intended size. Similarly, you can rotate these fonts, but they appear ugly in most unintended orientations.

If your printer has a close match to a raster font, you can print it satisfactorily. The key here is "close match," a rather nebulous term and one utterly unsatisfactory for exacting work. To resolve the problem of making a printed sheet look just like the Print Preview screen, some applications convert the entire document to a huge bitmap and then send it down the wire to the printer. This process ensures that the preview and the actual printed image match exactly, but it increases rendering and printing time.

Vector fonts installed in Windows 2000 reside in a series of GDI (Graphic Device Interface, that part of Windows responsible for the display) calls. Although accurate and easily scaleable, they take a long time to generate because the computer must process strokes.

Open Technology

Open is a special type of font technology. Rather than the font shape being stored as a bitmap as with raster fonts or being generated by calls like vector fonts, Open fonts are stored as glyph primitives or glyph shapes. That is, they are a series of points and scaling hints. When an application requests a font, Windows 2000 responds by supplying the hinted shape at the requested size.

The first call for a particular Open font causes Windows 2000 Professional to generate that font (from its outline and hints) to a bitmap. That bitmap gets placed in a cache for later use. This process works similarly to a disk cache. As long as the cache space isn't exceeded, subsequent requests for the font come from the cache and therefore require much less processing than the first call. This caching capability makes Open font use quite efficient.

Windows 2000 Professional uses Open fonts both for screen display and printer output. The fonts used for both are the same, giving true matching between the screen and printer when the fonts are used exclusively. If a document has non-Open fonts mixed in, the result can be a mismatch between the screen and output.

13

WINDOWS 2000
FONTS

The Installed Fonts

You can see the fonts available for your workstation by opening the `[%windows32%]\fonts` folder. Figure 13.6 shows a listing for one system.

You can see a more useful list of the fonts through the Control Panel. To see it, open the Control Panel by choosing Start, Settings, Control Panel and then double-click the Fonts applet (folder icon). Figure 13.7 shows this display with the menu choice View, List Choice by Similarity selected. This lists fonts proximate to other fonts that they resemble. Using this facility, you can see what duplicate fonts you have masquerading under different names and also get an education on font relationships. If you have the toolbar open, this button is the second from the right with an AB icon.

FIGURE 13.6
*You can see a file
listing for fonts in
the Fonts folder.*

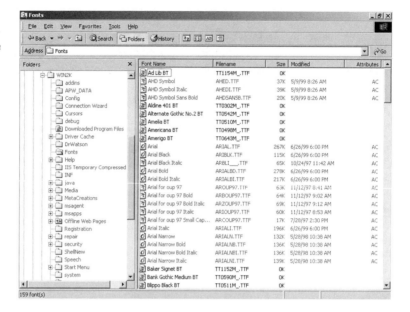

FIGURE 13.7
*You can view your
installed fonts
sorted by simi-
larity. You select
the font you want
compared in the
combo box that
currently shows
Arial.*

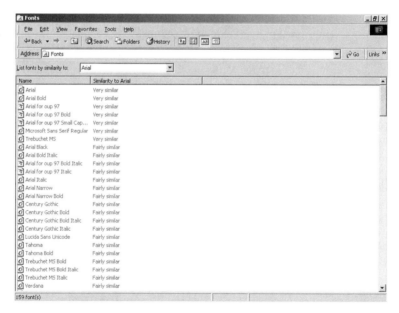

Windows 2000 provides an icon telling you what kind of font each is in the listing. Most of the icons to the left of the font name show that the fonts listed in Figure 13.7 are Open or Outline fonts (there are some TrueTypes listed as well). The icon for these is the one with the letter O on it, but it might be difficult to make that out in this screen shot. Other font types are available for this computer, but they are all below the bottom font shown in this figure.

You can see a good display of the font by double-clicking its entry in the screen shown in Figure 13.7. Figure 13.8 shows the display for Arial font.

FIGURE 13.8

You can see usage examples of fonts by double clicking their entries in the Fonts folder display.

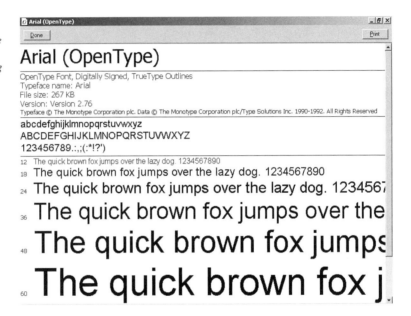

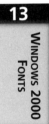

Figure 13.9 shows the result of changing the font chosen for comparison to Tahoma. Figure 13.10 shows two very similar fonts side by side in windows, similar to the display in 13.8. Figure 13.11 shows the same display for a font that's not similar to Tahoma.

FIGURE 13.9

Tahoma has a different set of very similar looking fonts than Arial, which is only fairly similar.

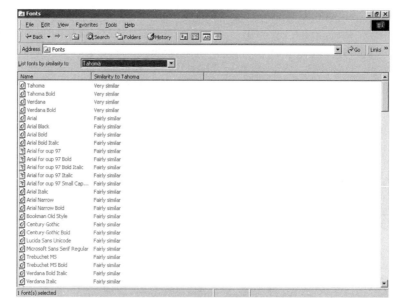

FIGURE 13.10

Even this small screen shot makes the similarity between these fonts obvious.

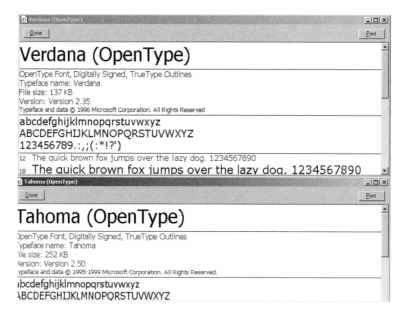

Figure 13.11

This fairly similar font is, for most purposes, the same font as the example font Tahoma.

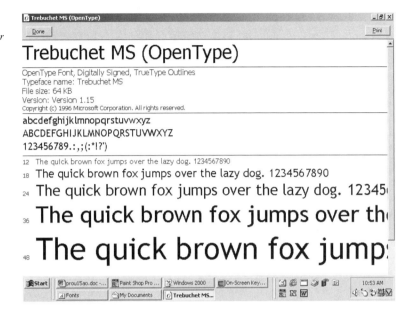

Webdings font (a decorative font), listed as "Not Similar" in the Fonts listing, is obviously not at all similar to Tahoma. Figure 13.12 shows this font in the expanded Fonts display.

Figure 13.12

A decorative font like Webdings isn't at all similar to Tahoma and looks it.

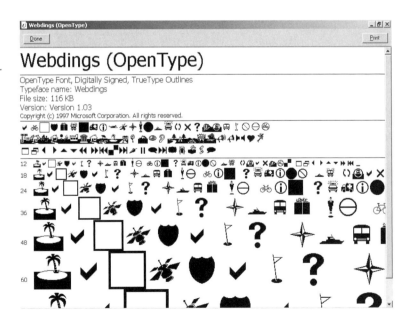

When viewing these fonts in separate screens, most people see little or no difference between the fonts. Figure 13.13 shows four fonts similar or fairly similar to Arial displayed in 24-point size in one document.

FIGURE 13.13

Windows 2000 looks at the font information and tells you what it's similar and dissimilar to. If you want to see the specific differences, nothing is as illustrative as putting the various fonts on the same page.

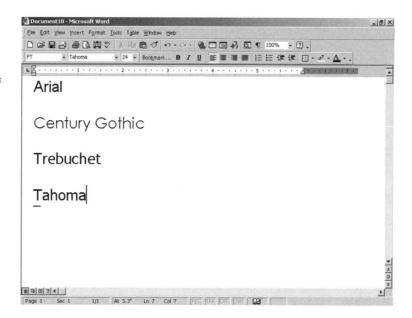

While each one of these fonts is different, there are similarities that outweigh these differences. If you mixed the top two fonts in a word or even a paragraph, it'd be obvious that you did because the use of these fonts is the same. A document that looks good in Arial will look good in Century Gothic too.

When you're looking at these screens, remember that the printed versions of these fonts lay out the same as the screen but look significantly smoother because of screen display limitations.

Going All Open or Open

Windows 2000 Professional needs some non-Open (outline) fonts for system use, but most people can live very comfortably choosing only Open fonts for their documents. Using only Open fonts speeds processing and assures that your screen layouts print as you expect them to. Also, installing Open fonts exclusively (other than Windows 2000's system fonts) takes up less disk space because the fonts are scaleable. Therefore, one font file has the information available in it to create many fonts effectively. What's really occurring is that the system scales a font to different sizes with different characteristics.

> **Note**
>
> The older TrueType and the new Open fonts are quite similar in technology in that they're both vector (outline) fonts described by math rather than a bitmap. For most applications, you can interchange the words Open and TrueType.

To instruct Windows 2000 Professional to display only Open fonts in your applications, choose Tools, Folder Options from the Fonts menu display, select the TrueType tab shown in Figure 13.14, and check the box Show only TrueType fonts.

FIGURE 13.14

You can opt to show only Open fonts in your applications. This option is good for most users to choose.

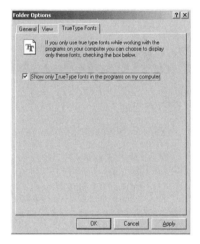

You need to restart your computer before this option takes effect.

> **Note**
>
> Instructing Windows 2000 Professional to display and use only Open (or TrueType) fonts won't affect the system's use of specialized raster (bitmap) fonts for its own use. It will only affect the fonts available to applications.

Installing and Deleting Fonts

Unless you have very exacting or special needs, you reduce your system overhead by eliminating appearance-like fonts and telling Windows 2000 Professional to use only Open fonts.

13

WINDOWS 2000 FONTS

The former action frees some disk space; the latter makes your machine most efficient by using the most efficient font technology.

To delete a font, right-click it and then choose Delete from the context menu. Figure 13.15 shows the confirmation dialog box opened when you choose this option.

FIGURE 13.15

Deleting a font from the Fonts list deletes the entry from Fonts and from your application font selection list.

> **Note**
>
> Removing a file from the Fonts folder doesn't move the file into the Recycle Bin. This action makes the deletion permanent unless you maintain a backup or have a distribution list.

To add fonts from the Fonts display, choose File, Install New Fonts. You need to browse to find the fonts. Figure 13.16 shows how to browse for new fonts to install.

FIGURE 13.16

You need to have the fonts you want to install on hand. After you do, installing them is as easy as browsing for them and choosing the ones you want to have available to your programs.

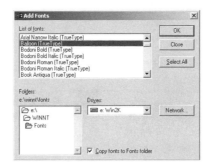

Many installation or setup programs install their own set of fonts either after seeking your approval or by stealth. Unfortunately, some of these programs either complain or even refuse to run if they don't find the fonts they expect when they launch. If you've deleted these fonts, you might run into problems, even though the programs have identical (if not identically named) fonts available to them. If one of these programs is especially cranky, you might need to re-install it, accepting the overhead of the extra fonts as some additional cost of the program.

Extra Symbols and Decorative Fonts

Any given font or typeface contains only certain characters. Most contain the letters from a to z in both lower- and uppercase plus all the numbers and common punctuation marks. They take up only part of the available characters in a set. What's left is up to the vendor. Take a look at the following two lines. They are the same ASCII characters. The first line is in Courier New. The second is in Symbol.

> This is a line of text.
> Τηισ ισ α λινε οφ τεξτ.

As you can see, Courier New uses the Roman or common U.S. English character set, and the Symbol font uses the Greek alphabet.

The Character Map, which is an applet within Windows 2000, displays the entire character set for a font. Figure 13.17 shows the Character Map for Courier New.

FIGURE 13.17

The Character Map shows all the available characters for any given font. Using this applet is a quick way to know what's available for each font and to get a special character into your document.

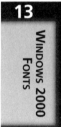

To see the Character Map, choose Start, Programs, Accessories, System Tools, Character Map. If you don't see the Map, it likely wasn't installed as part of your Custom option or push install. You can install the Character Map from your Windows 2000 CD-ROM through the Setup program.

Note

The Insert Symbol (or similar function) in many applications works the same as the Character Map.

13

WINDOWS 2000
FONTS

You can get a special character (non-keyboard) into your document from the Character Map or the font set in the following three ways:

- Double-click the character you want to insert.

- Click the character in the Map, and then click Select or press the Enter or Return key on your keyboard.

- Enter the ASCII code for the character by holding down the Alt key and then entering the numeric code from the numeric keypad (not the keys above the regular key set). When you click a character (really a character place) in the Character Map, the status line tells you what the ASCII code for that character is.

Note

Character selection and mapping vary with font set. For example, Alt+174 is the ™ (trademark) symbol in Tahoma. It won't be in all font sets. In Arial, Alt+174 is the double chevron «.

Using the first two techniques, you then need to click the Copy button to copy the character or characters to the Clipboard. From there, you can paste them into your application.

Each font has its own set of special characters. Figure 13.18 shows the Pi6OUP MT font. Note that this font has no common alphanumeric characters at all, and that the selected symbol is character 21. You can tell by examining the status bar at the bottom right of the Character Map.

FIGURE 13.18

Some fonts, such as Pi6OUP MT and Symbol, have no ordinary alphanumeric characters. These fonts exist only to supply special characters for your documents.

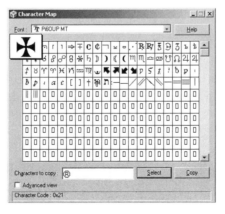

The limit of what you can do with fonts is limited only by your imagination. Figure 13.19 shows some Pi6OUP MT characters entered into Word 2000 and manipulated to give them an interesting look. Using fonts this way, you can take a simple font character and change it to a minor work of art.

FIGURE 13.19

Fonts can be fun. You can start with the basic font and alter it in anyway if you have the software.

On Screen Keyboard

The On Screen Keyboard was created for people with disabilities. Using it, you can enter characters normally entered via keyboard by using pointing devices like mice or mouth sticks. Using the On Screen Keyboard combined with certain font sets allows you to enter characters using the keyboard and your mouse. To see the On Screen Keyboard choose Start, Programs, Accessories, Accessibility, On Screen Keyboard.

Private Character Editor

Windows 2000 has a little-known feature enabling you to create your own font or full font set. Windows 2000 Professional's capacity for custom characters made by using the Private Character Editor (PCE) is more than 6,000 characters. To see the PCE, choose Start, Run, and then enter **eudcedit** in the resulting dialog box. Figure 13.20 shows the editor launched.

FIGURE 13.20

The Private Character Editor launched and ready to design a font character.

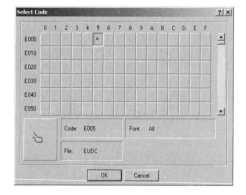

The editor starts with a grid showing boxes allowing you to select a code for a new bitmap. Double-click a square, which opens up a bitmap editor similar to Painter with similar tools such as various outlines, a "pencil" tool, a paintbrush-like tool, and so forth. Edit the code using this Paint-like editor shown in Figure 13.21.

FIGURE 13.21

Select a square and then edit the bitmap to appear in the square.

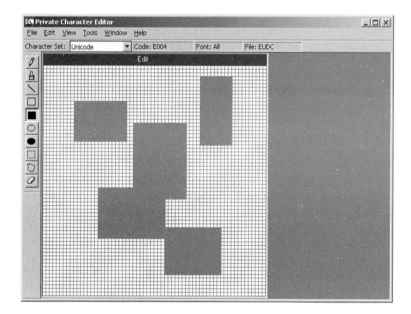

You can advance to the next square or retreat a square (to edit it) by choosing the menu selections View, Next Code or View, Previous Code. You can jump to other codes in the first window (Figure 13.20) by choosing Edit, Select Code or pressing Ctrl+O.

When you're done editing, you can save your creation using the File menu. The editor will also prompt you for a save when you exit the bitmap editor. Figure 13.22 shows the Select Code window with two bitmaps edited. The bitmaps will be difficult to see in the screen shot within their squares, but you can see it expanded in the Select Code dialog box at the bottom left.

FIGURE 13.22

After saving in the bitmap editor, your art appears in the select code dialog box.

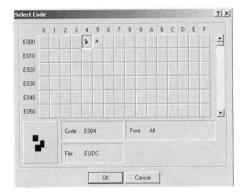

An important feature of the editor is the link feature. By linking to an existing font, your custom character will be available in these font sets.

Note

Most people use the PCE to create logos for insertion in their documents.

Summary

Windows 2000 Professional can use a variety of fonts. Raster, vector, and Open outline fonts are all equally at home in Windows 2000. However, the technology behind Open fonts makes them the right choice for the vast majority of uses. Many users need only Open fonts for their applications, although Windows 2000 itself requires some ASCII and Symbol fonts.

You can add or delete fonts through the Fonts applet and also see what fonts you have and their similarity to each other. Some applications rudely add fonts to your system without your approval. In some cases, these applications don't run without such fonts.

13

WINDOWS 2000 FONTS

The Character Map is a good place to view all the character symbols for each font. Using a bit of creativity and a drawing program, you can exercise quite a bit of latitude on how you display fonts and where you can use them.

The Private Character Editor is an almost unknown tool supplied with Windows 2000 Professional that will let you create custom fonts or font sets. Most people use the PCE for logo creation.

Using Windows 2000 on Laptops

Why Use Windows 2000 on Your Laptop?

Mobile executives, consultants, students, sales representatives and others are increasingly relying on laptop technology today. Mobile executives are required to "stay in touch" with the office while on the road, while sales representatives rely on current pricing and product information. Laptop technologies are continuing to become more powerful and cost less, which is allowing more companies to "laptop-enable" more of their workforce for customer visits and travel.

In the past, however, information on laptops has traditionally been difficult to manage and synchronize with network file servers back at the office. It was not uncommon in the past to overwrite updated files with old ones after returning to the office. One of the biggest benefits for the mobile user in Windows 2000 Professional is the ability to more easily manage offline files and folders. Advanced Windows 2000 Professional features allow mobile laptop users to easily take files and folders on the road and to then synchronize the files when plugging back into the local area network.

Other features built in to Windows 2000 Professional include viewing Web content easier while offline, advanced power management features for extended battery life, plug-and-play support, advanced docking station support, hardware profiles, wizards, and more. This chapter will explore these topics in-depth and offer step-by-step instructions for using these advanced features.

Installing Windows 2000 on Your Laptop

Just like the earlier versions of Windows NT, it is necessary to do some preparation and research prior to installing Windows 2000 Professional. A little bit of research in the beginning may help avoid headaches during the installation process. The key to this preparation is to make sure your hardware is compliant with Windows 2000. This not only includes the laptop but any other peripherals—adapter cards, external storage devices, and so on. The Microsoft site to check the hardware compatibility is http://www.microsoft.com/hcl/. Microsoft states that there are compatible devices that might not be listed on the Hardware Compatibility List, but you will have to test whether they are acceptable yourself. Also, this list does change periodically, so if your laptop or device is not on the list, check back periodically.

Next, check your laptop to see if it meets the minimum hardware configuration. Table 14.1 shows both the minimum and recommended configuration to run Windows 2000 properly.

TABLE 14.1 Minimum System Requirement for a Windows 2000 Professional Installation

	Minimum	*Recommended*
CPU	Pentium	Pentium II or better
RAM	32MB	64MB
Drive Space	1GB	2GB

> **Tip**
>
> Make sure that the volume where Windows 2000 Professional will be installed has *at least* 576MB of free space. If not, you will get a third of the way through the installation and the installation software will force you to exit, free up space on the hard drive, and then start over.

Installation

After you have checked the hardware compatibility list and determined that your machine meets or exceeds the minimum hardware requirements, it is time to take a close look at the Windows 2000 Professional installation procedure. Microsoft continues to forge ahead and make this operating system simple to install and easy to configure.

To install Windows 2000 Professional, first insert the Windows 2000 Professional CD-ROM in the CD-ROM drive. If your machine is currently running a previous version of Windows NT Workstation or Windows 95/98, the screen shown in Figure 14.1 appears.

FIGURE 14.1

Default installation prompt on Windows NT Workstation and Windows 95/98.

If you choose No, the first dialog box will disappear and you will have the choice of launching the Windows 2000 install, browsing the CD-ROM, or exiting. To continue with the upgrade, choose Yes. At this point, because you are running a compatible operating system, Microsoft is going to recommend that you upgrade your current version to Windows 2000. By upgrading your version, Windows 2000 will migrate your existing operating system's configuration. If you choose to run a Clean Install, you will be able to boot to this instance of Windows 2000 Professional in addition to the other operating systems on the machine.

If you are running a machine that you want to perform a clean install on, perform the following steps.

Note

If your laptop currently has Windows NT Server installed, you will not have the option to upgrade because there is no upgrade path from Windows NT Server to Windows 2000 Professional. In this case, you will have to run a clean install.

1. Choose Install a New Copy of Windows 2000 (Clean Install) as shown in Figure 14.2, and then click Next.

FIGURE 14.2
Choosing the clean install in Windows 2000.

2. The installer will now prompt you to take the oath and accept its license agreement. Select the I Accept This Agreement radio button and then click Next.

3. The next option is to choose from the Select Special Options. The defaults for these settings are shown in Table 14.2.

TABLE 14.2   Default Installation Options

Category	Setting	Default
Language Options	Primary Language and region	English (United States)
Language Options	Additional languages	(None)
Advanced Options	Location of Windows 2000 files	`<cd drive>:\i386`
Advanced Options	Windows Installation folder	`\WINNT`
Advanced Options	Copy all Setup files from the Setup CD to the hard drive	Not selected
Advanced Options	I want to choose the installation partition during Setup	Not selected
Accessibility Options	Magnifier	Not selected
Accessibility Options	Narrator	Not selected

To change any of these default settings, click the button corresponding to the category as shown in Figure 14.3. Then alter your selection in the screen that appears. When finished, click the Next button to proceed with the installation.

FIGURE 14.3

Special Options dialog box.

4. The next dialog box is very important. Deciding whether to upgrade the file system to NTFS is similar to making the decision of whether to go professional (all puns intended) or stay amateur. Going professional is a good thing, but once you accept your first prize money, there is no turning back.

   NTFS has many advantages over the FAT file system, such as security, reliability, and so on. However, MS-DOS and Windows 95/98 will not run on NTFS. If you choose to stay with the FAT file system for that reason, you can always convert to NTFS at a later date if you decide you need it. I recommend using NTFS wherever possible.

   Choose to either upgrade or not upgrade, and then click Next.

5. The setup will now start copying the installation files to your local hard drive. When finished, it will restart your machine and enter the text-based portion of the installation.

6. The Welcome to Setup will now appear. Press Enter again to begin the set up of Windows 2000 Professional.

7. Setup will now look for other installations of Windows. If it finds one, it will ask if you want to repair an old version or continue with installing a fresh copy. Press ESC to continue with the fresh copy.

8. A screen appears with the existing partitioned and unpartitioned space on your local computer. Choose where you want the install to be done and then press Enter proceed.

9. If you chose a drive with less than 576MB of free space, you will get a message to return to the previous menu and choose another location. Choose a volume with at least 576MB of space and proceed to the next step. If no partition has that much space, it will be necessary to exit the Setup program, reboot to your old installation (or an MS-DOS floppy if you have the FAT file system installed). After reboot, take the appropriate steps to clear the installation partition to meet the space requirements.

10. If you chose to install Windows 2000 on a partition that contains another version of Windows, you will now be warned. The warning states that the other version of Windows may not function properly once Windows 2000 Professional is installed. This is a warning that should be thought about carefully. Windows 2000 may change some settings in the boot process or system configuration that may cause other operating systems not to function. Click C to Continue.

11. If you chose to install Windows 2000 to a folder that already had a version of NT, you will be prompted to either use the folder and clear its contents or choose a different directory. Press L to use the existing folder or ESC to choose a different folder.

12. Setup will now examine the disk and, if you chose to overwrite your existing version of Windows, will take a minute to delete the files associated with that version.

    Following the file deletion, Setup will begin to copy the necessary files from the CD-ROM to the installation folder. When finished, your machine will be rebooted and Setup will continue.

    Following the reboot, you will enter the graphical portion of Setup. The Wizard will display a Welcome screen. Click Next.

13. The next step is where Microsoft has made some real improvements over previous versions of Windows. The setup program will now begin installing devices by inspecting your laptop. Keyboard, mouse, and video drivers will all be installed at this point. It will take several minutes, but it is worth the wait because this portion didn't miss anything on several machines on which I ran the install.

    When Setup concludes the hardware inspection phase, a Regional Settings dialog box will appear. By customizing your regional settings, you can control how numbers, currencies, and dates appear based on your locale. When you click the Customize button, you will see another dialog box on which you can specify which languages your system can read and write to, how numbers should appear (decimal symbols, and so on), what currency symbol to use, and how you want the date and time to appear. Click Next to accept the regional settings.

Year 2000 Note

Under the Date tab, there is a calendar section for specifying how 2 digit years should be handled. The default is that any years entered into the system with only 2 digits should be interpreted between 1930 and 2029. For example, suppose you are running a program to balance your checkbook in the year 2001. You pay a bill on 2/5/2001 but enter it as 2/5/01. The system will look into your regional settings and see that 01 should be 2001 and not 1901. This is a catchall that hopefully will help the noncompliant programs that may still accept 2 digit years. This setting can be changed. For instance, if your company deals with mortgages that may be entered and matured in 30 years, the default settings may not have a large enough range because in the year 2005, you do not want to enter a two digit maturity year of 1935. In this case, you can update the system to a range of 1951 to 2050.

14

USING WINDOWS
2000 ON
LAPTOPS

14. To personalize your software on the next screen, type in your name and organization and then click Next. You are required to at least type in your name. The organization is optional.

15. The next dialog box will prompt you for a computer name and Administrator password. The computer name has to be unique on your network. Check with your network Administrator to see if standards have been established. If so, follow the standards and enter the specified name in the Computer Name text box.

    Also, enter an Administrator password in the space provided. This password should be something unique but easily remembered. The Administrator account has complete access to your machine and is allowed to delete files and programs. Click Next to continue.

16. After you enter the security information, Setup will prompt you for some modem dialing information. Select your country or region, your local area code, and any numbers that must be dialed to get an outside line. As soon as the area code is entered, you will be able to click Next and continue to the next screen.

> **Note**
>
> These settings can be overwritten later based on where you and where your laptop will be dialing in to. These setting are merely the default for all new dialup connections.

17. You are now prompted for date and time settings. Enter the correct date and time and specify the time zone where you are located. If you will be traveling internationally, you may not want to check the box to automatically adjust for Daylight Savings time. Some regions do not participate in Daylight Savings time, so you may want to manually change the time based on where you and your laptop are. Click Next to continue.

18. Setup will now begin installing the network components. You are prompted to choose the typical Windows 2000 Professional network settings or to customize. Choose Custom Settings, and then click Next.

19. The next dialog box will display the networking components that Setup was able to locate. If your laptop has a network card installed, you should see the name of the card in bold as well as the MAC Address. The default here is to install Client for Microsoft Networks, File and Printer Sharing for Microsoft Networks, and Internet Protocol (TCP/IP). I recommend at least installing Client for Microsoft Networks and the Internet Protocol (TCP/IP). To ensure a secure laptop, you can deselect File and Printer Sharing for Microsoft Networks if you will not be creating network or printer shares on your machine. By deselecting this check box, no user will be able to connect to your machine and manipulate your files.

At this point you can also install additional protocols or reconfigure the default settings. You will still be able to add protocols and clients later. Say, for example, you are on the road at a customer site that runs NetWare with the IPX protocol. If you left the default configuration, you would not be able to successfully log on to the network. At that time, you could alter your configuration and add the proper client and protocols.

If your network is still configured with static IP addresses, click Internet Protocol (TCP/IP), click the Properties button, enter the proper TCP/IP configuration, and then click OK. Click Next to continue the installation.

20. Now you will enter how your laptop will participate in the network. This is another setting that can be changed later, based on your location. If your laptop should log in to a Windows domain, click the Yes radio button and enter the name of the domain. If your laptop will not log in to a domain, click No and type in the name for the workgroup in which to participate. If you do not know how this should be configured, click Next to accept the default settings.

21. Setup will now install Windows 2000 components and then prompt you to remove the CD-ROM from the drive in preparation for a reboot. Click Finish to reboot your laptop.

22. After your laptop completes the reboot, you will be in Windows 2000 Professional. Take a few moments to register your software and then insert the CD-ROM again and run the Discover Windows program to get an overview of your new operating system.

Performance Tuning for Laptops

Windows 2000 performance tuning has been simplified from the old tweaking of the AUTOEXEC.BAT, CONFIG.SYS, WIN.INI, and SYSTEM.INI. Today, there are only a few simple configuration adjustments that can be made. Windows NT 3.1 and Windows 95 did away with a lot of the decisions in the configuration. Does any one miss loading device drivers into high memory to save a few KB?

Out of the box, Windows 2000 Professional should be adequately configured for all but a very few circumstances. About the only thing to worry about and monitor is if you have enough RAM to reduce disk thrashing, which could bring your machine to a grinding halt in some instances. To find out what you need in terms of memory, I recommend buying every last megabyte of RAM you can afford. Windows 2000 likes memory and will use as much of it as available.

In Windows 2000, one of the quickest ways to check both your CPU and memory usage is to bring up the Task Manager and look at the graphs.

To bring up the Task Manager

1. Press Ctrl+Alt+Delete and then click Task Manager.
2. Click the Performance tab (see Figure 14.4).

FIGURE 14.4

Monitoring CPU and memory usage from the Task Manager.

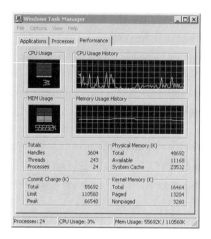

As you can see, my CPU reading is low and my average across the graph is also fairly low. Physical memory unfortunately is low also. Of the 48MB of memory on my machine, I only have 11,168KB available. After that memory fills up, the paging file on disk is going to be used for virtual memory. While virtual memory is a nice thing because it will save my computer from crashing, it does have a downside. The downside is that once I start using the page file on disk, my machine begins to slow down. This slow down is usually very noticeable even to the untrained eye. During periods of time, the hard drive will race to keep up with your requests.

This is a simple thing to monitor over a period of time through normal use. If the performance on you machine is suffering due to lack of memory, it is advisable to keep as few applications open at any one time. Too often users complain of poor system performance only to find out that they have too many applications running at one time. If having many applications open at the same time on your laptop is part of your job, I would advise you to add more memory to the machine. The performance improvements are worth the money.

The Performance Monitor is another tool that can be used to identify bottlenecks, resource shortages, and other performance indicators on your laptop. This tool is much more sophisticated than the limited Task Manager, and it can produce alerts when values are exceeded.

To start the Performance Monitor

1. Click the Start button and then click Settings.
2. Click Control Panel and then double-click Administrative Tools.
3. Double-click the Performance icon to open the Performance Monitor application.

To view some sample values and indicators

1. Click the Performance Monitor label under the main Performance folder.
2. Click the plus (+) sign on the toolbar of the Performance monitor to a value to graph.
3. Under the Performance objects, choose an object to monitor. For this example, choose Memory.
4. A list of performance counters appear that are specific to the Memory performance object. If you are unsure of what the counter refers to, click the Explain button and a description will appear.
5. Select Pages/Sec, and then click Add.
6. Click Close to close the Add counters dialog box.
7. As you can see, the graph will now begin recording numbers at one (1) second intervals.

Repeat this process to add additional counters. This tool is invaluable for tracking down performance-related problems on your machine.

Setting Up Hardware Profiles

Windows 2000 Professional allows laptop users to create specific hardware profiles for any hardware configuration that their laptops may use. For example, you will now be able to save the configuration specific to your network connectivity (plugged into the local area network or using a network card or modem) and the specific docking station to which you are connected. The default Hardware profile created for laptops is named Undocked Profile, which recognizes that the computer is a laptop and is undocked.

To create and use an additional hardware profile, perform the following steps:

1. Open the Control Panel and double-click the System icon.
2. Click the Hardware tab and then click the Hardware Profiles button to bring up the Hardware Profiles dialog box, as shown in Figure 14.5.

14

USING WINDOWS
2000 ON
LAPTOPS

FIGURE 14.5

Default hardware profile settings.

This dialog box shows the available hardware profiles on your laptop. Displayed is the current profile from the last boot of the system.

3. Select Undocked Profile (Current) and then click Copy.

4. Another dialog box will now appear. Key in a name for the new profile, as shown in Figure 14.6. Click OK to proceed.

FIGURE 14.6

Creating a new hardware profile.

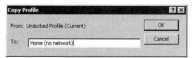

5. Double-click your new profile and then check the box to include this profile as an option when Windows starts.

6. Click OK and repeat step 5 on the Undocked Profile, and then restart your laptop.

7. After choosing to start with the Microsoft Windows 2000 Professional operating system, you will be prompted for a hardware profile. You should have two profiles from which to choose. Choose the new profile Home (no network), and then press Enter.

8. Because you have copied the default profile, your laptop will now boot with the exact same hardware profile as before. To make a change to this profile to disable the network card, launch the Control Panel and then double-click Administrative Tools.

9. Double-click the Computer Management icon to load the Microsoft Management Console.

10. Double-click System Tools, and then click Device Manager. This will display all the devices attached to your computer, as shown in Figure 14.7.

FIGURE **14.7**

Device Manager.

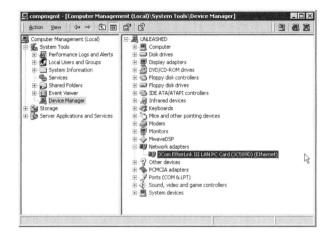

11. Locate the Network adapters and then click the plus (+) sign to the left of the net-work card icon. Locate and double-click the network card.

12. Under Device Usage, choose Do Not Use This Device in the Current Hardware Profile (Disable), as shown in Figure 14.8.

FIGURE **14.8**

Configuring hard-ware profiles.

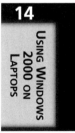

13. Click OK and then restart your laptop. If you chose the new hardware profile, the drivers for the network card will no longer be loaded on startup.

This same method applies to any of the devices listed in Device Manager. Use this feature to customize your environment to allow for specific configurations, whether you are on road or in the office.

Remote Computing Features

Point to Point Tunneling Protocols provide a way to securely communicate between a client computer to a corporate server. This communication is done through a virtual private network (VPN). For example, a laptop user with Windows 2000 Professional can dial into an Internet Service Provider (ISP) while on the road and establish a secure connection to a server back at the corporate headquarters. Although your laptop will be connected over public Internet lines, the established connection to your corporate service will be private and your own. The laptop mobile user benefits by not paying expensive phone charges by dialing directly into the corporate office, and the MIS staff at the corporate office benefits from not maintaining a large modem bank set up specifically for mobile users. Explore the VPN options in Windows 2000 to securely communicate over a common infrastructure already in place. See Chapter 20, "Remote Computing with Remote Access Service," for more information on remote computing features.

Support for Offline Use

A very important new feature in Windows 2000 Professional for laptop users is the ability to better manage and synchronize the files you take with you while on the road. The new features will easily allow you to make network directories available while you and your laptop are on the road and then easily synchronize that same directory when you return to the office. This section of the chapter will explore these new features and will walk you through a somewhat typical scenario.

Making Information Available Offline

To take a file or folder offline prior to leaving the office, perform the following steps:

1. If this is the first time you have attempted to work with offline files, go to My Computer and choose Folder Options from the Tools menu.

2. Choose the Offline Files tab and make sure the Enable Offline Files box is checked to enable this feature (see Figure 14.9).

   When you select to Enable Offline Files, the Synchronize All Offline Files Before Logging Off and Enable Reminders are selected by default. You are also given the ability to limit the space used by temporary offline files to prevent taking more than your machine can handle. Buttons are also provided to allow you to delete local copies of files, view file properties, and even to specify options for specific computers that become offline.

FIGURE 14.9
Enabling offline files.

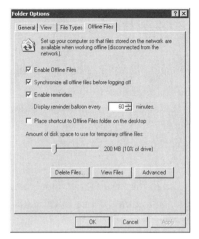

Click OK to accept the setting. Now you can proceed and when any network volume, file, or directory is right-clicked, it will have the Make Available Offline option.

3. Locate a network file share, file, or folder that you would like to take with you.

4. Right-click the objects and choose Make Available Offline from the pop-up list box, as shown in Figure 14.10.

FIGURE 14.10
Making a folder available offline.

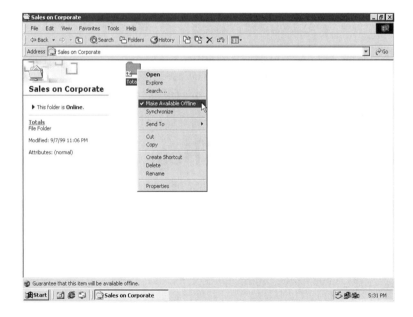

14

USING WINDOWS
2000 ON
LAPTOPS

The Offline Files Wizard box will now appear. Click Next to Continue.

5. Windows 2000 will then give you a brief description of how the icon on the folder will be marked. At this point, you have the option to automatically synchronize your offline files when you log on and off of the computer. Click Next to continue.

6. The Wizard will now prompt you for a reminder to let you know when you are offline. You will have the option to create a shortcut to this folder you have made available offline.

   Make your selections and click Finish. The Wizard will now finish by synchronizing the files.

7. A small computer icon now appears in the system tray. Double-click this icon. Figure 14.11 shows a screen representing the Offline Files Status.

FIGURE 14.11

Offline Files Status.

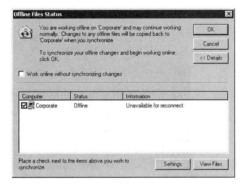

This screen summarizes my offline experience. It tells me that I am working offline on "Corporate" machine, and that everything is OK. It states that my connection is offline and that, presently, it is unavailable for reconnect.

8. Click OK to continue.

Back at the Office

When you return to the office, it will be necessary to re-establish a network connection and synchronize your files (especially if you made changes to any of them). After reconnecting, perform the following steps:

1. Double-click the Offline Files icon in the system tray and then click OK to synchronize your changes. Notice, in Figure 14.12, that one file is modified, as displayed under the Information column of the grid.

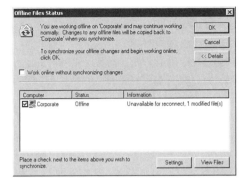

FIGURE 14.12

Synchronizing offline files.

2. Click OK to synchronize the files. The synchronization manager notices that my copy of the file was modified after the file on the network server and therefore updates the file server. Now all copies are the same.

Note

The folder specified is still scheduled to be synchronized and still displays the Offline Synchronization icon on the bottom-left corner. However, the properties for the folder now display that the folder is Online and, therefore, all changes made to the file will be made on the server. After your connection to the network has terminated, Windows will notify you that you are back offline.

Remote Web Content

In addition to taking network files on the road, Windows 2000 gives you the ability to take Web content on the road. Much like taking your files on the road, you will now be able to browse an Internet site while not connected directly to the Internet. This may come in handy for training, presentations, and research. Imagine that you don't have enough time at the office to research your competitor's products before catching your next flight. Instead of missing your flight, you can now download portions of your competitor's Web site and take it with you on the plane.

Working offline with Web content is easy.

1. Open Internet Explorer and locate the Web site you want to take with you.

2. Click the Favorites drop-down list box and then click Add to Favorites. The dialog box shown in Figure 14.13 appears.

FIGURE 14.13

Adding a Favorite in Internet Explorer.

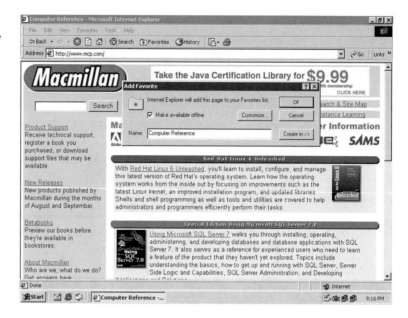

3. Select Make Available Offline, and then click Customize.

4. A wizard appears to help guide you. Choose the level of content you want to download. Click Next to Continue.

5. The next dialog box asks whether to also download any links on this page. If you choose Yes, you can then specify how many levels deep to download. Make your selection and then click Next.

6. You will now be prompted for synchronization settings. The two choices are to manually kick off the synchronization process or to have the synchronization process happen on a schedule. I recommend manually running this synchronization process. If you schedule it, you may find that it runs at inopportune times when you are trying to get some other work finished. Make your selection and then click Next.

7. If the site you are using requires an account and password, enter that information in the next screen.

8. Click Finish to complete the Customization Wizard.

9. Click OK to add the favorite. The synchronization process will now begin. Depending on the settings you use, this process could take quite a bit of time. If you chose to download links, you will see the process go through each link in turn. As you can see in Figure 14.14, there is also a button to skip the current site if you don't need an update at that time.

FIGURE 14.14

Synchronizing offline Web pages.

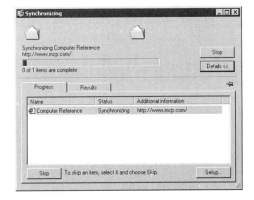

10. Now that the Web site of choice has been downloaded, you may want to update it when you return to the office. To do this, simply start Internet Explorer and choose Synchronize from the Tools menu. Depending on your network speed, this could take quite a while.

This feature is interesting and has many benefits. Use it as often as possible before going on the road. Don't get caught without all the information you need to do your job!

Advanced Power Management

Many users I talk to complain about battery life in their portable computers. Microsoft included some additional features in Windows 2000 that will help you get the extra nudge from your battery. Windows 2000 supports the Advanced Configuration and Power Interface (ACPI) hardware. With this hardware, Windows 2000 is better able to manage the power in laptops via applications and device drivers. Specific applications can now interface with the power management of the computer and notify the interface not to power down during long periods of processing. Most laptops today will power down no matter what is running on the machine. This new feature should improve use and functionality.

To view the power management options, perform the following steps:

1. Click the Start key, and then click Settings.

2. Click the Control Panel.

3. Double-click Power Options.

4. The Power schemes are shown in Figure 14.15. These schemes allow you to customize your power management options depending on your situation.

FIGURE 14.15

Power Options Properties.

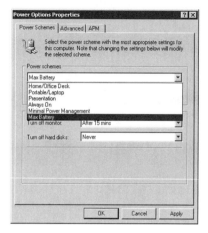

5. Choose one of the power schemes from the list or add a new power scheme to better suit your needs.

Summary

Microsoft has made "being on the road" a little easier with its new release of Windows 2000 Professional. For IS managers and support personnel, the installation and customization are powerful. For the end user, the new advanced features will help you spend less time worrying about hardware configurations and file synchronization and more time getting your work done.

Windows 2000 Goes to the Internet

PART
IV

IN THIS PART

Talking to Another Computer: Direct Cable Connections

CHAPTER 15

Sometimes network situations call for a quick method of connecting computers together without all the hassle of installing network cards while ensuring they are configured properly. Direct Cable Connection offers a fast, inexpensive method to hook two computers together. Using Direct Cable Connection, Windows 2000 will connect to Windows 95, Windows 98, and Windows NT using a Point to Point (PPP) connection. In addition, Windows 2000 will connect to UNIX systems using an older Serial Line Interrupt Protocol (SLIP) connection. This situation is often used in home environments or for computers that do not often require network connectivity. Direct Connection acts the same as a network adapter connection, allowing access to printers, folders, and files. This chapter steps through hooking up a Direct Cable Connection and explains the confusing terminology found in cabling. For further details on Remote Access Service, protocols, and networking refer to Chapter 20, "Remote Computing with Remote Access Service" and Chapter 21, "Windows 2000 Networking Protocols."

Ports

To provide a better understanding of Direct Cable Connections, ports must first be described. Computers have different types of ports, some of which are external, some internal. In simple terms, a *port* is an outlet used to pass data in and out of a computing device. Think of the inside a house, where the outlets in the wall pass information to devices inside the house from outside the house, and vice-versa. A house has outlets for the television cable, the telephone, and any electrical devices. Computers, like houses, have many different types of outlets, called ports. The type of port used for communicating is called a COM port, otherwise known as a *serial port*.

> **Note**
>
> What is the difference between serial and parallel communication? Serial ports pass data into and out of the computer one bit at a time. They act like a one lane road on which each car on the road is a bit of data. As with single lane traffic, this method of communicating is very slow when traffic is busy. Parallel ports transfer information eight bits at a time. Using the road analogy, parallel ports would be eight lane highways, each car again acting as a bit. Because of the different methods for communicating, parallel ports are much faster than serial ports.

Windows 2000 allows a Direct Connection using a serial null modem cable (RS232) or a parallel cable. Windows 2000 uses a featured driver called a DirectParallel driver for communicating over parallel ports. The parallel cable has to be one of the following types, which can be purchased at most computer stores:

- *Standard or Basic 4-bit cable*—These cables are early versions of cables. Generally not used as much because of their slow speed.

- *Extended or enhanced capabilities port (ECP) cable*—Ten times faster than standard cable. Not all computers have ECP-enhanced parallel ports, and it must be enabled in BIOS.

- *Universal Cable Module (UCM) cable*—This type of cabling is similar to ECP cabling and uses ECP ports but provides a much faster communication speed.

> **Note**
>
> Determining which port connection is which on the back of a computer can be tricky. Here are some guidelines. A serial port is a male 9-pin connection from the computer. This means that on the back of the machine, an outlet that has five pins in one row and four pins in a row underneath is a serial port. A parallel connection has a male 25-pin connector. Again, the outlet on the back of the machine will have two rows, the top with thirteen pins and the bottom with twelve. This connection can be confusing because most computers will also have a 25-pin male connection used for connecting printers.

Ports have to be configured on both machines to enable communication. Windows 2000 changes the location and format for ports and the attached modems from previous Windows NT versions. First of all, the location for configuring a modem's port settings (such as choosing which COM port to use) depends on whether the port settings were configured during modem setup—as is the case for most Plug and Play modems—or Device Manager assigned the port settings. For certain modem installations, the port setting can be changed from the Advanced Port Setting properties window found under Phone and Modem Options in the Control Panel. If the port settings are not in this location, they can be accessed in the Device Manager. One item to remember when configuring ports: Windows 2000 has the modem's port settings, which sets the properties for communication between the computer and the modem. Each modem will have a maximum port speed, which will match the port speed. Windows 2000 will also have settings for each port, also found in the Device Manager. Each port's properties will set the communication between the computer and the port, not knowing what is attached to the port. Many computers have modems set to one speed and the port set to another. Figure 15.1 shows the listed ports found in Device Manager.

15

DIRECT CABLE CONNECTIONS

FIGURE 15.1

The ports listed in Device Manager.

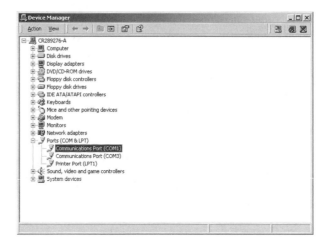

To change the port setting for a particular COM port, right-click the port and choose Properties. The Communications Port Properties dialog box will display four tabs; choose the Port Settings tab (see Figure 15.2).

FIGURE 15.2

The properties for Com Port 1.

The following list describes the features for the COM port properties:

- *Bits per Second*—This is the maximum rate of data transmitted through the port. Windows 2000 supports up to 128,000 bits per second (bps), null modems are usually set at 19,200bps.

- *Data Bits*—The amount of bits used to represent each character transmitted through the port. Usually Data Bits is set at eight, but Windows 2000 accepts from four through eight as valid settings.

- *Parity*—Used for error checking on data sent between two computers. When transmitting information, an extra bit can be added for parity if necessary, which can help rebuild any lost data during the data transfer. Parity is usually set to none.

- *Stop Bits*—Because data is sent over serial ports one bit at a time, a start and stop bit must be set to tell the receiving computer when a character is sent. This setting states the amount of bits the stop will be in between characters. The default setting is one.

- *Flow Control*—Different communication devices will have different speeds for sending information. A receiving computer needs a way to control the speed, or *flow*, of communication and a method of telling a sending computer to slow down. Windows 2000 supports a software method of flow control called *Xon/Xoff* and a hardware method, simply called *hardware*.

- *FIFO buffers*—Listed under the Advanced port settings, first in/first out (FIFO) buffers is a component found in serial ports that stores incoming data for later processing and, if a modem line is busy, stores outgoing data for later transmission.

> **Note**
>
> The Parity, Stop Bits, and number of data bits must be the same on the sending and the receiving computer; otherwise, errors will occur.

Port setting can be configured before or after installing a null modem, but should be checked at some point before opening communication.

Null Modem Cables

Null modem cabling offers an economical and immediate method for physically connecting two computers together to pass information. This method uses a specialized 9- or 25-pin serial or parallel cable, commonly referred to as a *null modem cable* or a RS-232 serial device, and a COM port on each machine. A null modem cable has swapped particular lines so that what is sent from one machine is received on the other. Table 15.1 illustrates the cabling structure for a 9- and 25-pin null modem cable. In effect, this cable emulates a modem between the two computers.

15

DIRECT CABLE CONNECTIONS

TABLE 15.1 Cabling for 9-pin Null Modem Cables

Cable Line Signal	Host Computer	Calling Computer
9-Pin Cabling		
Transmit Data	3	2
Receive Data	2	3
Request to Send	7	8
Clear to Send	8	7
Data set ready and Carrier detect	6, 1	4
Signal ground	5	5
Data terminal ready	4	6, 1

Cable Line Signal	Host Computer	Calling Computer
25-Pin Cabling		
Transmit Data	3	2
Receive Data	2	3
Request to Send	4	5
Clear to Send	5	4
Data set ready and Carrier detect	6, 8	20
Signal ground	7	7
Data terminal ready	20	6, 8

Warning

The cabling for null modem cables has to be as listed in Tables 15.1. Many retail stores sell serial cables as null modem cables, but they do not have the specialized wiring. Be sure when purchasing a null modem cable that it is an RS232 cable with the proper wiring. A null modem cable should cost approximately ten dollars.

Before purchasing a null modem cable, determine what COM ports are available on each machine. Also, null modems will not work for lengths of over fifty feet, so be certain that the physical location of these computers does not rule out this connection type. The next section describes how to install a cable to the port.

Installing a Null Modem Cable

After the proper null modem cable has been attached to each machine, the cable must be installed and the COM ports must be configured on each computer. To create a serial connection between two computers, use the following steps.

1. Open Phone and Modem Options. Windows 2000 has integrated all modem and phone features into one applet in the Control Panel. Figure 15.3 shows the Phone and Modem Options applet.

FIGURE 15.3

The Phone and Modem Options applet in the Control Panel.

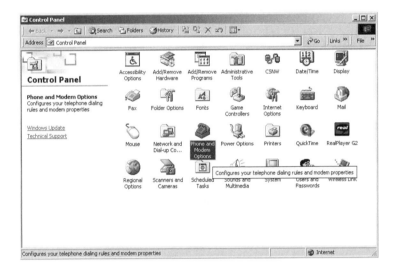

2. Choose the Modems Tab from the Phone and Modem Option Properties dialog box.

3. Click Add to install a new modem. An Install New Modem Wizard appears (see Figure 15.4).

FIGURE 15.4

The Install New Modem Wizard.

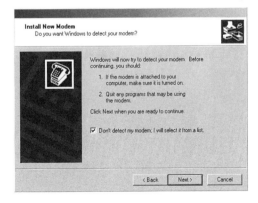

15

DIRECT CABLE CONNECTIONS

4. Check the box for the option "Don't detect my modem; I will select from a list." Click Next.

5. The next step in the Wizard process lists all the manufacturers and the modems they make. Choose Standard Modem Types from the list of manufacturers and Communications Cable between Two Computers and the model. Click Next. Figure 15.5 shows this step in the Install New Modem process.

FIGURE 15.5

The Install New Modem Wizard with a list of manufacturers.

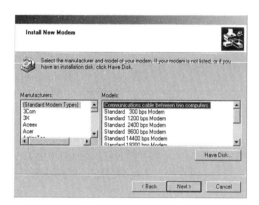

6. The next step presents a list of available COM ports. Click either All Ports to install a Direct Connection for each available port or click Selected Ports and choose the appropriate port. Click Next. Figure 15.6 demonstrates this step. Determining which port is which can be tricky. Most computers now come with labeled ports on the back of each machine. However, some older machines may require examining the motherboard to port connection to see which COM port is which.

FIGURE 15.6

The list of available ports in the Install New Modem wizard.

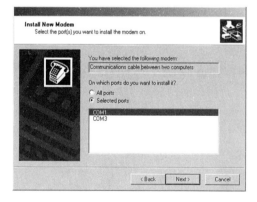

7. Click Finish and the computer will install the null modem cable.

This procedure must be completed on both machines on which you are setting up Direct Connection.

Setting Up Direct Connections

Once the null modem has been installed, the next step is to make a direct cable connection. To establish a Direct Connection, follow these steps:

1. Open the Control Panel and choose Network and Dial-up Connections.

2. Double-click the Make New Connection to start the Network Connection Wizard. Figure 15.7 illustrates the Network Connection Wizard.

FIGURE 15.7

The Make New Connection Wizard.

3. Click Next. A list of connection methods will appear (see Figure 15.8). For Direct Connection, choose the Connect Directly to Another Computer option. This choice allows a choice of COM ports to use.

FIGURE 15.8

Choose to Connect Directly to Another Computer.

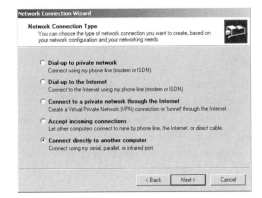

15

DIRECT CABLE CONNECTIONS

> **Note**
>
> Unlike Windows 95 or Windows 98, Direct Connection is automatically installed in Windows 2000.

The next step has two options that ask the computer's role in the cable connection (see Figure 15.9). When establishing a connection, one computer acts as the *host* and one as the *guest*. These roles determine which computer is calling the other (the guest computer calls the host computer) and allows the host computer to use user accounts for authenticating direct cable connections. Only administrators or users with administrator-level rights can create a direct network connection that acts as a host. Guest direct network connections do not require administrator-level rights.

FIGURE 15.9

Choose to act as the Host or the Guest.

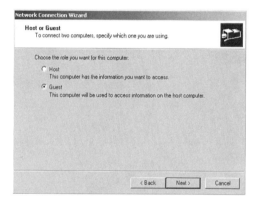

> **Note**
>
> Regardless of whether a computer acts as a host or as a guest, both computers will be able to access resources on the other machine.

Host Computers

One window in the Network Connection Wizard process asks if the computer will run as a host or as a guest. A host computer has resources, such as files or printers, that it provides to the guest computer. To have a computer act as the host, choose Host. The next step asks what device is used to make this connection. An option to configure the properties for each device is also available in the host connection. If this is the first time installing a particular connection, the device will be disabled, so configuring the device will not be possible until after that wizard completes. Figure 15.10 shows the device connection type for a host machine.

FIGURE 15.10

The list of available devices for a host machine.

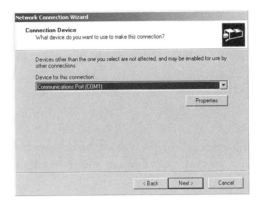

Choose the device that the null modem cable is using, and then click Next. The next step presents a list of user accounts for the host machine. These user accounts are based on the list created in the Users and Passwords applet on the Windows 2000 Professional computer. User accounts can be created, deleted, or configured at this point. Authentication can be disabled, which can be useful for palmtop computers, but not during the setup process. To bypass authentication, after the direct connection is established, go into the Incoming Connection properties. Figure 15.11 shows a list of user accounts in the Network Connection Wizard.

FIGURE 15.11

A list of user accounts in the Network Connection Wizard.

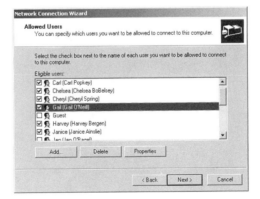

15

DIRECT CABLE
CONNECTIONS

Once the appropriate eligible users have been selected, click Next to proceed to the last step for the Wizard. This last window specifies the name for the connection, which for host computers is called Incoming Connections. Click Finish to complete the Wizard. If any options need to be edited after the Wizard process, selecting Incoming Connections for Host machines or Direct Connection for Guest machines and choosing properties from file in the menu bar (or right-clicking the object) will show all of the options from the Wizard process.

Guest Computers

If the computer is acting as a guest computer for the Direct Connection, choose Guest for the third step in the Network Connection Wizard. A guest computer will access resources (files and printers, for example) located on the host machine. More importantly, the user setting up the guest computer does not require administrative privileges. Click Next to proceed to the next step in the Wizard.

The next window in the Network Communication Wizard is the same as host connections (see Figure 15.10). Select the device that the null modem cable is using and click Next.

If a user with administrative privileges is creating the network connection, the next window asks whether this Direct Connection should be available for all users or just for the user currently logged on (see Figure 15.12). While other users can create their own Direct Connections, choosing All Users sets up the connection for them. By doing this, users who may be unfamiliar with the setup process can use the existing connection. If a user who does not have administrative privileges is establishing a connection between the two machines, this step is skipped.

FIGURE 15.12

Administrators can choose the connection availability in the Network Connection Wizard.

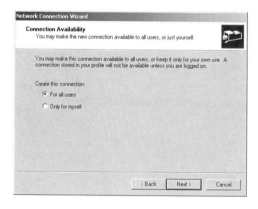

After you have chosen an option for connection availability, click Next. The last window in the Wizard specifies the name for the connection, which for guest computers is called Direct Connections. Click the Finish button to complete the Network Connection Wizard process.

Direct Connection Properties

Once the ports and Direct Connections have been configured, the Network and Dial-Up Connection applet will have options to connect to another machine for guest connections in the Direct Connection object or to observe any connections to a host machine from the Incoming Connections object. To connect to another machine using the guest option, right-click the Direct Connection object and choose Connect. Figure 15.13 shows the Connect Direct Connections dialog box with options for name, password, and domain and phone number. These options can be bypassed through the Direct Connection properties, which are explained in the following paragraphs.

Figure 15.13

The Connect Direct Connection dialog box.

To change to properties for connections, either choose Properties from this dialog box or right-click of the Direct Connection object and choose Properties. The Properties dialog box displays some general properties such as the modem type and dialing phone number, which is not applicable for direct connections. Figure 15.14 demonstrates the General properties tab for Direct Connections.

The Options tab displays all the features for the Direct Connection Properties dialog box. This window has prompts for displaying the dialing process, authentication methods, and the phone number to use for modems. Also, if a line is busy, there are options for how long the Direct Connection should wait before redialing and how many attempts it should make before quitting. There is also an option for any X.25 connections. Figure 15.15 shows the Options window from the Direct Connection properties.

15

Direct Cable Connections

FIGURE **15.14**

*The General prop-
erties tab for
Direct
Connections.*

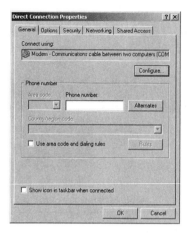

FIGURE **15.15**

*The Options prop-
erties tab for
Direct
Connections.*

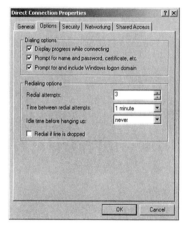

The Security tab has options for password protection and for any scripting or terminal
windows during session establishment. Users can log on to another computer using a
user account and password from a domain or local account. The passwords can use an
unsecured connection, a secured connection, or a smart card for authentication. Any
encryption settings will scramble (encrypt) the password from the guest computer to the
host computer (decrypt), which means that any device intercepting the logon process will
not be able to decipher the password. The typical setting allows unsecured passwords
during a PPP exchange, which is a good default setting for null modems due to throughput speed. Choosing the Advanced option and then the Customize button will display the
typical settings and also allow options to change the security settings.

Another feature in the Security tab is to activate a terminal window and script the logon process. This feature can be useful for dialing into remote systems or for any procedures that have a logon process that can be automated through scripting. Figure 15.16 shows the Security Tab for Direct Connections.

FIGURE 15.16

The Security prop-erties tab for Direct Connections.

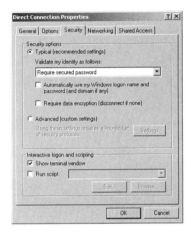

The Networking property tab displays all the client, protocol, and service information for the Direct Connection (see Figure 15.17). For further information about any of these items, refer to Chapter 21.

FIGURE 15.17

The Networking properties tab for Direct Connections.

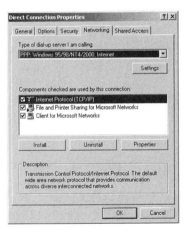

The last tab in the Direct Connections properties window has shared access options (see Figure 15.18). Sometimes, one of the computers in a direct connection has resources that need to be available to the entire network. The shared access option allows all other

15

DIRECT CABLE CONNECTIONS

computers participating on the network to use the Direct Connection to access resources on the other machine. This connection can be continuously open or available on demand. The Settings button can be used to allow specific applications or services to access information via the connection.

FIGURE 15.18

The Shared Access properties tab for Direct Connections.

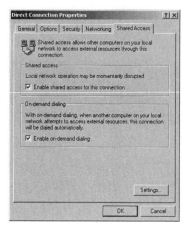

Logging On

Once the two computers have set up their respective roles, the guest machine can now log on to the host machine. The following steps describe the process for logging on the host computer.

1. On the guest computer, click the Start button, choose Settings, Network and Dial-up Connections, Direct Connection. There are other methods as well, but this method is the easiest to access.

2. A Connect Direct Connection dialog box appears. Type in the username, password, and Logon Domain information (see Figure 15.13). Click the Connect button.

3. The guest computer will now dial the host machine, verify that the user information is correct, and then register the guest computer on the network. Provided that no errors occur during these steps, a final message states that the guest computer has been authenticated, and then a Connection Complete Dialog Box appears (see Figure 15.19). Also, a new icon (if specified in the General tab of the Direct Connection Properties) will appear in the Taskbar tray with a bubble that displays the network speed in bits per second.

FIGURE 15.19

The Connection Complete dialog box.

At this point, the two computers are connected and can access each other's resources. If any errors occur during the connection process, see the "Troubleshooting Direct Connections" section in this chapter.

> **Note**
>
> A resource is a file (application or data), folder, or printer on a machine. Not all resources on a computer will be accessible through the Direct Connection—only those that have been shared. The "Sharing Resources" section describes how to create a share.

Accessing Resources

Once a connection has been established between the host and the guest computer, each computer can access the other's resources. There are a number of different methods for accessing resources. Some of the most common methods are discussed in the following sections.

My Network Places

Double-clicking the My Network Places icon located on the desktop displays three options: Add Network Place, Computers Near Me, and Entire Network. For Direct Connections, double-click the Computers Near Me icon. This method is not recommended because it searches for all computers that belong to the same workgroup and can take a long time to complete, or it will not complete at all and produce an error message. The connection between the two computers is fine—My Network Places is usually recommended for networks with high-speed bandwidth, not null modems with a maximum speed of 19,200 bits per second.

Universal Naming Convention

The Universal Naming Convention (UNC) can be used to locate the host computer without having to search for all computers. This method follows a specific format that searches for a computer name, a share name, and a filename. Each of these three names is separated by a blackslash (\), with two backslashes before the computer name to indicate that the UNC method is being used. The following is an example of a UNC method:

```
\\HostComputer\data\file1.doc
```

To use the Universal Naming Convention to access the other computer, click Start from the taskbar, and then choose Run. Type in two backslashes (\\) followed by the name of the other computer. Press Enter. This method locates the other computer directly without searching for all computers. If a share name and a filename are not included, Windows 2000 will return a listing of all available shares from the host computer.

Map a Drive

If the Direct Connection will be used frequently, map a drive letter to the shared resource on the other machine. Mapping a drive means assigning a letter to a shared folder that is commonly used. To map a drive, right-click My Computer or My Network Places. From the Shortcut menu, choose Map Network Drive. A Map Network Drive dialog box appears asking what letter to use and where the shared folder is located (see Figure 15.20). Type in the drive letter and UNC name for the host machine and click Finish.

Mapping network drives is a useful when one machine constantly accesses a resource on another machine. After this process has been completed, the drive letter will appear in the My Computer window along with the A and C drives. Other options in this window include connecting using a different name, which is useful to connect to a share that the Direct Connection user account does not have access to and for creating a shortcut to an FTP or WWW site.

FIGURE **15.20**

The Map Network Drive dialog box.

Sharing Resources

For another computer to allow a folder to be accessed through Direct Connection or any other network connection, the folder must first be shared. The following steps list how to share out a folder.

1. Click Start from the Taskbar, choose Programs, Accessories, Windows Explorer.

2. Expand the folders pane until the folder to be shared out is listed.

3. Right-click the folder to display the shortcut menu and choose Sharing.

4. A properties box for the folder appears with information displayed in the Sharing tab. Choose Share this Folder.

5. Type in a new share name or accept the default name (the same name as the folder). The Folder name and the Share name do not have to be the same.

6. Complete any other options such as user limit, permissions, and caching files for offline use.

7. Click OK. A hand will appear underneath the folder to indicate that the folder is now accessible to others on the network.

For more information on setting user and group permissions, see Chapter 22, "User and Groups."

Troubleshooting Direct Connections

As with most network connections, Direct Connections can be a tricky process. If an error occurs during the connection process, try the following:

15

DIRECT CABLE CONNECTIONS

- Make sure the cable is plugged in. Most network problems are caused by a physical connection, not by any software errors. Also, make sure that the cable is a null modem cable and is plugged into the appropriate port.

- Check that one computer has been set up as a host computer and the other as a guest computer.

- Are both computers using the same protocols? If so, is the protocol set up properly? The easiest way to avoid any protocol issues is to use NetBEUI on both machines. This protocol does not require any configuring and is guaranteed to work. For more information about protocols, see Chapter 21.

- Does the user on the guest machine have permission to log on to the host machine? A user account has to be created on the host machine and the user account has to be granted remote access rights. For further information about creating users, see Chapter 22. To grant a user remote access, right-click Incoming Connections and choose Properties. Select the Users tab and grant remote access to users.

- A message appears stating that a port has been disabled and therefore a connection cannot be made. Reboot the computer and try again. This happens if any other network settings have changed that require a reboot, but the computer has not been restarted.

- The connection works, but the host machine states that the user is an unauthorized user. In the Users tab for the Incoming Connections Properties dialog box, be sure that Require All Users to Secure Their Passwords and Data has been selected and that Always Allow Directly Connected Devices Such As Palmtops... is not selected.

These options should fix most Direct Connection problems. If the connection still will not work, the computer has a more serious issue not related to Direct Connections. Try the process on different computers, if any are available, or use a different null modem cable.

Summary

In circumstances where network cards are not available, Direct Connection offers a quick, inexpensive method for hooking up two computers. Direct Connections use null modems and serial ports to communicate between two computers. At times, direct cable connection can be difficult to install and connect, but following the procedures detailed in this chapter and checking the properties will eliminate most connection issues. This chapter discussed what a null modem cable does and how to use it on a Windows 2000 computer. Also, the various serial and parallel ports were examined, with steps on how to change their properties.

Setting Up Your Modem

In this chapter, you take a close look at the modem and how it works with Windows 2000 Professional. The modem has become an important tool over the last few years. The emphasis these days is on mobile users, telecommuters, and dial-up Internet users—none of which would be possible without the modem. Recently, we have seen the speed of modems rise to 56Kbps. If you are a mobile user, telecommuter, or simply a home user who dials an ISP for Internet access, you'll need to be familiar with installing, configuring, and troubleshooting your modem.

Windows 2000 Professional is, unlike previous operating systems using 2000 technology, fully Plug and Play (PnP). This should make setting up a modem as simple as just plugging it in and then starting up. Problems arise when PnP doesn't work as expected. This is usually due to the modem not being on the hardware compatibility list (HCL). Unlike most other hardware, Windows 2000 Professional seems to have special difficulty working with incompatible modems.

I had a modem that worked fine under Windows 98, Windows NT4, and even early preview releases of Windows 2000. For some reason I never determined, Windows 2000 wouldn't detect this modem. I took this as a challenge and a bit of an insult. I ended up spending a full day and a half trying to get this modem to work and never succeeded. In the end I bought a new modem for a cost, including tax, of $37.

Given the cost of hardware, I won't discourage you from fighting the setup fight, but I won't encourage you either. I'm glad I took the time to fight the modem fight, not for the try at saving $37, but for the lesson not to do it again.

Installing Your Modem

As I indicated, it's important when buying a modem to choose one that is included in the Hardware Compatibility List for Windows (HCL) or prepare for a fight. Installing your modem is done through the Phone and Modem Options applet, which is located in the Control Panel. To install a modem, follow these steps:

1. Double-click the applet, which is contained within the Control Panel (see Figure 16.1). The Control Panel can be accessed either by opening the My Computer program group or through the Start menu (that is, selecting Start, Settings, Control Panel).

FIGURE **16.1**

Accessing the applet.

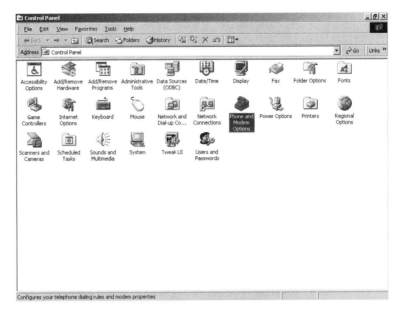

2. When you double-click the Phone and Modem Options applet, you are presented with the Phone and Modems Options dialog box (see Figure 16.2). This properties dialog box contains a large pane that lists all currently loaded modems. The Modems tab is where modem information resides. Currently, one modem appears in the list. To install a modem, click the Add button.

FIGURE **16.2**

The Modems tab of the Phone and Modem Options dialog box.

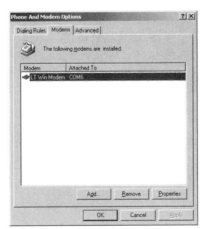

3. You are now presented with the Install New Modem Wizard (see Figure 16.3). The installation routine will attempt to detect your modem automatically unless you check the Don't detect… check box at the start of the Wizard. If this is your first time installing a new modem, let 2000 try to detect it. Only choose the manual setup (checking the box) if you're sure that Windows won't be able to "see" your modem. 2000 scans all the workstation's COM ports in turn for a modem. I prefer to manually select the modem, because I find that 2000 sometimes returns a standard modem as the result of its findings. At least when you select the modem yourself, you are forcing 2000 to install that modem. Click the Next button.

FIGURE 16.3

The Install New Modem dialog box.

4. If you choose the manual setup by checking the Don't detect… check box in the first Wizard screen and then click Next, you'll see the manual setup dialog box that lists all the modem manufacturers that 2000 supports (see Figure 16.4). Scroll down through the list of manufacturers and select the manufacturer of the modem you are about to install. When you select a manufacturer, that manufacturer's modems appear in the list on the right. Again, scroll down through the list of models and select your particular modem model. Once you have selected your manufacturer and model, click Next to continue. If you cannot find your manufacturer or model on the list, click the Have Disk button to be presented with the Install From Disk dialog box (see Figure 16.5). Enter or browse to the path of the manufacturer's distribution disk and click OK. You will now be presented with the manufacturer's list of models, as shown in Figure 16.4.

16

SETTING UP
YOUR MODEM

FIGURE 16.4

*Selecting the man-
ufacturer and
model of your
modem.*

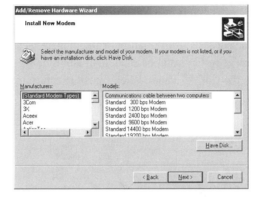

FIGURE 16.5

*The Install From
Disk dialog box.*

5. After you have selected a manufacturer and modem model, you are presented with
   the next dialog box in the setup (see Figure 16.6). On the top of the dialog box is
   the name of the modem you chose in the previous step. You must now select the
   COM port to which the modem is attached. Choose the Selected Ports radio button
   and highlight the COM port to which the modem is connected.

FIGURE 16.6

*Selecting a COM
port.*

6. After you have selected the correct COM port, click Next. 2000 now installs your selected modem on your chosen COM port. The final dialog box in the setup routine informs you of the successful installation of the modem (see Figure 16.7). You can change the properties of the installed modem at any time by selecting the Modem applet within the Control Panel. Click Finish to return to the Modems Properties dialog box.

FIGURE 16.7

Confirmation of a successful installation.

7. You can now see your newly installed modem listed in the Modems Properties dialog box (see Figure 16.8) as well as the COM port to which it is attached.

FIGURE 16.8

The newly installed modem.

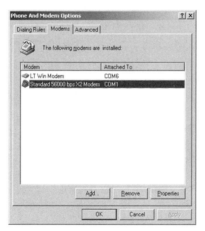

Configuring Your Modem

Sometimes when you install a modem, the COM port that the modem is attached to is also changed to reflect the speed of the modem. To confirm whether the COM port is set correctly for your modem, also use the Phones and Modems Options applet within the

Control Panel. Launch the applet, click the Modems tab and then the Properties button or double-click the modem for which you want to configure the port. You will be presented with a dialog box similar to the one shown in Figure 16.9.

FIGURE **16.9**

The Modem Properties dialog box.

You can also access port configuration information through the Device Manager. To see this, launch the System applet from the Control Panel, click the Hardware tab, and then click the Device Manager button. Locate the port you want to check the properties on in the resulting list and either double-click it or click it and choose Properties. Figure 16.10 shows the resulting dialog box for one port.

FIGURE **16.10**

Port settings from within Device Manager.

General

The dialog box accessed through the Phones and Modems Options dialog box
(Figure 16.9) has three tabs. The first of these tabs is the General tab; it is usually the
selected tab by default. Figure 16.11 shows you an example of the General tab with the
Maximum Port Speed combo box pulled down. The tab confirms the name of the modem
and the COM port to which it is attached. You can configure the volume of the modem
by positioning the speaker volume slider. You can also set the maximum speed of the
modem by choosing its speed from the Maximum Port Speed drop-down list located at
the bottom of the tab.

FIGURE 16.11

*The General tab
of the Modems
Properties dialog
box.*

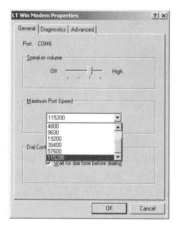

Connection

The next tab in the Modems Properties dialog box is the Diagnostics tab (see
Figure 16.12). You can use this tab to make sure your modem is talking to the system.
This diagnostic won't check the quality of your phone line.

To check out the modem, click the Query Modem button. Windows 2000 will try to communicate (query) the modem, expecting certain replies.

The results of the modem query/reply is reflected in the dialog box. If the system can't
find or query the modem, a failure dialog box will appear.

Advanced Tab

Click the Advanced tab to configure advanced connection settings, such as modem initialization strings. If your modem doesn't seem to be working right at startup, consult
your modem manual and see if you can address this using a different setup string.
Figure 16.13 is the Advanced tab of the Modem Properties dialog box.

FIGURE **16.12**

The Diagnostics tab of the Properties dialog box.

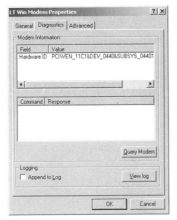

FIGURE **16.13**

The Advanced tab of the Properties dialog box.

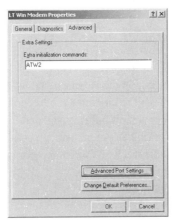

This dialog box allows you to drill further down to configure advanced options, such as port buffers, by choosing the Advanced Port Settings button. If you suspect that you're dropping bytes during your modem connection, you might try to increase or decrease the buffer size. After clicking the Advanced Port Settings button, you'll see a dialog box with two slider controls. This is how you configure your port buffers. Slide left for safety, or slide right for speed.

Change Default Preferences

The Change Default Preferences button on the Advanced tab will allow you to change rather esoteric settings such as hardware or software flow control and whether data stream compression is enabled or disabled. These options are best left at defaults for the vast majority of computers. In some cases, you'll need to change these settings if advised to by the modem vendor, but this is rare. Figure 16.14 shows the Change Default Preferences dialog box.

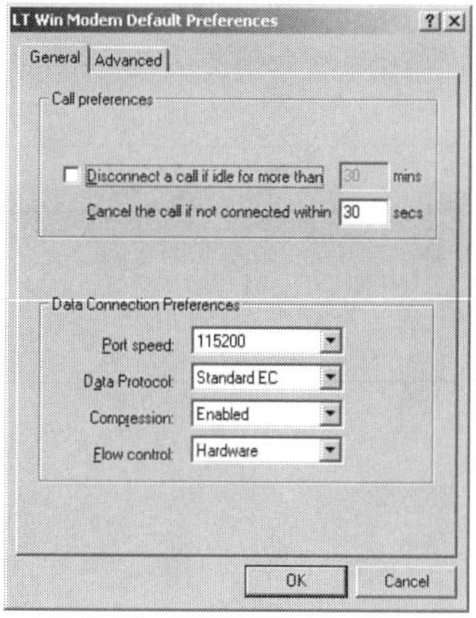

FIGURE **16.14**

Here is where you can change port default settings.

There is an important and little known setting on the Advanced tab of the dialog box shown in Figure 16.14—the option to change the modem's modulation. Certain HST and Bell modems won't work properly with the default industry standard modulation. If you have one of these modems and it's not working as you expect, give the modulation scheme option a try. Figure 16.15 shows this tab with the combo box pulled down.

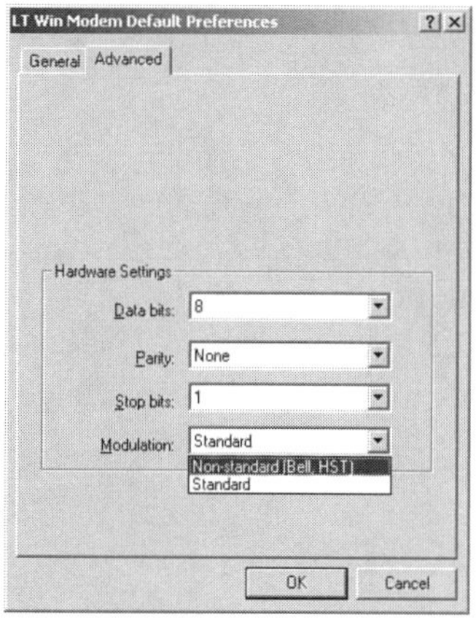

FIGURE **16.15**

Here is where you can change your modem's modulation scheme.

Dialing Properties

Previous versions of Windows had their dialing properties located within the modem configuration. Windows 2000 Professional is a departure from those versions. Instead, it has them placed in the new and, to my way of thinking more logical, location within Network Connections. This also is an applet in Control Panel. Once you've created a DUN (dial-up networking) connection, you can adjust its properties though the Control Panel. See Chapter 17, "Setting Up TCP/IP Protocol Access," for more information on this technology.

To access these properties, open the Network and Dial-up Connections applet in Control Panel, right-click the connection you want to edit or examine, and choose Properties. Figure 16.16 shows the resulting dialog box.

FIGURE 16.16

The Properties dialog box for a dial-up connection.

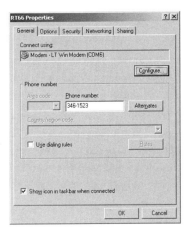

If you click the Configure button, you'll get yet another version of the modem properties. All the properties in Configure exist in the Phones and Modems Options applet, but in slightly different formats. The existence of the Configure button here is a convenience so you can tweak the modem settings without opening another Control Panel applet.

The Options tab is probably the most useful of the tabs in this dialog box. Figure 16.17 shows this tab.

FIGURE 16.17

The Options tab is arguably the most useful tab of this dialog box.

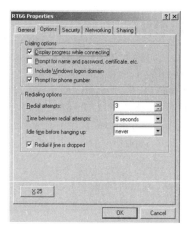

The following is a list of the options and what they do.

- *Display progress while dialing*—This controls whether Windows 2000 DUN will show you the stages of logging on to a server. Useful for figuring out just where a logon problem is when it occurs. Most people leave this checked on the theory of keeping an eye on what their computer is doing.

- *Prompt for name and password, certificate, etc.*—Forces request for interactive security information. Useful for several online accounts where there is one Windows 2000 logon but several DUN logon accounts. That is, several people or identities log on to Windows 2000 as the same user, but want to access individual accounts. When in doubt, leave it out.

- *Include Windows logon domain*—Requires manual prompt (immediately previous) option. This adds Windows domain information to the interactive security information asked for by the prompt for name and password, certificate, and so on options.

- *Prompt for phone numbers*—Allows you to enter and choose several phone numbers for any DUN account. I use this extensively because my ISP is unreliable at high speed. When I have problems accessing it, I tell Windows 2000 to use the lower speed access number. If left unchecked and you put in several phone numbers for a DUN account, Windows 2000 will use them serially.

- *Redialing options*—These are self evident with no subtleties or surprises.

- *X.25*—A button allowing you to configure X.25. This is a set of standards for doing an end run around POTS (plain old telephone service) using a packet switching network. The purpose of X.25 is to find higher quality connections than POTS. You will need access to the network and have an X.25 adapter to use this standard.

I suggest to my clients that they check the Display Progress While Dialing check box. The default is to not show progress, which makes the process of dialing up a blind one. If you have more than one connection number, having 2000 show a choice of telephone numbers is almost mandatory. I have several dial-up connections that have a fast connection number and a slow, but more reliable one. During bad connection times (like when it rains, which knocks out my local phone system) I jump to the slow connection number, because experience has shown me that it's just a waste of time to try the fast line.

The Security tab is one that you may need to adjust for your users who dial into your company from the field.

Internet Connection Sharing is an intriguing feature partly enacted first in Windows 98SE during 1999. This will allow connecting through a LAN to use a dial-up connection on a modem-equipped computer. That is a workstation with a modem and a dial-up account that can share those resources with any other computers on the LAN (local area network). Figure 16.18 shows the tab allowing the enabling of this feature as well as the Settings dialog box accessed by the Settings button.

FIGURE 16.18

Internet Connection Sharing enables DUN/RAS resource sharing on a LAN.

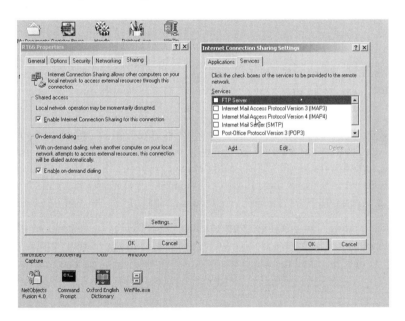

The settings in the dialog boxes shown in Figure 16.18 are somewhat esoteric. The proper entries depend heavily on your network specifics and sharing needs. If you're setting this up and have any questions about what's needed here, consult with your Internet system administrator or specialist.

A critical dialog box, but one that's usually done properly by default, is on the Networking tab. Here is where you tell Windows 2000 Professional what protocols to use when connecting using a dial-up account. Having unnecessary protocols will increase the time it takes to connect and will often generate spurious error messages or even prevent such a connection from occurring. Figure 16.19 shows this tab.

FIGURE 16.19

It is critical to only have DUN try to connect using the minimally required protocols.

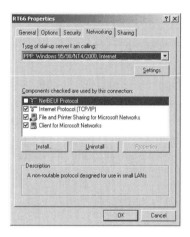

The dialog box in Figure 16.19 shows the NetBEUI protocol left unchecked because it's unnecessary for this Internet connection. The reason the protocol appears at all is because this computer participates on a LAN that uses NetBEUI as well as TCP/IP.

If the NetBEUI protocol were checked here, this dial-up connection would attempt a connection to the Internet using not only TCP/IP, but also NetBEUI. As that wouldn't be compatible (or sensible), it would delay or prevent a dial-up connection from occurring. Figure 16.20 shows the pull-down or combo box for type of server. Today most dial-up servers are PPP, but the previously dominant SLIP is still seen in some cases.

The Settings button on the Networking tab configures the settings for the server type protocol. If you're having trouble with connections to an Internet Service Provider (ISP), you may be asked to change one or more of these settings. They are

- *Enable LCP extensions*—Settings for various technical settings in a link such as frame size.

- *Enable Software Compression*—By compressing data you can send it more quickly (because it's smaller) than your connect speed would normally allow. Some modems (matched at both ends) handle this better between themselves than using the software method here. If you use this, uncheck the box telling your modem to use hardware compression (if it's an option). You can't compress already compressed data. Trying to do so only slows things down.

FIGURE 16.20

Dial-up networking will default to the common PPP (Point to Point Protocol), but SLIP is an option.

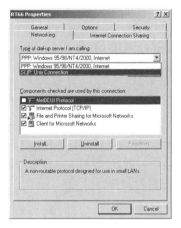

- *Negotiate Multilink for Single link connections*—If available, use two channels at the same time for data exchange. This is enabled by default if you have the relevant connection type (such as ISDN).

Having to change these settings is rare. I include the list only to show you where they are in case your ISP suggests adjusting them.

If you have a need to install a new protocol for a dial-up connection, you can do so by clicking the Install button. Do not install any unneeded protocols. For example, if you needed to log on to a NetWare-only server, you'd remove the TCP/IP protocol and add a NetWare (NWLink) protocol. You'd also need to install a NetWare client.

Note

The chief reason for long dial-up logons or failed connections is the existence of unnecessary installed protocols. Remember: You don't need all protocols for all connections. For example, many folks are on a NetBEUI LAN and a TCP/IP dial up. The dial up doesn't need (and can't use) the NetBEUI protocol—it will only cause delays and trouble. Similarly, the LAN can't use TCP/IP, and its existence is superfluous.

ISDN and Beyond

Integrated Services Digital Network, or ISDN, is a set of standards for Dial-up Networking that's roughly 20 years old at this point. While once its 64Kbps per channel speed was blinding, today it's not all that special. Still ISDN allows a faster connection speed than any standard POTS (Plain Old Telephone Service) modem connection. Using two channels, its speed of 128Kbps is remarkably faster than POTS. ISDN connections also offer a much faster connect to server time than a POTS modem. For most people, there is no real time (perceived) difference between the ISDN connect time and instantaneous—it's like having a connection on demand or being online always. The sense is the same as being connected constantly as through a gateway on a LAN.

ISDN connections have properties accessed the same as standard modem networking. To set up a new ISDN account, double-click the Make a New Connection in the Control Panel's Network Connections applet, and then choose the first or second option in the resulting dialog box, depending on if you want to connect to a private server or the Internet.

Figure 16.21 shows the Network Connection Wizard dialog box.

FIGURE 16.21

ISDN is a private network, even if it uses a public service provider.

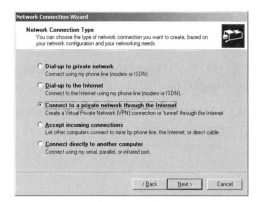

There is a host of other proprietary networking, some of which use modems or modem-like devices, such as a satellite connection. The variety of these connection devices is wide and varies almost daily. Each of these connections requires specialized setup, and many don't work very well. I've wasted many hours trying two different satellite dish schemes only to give up on them, not only for the new Windows 2000, but the supposedly established Windows 98 and 95.

My only advice to you here is that if you try one of these new schemes and have trouble, the problem might not be solvable. Someday this will be as simple as setting up a printer is today, but that day isn't here yet (as of this writing).

Summary

In this chapter, you explored the installation and configuration of a modem under Windows 2000. You also stepped through the configuration of the modem, drilling down to the level of error control and flow control settings. In each country, dialing properties are different. To meet these differences, 2000 allows you to create and call up dialing location settings that suit your present location.

Setting Up TCP/IP Protocol Access

IN THIS CHAPTER

CHAPTER 17

In the 1960s, the U.S. Department of Defense and a group of educational institutions formalized a set of standards that would enable various types of computers to communicate with each other. Transmission Control Protocol/Internet Protocol (TCP/IP) is the result of this development, and, due to the exploding popularity of the Internet, TCP/IP has grown to become the world's most-used protocol. No specific company owns the TCP/IP protocol; rather, the Internet community as a whole governs it. Although Microsoft implemented the protocol in earlier operating systems, their entrance into the TCP/IP forum began with a completely rewritten TCP/IP stack for its Windows NT 3.5 operating system in 1993. Since that release, each new operating system continues to advance this protocol. Windows 2000 is no different, with many new features and services designed to improve performance, reliability, and administration.

This chapter examines the substance behind the acronym by describing the TCP/IP layering process for communication and defines IP Address properties. Lastly, this chapter points out some important troubleshooting tools. For details on the steps for TCP/IP installation, refer to Chapter 21, "Windows 2000 Networking Protocols."

Protocol Layering

To make a network administrator's eyes roll around, ask him or her to describe the OSI model, giving examples of what devices act at what level. Developed by the International Standards Organization (ISO), the Open Systems Interconnection (OSI) model is a protocol-layering model that serves as an outline for communicating between devices. As data is sent from the source computer, each layer in the OSI model adds its own header information that describes the operation performed at that layer. The destination computer strips off this information at each layer that is used to reassemble and decipher the data sent. The OSI model is a conceptual model only, and, as with most protocols, the TCP/IP protocol does not map directly to each layer (see Figure 17.1). However, the functionality of the OSI model is the same in the TCP/IP model.

FIGURE 17.1

The OSI and the TCP/IP models.

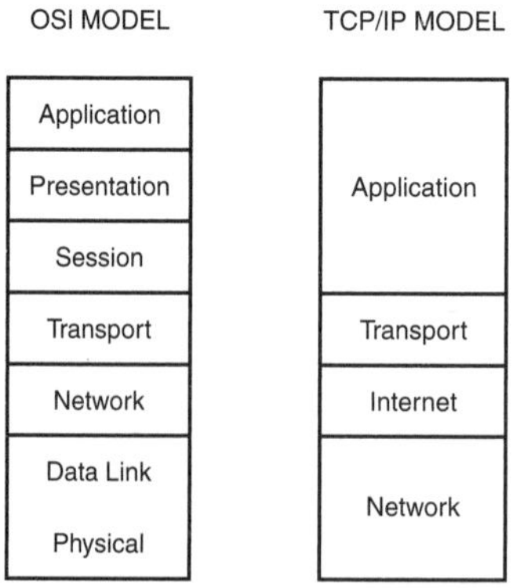

OSI MODEL

| Application |
| Presentation |
| Session |
| Transport |
| Network |
| Data Link |
| Physical |

TCP/IP MODEL

| Application |
| Transport |
| Internet |
| Network |

TCP/IP is not one protocol, but a number of protocols *stacked* one on top of another—each with a defined purpose. The Internet community supports these protocols through RFCs (Request for Comments), which are series of proposals, recommendations, and standards for protocols and services. Table 17.1 lists some of the common RFCs supported by Windows 2000.

TABLE 17.1 Common Request for Comments supported by Windows 2000

RFC	Title
768	Users Datagram Protocol (UDP)
791	Internet Protocol (IP)
792	Internet Control Message Protocol (ICMP)
793	Transmission Control Protocol (TCP)
826	Address Resolution Protocol (ARP)
894	IP over Ethernet
959	File Transfer Protocol (FTP)
1001,1002	NetBIOS Service Protocols
1034, 1035	Domain Name System (DNS)
1112	Internet Group Management Protocol (IGMP)
1541	Dynamic Host Configuration Protocol (DHCP)

17

SETTING UP TCP/IP PROTOCOL ACCESS

The TCP/IP model (also referred to as the Department of Defense model) has four layers. The following section describes each layer in turn, pointing out any new additions incorporated into Windows 2000.

Application Layer

The highest layer in the TCP/IP protocol stack has many different functions, but its primary responsibility is to define how an application communicates with another application through a network using TCP/IP. This definition includes what method the application should use to communicate using TCP/IP and what services are required to share resources on the sending computer and to access resources on the destination computer. The Application Layer compiles this information and provides it to the next layer in the TCP/IP protocol stack, the Transport Layer.

> **Note**
>
> For this chapter, an application is a type of program that can interact with other programs that reside on other computers in a network. This type of application is commonly referred to as a *distributed application*.

Think of the following example to better understand the purpose of the Application Layer. You want to send information to a friend who lives a long distance away. What method should you choose to send this information? What services are available to you and your friend? You may decide to call on a telephone and tell her this information, or you may decide to send a letter through regular mail. These examples are two different methods for transmitting information. Before using these methods, you must be certain that the services (telephones or mail) are available to you and your friend. Applications function in the same manner. They have a way that they send information to another application through a network. Using TCP/IP, two main methods implemented in Windows 2000 are Windows Sockets and NetBIOS over TCP/IP. Which method is used depends on the application itself. Figure 17.2 illustrates the two application interface methods.

FIGURE 17.2

A model of Windows Sockets and NetBIOS over TCP/IP.

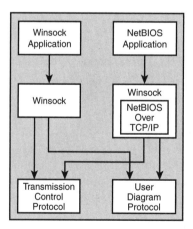

> **Tip**
>
> A *service* is a routine, process, or program that carries out a specific system task. Services are used to support programs installed on top of Windows 2000 or to execute a function in Windows 2000 programs. Two examples of services are the MS SQLServer Service, which supports MS SQL installed on a Windows 2000 machine, and the Event Log Service, which supports a built-in Windows 2000 program called Event Viewer. Services are run at a low level, meaning they interact closely with the hardware.

Windows Sockets

Windows Sockets (Winsock) are used by applications to establish connection points on the two communicating machines that create a bi-directional communication path for sending and receiving data. Each connection point is called a socket, and, for the TCP/IP protocol, is comprised of an Internet address and a port number. Winsock applications can connect using two different types of sockets: stream sockets, which use TCP as a transport protocol, and datagram sockets, which use UDP as the transport protocol. Further information regarding the two types of sockets and the transport protocol can be found in the "Transport Protocols" section of this chapter. Regardless of the type of socket used by an application, WinSock's primary advantage over the other application interface, NetBIOS over TCP/IP, is that the communicating computers can send packets directly to each other through this bi-directional path, which saves time and bandwidth.

> **Note**
>
> Examples of Winsock applications are Internet Explorer, FTP programs, Microsoft Outlook, DNS, and SNMP programs.

An Internet address (IP address) is a unique 32-bit address that identifies a computer on the network. IP addresses are discussed in greater detail in the "Internet Addresses, Subnet Masks, and Default Gateways" section later in this chapter. Port numbers are logical connection points used to distinguish different services and protocols on computers. For example, services will wait and listen for traffic on certain port numbers. The WWW Publishing service, a service for a Web server program, will wait for communication on port 80. The MSSQLService, a service for the MS SQL database program, will wait for traffic on port 1433. Applications that want to communicate with these services can direct information to these particular ports.

> **Note**
>
> For Windows Sockets, think of having a phone in your house, and each room has a phone jack. You want to make a call from your kitchen to discuss a recipe with a friend. What do you need before you make this telephone call? You need the telephone number and a wall jack in the kitchen. Once you plug in the phone and dial the number, you can make a connection to your friend's phone. In this case, the telephone is the IP address, the wall jack is the port number and the connection is the socket. Also, the phone is in the kitchen, which provides a particular service (making dinner) that is different than a phone located in the garage (fixing your car). Port numbers define which program (and its supported service) is communicating with another.

Windows Sockets is an industry standard application programming interface (API). When called by a service or an application, it will perform a set of routines that define how and where to send data. To summarize this process, Winsock performs the following to establish communication between two machines.

1. Services register port numbers with Winsock. By registering, the service can wait and listen for any communication being sent to the port. Through registering, Winsock is aware of the protocol, IP address, and port number necessary to communicate with the service.

2. On other computers, applications provide the protocol, IP address, and port number required to establish the socket connection to Winsock. Unlike services, applications do not register specific port numbers; instead they select any free port number higher than 1024.

3. Winsock determines what type of socket connection is being made, a stream socket or datagram socket, and creates a socket connection.

4. Winsock passes information about the socket connection to the underlying layers, which establishes a connection between the two computers.

5. On the receiving computer, information is sent up through the TCP/IP layers to the service's port number. Winsock provides the service with the socket number (containing the IP address and port number) of the sending computer's application.

6. Both computers use the open sockets to pass data back and forth.

> **Note**
>
> Application programming interfaces and services are often described as running at different levels. These levels are determined by how closely they interact with the operating system and hardware. Programs and their supported services that are installed as a part of Windows 2000, such as DNS (described later in the "DNS" section later in this section), function at a lower level than other programs that are installed on top of Windows 2000. Internet Explorer's API (WinInet) is an example of a higher-level application programming interface. The level of an API does not determine whether it uses Windows Sockets or not. This is determined when the program is written.

Windows sockets use IP addresses and port numbers to send information to another computer. However, applications often send information using a hostname, which is a user-friendly name for a computer. People type a fully qualified domain name (FQDN), such as www.microsoft.com (www is the hostname of a computer on the microsoft.com domain), on the Internet to send and receive information. Therefore, the application layer is also responsible for translating these hostnames into IP addresses, so that the lower layers can send the data properly. This application layer function is called *hostname resolution*.

Hostname Resolution

TCP/IP assigns each computer a unique, hierarchical name that allows users to identify the computer on the network. An email server's IP address is not commonly known to users; however, they may know that email is sent through a computer called mail.abccompany.com. As mentioned in the preceding paragraph, this computer has a hostname (mail) and a domain name (abccompany.com). This means that the email server has a unique name called mail that it is referred to on a network. The Windows Sockets API runs a routine called the gethostname or gethostbyaddr function (which function is used depends on the application) that resolves this hostname into an IP address, which then allows WinSock to open a socket for communication. To resolve the hostname into an IP address, the function will check in a text file called hosts, then, if no hostname resolution is found, query a Domain Name Service (DNS). If the hostname cannot be resolved using these two methods, this function will try the NetBIOS name resolution methods. Hosts and DNS are discussed in the next two sections respectively, and NetBIOS is discussed in the "NETBIOS over TCP/IP" section later in this chapter.

Hosts File

A HOSTS file is a simple text file that contains a list of IP addresses and the associated hostname or fully qualified domain name. Hostnames can be up to 255 characters in length and do not have to be the same as the computer name. Because a computer can serve in more than one capacity on the network, an IP address can have more than one associated hostname listed in the HOSTS file. For example, a computer can function as a Web server and require a hostname of WWW and function as an FTP server requiring a name of FTP. Both WWW and FTP can be placed as hostnames next to the same IP address in a host file. Figure 17.3 displays a common host file.

FIGURE 17.3

An example of a HOSTS *file.*

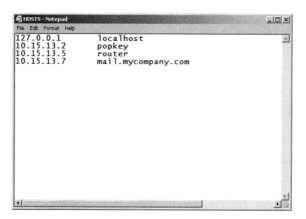

> ### Tip
>
> A common oversight is to name the HOSTS file `hosts.txt`. A HOSTS file will not work if it has any file extension. The HOSTS file is located in the following path: `\systemroot\system32\drivers\etc`.

Windows Socketswill first attempt to resolve a hostname into an IP address using the HOSTS file. If not successful, it will then query a Domain Name System (DNS) server.

DNS

DNS is a fundamental part of Windows 2000 and its Active Directory Services (ADS). ADS is the directory services database for Windows 2000 that stores information about network objects (such as users, groups, organizational units, and computers), provides a single login process for users, and controls their access permissions for resources.

A DNS server can be configured to replicate its database containing hostnames, FQDNs, and IP address into the ADS database.

A Domain Name System server contains a database of hostnames or fully qualified domain names (FQDNs) and their IP addresses. Winsock queries a DNS server with a hostname or a FQDN, and asks DNS to convert the hostname or FQDN into an IP address in a process called *forward lookup*. If the DNS server does not contain an entry for a fully qualified domain name, it can forward the query to other DNS servers to resolve into an IP address in a process called a *recursive forward lookup*. Also, a DNS server can be queried to perform a *reverse lookup*, which will convert an IP address into a hostname. Reverse lookup queries are often used to negate any security breaches caused by a computer impersonating another computer by using its IP address. Using reverse lookup queries will ensure that the proper hostname is using the IP address. Figure 17.4 demonstrates a common DNS server.

17

SETTING UP TCP/IP PROTOCOL ACCESS

FIGURE 17.4

A Windows 2000 DNS Server.

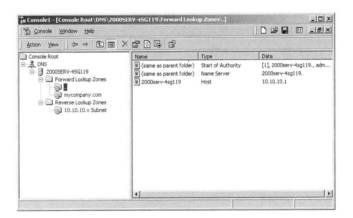

Dynamic DNS and DHCP

In Windows 2000, a DNS server can be dynamically updated through Dynamic Host Configuration Protocol (DHCP). A DHCP server manages IP address settings for DHCP clients. When a DHCP client computer boots on to the network, it sends a broadcast asking for an IP address from a DHCP server. The DHCP server can "lease" an IP address to the client and provide other information such as a subnet mask, a default gateway's IP address, and a DNS server's IP address. A *lease* is an IP address that has been given to a DHCP client for a limited time, with three days as the default time. Using DHCP servers, all IP information can be centrally managed and dynamically distributed for clients on the network.

> **Note**
>
> A DHCP client is any computer configured to request IP address information from a DHCP server. Windows 95, 98, NT and 2000 computers can all act as DHCP clients.

DHCP can be used to update hostname information in a DNS server. The following steps illustrate how this process works.

1. A DHCP client sends a broadcast called a DHCPDISCOVER message requesting an IP address from a DHCP server.

2. Each DHCP server that receives the DHCPDISCOVER will respond to the client with a DHCPOFFER message, offering an IP address to the DHCP client.

3. The DHCP client responds to the DHCPOFFER message (usually the first one it receives), and sends a DHCPREQUEST message requesting the offered IP address.

4. The DHCP server sends a final DHCPACK message to the DHCP client, which contains the IP address, subnet mask, lease duration, and other DHCP options such as default gateway IP address and the DNS server's IP address.

5. The DHCP client is now responsible for registering its fully qualified domain name. The next time the DHCP client contacts the DHCP server, it requests that the DHCP server register the client's FQDN with a DNS server.

6. The DHCP server sends the client's FQDN to the DNS server, and a host record (referred to as a *record*) is registered in the DNS database. The host record contains the DHCP client's FQDN and IP address.

7. Included with the host record registration is a request for the DNS server to register a reverse record on the client's behalf. The reverse record is referred to as a *PTR record*. This reverse record will allow reverse lookup queries to be performed.

8. Any changes or renewals to the client's IP address information will cause a new registration to be sent to the DNS server.

> **Note**
>
> A DNS server and DHCP server can only be installed on Windows 2000 Server.

For dynamic DNS updates, the DHCP server must have the Enable Dynamic Update of DNS Client Information option selected (see Figure 17.5).

FIGURE 17.5

*DHCP Properties
Dynamic DNS tab.*

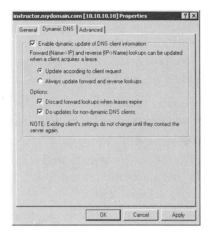

DNS Resolver Cache Service

Another feature on Windows 2000 is the DNS resolver cache service. When a Windows 2000 Professional computer queries a DNS server to resolve a fully-qualified domain name into an IP address, the computer stores the result locally in DNS cache. The query result includes a Time to Live (TTL) that specifies how long the entry will be saved locally in cache. Any future queries by the Windows 2000 Professional computer do not need to contact the DNS server, thereby reducing traffic on the network. The DNS cache service will also store negative responses from queries that responded back with no IP address for the given hostname, or from queries that do not receive any response at all; thus, future time-outs will be avoided for negative responses. The DNS caching feature runs as a service on Windows 2000 Professional and can be started, paused, and stopped like any other service. Figure 17.6 illustrates the DNS cache service.

FIGURE 17.6

*DNS cache
service.*

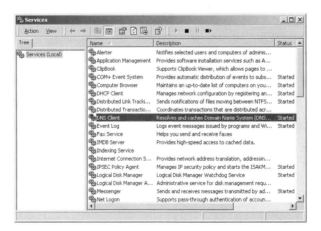

NetBIOS over TCP/IP

The term NetBIOS over TCP/IP (NetBT) is the union of two separate functions—NetBIOS and TCP/IP. NetBIOS is not a protocol; rather, it is an broadcast-based application interface that provides three functions to Windows:

- *Name Management*—For applications to communicate with services, each computer requires a NetBIOS name (computer name). NetBIOS names give an identity to each machine for data transfers
- *Data Transfer*—NetBIOS uses a transport protocol to send and receive data. The transport protocol must handle connection-oriented protocol, meaning the transport protocol must be able to guarantee delivery of data.
- *Session Management*—Two communicating computers must establish a session to stipulate the conditions for connection-oriented data transfers.

NetBIOS natively uses the NetBEUI protocol to transport data. TCP/IP can handle NetBIOS data transfers using the TCP and UDP transport protocols (discussed in the "Transport Layer" section of this chapter). Also the TCP protocol can establish and manage NetBIOS sessions. However, TCP/IP did not have a method for interpreting NetBIOS names. Many Windows networking services, such as the Server and NetLogon services (see Chapter 21, "Windows 2000 Networking Protocols," for details on these services) function using NetBIOS names. Microsoft resolved this incompatibility by forming NetBIOS over TCP/IP (NetBT).

The Client for Microsoft Networks component is the equivalent of the Workstation service in Windows NT 4.0.

NetBT handles name management by registering NetBIOS names through ports 137, 138, and 139. For example, when a computer with a NetBIOS name of Popkey1 boots, NetBT registers this name by placing a broadcast through port 137. All other NetBIOS systems will know that Popkey1 can be accessed through this port. When the computer is shut down, another broadcast releases this name, allowing other computers to use this name if they choose.

NetBT must have a method for handing information to the underlying layers. A NetBIOS application uses NetBT to transmit information, and NetBT uses a Transport Driver Interface (TDI) to transfer information to the Transport Layer. TDI is a primitive conduit that acts as a bridge between the NetBT client (the NetBIOS application) and the Transport Layer. TDI is also used by Windows Sockets.

> **Note**
>
> The Workstation and Server Service allow computers to send information (Workstation Service) to the network and receive information (Server Service) from the network. Although these services are NetBT clients, they do not utilize NetBT; instead they communicate directly with TDI. TDI is a kernel mode function, meaning it interacts directly with the operating system with a higher priority level. Interacting directing with TDI increases speed for these services.

NetBIOS Resolution

NetBIOS names can be 16 characters in length. The first 15 characters can be used for the computer name, while the 16th character is reserved to specify which service on the machine is transmitting information. For example, the 16th character for the Messenger server (a service that sends and receives messages) is the hexadecimal number 03. Before NetBT can send information to the Transport Layer, it must resolve the NetBIOS names of the receiving computer into an IP address. NetBT uses many different methods to resolve a NetBIOS name into an IP address. These methods are as follows:

- *NetBIOS Name Cache*—When a NetBIOS name is resolved into an IP address, the information is held in cache for two minutes. If the name is used within the two minutes, it will be held in cache for ten minutes.

- *Windows Internet Name Server (WINS)*—An additional service installed on Windows 2000 Server that dynamically records all NetBIOS names. WINS clients can communicate directly with a WINS Server to resolve these names into IP addresses. A WINS Server is primarily used for backwards compatibility.

- *Broadcast*—NetBIOS's design was based on broadcasts, which is its fundamental limitation in that broadcasts will not pass through a router and increase network traffic. If a WINS server does not resolve a NetBIOS name into an IP address, NetBT will send a broadcast asking the receiving computer to broadcast back the IP address.

- LMHOSTS *file*—Similar to the HOSTS file, a LMHOSTS file is a text file that lists IP addresses and their NetBIOS names. By placing a #PRE at the end of an entry, the name and IP address can be permanently placed in the NetBIOS Name Cache. The LMHOSTS file is located in the \\systemroot\system32\drivers\etc path and cannot have a filename extension.

- HOSTS *file*—If enabled, NetBT will attempt to resolve a NetBIOS name into an IP address. The EnableDns registry parameter enables the HOSTS file. This parameter can be added in the following registry key: HKEYLOCALMACHINE\SYSTEM\CurrentControoSet\Services\NetBT\Parameters.

- *DNS*—If enabled, NetBT will also query a DNS Server to resolve NetBIOS names into IP addresses. The EnableDns registry parameter must be added to use this method.

NetBIOS in Windows 2000

The line between host applications and NetBIOS applications becomes murky in Windows 2000. New features include connecting to other TCP/IP devices using FQDNs from NetBIOS commands. For instance, the net use command maps a drive letter to a shared resource on another machine. Drive letters can now be mapped to FQDNs. For example,

- net use x: \\www.microsoft.com\windows2000

- net use v: \\10.16.0.10\home

Other commands, such as dir, net view, and many administrative programs can also use fully qualified domain names.

In addition, a new Windows 2000 feature is direct hosting, which allows applications that previously used NetBIOS broadcasts to instead communicate directly to each other, similar to the Windows Sockets method. Direct hosting uses DNS for name resolution instead of broadcasting, which simplifies the protocol and allows more bandwidth for other applications. However, direct hosting only works when communicating with other Windows 2000 operating systems. For communicating with previous operating systems, such as Windows NT 4 or Windows 98, broadcasts or WINS will be used for resolving NetBIOS broadcasts.

If an administrator does not want to use NetBIOS, it can be disabled completely using the Network Connections dialog box.

Transport Layer

The Transport Layer is responsible for data delivery and for establishing a connection between the two computers. The Application Layer passes down information in a data segment to the Transport Layer. The Transport Layer adds header information to the data segment that includes which protocol is being used, TCP or UDP, and the sending and receiving computer's IP address. TCP headers will include additional information because of the nature of the protocol. The TCP/IP Transport Layer can use TCP or UDP, both of which are discussed in the following sections.

Transmission Control Protocol (TCP)

Transmission Control Protocol (TCP) is a connection-oriented protocol that guarantees reliable delivery of data by using acknowledgements and checksums. A *connection-oriented protocol* is a protocol that must establish a connection and formalize the communication process before any data can be sent. TCP uses byte-streaming, which means that data is sent in a stream of bytes, sections at a time, without considering any boundaries for the data. Computers are able to manage a continuous byte stream using sequence numbers. TCP headers are attached to the data being sent that include sequence numbers and other fields that ensure reliable data delivery. TCP headers determine how the sending computer sends information and how it expects to receive information. Some key fields included in the TCP header are as follows:

- *Source Port*—The port number of the sending computer.
- *Destination Port*—The port number of the destination computer.
- *Sequence number*—The sequence number for the first byte of data in the TCP segment. TCP segments are determined by the window size.
- *Acknowledgement number*—The sequence number the source computer expects to receive from the destination computer.
- *Control Bits*—Pointer flags used for special data being sent. An example of a control flag is a FIN pointer that indicates that no more data is being sent and the connection is closed.
- *Window*—The number of bytes the computer can receive (buffer) at one time. This field specifies the TCP receive windows size, which is discussed in greater detail in the "TCP Sliding Windows" section of this chapter.
- *Checksum*—An error control checksum number that verifies the integrity of the data sent is intact.

Before data is sent between the source and destination computer, they must first establish a connection through the three-way handshake process.

TCP Three-Way Handshake

The three-way handshake process synchronizes the sequence and acknowledgement numbers for the two computers and specifies the windows size for each computer. This process has three steps:

1. The source computer sends a TCP segment, which includes the beginning sequence number and a TCP receive window size.

2. The destination computer returns a TCP segment that includes its beginning sequence number and TCP receive window size and an acknowledgement of the source computer's TCP segment.

3. The source computer sends a TCP segment that acknowledges the destination computer's sequence number.

Using this process, each computer now knows the sequence number and window size of the other computer. A similar process will close the connection.

TCP Sliding Windows

Each computer has a TCP send and receive window size. During the three-way handshake process, each computer specifies the TCP receive window size, which indicates how many bytes the computer can receive at one time. For example, the source computer may send a window size of 16KB, stating it can only receive 16 kilobytes at one time. The destination computer will set its TCP send window size to 16KB. Therefore, the destination computer will not send more bytes than the source computer can handle. This process is necessary because computers participate on various types of networks on the Internet, and each network can have a different window size. The TCP receive window size is automatically configured by Windows 2000 and should not require any changes. The size is displayed in the registry `HKEYLOCALMACHINE\SYSTEM\CurrentControlSet\Services\Tcpip\Parameters\(Interface)\TcpWindowSize` parameter.

Earlier operating systems were limited to a maximum of 64KB. However, Windows 2000 can support a TCP receive window size of up to 1GB using scaling windows. During the handshake process, TCP can use the `SYN` control flag to indicate it supports scaling windows and specify how much to scale. Scaling uses a logarithmic formula to scale up the regular receive windows size to a new size. Both computers must be able to support windows scaling, which is very useful in high-bandwidth environments. For further information on windows scaling, refer to Request for Comments (RFC) 1323.

Once the source computer knows the TCP receive window size of the destination computer, it sets its own TCP send window size to the same amount of bytes. The source computer will only send out that amount of bytes and then wait for an acknowledgement from the destination computer. If the destination computer does not send an acknowledgement within a specified acknowledgement time, the source computer resends the bytes. When the source computer receives an acknowledgement, it *slides* the TCP send window up to the next data that is to be sent.

Many things can happen to data sent between two computers. It can be lost, broken up into smaller segments, or arrive on the destination computer out of order. If the destination computer only receives some of the bytes sent, it will place a delayed-acknowledgement timer on the remaining bytes. If the remaining bytes are not received within that time, the destination computer sends acknowledgements for the bytes it did receive, and the source computer will re-send the missing bytes. To reduce the amount of network traffic, if data is sent and received properly between the source and destination computer, acknowledgments are now returned on every other data segment. Windows 2000 also supports Selective Acknowledgements (SACK), which are useful for large window sizes. SACKs can acknowledge not only the one data segment received, but also other data segments that have been received. This method allows destination computers to acknowledge blocks of data segments at one time or acknowledge data missing from these data segments.

User Datagram Protocol (UDP)

User Datagram Protocol (UDP) is a connectionless-oriented, unreliable protocol operating at the Transport Layer. UDP does not have to establish a connection or window size to send information (thus connectionless). Therefore, UDP headers are much smaller than TCP headers, and data is sent much faster because there is no waiting for acknowledgements. UDP headers are referred to as datagrams and are used when programs include their own method for guaranteeing reliable data delivery. Microsoft logons, name resolutions, and multicasting (discussed in the "IP" section of this chapter) are some examples where UDP is used.

Internet Layer

The Internet Layer provides connectionless-oriented protocols used to determine what route data will take when transmitted from the source computer to the destination computer. The Internet Layer will address and package the data in IP datagrams and handle all routing communication that occurs between the source and destination computers.

Some of the protocols of the Internet Layer are Internet Protocol (IP), Internet Control Message Protocol (ICMP), Internet Group Management Protocol (IGMP), and Address Resolution Protocol (ARP). These protocols are discussed throughout this section.

Internet Protocol (IP)

The Internet Protocol's primary responsibility is to determine the route data will take to go from the source computer to the destination computer. An IP datagram contains information required for the data to be routed and delivered to the destination computer.

> **Tip**
>
> Think of IP as the post office delivery service. Suppose you send a letter to a friend living on the other side of the country; you write the letter and drop it off in a mailbox. From that point, the letter may go through several cities before reaching your friend, but the postal company is responsible for routing the letter to its final destination. IP works the same way. It routes data through several routers to arrive at the destination computer. Just as the postal company may take different routes depending on the weather, the IP protocol uses several routers depending on the network traffic.

IP Header information contains the following:

- *Version*—The format of the IP header for IP addressing. IP version 4 is the current version, but Windows 2000 does support some DNS extensions for IP version 6. IP version 6 is proposed in RFC 1886.
- *Identification*—If IP datagrams are broken down into smaller fragments, the fragments are listed in this field to be reassembled on the destination computer. Fragmentation is discussed in greater detail in the "IP Datagram Fragmentation" section of this chapter.
- *Fragment Offset*—If IP datagrams are broken down into smaller fragments, this field indicates which fragment is currently being sent.
- *Time to Live (TTL)*—The maximum amount of time the fragment can live on the network. This number decrements by one or more whenever it passes through a router. If a TTL didn't exist, all undeliverable data would continue to circulate on networks.
- *Protocol*—What protocol was used at the upper layer: TCP or UDP.

- *Checksum*—Used to ensure the data arrived intact.
- *Source Address*—The IP address of the source computer.
- *Destination Address*—The IP address of the destination computer.

IP Routing

IP routing is the process of sending data through routers to arrive at the destination computer. A router is a computer or device that routes data to different networks. Routers use routing tables to determine the best route to pass on data. Routing tables have entries for the networks either directly attached to the router or for indirect networks that are located through another router.

Tip

Think of driving across a city to get to a friend's house and the intersections you have to cross. Some intersections may be busy and therefore avoided. Routers are like intersections—they direct traffic along the best route to arrive at a destination computer. Each street is like a network.

When an IP datagram is passed to a router, the router consults the routing table to determine the next step. The router can forward the datagram to another router, send it to a particular IP address on an attached network (the destination address), or discard the datagram (if the TTL is set to zero). The routing table contains four different types of entries.

- *Host*—IP addresses for specific computers on a network. An example of a host entry would be the IP address of the router.
- *Subnet*—A routing entry to a portion of a network. Subnets are described in greater detail in the "Subnetting" section in this chapter.
- *Network*—A routing entry for an entire network. Used for broadcast addresses.
- *Default*—A routing entry used when all other entries do not match. This entry usually points to another router.

Routing table entries can be manually entered for static routing or automatically entered for dynamic routing. For dynamic routing, an addition protocol must be used. Windows 2000 supports two routing protocols, Routing Information Protocol (RIP) and Open Shortest Path First (OSPF).

> **Tip**
>
> A Windows 2000 server that functions as a router is referred to as a multihomed computer. Multihomed computers must have more than one network installed, each with separate IP address, or one network card with multiple IP addresses. To enable routing, the following registry parameter must be set to a value of 1: HKEYLOCALMACHINE\SYSTEM\ CurrentControlSet\Services\Tcpip\Parameters\ IPEnableRouter.

Routing Information Protocol (RIP)

The Routing Information Protocol allows routing table information to be exchanged among routers. RIP is a distance-vectoring protocol, meaning that it will find the best route for data to travel from the source computer to the destination computer by considering the amount of hops different routes will need. The hop count (called a *metric*) is how many routers the data will have to travel through to arrive at the destination computer. RIP supports a maximum hop count of 15.

RIP functions by broadcasting its routing table every thirty seconds. Other routers will record any new entries from this broadcast into their own routing tables, and then, in turn, broadcast their routing tables to other routers. When a new routing table entry is inserted, the hop count is also recorded. New entries will only be inserted if they do not already exist or if the hop count is lower than an existing entry.

RIP is not normally used in large network environments for a couple of reasons. Routers broadcast their routing table entries every thirty seconds, which can quickly saturate the bandwidth on WAN links. However, RIP version 2 (Windows 2000 supports version 1 and 2) improved this method of communicating by using IP multicasting to send routing table information instead of broadcasts. Another problem with RIP is that routing table entries are stored for three minutes past the time that the last update occurred. This means that if a router is taken off the network, its routing table entries would remain in other routers for three minutes past the expected broadcast from the offline router. Therefore, it can take several minutes for a network to adjust to the new routing paths, and information sent during this time can become undeliverable. This problem is called a *slow convergence*.

RIP has some advantages over OSPF in that it is much easier to install and design and is widely used on small to medium sized networks. RIP version 2 can only be installed and configured on Windows 2000 server under Routing and Remote Access. Windows 2000

Professional can only act as a RIP listener (silent RIP), which means the computer will listen for any new routing table entries and update its own routing table, but will not broadcast its own routing entries.

Open Shortest Path First (OSPF)

Like RIP, Open Shortest Path First (OSPF) was designed to allow routers to exchange routing table information with other routers. However, OSPF functions very well and is widely used on larger networks. Instead of broadcasting routing table entries every thirty seconds like RIP, OSPF retains a map of the entire network and only transmits routing information to other routers when changes occur to this map. The map is kept in a link state database, which is synchronized with all other OSPF routers on the network.

To maintain a synchronized link state database (LSDB), each router distributes a Link State Advertisement (LSA) to other routers. The LSA consists of the router, its attached networks, and the cost for communicating with these networks (metric hop). Routers compile a LSDB by receiving all LSAs from other routers in a process called *flooding*. If any changes occur to a router's connected networks, the router redistributes its LSA. This method of distribution avoids any slow convergence issues.

After a router compiles its LSDB, it calculates the shortest path to send information to other networks. Large networks can cause this database to become unmanageable, so OSPF splits the network into areas that are connected together through a backbone area. Each router is assigned a 32-bit number that acts as a unique router ID. When a router distributes its LSA, other routers know what area and router the LSA belongs to and can adjust their LSDBs accordingly.

OSPF functions very well on large networks because it allows instant routing updates through the flooding process, and it does not have the broadcast costs associated with RIP. However, OSPF requires much more network planning and designing and has more installation steps. OSPF can only be installed on Windows 2000 Server in Routing and Remote Access.

IP Datagram Fragmentation

Routing tables may not be able to handle the size of IP datagrams, so they will fragment the packet into smaller sizes and forward the packets to their final destination. The destination computer must reassemble all the fragmented pieces. This process works as follows:

1. The source computer places a unique number in the identification field of the IP datagram and sends the packet to the router.
2. The router receives the packet and determines the best routes to forward the packet.

3. The router then consults the maximum transmission unit (MTU) for the network. The MTU determines the largest packet size the network will accept.

4. If necessary, the router fragments the packet into smaller packets. Each fragment will contain the unique identification number, a More Fragments Flag, indicating that more fragments will follow (except for the last fragment), and a Fragment Offset that specifies which number the fragment is in the group.

5. The router then forwards the fragments onto the appropriate network.

6. When the fragments are received on the destination computer, the computer uses the identification number and the fragment offset to reassemble the fragments into one IP datagram.

Fragmentation and the resulting reassembling is common for IP datagrams, especially for any Internet connections.

IP Security (IPSec)

IP Security is a cryptography-based method functioning at the Internet Layer that provides security against any unauthorized network monitoring attacks or active attacks designed to change or destroy data. There are a number of different types of attacks on a network, most occurring from within the network. Some of the more common attacks are

- *Eavesdropping*—One of the most common types of attacks in which a user runs a network monitoring program to listen to information being sent across the network. Any unsecured data or clear-text passwords can be intercepted.

- *IP Spoofing/ Data Origin Authentication*—Users who use a false or stolen IP address to gain access to a network resource.

- *Data Alteration/ Corruption*—Unsecured documents that are altered or destroyed by a third party. This type of attack could also be a middle person altering database entries that are entered on a client machine, changed by the middle person, and then submitted to a server.

- *Identity Protection*—Some applications do not secure the identity or password of their users, and therefore are open to attackers. Attackers can use this information to log on to applications.

- *Denial of Service*—A favorite pastime for experienced attackers, this type of attack terminates a service or saturates networks, rendering them unusable.

IPSec is designed to protect packets and defend them against these types of attacks by creating an Internet Layer level of security that is available to the upper TCP/IP layers and applications. Each IP datagram sent on the network is screened by a security policy to ensure that only legitimate data is filtered through and forwarded on the network. IP Security Policies are configured under IP Security Policy in the Microsoft Management Console. To access the IP Security Policy, click Start from the taskbar, choose Run, enter mmc / a, and click on the IP Security plug-in. Add the plug-in if it is not already installed.

Three IP Security types are configured by default, which can be customized, or others can be created. Also, the IP Security Policies can be set for the local machine, another computer, or an Active Directory Domain. The three default security policies are as follows:

- *Server*—Requests security from all network traffic. If none can be negotiated within forty seconds, it will accept unsecured communication.

- *Secure Server*—Requires security for all communications. Any unsecured data is rejected.

- *Client*—Usually sends unsecured information but can respond to any security requests using IPSec.

To create a new IP security policy, right-click the IP security policy object and choose Create IP Security Policy (see Figure 17.7). This option will open the IP Security Policy Wizard, which creates a rule carried out for the policy. Policies can be comprised of multiple rules. Click Next to begin the new IP Security Policy Wizard process.

FIGURE 17.7

Creating a new IP security policy.

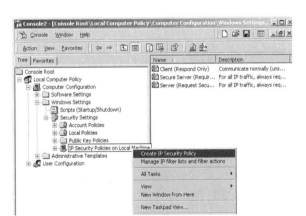

Type in a name for the policy and a description of the policy's purpose. Figure 17.8 displays the IP name window of the IP Security Policy Wizard. Click Next to continue the Wizard.

FIGURE **17.8**

Entering the IP Security Policy name and description.

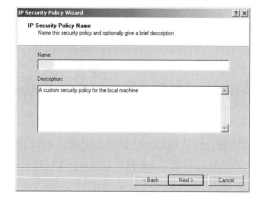

The next window specifies how Windows 2000 Professional should respond to any security requests. An option is set to activate the default response rule. If this option is set, the default response rule can be set in the next window; otherwise, the Wizard will be finished at this point. Leave the check mark in the Activate the Default Response Rule check box and click Next (see Figure 17.9).

FIGURE **17.9**

Default response rule for IP Security Policy.

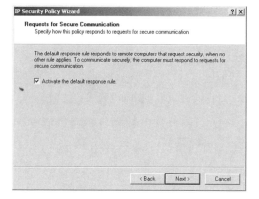

At this window in the IP Security Policy Windows, the authentication method must be chosen. Only one type of authentication method can be configured using the Wizard; however, other authentication methods can be added afterwards in the Security Policy properties. The three types of authentication methods are

- *Kerberos v5*—Named after the Greek mythological dog that guarded the door to the Underworld, the kerberos protocol is the default security method for security policies and is widely used in Windows 2000. Before data is sent between two computers, the source computer encrypts a shared key with information specific to the source computer. The destination computer decrypts the key and analyzes the information. If the key appears to have come from the source computer, the destination computer will encrypt a response, which includes one piece of information from the source computer, and return the key. The source computer analyzes the response, determines that the destination computer is authentic, and begins communication. For both computers to trust each other, they use an intermediary called the Key Distribution Center (KDC). The KDC is a service running on a secure computer that maintains a database of account information for all computers within its realm.

- *Certificate Authority*—This authentication method uses certificates to confirm that users are not masquerading as someone else. When a policy is applied against data, the user must supply a certificate to confirm his or her identity. Certificates have to be requested from a Certificate Authority, which is a company that will investigate clients to ensure they are not imposters. This authentication method is commonly used for Internet or remote communication.

- *Pre-shared key*—This authentication method uses a predetermined key to authenticate users. A pre-shared key can be a word or a phrase that is known to both users. Pre-shared keys do not encrypt data, they just ensure that the two communicating parties trust each other. This method is useful for authenticating non-Windows 2000 computers, but is not recommended for use if kerberos or certificates are available options.

Figure 17.10 displays the different authentication options. This example is using the Verisign Certificate Authority as an authentication method.

FIGURE 17.10

Authentication Methods for IP Security Policies.

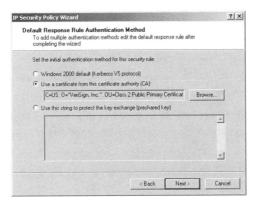

Clicking Next proceeds the last step in the IP Security Policy Wizard. An option to edit the properties is available, which is useful for adding additional authentication methods. Click Finish to complete the Wizard.

After a policy has been created, it must be activated. To activate the policy on Windows 2000 Professional, right-click the policy and choose Assign (see Figure 17.11). Only one policy can be assigned at a time.

FIGURE 17.11

Assigning an IP Security Policy.

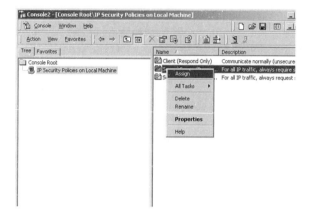

Windows 2000 includes a monitoring program for IP security connections. To view the IP Security Monitor, type `ipsecmon` from the Run dialog box. IP Security promises to be a powerful, complex security method that will quickly become the mainstay for all secure communications.

Internet Control Message Protocol (ICMP)

ICMP is an Internet Layer maintenance protocol used to send messages between routers. ICMP messages are used for the following functions:

- *Build and maintain routing tables*—When better routes become available for network traffic, ICMP Redirect messages inform machines of the better route.

- *Command routers to slow down data transmissions*—ICMP maintains flow control by sending messages to a router that is saturating another.

- *Diagnose network problems*—ICMP is used in the `ping` and `tracert` commands, discussed in the "Troubleshooting TCP/IP" section of this chapter.

- *Dynamic router discovery*—ICMP utilizes another protocol, Internet Routing Discovery Protocol (IRDP), to allow computers to dynamically discover default gateways.

Internet Group Management Protocol (IGMP)

Applications that simultaneously communicate to more than one computer in a process called multicasting use the Internet Group Management Protocol. IGMP manages the computers, called *hosts*, in a IP datagram group. Hosts can leave the group or be added to the group at any time, and the group can grow to be of any size. NetShow is an example of a program that employs the IGMP protocol.

Network Access Layer

The bottom layer of the TCP/IP protocol stack—the Network Access layer—characterizes the physical media, the network interface cards (NICs), and driver information. In a nutshell, at this level, the network adapter card groups bits into frames and sends these frames across the physical media to the receiving computer or computers. The most significant advancement at this layer is Windows 2000's use of Network Driver Interface Specification level 5 (NDIS 5.0). In earlier versions, NDIS allowed operating systems to bind any or all protocols to any network adapter. NDIS 5.0 builds on earlier versions with the following extensions:

- *Plug and Play capability*—Plug and Play is not a new subject, but it is new to the Windows NT versions. Changes to the network interface can occur anytime, and the Windows 2000 drivers have been modified to adapt to these changes.

- *NDIS Power Management used for network wakeup*—Network adapters cards can sleep and wake up depending on network use.

- *Support for single INF format for all Windows operating systems*—INF files contain installation information that Windows 2000 references to setup new software. These files can be viewed using any text-editor program, but usually should not be modified.

- *Support for Windows Management Instrumentation (WMI)*—Windows Management Instrumentation allows administrators to manage all components of a business environment from one location by providing a uniform view of the environment.

Internet Address, Subnet Mask, and Default Gateway

Computers using TCP/IP must have an IP address and subnet mask to communicate with others on their own subnet. A *subnet* is a portion of a network that is located on its own physical segment and is usually separated from other computers by a router. To send information through a router beyond their own subnet, they must also have a default gateway. Understanding what an IP address is and how the computer sends information, either locally or remotely, is essential to TCP/IP networks. An IP address is a 32-bit binary number that identifies on which subnet a computer resides and the unique number of the computer on that subnet. For your convenince, this number is converted into four decimal numbers ranging from 0 to 255. An example of an IP address displayed as a decimal number and its matching 32-bit binary number is as follows:

Four Decimal numbers: `207.219.170.193`

32-bit Binary number: `11001111.11011011.10101010.11000001`

To convert a number from binary to decimal or decimal to binary, the following simple chart will aid in example.

1	1	1	1	1	1	1	1
128	64	32	16	8	4	2	1

This chart shows the possible combinations for the number of bits used starting from the right (the least significant bit). For example, two bits will have four possible combinations:

00
01
10
11

However, to start counting these combinations, you must start at *zero*, not one. Therefore, the numbers converted back into decimal will be 0,1,2,3. To write the number 4 in binary, you must use another bit. The following is an example of using the chart to convert binary to decimal.

1	1	0	0	1	1	1	1

$128 + 64 + 0 + 0 + 8 + 4 + 2 + 1 = 207$

But what does an IP address do? The IP address defines a network address and a host address for each machine. Computers that communicate with each other on the same side of a router all have an identical network number, meaning that the first portion of the IP address is exactly the same. The last portion of the IP address is unique for each device. This is similar to going out for a stroll to visit a neighbor. You are going from your house, which has a unique number on the street to a neighbor's house, which has his or her own unique number on the street. However, both addresses are located on the same street. To go to a different street, you have to go through an intersection or intersections to get there. Crossing through these intersections is similar to using a default gateway to tell the computer how to send information beyond your own subnet.

The Subnet Mask defines which portion of an IP address is the network address and which part is the host address. It does this by masking out the network portion of an IP address with binary ones. The following is an example of an IP address and a subnet mask:

Four Decimal number: `207.219.170.193`

Subnet Mask in Decimal: `255.255.255.0`

32-bit Binary number: `11001111.11011011.10101010.11000001`

Subnet Mask in Binary: `11111111.11111111.11111111.00000000`

The three decimals numbers, or the first 24 bits, have been masked out, meaning that they are the network numbers, and the last decimal number, or eight bits, is left for the host address. Subnet masks are used to determine if a destination device is on the same subnet as the source device or remote. If it is remote, the computer will send the information to the IP address listed in the default gateway. This decision is processed by a term called ANDing. ANDing is using a binary comparison of the source device's IP address with the subnet mask and the destination device's IP address with the same subnet mask. If the results are the same, the destination device must be local. If they are different, the destination device must be remote. For the comparison, whenever the IP address and the subnet mask are both ones, this is represented by a one; any other combination is represented by a zero. For example, a computer with the IP address of `207.219.170.193` is sending information to another computer with an IP address of `207.219.170.129`. Both have a subnet mask of `255.255.255.0`. Is this a local computer or a remote computer beyond the router? The naked eye can tell the difference quickly, but for a computer, the ANDing process will determine a local or remote destination. The ANDing process is as follows:

Source IP Address: `207.219.170.193`

Subnet Mask: `255.255.255.0`

17

SETTING UP
TCP/IP
PROTOCOL ACCESS

Source Binary number: `11001111.11011011.10101010.11000001`

Subnet Mask in Binary: `11111111.11111111.11111111.00000000`

ANDing process: `11001111.11011011.10101010.00000000`

Destination IP Address: `207.219.170.129`

Destination Binary Address: `11001111.11011011.10101010.10000001`

Subnet Mask in Binary: `11111111.11111111.11111111.00000000`

ANDing Process: `11001111.11011011.10101010.00000000`

The two ANDing process numbers are identical, so the destination device is local.

IP addresses usually follow one of three different classes. Although it is very difficult to receive a class of IP addresses at present, many companies are choosing to create their own internal IP structure for intranets and using proxy server to communicate to the Internet. A *proxy server* is a computer that accepts requests from other computers to communicate beyond the network and processes these requests on their behalf. Proxy servers also have some security management and packet filtering capabilities. The main advantage to a proxy server is that while it must have a valid Internet IP address, devices behind the server can adhere to whatever IP class the administrator wants to use. The following are the different types of IP classes:

- *Class A*—The first binary number in a class A IP address range must be a zero (0). Along with the first binary number, the next 7 bits are reserved for the network address, and the remaining 24 bits are reserved for the hosts addresses. Thus, the first decimal number can be from 0—127, for a total of 128 possible class A IP ranges; however, in reality only 126 exist—two numbers are reserved for special purposes (discussed later in this section).

  Class A IP network in decimal: `1.0.0.0` to `126.0.0.0`

  Class A IP network in binary: `00000001.00000000.00000000.00000000` to `01111111.00000000.00000000.00000000`

- *Class B*—A one (1) must represent the first binary number, and a zero (0) must represent the second number. These two and the next 14 bits are reserved for the network number. The remaining 16 bits are used for hosts. Therefore, 16,383 possible Class B networks can be used, each with 65000 hosts.

  Class B IP network in decimal: `128.0.0.0` to `191.255.0.0`

Class B IP network in Binary: 10000000.00000000.00000000.00000000 to
10111111.11111111.00000000.00000000

- *Class C*—The first two bits must be a one (1) and the third bit must be a zero (0). These 3 bits plus the next 21 bits are reserved for the network number and the remaining eight bits are used for the hosts. The possible Class C IP networks are 2,000,000 Class C networks with 254 hosts each.

  Class C IP network in decimal: 192.0.0.0 to 223.255.255.0

  Class C IP network in Binary: 11000000.00000000.00000000.00000000 to
  11011111.11111111.00000000.00000000

A Class D and Class E network also exist, but are not used for general Internet addresses. Also, certain numbers are withheld because they hold special meaning. An IP address that begins with 127 is also not valid. This IP network is reserved for a *loopback* control. The loopback address of 127.0.0.1 is used to test the functionality of your network adapter card and TCP/IP. If a valid response is returned when pinging this IP address, the network adapter card can function using TCP/IP, but does not necessarily have an IP address at that time. The 10.0.0.0 network is also a special reserved IP address range because Internet routers do not forward this address. Therefore, companies are free to use this network number without taking someone else's IP numbers. Other IP addresses available for internal use are listed in Table 17.2. For further details, refer to RFC 1918.

TABLE 17.2 Available IP Addresses

IP Address	Subnet Mask
10.0.0.0	255.0.0.0
172.16.0.0- 172.31.0.0	255.255.0.0
192.168.0.0- 192.168.255.0	255.255.255.0

One detail concerning issuing IP addresses: a network number or a host number cannot display all zeros or all one in binary. All zeros represent "this network," while all ones represent a broadcast address. This does not mean that a zero or 255 (the decimal equivalent) cannot be a part of the IP address. For example, an IP address of 128.0.0.1 with a subnet mask of 255.255.0.0 is a valid IP address because the network address (128.0) and the host address (0.1) both contain a one when converted to binary.

Subnetting

While IP classes are useful, circumstances may require that you further break down an IP class into a more manageable size. For instance, Popkey Enterprises Co. has been assigned a Class C network of 192.168.112.0 —. This gives them a total of 254 (256 minus all zeros and all ones) host addresses that can be used for computers, printers, and routers (even their fridges if they choose!). However, their company covers five floors in a building, and each floor's network is separated from the other by a router. Figure 17.12 displays the network diagram of Popkey Enterprise's building. Because of the ANDing process, explained earlier in this chapter, a computer on the fourth floor sending information to another computer on the second floor will be unsuccessful, because the subnet mask will determine that the address is remote, thus ignoring the routers altogether. Further subnetting an IP network resolves this issue.

FIGURE 17.12

A network diagram of a five-story building for Popkey Enterprises.

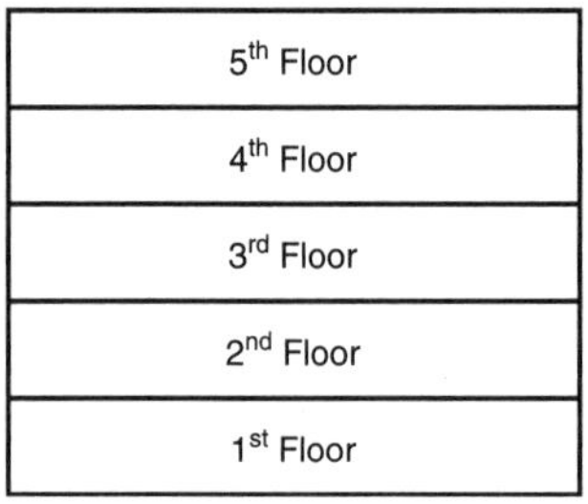

5th Floor
4th Floor
3rd Floor
2nd Floor
1st Floor

Subnetting requires taking bits from the host portion of the IP address and using them for the network portion. In the preceding example, Popkey Enterprises needed to divide its Class C network into six smaller networks (five floors plus one for the other side of the router). By taking the first three bits from the left side of the host address, this will give them enough possible combinations to have six smaller subnets. The following demonstrates the six possible combinations. Note that a space has been left between the network portion, the subnet portion, and the host portion for emphasis only.

Before Subnetting:

Network in decimal: 192.168.112.0-
Network in binary: 11000000. 10101000. 1110000.00000000

Subnet Mask in decimal: 255.255.255.0

Subnet Mask in binary: 11111111.11111111.11111111.00000000

Subnetting Combinations:

Binary	Decimal
11000000. 10101000. 1110000. 001 00000	192.168.112.32
11000000. 10101000. 1110000. 010 00000	192.168.112.64
11000000. 10101000. 1110000. 011 00000	192.168.112.96
11000000. 10101000. 1110000. 100 00000	192.168.112.128
11000000. 10101000. 1110000. 101 00000	192.168.112.160
11000000. 10101000. 1110000. 110 00000	192.168.11225.192

Note that a subnet of all zeros and all ones has been left out because of the same reasons network numbers and host numbers cannot be all zeros and ones. Also, this subnet leaves five bits to use for hosts. Therefore, each subnet will have a valid range of host addresses that can be handed out to the computers, routers, and so on that are on that floor. The following illustrates the first subnet's valid host range for IP addresses.

Binary	Decimal
11000000. 10101000. 1110000. 001 00001	192.168.112.33
to	to
11000000. 10101000. 1110000. 001 11110	192.168.112.62

> **Note**
>
> Each subnet created will cause two IP addresses to be unusable. This occurs because each subnet cannot use the host address of all zeros and all ones. An address of all zeros is used to represent the network, while an address of all ones is used for broadcasts. Also, the first and last subnet option displays all zeros and ones, thus they are illegal as well.

Once again, the network, subnet, and host portions of an IP address cannot be all zeros or all ones. Figure 17.13 shows the same five-story building, now with subnets and valid hosts per subnet.

One last question must be answered before being able to send information between devices. What is the subnet mask? As previously explained, the subnet mask is used to specify what part of the IP address is the same for everyone on the network and what is the unique host address for each IP address. A better word, instead of network, for the last sentence is subnet, since that has what has happened to the Class C network.

The networked portion is then represented as ones in the subnet mask. In this case, the first 24 bits were already ones and could not be changed. However, the next three bits have been added to the network portion, leaving five for the host address. The subnet mask for Popkey Enterprises will be as follows:

Binary: 11111111.11111111.11111111.11100000

Decimal: 255.255.255.224

FIGURE 17.13

A network diagram of a five-story building for Popkey Enterprises that shows subnets and valid hosts per subnet.

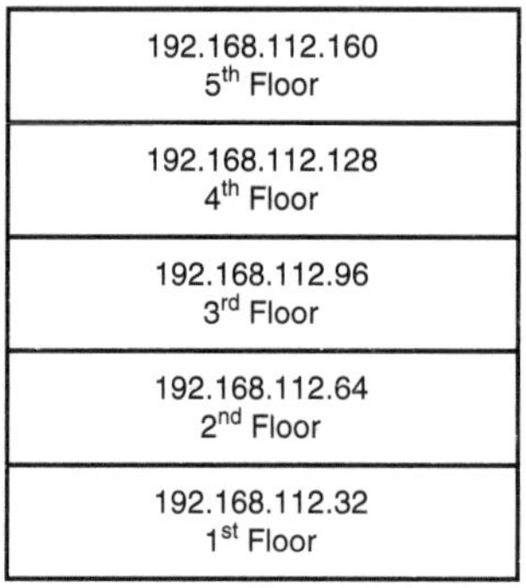

| 192.168.112.160
5th Floor |
| 192.168.112.128
4th Floor |
| 192.168.112.96
3rd Floor |
| 192.168.112.64
2nd Floor |
| 192.168.112.32
1st Floor |

Table 17.3 shows subnet masks, the subnet, and hosts for a Class A, B, and C network. All subnets that show invalid mean that no possibilities exist or that the possibilities are only all zeros or all ones. This table can be used for future reference whenever you need to split up an IP address into subnets.

TABLE 17.3 How Subnet Masks Divide a Class A, B, and C Network

Subnet Mask	Subnets	Number of Hosts per Subnet
Class A		
11111111.00000000.00000000.00000000	1	16,777,214
11111111.10000000.00000000.00000000	Invalid	Invalid
11111111.11000000.00000000.00000000	2	4,194,302
11111111.11100000.00000000.00000000	6	2,097,150
11111111.11110000.00000000.00000000	14	1,048,574
11111111.11111000.00000000.00000000	30	524,286
11111111.11111100.00000000.00000000	62	262,142
11111111.11111110.00000000.00000000	126	131,070
11111111.11111111.00000000.00000000	254	65534

Subnet Mask	Subnets	Number of Hosts per Subnet
11111111.11111111.10000000.00000000	510	32,766
11111111.11111111.11000000.00000000	1,022	16,382
11111111.11111111.11100000.00000000	2,046	8,190
11111111.11111111.11110000.00000000	4,094	4,094
11111111.11111111.11111000.00000000	8,190	2,046
11111111.11111111.11111100.00000000	1,6382	1,022
11111111.11111111.11111110.00000000	32,766	510
11111111.11111111.11111111.00000000	65,534	254
11111111.11111111.11111111.10000000	131,070	126
11111111.11111111.11111111.11000000	262,142	62
11111111.11111111.11111111.11100000	524,286	30
11111111.11111111.11111111.11110000	1,048,574	14
11111111.11111111.11111111.11111000	2,097,150	6
11111111.11111111.11111111.11111100	4,194,302	2
11111111.11111111.11111111.11111110	Invalid	Invalid
11111111.11111111.11111111.11111111	Invalid	Invalid

Class B

Subnet Mask	Subnets	Number of Hosts per Subnet
11111111.11111111.00000000.00000000	1	65534
11111111.11111111.10000000.00000000	Invalid	Invalid
11111111.11111111.11000000.00000000	2	16,382
11111111.11111111.11100000.00000000	6	8,190
11111111.11111111.11110000.00000000	14	4,094
11111111.11111111.11111000.00000000	30	2,046
11111111.11111111.11111100.00000000	62	1,022
11111111.11111111.11111110.00000000	126	510
11111111.11111111.11111111.00000000	254	254
11111111.11111111.11111111.10000000	510	126
11111111.11111111.11111111.11000000	1,022	62
11111111.11111111.11111111.11100000	2,046	30
11111111.11111111.11111111.11110000	4,094	14
11111111.11111111.11111111.11111000	8,190	6

17

SETTING UP
TCP/IP
PROTOCOL ACCESS

continues

TABLE 17.3 continued

Subnet Mask	Subnets	Number of Hosts per Subnet
11111111.11111111.11111111.11111100	16,382	2
11111111.11111111.11111111.11111110	Invalid	Invalid
11111111.11111111.11111111.11111111	Invalid	Invalid
Class C		
11111111.11111111.11111111.00000000	1	254
11111111.11111111.11111111.10000000	Invalid	Invalid
11111111.11111111.11111111.11000000	2	62
11111111.11111111.11111111.11100000	6	30
11111111.11111111.11111111.11110000	14	14
11111111.11111111.11111111.11111000	30	6
11111111.11111111.11111111.11111100	62	2
11111111.11111111.11111111.11111110	Invalid	Invalid
11111111.11111111.11111111.11111111	Invalid	Invalid

Troubleshooting TCP/IP

Effective troubleshooting of Windows 2000 requires a firm grasp of the TCP/IP utilities and the strategies that aid a logical approach to the problem. Three important questions to ask when troubleshooting are

- What is not functioning properly?
- What is functioning properly?
- What has changed?

Asking these questions and using the proper tools can answer most TCP/IP difficulties. Two common areas that cause problems on a network are

- Cable problems
- Network adapters

Cable Problems

Physical wiring has improved over the past couple of years and is not the issue it once was; however, if a user reports any communication problems, checking the physical layer is always a good idea. Troubleshooting this area includes checking for the correct light signals on Hubs and MAUs (the token ring equivalent of a hub), checking that the cabling is securely plugged in at both ends, and checking that the adapter card has not become jarred loose. If time permits, try replacing the cabling; if still unsuccessful, replace the adapter card. Be sure the replacements are functional. Usually, administrators move on to other steps before replacing devices, and if no answer is found, they will come back to this step.

Network Adapters

Network adapters with conflicting IRQ or I/O settings have caused a few late nights for inexperienced troubleshooters. Windows 2000 significantly improves network card installation with the advance of Plug and Play. As with the Windows 95 and 98 operating systems, Plug and Play network cards can be automatically detected and configured without any conflicts. Windows 2000 goes one step further by using digital signatures from manufacturers, ensuring that the device will be configured properly by the operating system. However, ISA legacy cards will still cause difficulties and may require configuring `.inf` files for proper installation. The problem here lies within the dated cards and not the operating system itself.

After the physical cabling is complete and the network card is installed and configured properly, using the following troubleshooting tools will help diagnose the majority of the remaining TCP/IP problems.

- `ipconfig`
- `ping`
- `ipkern`
- `arp`
- `tracert`
- `netstat`
- `nbtstat`
- `nslookup`
- Performance Monitor
- Network Monitor

These tools are described in more detail in the next sections of this chapter.

ipconfig

The `ipconfig /all` utility reports configuration parameters for all network adapters and serial ports (RAS) installed on a computer. This utility displays the IP address, subnet mask, and default gateway for each interface. Empty IP address information indicates one of many possibilities. A duplicate IP address may exist on the network, although DHCP's advanced features reduce this occurrence. TCP/IP may be corrupt and need to be reinstalled. The adapter card may have incorrect drivers installed, or conflicts may be occurring. However, don't overlook the obvious—someone may have forgotten to type in an IP address. Typing **ipconfig /all** from a command prompt (now located in the Accessories folder) displays information like the following:

```
C:\>ipconfig /all
```

Windows NT IP Configuration

Host Name	Home
Node Type	Broadcast
IP Routing Enabled	No
WINS Proxy Enabled	No
DNS Suffix Search List	home.widgets.com

Ethernet adapter Local Area Connection:

Adapter Domain Name	home.widgets.com
DNS Servers	10.16.15.3
	10.16.15.4
Description (3C905B-TX)	3Com EtherLink XL 10/100 PCI TX NIC
Physical Address	00-10-4B-62-15-BA
DHCP Enabled	No
IP Address	10.16.10.15
Subnet Mask	255.255.0.0
Default Gateway	10.16.0.1

This command is useful because it displays all TCP/IP information. If information that is supposed to be included is not, you can isolate the problem to this missing data area. Typing **ipconfig** without any command options will display the adapter domain name, DNS servers, IP address, subnet mask, and default gateway.

Ping

Ping is the most effective and simple utility for troubleshooting TCP/IP connections. Packet Internet Groper (PING) sends out four ICMP packets (a messaging protocol acting at the Internet layer) to a destination computer and, if successful, receives four echo replies in return. To ensure that two computers can communicate, four pings can be sent. The following are these four separate pings and their purposes:

- *Ping the loopback address*—As previously mentioned, the IP address of 127.0.0.1 has been set aside for testing network cards. By pinging this loopback address, this informs you that the network card has been installed properly, but the IP address or subnet mask may need attention.

- *Ping an IP address of the near side of the router*—This will ensure that your IP address and your subnet mask are functioning properly.

- *Ping the IP address of the far side of a router*—Administrators always have one or two IP addresses they know are always functioning and can use these IP addresses as test IP addresses. Replies will indicate that the default gateway is functioning properly.

- *Ping another computer by hostname*—The first three pings check the communication between two computers. This last ping checks whether the computer can resolve a hostname to an IP address. Windows 2000 will first check the local hostname of a machine to see if the ping is for itself, and then it checks the hosts file, and last it checks DNS. If a response for a host name is not returned, one of these three areas will not be functioning. As previously listed, Windows 2000 also includes a caching DNS resolver service, which caches name queries for a specified amount of time. Future name queries can be resolved by cache.

Of course, many administrators will jump to the fourth ping, because a correct response by hostname indicates that the other three pings will also be successful.

The following is an example of a ping to an IP address:

```
C:\>ping 10.16.10.15

Pinging 10.16.10.15 with 32 bytes of data:
Reply from 10.16.10.15: bytes=32 time<10ms TTL=128
Reply from 10.16.10.15: bytes=32 time<10ms TTL=128
Reply from 10.16.10.15: bytes=32 time<10ms TTL=128
Reply from 10.16.10.15: bytes=32 time<10ms TTL=128

Ping statistics for 10.16.10.15:
    Packets: Sent = 4, Received = 4, Lost = 0 (0% loss),
Approximate round trip times in milli-seconds:
    Minimum = 0ms, Maximum =  0ms, Average =  0ms
```

17

SETTING UP TCP/IP PROTOCOL ACCESS

This data indicates that the source computer can successfully communicate with the destination computer (`10.16.10.15`). The next step would be to `ping` the hostname of the computer. If a hostname `ping` is not successful, you can isolate the problem to hostname resolution and not a communication problem.

By default, a `ping` command sends 64 bytes in four packets and waits one second for each response. Typing **ping** by itself will display the available command-line options to change these defaults. The following are some useful options:

- `-t`   Allows a continuous ping until interrupted by CTRL+C. This option is useful when downloading files and you need to keep a continuous connection open.

- `-w`   Changes the response time for each reply. An administrator can ping a computer on the next desk or ping a device located on another continent across a high-delay link. In addition, security links may need to be established. Increasing the response time using the `-w` option allows a longer time period than one second for echo replies.

- `-n`   The number of echo requests to send.

- `-a`   Resolves IP addresses into hostnames.

A ping will either generate a successful response in return as shown in the previous examples, or it will return an error message. The following are the possible error messages and their definitions:

- *Bad Host Address (Hostname)*—The hostname provided could not be resolved into an IP address. Check the hosts file and listed DNS server.

- *Destination Host Unreachable*—The ping command either could not find the default gateway or found the proper network address for the requested IP address, but no IP address existed.

- *Request Timed Out*—Not enough time was given for an echo reply. Increase the response time using the `-w` option.

- *Hardware Error*—A device or media interrupted the ping command, so a successful response could not be given.

- *??? is not recognized as an internal or external command, operable program or batch file*—Ping was spelled incorrectly or a space was not left between ping and the IP address or hostname.

ipkern

The `ipkern` utility combines features found in the `route`, `ipconfig`, and `ARP` commands together to provide statistical information about routing. ARP and route are discussed in further detail later in this section of this chapter. Although the `route` command may still be used, `ipkern` gathers a more detailed representation for routing information and performs the same manual tasks as the route command. For example, `ipkern` will manually update routing tables.

The following is an example of `ipkern` displaying a routing table:

```
C:\>ipkern route print
```

Destination	Mask	Next Hop	Interface	Metric	Protocol
0.0.0.0	0.0.0.0	10.16.0.1	2	1	2
10.16.0.0	255.255.0.0	10.16.10.15	2	1	2
10.16.10.15	255.255.255.255	127.0.0.1	1	1	2
10.255.255.255	255.255.255.255	10.16.10.15	2	1	2
127.0.0.0	255.0.0.0	127.0.0.1	1	1	2
224.0.0.0	224.0.0.0	10.16.10.15	2	1	2
255.255.255.255	255.255.255.255	10.16.10.15	2	1	2

This information can be used to determine what route data is taking to arrive at destination computers. `ipkern` is a Windows 2000 command and is not used as often as the other troubleshooting tools.

ARP

The `ARP` utility can be used to display IP address to Media Access Control (MAC) address resolution. A MAC address (commonly referred to as a hardware address, physical address, or Ethernet address) is a unique address consisting of six hexadecimal number hardwired into every network adapter. Devices must acquire the destination device's MAC address before a session can be established. Once a computer obtains the other computer's MAC address, it is stored in the ARP cache for two minutes. If the address is referenced again during those two minutes, it is stored for ten minutes before it is flushed.

The `ARP` command allows an administrator to view ARP cache information. The `-a` command displays the current entries held in cache. The `-s` option will place a static entry in cache, which can be deleted using the `-d` option. The following is a typical `ARP` command:

```
C:\>arp -a

Interface: 10.16.0.230 on Interface 0x2
  Internet Address      Physical Address      Type
    10.16.0.1           00-06-29-05-8e-7e      dynamic
    10.16.0.236         00-60-94-05-ef-26      dynamic
```

This ARP entry displays computers by their IP and MAC addresses with which the source computers has recently communicated. This information can be used to discover the MAC address of another computer. For a complete listing of command options, type ARP /? from a command prompt.

tracert

tracert is trace-routing utility that allows you to view what route an IP address will take from one device to another. At each router, an ICMP packet will be sent back. The following is an example of using tracert:

```
C:\>tracert 10.16.0.1

Tracing route to ZEUS1 [10.16.0.1]
over a maximum of 30 hops:

  1   <10 ms   <10 ms   <10 ms   ZEUS1 [10.16.0.1]

Trace complete.
```

In large companies and on the Internet, this tool allows you to determine at what point a message could not continue, thus pinpointing the breakdown in communication. A tracert command will report a destination host unreachable message at the point in which communication broke down. Administrators can then check the failing device.

netstat

netstat discloses protocol statistics and current TCP/IP connections by IP address and port numbers. netstat also displays the state of the connection and the type of transport protocol used. The following is an example of netstat output:

```
C:\>netstat

Active Connections

  Proto  Local Address          Foreign Address        State
  TCP    LIFE-90FNXXFTU5:1033   ZEUS1:netbios-ssn      ESTABLISHED
```

This information shows that a TCP connection using port 1033 has been established to a NetBIOs session on a destination computer called Zeus1.

nbtstat

The `nbtstat` utility troubleshoots NetBIOS name-resolution problems. The following lists a number of command line options that display useful information:

- `nbtstat -c` Displays all NetBIOS names in cache.
- `nbtstat -R` Purges all entries from cache and reloads entries from the `LMHOSTS` file that display a `#PRE`.
- `nbtstat -RR` Re-registers all names with the name server. This option is new for Windows 2000.
- `nbtstat -n` Lists all local names registered on the system.
- `nbtstat -r` Lists how names are resolved, by broadcast or through WINS.

The following is an example of `nbtstat`:

```
C:\>nbtstat -RR
    The NetBIOS names registered by this computer have been refreshed.
```

This example will purge all NetBIOS cached entries and reload entries from the LMHOSTS file. For a complete listing of nbtstat commands, type **nbtstat /?** from a command prompt.

nslookup

`nslookup` is an extremely useful tool for querying a DNS host database for name resolution. By typing `nslookup`, the DNS server and DNS IP address is displayed. Typing a hostname will return its IP address through a query of the default DNS server. `nslookup` resolves an IP address through a procedure called the *domain name devolution method*. Typing a host name causes `nslookup` to attach the domain suffix to the host name (an example would be `bc.niceweather.ca`) and query the DNS. If no entry exists in DNS, `nslookup` removes one label from the domain suffix. Windows 2000 computers will not reduce names further than the second level domain (`niceweather.ca`). Therefore, if `nslookups` cannot be resolved to the second domain level, the lookup will fail. Querying DNS for hostname entries that exist outside the home domain requires a fully-qualified domain name.

Performance Monitor

Performance Monitor installs as a Windows 2000 MMC snap-in that monitors processing, memory, disk, and network information. This tool monitors protocols such as IP, TCP, and UDP to examine what is happening at each layer and determine if any bottlenecks occur. Performance Monitor charts current details or logs information for later analysis.

Network Monitor

Microsoft Network Monitor is not a tool to use for verifying connections between two devices. Network Monitor captures all frames being sent to and from the monitored computer. The information captured in the frames displays how devices are communicating and the type of traffic on the network. Windows 2000 Advanced Server installs with a limited version of Network Monitor that only captures frames to and from the one computer. Microsoft Systems Management Server includes a complete version, allowing all frames, regardless of their origin, to be captured. Network Monitor displays a large amount of information, and time should be spent learning this important tool. Understanding the TCP/IP protocol stack is essential for this tool.

Summary

TCP/IP networking can be a very complex procedure. Large networks are bound to have communication problems, but a proper understanding of the protocol layers will make these problems only minor ones. Subnetting helps break up large IP addresses, and TCP/IP tools provide useful information for any networking questions. The information printed in this chapter and experience using TCP/IP will assist with a smooth TCP/IP implementation on a Windows 2000 operating system.

Using Microsoft Internet Explorer

For some time now, the battle of the browsers has raged as Microsoft redirected its corporate focus toward the Internet. Because enough has already been written on this epic struggle to capture the browser market, this chapter concentrates on the task of investigating the nuts and bolts of Internet Explorer 5, Microsoft's latest offering into the Web browser arena.

If you're not familiar with browsers or the Web, let me give you a little background. The World Wide Web (WWW) is primarily an information service on the Internet. Web sites dotted around the Internet store information, text, graphics, sounds, and so on. These sites use an underlying technology called HyperText Markup Language (HTML) to format and present the information. On most users' desktops is a browser, which is an application that can request information from a Web site, interpret it, and present it to users in a nice, graphical fashion. Information is transferred from the Web site to the user desktop via an IP protocol called HyperText Transfer Protocol (HTTP).

Starting Internet Explorer 5

Version 5.0 of Internet Explorer (IE) comes pre-installed with Windows 2000 Professional. By the time you read this there might be a newer version available because Microsoft is continually improving and re-issuing this program. You can download newer versions as they become available at various sites including Microsoft's. At the time of this writing, the home Web site for IE is www.msn.com. IE comes installed both on the Start menu through Start, Programs, Internet Explorer and on the Desktop. Figure 18.1 shows the Start menu way into IE.

FIGURE 18.1

Accessing IE5 from the Start menu.

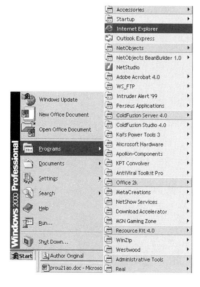

If this is the first time you have started IE5, you will be presented with the Internet Connection Wizard dialog box, shown in Figure 18.2. If you (or someone else) has used Internet Explorer on your computer, it will start using the user-defined defaults set.

FIGURE 18.2

The Internet Connection Wizard. You can launch this Wizard later through Start, Programs, Accessories, Communications.

In this first dialog box, you can define how your copy of Windows 2000 Professional will connect to the Internet. Choose your preferred connection method and click Next to proceed.

If you choose to connect via a modem, the Internet Connection Wizard takes you through the detection, installation, and configuration of the modem and, if necessary, the installation and configuration of the Remote Access Service (RAS) client. For more information on adding a modem and RAS, refer to Chapter 16, "Setting Up Your Modem," and Chapter 20, "Remote Computing with Remote Access Service."

If you choose to connect via a LAN, you are asked whether you connect via a proxy server (see Figure 18.3). Choose the correct option and click Next to continue.

Enter the name or IP address of the proxy server in the Proxy To Use column and enter the port number in the Port column for that service (see Figure 18.4). After you enter your proxy settings, click Next to continue. You can save a lot of time by telling the Wizard to use the same value for all services—if this is what is valid for your server.

18

USING MICROSOFT INTERNET EXPLORER

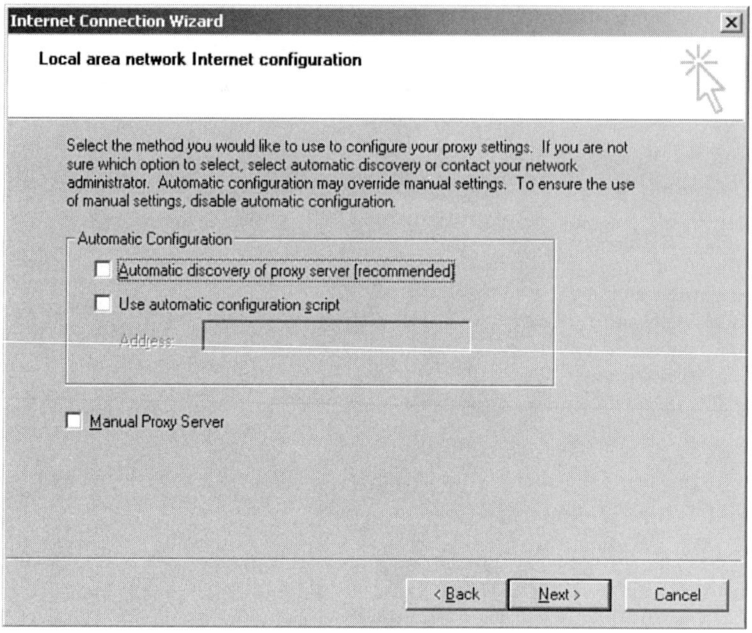

FIGURE 18.3

Are you using a proxy?

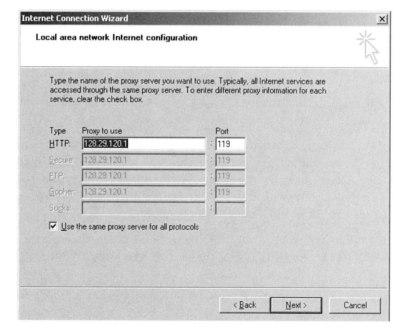

FIGURE 18.4.

Enter the Proxy values. The example here does not use valid values for these fields.

You can choose to exclude certain services from this account and then move on to the next dialog screen where the modem and LAN wizard converge asking whether you want to set up your Internet mail account (see Figure 18.5). To set up your account now, choose Yes and then click Next to continue. Your email account, as with all other IE5 settings, can be configured later if you choose.

FIGURE **18.5**

Set up your email account.

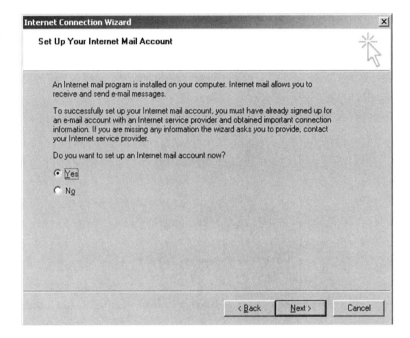

If you choose Yes, the next dialog box requests your Internet mail account name (see Figure 18.6). You can enter any name you want to represent your Internet service. Enter a descriptive name and click Next to continue.

The next dialog box, shown in Figure 18.7, requires you to enter your full name. This name will be displayed in the From field of all your outgoing messages. Enter your name and click Next to continue.

In the next dialog box, shown in Figure 18.8, you must enter your email address. After you're done, click Next to continue.

In addition to your email address, the Wizard requires you to enter the type of mail server you're using (see Figure 18.9). Select the correct type of mail server from the drop-down list. Also enter the name or IP address of your incoming and outgoing mail servers. Then click Next to continue.

FIGURE **18.6**

*Enter your
Internet mail
account name.
This example
already has two
existing email
accounts.*

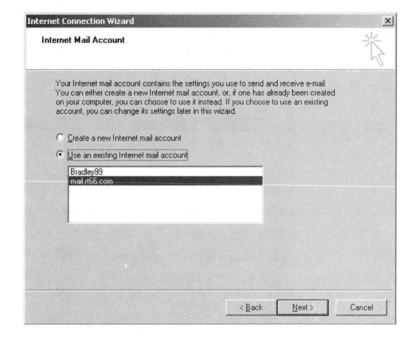

FIGURE **18.7**

*Enter your display
name.*

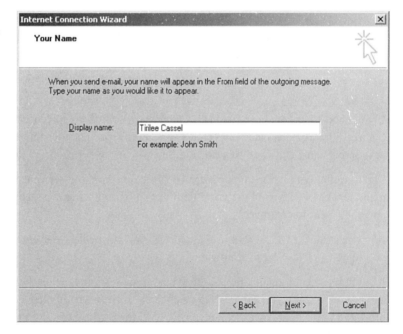

FIGURE 18.8

Enter your email address.

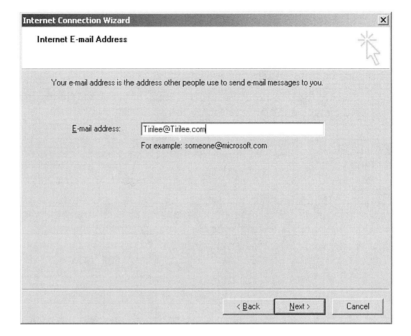

FIGURE 18.9

Enter email server addresses. You can use either IPs or domain type names. I've shown both here.

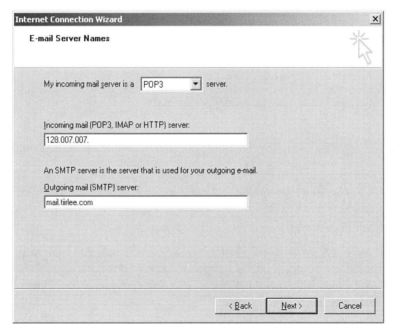

After you enter the email server details, the next dialog box requires you to choose how you will be authenticated by the email server (see Figure 18.10). You can choose from two possibilities:

- Log on using a username and password.
- Log on using Secure Password Authentication (SPA). This capability has to be supported by your ISP.

FIGURE 18.10

Internet Mail Logon.

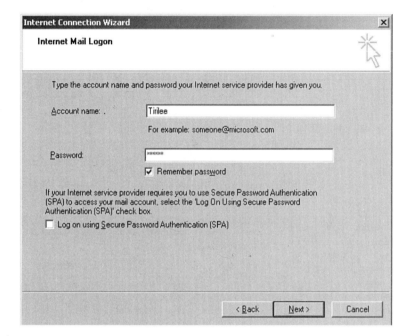

After you choose how you will log on, click Next to be presented with a completion dialog box (see Figure 18.11).

If you choose to connect through a modem and find an ISP, Windows will locate a toll free access number (if you're in a participating area) and dial that number. Figure 18.12 shows the dialog box.

If there are no providers in your area, or you want to set up a non-participant provider, you'll have to supply certain information manually. Figure 18.13 shows the first dialog box for the manual configuration of a modem connection where you supply the ISP's phone number.

FIGURE 18.11

That's all there is to setting up an email account.

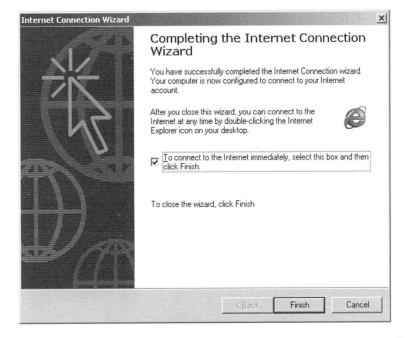

FIGURE 18.12

Microsoft has developed a network of participating ISPs to make your account setup even easier. If you live in a participating area, you can take advantage of this service.

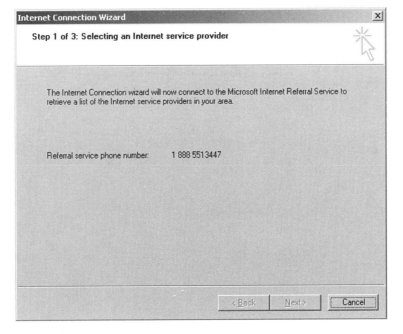

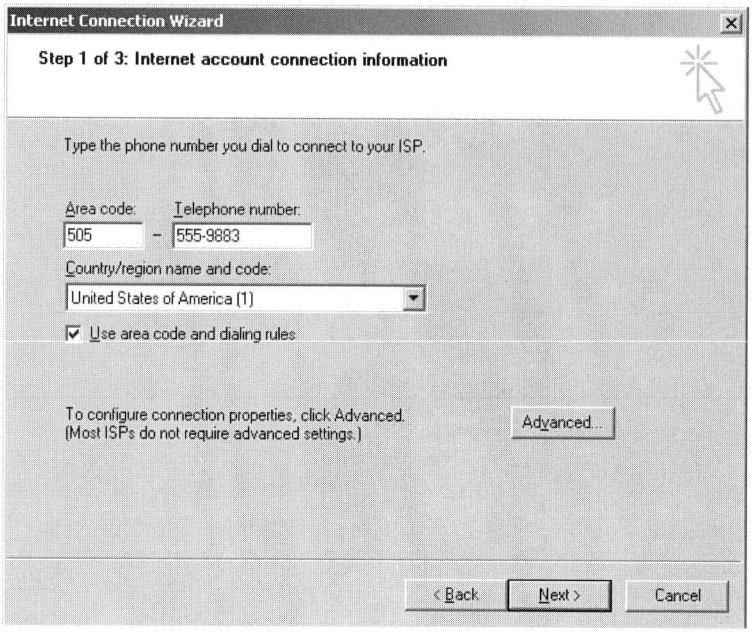

FIGURE 18.13

The first and fore-most piece of information for a dial-up connection is the phone number to dial up.

You'll then need to supply your username, password, and a display name for this dial-up connection (see Figure 18.14).

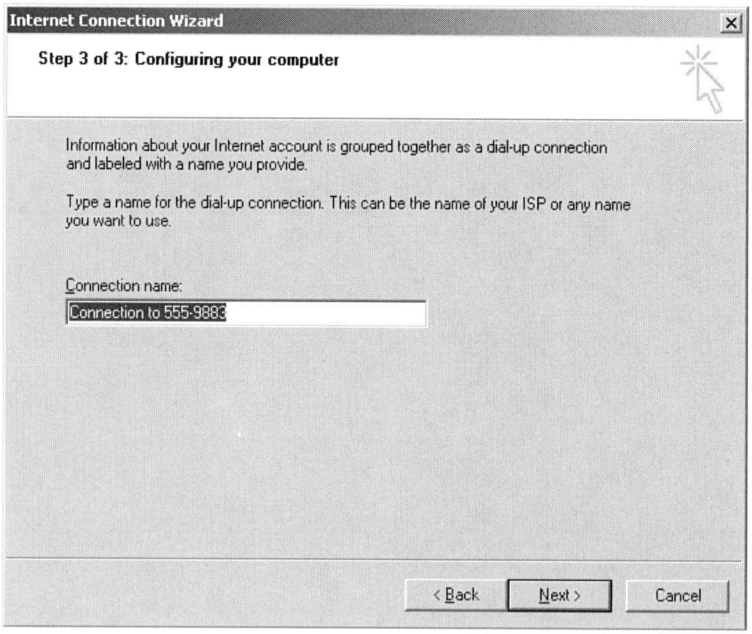

FIGURE 18.14

Here you can supply a friendly display name for the dial-up account you just established.

The steps for setting up a dial-up account are the same whether you're connecting to the Internet using an ISP or connecting to a company server. The details will vary somewhat with a company server, especially if it doesn't use TCP/IP as its Dial Up Networking (DUN) protocol. If you're not the one setting up the DUN/RAS on a server, you'll need to get these details from that person.

When you start IE5 again, you go to the IE5 section of the Microsoft Web site.

Examining the Internet Explorer 5 User Interface

Before going any further, let me explain the main areas of the IE5 User Interface (UI). These areas include the following:

- *Address*—In the Address list box, you can enter locations of Web sites you want to see. The Address list box keeps a history of the sites you have entered into the Address box. To revisit any of them, simply scroll down the list and select the one you want.

- *Toolbar*—Below the menu bar is the toolbar. The toolbar contains buttons that represent many of the menu options.

- *Menu bar*—The menu bar located at the top of the UI allows you to configure and use the browser by selecting entries from the appropriate menu.

- *Page*—Below the Address is a large pane. This pane is used to display the information sent back from the Web site. Web sites divide their information into pages.

- *Status bar*—At the base of the UI is the status bar that displays the current status of the browser. The status bar displays information, such as the page it is accessing, what percentage of the page is left to download, and so on.

- *Logo*—Another area of the UI is the logo that is located on the top right-hand side of the browser. This logo also represents the status of the browser. If the browser is downloading or opening a page, the logo moves. If the browser is inactive, the logo is static.

- *Links*—The Links bar is used to store preselected Web sites. You can toggle between the Address list and the Links bar by clicking either the Address or Links button.

Address List Box

To access a Web site, you must enter its address in the Address list box. Web sites are represented by Uniform Resource Locators (URLs). These URLs can be as general or as specific as you require. Through URLs, you can specify either an entire Web site, or you can drill down and specify a particular page within it. A URL is always preceded by a prefix to define the data type it represents. For example, if a URL is preceded by the `http://` prefix, it signifies a scheme of HTML files. Other schemes are outlined in Table 18.1.

TABLE 18.1   URL Definition Schemes

Scheme	Data Type	Example
file	Data files	`file://ftp.microsoft.com/download/ie6.exe`
http	HTML files	`http://www.mrshowbiz.go.com`
news	Newsgroup	`news:news.suntimes.com`
telnet	Telnet	`telnet://hp1.unm.edu`
wais	WAIS	`wais://wais.unm.edu:8080`

As you can see from Table 18.1, a URL consists of a scheme prefix, a host, and an IP domain name. A host and IP domain name is a means of representing an IP address in a more intuitive way. For example, a machine might have an IP address of `192.168.12.10`, yet might possess a DNS name of `myhost` and might be a member of the `mydomain.com` IP domain—for example, `myhost.mydomain.com`. As you can see, a DNS name is easier to remember than an IP address. There is nothing stopping you from entering an IP address for a URL instead of a DNS name. For more information on DNS, see Chapter 21, "Windows 2000 Networking Protocols."

Look at the example of the `http` entry from Table 18.1— `http://www.mrshowbiz.go.com`. This general URL points to the index page for the entire site, as you can see in Figure 18.15.

To drill down further, you either need to enter a more specific URL, as shown in the Address list box in Figure 18.16, or follow a hypertext link.

As mentioned previously, the Address list keeps a history of the sites you visit. To go to any of these sites, scroll down through the list and select a site you want to visit.

Toolbar

The toolbar, which is located beneath the menu bar, is useful for quickly accessing various tools and features within IE5. Toolbars are primarily used to present menu options to users in a graphical fashion. When the main menu options are displayed in a prominent position on the toolbar, users can select options quicker. The main toolbar buttons are outlined later in this chapter. The IE5 toolbar contains navigation buttons that allow you to navigate your way through sites. You can use the Back and Forward buttons (far left) to navigate between pages you have previously visited. Webmasters usually place hypertext links to preceding and succeeding pages within the pages themselves. You use the Stop button to interrupt the loading of a page, site, file, or other multimedia object.

FIGURE 18.15

A general URL or home page.

FIGURE 18.16

A specific URL or a page on a site.

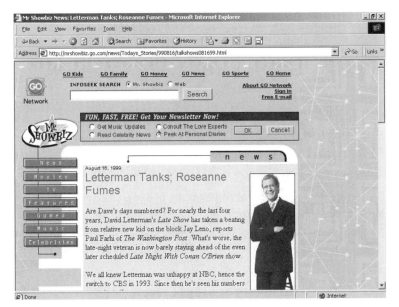

To refresh the display, click the Refresh button. This action builds the page from IE5's cache. To force IE5 to reload from the site directly, hold down the Shift key and click Refresh.

The Home button, when clicked, takes you to your user-defined home page (initially the Microsoft Web site). When you start IE5, it always loads this home page. Later in this chapter, in the "Options" section, you learn how to set this page to be whatever you want.

The Search button splits your page and displays a search page (see Figure 18.17).

FIGURE 18.17

The search facility splits the screen between search criteria and display.

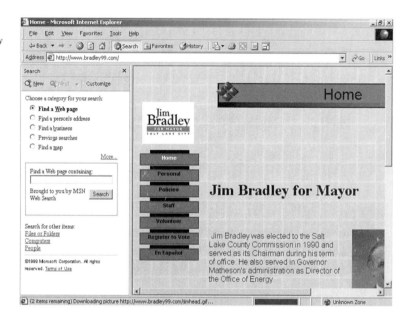

This search page contains a list of possible search types. You can customize the search engine by clicking Customize in the upper-right section of the Search pane shown in Figure 18.17. This will display the dialog box shown in Figure 18.18 where you can specify search engines to use or let IE manage things for itself (default).

To find a resource (the name for anything online), enter what you're looking for as a criteria in the supplied text box in the Search pane. I'll enter my surname to see what happens and leave the choice to finding a Web page. Click the Search button and the engines will go to work. Figure 18.19 shows one return I got from entering this criterion.

FIGURE 18.18

Customizing the search engines.

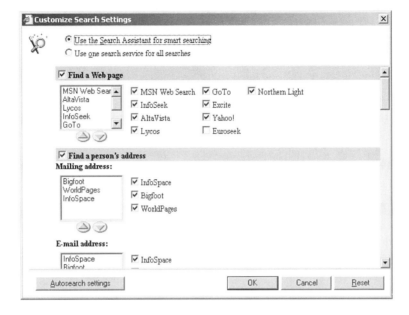

FIGURE 18.19

One return from a simple criterion.

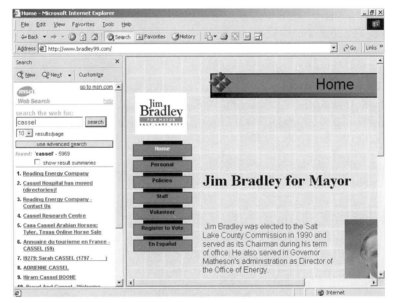

To go to any of the sites listed in the Search pane, click the link and it'll appear in the right pane. Figure 18.20 shows one such link's page.

FIGURE **18.20**

You can display the linked resource in the right pane.

To close the Search pane, click its toolbar button or click the close button (×) on the upper-right corner.

Favorites

The Favorites button on the toolbar contains a pane for configuring and selecting your favorite sites. Click it to activate the pane shown in Figure 18.21. You can also use the menu bar Favorites selection to see the entries in this pane in a slightly different presentation. All the facilities of the Favorites pane exist in the menu selection.

To add the current URL to your list of favorites, simply choose Add to Favorite from the menu.

You can manage your favorites by choosing the Organize option. This displays the Organize Favorites dialog box (see Figure 18.22).

Your favorites are stored within the Favorites folder of your profile folder. The buttons at the base of the Organize Favorites dialog box can help you manage your favorites.

The Move to Folder button allows you to move a selected favorite to a subfolder underneath the Favorites folder. After you choose the Move to Folder button, the Browse for Folder dialog box appears, as shown in Figure 18.23. You can select a new destination for your folder in this dialog box. After you decide on a destination, click OK to return to the Organize Favorites dialog box.

FIGURE **18.21**

The Favorites menu.

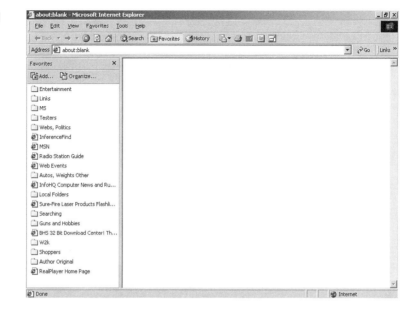

FIGURE **18.22**

The Organize Favorites dialog box.

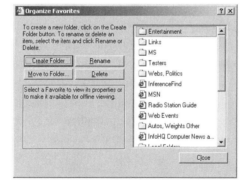

18

USING MICROSOFT INTERNET EXPLORER

The Rename button in the Organize Favorites dialog box allows you to rename a selected favorite to whatever name suits you. Choosing the Delete button removes the favorite from the list. Remember: You can save your Favorites folder (and other elements of Internet Explorer) by backing up or making copies of their folders.

You can also create a folder to contain links or other folders by using the Create Folder button. To go to any Favorite in the right pane, click it or, in the case of a folder, click it to open and show its contents (usually links or other folders).

FIGURE **18.23**

Moving a folder in Favorites.

Offline

There is an option on Organize Favorites to make a link (a favorite) available offline. This feature was known as Subscriptions in previous versions of IE.

Through this facility, you can subscribe to a Web site and configure IE5 to pull down any updates to the site automatically. This feature is useful because you can download the pages at night or when Professional is idle. You can view the updated site either online or offline at your convenience.

To subscribe to a site (make it available offline), simply choose the check box from the Organize Favorites dialog box. Doing this brings up a button for Properties for the subscribed to link. Figure 18.24 shows the tabbed Web Events Properties dialog box for offline sites.

This dialog box lists the details of the subscription. The two critical tabs are Download and Schedule. The Download tab is shown in Figure 18.25. This lets you detail how the site will be downloaded for later offline viewing.

On the Schedule tab, shown in Figure 18.26, you can define when IE5 seeks an update from the site.

You can set IE5 to update only when you force a synchronize (top option button), or you can customize IE to update when you require. If you select the second option, you'll need to set up a schedule using the Add button. The dialog box for adding a schedule is shown in Figure 18.27.

FIGURE 18.24

The Web Events Properties dialog box for offline sites.

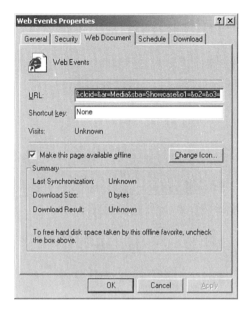

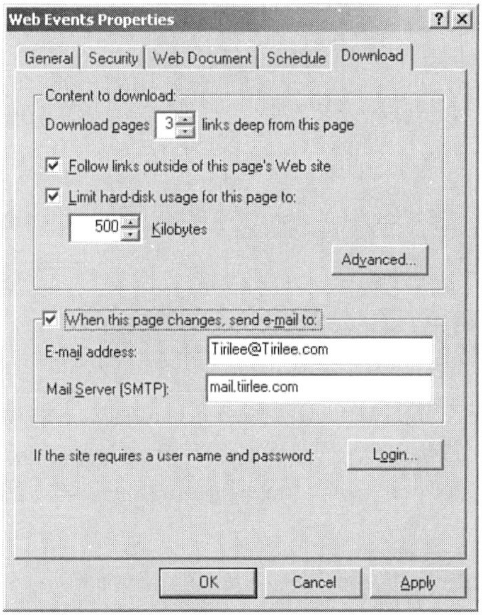

FIGURE 18.25

The Download tab of the Web Events Properties dialog box.

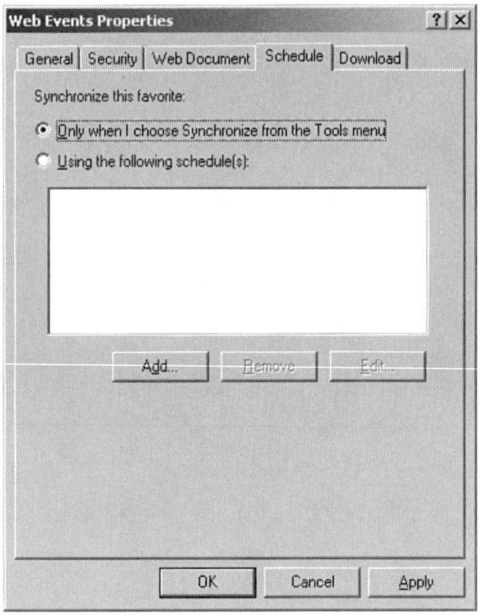

FIGURE 18.26

The Schedule tab.

FIGURE 18.27

The New Schedule dialog box.

You can get more specific here with scheduling and download when it best suits you. Select a schedule and click OK to return to the Web Events Properties dialog box. Note you can also have the Scheduler dial up for those installations that aren't always connected to the Internet.

You need to set one final configuration option on the Download tab of the Web Events Properties dialog box. If the remote site requires a username and password, click the Login button on the Download tab. The Login Options dialog box appears (see Figure 18.28).

FIGURE **18.28**

The Login Options dialog box.

In this dialog box, enter your username and password (then confirm) for the site. Click OK to return to the Web Events Properties dialog box.

The Advanced button in the Download tab allows you to restrict the download contents. This is important if you want to download only text and links instead of all that a site might have (such a multimedia content). Figure 18.29 shows the Advanced Download Options dialog box for this button.

FIGURE **18.29**

The Advanced Download Options dialog box of the Download tab will allow you to prevent unwanted download content.

The Security tab within the Web Events Properties dialog box is shown in Figure 18.30.

This is the standard Security dialog box allowing you to change, view, delete, or add permissions for users and groups if you have the security permissions yourself to do so.

If you have set the update schedule to only when you synchronize, you'll have to sync from time to time or your content will never get updated. To do this choose Tools, Synchronize from the main menu. This will result in the Items to Synchronize dialog box shown in Figure 18.31.

FIGURE **18.30**

The Security tab of the Web Events Properties dialog box.

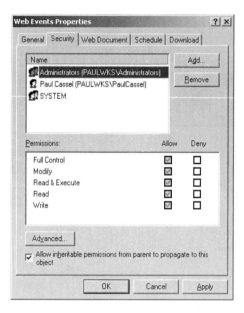

FIGURE **18.31**

The Items to Synchronize dialog box.

The Setup button on the Items to Synchronize dialog box allows you to set up global update options for your offline (subscribed to) sites. Figure 18.32 shows the dialog box that displays when you choose this button.

FIGURE 18.32

The Synchroniza-tion Settings dialog box.

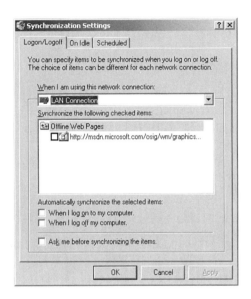

File Menu

In addition to the toolbar, a user can choose to use the menu bar located at the top of IE5. The first menu on the menu bar is the File menu. By choosing the Open option from the File menu, you can open a URL. This approach is equivalent to entering the URL in the Address list box or pressing Ctrl+O and then entering the URL directly.

When you choose Open, the Open dialog box appears (see Figure 18.33). Here, you enter the URL for the site you want to visit and click OK. Notice that the Open dialog box keeps a history of URLs you have previously entered within its drop-down list. A history list containing previously visited sites is also maintained within the File menu itself. You can also browse to a saved URL by choosing the Browse button. To save the current URL you're visiting, simply choose File, Save. You can also choose the Save As option to determine where and in what format the URL is saved.

FIGURE 18.33

The Open dialog box.

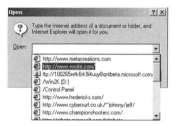

If you choose File, Properties, the Properties dialog box for the currently displayed URL appears (see Figure 18.34). The General tab of the Properties dialog box lists the page header, its protocol, its document type, its URL, its size, and when it was created, modified, and updated.

FIGURE 18.34

The Properties dialog box for a page.

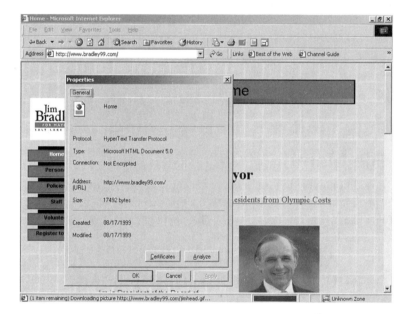

The Certificates button of the Properties dialog box shown in Figure 18.34 lists the security information for the current page. The Analyze button analyzes the page for errors. Figure 18.35 shows an error free page analysis. To close the Properties dialog box, simply click OK.

The Work Offline option on the File menu allows you to traverse through pages that you downloaded earlier through a scheduled update. You do not have to be online because these pages are all on your local computer.

If you have Microsoft FrontPage installed, it will modify the File menu to include an option to edit the current page using that program. You must have requisite permissions to do this, of course. The other entries on File, such as Print, are self evident.

FIGURE 18.35

This page has no errors detectable by Internet Explorer.

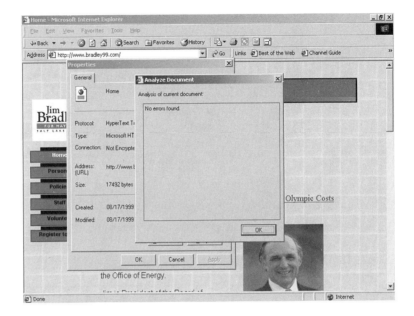

Edit Menu

The Edit menu allows you to cut, copy, and paste selected objects to and from pages. You also can choose the Find option, which searches the current page for a word or phrase you enter.

View Menu

You use the View menu to enable or disable the toolbar and status bar. You can also use it to view the source of a page in raw HTML format. Figure 18.36 shows the HTML equivalent of the page shown in Figure 18.33. Note that to do this IE loads the page in Notepad.

You can view a site or the Web in full screen by choosing this option from the View menu or by pressing F11 (toggle). Figure 18.37 shows a page in Full Screen view.

FIGURE 18.36

*A home page in
raw HTML.*

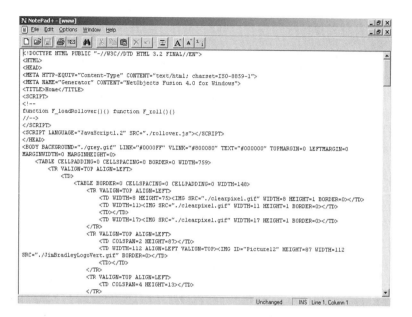

FIGURE 18.37

*The same home
page as Figure
18.36 shown in a
browser.*

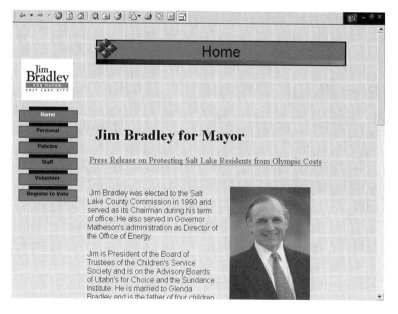

Tools Menu

The Tools menu allows you to access Internet Options, access mail and news (based on the Programs tab in Internet Options), send a link, find related links, and access the Windows update site where you can find the latest updates to Windows 2000 Professional.

Internet Options

By choosing Tools, Internet Options, you can configure IE5 to a look and feel that suits you. Figure 18.38 shows the General tab of the Internet Options dialog box that appears.

FIGURE 18.38

The General tab of the Internet Options dialog box.

The Security tab (see Figure 18.39) allows you to set how much security your browser will use. To summarize Microsoft's security concept here, this tab and its slider will configure IE for different modes on what IE will allow or allow with user notification. For example, the lowest security setting will allow downloading of almost all content without notification. This makes it easy for you to get into trouble, but it also provides seamless browsing of the Web. The highest security setting will be quite intrusive because IE will either not download or ask you before doing so.

To use this tab, first select an area to secure in the top icon pane and then set the slider for whatever security you want to apply.

The Content tab's Content Advisor (button) will allow you to filter content by predefined criteria. This tab's main purpose is to allow parents to configure IE for their children's unsupervised use—to filter out pornography or other objectionable material. To use this facility, first you enable it, secure the settings with a password, and then set the access level you want from fairly mild to fairly risqué. Figure 18.40 shows the Content Advisor dialog box.

FIGURE **18.39**

Setting security for a local intranet.

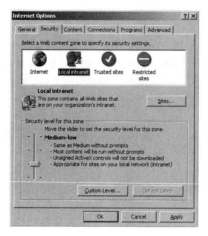

You can also enter or change your profile and set whether IE autocompletes URLs you've visited (from the History) on the Content tab. There are also buttons for setting Certificates (positive IDs) and Publishers of such certificates to set up a trusted site. A trusted site is a Web site or provider whose content can pass security.

FIGURE **18.40**

Protecting yourself or your users from objectionable sites using the content filtering that's part of IE.

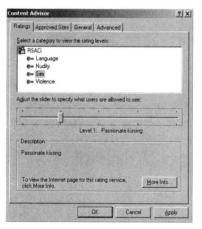

The Publishers button in the Certificates dialog box allows you to define what publishers of software you trust. The Authenticode Security Technology dialog box displays when you choose the Publishers button. You can trust all publishers by selecting the Consider All Commercial Software Publishers Trustworthy check box. Click OK to return to the Content tab.

On the Connection tab of the Internet Options dialog box (see Figure 18.41), you can call up the Internet Connection Wizard and set how and if IE will trigger dial-up networking if you're connected through a modem. There are also analogous settings for a LAN connection.

If you choose the LAN Settings button, the Proxy Settings dialog box displays (see Figure 18.42). On this dialog box, you can enter proxy values for services. You should be aware of the ports these services use. Click OK to return to the Internet Options dialog box.

FIGURE **18.41**

The Connection tab.

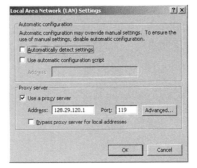

FIGURE **18.42**

The LAN Settings dialog box contains access to proxy server settings.

The Programs tab will tell IE which programs to use for non-browser work. For example, in Figure 18.43, the Programs tab has no entry for HTML Editor so IE uses the default program (Notepad). If you have a dedicated HTML editor, such as Home Site, you may prefer to tell IE to use this instead. There are also entries for email, newsgroups, and other related services.

18

USING MICROSOFT INTERNET EXPLORER

The Advanced tab is loaded with a plethora of check boxes to fine tune IE's functioning. The entries here are self-explanatory for the most part, especially if you're somewhat familiar with Web technology. If not, highlight an entry you have a question about and then press Shift+F1 for context-sensitive help.

FIGURE 18.43

The Programs tab asks what programs you want to use to support IE's non-browser functions.

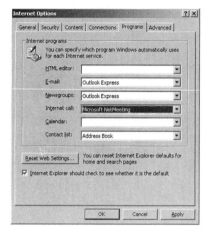

These entries are classified into functional categories to make wading through them somewhat easier. Figure 18.44 shows this tab with a context help up for an entry.

FIGURE 18.44

Context help is available to clarify even the most obscure entries in the Advanced tab.

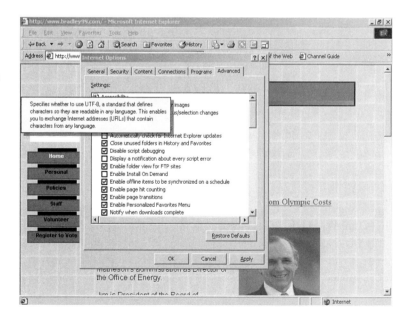

Favorites Menu

The Favorites menu on the menu bar is similar in function to the Favorites menu within the toolbar.

Links

To access a number of sites quickly, you can use the Links bar. The Links bar shares the same area on the user interface as the Address list box. You use the resize section of the Links toolbar to make it bigger (drag it left) or smaller (drag it right).

Figure 18.45 shows the IE5 UI with Links dragged left to make it bigger.

FIGURE 18.45

The Links bar.

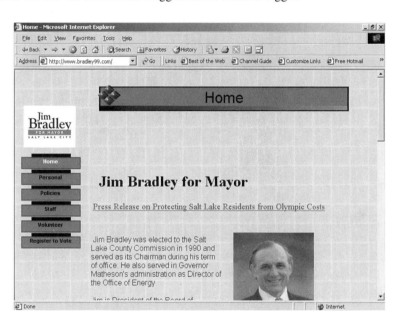

IE5 Tips and Tricks

To complete this look at IE5, I'll give you some tips and tricks to help you to get more from your browsing.

Drag to Links

You can drag a URL from a page and drop it on your Links bar. You can change the link's settings later by choosing Tools, Internet Options.

Context Menu

Right-clicking any page gives you the right-click, or context, menu (see Figure 18.46). With the right-click menu, you can traverse backward and forward, select all, create shortcuts, add the current page to your Favorites, view the document source, select the default language, print the current page, refresh the current page, and view the properties of the current page.

FIGURE **18.46**

The context menu.

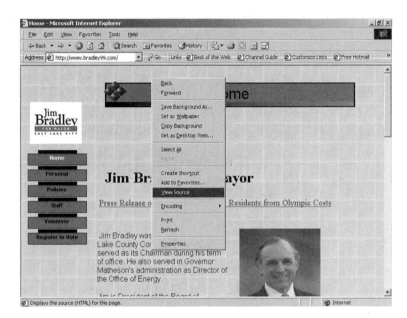

Powerful Printing

In IE5, options have been added to the standard print facility on the Options tab of the Print dialog box. Figure 18.47 shows the Print dialog box on the Options tab. The Print Frames area allows you to print either the select frame or all frames. This capability is useful if you're visiting a site with HTML frames. The Print All Linked Documents button allows you to print all linked documents also. Be careful with this option because your current page could be linked to many more pages. You can also print an index to the links along with the linked pages.

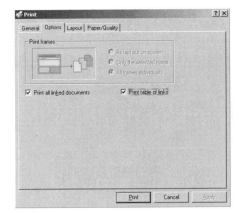

FIGURE **18.47**
*Extra print
options.*

Moving Favorites

You can drag and drop favorites within the Favorites menu and the Favorites toolbar entry. If you have several favorites, you can organize them so that the most popular ones are always on top.

Back and Forward

If you right-click the Back or Forward buttons, you get a list of the recent sites you visited. Select one, and IE5 takes you directly there.

Dragging Bars

By default, the Address and the Links bar share the same space. You can move either one of them to a separate line by clicking its left side and dragging and dropping it, as shown in Figure 18.48.

Express Searching

To enter a search criterion or criteria without opening the Search panel, choose File, Open or press Ctrl+O and then enter a question mark before your criterion. IE will take your entered criterion, open the Search panel, and then enter the criterion into the panel and start the search. This is enormously faster than the open and enter method of searching the Web.

FIGURE **18.48**

Dragging bars.

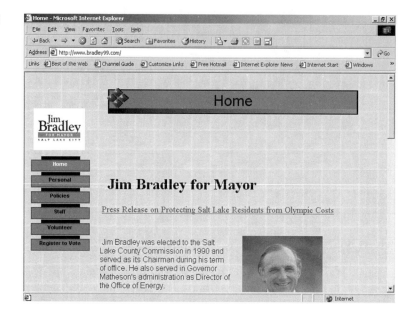

Summary

As the battle of the browsers rages, Microsoft's latest response comes in the form of Internet Explorer 5 (IE5). This chapter covered the initial setup of IE5 and took you through this feature-rich browser. The chapter concluded by covering some tricks and tips you can employ to leverage off IE5's many features.

Using Microsoft Outlook Express

CHAPTER 19

Outlook Express, or OE, is an extension of Internet Explorer. It is a news and email client with rudimentary facilities for management of messages. While other more sophisticated clients exist, many people find OE meets their needs so well that they use it exclusively.

I'm going to dance lightly over OE and its various aspects in this chapter. Microsoft has made a great effort to make this program's features discoverable to someone who has the basics. So what I'll do here is to show you the basics and then mention some of the features I've found people tend not to discover on their own rather than bog the chapter down with items almost everybody finds obvious.

Outlook Express Interface

The OE interface is the familiar right/left pane layout of Internet Explorer and Windows Explorer. The left pane holds information about subscribed to servers and user-defined and default folders (both for storing messages). The right pane is further divided top and bottom with the top for storage of headers (subject lines) and the bottom for display of message text. Figure 19.1 shows OE's three panes.

FIGURE 19.1

*Outlook Express'
three panes.*

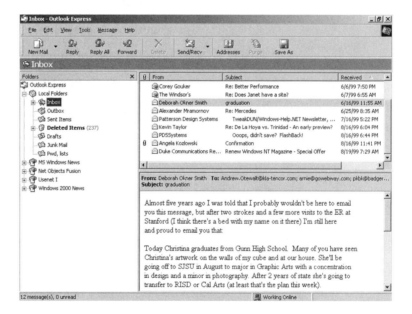

On the left, you can see topmost several entries starting with Local Folders. These are folders, some of which came defined with OE and some of which I've made for my convenience—for storage (archiving) of email or news messages. The Inbox folder has focus in Figure 19.1, meaning the contents of that folder will appear in the top section of the right pane.

Note on the right pane that I've highlighted a message. You may be able to make out that it's from Deborah Okner Smith and the topic (subject line) is "graduation." The bottom frame of the right pane shows the contents of this message, which is about Debbie's recovered health and her daughter's high school graduation.

When you first launch OE, you'll find a message or two from it and Microsoft, so even if you've never used OE before, you will have a message waiting for you. A little experimentation will give you the feel for the left, right, and double panes of OE.

Folder Management

Usually the default folders work fine for one just starting out in OE, but soon you'll want to create your own folder structure for message storage. You can also set message rules that will watch for certain senders or subject line words and route messages to particular folders. I, for example, have several businesses and don't like to mix email pertaining to them, so I set message rules (see the "Message Rules" section later in this chapter) to route messages according to sender and subject.

Creating and deleting new folders is the same in OE as in Windows Explorer or any other Windows 2000 facility. You have the familiar choice of menu or context menu choice. Here's how to do this from the context menu.

Locate the folder you want to be the parent to the folder you're creating. Right click it. Choose New Folder from the context menu (see Figure 19.2).

Name the folder and you're set. You can also drag and drop folders to make them equals, parents, or children of existing folders. Once you have a folder hierarchy, you can expand the tree or collapse it just as you can in Windows Explorer. As in that applet, a collapsed tree has a plus sign at its parent folder and a minus sign when expanded.

19

USING MICROSOFT
OUTLOOK
EXPRESS

FIGURE 19.2

Creating a new folder in OE is the same as creating a new folder in Windows Explorer.

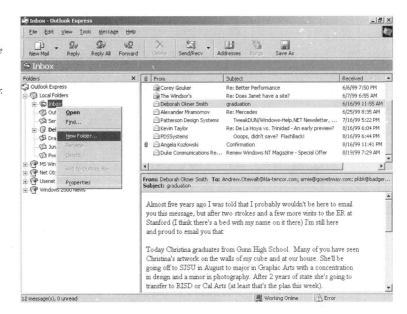

Message Management

You can drag and drop messages between folders. Dragging and dropping moves a message, while holding down Ctrl when dragging will copy a message. Generally speaking, operations in OE are the same as in Windows Explorer only falling apart when there isn't an analogous operation in one or the other.

You can also export messages from OE to a discrete file. To do this, select a message or open it, and then choose File, Save As from the menu. You will have the choice of saving the message in text, Unicode text, email (.eml), or HTML format. There is also a Save As button on the standard toolbar.

Note

The email format (.eml extension) is readable by OE, but not by general application packages such as Word 2000. Use a text format if you want your files to be generally usable.

Account Management

You'll need to establish at least one account before making any use of OE. An account is either an email account or a connection to a news server.

The Internet Connection Wizard has a section for creating an email account. You can run this Wizard to create an account (it'll appear in OE after you finish the Wizard) by choosing Start, Programs, Accessories, Communications, and then the Wizard, or do it faster using the new account method within OE.

> **Note**
>
> Chapter 17, "Setting Up TCP/IP Protocol Access," covers many aspects of Internet protocol. If this protocol or its details aren't familiar to you, I suggest you review this chapter before proceeding. The Glossary also contains explanations for some terms used here, but which aren't in the general computer lexicon.

To use the manual method within OE, choose Tools, Accounts, which will bring up a dialog box containing all your current accounts (if any). You do not have to be online to create an online account. Choose the Add, Mail Entry from the submenu to do an email account (see Figure 19.3).

FIGURE 19.3

Creating a new email account starts here.

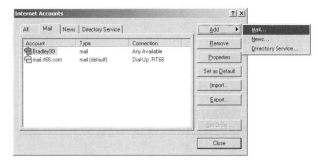

The creation process for an account is a wizard that launches as soon as you choose which type of account you're creating. You'll need to know the IP (Internet Protocol) or domain name for your outgoing and incoming server, your email address, logon name, and password to set up this account.

> **Note**
>
> Outlook Express' use is so widespread that many Internet Service Providers (ISPs) have distribution sheets telling you specifically what to enter in each text box of the New Account Wizard. If you have any doubts about what goes in which box, ask your ISP or your System Administrator (sysadmin).

> **Note**
>
> Setting up an email or news account is separate from setting up a dial-up account (RAS or DUN). You need to set that up too if you're connecting using a modem of any type. Chapter 17 covers many aspects of TCP/IP protocol. If this material is unfamiliar to you, I suggest you review that chapter.

News Accounts

Setting up a news account is similar to an email, but it's usually a bit simpler especially if you're logging on to a public server like the linked servers that form the Usenet.

You start out choosing Tools, Accounts (as with email), but choose the News option from the Add submenu. This launches the Internet Connection Wizard. Public servers (or services), such as the Usenet, or commercial servers, such as news.Microsoft.com or news.Netobjects.com (for the Net Objects company's products), don't require any logon, so the only thing you must tell OE is what the server's name is and what to use for your display name and email address (for those people who may want to email you off the server).

> **Tip**
>
> You can spoof public servers easily enough by using false email addresses or a handle (alias), and they'll still work just fine for news groups. People sometimes do this to prevent unsolicited (spam) email from utilities that collect user information from public servers. Sometimes people just prefer their identity to be a secret.

There are also private news servers that require you to log on. Figure 19.4 shows the dialog box in the Internet Connection Wizard's new news account where you tell it whether this is a private server requiring logons. If you check the box in the lower left, you'll get a dialog box with a user ID and password field when you launch the dial-up account. If you don't, you won't.

FIGURE **19.4**

Checking this box will branch you to a section of the Wizard where you can tell it your user name and password for private or secured servers.

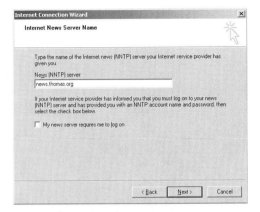

> **Note**
>
> Throughout both account setups, you'll get an option to use secure logons rather than the standard ones. Don't check this box unless you are sure your server uses this facility. Checking the secure logon box when your server can't comply won't make your logons more secure—they'll become impossible. When in doubt, leave it unchecked. You'll need to contact your System Administrator to know if your server uses this technology. This isn't the same as a user ID and password logon scheme.

Options

OE can be easily configured to suit your needs and style. The defaults suit most users, but it's a good idea to see what you can do to modify these defaults before you start working with OE.

To see these options, choose Tools, Options from the main menu. This displays the tabbed Options dialog box shown in Figure 19.5.

All these options other than the ones in Maintenance and Security are self-explanatory. I'll get to them in a moment.

I do want to discuss one item, even if it's obvious. The Send tab allows you to specify whether to use HTML or text-only messages for news and email.

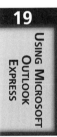

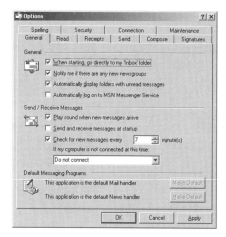

FIGURE 19.5

The Options for Outlook Express dialog box.

Note

Sending an email in HTML is the same as sending a Web page.

Text-only makes your messages smaller and also assures that they will be able to be displayed on all servers and all machines. HTML is pretty and also allows you to specify Stationery, but takes up much more bandwidth than text.

Tip

I'd say it's generally a bad idea to use HTML for news postings and a marginal idea for email unless you are sure your correspondents can read HTML (they can if they use OE) and don't mind the use of bandwidth and the attendant additional download time. When in any doubt, use text-only.

The Maintenance tab allows you to specify where to store the folders containing your messages. Many people, I think too many, lose their messages after a restore from backup due to not knowing where the messages were stored. Use this tab and the Store Folder button to tell OE where to store your messages. I find this option not to be very obvious because most folks don't recognize that the Store Folder button has anything to do with where the storage occurs.

Figure 19.6 shows the results of clicking the Store Folder button.

FIGURE 19.6

Telling OE where to store your messages. You can also point this to another place and then back again for a quick backup.

You'll have to restart your computer before your store folder change takes place.

There is also a Clean Up Now button on the Maintenance tab. OE will delete your news messages after an interval you specify here on the Maintenance tab, but you may want to compress or delete messages manually. Use the Clean Up Now button to do this.

> **Tip**
>
> OE will, by default, store sent messages in the Sent folder and deleted messages in the Deleted folder. You can change these options, but if you choose to keep them as they come from Microsoft, you should check in these folders from time to time to delete older messages because these folders can become enormous over time.

The Security tab offers various ways to secure your email by use of encryption and certificates (digital IDs). Certificates assure the recipient, by use of public and private key encryption, that a message is really from the stated sender. There is no such assurance in regular email and in fact spoofing, or sending a false return person or email address, is quite prevalent on the Internet. It only takes a few seconds to create a false identity in OE or similar programs.

A sophisticated user can determine that he or she has been spoofed by examining the header information, but most people will be fooled by this simple maneuver. The details of certificates are fairly complex, but Microsoft, understanding this, has created a good essay on the topic. To see this essay, choose the Security tab, and then choose the Tell Me More button. This will give you a very good overview of what this technology is about and how to use it if you so choose.

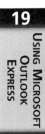

19

USING MICROSOFT
OUTLOOK
EXPRESS

> **Tip**
>
> I suggest strongly that you use this facility for all email of any critical nature and that you also not trust conventional (non-certified) email (especially the weird stuff) out of hand. It's just too easy to spoof folks.

There is also an Advanced tab for encryption. OE comes with the option of 56- or 40-bit encryption, which is secure for most transactions, but not if someone who knows what he is doing is trying to intercept your messages.

For this type of real security you'll need 128-bit encryption. This is somewhat controversial because the U.S. government claims it can't decrypt such code and is reluctant to let its untrusted citizens (non-government employees fall into this category) use it and also won't let it leave the country. This hasn't stopped many people from downloading the updates from the Microsoft site and installing them—a simple process.

Depending on the state of the state at any time, you might be able to download an extension to OE allowing full 128-bit encryption from the Microsoft Web site. It's worth a look. If you can get it, do so.

Outlook Express in Operation

The fundamental use of Outlook Express is stone-cold simple—electronic communications. Most of the operations are automatic, make use of the toolbar/menu, or are drag-and-drop. Everything available on the toolbar is also available in the menu system. Also, OE is context-sensitive. That is, when you have a news server highlighted, a new message will be a news message. When you have an email section highlighted, you'll get an email composer dialog box. The next sections are a quick run through of basic OE usage.

Send or Receive Messages

Click the Send/Receive button on the toolbar. This will send all messages in your Outbox (both email and pending news messages) and put all incoming messages in your Inbox or wherever you have them routed through your established Message Rules (see "Message Rules," later in this chapter).

Note

When you choose Tools, Options, and then select the Send (tab), you'll see an option (check box) to send messages right away or place them in your Outbox for later transmission. Even if you have your option set to send right away, you can place your messages in the Outbox by choosing the menu options File, Send Later after composing your message.

View Email Messages

Click the Inbox or the folder where the message exists. OE will display a list of stored messages by sender, date, and subject (and more) in the upper-right pane. Click the message you want to display in the lower pane. You can also double click the message to display it in it's own window (Multiple Document Architecture or MDA).

Compose a New Email

Highlight (click on) the Inbox folder or any mail folder. Click the New Mail button (far left) on the toolbar. Fill in the recipient's name (OE will auto-complete the address if it's in your Address Book), the Carbon Copy line and the Blind Copy line (both other email addresses and optional), and the Subject line (also optional). Then create your message in the large text box below. For more information on the Address Book, see "The Address Book" section later in this chapter.

Note

OE doesn't have a built-in spell checker but instead uses a checker from another compatible program or suite, such as Microsoft Office 1900. If you don't have such a program installed, you won't have any spell check capacity in OE.

19

USING MICROSOFT OUTLOOK EXPRESS

Note

A *blind copy* (bcc) is a copy of the message, but the original recipient (addressee) and other blind addressees don't see that it's copied to another. A *carbon copy* (cc) is also copied, but that information is shown to the addressee.

When you're done composing your email, you can send it by clicking the Send/Receive button, if you're online, or choose File, Send Later to store it in your Outbox for later transmission. You can also use File Save (As) to save a draft of your message in the Drafts folder. This is handy for longer edits or for storing messages you're not sure you want to send ("Take this Job and … it").

> **Caution**
>
> OE will send all messages in the Outbox at its send/receive interval or when you click Send/Receive on the toolbar. Do not store messages you don't want to send or are unsure of in the Outbox. More than one dispute has been triggered by such an innocent error.

Reply to Email

Highlight the message you want to reply to and then click Reply or Reply All on the toolbar. Reply will reply only to the sender, Reply All will reply to the sender and all copied parties. Compose your reply in the composer.

You have an option in Tools, Options, Send to include the original message in your reply. The email term for including the original message in your reply is *to quote*.

Forward an Email

Highlight the message or messages you want to forward to another (bounce) and then click the Forward button on the toolbar. Add an email address to forward to and then click the Send button or File, Send Later menu choices.

Using Newsgroups

Even after establishing an account with a server, you must tell OE from which groups within that server (really on that server) to see messages. OE must contact and then download the list of groups from every server in its news accounts. It will try to do this to new news accounts when you first use them.

Most message operations are available from the menu, the toolbar, or by context menu.

Getting the Group List and Subscribing

Figure 19.7 shows the process of OE downloading a server's newsgroups. The first time you're online and click a news server, OE will offer to download its newsgroups. You can't see messages in a server until you've downloaded this list.

Figure 19.8 shows the resulting list box with the groups in it.

FIGURE 19.7

Outlook Express will download the list of newsgroups the first time you log on to a news server.

FIGURE 19.8

This is the list of news groups on this server. There can be thousands of groups on large server systems, such as the Usenet.

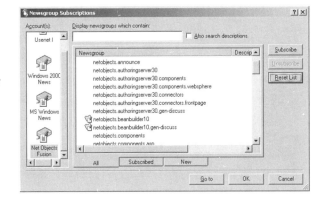

The download process is automatic once you've invoked it. When you've downloaded the list of newsgroups, you can subscribe to any group by double clicking it. A subscribed to newsgroup is one that appears persistently as a sub-entry under a server.

Figure 19.8 shows several subscribed to groups. They are the ones with a small folder-like icon to the left of the group name.

You can also see the group list filtered by subscribed to and new groups only by clicking the appropriate tab. To unsubscribe to a group, double click it again.

A subscribed to group is one that appears under the server for easy and fast use. There is no cost or obligation to such subscriptions.

19

USING MICROSOFT
OUTLOOK
EXPRESS

Newsgroup Message Reading

To see a list of newsgroup messages, locate the server (account) you want to access, and then click the group from which you want to see messages. Figure 19.9 shows me viewing messages from the server maintained by Net Objects company, the group is about Web design and one message is highlighted and appears in the lower window of the right pane.

FIGURE 19.9

Viewing or reading messages in newsgroups is almost identical to doing so in email. This message will be part of a thread if folks reply to it.

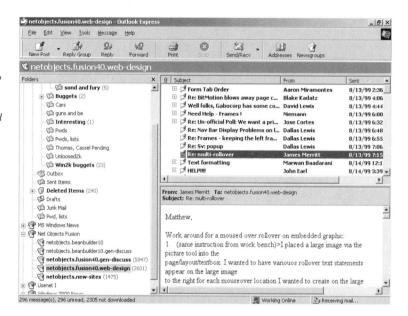

Newsgroup messages follow *threads*, which are messages and replies to those messages. To see an entire thread, click the plus sign next to the message in the upper-right pane. The highlighted message in 19.9 isn't part of a thread. Figure 19.10 shows a thread expanded with a message displayed.

Replying to and Forwarding News Messages

To reply to a newsgroup message, highlight the message and click the Reply or Reply Group button. A Reply is an email message. A Reply Group posts the message as part of the thread.

You can also forward a message by clicking the Forward button.

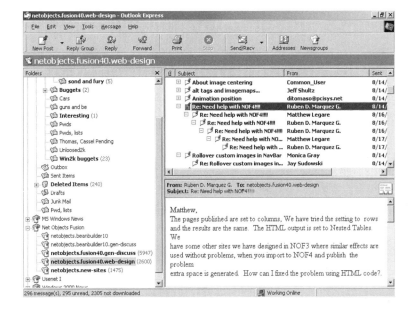

FIGURE **19.10**

Here is a thread expanded to see the original message and its replies.

Archiving Messages

You can copy news messages to a folder by right clicking the message and choosing the Copy to Folder option. Because OE will delete messages at your preset time, be sure to do this if you want to archive a message from a newsgroup.

The Address Book

You can manually enter email addresses or use the Address Book, which not only contains email information but general contact information as well. To launch the Address Book, click the Addresses icon on the toolbar.

By default, OE will enter all messages you reply to in your Address Book. You can turn off this option on the Send tab of Tools, Options.

Adding Contacts

To add an entry in Address Book, open it, click the New button on the toolbar, and choose New Contact from the pull-down menu.

Enter a person's information in the spaces provided and click OK to commit the entry to the database. Figure 19.11 shows an entry being made to the database for Nancy Allf.

FIGURE 19.11

Here is Nancy's contact information being entered in the database.

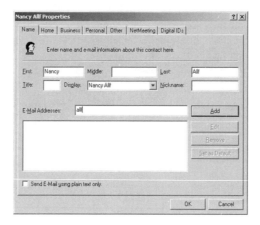

Nancy's email address is `xyaisk@allf.com`. After you enter her in the database, OE will attempt to auto-complete her address when entered as a recipient of an email. For example, if she's the only name that begins with "Na," it'll auto-complete her address after I enter those letters on the recipient line. She is surely the only person with an email address that starts with an `xy`, so entering `xy` will likewise auto-complete her address. This saves a lot of time and energy.

OE has an option in Tools, Options, Send (tab) to automatically place anybody you send messages to in your Address book. This is handy, but, if you often reply to news messages, it can bloat your Address Book alarmingly.

Groups

You can also create groups of contacts to which you can send mass mailings. To create a group, first enter all the contacts. If you forget a few, you can enter them on-the-fly using the New Contact option in the Group Creation dialog box.

Choose New from the Address Book toolbar and choose New Group. Click Select Members, which will bring up a list of what's in your Address Book. Highlight the members (or established groups) you want to add to your new group and then click the Select button to move them into the group. Click OK to commit the changes. Figure 19.12 shows a group in the first New Group dialog box. There is a details page allowing you to enter contact information for the group just as you would an individual contact.

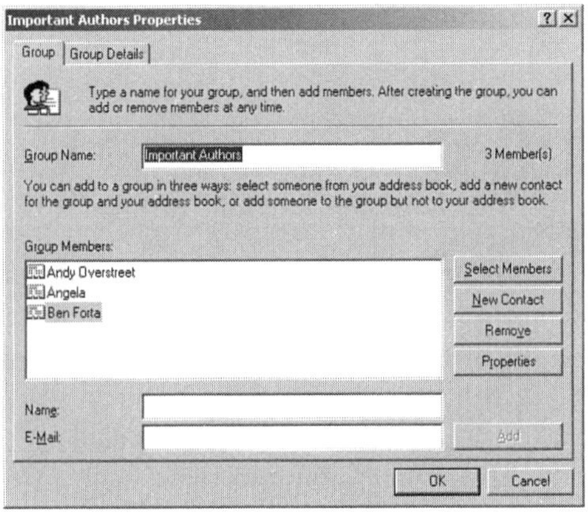

FIGURE 19.12

Groups are a fast and easy way to send mass mailings.

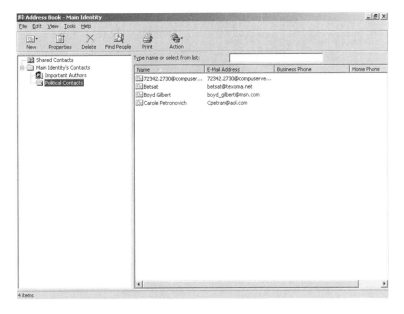

Folders

You can also organize your contacts in folders using the New Folder option in New. After you create a folder, you will have an Address Book organized into a left and right pane. You can drag and drop contacts from your main folder to private folders. You can also drag and drop into groups. Figure 19.13 shows the look of the Address Book with folders added.

FIGURE 19.13

Folders create the right and left pane look to Address Book.

You can also right click entries (or use the menu) to copy entries from folder-to-folder or group-to-group-to-folder.

Message Rules

You can tell OE to treat messages meeting certain criteria or a criterion in specific ways. Most people use this feature to filter out messages of objectionable material or from objectionable people. I use this facility to route my email into discrete folders according to the sender or subject and also to filter out objectionable people's mail.

Message Rules are on the Tools menu with three entries for the submenu, depending on whether you want to create a rule for email, news, or modify your blocked sender list. Creating a rule is as simple as setting criteria and then setting an action when that criteria is met. Figure 19.14 shows a rule being created for an email.

FIGURE 19.14

Here I'm making a rule to delete email messages bearing what I think will be objectionable content.

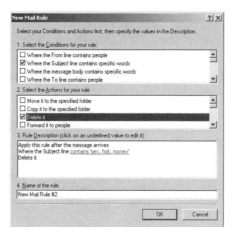

It might be tough to read, but in this rule I'm telling OE to filter out any email with the words "hot" or "sex" or "money" on the subject line and to then delete them without me even seeing them.

You can create a fast track rule by finding a message with some matching criteria and choosing Message, Create Rule from Message from the menu. This is the fast start to making a rule and also lets you quickly create a rule almost on-the-fly.

Blocking Senders

You can avoid the pain of seeing messages from any objectionable sender by blocking him or her in email, news, or both. You can do this either from the Message Rules Blocked Senders tab or by highlighting an email or news message from the sender and choosing the menu items Message, Block Sender. You can edit this list from Message Rules, Blocked Senders tab. Figure 19.15 shows my blocked senders list. Note most of the blocked ones are from newsgroups.

FIGURE 19.15

Blocking senders is a relief from the nonsensical. A sender block is also known as a twit filter.

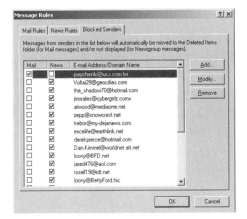

Identities

Identities are a way for more than one person to use OE or for one person to assume different identities while online. Different identities have different accounts and discrete Address Books.

To create a new identity, choose File, Identities, Add New Identity from the menu. Identities have passwords (optional) and can be secured through the usual Windows 1900 Professional security protocols.

You can also switch and manage identities using the menu items File, Switch Identities or File, Identities, Manage Identities.

Summary

This has been a quick tour of Outlook Express covering the basics and even some advanced subjects. The items in this chapter represent approximately 95 percent of what 95 percent of the users do using OE.

While Outlook Express is all most users need in either an email or news client, it's not meant to be everything to everybody. There are dedicated email programs such as Eudora, many dedicated news readers, like Agent, and even Microsoft's Outlook (from Office) has features lacking in Outlook Express.

But for just getting the job done in a quick and easy manner, it's hard to beat Outlook Express.

CHAPTER 20

Remote Computing with Remote Access Service

RAS stands for Remote Access Service. RAS is the Windows 2000 facility that is used to establish connections with other networks through either modems or LAN connections.

In this chapter, we will focus on the most common use of RAS today—a client connection to an Internet Service Provider (ISP). For those readers upgrading from Windows 95 or Windows 98, you will see a vast change in the number of features in "Dialup Networking." Because Windows 2000 Professional was built on the Windows NT technology, you will now have access to the options and diagnostic tools that were previously available only to the NT users.

For those readers upgrading from Windows NT 4.0, you will see some new features added to RAS, most notably the modem log. You will also see that the configuration screens for remote computing have taken on the Windows 95/98 look and feel and are not so intimidating for novices.

OK, let's get to some real work setting up your computer for remote dialup. In this chapter, we assume nothing automated has occurred. We assume that Windows did not detect your modem on its own and you have to install it manually. We also assume that your ISP needs all the DNS information added manually. With that in mind, we should be able to cover just about every situation out there for readers configuring RAS.

This chapter starts off the chapter with the installation of the modem driver and the configuration of the modem. Then we move into the setup of the dial-up connection to an ISP. In the example, we create a connection to my ISP, Mindspring. We finish up the chapter with a look at some tools that are available to you for troubleshooting, and we take a quick look at the other types of remote connections that RAS can handle.

Installing the Modem

As you read in the introduction, we are going to assume nothing as far as autodetection of the modem goes. In my particular case, I bought a new U.S. Robotics 56K Sportster, which my Windows 2000 beta version did not recognize. I had the added bad luck of no driver disk being included with my modem. I was able to use my older system to log on to the Internet, go to the U.S. Robotics Web site and download the drivers from there. Let's get started with the modem installation.

The first thing to do is pull up the Control Panel and select the Phone and Modem Options icon and shown in Figure 20.1.

FIGURE 20.1

Like all other Windows devices, modems are added, removed, and configured through the Control Panel.

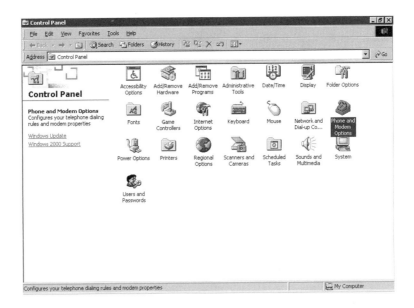

For new installations of Windows 2000, you will first be presented with the Location Information window, which will be used to configure the computer with your local telephone information. When you are done, this information will be used for your My Location default location.

The first location information window is shown in Figure 20.2.

FIGURE 20.2

The author's local telephone information.

The first drop-down list contains a list of most of the countries/regions in the world. For this selection, pick the country in which you live. The next piece of information you need to enter is your area code. In Figure 20.2, you see 203, which is the author's area code given that he currently lives in Connecticut.

The next box is interesting. It asks that you enter any numbers you normally dial to access an outside line. Because most people will be configuring RAS from home, this field can be left blank. In my case, however, I used the field to enter *67, which is my local phone company's code for disabling Caller ID boxes from seeing my phone number. Many companies can track the phone numbers of the people calling them through Caller ID. This little trick is just one small way of protecting your privacy. In the new millenium, you should take privacy wherever you can get it.

> **Tip**
>
> This does not work with toll free numbers—*67 has no effect.

The last question asks you if you use Tone or the older Pulse dialing on your phone. For the few people that don't know what this means, Tone means you are using a Touch Tone phone, and Pulse means that you are using the old style rotary phones. When you finish filling in the fields, click OK to continue.

After clicking OK, you will see the Phone and Modem Options window shown in Figure 20.3.

FIGURE 20.3

The Phone and Modem Options window with the new location displayed.

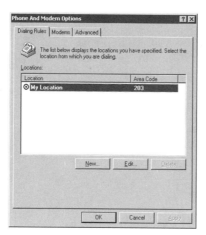

This window has three tabs: Dialing Rules, Modems, and Advanced.

The Dialing Rules Tab, shown in Figure 20.3, is the window you use to add and edit location information. New installs of Windows 2000 will display only one entry called "My Location." If you click Edit in this window, you will see all the location information you entered during the previous few paragraphs. To add a new location, simply click the Add button and follow the instruction dialog boxes.

Because our location information is already set, let's skip over Dialing Rules and click the Modems tab. The Modems tab is shown in Figure 20.4.

FIGURE 20.4

The Modems tab before the new modem is added.

If you take a look at Figure 20.4, you will see that there are no modems installed. It is not possible to configure RAS unless you have at least one modem installed and working. At this point, click the Add button.

Next you will see the Add/Remove Hardware Wizard. This Wizard can poll your system's communications ports in an effort to autodetect your modem. The first window in the Wizard is shown in Figure 20.5.

FIGURE 20.5

The Add/Remove Hardware Wizard.

For this chapter's purposes, we are assuming that you are using a modem new enough that Windows will not detect it. So, click the Don't Detect My Modem; I Will Select It from a List check box. Then click the Next button.

> **Tip**
>
> Before clicking the Next button, be sure that you have closed all other applications that could possibly be using the modem. Also, be sure that the modem is turned on and that the serial cable is properly connected to both the modem and your computer's serial port.

The second window in the Add/Remove Hardware Wizard contains a list of all the modems that Windows supports natively, as shown in Figure 20.6. They are grouped by manufacturer. If Windows did not detect the modem automatically, your modem is most likely on this list. If this is so, as it was with my USR 56K modem, and you have a driver floppy, place your driver disk in your floppy drive and click Have Disk. If you do find your modem in the list, select it and click Next.

FIGURE 20.6

Supported modem manufacturers and model names.

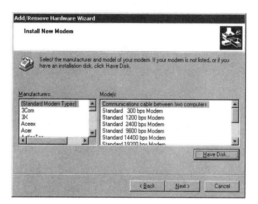

If you clicked Have Disk, you will see the Install From Disk window, as shown in Figure 20.7.

FIGURE 20.7

Modem driver location selection window.

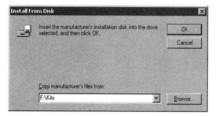

In this window, you can either type in the location of the driver files or click Browse to locate the files by exploring the disk. You need enter only the directory name. When you have identified the location of your driver files, click OK. If you look at Figure 20.7, you will see that I specified F:\Kits as my driver directory. If U.S. Robotics had given me a driver floppy, that field would most likely have been filled with the name of my floppy drive: A:\. Because I downloaded the drivers from the U.S. Robotics Web site, I simply specified the directory into which I downloaded the driver; no need to know or remember the filename of the driver file.

After you have successfully located and specified your driver directory and clicked OK, you will see the window displayed in Figure 20.8.

FIGURE 20.8
The 56K modem device driver found in the F:\Kits *directory.*

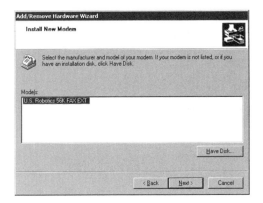

The Wizard will display all modem driver files in that directory. I had only one in my Kits directory and, as you can see from the figure, it was the device driver for my 56K modem. Highlight the name of your modem from the list, and click Next.

The next window you will see is shown in Figure 20.9. After you have selected your modem driver, the Wizard will ask you on which communications port to install the modem. Because I had my modem (which is an external modem) connected to COM1, I selected that. You also have the option of selecting All Ports, which will install the driver to run on all your serial communication ports. When you are done with this window, click Next.

When the driver is installed, you will once again be presented with the Phone and Modem Options window, with the Modems tab selected. Now however, instead of an empty list, you will see your newly installed modem. This is shown in Figure 20.10.

With this process completed, you are now able to configure network and dial-up connections to create new network connections.

20

REMOTE COMPUTING WITH REMOTE ACCESS SERVICE

FIGURE 20.9

The modem port selection window.

FIGURE 20.10

The newly installed modem.

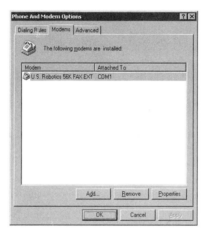

Creating a Dial-up Connection to the Internet

There are many different ways to use RAS to create network connections. In this part of the chapter, we detail how to make the connection between your home computer and the Internet through the use of an ISP. The other possible uses for RAS will be discussed later in the chapter.

Creating Your Dial-up Connection

Now that you have your modem installed and ready to go, you need to tell Windows 2000 about the ISP you use.

The first thing you want to do is pull up the Network and Dial-up Connections window (see Figure 20.11). This window is accessed from the Control Panel.

FIGURE **20.11**

The Network and Dial-up Connections window.

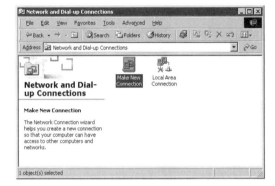

You will see a list of your already configured connections (if any) and an icon named Make New Connection.

Windows 2000 provides the Network Connection Wizard to help you configure RAS to get you connected to the Internet. Double-click the Make New Connection icon to start the Wizard. This icon is highlighted in Figure 20.11.

You will see the window shown in Figure 20.12. This is simply a banner window and there is nothing to do here except to click Next to continue or cancel to exit out of the Wizard.

FIGURE **20.12**

The Network Connection Wizard.

You will see the Network Connection Type window. This is where you select the type of network connection you want to create. For all dial-up connections to ISPs, select the second option, Dial-up to the Internet, as shown in Figure 20.13. After you have done that, click Next to continue.

FIGURE 20.13

The Network Connection Type window.

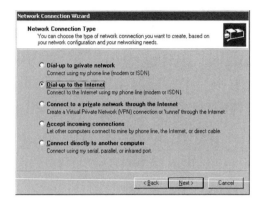

You will see that the Internet Connection Wizard has started. The Internet Connection Wizard is used specifically to configure dial-up connections to the Internet. As you can see from Figure 20.14, you have four options to define your ISP connection information.

FIGURE 20.14

The Internet Connection Wizard.

The first option helps you sign up for a new Internet access account if you don't already have one. If you select this option, and your newly-configured modem is working, your Windows 2000 system will dial up the Microsoft Internet Referral Service through a toll-free number and will download a list of the ISPs in your area. From that point, you can pick one and sign up, or you can cancel out of the Wizard.

The second option is I Want to Transfer My Existing Internet Account to This Computer. This option also dials the Microsoft Internet Referral Service and then creates a list of ISPs in your area. All you have to do is click your current ISP and the Wizard will dial up the ISP. You then follow the Wizard to reregister your account.

The third option, I Want to Set Up My Internet Connection Manually, is the one we will use. If you have trouble with either of the first two options, you will have to configure your Internet connection with this part of the Wizard. When you select this option, you are asked a series of questions about your ISP. When done, an icon is created in the Network and Dial-up Connections window that will put you one click away from the Internet. To exit out of the wizard now, click Cancel. Otherwise, select I Want to Set Up My Internet Connection Manually option and click Next to continue.

The next window you will see is shown in Figure 20.15. On this window, you select the path you will be taking to the Internet: either through a modem or across a local network. Because we are using a modem, select the I Connect Through a Phone Line and a Modem option and click Next to continue.

FIGURE 20.15

Setting up your Internet connection window.

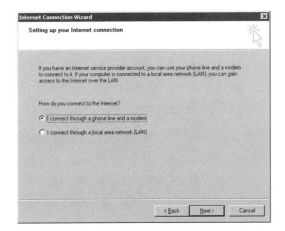

The next window is the dial-up connection step 1 of 3 window. On this window, enter the phone number (including area code) of your ISP's modem pool. As you can see in Figure 20.16, I have entered the local number for my ISP. You will see a note at the bottom of the window saying that most ISPs do not require you to enter connection property information.

This type information is a static IP address, should you have one, and the IP addresses of the primary and secondary DNS. For our purposes, we will assume that this information must be entered. If you have this information, click Advanced. If not, you can skip this step and come back to it should your ISP require manual entry of this information.

If you have clicked the Advanced button, you will see the Advanced Connection Properties window shown in Figure 20.17.

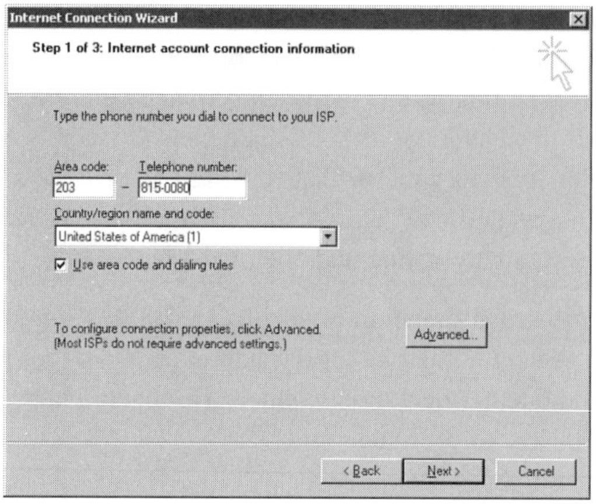

FIGURE 20.16

Step 1 of 3—
defining telephone
connection
information.

FIGURE 20.17

The Advanced
Connection
Properties con-
nection dialog
box.

This window has two tabs. On the Connection tab, you have the connection type and logon procedure information. For most ISPs, you can take the default of PPP (point-to-point) for your protocol setting. SLIP and C-SLIP are older and are most likely there for compatibility with older systems.

The other option you have on this tab is how you want to log in. If you select None, Windows 2000 passes your username and password to the ISP. If the information is correct, you will see the network connection icon appear at the bottom of the screen on the taskbar, and you are on your way. If the log on did not work (because of an invalid password, for example), you will promptly be told that an error has occurred.

I recommend that you choose the Log On Manually option when first setting up your dial-up connection. What this option does is after the modem has dialed your ISP, Windows 2000 will pop up a terminal window and display the login prompt from your

ISP's system. You then manually type in your username and password. If correct, you will see a message that the PPP session has started, followed by some garbage characters. This is good. Simply click Done and you're on your way. If there was an error, you will see the exact error text from the ISP right on your screen. This is a great debugging tool and will also let you know if you have dialed the wrong computer.

The last option for login procedure is the Use Login Script option. This option usually is used by people connecting to systems that require the entry of multiple passwords and commands. The text of the script is stored in the specified file. You will not need to use this option to connect to an ISP.

Now, click the Addressees tab on the Advanced Connection Properties window. This tab is shown in Figure 20.18.

FIGURE 20.18

The Advanced Connection Properties window Addresses tab.

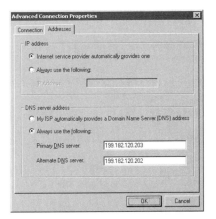

On this tab, you can manually enter in two types of information. The first type is your IP address. Most ISPs share a group of TCP/IP addresses, and you are assigned one of the free ones when you log on. If that is the case, select the Internet Service Provider Automatically Provides One option. If you have a static IP address, if you have the same IP address every time you log on, you would enter that number here. If you are unsure, don't use this option. Internet users that have static IP addresses know what they are and are paying big bucks for them.

On the bottom of the tab you will see the DNS connection information. This is where you enter the IP addresses of the primary and alternate (secondary) DNS servers.

DNS stands for Distributed Name Service, and it contains a list of all the Internet domain names and the IP addresses that correspond to them. You will need DNS to access anything on the Internet. Communication over the Internet is done through the IP addresses and not by the name. For example, if you start a browser and enter the URL `http://www.joeduer.com`, the browser does not open a connection to `joeduer.com`. If you look at the bottom of the screen, you will see the message "Looking up joeduer.com." This means that the browser is calling DNS to get the IP address of `joeduer.com`. When the DNS returns the information (209.111.242.39) to the browser, the browser says connecting to 209.111.242.39, and it opens a connection to the Web site.

If you look again at Figure 20.18, you will see the DNS information for Netcom/Mindspring entered on the window.

When you are done with this tab click OK to close the Advanced Connection Properties dialog box.

Step 2 of the Internet Connection Wizard is the entry of the username and password of your ISP account. This window is shown in Figure 20.19.

FIGURE 20.19
Step 2 of 3— defining your ISP account information.

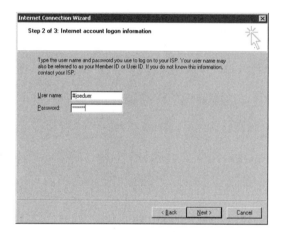

There is not too much to this step, simply enter your username and password in the fields as shown. If you do not know your username and your password, contact your ISP's customer service department and ask them what they are. When you have entered this information correctly, click Next to continue.

Now you will see step 3 of the Internet Connection Wizard. On this window (shown in Figure 20.20), all you have to do is type in a name for the connection. You can type in whatever you want, the information you type in here is what you will see on the Network and Dial-up Connections window. So, you will want to be descriptive about the type of connection the icon represents. If you look again at the figure, you will see that not only did I enter the name of the ISP, but also the location of the modem I am dialing. By doing this, when I travel, I can copy that connection icon, change the phone number, and have one-click local-call access to my ISP from wherever I am.

FIGURE 20.20

*Step 3 of 3—
Creating the net-
work connection
icon.*

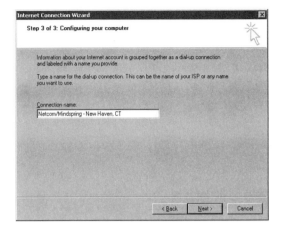

When you are done with this, click Next to continue.

Configuring Email

The next part of the Wizard allows you to enter your email server information. If you do
this, you can use the Microsoft tools to read your email right off the Internet. If this is
what you want to do, click Next to continue. If you use a different email client, such as
Eudora, you can click Cancel here and then configure Eudora separately.

You are given this option right on the Wizard, as shown in Figure 20.21.

FIGURE 20.21

*The Internet
Connection
Wizard's email
option.*

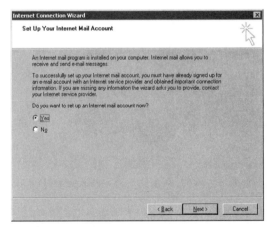

The single question on this Wizard window asks if you want to set up an Internet mail
account now. If you do, click Yes and then Next to continue. If not, you can click Cancel
and proceed to the next section of the chapter.

The first step in configuring your Internet email is to enter your name, as shown in Figure 20.22

FIGURE 20.22

Type your name here.

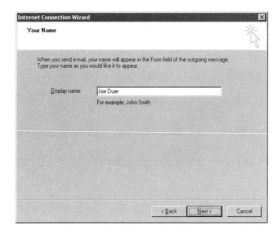

The name you enter here should be your actual name, not your account name. This is the name that appears in the From: column of all your email messages. As you can see from the figure, I entered my real full name.

When you have completed this task, click Next to continue.

Figure 20.23 shows the next window you will see of the Internet Connection Wizard— the email address window. On this window, you should enter your email address so that the people that receive your mail can reply to it.

FIGURE 20.23

Specifying your email address.

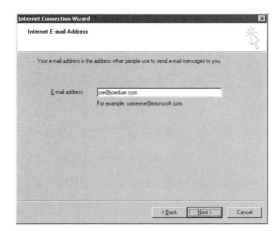

In reality, you can enter anything you want. If you do enter bogus information, such as x@y.z, this will appear in the Reply to: field of your email message, and your recipient will not be able to reply to your message. So, enter your real email address and double check it to make sure it is correct. When you're done, click Next to continue. If you spell something wrong in your email address, your email will still work without problem, you just won't get any responses to your messages.

The next step in defining your email information is specifying the names of your incoming and outgoing mail servers. You get this information directly from your ISP. This Wizard window is shown in Figure 20.24.

FIGURE 20.24

Defining the incoming and SMTP (outgoing) email servers.

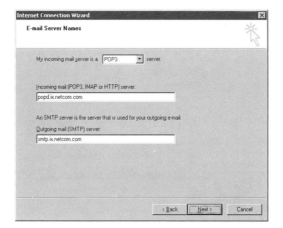

The first thing you have to define is the type of email server from which you will be retrieving your mail messages. You have a choice of POP3, IMAP, or HTTP servers. Most ISPs use POP mail, and that is the default. You select the server type and enter the server name in the field. For example, my POP3 server is located at popd.ix.netcom.com.

The other thing you have to configure on this window is how you are going to send mail. Sending mail over the Internet is done universally though a SMTP server. All you have to do on this part of the window is enter the name of the SMTP server your ISP provides for you. As you can see in Figure 20.24, the SMTP server that Netcom uses is smtp.ix.netcom.com.

When you are done entering this information, click Next to continue.

The next window you will see is the Internet Mail Logon screen, shown in Figure 20.25. All you need to do here is enter your ISP username and password (the same as you did before) so that your email software will be able to dial up the Internet and get your email on its own without having you connect to the Internet first. This is an easy task, and when you have completed it, click Next to finish up.

FIGURE 20.25

*ISP account user-
name and pass-
word information
for the email
client.*

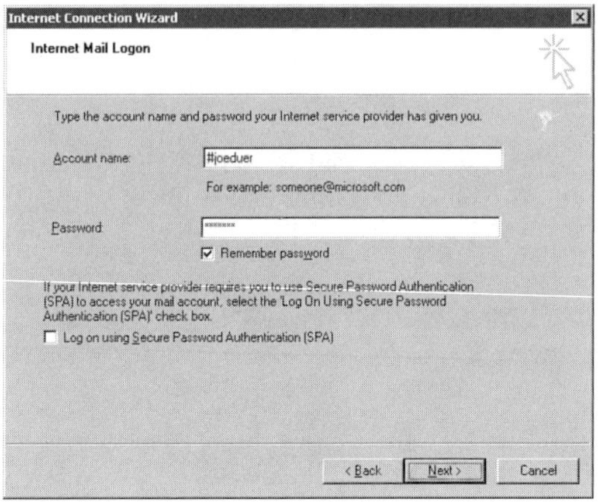

You have now successfully reached the end of the Wizard! The last window you will see is shown in Figure 20.26.

FIGURE 20.26

*Exiting the
Internet
Connection
Wizard.*

This window simply states that you are done and that it will activate the connection immediately if you select the check box on the window. This would be a good test of your new connection. Whichever way you decide, click Finish to exit the Wizard.

When you double-click the icon for Internet dial-up, you will see the window displayed in Figure 20.27.

FIGURE 20.27

Login box for Dial-up Networking.

This is a basic dialog box that is prompting you for your Internet username and password. The defaults that are shown are the username and password you entered while running the Wizard. There is a check box on the window that will save your password from day to day, so you don't have to constantly retype it. If this is a security issue for you, uncheck the box, and that will tell Windows to ask you for your password each time you dial into the Internet. Your username will be saved from day to day regardless.

If you select the Properties button at the bottom of the window, you will go to a window with multiple tabs that will allow you to change any of the information you entered in the Wizard during the creation of the Internet connection. You would correct any mistakes or do any customizations here.

Lastly, when you click the Dial button, Windows 2000 will dial the modem and connect you to the Internet. When successful, you will see a small icon on your taskbar showing that the connection is active. When you see that icon, you can run email, start a Web browser, connect to IRC chat, or do anything else you want on the Internet.

Other Features of RAS

In this part of the chapter, we will take a look at the lesser-known and seldom-used features of the Remote Access Service. These include different types of network connections other than Internet ISP dial-up. Also included in this section are some troubleshooting tools for debugging dial-up connections and how to use the command line version of RAS to dial up the Internet right from a console prompt. We close this section with the details of the RAS autodial feature.

Other Types of RAS Connections

With all the text and figures you have seen in setting up the dial-up connection to the Internet, it is hard to imagine there is much more to RAS, but there is. Take a look back at Figure 20.13. You remember that we only discussed in detail the Dial-up to the

20

REMOTE COMPUTING
WITH REMOTE
ACCESS SERVICE

Internet option. Let's take a quick look at the other types of RAS connections available to you.

Dial-up to Private Network

You use this option to connect to a private network. When you select this option, the Wizard asks you for the telephone number of the network you are calling and if you want to make it public or not. If you choose not to make it public, the icon will appear only on your desktop and will not appear for other users that use your system.

Connect to a Private Network Through the Internet

You select this option to connect to a private network after first dialing the Internet. When the Wizard runs, you are asked for which dial-up connection to use to first get on the Internet, and then you are asked for the TCP/IP address of the system or private network to which you will be connecting. This is shown in Figure 20.28. Lastly, you also have the option of keeping the icon private or global to all users on your system.

FIGURE 20.28

Using the Network Connection Wizard to connect to a private network through the Internet.

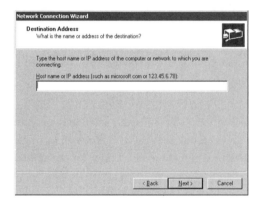

Accept Incoming Connections

You can also configure RAS to answer the modem and let other users create a network connection to your system. The configuration of this option is the most complicated of the network connection options.

After you select the Accept Incoming Connections option, you need to specify which devices you want to listen for the incoming connections. You will be presented with a list of all computer ports and devices that support incoming RAS connections.

After you have selected the device or devices (usually modems), you will see a window that will ask if you want to allow virtual private connection to your computer. This type of connection is only possible if you have a static IP address, so, in most cases, you would select the option to not allow private connections.

The next window you will see is the Allowed Users window. On this window you specify which of the system's users will be able to make incoming connections from the outside. You can select any or all of the users that have accounts on your system.

After that is the Networking Components window, shown in Figure 20.29. On this window, you select the network protocols that will be supported by the incoming connection.

FIGURE 20.29

Configuring RAS for incoming connections.

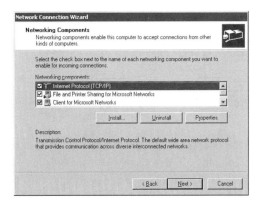

Lastly, you have to give the incoming connection listener a name, and an icon will be created on the Network and Dial-up Connections window.

Connect Directly to Another Computer

When you select this option, you can configure two systems to be connected directly together, either by cable or by infrared device. You define one computer as the Host, and the other as the Guest. The Guest creates a link into the Host's system. Once again, you define which user accounts on the Host system will be able to start the connection. On the Guest system, you decide whether to make the connections public or keep them private.

RAS Auto Connection Manager

The Auto Connection Manager of RAS is a great facility. This is a great tool for when you only want to connect to the Internet whenever you are accessing Internet objects.

The Auto Connection Manager monitors the system for any DNS or IP address connection requests that are outside of the local system. It then dials the network automatically, so the IP request can be fulfilled. The configuration of the Auto Connection Manager is done from the Computer Management window, as shown in Figure 20.30.

FIGURE 20.30

The Computer Management window.

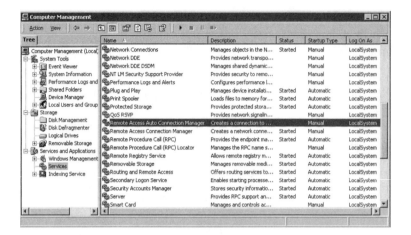

Please note that the default for the Auto Connection Manager service is Manual Startup. If you don't want to use this facility, go into Computer Management and set the startup type for this service to be Automatic. Then it will come up with each reboot of your system.

rasdial Command

The rasdial command is used in place of the Network and Dial-up connections window. You use this command if you want to initiate a network connection from the command line. The rasdial command (help selected) is shown in Figure 20.31.

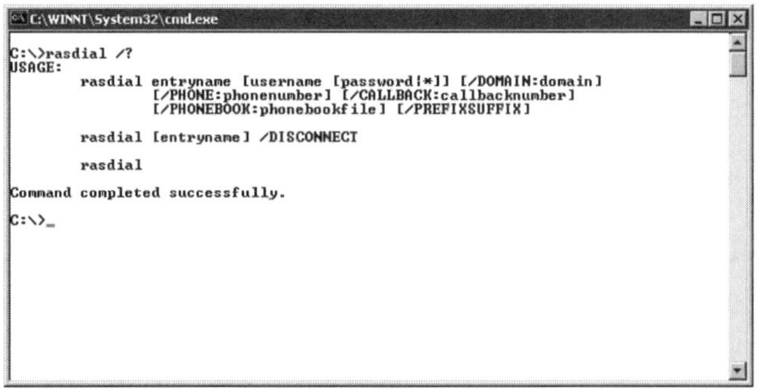

FIGURE 20.31

Example of the rasdial console command.

```
C:\>rasdial /?
USAGE:
        rasdial entryname [username [password|*]] [/DOMAIN:domain]
                [/PHONE:phonenumber] [/CALLBACK:callbacknumber]
                [/PHONEBOOK:phonebookfile] [/PREFIXSUFFIX]

        rasdial [entryname] /DISCONNECT

        rasdial

Command completed successfully.

C:\>_
```

If you take a close look at the figure, you will be able to figure out the syntax the command requires. For the most part, simply entering rasdial and the name of the dialup connection you want to activate will do the trick.

RAS Troubleshooter

Windows 2000 provides a troubleshooter for the Remote Access Service. You can find the troubleshooter yourself by clicking Start, Help, Remote Access. You start up the troubleshooter by selecting it from the list as shown in Figure 20.32.

FIGURE 20.32

Front screen for the Windows 2000 troubleshooters.

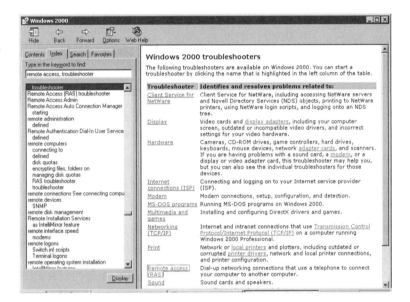

You move through the troubleshooter by answering simple questions and performing a few tests the troubleshooter asks you to perform. In most cases, you will be able to resolve your problem by using the troubleshooter. It cannot handle advanced problems though; you will have to read the help page for that.

A sample troubleshooter page dealing with misconfiguration of the modem used with RAS is shown in Figure 20.33

The Modem Log

There is a new feature in Windows 2000 that will help greatly with the diagnosis of modem problems—the modem log. Each modem that is installed on your system will have its own log of all the commands sent to it and all the responses. You can use the modem log to verify that a modem is dialing a number correctly and to verify the connection baud rate and serial port speed.

The modem log is accessed through Control Panel, Phone and Modem Options, Modems, Properties, Diagnostics. A sample log is shown in Figure 20.34.

20

REMOTE COMPUTING
WITH REMOTE
ACCESS SERVICE

FIGURE 20.33

The Windows 2000 RAS troubleshooter.

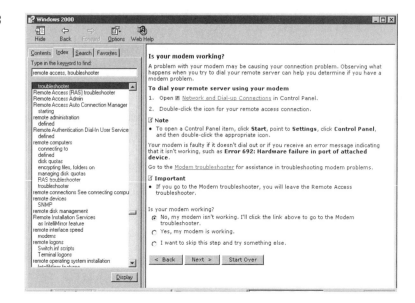

FIGURE 20.34

The Windows 2000 modem log file for the USR 56K modem.

As you can see from the figure, each entry is timestamped to the 1/1000th of a second and the logging is very verbose. It will definitely be a handy tool for the situation where you are trying to figure out if your ISP is having a problem or if your system is misconfigured.

Summary

In this chapter, you learned how to configure the Remote Access Server (RAS) software that comes with Windows 2000. You learned how to set up a connection between your computer and the Internet, and also about all the other network connection options available, including listening for incoming network connections.

You also learned about the command-line version of RAS and about the diagnostic tools available for monitoring and troubleshooting network connection problems.

20

REMOTE COMPUTING WITH REMOTE ACCESS SERVICE

Networking Windows 2000 Professional

PART
V

Windows 2000 Networking Protocols

IN THIS CHAPTER

One of the most important administrative tasks for Windows 2000 is installing and configuring the networking components. All network designs include unique hardware and software components; what may work for one environment may not be an ideal choice for others. This chapter discusses the networking features for Windows 2000 Professional by first examining the network device installation procedures, followed by the network property details, which have changed dramatically from earlier versions. Finally, this chapter concentrates on different protocol features and installations.

Installing Networking

Plug-and-play support has now been incorporated into the Windows code base and is administered by a new Plug and Play Manager included in Windows kernel mode executive services. As a result, Windows 2000 Professional will automatically detect plug-and-play network interface cards and install their network settings during installation. If a network card does not support Plug and Play but the associated drivers do, Windows 2000 will not automatically recognize the new device, but it will handle its resource management. Thus, IRQ conflicts will be greatly reduced. For more on plug-and-play features, refer to Chapter 3, "Installing Windows 2000 Professional."

This chapter steps through installing a network adapter card manually. However, the majority of the time, Windows 2000 will automatically detect any new devices during installation, system boots, or runtime hardware events (docking and undocking a laptop). Circumstances that may cause a manual installation are legacy devices and drivers or non-plug-and-play network cards with plug-and-play drivers.

An important consideration when purchasing network adapter cards for Windows 2000: Ensure the cards are listed on the Hardware Compatibility List published quarterly by Microsoft. If the network cards are not listed, contact the card's manufacturer's Web site to see if they have created Windows 2000 plug-and-play drivers. This check can be the difference between a headache and an inconsequential part of the installation process.

> **Note**
>
> Microsoft's Hardware Compatibility List is located at `www.microsoft.com/hcl`.

Another addition to Windows 2000 is *digital signatures*. When a company manufactures a new product that will operate on a Windows 2000 computer, it can submit the product's driver files to Microsoft for examination through a test submission process. As a part of this process, the drivers undertake a Windows Hardware Quality Labs (WHQL) test, which ensures that the drivers meet a certain level of standards. If the testing is successful, a catalog file (`*.cat`) is created for the drivers. This file contains a Microsoft-signed digital signature. When the new device is installed on a Windows 2000 machine, an `*.inf` file (a file that provides information to the operating system on how to set up the product) informs Windows 2000 that a catalog file exists for the device. The system uses this information to maintain the drivers for the product in the future. This process guarantees that the driver files will not be overwritten or altered by any future device or program installations.

> **Note**
>
> When a student finishes college, he or she receives a certificate that is signed by the college. This signature certifies that the student enrolled in the college and met the requirements for their program. Digital signatures have the same function, except they are signed electronically. These signatures ensure that a hardware device has met a certain quality level. Digital signatures are also used in cryptographic technology (a method that scrambles data between a sending computer and a receiving computer) to allow one computer to verify the identity of another computer.

Hardware Wizard

Windows 2000 uses a hardware wizard found in Windows 95 and 98 to install all new devices. To install any new devices, the user account logged on must have administrative privileges. The Add/Remove Hardware Wizard, accessed from the Add/Remove Hardware applet in the Control Panel, serves a dual purpose—add/troubleshoot a device or uninstall/unplug a device (see Figure 21.1). As a result, Windows 2000 centralizes all device management to one area.

Windows 2000 detects any new plug-and-play devices during installation and system boots, which, if successful, will proceed to install the device without any further information from the installer. The Network Wizard will perform this step routine upon running. Figure 21.2 illustrates the Network Wizard installing a new network interface card. As a next step, the Wizard confirms all new devices installed. Windows 2000 also configures the protocol settings for the new device, which are described in more detail in the TCP/IP, NWLink and NetBEUI protocols section of this chapter. In most networking environments, these steps will be all that is required.

FIGURE 21.1

Choosing a Hardware Task in the Add/Remove Hardware Wizard.

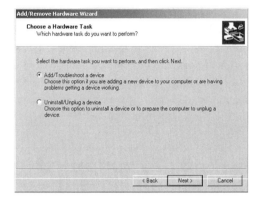

FIGURE 21.2

The Hardware Task detecting a new network adapter card.

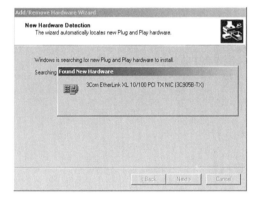

For non–plug-and-play network cards (with or without PnP drivers), the Add/Remove Hardware Wizard steps through the manual installation process.

Installing a Network Adapter Card

If the Add/Remove Hardware Wizard does not detect any new devices, it will display all currently installed devices for any troubleshooting. One option in the list of new devices is to add any new devices (see Figure 21.3). Choose to add a new device and click Next. The Wizard will ask if it can detect any new devices. Choose No and click Next. At this point, you will see a list of all the devices. Choose Network Adapters and click Next. Windows 2000 compiles a list of all recognized network adapters cards. This step usually takes some time to complete. The next screen displays a list of all manufacturers and the networks cards they produce (see Figure 21.4). Choose the correct card from the list and click Next. At this point, the Add/Remove Hardware Wizard will install the network device.

FIGURE 21.3

The Add/Remove Hardware Wizard showing a list of all installed devices, with an option to add a new device.

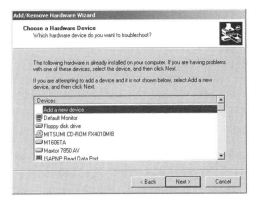

FIGURE 21.4

The Add/Remove Hardware Wizard showing a list of manufacturers and network adapter cards. The Have Disk option is useful for installing the latest drivers from a floppy disk or CD-ROM.

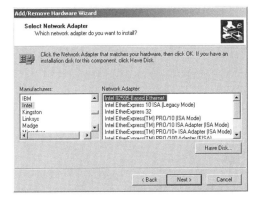

Tip

One option at this point during the installation process is Have Disk (refer to Figure 21.4). Whenever possible, use this option to install the most recent version of any drivers for network adapter cards. Retail computer stores will often sell network adapters without any drivers, leaving Windows 2000 to detect and install the proper drivers. While there is nothing wrong with this procedure, when purchasing an adapter, ask for any updated drivers. If this is not possible, manufacturers will have driver information on their Web sites.

Using the drivers from either the Have Disk option or from the list provided, the Add/Remove Hardware Wizard will now install and configure the new device. Usually the process does not require the Windows 2000 Professional CD-ROM or a system reboot.

Installing an Infrared Device

One viable option for network communication is using infrared technology. Once considered only for extraordinary circumstances due to the cost of hardware, infrared networks have become more commonplace for connecting two devices together. Infrared communication will not replace regular cabling media, but will be used in places where wiring is not possible or not installed for aesthetic reasons. An example of a use for wireless communication is in historical buildings where installing a cabling system is not possible.

As with network adapter cards, the Add/Remove Hardware Wizard can be used to install an infrared device. The steps are similar, except instead of installing a network adapter, choose an infrared device. Figure 21.5 displays the Add/Remove Hardware Wizard during the Choose Device step.

FIGURE 21.5

The Add/Remove Hardware Wizard during the device installation step.

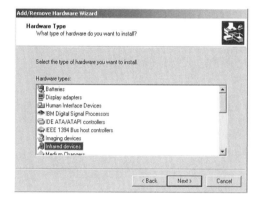

The Add/Remove Hardware Wizard will use default settings to automatically configure the infrared device.

> **Note**
>
> Infrared devices use an IrDA (Infrared Data Association) protocol to communicate. If a computer has built-in IrDA hardware, Windows 2000 will automatically detect and install the device using the default settings. No other settings need to be configured. Windows 2000 is equipped with additional programs, such as the Wireless Link file transfer program, infrared pointing capability, and image transfer capability. These installed programs allow Windows 2000 to detect, configure and use infrared devices. If the computer is not equipped with IrDA hardware, an IrDA transceiver can be attached to a COM port to install the infrared device.

Network and Dial-up Connections

Windows 2000 has one central location for all network connections. Therefore, any network connections from a modem, network adapter card, or infrared device are all managed from one area, making configuration settings easier to find. The Network and Dial-up Connections applet in the Control Panel displays different methods that the computer can use to communicate to other devices. Information about these connections is on the left side of the window. Each network adapter will have its own connection object in this window. Figure 21.6 demonstrates a typical Network and Dial-up Connections window.

FIGURE 21.6

The Network and Dial-up Connections window.

Note

Network settings can be accessed through the Control Panel or using the shortcut of right-clicking on My Network Places from the desktop and choosing Properties.

The Network and Dial-up Connections window has many options. One option is to make a new connection using one of the previously installed devices. As with installing plug-and-play network devices, this option will automatically be done by the operating system. For establishing a new connection via a modem, ISDN, Virtual Private Network (also called a VPN, which is a method for connecting computers through the Internet), or a port device, double-click the Make New Connection icon to begin a Network Connection

Wizard that will step through the connection process. Another option in the Network and Dial-Up Connection Window is to examine the properties for each network connection. This window is also used to identify the computer on the network identification option and to add any additional network components. These options are described in more detail in the following sections.

Network Identification

Choosing the Network Identification option from left side of the Network and Dial-up Connections window displays the Network Identification tab from the System Properties dialog box (see Figure 21.7). Be sure not to select any of the network connections; otherwise the left side will display information about the selected connection. The System Properties dialog box can also be accessed by right clicking the My Computer icon from the desktop or through the Control Panel. This Network Identification tab in the System Properties dialog box displays the full computer name, which can be entered manually or randomly generated during installation, and the workgroup or domain to which the computer belongs. The computer name can be up to 63 characters if TCP/IP is installed; otherwise the name can only be up to 15 characters in length. The name can use any of the following characters: A–Z, a–z, 0–9, and hyphens. Other characters can be used, but will not be recognized from all computers on the network. Changing the full computer name of the workgroup/domain information will prompt Windows 2000 to start the Network Identification Wizard.

FIGURE 21.7

The Network Identification tab from the System Properties dialog box.

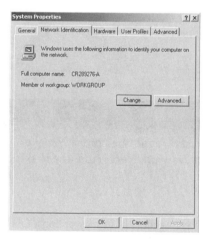

Before discussing this Wizard, workgroups and domains in Windows 2000 network environment should be provided.

Workgroups

Windows 2000 Professional can function in either a workgroup or a domain. Both will behave in a similar, logical fashion. They operate in a network environment in which the computers will communicate with each other. Also, both workgroups and domains have some form of security, although log on information can be disabled for workgroups (for more information about logons and users, see Chapter 22, "Users and Groups"). However, administering a workgroup network with regard to security and logon authentication is much different that administering a domain network.

Workgroups are usually a small group of computers performing similar functions or related for some purpose. Usually the computers are located within close proximity to each other, although this is not a requirement. An important distinction between workgroups and domains is who manages user and group accounts. In a workgroup environment, each computer manages its own user and group accounts. For instance, if ABC Mapmakers, Inc. creates an account for Janice on one machine in the workgroup, she can log into only that machine, because the user account only resides on one machine. Also, if she accessing a resource such as a file or a printer that is located on another machine, she will not be able to because she has not been authenticated on that machine. Each computer must be administered separately and will only authenticate users for that machine.

Because of the high level of maintenance associated with administering a workgroup, they are only useful in small environments, usually ten or less computers, or in environments that never change, which is rare. For larger networks, a domain environment offers much simpler methods for administering authentication and security.

Domains

Domains can be used for large environments. In fact, the environment could be all of the computers that are logically networked together for a similar purpose, located anywhere in the world. As with a workgroup, computers do not have to be physically near each other; in a domain, they usually aren't. In Windows 2000, there is virtually no limit to the size a domain can grow to become.

A domain structure means that all user and group accounts are administered centrally as opposed to all on one machine. If a user account for Janice was created in a domain environment, she would be able to log on from any machine in the domain. In addition, once she is authenticated, she can access any resource in the domain, providing she has the appropriate permissions.

Windows 2000 has greatly enhanced the domain structure with the introduction of Active Directory Services (ADS). In an ADS organization, user, group, and computer accounts can be grouped together into organizational units for easier administration. Also, a domain structure can be divided into forests and trees, again for easier administration.

For Windows 2000 Professional, users can log on to a domain controller. A domain controller has an additional role of storing a copy of all user accounts that can log on to a domain. Therefore, when Janice logs on, her log on information is passed to a domain controller. The domain controller checks in a directory database to ensure that the user account for Janice exists and that the password is correct, and then allows her to log on the domain. Unlike earlier Windows NT operating systems, no single domain controller acts as a primary computer. Instead, all Windows 2000 domain controllers contain a copy of the directory database that can be modified. Only Windows 2000 servers can function as domain controllers.

Network Identification

The Network Identification tab has two features to change any computer or workgroup/domain properties. By choosing the Change button (refer to Figure 21.7), the Network Identification Wizard starts and asks questions concerning the purpose the computer will be performing. Another option is the Advanced button, which displays computer and workgroup information without a wizard. This section first describes the Network Identification Wizard, and then discusses the advanced properties.

The Network Identification Wizard attempts to determine the function of the computer. The first step asks whether the machine is in a part of a business environment or is for home use (see Figure 21.8).

FIGURE 21.8

The Network Identification Wizard.

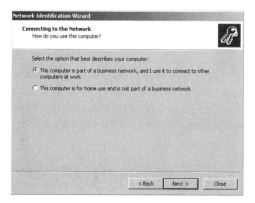

The home option will place the Windows 2000 Professional computer in a workgroup and then ask who can log on to the computer. One option is for separate user accounts for each user who logs on. User accounts cannot be created as a part of the Wizard steps; this is done later in the Users and Passwords applet in the Control Panel. This provides security for the machine because each individual has to log on and be authenticated by

the directory database on the machine. This format is similar to the Windows NT Workstation operating system. Figure 21.9 illustrates the Network Identification Wizard step for setting who can log on.

FIGURE 21.9

The Network Identification Wizard with options for who can log on to the computer.

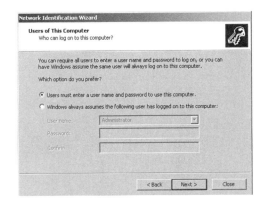

Similar to Windows 95 or Windows 98, another option during this step in the Wizard has all users log on using the same user account. The log process can be disabled altogether through the User and Passwords applet in the Control Panel. For either of these two options, the computer must be restarted to initialize under the new network settings.

If the machine is identified for business use, the Network Identification Wizard will ask whether the computer is participating in a domain or not. If not, the Wizard will ask for the name of the workgroup and finish. If the computer is a part of a domain, it will ask for the necessary information to join the domain (see Figure 21.10). To have the computer join the domain, a user account and password that have administrative privileges must be provided. Also, the domain name and possibly the computer name and domain may be needed. When this information is provided, the Wizard will contact a domain controller for the assigned domain to determine if the user has permission to create a computer account. If the information is correct and authenticated properly, the Wizard finishes. As with all of the possibilities within the Network Identification Wizard, the computer must be rebooted before these changes will go into effect.

The Advanced feature assumes that the purpose of the machine has not changed. Instead, this option can be used for computer name changes, and for domain or workgroup changes (see Figure 21.11). The necessary authentication procedures that apply in the Wizard will also apply to any changes made in the Identification Changes window.

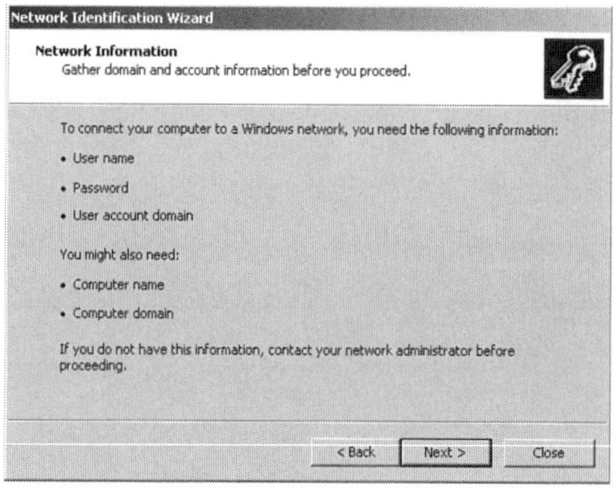

Figure 21.10

The Network Identification Wizard during the domain joining process.

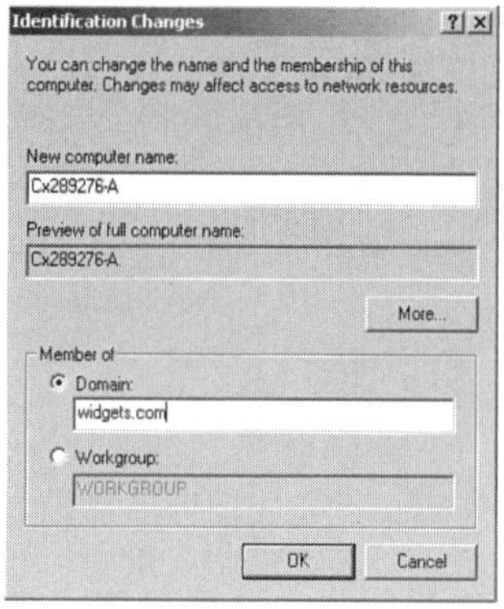

Figure 21.11

The Identification Changes window.

The More button on the Identification Changes window displays another window used to provide DNS information. In a domain environment, Domain Name System servers can be integrated with the computer accounts. DNS is discussed in more detail later in this chapter in the section titled "Installing and Configuring TCP/IP."

Add Network Components

Another feature in the Network and Dial-up Connections window is to install additional network components. These components are not required for regular network use and should not be installed except for a specific purpose. The additional components are divided up into four categories. The categories and the components are as follows:

- *Management and Monitoring Tools, Simple Network Management Protocol*— SNMP is a protocol used for managing devices on a network. On Windows 2000 Professional, this option installs an agent that can report network details to an SNMP Manager. An example of information to report from the SNMP agent would be the IP address of the network adapter.

- *Networking Services, RIP Listener*—Windows 2000 Server uses two IP routing protocols: RIP and OSPF. Computers and routers have routing tables that contain network information used to direct data to other computers and networks. The two routing protocols, RIP and OSPF, allow routers to share their table information with other routers. Routing Information Protocol (RIP) is a distance-vectoring protocol used for dynamic routing on small to medium sized networks. Open Shortest Path First (OSPF) is a link state routing protocol used for large networks. A Windows 2000 Professional computer can listen for any route updates from routers using RIP v.1. when this feature is installed.

- *Networking Services, Simple TCP/IP Services*— This option can be installed to support four optional TCP/IP services: Character Generator, Daytime Discard, Echo, and Quote of the Day. These options are not a part of the regular TCP/IP protocol suite and are classified as elective (meaning they can be chosen if a user wants to) services.

- *Other Network File and Print Services, Print service for UNIX*—This option allows UNIX clients to send LPR and LPQ commands to a Windows 2000 Professional computer.

Local Area Connection Properties

The Network and Dial-up Connections window places a network area connection properties object for each installed network adapter. These objects can be renamed for easier identification, and they can be connected or disconnected at any time. Also, a status window provides connection information such as duration, speed, and packets sent and received from this connection (see Figure 21.12). An option found under the Local Area Connection Properties can also have an icon displayed in the bottom-right corner of the taskbar (see Figure 21.13). A new convenient feature for each properties dialog box is the helpful description of each item when selected. Although most descriptions only run one sentence, they summarize the feature without having to select a help window. For configuring the Local Area Connection, right-click the object and choose Properties.

The Local Area Connection Properties dialog box displays all network adapter, client, service, and protocol information for the local area connection. With the exception of adapter information, adding a component for one local area network will in turn add the component to all of the local area networks.

FIGURE 21.12

The status window for a local area network.

FIGURE 21.13

The Local Area Connection Properties dialog box.

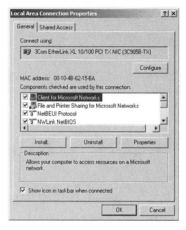

In the Local Area Connection Properties dialog box, there is an option for configuring network adapters. Figure 21.14 displays the network Properties window. The network configurations window has four tabs:

FIGURE 21.14

The network configuration dialog box.

- *General*—The General tab displays the device type, manufacturer, and location. If the device is encountering any difficulties, the device status window displays relevant information and has a troubleshooting option. The troubleshooter starts the Windows 2000 help screen, but displays specific details concerning the device in a manner similar to a Windows wizard. Lastly, the General tab has an option to enable or disable the network device.

- *Advanced*—The Advanced tab displays device-dependent settings such as duplex mode, media type, and network address. These settings should not be changed except for specific reasons. Depending on the device installed, this tab may not appear.

- *Driver*—The Driver tab presents driver information such as the date, version, and digital signer. This information is useful for determining whether or not to update drivers. The Driver Details button displays the driver files, and the Driver tab also allows driver updating.

- *Resources*—Similar to a Windows 95 or Windows 98 dialog box, this tab displays resource settings such as IRQ and I/O settings. These settings can be manually adjusted if the device is a plug-and-play device. Otherwise, the settings must be changed using the device configuration program provided by the manufacturer.

Client Options

A *client* allows the computer to communicate with other computers and their resources on the local area network and is represented by a computer icon in the Properties dialog box. By default, local area connections will install the Client for Microsoft Networks. The install option under the local area connection properties window has an option for Client Service for NetWare networks. This client is necessary for accessing resources on a NetWare server and replaces the Client Services for NetWare option found under Windows NT Workstation.

The properties for Client for Microsoft Networks Properties window provide choices for the service provider name for Remote Procedure Calls (see Figure 21.15). Distributed applications use the RPC communication mechanism to pass messages to other computers on the network. They essentially make a call to a remote computer to perform a function. Unless circumstances call for an intermediary device for these calls, such as the DCE Cell Directory Service, the default Windows Locator should be selected. An option for RPC support also is enabled from the properties window.

FIGURE 21.15

The Client for Microsoft Networks Properties window.

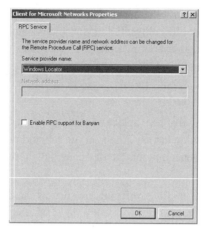

Interestingly, upon installing Client for NetWare Networks, the properties will be controlled through a CSNW applet in the Control Panel, not through the Network and Dial-up Connections window. However, the options displayed under CSNW will also appear during client installation. Figure 21.16 displays the options for connecting to a Novell server. Select a preferred server for any NetWare 3.x servers or type the default tree and context for NetWare 4.X servers. Login scripts can be selected to run from this window. Scripts perform command-line activities when a user logs on a machine. Windows also has this feature, which can be activated for users through the Users and Passwords applet.

FIGURE 21.16

The Select NetWare Logon dialog box.

Although installing a client from one local area network will install to all local area networks, each network properties dialog box has check mark options. These check boxes allow a choice for what client, service, or protocol should be enabled for each local area network.

Services

Windows 2000 Professional has three services available from the Local Area Connection Properties window. The first service, File and Print Sharing, installs by default. Two other services are available through the Install feature in the Local Area Connection Properties window. These three services are described next in detail.

- *File and Printer Sharing for Microsoft Networks*—This service allows others to access resources located on the computer. The equivalent of the Server service, file and print services must be enabled for sharing. A folder may appear to be shared regardless of this setting; however, users connecting will receive a message stating the Server service has not been started. On disabling this feature, no new connections will be made, but any existing sessions open will continue to be available. Existing sessions can be closed through the shared folders node from the computer management console.

- *QoS Packet Scheduler*—Quality of Service technology is used to manage media-rich applications utilizing the network. With the advent of video-streaming and real-time audio, QoS gives networks managers complete control over how much bandwidth these applications receive, thus ensuring that one application will not saturate the network. The packet scheduler feature retrieves packets from the network, applies any QoS parameters, and then retransmits them.

- *SAP Agent*—The SAP Agent provides support for the Netware Service Advertising Protocol. This protocol broadcasts resources such as shared folders, files, and printers on a network. The SAP Agent determines the available network resources (primarily used on IPX networks to access resources on Novell servers).

All installed services have an icon of a computer with a hand underneath. For a full listing of services and their current status in Windows 2000 Professional, run Computer Management from the Administrative Tools menu and select Services.

Installing and Configuring TCP/IP

In today's business world, network managers face a daunting task of administrating various operating systems that continuously require reorganization and integration without a loss of performance. Fortunately, Transmission Control Protocol/Internet Protocol (TCP/IP) emerged as a flexible and reliable communication protocol that operates in almost all environments and with most technologies. A large part of TCP/IP's popularity can be attributed to the growth of the Internet and its open protocol standards. Microsoft 2000's TCP/IP implementation includes many new features that greatly improve the protocol's security, reliability, and performance.

This section describes the installation process and defines all configuration properties for TCP/IP. For a more detailed definition on TCP/IP, refer to Chapter 17, "Setting Up TCP/IP Protocol Access."

Installing TCP/IP

TCP/IP installs automatically during installation, but can be configured, removed, and reinstalled at any time. Configuration settings are located in all local area connection Properties dialog boxes. The following steps describe how to install TCP/IP.

1. From Start, choose Settings, Control Panel.
2. In the Control Panel, double-click Network and Dial-up Connections.
3. In the Network and Dial-up Connections window, right click any Local Area Network object and choose Properties from the shortcut menu.
4. From Properties, double-click Install and then select Protocol. Click Add.
5. From the list of protocols, select TCP/IP and click OK. TCP/IP will install without requiring a system reboot.

TCP/IP will not ask for an IP address to be configured. This setting will automatically be assigned by using DHCP. This feature is described in more detail under the "DHCP" section, later in this chapter. Users do have an option to manually add the IP address and subnet mask after TCP/IP has been installed. To manually set this option, choose TCP/IP properties from the Networking Tab of any network connection properties dialog box. If TCP/IP is removed from the system, Windows 2000 Professional will need to reboot to reinitialize with the new settings.

General TCP/IP Properties

The Internet Protocol (TCP/IP) General Properties dialog box has options to manually install IP settings such as IP address, subnet mask, and default gateway (see Figure 21.17). By default, TCP/IP obtains an IP automatically from a DHCP server. However, for clients requiring static IP addresses, a radio button switches from dynamic to static IP addresses.

New to Windows operating systems is an option to automatically obtain the IP address of DNS servers. DNS has a more significant role in the Windows 2000 family and is discussed later in this chapter in the section titled "DNS." TCP/IP can automatically assign a DNS address or a primary and secondary can be assigned manually. For any further changes to TCP/IP, choose the Advanced button. The Advanced button allows more settings for DNS, WINS, TCP/IP Security, and IP Security, which are discussed in more detail throughout the remainder of this chapter.

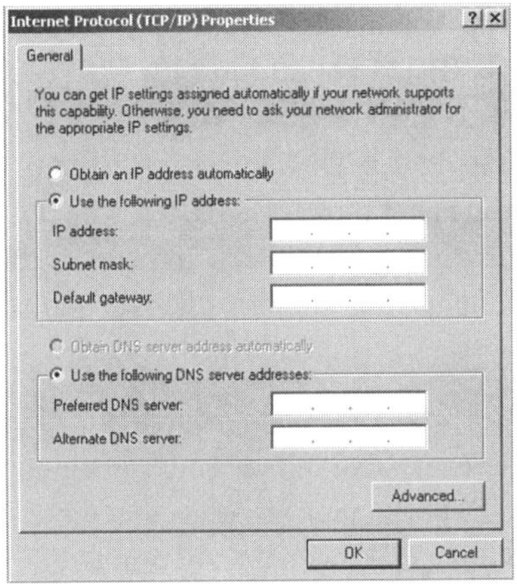

FIGURE 21.17
*TCP/IP general
properties.*

DHCP

Dynamic Host Configuration Protocol (DHCP) has one of the most important roles in
TCP/IP. Rather than manually assigning an IP address and other TCP/IP settings to each
computer on a network, all IP address information can be centralized and managed from
a DHCP server. A DHCP server contains a pool of IP addresses (referred to as a *scope*)
to be handed out to all computers acting as DHCP clients. A list of options a DHCP
server can hand out to clients include an IP address, subnet mask, default gateway IP
address, DNS, and WINS IP address. Therefore, a client can receive from the DHCP
server all the information required to communicate on a TCP/IP network.

When a DHCP client boots to the network, it will request an IP address from a DHCP
server. Windows 2000 Professional installs as a DHCP client. The DHCP server can offer
to lease an IP address, subnet mask, and other settings to the client for a specific amount
of time. By leasing the IP address, the client only has the address information for a certain amount of time before asking for a lease renewal. The client can accept this information and now communicate with other devices using TCP/IP locally or remotely. The
DHCP server then confirms that the client has accepted the TCP/IP settings and no
longer offers that IP address to other machines.

> **Note**
>
> A DHCP server may be remote to the subnet, meaning it can be located on the
> other side of the router or many routers away. A DHCP Relay Agent forwards
> client requests through routers to the DHCP server.

A new feature to Windows 2000 is the Automatic Client Configuration. When a computer boots to the network, it requests IP address information from a DHCP server via a broadcast. If no DHCP server replies to this broadcast, the DHCP client automatically configures an IP address using the `169.254.0.0` Microsoft-reserved class B network address range with `255.255.0.0` as a subnet mask. The DHCP client will make certain this IP address is not already in use by issuing an ARP command. If the IP address is in use on the network, the Automatic Client Configuration chooses another IP address and repeats the process.

In case a DHCP may have been offline temporarily, the Automatic Client Configuration feature will check for a DHCP server every five minutes after assigning an IP address from the `169.254.0.0` network. If a DHCP server responds to a request, the previously assigned information is removed, and the client can then accept the DHCP offer.

> **Tip**
>
> To disable the auto client configuration feature on Windows 2000 Professional, add an `IPAutoconfigurationEnabled` entry to the Registry with a value of `false`. Other values, `IPAutoconfigurationSubnet` and `IPAutoconfigurationMask`, will control the subnet and the subnet mask for this feature. These registry values are located under the registry key `HKEY_LOCAL_MACHINE\SYSTEM\CurrentControlSet\Services\TCPIP\` parameters.

DNS

Using the TCP/IP protocol, computers communicate to other devices via IP address. However, IP addresses are difficult to remember, so a more user-friendly method, called hostnames, was created. A hostname is a more commonly recognized computer name like Sales1 or SusanP. A Domain Name System (DNS) is a service that resolves these hostnames into IP addresses.

> **Caution**
>
> Microsoft Windows calls a centralized grouping of networked computers a *domain*. This definition is completely separate from a TCP/IP domain name that a DNS server resolves. TCP/IP domain names are used on the Internet in programs such as Internet Explorer. Microsoft domains are internal to a company.

Windows 2000 Networking Protocols

CHAPTER 21

579

21

WINDOWS 2000
NETWORKING
PROTOCOLS

Windows 2000 has improved DNS to include dynamic updates through a DHCP server. When a Windows 2000 DHCP server leases an IP address to a Windows 2000 DHCP client, the client sends its fully-qualified domain name (FQDN) to the server and requests that this name be registered on a DNS server. A fully-qualified domain name is the computer's hostname and the domain to which it belongs. The DHCP server will then register a host record and a PTR reverse lookup record on the DNS server. A PTR reverse lookup record is used to perform reverse lookups, which means the DNS server will provide the hostname for an IP address instead of an IP address for a hostname. These kinds of records are commonly used for email servers. By using the DHCP server to register FQDNs, the DNS database remains consistent with all IP addresses leased to DHCP clients. The same procedure also occurs for an IP address renewal.

If a Windows 2000 DHCP client leases an IP address from a DHCP server that does not handle dynamic DNS updating, the DHCP client will register with the DNS server itself. Static IP address entries for non-DHCP clients continue to be entered manually into a DNS server.

Another feature on Windows 2000 is the DNS resolver cache service. When a Windows 2000 Professional computer queries a DNS server to resolve a fully-qualified domain name into an IP address, the computer stores the result locally in DNS cache. The query result includes a Time to Live (TTL), specifying how long the entry will be saved locally in cache. Any future queries by the Windows 2000 Professional computer do not need to contact the DNS server, thereby reducing traffic on the network. The DNS cache service will also store negative responses from queries that responded back with no IP address for the given hostname, or from queries that do not receive any response at all; thus, future time-outs will be avoided for negative responses. The DNS caching feature runs as a service on Windows 2000 Professional, and can be started, paused, and stopped like any other service. Figure 21.18 illustrates the DNS cache service.

By default, a DHCP server provides the IP address for the DNS server or servers and therefore no other information is required. However, the Advanced tab for TCP/IP properties includes some configurable DNS settings. Figure 21.19 shows the DNS configuration settings. The following are the options for the DNS tab found in the Advanced TCP/IP properties:

FIGURE 21.18

*DNS Cache
Service.*

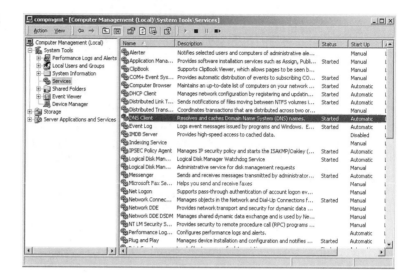

- The first option lists all DNS servers; listed in the order they are searched, used for IP address queries.

- Another option changes the DNS search parameters. When an application causes DNS to resolve a hostname to an IP address, the query appends the parent domain name to the hostname. For example, typing `ftp sales1` will require a DNS server to be queried to resolve the hostname into an IP address. Before the query is sent, the client computer will attach the domain name to the hostname of `sales1`. If the domain name for `Sales1` is `popkey.com`, the query will be `sales1.popkey.com`. The domain name can either be provided in a DHCP lease or typed in the Domain Name field in the DNS properties. This tab has options for appending the domain name or for querying a DNS server using the specified domain names listed.

- Other options include registering the hostname and domain name to a DNS server via a DHCP server. This option is discussed in the "DHCP" section of this chapter.

FIGURE 21.19

DNS tab from advanced TCP/IP properties.

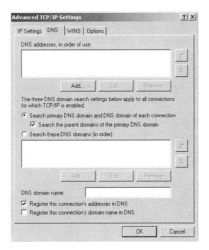

NetBIOS and WINS

In earlier Windows operating systems, each computer needed a NetBIOS (Network Input/Output System) name for communicating through programs such as Network Neighborhood and Net View. NetBIOS names are used by Windows applications to communicate with other computers. Like hostnames, a NetBIOS name was resolved to an IP address. However, NetBIOS names were resolved through broadcasts, which saturated large networks. A Windows Internet Name Service (WINS) decreases broadcast storms by providing a service that resolves NetBIOS names into IP addresses by communicating directly to the clients as opposed to broadcasts. WINS is a database of NetBIOS names and their IP addresses that are stored on a Windows 2000 Server that is running the WINS service. The Windows 2000 NETBIOS names and WINS service functionality have been enhanced from the prior Windows NT versions.

A new Windows 2000 feature for NetBIOS names is *direct hosting*, which allows applications that previously used NetBIOS broadcasts to communicate directly to each other instead, similar to the Windows Sockets method. Direct hosting uses DNS for name resolution instead of broadcasting, which simplifies the protocol and allows more bandwidth for other applications. However, direct hosting only works when communicating with other Windows 2000 operating systems. For communicating with previous operating systems, such as Windows NT 4 or Windows 98, broadcasts or WINS will be used for resolving NetBIOS broadcasts.

> **Note**
>
> A Windows socket is a method of communicating directly with another computer using an IP address and a port number. IP addresses identify which network the computer is residing on and which number the computer is on the network. Try this analogy: people live in houses located on streets. Each house must have a number to make it unique to that street, each street must have a name to make it unique in the city. An IP address is a street name and a house number. Sockets also use ports. A port identifies with which process in the destination computer the sending computer is communicating. For example, a computer is acting as an FTP server and a Web server. Other computers must know which service to communicate with—FTP or HTTP. Ports make each service unique to the computer (port 21 for FTP and port 80 for HTTP). A port is like an apartment number for the building on the street. The IP address and the port number make up a Windows Socket. This way, computers can communicate to a specific service on another computer.

The line between host applications and NetBIOS applications becomes murky in Windows 2000. New features include connecting to other TCP/IP devices using FQDNs from NetBIOS commands. For instance, the net use command maps a drive letter to a shared resource on another machine. Drive letters can now be mapped to FQDNs. For example,

- Net use x: \\www.microsot.com\windows2000
- Net use v: \\10.16.0.10\home

Other commands, such as dir, net view, and many administrative programs also can use fully-qualified domain names. If an administrator does not want to use NetBIOS, it can be disabled completely using the Network Connections dialog box.

The Windows 2000 WINS service also has improved functionality for both the server and client. Windows 2000 Professional can list up to 12 WINS servers for increased fault tolerance and changes to the WINS properties will not require a system reboot. To change any features for WINS information, the Advanced button for TCP/IP has a WINS tab. Figure 21.20 shows the options for the WINS tab.

FIGURE 21.20

The WINS properties tab.

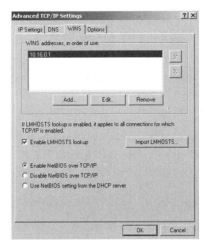

The WINS tab has the following options:

- *Manually type in WINS addresses*—Windows Professional computers require a WINS address to have the WINS server resolve NetBIOS names, which can be manually entered or provided with the DHCP lease information.

- *Enabling the Lmhosts file*—An Lmhosts file acts similarly to a hosts file in that it lists names and their IP address, but an Lmhosts file resolves NetBIOS names.

- *Changing the NetBIOS settings*—NetBIOS can be disabled altogether for networks that implement hostnames and do not use NetBIOS-based applications.

IP Security

IP Security (IPSec) is a cryptography-based authentication and encryption service that functions at the Internet layer of the TCP/IP Protocol stack. A new feature for Windows 2000, IPSec fills in a security gap in many networks that allowed clear text to be sent across an intranet or extranet. A malicious user only needed to access a physical machine on the network to intercept password information. Two methods to prevent any security breaches are computer authentication and data encryption. Each machine can now use the following authentication methods:

- *Certificate of Authority (CA) exchange*—For users to be authenticated, a certificate must be provided that contains a public key. A certificate ensures that the user is who he or she states he or she is and isn't an imposter. Public keys are used with private keys as a method for encrypting and decrypting password information.

- *Kerberos authentication*—This option is the default option for authentication. The Kerberos V5 protocol encrypts passwords sent across networks during authentication.

- *Key-based exchange*—This authentication method encrypts password information using a pre-shared secret key. The user must already have this key to be authenticated.

IPSec uses data encryption using a variety of Data Encryption Standards. Encryption will slow network traffic and should be used prudently. Other options, such as offloading the encryption processing to a hardware device, can reduce the effects on the network.

IP Security policies are created in the Computer Management under the group policy node on a Windows 2000 Server and then enabled through the TCP/IP Advanced Other tab. Enabling this option allows Windows 2000 Professional to act on a response mode for IP Security.

TCP/IP Filtering

The TCP/IP filtering feature controls which ports can send information to computers by applying a packet-level filter to the TCP, UDP, and IP protocols. The default settings permit all port numbers to transmit data, but choosing the Permit Only radio button and then typing in only the accepted ports can change this setting. Figure 21.21 shows a TCP/IP filtering dialog box with only the HTTP port 80 allowed for communication.

> **Note**
>
> User Datagram Protocol (UDP) is a transport protocol that provides connection-less delivery of data to a receiving computer. What this means is that it will not guarantee that the data arrives intact (the opposite of TCP). However, because of this, it has much less overhead than TCP and is therefore a quicker protocol. An example of communicating using UDP as the transport protocol is pinging another machine.

TCP/IP filtering provides an excellent security measure against illegal port attacks or to restrict access to only certain programs.

> **Note**
>
> Port numbers 1–1023 are reserved as "well-known" port numbers. TCP and UDP port numbers are based on the Winnt\System32\Drivers\Etc\Services file, which lists the well-known port numbers and their names. IP port numbers can be found in the \systemroot\system32\drivers\etc\ protocols file. Use these lists to determine which ports to allow.

FIGURE 21.21

The TCP/IP filtering dialog box.

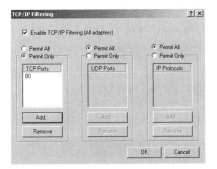

To specify which port numbers will be blocked out, click Add for one of the TCP, UDP, or IP protocols. Type in the port number that will be filtered out. Figure 21.22 displays the TCP Port 25 being filtered out. Port 25 is used for emails sent between SMTP servers.

FIGURE 21.22

The Add Filter dialog box. This filters out unwanted ports.

Testing TCP/IP Connectivity

Ping is the most effective and simple utility for troubleshooting TCP/IP connections. Packet Internet Groper (PING) sends out four ICMP packets (a messaging protocol acting at the Internet layer) to a destination computer and, if successful, receives four echo replies in return. To ensure that two computers can communicate, four pings can be sent. For more information on pinging, see the TCP/IP troubleshooting section from Chapter 17, "Setting Up TCP/IP Protocol Access." The following are the four separate pings and their purposes:

- *Ping the loopback address*—As previously mentioned, the IP address of 127.0.0.1 has been set aside for testing network cards. By pinging this loopback address, this informs you that the network card has been installed properly, but the IP address or subnet mask may need attention.

- *Ping the IP address of the near side of the router (Gateway Address)*—This will ensure that your IP address and your subnet mask are functioning properly. The default gateway IP address usually never changes or is taken offline, and therefore is a good choice to use for a test.

- *Ping the IP address of the far side of a router*—Administrators always have one or two IP addresses they know are always functioning and can use these IP addresses as test IP addresses. Replies will indicate that the default gateway is functioning properly.

- *Ping another computer by hostname*—The first three pings check the communication between two computers. This last ping checks whether the computer can resolve a hostname to an IP address. Windows 2000 will first check the local hostname of a machine to see if the ping is for itself, it then checks the hosts file, and then it checks DNS. If a response for a hostname is not returned, one of these three areas will not be functioning. As listed earlier, Windows 2000 also includes a caching DNS resolver service, which caches name queries for a specified amount of time. Future name queries can be resolved by cache.

Of course, many administrators will jump to the fourth ping because a correct response by hostname indicates that the other three pings will also be successful.

The following is an example of a ping to an IP Address:

```
C:\>ping 10.16.10.15
Pinging 10.16.10.15 with 32 bytes of data:
Reply from 10.16.10.15: bytes=32 time<10ms TTL=128
Reply from 10.16.10.15: bytes=32 time<10ms TTL=128
Reply from 10.16.10.15: bytes=32 time<10ms TTL=128
Reply from 10.16.10.15: bytes=32 time<10ms TTL=128

Ping statistics for 10.16.10.15:
 Packets: Sent = 4, Received = 4, Lost = 0 (0% loss),
Approximate round trip times in milli-seconds:
 Minimum = 0ms, Maximum = 0ms, Average = 0ms
```

NWLINK

NWLink is a Microsoft implementation of Novell's IPX/SPX protocol. IPX/SPX is similar to TCP/IP in that it is a reliable, 32-bit routable protocol. However, Novell privately owns the protocol suite, and therefore it has not been as widely used as TCP/IP. For networks that do not require access to the Internet or that go through a firewall or proxy, NWLink is a good alternative to the broadcast-based NetBeui. Also, NWLink is often used for large client installations as a protocol initially connecting to a distribution server.

Windows 2000 Networking Protocols
CHAPTER 21

587

21

WINDOWS 2000
NETWORKING
PROTOCOLS

To install NWLink on Windows 2000 Professional, use the following method:

1. From the Local Area Connection Properties dialog box, choose Install (see Figure 21.13).

2. Choose Protocol and click Add.

3. For the list of uninstalled protocols, choose NWLink IPX/SPX Compatible Transport Protocol and select OK.

NWLink properties controls which frame type to use on the network. Novell 3.11 servers and earlier used the 802.3 frame type; Novell 3.12 and later servers used an 802.2 frame type. A *frame type* is how information is formatted to be sent on the network. Devices must use the same frame type to communicate. NWLink defaults to Auto Detect, which means the computer chooses the appropriate frame type settings. If NWLink detects more than one frame type on a network, it will choose 802.2. The Properties window allows manual setting if the frame type does not default to the desired type.

Another setting in the NWLink properties windows is choosing an internal network number. Internal network numbers, also called *virtual numbers*, specify a unique number for computers with multiple adapter cards connected to multiple networks. Figure 21.23 displays the settings for NWLink properties.

FIGURE 21.23

The NWLink IPX/SPX Compatible Transport Protocol dialog box.

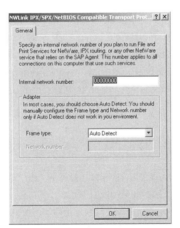

> **Note**
>
> When NWLink is installed on a machine, two settings are listed in the Local Area Connection Properties. The NWLink NetBIOS configures NetBIOS over IPX. This setting provides support for NetBIOS names and applications on Microsoft and Novell computers.

NetBEUI

NETBIOS Enhanced User Interface (NetBEUI) is a small, fast, and efficient protocol that has found a place in small business or home networks that either do not communicate outside the network or do so through a proxy server. The protocol will not expand beyond small networks, even though it has a very low overhead and zero administration because of some design limitations. NetBEUI is not a routable protocol with the exception of some specific non-mainstream networks, and it is a broadcast-based protocol.

> **Note**
>
> NetBEUI and NetBIOS are often confused with each other. NetBIOS is a set of commands and standards outlining how to transmit information between various systems. Originally developed by IBM, NetBIOS runs as an Application Programming Interface (API) that requests low-level services to handle these commands. NetBEUI is a protocol that carries out 17 of the NetBIOS commands and is the Microsoft implementation of IBM's NetBIOS standards.

NetBEUI was designed to operate on networks connected via bridges and therefore not specifically designed for routers. Contemporary networks almost always require some form of routing and, therefore, cannot use NetBEUI. Also, devices using NetBEUI communicate through broadcasts and, consequently, when a computer sends information, every computer on the network must process it. Larger networks become saturated with broadcasts and must either implement bridges or switch to a direct point-to-point communication protocol such as TCP/IP or IPX/SPX.

Other Protocols

Windows 2000 offers some additional protocols usually used as add-on features to one of the three protocols listed in this chapter. One key rule to using protocols on networks is to install as few as possible. A sending computer will attempt to establish a session with the receiving computer using all installed protocols. Installing only the necessary protocols eliminates extra overhead created by these attempted session establishments. Other protocols will place additional stresses on a computer's memory and CPU. The following are the additional protocols:

- *AppleTalk Protocol*—A protocol used to communicate with Apple Macintosh computers
- *Data Link Control (DLC) Protocol*—A non-routable protocol used to communicate with IBM mainframes and network printers

- *OSI-LAN Protocol*—Installs drivers that map to the Transport and Network layer of the OSI model, commonly used in mail and x.400 integration

- *Network Monitor Driver*—Installs the network monitor agent, which enables frames to be received and viewed in Network Monitor

- *Streams Environment*—Used to enable transport drivers from a UNIX-based streams environment to Windows

For further information about these protocols, refer to the Microsoft Technet-Technical Information Library.

Summary

This chapter discussed how to install network adapters and infrared cards. Next, it examined the new method for configuring the network settings. Finally, this chapter described the different protocols that can be installed on Windows 2000 Professional.

Users and Groups

CHAPTER 22

IN THIS CHAPTER

Microsoft designed Windows 2000 Professional to have flexible authentication methods. Administrators can choose to have all users provide a username and password in a Log on to Windows 2000 dialog box before accessing any applications, or allow all users access without logging on at all. This chapter examines user accounts, groups, and authentication methods, as well as properties for users such as profiles, login scripts, and home directories. Finally, this chapter covers some administrative tasks like account policies and disk quotas.

User Accounts

For environments that have multiple users who require different levels of permission for files and/or network access, Administrators can create user accounts. User accounts contain a username, which identifies the user to Windows 2000, and a password, which is a secret set of characters that confirms the person logging on is indeed the username provided. In keeping with the previous version of Windows NT Workstation, Windows 2000 has two built-in user accounts after installation. The Administrator must create all other user accounts.

Administrator

The first account created during Windows 2000 installation, the Administrator, has complete control over all aspects of the computer. This account is designed to have special privileges, and therefore it cannot be removed, disabled, or locked out. Some of the Administrator's special rights are as follows:

- Create and manage all other user accounts.
- Create and manage all domain local groups.
- Install all software and hardware.
- Create Shares for folders, files, and printers.
- Create group policies.

The Administrator is automatically assigned to the Administrators Local Group (discussed later in this chapter). For security reasons, one of the Administrator's first tasks should be to rename the Administrator account to a username that is less obvious.

Note

Windows 2000 actually has two Administrator accounts. The *domain administrator* controls every device that is a part of the domain. This Administrator can delegate administrative control for objects within the domain. For each machine in the domain, or for computers that participate within a workgroup, another Administrator account, called the *local administrator account*, has administrative control over the individual machine. When logging on a machine as an Administrator, be sure to choose the appropriate administrator account.

Guest

The Guest user account provides access for users who normally do not log on the computer. Usually, this account has very limited permissions and is disabled by default. This account is useful for when Uncle Bob comes to town and wants to use the computer.

Groups

User accounts that share common permissions can be organized into groups. Therefore, an Administrator does not have to apply permission for each individual user account; instead, permissions can be applied once for a group of user accounts.

At a domain level, Windows 2000 supports two types of groups to organize user accounts: security groups and distribution groups. Each type of group can be further divided into universal, global, and domain local groups. Security groups are used to apply permissions to user accounts. Distribution groups are used for applications, such as for a Microsoft Exchange Server. Windows 2000 Professional uses security groups. In particular, Administrators can organize user accounts into domain local groups for domain environments, or simply called local groups for a workgroup environment.

> **Note**
>
> Windows 2000 Domains use global and universal groups to organize user accounts. These groups can then be placed into local groups. However, Windows 2000 Professional computers can only create local groups, regardless of whether the machine participates in a domain or in a workgroup. Therefore, this chapter concentrates on local groups only.

Built-in Groups

Windows 2000 has six built-in local groups that can be administered through the Computer Management console (see Figure 22.1). By default, these built-in groups have a collection of rights and abilities.

- *Administrators*—Any group member has full administrative rights over every aspect of the computer. In effect, this user account is another administrator. The Administrator user account is a member by default and cannot be removed.
- *Backup Operators*—When using a backup program, any member of this group can back up files and folders, even if they do not have access rights to the file or folder. This group is useful for delegating responsibility for backups to another user without affecting file permissions. This group has no members by default.

FIGURE 22.1

The Computer Management console displaying built-in local groups.

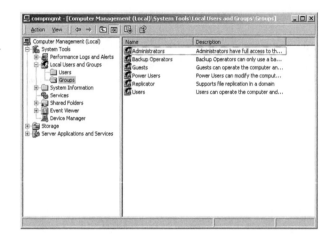

- *Guests*—This group is used for providing limited access to files and folders. Members of this group do not change machine settings, install new applications, or administer user accounts.

- *Power Users*—Similar to the account operators global group, except members only hold privileges on the local machine. Members can create user accounts and, for the accounts they create, a power user can modify and delete accounts. Members are not able to change computer settings. Power users cannot modify the Administrators or Backup Operators group.

- *Replicators*—This group is used explicitly for directory replication, and should not have any user account other than one used to log on to perform the replication service. Normally used as a part of domain replication.

- *Users*—Similar to the Power Users group, but with less abilities. Members can access files and shut down the computer, but they cannot share files or create user accounts.

Unlike Windows NT 4.0, all built-in groups can be renamed, but they cannot be deleted. Renaming a group does not change the group's functionality. One interesting addition to Windows 2000 from Windows NT is when you create a user account using the *Users and Passwords* (discussed in the next section) applet located in the Control Panel. You can chose to have the account be a member of the Power Users group, the Users Group, or specify another group of your choice. If you create the account using the local user manager snap-in, the user account is automatically added as a member to the users group.

Users and Passwords Applet

The Users and Passwords applet, located in the Control Panel, has been continued from Windows 98 to Windows Professional (see Figure 22.2). Used primarily for workgroup environments, this program creates user accounts and adds the user accounts to groups.

FIGURE 22.2

The Users and Passwords Applet in the control panel.

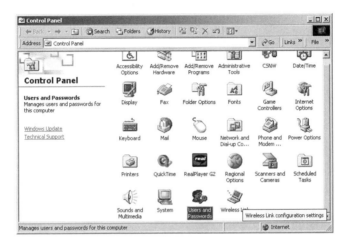

Domain user accounts cannot be administered through this program. User accounts created in Users and Passwords are local, and therefore cannot be used for logging on to other machines. Passwords and other properties only affect users logging on to the machine the user account that was created. Groups are not created in Users and Passwords, but user accounts can be placed in groups in this program. Domain user accounts can also be added to groups through the Users and Passwords applet.

> **Note**
>
> Only members of the Administrators group can use the Users and Passwords applet.

The Users and Passwords applet has two tabs: Users and Advanced. The Users tab lists user accounts and their group membership (see Figure 22.3). One feature in this tab is to allow users to log on to the computer without entering a username and password. This option makes Windows Professional useful for home environments or for businesses that do not require any authentication to access the programs.

FIGURE 22.3

The Users tab.

The Users tab also displays a list of user accounts and the group for each account. To change a password for a user account, select the account and click the Set Password button. As with most password settings, the password has to be entered twice.

Note

The Users and Passwords applet only displays a list of users who are member of groups. If a user account is not a member of the group, the account will be displayed in the Computer Management snap-in, but not in the Users and Passwords applet.

New user accounts can be created through an Add New User Wizard. The username used for logging on must be entered along with some optional fields for the user's full name and description. Figure 22.4 displays the first screen for creating a user account.

FIGURE 22.4

The Add New User Wizard.

The next step for adding a new user is to type in the user's password twice. Although this entry can be left blank, it is recommended that a password that combines numbers and upper- and/or lowercase letters be entered for increased security. Characters typed in will be displayed as asterisks, thus hiding the password from anyone looking over your shoulder. An eight-character password entered for Maxwell is shown in Figure 22.5.

FIGURE 22.5

Password entries for a new user.

The last step for adding new users is to specify the level of access for the new user account. In effect, this step places the user account into a group, each with different levels of access. The standard user level places the user account into the local Power Users group, giving the user some administrative rights. Most users will be placed into the second category—Restricted User. This allows users to log on the computer and save files, but they have no administrative privileges. Another option is to create a user-defined group and place user accounts into this group. The group must be created in the Computer Management snap-in. Figure 22.6 displays the last step for creating a new user account.

FIGURE 22.6

Choosing an appropriate access level for a new user account.

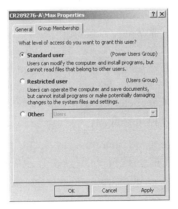

After user accounts have been created, selecting the targeted account and choosing properties can modify them. The properties allow changes to the username, full name, and description through the General tab, and changes to the access level through the Group Membership tab.

The second setting for Users and Passwords is the Advanced tab. This tab displays options for certificate management, advanced users management, and secure boot settings. Figure 22.7 shows the Advanced Users and Passwords tab.

FIGURE 22.7

The Advanced tab in the Users and Passwords dialog box.

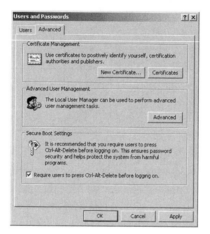

Certificates are used to ensure the parties involved in communication are not impersonating someone else to gain important information. A party can issue a certificate to declare that he or she has been certified by a trusted authority and can provide a secure method for authentication and data encryption. Certificates use a public key-private key algorithm that guarantees only the sending and receiving parties can decipher the data. Certificates can be mapped to a computer, a service or a user. The Certificate Management option allows the creation of new certificates if the computer can contact a certificate authority, and this option displays a listing of all certificates used for client authentication, securing email, and other purposes. Figure 22.8 illustrates a list of trusted root authorities for client authentication. Certificates can be administered using a certificate snap-in for the Microsoft Management Console.

The Advanced button in the Certificate Manager dialog box opens the Local User Manager snap-in, which is discussed next in this chapter. Local User Manager has advanced properties for user accounts, and administrators can create groups.

FIGURE 22.8

The Certificate Manager dialog box displaying a list of trusted root certificate authorities.

Secure Boot Settings enables Windows 2000 Professional's log on procedures to mirror that of Windows NT Workstation as opposed to Windows 98. For secure authentication, users should press Ctrl+Alt+Delete before logging on. Secure boot settings requires users to provide a user account and password before logging on, and that no other programs can run without a user logging on, thus stopping certain types of Trojan horse viruses from collecting user account information.

Local User Manager

Local User Manager is the main administrative tool for creating and managing users and groups. The snap-in for this program can be accessed through many different methods. All will open in the Microsoft Management Console (MMC).

1. From the Users and Passwords applet, choose the Advanced tab, and then click the Advanced button.

2. Select Start, Run, and type MMC. This will open the MMC program. From the console in the menu bar, select Add/Remove Snap-in. Click Add and select the Local Users and Groups snap-in. Choose Add, and then OK to close the dialog boxes.

3. Select Start, Programs, Administrative Tools, Computer Management. Computer Management displays a series of snap-ins, all used for managing computers (thus the name!). By default, Administrative Tools is not listed in the Programs menu; however, it can be added from the Advanced Tab of the Taskbar and Start Menu Properties dialog box.

Whichever method is used to access this snap-in, the Local User Manager has two items: Users and Groups. These items will display a list of user accounts or domain local groups, respectively. Figure 22.9 displays the Computer Management console showing a list of user accounts. Local user accounts display an icon that has a person with a computer behind them. From this window, Administrators can manage all user and group information.

FIGURE 22.9

Local User Manager displaying user accounts.

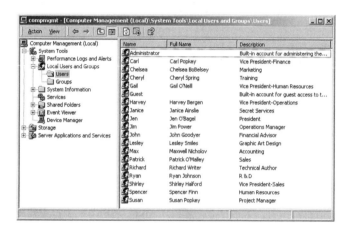

Creating and Managing User Accounts

To create a new local user account, right-click Users and select New User. This method for creating a new user has additional features not found in the Users and Passwords applet. The Create New User window has the options listed next. These options are also available from User properties after a user account has been created.

- *Username*—The logon name for each user account. This name must be unique from any other username and group, and can be as many as twenty characters in length. Certain characters that are not allowed (they are reserved for the operating system) in usernames are as follows: /, \, [,], <, >, ;, :, *, =, +, |, ,, *, ?.

- *Full name*—A field used to provide the user's full name.

- *Description*—A field to enter the user's business department or description.

- *Password*—A secret phrase or set of characters used to authenticate the user. Always put in a password, even if users will change it at a later time. A password can be up to fourteen characters in length and is case sensitive.

- *Confirm*—A field used to confirm the password in the event of accidentally typing an incorrect entry for password.

- *User Must Change Password at Next Logon*—A lot of Administrators will enter a default password for new users and then select this option. This ensures that the user changes his or her password to something he or she can remember, and that the only person who knows the password is the user. This option is also set when a user forgets his or her password, and an Administrator resets the password back to the default. This option overrides (and thus shades out) the options for User Cannot Change Password and Password Never Expires.

- *User Cannot Change Password*—This option can be set to allow only users with administrative rights to change the password for the user. This removes password control from users. This option has no effect on users who have administrative rights. Also, this option overrides User Must Change Password at Next Logon.

- *Password Never Expires*—This option is usually selected for user accounts that log on as services and therefore are not actually users. Selecting this option overwrites any password age restrictions set in Group Policies (discussed later in this chapter). Also, this option overrides the User Must Change Password at Next Logon option.

- *Account Disabled*—This option stops further logons for the user account. Usually this option is selected when a user is no longer working for the company, and the account is disabled until another person fills the position. A disabled account is represented by a local user account icon with a red X, as shown by the Guest account in Figure 22.9.

- *Account Locked Out*—One option that can be established in Group Policies is to give a user a certain number of chances to log on to the computer. If the user does not log on in the specified attempts (because they left the CAPS lock on for passwords), the user account is locked out. This option will only be available when an account is locked out. If an account is not locked out, the option is shaded out, meaning that it cannot be manually set. A similar function to locking out an account is to disable the account. The Administrator account cannot be locked out, but will have a check mark next to it if a user unsuccessfully attempts to log on using the account more times than allowed in Group Policies. This option will not be displayed when creating a new user account because it has no meaning at that time.

Figure 22.10 displays all of the previously listed user settings.

After a user account has been created, other properties can be set. To display a list of properties for a user account, right click the account (see Figure 22.11).

22

USERS AND
GROUPS

FIGURE 22.10

The general properties for Spencer's user account.

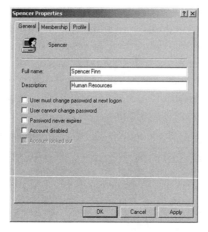

FIGURE 22.11

Options for all user accounts.

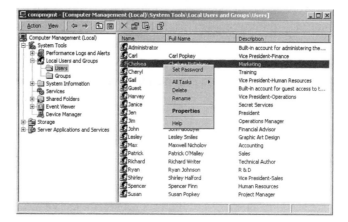

A user account's name can be changed without any repercussions for permissions or logons. Windows 2000 identifies user accounts by a security identification number (SID), not the username. Groups are also identified using SIDs. Right-clicking the user account can change this option. The account also can be deleted using this method. Because Windows 2000 uses SIDs to identify user accounts, if a user account is deleted and then recreated using the same username, all permissions must be reassigned.

The Properties option for user accounts displays two additional tabs along with the General tab displayed when creating a new user. These two options are Membership and Profiles. The Member Of tab provides a list of groups to which the user account belongs (see Figure 22.12).

FIGURE 22.12

The Member Of tab displaying a list of groups for Margo's user account.

To add the user account to a new group, select Add. This opens a Select Groups window. The top portion of this window displays a list of containers (local domains, trusted domains, and the local computer). After choosing from this selection, below this option is a list of groups. A group name can be typed in the name field or selected from the group list, and then click Add to make the user account a member of the group. Figure 22.13 displays the Marketing local group being added to a user account.

FIGURE 22.13

The Marketing Group being added to Chelsea's user account.

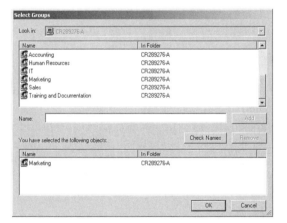

The third tab for user account properties is Profile. Profiles are discussed later in this chapter.

Creating and Managing Groups

The Local User Manager snap-in also has options for creating and managing local groups. Creating a new group is similar to creating a new user. Right-click the Groups option and choose Create Group. The fields for creating a new group are as follows:

- *Name*—The name of the local group. This name must be unique from any other local group or user account name and can be up to 256 characters. Group names cannot contain certain characters that user accounts cannot use, but they can include spaces. After a group has been created, it can be renamed, including the built-in local groups.
- *Description*—The description of the local group.
- *Members*—Lists all members of the group.
- *Create*—Creates the group. This option must be chosen to create the group. Clicking the Close button will close the windows without creating the group. The Create button is shaded out until a name has been typed for the group.

Figure 22.14 displays the Create Group window.

FIGURE 22.14

The Create Group window.

When Windows 2000 Professional is operating in native mode (only with other Windows 2000 computers), user accounts, universal groups, global groups, and other domain local groups can be members of domain local groups. If Professional is operating in mixed mode (with Windows NT computers), only user accounts and global groups can be added to domain local groups. Figure 22.15 shows adding user accounts and groups to a local group.

System Groups

One other type of group that has not been discussed is a System group. These groups can't be administered directly—user accounts are either members of these groups or they are not members.

The following is a list of all System groups and their descriptions:

- *Everyone*—A list of all users who can access the computer via the network or by logging on locally.

FIGURE 22.15

The Select Users and Groups window.

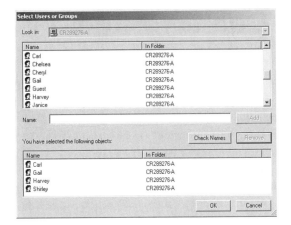

- *Authenticated Users*—A Windows 2000 version of the Everyone group. This group contains all users who can access the computer via the network or by logging on, except anonymous logons.

- *Anonymous Logon*—All users who log on to the computer anonymously. These users could be logging on an FTP server or a Web server.

- *Batch*—A process, user account, or service that is accessing the computer through a batch file.

- *Creator Owner*—The owner of a resource. When a user creates a file or folder or adds a new printer, the user owns that resource. If permission is granted, an owner can control the resource or allow someone else to take ownership from them.

- *Dialup*—All users who have permission to dial in to a RAS server are members of the dial-up group.

- *Interactive*—The user who logs on locally to the computer is a member of the interactive group.

- *Network*—Any user who accesses the computer through the network is a member of the Network group.

- *Service*—User accounts that are used to log on as a service.

- *System*—Any programs that require authentication through a system account.

- *Terminal Server User*—Any members who are terminal server users.

22

USERS AND GROUPS

Dos and Don'ts for the Administrator Account

Aside from the obvious security precautions, such as changing the Administrator account's username and assigning the account a complex password, Administrators can utilize some of Windows 2000 additional features to increase the security for the most important user account. Ideally, Administrator accounts should only be used to install new hardware or software and to perform any repairs to the operating system. Other user accounts and built-in groups should perform all other administrative tasks. Furthermore, only a select few should be added to the Administrators local group. Most administrative tasks can be delegated to other built-in groups, such as the Account Operators, Server Operators, Printer Operators and Power Users group.

Maintaining a computer while logged on as Administrator poses various security risks. Trojan horse viruses could intercept account information and be used to attack the system. Routine tasks, such as visiting Web sites, can spell disaster if a user is logged on as an Administrator.

Windows 2000 allows Administrators to log on as a regular user who can, in turn, perform most day-to-day administrative tasks. If a task must be performed that requires administrative rights while logged on as a regular user or power user, a special Run As feature allows a program to be opened as another user. The following steps describe this procedure:

1. Open Windows Explorer and find the executable file or an `.msc` file that can be used for the administrative task.
2. Right-click the file and select Run As. Figure 22.16 demonstrates this step. A dialog box will appear with two options for opening the application.

FIGURE 22.16

Selecting Run As.

3. You can log on with the present account or start a secondary logon using a new account. Figure 22.17 shows this step.

FIGURE 22.17

Starting an application as another user.

Using the Run As feature, an Administrator can log on using his or her own regular user account, and then open an application that requires administrative rights using a secondary logon. This secondary logon is only in effect for the one application.

A command-line utility called Runas will perform the same function. The following shows all the parameters for the Runas command:

```
RUNAS USAGE:
RUNAS [/profile] [/env] [/netonly] /user:<UserName> program

    /profile        if the user's profile needs to be loaded
    /env            to use current environment instead of user's.
    /netonly        use if the credentials specified are for remote access only.
    /user           <UserName> should be in form USER@DOMAIN or DOMAIN\USER
    program         command line for EXE.  See below for examples

Examples:
> runas /profile /user:mymachine\administrator cmd
> runas /profile /env /user:mydomain\admin "mmc %windir%\system32\dsa.msc"
> runas /user:user@domain.mycompany.com "notepad \"my file.txt\""
```

> **Note**
>
> Enter user's password only when prompted.
>
> USER@DOMAIN is not compatible with /netonly.

The Runas command or the option displayed when right-clicking does not have to be used for administrative duties only. This feature can be used whenever opening a program using a secondary logon.

The secondary logon feature runs as a service. As with other services, the secondary logon service must be started. Figure 22.18 shows the Secondary Logon Service.

FIGURE 22.18

*The Secondary
Logon Service.*

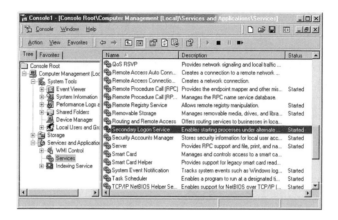

Profiles

Profiles allow each user to maintain their own settings. When a user logs on to a computer for the first time, a profile is created for that user. For example, Ed regularly uses the computer to check for email and surf the Internet. He decides to look around and finds the display settings. He changes the background settings to Coffee Bean and changes the screen saver to 3D Pipes (not a good screen saver for servers!). When he logs off the computer, these changes are saved to his profile. Therefore, when anyone else logs on to the computer, they do not get stuck with his customized settings. So if Elaine wants to use the computer to check for stock quotes, she will not have use his settings. In fact, she can create her own customized profile.

Each user will receive his or her own profile because when a user logs on to a computer for the first time, Windows 2000 copies a default profile to create a profile for that user account. All changes are stored in the new profile. Profiles are stored in a folder called Documents and Settings. Figure 22.19 shows Windows Explorer opened to show a profile for Cliff.

Profile Paths

Windows 2000 has additional features for user profiles. When users log on to one computer, profiles can run without any problem. However, if the users are a part of a domain, customizing a profile on one machine will not carry over to all other computers by default. Suppose that Jackie logs on to one computer and customizes her desktop environment, and then logs on to a different computer. Her user profile will not be displayed on the other computers. The Profiles tab under the User properties allows profiles to be saved and displayed regardless of the computer to which a user logs on. This tab has a field for typing in the location of a user's profile. After a user is authenticated on a computer, Windows 2000 looks for the path that is typed in this field for that user's profile. Figure 22.20 displays a profile path for Gail.

FIGURE 22.19

The Documents and Settings folder.

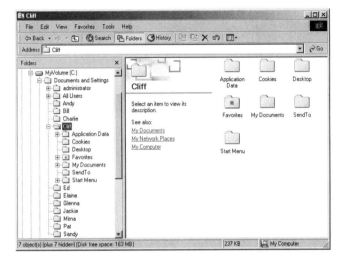

FIGURE 22.20

The profile path in User properties.

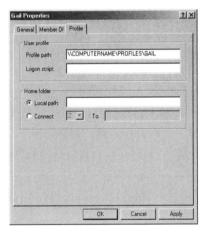

The location for profiles follows the standard universal naming convention (UNC), which means that path uses the computer name that the profile exists on, the name of the shared folder, and the name of the individual profile. These three items are separated by backslashes (\), with two backslashes at the beginning to indicate that UNC is being followed. A generic example of a universal name for profiles is as follows:

```
\\computername\sharename\profilename
```

By typing in the profile path, a roaming profile is created. Therefore, when Jackie moves from one machine to another, she can change her profile, and the changes will be saved for her next logon.

> **Note**
>
> Roaming profiles are only useful in domain environments. Also, roaming profiles should not be implemented on slow networks because they require extra bandwidth to download the profile to each machine.

Before roaming profiles will work, the Documents and Settings folder must be shared out and appropriate permissions must be applied. A common share name for this folder is Profiles. Administrators can also make these roaming profiles mandatory, which means that any changes to the profile are not saved when a user logs off a computer. Therefore, the next time a user logs on, he or she will receive the same profile.

Logon Scripts

Another setting under the Profile tab for user account properties is logon scripts. This field can be used to automate any commands when a user logs on. The automated steps are usually performed through a batch file and provide a very powerful tool for updating all machines in a domain. For example, instead of manually updating all machines for items such as service packs and anti-virus software or minor fixes to applications, these updates can be placed in a batch file that can be run the next time a user logs on.

To implement logon scripts, type in a local path to the location of these scripts, or follow the universal naming convention and include a filename for the batch file. Figure 22.21 shows a logon script path for Gail.

Logon scripts can also be implemented as a part of group policies.

Home Directories

A home directory is a folder for each user that contains information only for that user. In effect, a home directory is an area specified for each user to store his or her files. This folder can be located on the local machine. For domain environments, the folder can be located on a server. Figure 22.22 shows a home directory location.

FIGURE 22.21

The logon script path in User properties.

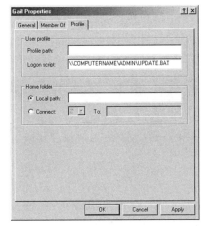

FIGURE 22.22

The Home Directory field in User properties.

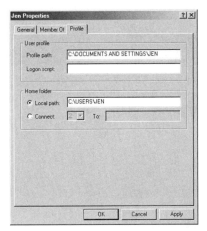

Home directories have a couple of advantages. First, some programs will use the home directory location as their default for opening and saving files. This feature is similar to the My Documents folder. Another feature of home directories is that each user can assign permissions to state who has access to their folder and who does not have access. To create a location for home directories, type in a location using one of the following parameters:

- A network path, such as:

  `\\computername\users\Carl`

- A local path, such as:

  `c:\users\John`

- Use a variable substitution, such as %username% instead of a username. An example is as follows:

```
\\SmithsFalls\users\%username%
```

> **Note**
>
> To use home directories located on other computers, a folder must be shared out first. This method for home directory locations is useful for centralizing user data for backing up.

Another option for home directories is to assign a letter for the location. Using this option maps a drive letter to the home directory, thus making it easier for users to locate and ensuring a continuous connection between the two machines.

> **Tip**
>
> If possible, avoid using the default drive letter of Z because many Windows 2000 log on procedures will temporarily use this letter during the authentication process. A good drive letter to use is H (for home).

Figure 22.23 demonstrates mapping a home directory to the letter H for Jen.

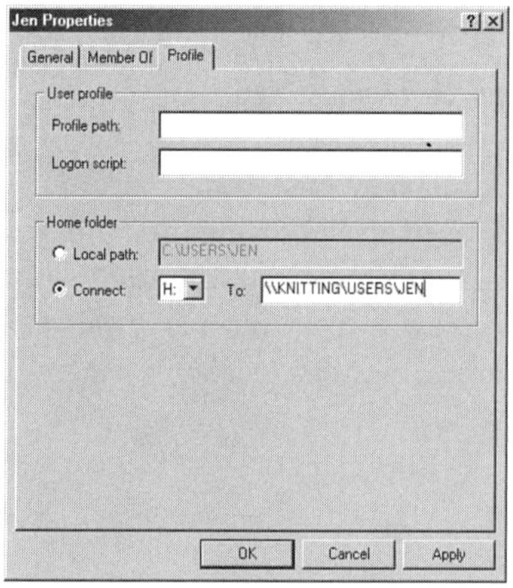

FIGURE 22.23

The mapped home directory field in User properties.

Mapping home drives can allow a consistent location for all users to store their files, thereby making file storage procedures easier for users. Also, backup procedures are simplified because all data is stored in a central location.

Group Policies

Group policies represent a major change for administrative management over desktop configurations. They can be used to enforce a set of requirements for users and computers and replace system policies, auditing, scripting, and software installation previously used in Windows NT. Policies can be implemented for all Active Directory containers, such as sites, domains, or organizational units. The subject of Group Policies can span an entire book on its own. Therefore, this topic will be limited to Group Policy's effect on user account logging on to Windows 2000 Professional computers.

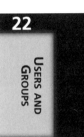

> **Note**
>
> Windows 2000 Group policies will not provide client support for previous operating systems such as Window 95, Window 98, and Windows NT. To implement policies for these computers in a domain environment, use the `poledit.exe` file, which can be found in the WINNT folder on your WIndows NT Server.

One of the main features of Group Policies is to apply configuration settings for computers and user accounts after a user has been authenticated to log on a machine. Group policies regulate what functions a user is able to perform and, more importantly, what they are not allowed to perform. These settings are based on the user account that logs on and to what machine the user logs on.

To create a local group policy, use the following steps.

1. Open the Microsoft Management Console from the Run command. Choose Console, Add/Remove Snap-in.
2. Select the Add button. From the list of snap-ins, choose Group Policy and click Add.
3. A window will appear asking to state the location for the group policy object. An object is a storage location for the group policies. For this example, leave the local group policy and select Finish. This will create a group policy object on the local machine.
4. Click Close to return to the MMC window.

After a group policy has been created, the MMC window displays some extensions for the computer and for the user (see Figure 22.24).

FIGURE 22.24

Local Group Policy in the Microsoft Management Console.

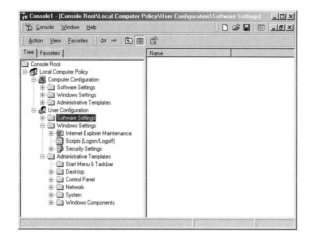

The following describes the Group Policy snap-in extensions:

- *Software Settings*—This provides a central area for any software installation management, including who can install, remove, and update software and on what computers software management can be implemented.

- *Security Settings*—This setting allows an Administrator to configure security for a group policy object in lieu of using a security template. Security settings include account policies, local policies (auditing and user rights), event log access, group restrictions, system service, Registry access, and IP security implementation. Security settings are discussed in more detail later in this chapter.

- *Scripts*—Scripts can be executed during computer startup and shutdown and during log on and log off. A script can be made using Visual Basic, Windows Scripting Host, or JScript.

- *Administrative Templates*—A Registry-based group policy that governs the desktop settings for users when logging on and the behavior of the system services and applications. This snap-in is described in further detail in the "Administrative Templates" section of this chapter.

The computer configuration settings and user configuration settings appear to have overlapping areas, and this is intentional. The computer configuration settings will initiate once a computer starts. When a user logs on, the user configuration settings will process. However, some applications set in one area will affect the other, such as the Run command. Use caution and experiment to find the proper settings for the network environment. The computer configuration settings are written to the Hkey Local Machine registry tree, and the user configuration settings are written to the Hkey Current User tree.

Account Policies

Account policies state what controls are applied for user account's passwords and account lockout restrictions for users logging on the computer. The following are the configuration options for the first parameter, Password Policy:

- *Allow Storage of Passwords Under Reversible Encryption*—Enabling this option allows a decryption key to transform an encrypted password back to plain text. Disallowing this option forces Windows 2000 to use a strong cryptographic algorithm to make a reverse encryption process virtually impossible. Disabled by default.

- *Enforce Password Uniqueness by Remembering Last*—Some users aren't particularly fond of the idea of changing passwords, and therefore spend a lot of time and energy attempting to change a password back to its original state. This option keeps a history of previously used passwords and prevents users from changing back to the password for a given amount of time. The default is no history of passwords.

- *Maximum Password Age*—The length of time a password can be used before it must be changed. The default is 42 days.

- *Minimum Password Age*—After a user changes his or her password, this option sets the minimum amount of days before a user can change the password again.

- *Minimum Password Length*—The minimum amount of characters a password can be. A good password should always be no less than eight characters.

- *Passwords Must Meet Complexity Requirements of Installed Password Filter*—First introduced in Windows NT SP3, this option forces complex passwords to be used.

- *Users Must Logon to Change Password*—This option forces users to use the Windows Security dialog box to change passwords. Users who do not change their passwords when the maximum password age has expired are effectively locked out.

An illustration of the different password policies is shown in Figure 22.25. The example shown is changing the minimum password age to 4 days.

Account policies also control how many chances a user has to log on before he or she is locked out. The options for account lockout policies are as follows:

- *Account Lockout Count*—This option maintains how many unsuccessful logon attempts users have before their accounts are locked out. The default is unlimited.

- *Account Lockout For*—How long a user account will be locked out. The default value is thirty minutes after the account lockout count has been set.

22

USERS AND GROUPS

FIGURE 22.25

Password Policies.

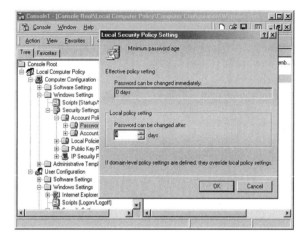

- *Reset Account Lockout Count After*—This option states how long before the account lockout count resets back to zero. For example, if Shirley attempts to log on, but has two unsuccessful attempts, she can wait ten minutes for the reset count to return to zero.

In a domain environment, account policies will also include settings for Kerberos policies. The Kerberos protocol is used for IP security authentication and has options for ticket lifetimes and enforcement.

Figure 22.26 shows a user account that has been locked out because of the account policy. A user will have a defined number of attempts before he or she receives the following message:

```
Unable to log you on because you account has been locked out. Please contact
your administrator.
```

FIGURE 22.26

An account locked out.

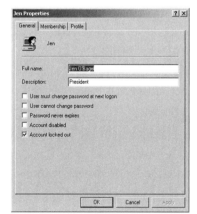

To unlock a user account, open the user's properties from the Local User Manager and remove the check mark from the Account Locked out field.

Local Policies

Windows 2000 has combined audit information, user rights, and security options into one area called local policies. Local policies are just that—they are local to the machine and can be set on a computer basis. Local policies override settings for user account policies.

The first option for local policies is Audit policy. This policy states what audit trail should be recorded in the Security Log by successful or failure. Figure 22.27 shows a list of all the audit events from local policies.

FIGURE 22.27

Audit Policies.

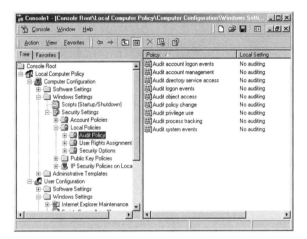

Each event can record the successful change of object or failed attempt. The list of audit events is as follows:

- *Audit Account Logon Events*—This option audits all users who successfully or unsuccessfully attempt to log on to a computer.

- *Audit Account Management*—Records successful or failed attempts for changes to user accounts and groups.

- *Audit Directory Service Access*—Audits any changes to directory services.

- *Audit Logon Events*—Audits any changes to logon procedures, such as account lockout.

- *Audit Object Access*—Audits accessing a file or a folder. This has to be enabled before setting audit events on individual files or folders.

- *Audit Policy Change*—Audits any changes to policies.

- *Audit Privilege Use*—Audits the use of any user rights.

- *Audit Process Tracking*—Audits low-level process information.

- *Audit System Events*—This policy generates a system event when the system event log is cleared.

User Rights

User rights define what privileges users or groups have on the local computer. Some rights determine who can log on the computer or access the computer via the network. Other user rights specify who has the right to back up files or restore files on a machine. Figure 22.28 shows a list of user rights.

FIGURE 22.28

User Rights assignment.

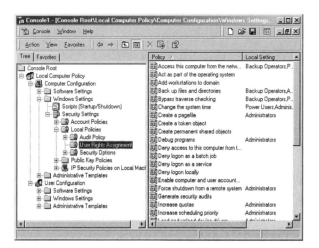

User rights can be added to individual user accounts or to groups. Any members of the group will inherit those rights. User rights may contain built-in local groups by default. The following is a list of user rights:

- *Access This Computer from the Network*—Who has the ability to access this machine over the network. By default, the Everyone, Users, Administrators, Power Users, and Backup Operators group have this ability.

- *Act as a Part of the Operating System*—What users or groups can perform as a secure part of the operating system. Usually granted to subsystems. This is an advanced user right usually used for developers.

- *Add Workstations to Domain*—Not applicable on Windows Professional computers that do not participate in a domain. No user has this right by default.

- *Back Up Files and Directories*—Who has the right only to back up files and directories, not restore. The Backup Operators and Administrators have this right by default.

- *Bypass Traverse Checking*—Users and groups who can change directories or access a directory (that they have permission to access), even if they do not have permission to access the parent directory. By default, the Everyone, Users, Administrators, Power Users, and Backup Operators group have this ability.

- *Change System Time*—Have the ability to change the system time. Power Users and Administrators have this right by default.

- *Create a Pagefile*—Users who can create or modify pagefile settings. By default, Administrators can create pagefiles.

- *Create a Token Object*—Permission to create an access token. Access tokens give users their rights and permissions when they log on, and this right is usually granted to the local security authority and not to users and groups.

- *Create Permanent Shared Objects*—Who can create a permanent shared object, usually to be used by the operating system and not by users.

- *Debug Programs*—Users who have the ability to debug low-level processes, such as threads. Administrators have this right by default.

- *Deny Access to This Computer from the Network*—Opposite of allow access. Used to explicitly deny users and groups.

- *Deny Log On as Batch Job*—Users who cannot log on as a batch job. This option defaults to none.

- *Deny Log On as a Service*—Users who cannot log on as a service. This option defaults to none.

- *Deny Log On Locally*—Users who cannot log on to the computer locally. This option defaults to none.

- *Enable Computer and User Accounts to be Trusted for Delegation*—This option defaults to none.

- *Force Shutdown from a Remote System*—Used to shut down a machine remotely. Administrators have this right by default.

- *Generate Security Audits*—Normally for processes that generate audit events in the security log. This right defaults to none.

- *Increase Quotas*—Users who can increase quotas. Objects have assigned quotas associated to them. This option defaults to Administrators.

22

USERS AND GROUPS

- *Increase Scheduling Priority*—Users who can increase priority levels for processes. Administrators have this right by default.

- *Load and Unload Device Drivers*—Users who can install and remove device drivers. Administrators have this right by default.

- *Lock Pages in Memory*—Users who can lock pages in memory so that they cannot be paged out. Administrators have this right by default.

- *Log On as a Batch Job*—What user account can log on and perform a job. The SQLAgentCmdExec has this right as a default. This account is used for jobs created in Microsoft SQL 7.0.

- *Log On as a Service*—User accounts that can log on as a service. Usually used for Microsoft BackOffice programs.

- *Log On Locally*—User that can log on locally. Windows 2000 Professional lets the Guest, Users, Power Users, Backup Operators, and Administrators have this ability by default.

- *Manage Auditing and Security Log*—Users who can manage and monitor events recorded in the security and audit log. This option defaults to Administrators. The system log is open to all users.

- *Modify Firmware Environment Values*—Users who can modify system-environment variables that are stored in nonvolatile RAM. Used for Alpha-based platforms. Administrators have this right by default.

- *Profile Single Process*—Users who can perform performance samples on processes. Power Users and Administrators have this right by default.

- *Profile System Performance*—Users who can perform performance samples on the system. Administrators have this right by default.

- *Remove Computer from Docking Station*—Used for laptops. Users who can remove the computer from a docking station and thus disconnect the computer from the network. Users, Power Users, and Administrators have this right by default.

- *Replace a Process Level Token*—Users who can modify access tokens. This is a dangerous right and should never be given to users, including the Administrator, unless specific circumstances warrant such use. The system uses this right.

- *Restore Files and Directories*—Users who can restore but not back up files and directories. Administrators and Backup Operators have this right by default.

- *Shut Down the System*—Users who can shut down the system. On Windows 2000 Professional, Users, Power Users, Backup Operators, and Administrators have this right by default.

- *Synchronize Directory Service Data*—Users that can synchronize directory service data. Directory synchronization usually occurs between different implementations of directory services, such as between NDS and ADS. Users usually do not perform this right on Windows 2000 Professional.

- *Take Ownership of Files or Other Objects*—Users who have the right to take ownership of files or other objects, even if they do not have permission to do so by the object owner. This right should only be granted to Administrators unless circumstances warrant such actions.

Most user rights are for advanced features and should not have their default option changed except for specific circumstances.

Administrative Templates

Administrative templates allow Administrators to configure desktop settings for users. These policies are all Registry-based; the computer policy will make changes to the Hkey_Local_Machine tree while the user policy will make changes to the Hkey_Current_User tree. These Registry settings are an important aspect when implementing administrative templates. Policies can be enabled, cleared, or left as the default. Enabling a policy will override any existing Registry entries and use the policy settings. Clearing a policy will remove any Registry entries, while leaving the default will not make any changes to the Registry. Policies are divided into six areas: Windows components, Start Menu & Taskbar, Desktop, System, Network, and Printers.

The windows components are further divided into categories: three categories for computer settings and five for user settings. User-configurable categories include Internet Explorer, Windows Explorer, Microsoft Management Console, Task Scheduler, and Windows Installer. The Internet Explorer category lists policies for various security zones and trust information. One nice addition for Windows 2000 is explanations for all administrative templates. To find out what a policy does and its available options, double click the policy. Figure 22.29 demonstrates an explanation for a policy.

The Windows Explorer category has many options for features within the Windows Explorer program. Folder options, File menu, mapping network drives, and the Search button can all be disabled using these policies. Figure 22.30 shows all the Windows Explorer policies.

FIGURE 22.29
Policy Explanations.

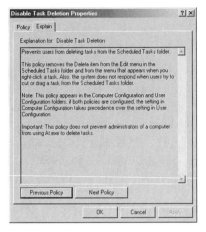

FIGURE 22.30
Windows Explorer policies.

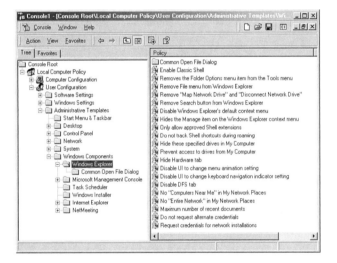

The Microsoft Management Console category includes options for restricting users from entering author mode and permitting only a specific list of snap-ins. These policies effectively state which snap-ins users can utilize and which they cannot.

The Task Scheduler category has policies for disabling features such as drag-and-drop and task deletion. There is also a policy for prohibiting browsing, meaning programs will not be able to use a Browse button for typing in pathnames. Property pages can also be hidden. Figure 22.31 displays the Task Scheduler policies.

FIGURE 22.31

Task Scheduler policies.

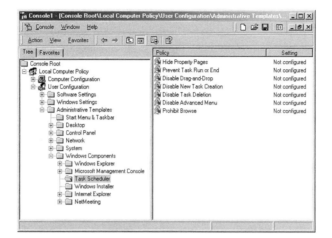

Windows Installer is a new method for installing software that replaces the use of `.inf` files with `.msi` and `.zap` files. Windows Installer Policies allow some configuration settings for installing new software, such as disabling rollback and search orders.

The second main category for user configurable Administrative Templates is Start Menu and Taskbar. This category lists many policies that can remove items from the Start menu, such as the Run and Search commands. Also, this category has policies for the disabling feature from the Start Menu, such as logging off, changing printers and control panel settings, and changes to the taskbar. With these policies, Administrators can lock down a workstation very tight. Figure 22.32 shows a list of the Start Menu and Taskbar policies.

FIGURE 22.32

Start Menu & Taskbar policies.

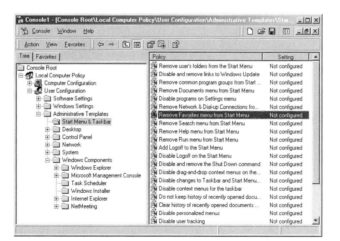

The next category has a list of permissions for the desktop. Administrators can hide objects such as Internet Explorer, My Network Places, or all icons from the desktop. In addition, active desktop features can be disabled. Figure 22.33 displays the Desktop policies.

FIGURE 22.33

Desktop policies.

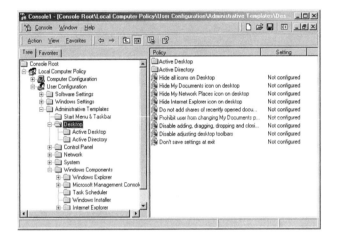

The Control Panel category has been further divided into three subcategories: Add/Remove Programs, Display, and Printers. The Add/Remove Programs displays a list of policies that hide components of the Add/Remove Programs applet in the control panel. Likewise, the Display policies hide the tabs from the Display applet. This usually aggravates users who like to change their screen savers. Figure 22.34 shows a list of Display policies. Printer policies have options for adding and deleting printers, displaying pages in the Add Printer Wizard, and default path when searching for printers.

FIGURE 22.34

Display policies.

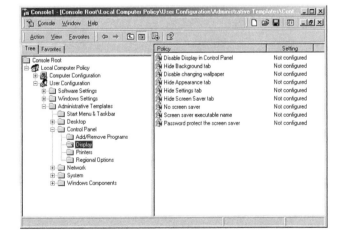

Network policies have two subcategories: Offline Files and Network and Dialup Connections. The Offline Files lists policies pertaining to synchronization procedures and balloon lifetimes. For more information about offline files and laptops, please refer to Chapter 14, "Using Windows 2000 on Laptops." The Network and Dialup Connections lists policies on enabling features to connect and disconnect to LANs and RAS connections. Different property tabs also can be enabled or cleared. Figure 22.35 shows a list of the Network and Dialup Connections policies.

FIGURE 22.35

Network and Dialup Connection policies.

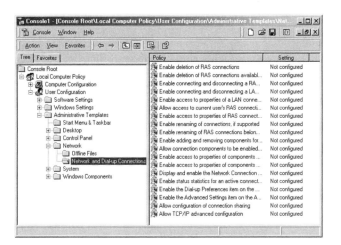

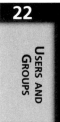

The last category for administrative templates is System polices. System policies allow Administrators to disable features from the Windows Security Dialog box, such as the Task Manager, Lock Computer, Change Password, and Logoff buttons. Also, logon and logoff scripts can be visible. Other system policies include group policy information. Figure 22.36 displays a list of logon/logoff System policies.

FIGURE 22.36

System policies.

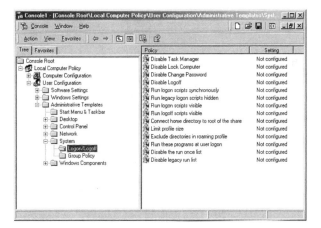

Account Templates can create a lot of damage on computers, and should be tested by an experienced user before being implemented on any production computers. Local group policies are only one small part of a domain-wide desktop configurable administration. Other areas allow for more advanced settings that can affect thousands of computers and users.

Disk Quotas

Disk quotas allow Administrators to manage file storage for all users on volumes. Users can be allocated a certain size for storing their data, and have warnings generated in the system log when they are near their limit. Disk quota characteristics and prerequisites are as follows:

- Disk quotas will only work on Windows 2000 NTFS volumes.

- Enabling disk quotas will slightly increase overhead, but this increase is minor compared to the administrative advantages the feature offers.

- File storage is based on object ownership. If a user copies a file, the new file is added to that user's quota. Likewise, if a user takes ownership of a file, the file is subtracted from the old owner's quota and placed in the new owner's quota.

- Disk quotas do not take into account file compression. Quotas are based on the uncompressed size of the file, not the compressed size.

- Each NTFS volume on a computer will have separate disk quotas.

- Disk quotas can prevent users from using further disk space or can be used as an administrative tracking procedure and still allow users to exceed limits.

Disk quotas can be enabled through the properties for each NTFS volume. Figure 22.37 displays the Quotas tab for the local disk D drive.

FIGURE 22.37

Quota Properties.

The following are the options for Quotas:

- *Enable Quota Management*—Enables disk quota limits for users.

- *Deny Disk Space to Users Exceeding Quota Limit*—Users cannot exceed the specified limit for saving files. No further files can be written to the volume and an "out of disk space" message appears.

- *Do Not Limit Usage*—Option for allowing unlimited disk storage space for users.

- *Limit Disk Space To*—Specify the limit each user is allotted for disk space.

- *Set Warning Level To*—The disk size that a user can fill before a warning message appears in the system log.

- *Log Event When a User Exceeds Their Quota Limit*—Generates a system event when a user exceeds his or her quota limit.

- *Log Event When a User Exceeds Their Warning Level*—Generates a system event when a user exceeds his or her warning limit.

A Quota Entries button can be used to monitor the various quota levels for users. This option opens a window displaying all users who have logged on the computer and where their current quota levels are. Figure 22.38 shows the Quota Entries for Local Disk window.

FIGURE 22.38

Disk quotas window.

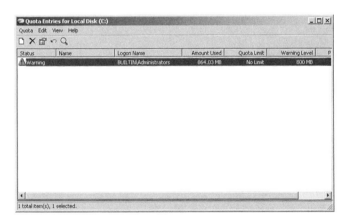

Disk quotas of individual users can be set through this window. To set an individual quota level, double click the user account. Figure 22.39 displays an individual disk quota level for the built-in Administrators group. Notice that Administrators do not have a limit.

FIGURE 22.39

Setting an individual user's disk quotas limit.

Summary

This chapter examined user accounts, groups, and authentication methods, as well as properties for users such as profiles, login scripts, and home directories. Finally, this chapter covered some administrative tasks, such as group policies and disk quotas.

CHAPTER 23

Internet Information Services (IIS)

Unless you have been living under a rock for the last five years, the Internet has impacted your life. You can't watch a TV show or read a magazine without being bombarded with Internet URLs for everything from the products advertised to the show or magazine itself. Everyone wants your email address, and it seems that everyone has a Web site to promote their home business, post pictures of their kids (or pets, the two are frequently interchangeable), or to post their resumé because they don't like their present job. It would appear that the Internet is here to stay. As the Internet continues to grow in popularity, Microsoft's commitment to providing easy-to-use, robust Internet applications will continue as well.

In Windows 2000 Professional, Microsoft's Internet application is the latest in the Internet Information Server (IIS) product line, Microsoft Internet Information Services 5. With Windows NT 4.0, the equivalent product was referred to as Peer Web Server for Windows NT Workstation. With Windows 2000, the application has the same name throughout the different operating systems, although functionality and features will vary from Windows 2000 Professional to Windows 2000 Server OSs. There are features included in Microsoft Internet Information Services 5 for Windows 2000 Server that are not available for the Windows 2000 Professional operating system.

Components of IIS

Let's look at what features are available in Microsoft Internet Information Services 5 under Windows 2000 Professional.

- *Common Files*—Required if any of the other IIS options are chosen. These are the core files to allow Microsoft Internet Information Services 5 to run on the system.

- *Documentation*—Documentation for all the services in HTML format for easy reading. If you have never worked with IIS or want to make sure you understand the latest version, be sure to select this during installation.

- *File Transfer Protocol (FTP) Server*—Implements the standard FTP protocol, which allows client machines to send and receive files from the server. The File Transfer Protocol (FTP) service provides clients attaching to your server the ability to transmit files to and from your Windows 2000 computer without the overhead of a network share. A veteran of the TCP/IP protocol suite, FTP has been used as the primary file transfer protocol for the Internet since its inception. Today virtually every operating system bundles an FTP client, and there are a number of third-party products available as well. All the Microsoft operating systems since Windows 95 include a character-based FTP client with their TCP/IP protocol stack. If you need to update any drivers on your Windows 2000 Professional computer, the odds are high that the vendor provides patches and updates via FTP.

For the Windows 2000 Professional user, an FTP site might be used to share documents for a virtual team, to trade MP3 files with people on the Internet, to make a new database client available to the field, or even catalog updates available to a customer.

- *FrontPage 2000 Server Extensions*—Extensions that are required for the IIS Server to publish Webs made with FrontPage 2000. If you are a Web developer, or even a Web developer to be, FrontPage 2000 Server Extensions can make your life much easier. What server extensions do is allow you to use FrontPage 2000 to develop and deploy your Web designs without going through the tedium of using FTP to transfer the files to the server. They also allow you to perform some management functions on the server from with the FrontPage application.

- *Internet Information Services Snap-In*—The IIS Snap-In allows IIS to be managed from within the MMC (Microsoft Management Console). This snap-in is not automatically added to the MMC and needs to be added manually. We will discuss adding the snap-in in the "Installing IIS" section, coming up next.

> **Note**
>
> While not strictly an IIS service, the Microsoft Management Console (MMC) is very important when discussing Internet Information Services 5. The MMC is an integral part of the Windows 2000 Professional operating system. This management framework, first introduced as part of Microsoft Internet Information Server 4 and the Windows NT 4.0 Option Pack, provides the next-generation management framework for managing Windows 2000 servers and services. Using management applications, known as snap-ins, the MMC provides a single interface for all Windows 2000 management applications. It also provides the main interface for managing your IIS 5 applications.

23

INTERNET INFORMATION SERVICES (IIS)

- *Personal Web Manager*—This allows all of the Internet services to be managed using HTML. If you are not a fan of the Microsoft Management Console interface, or you want to be able to manage Microsoft Internet Information Services 5 remotely from a Web browser, you should install this application.

> **Note**
>
> Personal Web Manager will only work if the WWW Publishing Service is running.

- *SMTP Service*—Allows the server to provide SMTP services, which is the Internet standard mail system. This allows mailboxes and forwarding routes to be set up on the system. The Microsoft SMTP Service uses the Simple Mail Transfer Protocol (SMTP) to send and receive email using TCP port 25 for operations. There are a number of clients available for reading SMTP mail, including Microsoft's Outlook Express, included with Internet Explorer 5. These clients allow you to send and receive SMTP mail, which is the primary mail type used on the Internet today. If you want to send email to Que Publishing to tell them how terrific this book is, you will need to send an SMTP mail message. The SMTP Service allows you to turn your Windows 2000 Professional workstation into an inexpensive Internet mail server. One additional feature of having a bundled SMTP service included with Microsoft Internet Information Services 5 is that you can mail-enable Web applications. Let's say you have written a guestbook for your personal Web site, and you want it to send you an email whenever a new entry is added. With the SMTP Service, your application can use the SMTP service to send the email to you.

- *Visual InterDev RAD Remote Deployment Support*—Allows Visual InterDev to remotely deploy applications (components and ASP pages) to the server. This is for the serious Web developer. If you are a Visual InterDev expert, you are already familiar with this. If you are not, there's nothing to worry about. Just stick with FrontPage and you'll be fine.

- *World Wide Web Server*—The WWW (World Wide Web) Server allows you to include HTML (Hypertext Markup Language) documents on your Web site and allow remote clients to reach them using a Web browser. You can also use a variety of other formats for these documents including Active Server Pages, Java applets, PERL scripts, and a variety of graphics formats. The WWW Server allows client machines to access information on the server via a Web browser (like Internet Explorer 5) using the HyperText Transfer Protocol (HTTP). HTTP is the protocol that is credited with the birth of the World Wide Web and the subsequent explosive growth of the Internet. The Web Server included with Windows 2000 Professional provides an excellent Web server for application development and testing, workgroup Intranet sites, or hosting small personal Web sites from home. This is not a good application for hosting a busy business Web site.

All right, you should be very comfortable with the components of Microsoft Internet Information Services 5 by this time. Let's look at how you install Microsoft Internet Information Services 5 on your Windows 2000 Professional computer.

Note

One thing you will notice is that the NNTP Service is not included in Microsoft Internet Information Services 5 for Windows 2000 Professional, which allows the server to operate as a network news transfer server. This is a functionality that Microsoft only includes with the Server version of the product.

Installing IIS

Now that you are familiar with the components of Microsoft Internet Information Services 5, let's discuss how you install IIS 5.

1. Making sure the Windows 2000 Professional CD-ROM is in the CD-ROM drive, open the Control Panel by going to Start, Settings, Control Panel.

2. After the Control Panel is open, double-click the Add/Remove Programs applet icon. This opens the Add/Remove Programs dialog box shown in Figure 23.1.

FIGURE 23.1

The Add/Remove Programs Dialog box shows installed applications and offers the ability to install, change, or remove applications and Windows 2000 components.

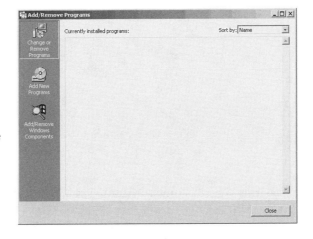

3. From the Add/Remove Programs dialog box, select the Add/Remove Windows Components icon in the left pane. This opens the Windows Components Wizard, pictured in Figure 23.2.

4. Select the Internet Information Services (IIS) Component. Notice that the different services that are included with this component are listed in the Description directly below the Components window. By clicking the Details button, you can see precisely what the components are and how much space each component uses. You can also customize which components can be installed. In this case, we will be

installing all the components discussed in the first section of this chapter, so click Next. This starts the Configuring Components portion of the Windows Components Wizard, shown in Figure 23.3.

FIGURE 23.2

The Windows Components Wizard is one of the many new wizards included as part of the new Windows 2000 Professional operating system.

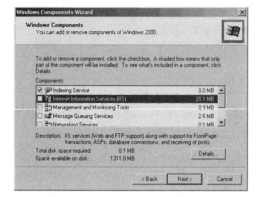

FIGURE 23.3

The Configuring Components portion of the Windows Components Wizard is where the setup process configures the components you have selected for installation.

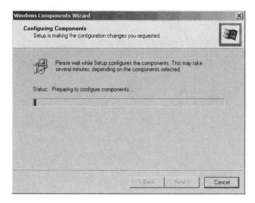

5. When the Components Wizard is complete (see Figure 23.4), click Finish to return to Windows 2000. The installation is complete.

FIGURE 23.4

After the IIS Component is installed, the Windows Components Wizard displays the successful completion dialog box. Clicking Finish returns you to the Windows 2000 operating system.

Installing IIS has always been the easiest part of bringing up a Microsoft-based Web application server. Windows 2000 has further simplified the process. Now comes the interesting part: managing the applications now that you have them installed.

Managing IIS

The first thing we need to discuss is how to manage this newly installed Windows 2000 component. The first step in this process is to understand the Microsoft Management Console framework for Windows 2000 management. By this point in the book, you should be conversant in its use, so we will not take any time to review it again. What we will do however, is look at how to add the IIS snap-in to the MMC framework. This snap-in must be added manually because it is not installed as part of the IIS installation process. To install the IIS snap-in to the Microsoft Management Console, perform the following steps:

1. Go to Start, Run, and enter the command **MMC** (see Figure 23.5). Then click OK to start the application.

FIGURE 23.5

Starting the Microsoft Management Console manually from the Run box.

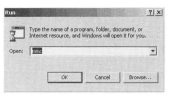

2. This will open the Microsoft Management Console shown in Figure 23.6. Your version of this view may differ from the figure, depending on the snap-ins you have installed on your machine. Note the absence of the IIS snap-in in this figure.

3. In the menu, go to Console, Add/Remove Snap-in menu. This opens the Add/Remove Snap-in dialog box, shown in Figure 23.7. This dialog box can also be opened using the keyboard shortcut Ctrl+M.

4. Click Add to open the Add Standalone Snap-in dialog box shown in Figure 23.8. Select the Internet Information Services snap-in and click Add.

5. Figure 23.9 shows the newly installed Internet Information Services snap-in. Click OK to return to the MMC main window.

6. Figure 23.10 shows the Internet Information Services snap-in expanded to show all the managed components in an expanded tree view. Notice that the display shows the snap-in, the managed computer, and the running services. In this case, these are all the services that were installed in the previous section.

23

INTERNET INFORMATION SERVICES (IIS)

FIGURE 23.6

The main screen of the Microsoft Management Console, shown in the tree view.

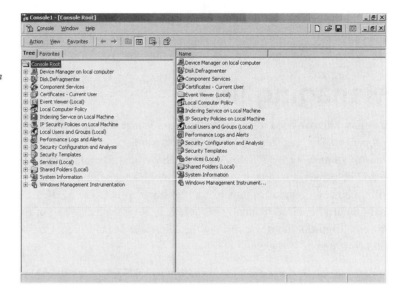

FIGURE 23.7

The Add/Remove Snap-in dialog box is used to manage all the installed snap-ins available on your Windows 2000 Professional workstation.

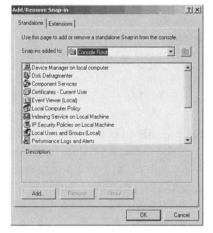

FIGURE 23.8

The Add Standalone Snap-in dialog box is used to select the snap-in(s) to be installed. This dialog box not only lists the snap-in but, where appropriate, also lists the associated vendor.

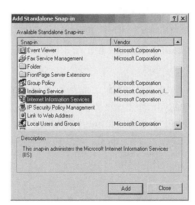

FIGURE 23.9

The Internet Information Services now appears as an installed snap-in in the Add/Remove snap-in dialog box.

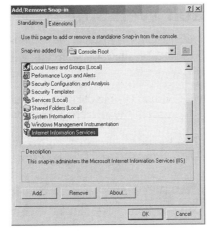

FIGURE 23.10

The expanded Internet Information Services snap-in shows the managed computer(s) and the available services that can be managed.

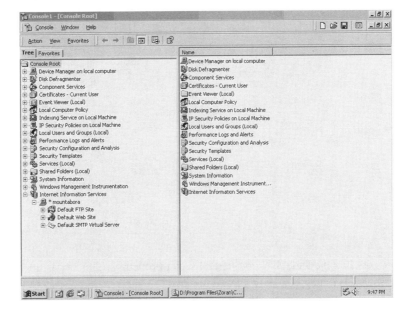

We will discuss the Personal Web Manager application in the "Additional IIS Configuration Tips" section of this chapter. Because the Microsoft Management Console is the major management framework for Windows 2000, we will discuss managing the Microsoft Internet Information Services 5 application from it, instead of via a Web browser. After you have mastered the MMC version of this management, the browser-based version should be very easy to familiarize yourself with. Now, let's create our first Web site.

23

INTERNET INFORMATION SERVICES (IIS)

Managing the Default Web Site

When Microsoft Internet Information Services 5 is installed on Windows 2000 Professional, it automatically creates your Web site for you. In this section, we will look at how to manage this Web site.

First, open the Microsoft Management Console. Double-click the Internet Information Services Snap-in. You should see the list of sites—Web, FTP, and SMTP (see Figure 23.10).

Double-click the Default Web Site. You should see an expanded tree in the left pane of the MMC and the files and directory listing in the right pane (see Figure 23.11).

FIGURE 23.11

The expanded Default Web Site shows all the files and directories installed by default.

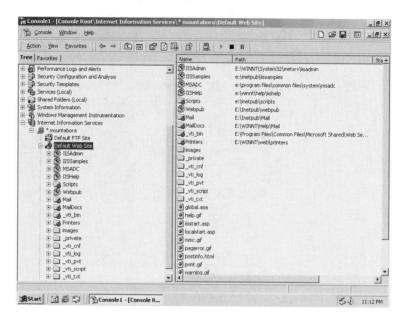

Right-click the Default Web Site and select Properties. This opens the Default Web Site Properties dialog box shown in Figure 23.12.

From the Web Site tab, you can set the following information:

- *Description*—This changes the description of the Web Site in the MMC.

- *IP Address*—If you have multiple IP addresses bound to your network interface card, you can select a specific address for your Web site, or the Web service will respond on all addresses by default.

- *TCP Port*—You can modify the TCP protocol port used by the Web service. By default, the TCP port for HTTP is port 80. Unless you are doing something that requires security or privacy, it is a good idea to leave this set to port 80.

FIGURE 23.12

The Properties dialog box for the Default Web Site opens showing the Web Site tab.

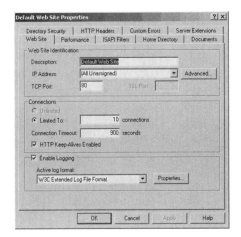

- *Connections*—Notice that with the Windows 2000 Professional version of Microsoft Internet Information Services 5 you are limited to 10 concurrent connections. You can reduce this number, but you cannot exceed this number.

- *Connection Timeout*—You can control the amount of time before the Web service drops a connection due to inactivity timeout.

- *HTTP Keep-Alives*—Enabled by default, HTTP Keep-Alives can be used to reduce the number of connections a client uses to make multiple requests to the Web server. Without Keep-Alives enabled, when a browser connects to a Web server and requests a resource, a connection is established with the server. When the request is completed, the connection is dropped. Because this is an expensive process in terms of server processing, enabling HTTP Keep-Alives can reduce or eliminate the need for multiple connections when clients make multiple requests for resources.

- *Logging*—From this tab, you can enable or disable logging, as well as determine the format of your log file. The selections are:
  - W3C Extended Log File Format (the default)
  - Microsoft IIS Log File Format
  - NCSA Common Log File Format

Depending on the analysis package you are using or the information you want to track, each format has its own benefits and drawbacks.

Click the Performance tab, shown in Figure 23.13. You will notice some of the advanced features are not available in the Windows 2000 Professional version of Microsoft Internet Information Services 5. Due to the limitation of 10 concurrent connections to a single

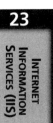

23

INTERNET INFORMATION SERVICES (IIS)

Web site, they are really not needed for this version. The enabled feature on this tab is Performance Tuning. This allows you to configure the Web server's performance based on the anticipated number of hits daily. For most Web sites running on Windows 2000 Professional, the default is more than adequate. With a limit of 10 concurrent connections, a hit count of greater than 100,000 is difficult to achieve.

FIGURE 23.13

The Performance Tab is used to set the site performance characteristics. In the Windows 2000 Professional version of Microsoft Internet Information Services 5, the advanced performance features are not available.

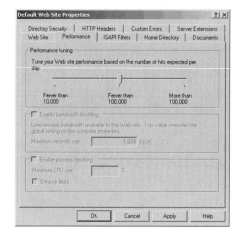

The ISAPI Filters Tab (see Figure 23.14) is used to install ISAPI filters on the Default Web Site. Internet Server Application Programming Interface (ISAPI) filters are DLLs written to the ISAPI interface of IIS. These filters can be used to enhance the functionality of your IIS server. ISAPI filters can intercept specific server events before the server itself handles them. When a filter is loaded, there is a specific set of event notifications it will handle, based on its function. If these events occur, the filter has the option of processing the events, passing them on to other filters, or sending them back to the server after it has dealt with them. Needless to say, use of ISAPI filters is an advanced Web application development activity, and is well beyond the scope of this book.

To add an ISAPI filter, click Add and browse to the filter you want to install.

The Home Directory Tab (see Figure 23.15) allows you to configure all the settings surrounding the Default Web Site's home directory. From this tab, you can configure the following parameters:

- *Content location*—The content of the home directory can come from a directory on the IIS server, a share located on another computer, or can be a redirection to another URL.

FIGURE 23.14

The ISAPI Filters tab is used to install ISAPI filters for your Web site. ISAPI filters can be used to increase the functionality of your Web site.

- *Local Path*—This parameter allows you to set the exact location of the home directory. If you have created a site you want to publish, but want to maintain the sample site installed with IIS for reference, you can place your developed site in another directory and then change the Local Path to point to the new directory.

- *Home directory permissions*—This tab allows you to determine what permissions guests will have on the site home directory. Those permissions can be any combination of the following:

  - Script Source Access
  - Read (enabled by default)
  - Write
  - Directory Browsing
  - Log Visits (enabled by default)
  - Index this Resource (enabled by default)

  If you are familiar with IIS 4, you will notice there are two additional check boxes enabled by default. While not strictly permissions, these control visit logging and resource indexing within this directory.

- You can also set some new parameters, including Application Name, Execute Permissions, and Application Protection Levels. These parameters are all geared toward advanced web application development.

The Documents tab (see Figure 23.16) allows you to set the Default Document and also allows you to add a Document Footer to the pages on the site.

The Directory Security tab (see Figure 23.17) allows you to secure your site, using three mechanisms:

FIGURE 23.15

The Home Directory tab allows you to configure the behavior of the Default Web Site's home directory.

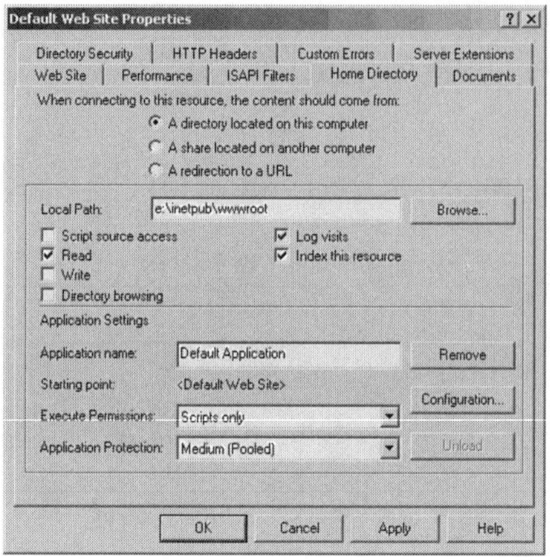

FIGURE 23.16

The Documents tab is where you set IIS to automatically load the file Default.htm *whenever someone connects to the Web site.*

- *Anonymous access and authentication control*—This allows you to enable or disable anonymous access to the site, as well as configure the preferred authentication mechanism, Basic or Integrated Windows Authentication. If possible, use the Integrated Windows Authentication. It is much more secure.

- *IP Address and Domain name restrictions*—These services are not available in the Microsoft Internet Information Services 5 version for Windows 2000 Professional. These are excellent tools for access control in the server version of the product.

- *Secure Communications*—This Certificate-based security mechanism relies on Secure Socket Layer protocol (SSL) to encrypt traffic to and from the server. You will need a certificate to use SSL.

FIGURE 23.17

The Directory Security tab allows you to secure your Microsoft Internet Information Services 5 Web site using Windows Authentication and SSL.

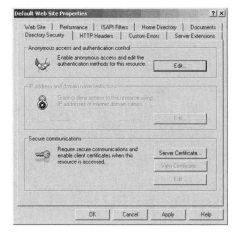

The HTTP Headers tab (see Figure 23.18) is used for advanced features of IIS beyond the scope of this book. The Content Expiration, Custom HTTP Headers, Content Ratings, and how to use MIME mappings options are more geared toward application/Web developers who will be hosting on a Windows 2000 Server platform. Be aware that these features are available, and more details are available in the IIS documentation.

23

INTERNET INFORMATION SERVICES (IIS)

FIGURE 23.18

The HTTP Headers tab allows you to con- figure advanced IIS settings like Custom HTTP Headers, Content Ratings and MIME mappings.

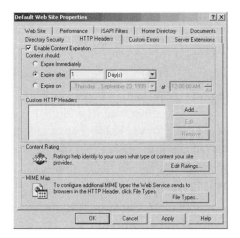

The Custom Errors tab allows you to do just what it describes. If you don't like the default Error 404 - Requested URL Not Found error, you can create your own error. By editing the properties of the 404 HTTP Error (highlighted in Figure 23.19), you can make that error page communicate any message you want.

FIGURE 23.19

*The Custom
Errors tab allows
you to customize
the error mes-
sages that your IIS
Web Site uses
when there is an
error generated in
the user's browser.*

The Server Extensions tab (see Figure 23.20) is a new tab for IIS. Server Extensions are a new feature that is included with Microsoft Internet Information Services 5, and this tab allows you to do the following:

- *Enable Authoring*—This feature enables Web designers and content authors to use FrontPage to access and modify Web site content. This was an add-on feature under IIS 4.0 and was known as FrontPage Extensions. If Enable Authoring is selected, you can configure Version Control, Performance (this is performance for authoring, not to be confused with the Web site performance features under the Performance tab), and what type of Client scripting to use on the site.

- *Options*—From this section, you can configure how the Web server will send email to visitors. An example of this might be a confirmation email when an order is placed. If you have Office Server Extensions installed, you can configure them here. This is unavailable if the Office Web Server is not installed.

- *Don't Inherit Security Settings*—By default, the root Web server inherits the security settings of the Web server. If you want to configure security for this Web site differently, this section allows you to set the logging of authoring actions, manage permissions manually, and require an encrypted SSL connection to perform authoring on the site.

By now you either have a thorough understanding of Web site management under Microsoft Internet Information Services 5, or you are thoroughly tired of the topic. So let's move on to managing the much simpler FTP site.

FIGURE 23.20

The Server Extensions tab allows you to configure how FrontPage authoring is handled by your Web site.

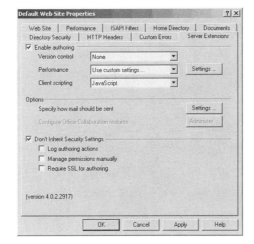

Managing the Default FTP Site

Managing the Default FTP site under Microsoft Internet Information Services 5 has not changed at all since the IIS 4 version of the application. If you are familiar with IIS 4.0, you can probably jump right past this section. If you are not familiar with IIS 4.0 or with FTP, please keep in mind that the main reason this hasn't changed is that FTP hasn't changed significantly in over 10 years. A staple of the Internet community, FTP servers are designed to be a simple method for transferring files. So while Web sites get more and more sophisticated, FTP sites tend to remain stable and reliable. The remainder of this section discusses how to manage the Default FTP Site.

First, open the Microsoft Management Console. Double-click the Internet Information Services Snap-in. You should see the list of sites: Web, FTP and SMTP (see Figure 23.10). Then, right-click the Default FTP Site and select Properties. This opens the Default FTP Site Properties shown in Figure 23.21.

From the FTP Site tab, you can set the following options:

- *Description*—This changes the description of the FTP Site in the MMC.
- *IP Address*—If you have multiple IP addresses bound to your network interface card, you can select a specific address for your FTP site, or the FTP service will respond on all addresses by default.

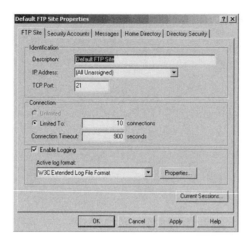

FIGURE 23.21

The Properties dialog box for the Default FTP Site opens showing the FTP Site tab.

- *TCP Port*—You can modify the TCP protocol port used by the FTP service. By default, the TCP port for FTP is port 21. Unless you are doing something that requires security or privacy, it is a good idea to leave this set to port 21.

- *Connections*—Notice that with the Windows 2000 Professional version of Microsoft Internet Information Services 5 you are limited to 10 concurrent connections. You can reduce this number, but you cannot exceed this number.

- *Connection Timeout*—You can control the amount of time before the FTP service drops a connection due to inactivity timeout.

- *Logging*—From this tab, you can enable or disable logging, as well as determine the format of your log file. The selections are:

  - *W3C Extended Log File Format (the default)*—This logging format is similar to the Microsoft IIS Log File Format because it too is created as ASCII text. It differs however because it is fully customizable. You can customize exactly what information is logged from a list of 30 different variables.

  - *Microsoft IIS Log File Format*— This logging format creates logs in a fixed ASCII format. It does not support customization and should be used if you are looking for the bare minimum of information.

  - *NCSA Common Log File Format*—This logging format is also a fixed ASCII log file but captures information based on NCSA's standards.

  Depending on the analysis package you are using, or the information you want to track, each format has its own benefits and drawbacks.

From the Security Accounts tab, shown in Figure 23.22, you can configure anonymous access to the site. You specify who can administer the site and set the site to accept only anonymous connections. While this may sound like a major security issue, anonymous-only access is, in fact, more secure than authenticating to the FTP site. FTP is a very old protocol and was written long before people were paranoid about security or privacy. All FTP traffic travels over the network as unencrypted (clear) text. This includes your passwords. If you use the same password to access FTP as you do to access your mail account at work, which do you think is the larger security issue? You obviously want to avoid placing sensitive data on an anonymous-only Web site, but for distributing files or something similarly innocuous, anonymous-only is an excellent solution.

FIGURE 23.22

The Security Accounts tab can be used to configure access security to the Web site, including anonymous access.

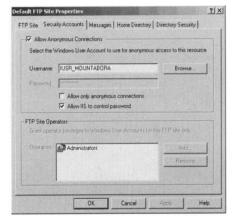

The Messages tab (see Figure 23.23) allows you to configure the Welcome, Exit, and Maximum Connections messages for the site.

FIGURE 23.23

The Messages tab allows you to configure the messages users will see when they connect to the FTP site.

23

INTERNET INFORMATION SERVICES (IIS)

The Home Directory tab (see Figure 23.24) allows you to configure the following:

- *Directory Location*—This can be either a local directory or a directory on a share. Unlike the Web service, it cannot be a redirected URL.

- *FTP Site Directory*—This is the actual directory path, as well as the permissions on the directory. Unlike the Web service, the permissions are limited to:
  - Read
  - Write
  - Log Visits

- *Directory Listing Style*—The directories an FTP user sees can be displayed in UNIX or MS-DOS format. They will appear as MS-DOS format by default.

FIGURE 23.24

The Home Directory tab allows you to configure the directory location, permissions and directory listing style for the FTP site.

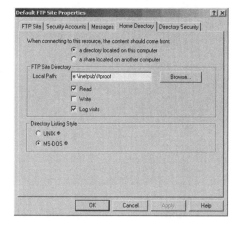

How do I enable Directory Security?

You don't. The Directory Security tab (see Figure 23.25) is not available in the Microsoft Internet Information Services 5 version for Windows 2000 Professional. It is only available in the Server versions of the product.

See, I told you FTP was much simpler than the Web site management. Let's look at how to configure the Default SMTP site.

FIGURE 23.25

Directory Security is only available in the Server version of Microsoft Internet Information Services 5, as is evidenced by the unavailable options shown in this figure.

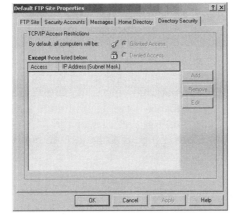

Configuring and Managing the Default SMTP Virtual Server

The Simple Mail Transport Protocol (SMTP) Site under Microsoft Internet Information Services 5 is the mechanism used for providing Internet standards-compliant messaging in conjunction with your Web site. One thing to keep in mind is the fact that the SMTP service is not meant to be a workgroup mail server. While Microsoft Internet Information Services 5's SMTP service can be used to mail-enable Web applications and relay SMTP mail, you cannot create users on the mail server, nor can you receive messages on it. It is for relaying only. With that in mind, let's look at some of the configurations for the virtual server.

23

INTERNET
INFORMATION
SERVICES (IIS)

If it's not an SMTP server, what is it?

Getting into the email business is a bit more complicated than just installing Microsoft Internet Information Server 5 on your Windows 2000 Professional workstation. You don't get to create mail accounts, you can't set up directories, you can't do much of anything, right? Wrong. If you want to write Web applications that generate email, this is an excellent application. Let's say you want to write an application that allows a visitor to ask for sales literature. Using Microsoft Internet Information Server 5 and the SMTP service, you can write a form that collects the user's information and sends it to you in an email.

What if you need a real email server?

If you need a true email server, it's going to cost you some money, and you will probably not run it on Windows 2000 Professional. Microsoft's solution for email, including SMTP email, is Microsoft Exchange on Windows 2000 Server. There are a number of competing packages, including Lotus's cc:Mail or Novell's GroupWise. If you are looking for just SMTP email, there are a number of companies that have them: Ipswitch, Eudora, and Netscape to name a few. This is by no means a comprehensive list, but it should be enough to get you started.

First, open the Microsoft Management Console. Right-click the Default FTP Site and select Properties. This opens the Default FTP Site Properties, shown in Figure 23.26.

FIGURE 23.26

The Properties dialog box for the Default SMTP Virtual Server opens showing the General tab.

From the General tab, you can set the following information:

- *Description*—This changes the description of the SMTP Virtual Server in the MMC.

- *IP Address*—If you have multiple IP addresses bound to your network interface card, you can select a specific address for your SMTP Virtual Server, or the server will respond on all addresses by default.

- *Connection*—From this section, you can configure not only the SMTP port (by default, port 25) but also the incoming and outgoing timeouts and connection limits. This service is not limited to the 10 connections the other services were because SMTP connections are not interactive.

- *Logging*—From this section, you can enable or disable logging, as well as determine the format of your log file. The selections are

    - *W3C Extended Log File Format (the default)*—This logging format is similar to the Microsoft IIS Log File Format, since it too is created as ASCII text. It differs however, since it is fully customizable. You can customize exactly what information is logged, from a list of 30 different variables.

- *Microsoft IIS Log File Format*—This logging format creates logs in a fixed ASCII format. It does not support customization and should be used if you are looking for the bare minimum of information.

- *NCSA Common Log File Format*—This logging format is also a fixed ASCII log file but captures information based on NCSA's standards.

Depending on the analysis package you are using, or the information you want to track, each format has its own benefits and drawbacks.

The Access tab (see Figure 23.27) allows you to configure the access restrictions to the server, through four main areas:

- *Authentication*—This allows you to enable or disable anonymous access to the site as well as configure the preferred authentication mechanism: Basic or the Windows Security Package. If possible, use the Windows Security Package, it is much more secure.

- *Secure Communications*—This Certificate-based security mechanism relies on Secure Socket Layer protocol (SSL) to encrypt traffic to and from the server. You will need a certificate to use SSL.

- *Connection Control*—This parameter is available for the SMTP Virtual Server, in large part to further control SPAM email traffic. It allows you to restrict the IP addresses and Internet domains allowed to connect to this service.

- *Relay Restrictions*—Taking the last parameter one step further, the Relay Restrictions parameter allows you to explicitly grant or deny relay restrictions.

23

INTERNET
INFORMATION
SERVICES (IIS)

FIGURE 23.27

The Access tab allows you to secure your Microsoft Internet Information Services 5 SMTP Server using Windows Authentication and SSL.

The Messages tab (see Figure 23.28) allows you to set the following parameters:

- *Limit Messages Size*—This parameter, when enabled, allows you to set the maximum message size in kilobytes.

- *Limit Session Size*—This parameter, when enabled, allows you to set the maximum session size in kilobytes.

- *Limit number of messages per connection*—When enabled, this parameter allows you to restrict the number of messages being sent or received during a single connection.

- *Maximum number of recipients*—This parameter limits the number of people who can receive a single message. This parameter was undoubtedly added to help combat SPAM emailings.

- *Non-delivery report*—If you are the site Administrator, you can have a report emailed to you of all the mail the server was unable to deliver.

- *Badmail directory*—This directory stores messages that cannot be sent or are invalid for some reason.

FIGURE 23.28

The Messages tab allows you to configure limits on the size and number of messages.

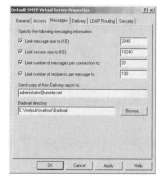

The Security tab (see Figure 23.29) allows you to grant Operator permissions to the appropriate users.

FIGURE 23.29

The Security tab is very similar to the security associated with the Default Web Site.

The Delivery tab (see Figure 23.30) is broken into the following sections:

- *Outbound*—This section contains the parameters that control how mail that cannot be delivered immediately is handled. It includes parameters such as Retry intervals, Delay Notification times, and message expirations for both Outbound and Local Delivery.

* *Outbound Security*—This controls the security for connections that the SMTP server must make to deliver mail. The options are very similar to the ones found on the Access tab but deal with connecting to other SMTP servers.

* *Advanced*—This button opens the Advanced Delivery Options, which allow you to configure the following:

    * *Hop Count*—This parameter limits the number of hops a message can take before it is aged out.

    * *Masquerade Domain*—If configured, this domain replaces the local domain on outgoing messages.

    * *Fully Qualified Domain Name*—This is the complete DNS name of the SMTP server.

    * *Smart Host*—This parameter allows you to route all traffic through a smart host instead of sending them directly to the destination domains. This can be used to route traffic over a cheaper connection to allow virus scanning or even content filtering of the mail before it is sent.

    * *Perform Reverse DNS lookup on incoming messages*—This parameter is used to ensure that email is originating from a registered domain before accepting it. This is another SPAM fighting tool.

FIGURE 23.30

The Delivery tab controls the parameters for connecting to other SMTP servers and how to handle undeliverable mail.

The LDAP routing tab is used to specify the location and properties of an LDAP (Lightweight Directory Access Protocol) server and is another advanced topic that can take up an entire book. Figure 23.31 is included for reference, and the Microsoft Internet Information Services 5 documentation includes more information on the topic.

23

INTERNET INFORMATION SERVICES (IIS)

FIGURE 23.31

The LDAP Routing tab is used to specify the location and properties of an LDAP (Lightweight Directory Access Protocol) server.

Summary

I'm sure by now we all realize how critical the Internet is to anyone who might be installing the Windows 2000 operating system. As we have discussed, Microsoft's premier application that enables a user to get involved with the Internet using Windows 2000 is Microsoft Internet Information Services 5.

In this chapter, we discussed the various components of Windows 2000 and their respective capabilities. We took a step-by-step look at installing Microsoft Internet Information Services 5 and then looked at how we added the IIS snap-in to the ubiquitous Microsoft Management Console framework. We also discussed how to manage the default Web and FTP sites created at installation. Finally, we discussed how to use the SMTP service to provide messaging capabilities within IIS.

This chapter should help emphasize Microsoft's commitment to providing cutting-edge applications to support the Internet not only on their premier server product line but also for the Windows 2000 Professional desktop operating system.

Setting Up an Intranet

CHAPTER

24

In previous chapters you learned about Windows 2000 networking protocols, network services, users and groups, and the Internet Information Services (IIS). These are all essential elements for discussing the next step, establishing your own intranet using Windows 2000 Professional. In this chapter, you will learn:

- What an intranet is and the costs and benefits of this rapidly growing technology
- Issues to consider when planning your intranet, including how to determine your audience, setting intranet use policies, and more
- How to incorporate Microsoft Office documents into your intranet
- Tasks that must be performed to keep your intranet healthy, current, and well used

Although there are many different choices available to you for creating and designing an intranet (see the "References and Suggested Reading" section later in this chapter for a partial listing), for this chapter, I will be using Microsoft Office 2000 and Microsoft FrontPage 2000 to show you how to set up a sample intranet.

Understanding Intranets

Simply put, an intranet is a finite, closed network of computers that uses Internet technologies to share data. An intranet can be a subset of the Internet, with access controls in place to keep out the uninvited. For that matter, an intranet doesn't have to be on the Internet at all.

Extranets: The Next Step

A new buzzword being heard over the conference room table in corporate planning meetings is "extranet." While intranets are intended to allow members of a company or organization to share information among themselves, an extranet goes one step further. Extranets are actually intranets that open their doors to an invited group of outsiders. One practical use of the extranet is to allow companies to share information with strategic partners, such as customers, shippers, or suppliers.

Intranet Benefits

Due to the relatively low implementation and maintenance costs associated with intranets, companies are realizing very high ROI (return on investment) values. Benefits include the following:

- Intranets are easy to use. Because the user interface of an intranet is the Web browser, training costs are very low.

- Intranets facilitate the dissemination of information to employees.

- Intranets reduce printing costs.

- Intranets add value to traditional documents. Documents and databases can be searched quickly by keywords, meta-tags, and other directory information.

- Intranets improve data accuracy. Having copies of outdated and possibly inaccurate documents in circulation can be dangerous.

Example Applications of an Intranet

The ways in which an intranet can help make the members of your organization more efficient and productive are just about endless. The following are some typical uses of intranet technology:

- *Human Resources*—More and more companies are circulating internal job advertisements, maintaining databases of employee skills, and distributing documents via an intranet.

- *Project Management*—Spreadsheets, Gantt charts, and status reports can be posted on the intranet where they can be viewed and updated by project members.

- *Inventory Tracking*—Inventory databases can be made available online, either in raw data format or as value-added applications.

- *Office File Management*—With Microsoft Office 2000, you have the ability to save all your documents directly to the Web, where they can be viewed, retrieved, and updated by your co-workers and employees. These files can include employee policy handbooks, corporate memoranda, PowerPoint presentations, and more.

24

SETTING UP AN
INTRANET

Tip

Microsoft Office 2000 can be very tightly integrated with your Web server through the use of the new Microsoft Office Server Extensions (OSE). This powerful addition to Office 2000 can be installed on any Internet Information Server (IIS) Web server. OSE lets Office 2000 users create discussions in published documents (Web Discussions), be notified via email when certain documents are modified (Web Subscriptions), and search and navigate through published documents. To learn more about OSE, as well as the other new features of Office 2000, please refer to the Microsoft Office 2000 Resource Kit at
`http://www.microsoft.com/office/ork/2000`.

If your Web server is running OSE, you can access the OSE Start page at
`http://localhost/msoffice`.

Read on to see how an intranet can drastically simplify your company's information publishing process while saving time and money.

Intranet Versus Paper Publishing

The typical corporation produces thousands of pages of information per year. The printing, reproduction, and distribution of this information translates into very high costs. And just think how much of this paper is tossed into a wastebasket or recycling box within hours of production! With an inexpensive intranet, you can immediately start publishing corporate documents there instead of on paper. The benefits of publishing over a corporate intranet are many.

- *Intranet publishing increases storage efficiency*—Using your intranet to store, disseminate, and share documents will allow you to keep all your documents in one place—namely, your intranet server.

- *Intranet publishing increases data accuracy*—Very soon after a paper document is printed, its content can become outdated. Within one office, there may be different versions of any given document floating around. Publishing your documents on the intranet will ensure that everyone is working with the same copy.

- *Intranet publishing increases data security*—Many corporate documents contain proprietary or confidential information that could be harmful in the wrong hands. Paper-based documents are easily lost or improperly discarded. You can implement password-protected directories on your intranet to prevent this. In addition, you should establish a company security policy for data security.

- *Intranet publishing allows quicker dissemination of information*—With the click of a button, you can update an important file and notify everyone of the change.

- *Intranet publishing saves on costs*—All of the previous examples involve costs of some kind that intranet publishing can help reduce. Studies also show that an intranet will help your employees work more efficiently and effectively.

Planning Your Intranet

There are several things you will want to think about up front to ensure that your intranet deploys and runs smoothly. Some things to consider are:

- Who are the decision makers? Who will administer the intranet?

- Who is your primary audience and what types of content will you be publishing to help them perform their jobs better?

- What will you need to get your intranet up and running?
- Will you need to create policies to control how the intranet is used?

All these things and more are covered in this section.

Administering Your Intranet

In a medium- or large-size company, the information technology (IT) department or network shop would typically be in charge of the intranet. If there is already a group in charge of your Internet Web server, it is likely the group to administer your intranet as well. But what if there is no IT shop? If you find yourself in this situation, someone will need to be appointed to be in charge. To set up a basic intranet using Windows 2000 Professional, this person (or group) will need a mix of the some of the following skills:

- A basic understanding of Windows 2000 networking (as discussed in previous chapters) and Internet Information Server (IIS) administration—your Web server environment.
- Web server installation and administration skills.
- Familiarity with an HTML (Hypertext Markup Language) editor, such as Office 2000 or FrontPage 2000 and other Web publishing skills.
- To make intranet publishing easy and effective, you also might want to take advantage of the new Web features built in to Office 2000.

You also will want to decide who will be making the decisions and policies with respect to your intranet. Typically this will come from upper management or from someone with the power to control the use of this corporate tool.

After the intranet is set up and running, you will want to appoint other members of your organization to post content. These Webmasters will be responsible for keeping the intranet current. It may be a good idea to appoint a separate Webmaster for each content or subject area.

Determining Your Audience and Content

The next step is to determine the audience or primary users of the intranet. With your audience in mind, you will need to look at the types of information you can put out there to help them perform their jobs more efficiently and effectively.

24

SETTING UP AN
INTRANET

Using Source Control

Anytime you have more than one Web developer (or programmer) working on a project, there is always the chance of conflict. For example, when two developers try to edit the same page at the same time, the results can be confusing at best. To avoid the conflicts, you may want to use some type of source control.

Two examples of this are FrontPage2000 and Microsoft Visual SourceSafe, a powerful version control package. SourceSafe provides functionality that will allow your Webmasters to track a file's editing history, see the difference between two versions of one file, and even recover a prior version.

FrontPage 2000 integrates well with Visual SourceSafe. With source control turned on, FrontPage provides basic version control along with a check-in and check-out facility that will keep your Webmasters from stepping on each other's toes.

There are a number of ways you can ensure source control for your intranet. For more information on integrating Visual SourceSafe with FrontPage, see the Microsoft FrontPage 2000 Server Extensions Resource Kit, which you can install from the FrontPage 2000 CD-ROM or get it online at `http://officeupdate.microsoft.com/frontpage/wpp/serk/`.

Tip

A useful tool at this stage in your intranet development is to create an intranet survey. This questionnaire is designed to help you gather information from other members of your organization about the types of information they would find beneficial on the intranet. This survey is also a good way to locate volunteers to assist with the setup and maintenance of your intranet.

Who is the audience for your intranet? While the answer to this question is company specific, there are some commonalties that most companies share. First of all, initially you will probably want to limit the use of your intranet to your information workers. Presumably these are the employees in your company who already spend most of their day working at a computer. These information workers will probably have the greatest need for the types of documents you will be posting to your intranet. Also, by initially limiting the use of the intranet to those employees who already have computer access and skills, you will be holding down your costs.

You might also consider deploying your intranet initially within one department or subject area. For instance, you might set up to handle only Human Resource and Personnel related issues and information.

Once you have your subject area and audience in mind, you need to start thinking about the information that needs to be on the intranet. Previous sections of this chapter have listed many specific benefits of intranet publishing, so you will want to keep those in mind as you plan for content. Table 24.1 lists some subject areas and content examples to help you brainstorm.

TABLE 24.1 Example Subject Areas and Content

Subject Area/Department	Typical Content
Human Resources/Personnel	Timesheets, Expense Reports, other forms, internal job listings, employee policy manuals, 401(k) information, promotion or new employee announcements, employee skills/qualifications database, discussion groups
IT Department	Contact information, Frequently Asked Questions (FAQs), database of common problems/solutions, help desk tracking system, white papers, online computer manuals, computer-based training (CBT), discussion groups
Project Management	Team roster, delivery schedules, timelines and Gantt charts, requirements and specifications documents, collaborative documentation, version control system, discussion groups
Generic Corporate Content	Messages from the president, mission statements, company newsletter, internal announcements (new employees, birthdays), upcoming events

After you have determined your audience and content, you can begin to consider what you will need in the way of tools to support your intranet.

Evaluating Your Hardware and Software Needs

Many intranets often began on an old surplus computer with free software and a team of volunteer Webmasters. There's nothing wrong with that, but using Windows 2000 to maintain your intranet will require a little more processing power. This section is designed to give you an idea of what you will need to get your intranet off the ground.

The Web Server

Your intranet does not necessarily need to have a dedicated server. However, having such a server would be ideal if you have one available. In this chapter, we'll be discussing how you can use Windows 2000 Professional to set up a small to medium-sized intranet. However, if your organization is larger or you require a dedicated server, the Windows 2000 family features Windows 2000 Server and Windows 2000 Advanced Server, which are designed to handle the heavy processing needs of a complex intranet.

If you already have an Internet Web server in your organization, that would be the perfect candidate. You will want to look into the load currently handled by that server and determine if the addition of the intranet will cause any performance problems. Also, if you choose to use your existing Internet Web server, you will want to be conscious of the security implications of doing so. You must ensure that your sensitive intranet information is completely segregated from your public documents. Refer to your Web server documentation or online help facility for more information on segregating and securing your internal data.

Most Web server software vendors recommend a Pentium class machine, something over 90MHz or 100MHz is good; higher is better. Windows 2000 has a slightly higher processing requirement, and this will vary depending on the amount of traffic your intranet will be handling. To use your Windows 2000 computer effectively as a Web server, you should meet the following recommended minimum hardware requirements:

- 166MHz Pentium or higher microprocessor (P5 or equivalent compatible microprocessor).
- 32MB of RAM (64MB recommended; 4GB maximum).
- 2GB hard disk with a minimum of 650MB of free space.
- A CD-ROM drive (12x or faster recommended).
- Windows 2000-compatible network adapter card and related cable (see the Hardware Compatibility List, Hcl.txt, on the Windows 2000 Professional CD-ROM).

As I mentioned, depending on the size, amount of content, and number of users on your intranet, you may want to consider a more powerful system.

Tip

If you're running a dedicated Web Server, and are truly pressed for processing power, you may want to consider running an operating system such as Linux. Linux is a low cost, UNIX-based operating system known for its performance in minimal configurations. Apache, an open source ("free") Web server, is available for Linux. Windows 2000 provides excellent support and integration with UNIX-based servers. For more information on Linux and Apache, see the following sites:

Linux: `http://www.linux.org`

Apache: `http://www/apache.org`

Web Server Software

Windows 2000 includes Internet Information Server 5.0, which is built in to the Windows 2000 operating system. Table 24.2 lists several of the most popular Web servers that can also be used to host an intranet or Internet site.

TABLE 24.2   Other Widely-Used Web Servers and Common Operating System Environments

Web Server	Windows NT/2000	Windows 95/98	Linux	Solaris	SunOS	HP/UX
Apache	X	X	X	X	X	X
Netscape Enterprise	X			X	X	X
O'Reilly Web site	X	X				
Microsoft IIS	X					
Microsoft Personal Web Server	X (NT)	X				

Note

Internet Information Server, and other features, are not installed by default when you install Windows 2000. To install them, use the Add/Remove Programs feature in Control Panel to add Windows Components.

For more information on the specific requirements, features, and costs of Web server software, please refer to the following sites:

- Webserver Compare, the definitive guide to HTTP server specs, at `http://webcompare.internet.com/`
- Server Watch, the ultimate guide to Internet servers and platforms, at `http://serverwatch.internet.com/index.html`

Client Software

After you have identified your intranet server platform, it's time to start thinking about the client software. One of the great benefits of intranets is that the client software is nothing more than a Web browser. However, due to the strong competition for browser market share between Netscape's Communicator and Microsoft's Internet Explorer, you still have a decision to make.

If you want to utilize the benefits of Office 2000 Server Extensions or the posting of Microsoft Office documents on your intranet, you will need Microsoft Internet Explorer 4.01 or later. IE 5.0 is included with Windows 2000 and is also downloadable from Microsoft's Web site at `http://www.microsoft.com/windows/ie/`.

To fully realize the benefits of the Microsoft intranet model, you will also want to have the Microsoft Office 2000 Web components incorporated into your network environment. For more information on these new features of Office 2000, refer to `http://www.microsoft.com/office/ork/2000`.

Policies and Procedures

Before you put your intranet into action, it is a good idea to consider creating and publishing a set of policies and procedures that provide your employees with guidelines for using the intranet. Acceptable use guidelines typically cover details such as the types of information that can and cannot be published. You may not mind if an employee uses a discussion group to advertise his used car. If you do, you should put it in writing.

Along with acceptable use, this set of policies and procedures should also provide your users with information such as

- Who to contact for help with intranet-related problems
- What subject areas, documents, and tools can be found on the intranet
- Rules and guidelines for protecting usernames and passwords
- Who to contact to report inaccurate or outdated information

Designing the Intranet

The design of your intranet will determine how easily and quickly your users are able to find the information they need. An intranet that is poorly designed and is hard to navigate will very likely not be used. On the other hand, an intranet with an intuitive layout can become a great resource for your employees.

One of the best intranet designs is probably one of the simplest. Think about the functional areas or specific subject areas you plan to incorporate into your intranet, and base your design on those. Figure 24.1 shows a simple intranet home page with a basic, functional layout.

FIGURE 24.1

Sample intranet home page depicting a functional layout.

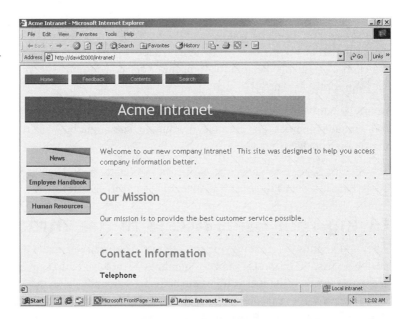

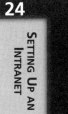

24

SETTING UP AN
INTRANET

Tip

A functional design will help your users efficiently and effectively navigate the intranet. However, tools like an up-to-date table of contents, site map, what's new page, and search engine are just as important. Most HTML editors, including Microsoft FrontPage 2000, provide tools and components to help you create these and keep them current.

Setting up and Accessing Your Intranet

Before you can begin publishing information to your intranet, you need to have a basic understanding of how to set up your Web server, in this case Internet Information Server 5.0, and how to give your users access to the new site.

Setting Up the Web Site

To put documents on your intranet, you need to first set up a Web site location on your server. By default, when you install Internet Information Server (IIS), a local Web site is created based on the name you gave your computer during the Network Identification part of the setup—in my case, `http://david2000/`. This is referred to as a root Web. You can choose to use this location for "housing" your new intranet site, or you can create a sub Web for the intranet.

Briefly, a sub Web is essentially a virtual directory within an existing Web that has it's own unique properties. For example, my intranet site might be `http://david2000/intranet/`.

The Internet Services Manager, as explained in Chapter 6, "Advanced Control Panel Tools," discusses how to set up and manage your Web site.

Giving Your Users Access to the Intranet

After you've finished creating your intranet site, you need to be able to tell your users how to access it. This process is very simple. All you have to do is tell them the URL or address of the Web site that you just created—for example, `http://david2000/intranet/`. Once they know the address of the intranet, they can simply type that into their Web browser to access it.

> **Note**
>
> For users to access your intranet, they must all be a part of the same Workgroup or Domain, have privileges to access shared files and directories on your drive, and you must grant them rights to access your Web in the Internet Information Services Manager.

Using Existing Documents as the Basis of the Intranet

Within your organization, there are likely hundreds of documents that your employees need to access. Some, like timesheets or progress reports, may need to be accessed daily or weekly. Others, like policy manuals, may be needed less frequently. But how can you get those documents and files onto the intranet? Microsoft Office 2000 has the tools built in to let you do it very easily. This section will walk you through the creation and population of an example intranet using your existing Office 2000 documents.

Building the Office 2000 Intranet: A Simple Example

Perhaps the easiest way to begin your Office 2000 intranet is to create a new Web and import into it the Office 2000 documents that you want to be available on the intranet. From there, you can create a simple navigation page to help your users quickly find the information they need.

In FrontPage, create a new Web for your intranet. Select New, Web from the File menu. From the New dialog box, select the template you want to use. It might be best to start with the One Page Web. Enter the location of the new Web and click OK.

In the new Web, create folders for each category of information you plan to import into your intranet. For this example, we will create three folders: `Forms`, `Memorandums`, and `Finance`.

Select Import from the File menu, and navigate to find the files you want to import. Typical forms you might want to include are employee timesheets, expense reports, purchase requests, and so on. Refer back to Table 24.1 for more ideas. Click Modify to modify the URL location for the imported files. You will want to specify that the files should be imported into the folders you just created. Click OK in the Import dialog box to import the files into their respective folders.

At this point, your intranet consists of some useful Office 2000 documents. However, it lacks a navigation page to help your users find them.

Create a new page (or, if you used the One Page Web template, use `Default.htm`). On the new page, enter text for each of the categories or folders. Create a hyperlink for each text item by selecting a text item and then selecting Hyperlink from the Insert menu. In the Create Hyperlink dialog box, select the folder to which you want the text to link. For example, for the text item Finance, select the `Finance` folder. Click OK to create the hyperlink.

Figure 24.2 shows the Web in FrontPage.

FIGURE 24.2
The simple Office intranet in FrontPage.

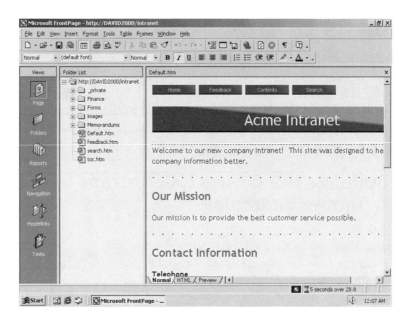

After you save the Web, you will have a simple intranet. It will consist of a navigation page and several folders containing pertinent Office documents that are ready to be used by your employees.

Depending on their software configurations, your users will view these new Web files in different ways. Users of Microsoft Internet Explorer 4.01 or later will be able to view the Office files directly in their browsers. Users of older versions of Internet Explorer or any other browser will have the option of either downloading the document to their local file systems for viewing or launching a viewer from their browsers.

From here you will want to consider incorporating other intranet tools and components discussed earlier in this chapter, such as a search engine and a table of contents.

The following sections will show you other ways you can incorporate Office 2000 files into your new intranet.

Incorporating Your Files

This section provides an introduction to posting your Microsoft Word 2000 files to your corporate intranet using Word and FrontPage 2000.

In previous sections, we've discussed the types of documents that should be posted to your intranet. One such document is the corporate memorandum. In this section, you will learn several ways to post a corporate memo to the intranet first using FrontPage and then using Word.

Posting the Corporate Memo Using FrontPage

You can use FrontPage to post your Word files. Simply opening your Word document in FrontPage (File, Open) will launch Word. From there you can post the page using the steps outlined in the following section. However, if you would rather insert the Word file into FrontPage and post from there, you can. In FrontPage, open a new document or an existing page into which you would like to insert the Word document. Select File from the Insert menu and navigate through the Select File dialog box to locate and select the file, and then click the Open button. The file will be converted to HTML and inserted into the FrontPage document. To post this file, choose File, Save or File, Save As and save the file to the Web or location of your choice.

This method results in your Word file being converted to HTML. If you prefer to leave your document in Word format, you can simply import the file into your Web.

With your target Web open in FrontPage, select Import from the File menu. In the Import dialog box, click the Add File button. Use the Add File dialog box to locate the memorandum. Once you have located and selected the memo file, click Open.

Back in the Import dialog box, click OK to import the file. This will result in the Word file being saved to your Web. You can also use the Windows drag-and-drop or copy/paste method to import files to your FrontPage Web.

Figure 24.4, later in this chapter, shows the completed memorandum retrieved from the intranet.

Saving the Word File to Your Web

The most basic method of publishing Word documents to the Web is simply to save them in Word format to the location of your Web in My Network Places. With your document open in Word, select File, Save As. This will open the Save As dialog box.

In the left frame of the Save As dialog box, click the My Network Places icon and open the destination Web folder by either double-clicking the name or selecting it and clicking Open.

In the Save as Type drop-down list, select Word Document. Enter the name you want to save the file as in the File Name area and click Save to save the document to the Web.

Depending on their software configuration, your users will view this new Web file in different ways. Users of Microsoft Internet Explorer 4.0 or later will be able to view the Word file directly in their browsers and, if they have Internet Explorer 4.01 or later and Microsoft Office Web components, they will even be able to modify the document and resave it to the Web. Users of older versions of Internet Explorer or any other browser will have the option of either downloading the document to their local file systems for viewing or launching a viewer from their browsers.

Posting the Corporate Memorandum from Word

The difference between this and the previous method is the target format. In the previous example, we simply saved a Word document to the Web. In this example, we will be converting the document to HTML.

With your document open in Word, select Save as Web Page from the File menu. The Save As dialog box will appear. Figure 24.3 shows the Save As dialog box.

FIGURE 24.3

The Save As dialog box for saving the memo as a Web page.

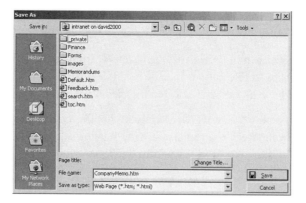

In the Save As dialog box, locate your destination Web folder or use the Create New Folder button from the toolbar to create a new Web folder. If you prefer to change the HTML title of the page, click the Change Title button and do so in the Set Page Title dialog box. Press OK to return to the Save As dialog box. Select a filename for your new Web page, and then click the Save button to post the memo to the Web.

Use your Web browser to locate and examine the document. If you need to make changes later, reload the document from the Web folder, change the memo, and resave using the File, Save menu item.

Figure 24.4 shows the intranet version of the memo using Microsoft IE 5.0.

FIGURE 24.4

*The intranet
version of the
corporate memo
in Internet
Explorer 5.0.*

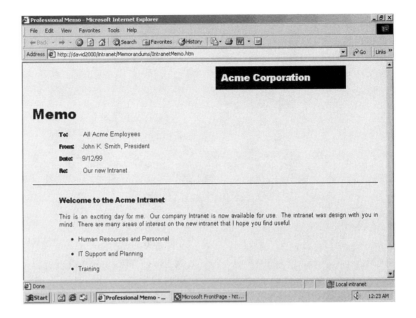

Posting PowerPoint Presentations

This section provides an introduction to posting your Microsoft PowerPoint 2000 files to your corporate intranet.

PowerPoint 2000 presentations can be imported into your FrontPage Web using the same steps outlined in the previous Word section. In summary, the steps to import files into a FrontPage Web are

1. Open the target Web in FrontPage.
2. Select File, Import.
3. In the Import dialog box, click Add File.
4. Navigate to the file you want to import and click Open.
5. Add files by clicking Add File, or modify the URL or file location by clicking Modify.
6. Click OK to import the file(s) into your FrontPage Web.

You also can use the Windows drag-and-drop or copy/paste method to import files to your Web.

Like Word, PowerPoint 2000 has simplified the process of posting to the Web. In PowerPoint 2000, select Save as Web Page from the File menu. The Save As dialog box will appear. Figure 24.5 shows the Save As dialog box.

FIGURE 24.5

Saving from PowerPoint to the Web.

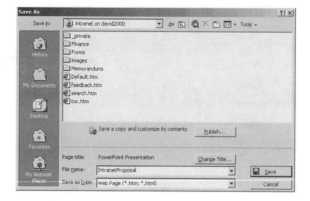

In the Save As dialog box, locate your destination Web folder or use the Create New Folder button from the toolbar to create a new Web folder. If you prefer to change the HTML title of the presentation, click the Change Title button to reach the Set Page Title dialog box. Press OK to return to the Save As dialog box. Select a filename for your new Web presentation, and then click the Save button.

Now use your Web browser to locate and examine the presentation. If you need to make changes later, reload the document from the Web folder, change the memo, and resave using the File, Save menu item.

Figure 24.6 shows the intranet PowerPoint presentation in Outline mode. Notice the navigation buttons at the bottom of the IE 5.0 window. The Full Screen Slide Show icon at the far right of the lower toolbar will launch your presentation into Slide Show mode.

FIGURE 24.6

Running the PowerPoint presentation in IE 5.0.

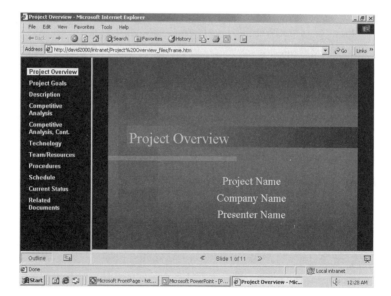

Adding Excel Worksheets

This section provides an introduction to posting your Microsoft Excel 2000 files to your corporate intranet.

Excel 2000 worksheets can be imported into your FrontPage Web using the same steps outlined in the previous Word and PowerPoint sections. In summary, the steps to import Excel files into a FrontPage Web are

1. Open the target Web in FrontPage.
2. Select File, Import.
3. In the Import dialog box, click Add File.
4. Navigate to the Excel file you want to import and click Open.
5. Add files by clicking Add File, or modify the URL or file location by clicking Modify.
6. Click OK to import the file(s) into your FrontPage Web.

You also can use the Windows drag-and-drop or copy/paste method to import Excel files into your Web.

Other methods are to insert Excel data into your page using Insert, File or to use the Microsoft Office Web components.

In the remainder of this section we will examine different ways to get your Excel worksheets onto your intranet. The first step is to launch Excel 2000 and open an existing worksheet.

Publishing as Static HTML

The simplest way to publish your Excel data to the Web is as static, non-interactive HTML. After the file is open in Excel and you have reviewed its contents, it is ready to be published. To preview how it will look in a Web browser, select Web Page Preview from the File menu. This will launch your browser and load the file. If you are satisfied with the way the page looks, the next step is to publish it to the Web.

In this example, we will publish a selected range of cells from the current worksheet, `inventory.xls`. First, select the range of cells you want to publish by dragging the mouse over the range with the left mouse button pressed.

Click File, Save as Web Page to bring up the Save As dialog box. Select the location to which you want to save the file. Click the Selection radio button to publish only the selected range. If you want to add an HTML title to the page, click the Change Title button. When you are ready, click the Save button to publish the file to the selected location. Figure 24.7 shows this process.

24

FIGURE 24.7

Saving an Excel worksheet to a Web.

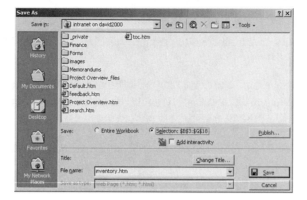

To save the entire worksheet, repeat the previous steps with no cells selected and, in the Save As dialog box, select the Selection: Sheet radio button. To save the entire workbook, select the Entire Workbook radio button from the Save As dialog box.

This example demonstrates how simple it is to publish your worksheets as static HTML. Figure 24.8 shows the finished product as it would appear in your Web browser.

FIGURE 24.8

The final product in non-interactive HTML format.

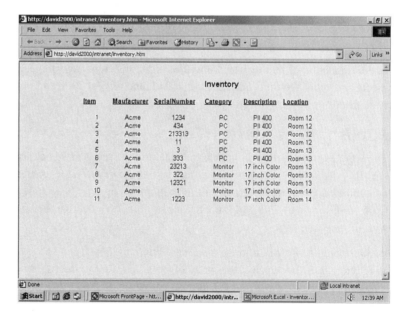

Publishing as an Interactive Excel Spreadsheet

Again, in this example we will publish a selected range of cells from the current worksheet, `inventory.xls`. First, select the range of cells you want to publish by dragging the mouse over the range with the left mouse button pressed.

Click File, Save as Web Page to bring up the Save As dialog box. Select the location to which you want to save the file. Click the Selection radio button to publish only the selected range. To make this version interactive, check the Add Interactivity check box. If you want to add an HTML title to the page, click the Change Title button. When you are ready, click the Save button to publish the file to the selected location.

To save the entire worksheet, repeat the previous steps with no cells selected. In the Save As dialog box, select the Selection: Sheet radio button. To save the entire workbook, select the Entire Workbook radio button from the Save As dialog box.

After the file is published to the Web, your users can begin to use the worksheet interactively as if it were running in Excel on their PCs. Figure 24.9 shows the finished page in Internet Explorer.

FIGURE 24.9

The final product in interactive format.

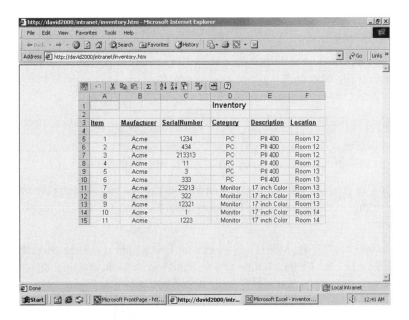

24

SETTING UP AN INTRANET

Note

For your users to realize the power of your interactive worksheets, they will need Internet Explorer 4.01 or later and Microsoft Office Web components (such as Excel 2000).

Accessing Databases via the Intranet

The next step for your intranet might be the incorporation of Web database applications. These applications can provide your users with the ability to search and retrieve data from large organizational databases. Examples of Web database applications are a personnel locator or telephone directory, an inventory tracking system, and a shopping cart application.

> **Note**
>
> This section is intended to provide a brief introduction to connecting your intranet to databases. For more details, refer to the "References and Suggested Reading" section later in this chapter.

FrontPage 2000 provides the ability to integrate powerful database applications into your Web pages. The FrontPage Database Connection Wizard will help you connect your Web to an Excel list, an Access database, or any other data source available. The following example demonstrates this through the creation of a simple computer inventory lookup application.

This example assumes that the database is already imported and integrated into the FrontPage Web. In FrontPage, open a new page or a current page that you would like to connect to your database.

Choose the Insert, Database, Results menu item to bring up the Database Results Wizard.

Check the Use an Existing Database Connection radio button and select the Inventory database from the drop-down list. Click Next to proceed to step 2.

In step 2, either select a record source from the database or enter a custom SQL query. For this example, select the Inventory record source. Click Next to proceed to the next step.

In step 3, click the More Options button. This will bring up the More Options dialog box. Click the Criteria button to set up the search form, and then click the Add button. This will bring up the Add Criteria dialog box shown in Figure 24.10.

FIGURE 24.10

The Add Criteria dialog box.

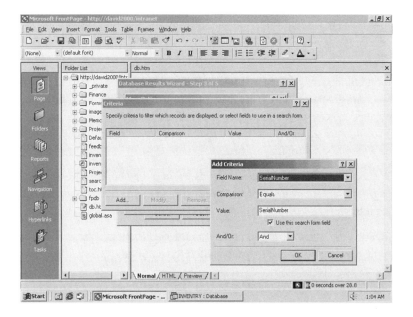

In this step, we want to specify the data field we will use to search our database. Select SerialNumber from the Field Name drop-down list. Select Equals from the Comparison list, and type **SerialNumber** into the Value text field. Check the Use This Search Form Field check box.

The And/Or drop-down list is used in the event that we have more than one criterion record. For this example, we will create only one, so leave it as it is. Click OK to continue. Click OK again to return to the More Options dialog box. Click OK again to return to step 3 of the Wizard. Click Next to proceed to the next step.

Step 4 (see Figure 24.11) is where the table for the result set is formatted. In the drop-down list, select the overall format for the results. Choices include a table, a list, or a drop-down list. For this example select Table One Record per Row.

24

SETTING UP AN INTRANET

FIGURE 24.11

The Database Results Wizard, step 4 of 5.

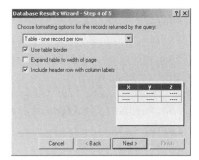

Check the Use Table Border check box and the Include Header Row with Column Labels check box. Uncheck the Expand Table to Width of Page check box. Click Next to proceed.

In the final step, you can instruct the Wizard to return the results either together or broken into smaller groups. This is helpful in the event that the query returns a large number of rows. For this example, check the Split Records into Groups radio button, and specify 5 records per group. Click Finish to complete the Wizard. The Database Results area will be added to the FrontPage page.

We can now add additional formatting around the Database Results area or publish the page as it is. The page must be saved with an .asp (Active Server Page) file extension for it to work.

Figure 24.12 shows the final product in Internet Explorer. The inventory manager, given the serial number, could use this application to identify the type and location of equipment.

FIGURE 24.12

The database application in Internet Explorer.

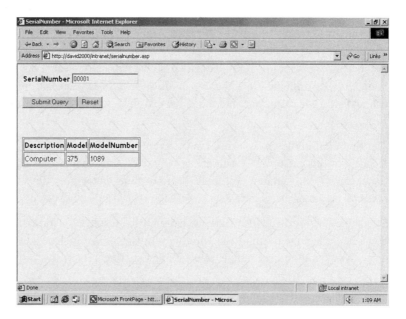

FrontPage's database connectivity tools are very powerful. However, there may be a case where you need something that FrontPage cannot do for you. There are a wealth of other tools and applications available that you can use to create Web database applications. Table 24.3 lists several of them, along with Web URLs to refer to for more information.

TABLE 24.3   Web Database Tools and Technologies

Tool/Technology	For More Information
Active Server Pages (ASP)	`http://www.aspsite.com/`
	`http://www.learnasp.com/`
	`http://www.takempis.com/`
	`http://www.kamath.com/`
ColdFusion	`http://www.allaire.com/products/` `ColdFusion/index.cfm`
iHTML	`http://www.ihtml.com/`
Visual Interdev	`http://msdn.microsoft.com/vinterdev/`
Drumbeat 2000	`http://www.drumbeat.com/`
Netscape LiveWire (server-side JavaScript)	`http://developer.netscape.com/tech/` `javascript/index.html?content=/tech/` `javascript/ssjs/ssjs.html`
Perl/DBI	`http://www.perl.org/` or `http://www.perl.com/`

All of these technologies can get you on your way to incorporating database applications into your intranet.

Other Applications of the Intranet

There are many other functions that your intranet can serve, beyond the sharing of Microsoft Office documents and data. This section will briefly introduce some intranet applications that you can put to use in your company or organization.

Surveys and Questionnaires

When was the last time you needed to collect information from your employees? Whether to determine the preferred day for the corporate picnic, to conduct a satisfaction survey (shown in Figure 24.13), or to establish a forum for anonymous reporting of theft or harassment, your intranet can help. Using FrontPage, you can quickly and easily build HTML forms using a range of form elements. You can configure your forms to send your data to a text file, a database, or even to your email inbox.

24

SETTING UP AN INTRANET

FIGURE 24.13

An intranet satisfaction survey.

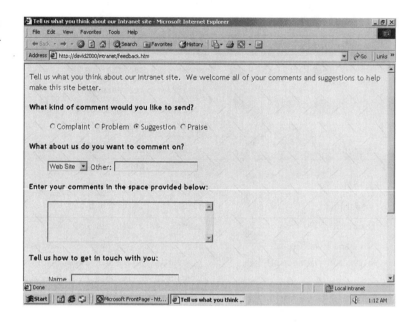

A Discussion Web

Discussion groups, mirrored after the bulletin board systems (BBSs) that predate the Internet, are gaining in popularity on intranets. These forums give your employees the opportunity to share ideas and information with other employees with common work interests. Discussion groups can also provide a great medium for your LAN support office or IT help desk to field questions and publish fixes to common problems.

The Project Web

Another great use of your intranet is project management. FrontPage provides a template for the Project Web. Using this template, you can set up a Web that will allow you to share status, delivery schedules, discussions, and so on with members of your project.

The Support Web

Yet another brilliant application of an intranet is in support of your customers. Regardless of your company's focus or product offerings, there is a very good chance that you are responsible for ensuring that your customers, either external or internal, are satisfied with what your company offers. If you work in the IT department of a large company, you are likely to be responsible for taking trouble calls from fellow employees.

Multimedia and Conferencing

As technology has increased, the ability to add multimedia presentations or conduct online conferencing has become easier to use and an important tool for conveying information over your intranet. For example, suppose you wanted to have all your employees take sexual harassment training. You could create a video and then convert it to streaming media using Windows Media technologies. Your employees could then watch the video on their PCs using the Windows Media Player. To get the most out of this technology, you may want to consider installing a Windows Media server. For more information about creating streaming media, see

`http://msdn.microsoft.com/workshop/imedia/windowsmedia/abc.asp`

> **Note**
>
> Another popular tool for creating and viewing streaming audio and video is the Real Audio/Video Player and Real Producer. Files created using Real Producer can be "streamed" without the need for a streaming media server. For more information, visit Real Network's site at `http://www.real.com/`.

You may also want to include the ability to have a departmental "conference call" via your intranet. Incorporating Microsoft's NetMeeting into your intranet can add another powerful feature.

There are so many other applications for your intranet that there is no way they can all be discussed or listed here. Talk to employees of other companies to see what they are doing with theirs, or search the Internet for case studies, white papers, and other information about intranets. Before long, you will be doing so much with your intranet that you will wonder how you ever got by without it. It won't take you long to realize how companies are achieving those extraordinarily high return-on-investment (ROI) values. Keep at it, and your company will achieve them, too.

Maintaining Your Intranet

You have now entered into one of the most important phases of your intranet lifecycle—maintenance. Intranet maintenance, or administration, is the task of ensuring that your intranet is staying secure, healthy, and up to date. This section will discuss several important chores, including intranet administration, security, and keeping your intranet data current.

24

SETTING UP AN INTRANET

Intranet Administration

Windows 2000 provides several tools to help you administer your Web site and Web server. For more information, check the section in Chapter 6, "Advanced Control Panel Tools," of this book titled "The Microsoft Management Console."

In addition, if you're using FrontPage 2000, you can obtain reports that can help you keep track of everything in your Web, from potentially slow or outdated files to broken links and unlinked files—all potential problems on an intranet.

FrontPage also includes a Tasks facility will help you keep track of the work that needs to be done and the workgroups or people responsible. Other FrontPage tools, such as the security manager and the site-wide spell checker, will help you keep a tight, clean intranet.

You will also want to perform some level of Web server Administration. This includes important tasks such as

- Ensuring that the intranet is backed up regularly. The FrontPage Publish command can help with this.
- Tracking log files to ensure that your intranet is secure and error free.
- Removing stale documents and old log files to save disk space.

Also, as your intranet grows, you might need to increase the capabilities of your intranet server by adding more memory and disk storage. As with most IT-related tasks, you don't want to wait until the intranet is having problems to begin thinking about this job.

> **Note**
>
> Detailed discussions of intranet administration and security are beyond the scope of this book. However, there are a number of books on the market that will assist you in keeping your site secure. Refer to your Web server manual or online help, or visit the Internet section of your bookstore to browse for titles.

Security

Security is something that must be taken very seriously, especially if your intranet is connected to the Internet. There are several ways you can help ensure that your intranet is safe from intruders. First and foremost is FrontPage Web security. FrontPage allows you to add users with three different levels of permission:

- Browse (read-only access to Web pages)
- Author (read and write access to Web pages)
- Administer (full access, including user administration)

Your Web server will also have a mechanism to keep outsiders out of your intranet. This mechanism is dependent on the type of Web server you are using and will probably require either a username and password or that intranet users be using a computer within a fixed network or subnetwork (for example, your company LAN). Use of this mechanism is the first step to ensuring that outsiders don't mistakenly stumble onto your intranet. It will also keep Internet search engines from cataloging your intranet and adding it to their sites.

Keep track of users or employees who leave your company or organization. Remove their access to the intranet as soon as possible.

If you ever open your doors to an outsider (such as turning your intranet into an extranet), be sure to keep track of who that person is, the reason he or she was granted access, how long his or her access is valid, and so on. In this way, you can be sure to close the door again as soon as this user has completed his or her business.

Monitor Web server log files on a daily basis. Your Web server will track access requests and errors. These log files should be viewed regularly and either archived or trimmed when they begin to take up too much disk space. Your Web server operating system will have its own access and system logs that will help you detect when someone is attempting to access your server. These should be monitored as well. The locations and names of these log files are operating-system dependent. Refer to your Web server manual or online help for more information.

Keeping It Current, or Ensuring That Content Gets Updated

The intranet has inherited many traits from the Internet. A trait of the utmost importance to your intranet is the need to keep it current. There is nothing more detrimental to your intranet than outdated information. This doesn't mean you need to update your policy manual every day for fear that your employees will stop reading it. They will refer to such documents when they need to. However, nothing can turn off an intranet user more than a Last Modified comment that dates back to the day you launched the intranet. You have to keep the data current and dynamic to keep your users interested.

Consider a What's New page that is regularly updated to indicate the new data or documents that have been posted since the last update. This page could also have a Current Events section in which you display newsworthy items of interest to your employees.

24

SETTING UP AN
INTRANET

Information about birthdays, new employees, promotions, and other announcements will keep your employees coming back for more.

Your search engine will also need to be updated regularly. Depending on the type and complexity of your search engine, it might be able to update itself automatically on a nightly or weekly basis. If it doesn't have this capability, you will need to update it yourself every time you add or delete documents. Think about how you feel when you do an Internet search and many of your returned documents result in 404 File Not Found errors. You don't want your users to feel like that, do you?

FrontPage 2000 also provides tools to automatically update your Table of Contents (TOC) pages and search engines. If you aren't familiar with these options, consider using a wizard like the Corporate Presence Web Wizard to set up the base of your intranet, or you can take a look at the Microsoft Office 60 Minute Intranet Kit at `http://www.microsoft.com/office/intranet/`.

References and Suggested Reading

The following resources are available to provide more information to help make your intranet a success story.

Office 2000

- Office 2000 Resource Kit:
  `http://www.microsoft.com/office/ork/2000`
- Using Microsoft FrontPage to Create and Manage an Intranet:
  `http://msdn.microsoft.com/workshop/languages/fp/dev/Intranet.asp`
- Integrating Microsoft Office with Your Intranet:
  `http://msdn.microsoft.com/library/officedev/office97/orkhtml/024.htm`

General Intranet

- Microsoft TechNet, Intranet Resources:
  `http://www.microsoft.com/intranet`
- *Intranet Design Magazine*, FAQ:
  `http://idm.internet.com/ifaq.html`
- Microsoft Office 60 Minute Intranet:
  `http://www.microsoft.com/office/intranet/`

- Improving Web Site Usability and Appeal: `http://msdn.microsoft.com/workshop/management/planning/improvingsiteusa.asp`

- *Intranets Unleashed*, by David A. Garrett. 1996, Sams.net Publishing.

- *Building a Corporate Internet Strategy: The IT Manager's Guide*, by Amit K. Maitra. 1996, John Wiley and Sons.

- *Practical Intranet Security   Overview of the State of the Art and Available Technologies,* by Paul Ashley & Mark Vandenwauver. 1998, Kluwer Academic Publishing.

- *Internet and Intranet Development for Business Advantage*, by Neil Fawcett and Terry Ridge. 1998, Digital Press.

Web Server

- Netcraft:
  `http://www.netcraft.com/`

- Webcompare:
  `http://webcompare.internet.com/`

- ServerWatch:
  `http://serverwatch.internet.com/`

- Apache:
  `http://www.apache.org/`

- Microsoft IIS:
  `http://www.microsoft.com/ntserver/web/exec/overview/overview.asp`

- Netscape Server Family:
  `http://home.netscape.com/servers/index.html`

- O'Reilly WebSitePro:
  `http://website.oreilly.com/`

- Microsoft Personal Web Server:
  `http://www.microsoft.com/windows/ie/pws/`

Web Browser Information

- Microsoft Internet Explorer:
  `http://www.microsoft.com/windows/ie/default.htm`

- Netscape Communicator:
  `http://home.netscape.com/download/`

24

SETTING UP AN INTRANET

Web Database Applications

- *Database Driven Web Sites,* by Jesse Feiler. 1999, Morgan Kaufmann Publishers.
- ColdFusion:
  `http://www.allaire.com/products/ColdFusion/index.cfm`
- ASP:
  `http://www.aspsite.com`
- iHTML:
  `http://www.ihtml.com/`
- Visual InterDev:
  `http://msdn.microsoft.com/vinterdev/`
- Netscape LiveWire, Server-Side JavaScript:
  `http://developer.netscape.com/tech/javascript/index.html?content=/`
  `tech/javascript/ssjs/ssjs.html`
- Perl/DBI:
  `http://www.perl.org/` or `http://www.perl.com`

Acceptable Use Policy Information

- *E-Policy: How to Develop Computer, E-Mail and Internet Guidelines to Protect Your Company and Its Assets,* by Michael R. Overly. 1998, AMACOM Books.
- `http://www.jmls.edu/cyber/statutes/email/policies.html`

Intranet Usage Case Studies

- `http://www.cio.com/forums/intranet/cases.html`

Summary

This chapter has discussed the numerous uses and benefits of an intranet. Typical intranet applications help companies and organizations save resources by simplifying the publishing of information and allowing their employees to work more efficiently and effectively. With Office 2000's increased integration with the Web, your intranet publishing options are practically endless.

In this chapter, we also walked through several examples that demonstrate the setup and population of a simple Office 2000 intranet. Starting with a FrontPage Web built around some existing Office 2000 documents, we then examined other methods of posting Office information such as memoranda, inventory spreadsheets, and presentations. We also examined the use of Excel databases to create powerful Web database applications.

Hopefully, all of this, plus a quick glance at a few other possible intranet applications, has armed you with the information and motivation you need to help your company or organization start to realize the benefits and investment returns that many others are already realizing today.

24

SETTING UP AN INTRANET

Linux and Windows 2000 Together

CHAPTER 25

You maybe wondering why there is a chapter on Linux in a Windows 2000 Professional book. Linux is finding its way into many corporate environments. As a user or Administrator of Windows 2000 Professional workstations, you may find yourself needing to work with or at least understand what Linux is all about.

The popularity of Linux has grown over the years, and proof of this comes in the rapidly increasing user base, wide spread press coverage, "Linux" shows, and the list of vendors jumping on the Linux bandwagon. Vendors, such as Oracle, Corel, Dell, have all made a commitment to Linux—not bad for a free operating system.

From an end user's prospective, the popularity of Linux will serve to our benefit. This only induces competition between Microsoft and the Linux camp, which will inevitably force each side to produce a better product. This will only result in one winner—end users!

For those of you who are not familiar with Linux at all, this chapter will serve as an introduction to the operating system. What you will not find in this chapter is a debate of any sort for or against Linux. We will strictly stay focused on the technical aspects of the operating system.

What Is Linux?

Linux is an operating system just like any other. However, the major difference between it and other operating systems is that there is no one company behind its creation or development. Linux fits into the category of Open Source software. *Open Source* software allows anyone access to the source code of that operating system or application. Other features of open source software include the free distribution of the software and ability of the end user to modify and redistribute the software.

The Linux operating system started off as a project of a 23-year-old by the name of Linus Torvlads. The project he was working on was one to expand the Minix operating system to a full clone of the UNIX operating system. The project took on a life of its own. Because of Linux's open source policy, there were countless numbers of developers hacking at the source code to create what is, in their eyes, the "perfect" OS.

This does not mean that you cannot buy Linux from your favorite software store. A number of companies for the past few years have been developing their own distributions of the Linux operating system using the standard kernel. One such company, Red Hat, which has become synonymous with the name Linux, has had several distributions of Red Hat Linux available for commercial sale. You can also find major software vendors like Oracle, Corel, and Netscape offering versions of their software to run on Linux.

> **Note**
>
> Just because a company has agreed to port over a version of their software to Linux does not mean that they have opened the source code to the general public. Companies such as Netscape have chosen to do so, however Oracle is still tight as a drum.

Key Differences Between Windows 2000 Professional and Linux

There are some key issues that differentiate Windows 2000 Professional from Linux. These may help you determine whether Linux is right for your own use or your company's environment. However, the differences could cause you to stay away from Linux because of weaknesses, maybe not with the operating system as much as with issues such as support from the distributor of the Linux you may choose. The following sections list some of these issues and key differences between Linux and Windows 2000 Professional.

Open Source

Microsoft does not have an open source policy for Windows 2000 Professional and we shouldn't expect it to. If Microsoft were to give away the source for the Windows 2000 operating system, it would be giving away the life blood of Microsoft. The Windows operating system is the foundation of Microsoft's success. This policy, in itself, is what makes Linux so popular among programmers who feel they have no freedom of choice or freedom of innovation with Microsoft.

Linux Has No One Qwner

Unlike Windows, Linux is not controlled, owned, or licensed as the creation of anyone particular company. No one software vendor can authorize or prevent hardware manufacturers from installing the Linux operating system on the machines they sell. With the Linux operating system, a programmer, no matter who he or she is or what group he or she may be affiliated with, can contribute to the Linux operating system, from developing applications to run under Linux to contributing to the next release of the kernel.

Linux Is Based on the UNIX Operating System

This fact alone may prevent Linux from becoming a widely-used operating system in the household the way the Windows operating system has managed to become. Secondly, some businesses may think twice about deploying Linux to its users' desktops because of the learning curve. Companies have invested millions of dollars over the years to train users in the Windows operating system, and they may not be able to justify the cost to retrain these same users in how to operate the Linux desktop.

Microsoft Has an Established Application Base

Even though many vendors have committed themselves to developing for the Linux operating system, Microsoft Windows still has the edge over Linux with regard to this. Its not the fact that Linux has no word processor or spreadsheet available; rather it is its interoperability that many are concerned about. If you create a document under Linux, will you be able to email it to your business partner and expect him or her to be able to convert it to a Microsoft Word format very easily? In today's corporate world, companies expect you to be running Microsoft Word on your desktop or at least be able to read Word documents sent to you in Word format.

Multiple Flavors of the Same Operating System

When you purchase Windows 2000 Professional, you are purchasing a product that is truly one of a kind. Windows 2000 Professional has only one manufacturer, only one company is behind the operating system. The Linux kernel is available freely to anyone who wants it. Free distribution of the product is just part of the General Public License (GNU) that Linux was developed under. However, software companies have created "distributions" of Linux. These distributions consist of enhancements to the core Linux product. Usually they are available in a form that can be packaged for consumer use.

There are a number of software companies with distributions of Linux. These include: Red Hat, Caldera, SuSE, and Mandrake.

Having this many choices for a operating system is a dilemma for some, while it's considered a freedom of choice for others. Having multiple vendors of the same operating system has been done before, UNIX being a case in point. You have Sun Solaris, HPUX, and IBM's AIX for you to choose from if you want to run on a UNIX platform. However, for companies who are looking to go with an operating system that has a single vendor, single distribution, Linux may not be the right choice. Corporate environments have additional concerns compared to the user at home. Corporations have to take into account training, support, and consistency of operating system versions across their environments. Linux is still young, and so are the vendors behind the product and vendor commitment. They don't have the dollars or support that Microsoft has. This will truly be a hurdle for many who are choosing to go with Linux as an operating system on their desktop or as their server.

You Get More Out of Linux

Many in the Linux world will argue (very strongly) that you get more out of the Linux operating system than you do with Windows 2000. They point out the fact that you can run Linux on a machine with a dated 486 processor and get the same performance and productivity as you would with a Windows 2000 workstation running a Pentium processor. This may be stretching the truth a bit, but they do have a case. Many have been able to load Linux on older, slower machines and make some use of it. They may put it to use as a router on their network, a firewall to enhance security, or even an LDAP server. Linux does have an edge over Windows 2000 in this respect.

This capability to run Linux on lesser machines is what makes it the perfect NC (Network Computer). We are seeing this trend in many enterprise networks, where everyone is developing applications to run in a three-tiered architecture in an attempt to decrease the amount of horsepower needed at the desktop.

Installing Linux

As previously mentioned, there are several distributions available for the Linux operating system. Therefore the question arises as to which distribution you should install. One way to reach a decision is to compare features of each company selling Linux in a commercial form. One company may have a better support policy than the other or a slew of more additional components than the other guy. For the purposes of this chapter, I have chosen to discuss Red Hat's distribution of Linux. Red Hat is one of the more popular vendors of Linux, and its OS is free. You can download it from several FTP sites on the Internet.

> **Note**
>
> Red Hat has a list of download sites from which you can get Red Hat 6.0. You should understand that the version you download from these sites is not supported by Red Hat. Red Hat cannot guarantee that changes have not been made to the software. The only way to call or contact Red Hat for support is to purchase a copy of Red Hat Linux. The list is there as a matter of convenience for you. You can find this list at
> `http://www.redhat.com/download/mirror.html`.

Before we delve into the installation procedure, let's review the basic hardware requirements.

Hardware Requirements

Red Hat Linux will run on three distinct platforms: Intel, Alpha, and SPARC. Depending on which platform version you intend to install onto, your hardware requirements will differ. The following lists the basic requirements to run the Intel version according to Red Hat:

- *CPU Requirements*—Intel 386 through Pentium III.
- *Memory Requirement*—8MB of memory (I would strongly recommend at least 32MB).
- *Disk Requirements*—You can run Linux in two modes; character mode or with X Window. The character mode requires 320MB of hard drive space and the X Window install 450MB.
- *Floppy Drive*—3 1/2 inch disk drive.
- *CD-ROM*—IDE or SCSI CD-ROM.

> **Note**
>
> If you downloaded Red Hat from the Internet, you will still need to create a boot disk to begin the installation process. You will not need a CD-ROM if the source files are located on a local hard drive.

> **Note**
>
> Red Hat provides a hardware compatibility list where you can see if your hardware is supported. You can find the list at http://www.redhat.com/corp/support/hardware/index.html.

Prepping a Volume for Linux

Volume preparation is important no matter what operating system you are installing, be it Linux or Windows 2000. Things you need to determine are where the Linux OS will be started from, if it will be the only operating system installed, and, if so, what type of bootloader you will use.

Determining where to start the operating system is especially critical if you have other operating systems already installed on the system. During the installation of Red Hat Linux, you will be given the choice of startup loader locations. The choices are: Master Boot Record (MBR) or First Sector of Boot Partitions. If you select the MBR, you will overwrite any existing loaders present. This will, in turn, stop previously loaded operating systems, such as Windows 98, from loading. If you do not want to replace another bootloader, select the first sector of boot partitions.

Problems with Booting Up

When installing Linux, I have found that most of the problems with starting the operating system stem from incompatible hardware or problems with the bootloader.

When tracking down hardware configuration problems, one of the first places you should start is with the compatibility list for the Linux distribution you are installing. Next, check the BIOS of your machine to ensure that it's booting off the correct drive. You should also check the kernel you may have installed. For example, if you have a SCSI drive, make sure you installed the SCSI kernel and not the IDE kernel.

Bootloaders manage the multiple operating systems you may have loaded on your system. By installing Linux and LILO (the Linux loader), you may have wiped out another bootloader that was present on your MBR. This will stop other operating systems, such as Windows 2000, from loading correctly. If you find LILO is incompatible with your hardware or other operating systems loaded on your machine, you have the option to go with commercial loaders, such as Partition Magic or V Communication's System Commander.

> **Note**
>
> If you plan to install Windows 2000 Professional on the same machine where Linux will reside, STOP. It is recommended that you install Linux after installing Windows 2000 Professional. This way, you can set Linux to be started from the first sector of boot partitions. If you selected Linux to be started from the MBR, Microsoft Windows will not start, and you will need to either re-install Windows 2000 or use a third-party bootloader. You should also be aware of which partition you are installing Linux to; if another operating system resides at that partition, choose a different partition.

Whichever loader you go with, check its compatibility with all operating systems currently loaded on your machine. One option that may not be feasible because of lack of hardware is to install Linux on a dedicated machine. This way, you rule out any problems with loaders or having to manage multiple operating systems. I have found myself breaking down and doing this because of the number of times I find myself reloading Linux. There is always some other distribution I want to try, or my constant poking around with the system requires me to re-install.

The Installation Procedure

Before you install the software, you need to get your hands on it. One obvious way is to purchase it (you can buy online from www.redhat.com) or download it from the many FTP sites on the Internet. You can find the list of FTP sites at http://www.redhat.com/download/mirror.html.

When you connect to any of these FTP sites, you should see a Red Hat directory with sub-directories of the latest version of Red Hat and previous versions of the software. Be sure to download all of the directories and files for the version you choose.

There is more than one way to install Red Hat Linux. The method we will use involves creating a startup disk. The startup disk will be used to boot the machine on which Linux will be installed.

To create the floppy disk

1. Under MS-DOS, switch to the Images directory. When you downloaded Red Hat 6.0, the Images directory should have been part of the files and directories you downloaded.

2. From the Images directory, type the following:

   f:\images /dosutils/rawrite.exe

   and press Enter.

3. The rawrite program will ask for a filename for the disk image. Type **boot.img** and press Enter (see Figure 25.1)

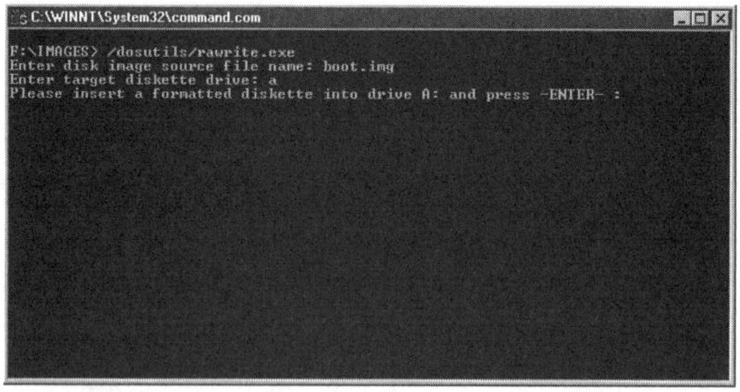

FIGURE 25.1

The rawrite *program creates the disk images needed to begin the install of Red Hat Linux.*

4. Insert a blank formatted disk into your floppy drive.

5. You will be asked for a disk to write to, type **A:** to specify the A: drive and press Enter. (If your floppy drive is one other than A:, enter the appropriate drive letter.)

The next part of the installation requires that you boot the machine using the new startup disk you just created. Insert the startup disk in the machine and power up the PC. Once the machine has booted up, you will be presented with a Welcome to Red Hat Linux! screen. Simply press the Enter key to proceed. The image will be read from the floppy disk and you will be presented with yet another Welcome to Red Hat Linux! screen, press Enter to proceed.

> **Note**
>
> If you do not select an option at this point, the install program will automatically begin to load the image from the floppy disk.

1. At the next screen you will be given a choice of languages, press Enter to select the default choice of English.

2. The next screen asks the keyboard configuration you would want. Press Enter to select the default of U.S., or scroll up and down for other choices.

3. In the next screen, you need to specify the location for the packages to be installed. If you downloaded the Red Hat files to the local hard drive, select Local Hard Drive as the location. If you have a CD-ROM with the Red Hat Linux on it, specify Local CD-ROM.

> **Note**
>
> If you are using a DOS file system, you need to create a directory called **RedHat** at the top level of the directory tree. Next, copy the BASE subdirectory over to the RedHat directory. Finally, create another subdirectory in the RedHat directory and name it **RPMS**. All the packages you want to install should be copied to the RPMS directory. The directory tree structure should look like the following
>
>   D:\RedHat
>
>   \BASE
>   \RPMS
>
> assuming D: is the local hard drive. The partition of the local drive where you choose to copy these files should not be needed for the install procedure. It should be a partition used strictly for data storage, not system files.

25

LINUX AND WINDOWS 2000 TOGETHER

4. After specifying the location for the packages, the install program will ask whether you want to conduct a new Install or Upgrade. Select Install and press Enter.

5. Next, you specify the class of installation: Workstation, Server, or Custom. Select Custom and press Enter.

6. A dialog box appears asking which tool you want to use to partition the drives. The default selection is Disk Druid. You have the choice of selecting `fdisk`; however, I have found Disk Druid to be more user-friendly. Press Enter to continue.

> ### Note
>
> In the next step, you will run the utility to partition the drive(s). You must take note of any existing operating systems, so you do not mistakenly partition the incorrect drive(s).

7. Disk Druid launches and you will be presented with the current partition configuration. You will want to create new partitions and then specify mount points. A mount point indicates where the partition will be mounted once Linux is up and running. Linux requires that you have at least one / mount point created. To do this; tab over to the Add button and press Enter.

8. A dialog box appears. Fill in each field appropriately. For the Mount Point field type / and press the Tab key. Type the size in megabytes. The suggested size for / is between 100–200MB. Tab over and press the spacebar to place a check mark in the box. Placing a check mark in the box will allow the partition to fill all available space on the hard disk, otherwise the size will be considered its exact size.

9. Tab over and select the partition type for the partition. When you press Tab once more, you can select the drive where the partition is created (if you have more than one drive). To create the partition, tab to the OK button and press the Enter key. In addition to the / mount point, you must create a mount point for swap space. It is recommend that you create the following mount points:

Mount Point	Size (Recommended)
/	200MB
/usr	1024MB
/var	100MB
/home	Depends on the amount of space required by your users.
Paging Space (swap size)	Depends on RAM and applications you plan to run.
	For a 64MB machine, 32MB of swap space would suffice.

Create the remaining mount points as instructed in steps 8 and 9.

10. When you are finished adding and configuring the mount points, tab to the OK button and press Enter. You will be asked to save the partition table, select YES and press Enter to continue.

11. The next screen will ask which partition you want to use as swap space. Select OK to continue or Back to confirm the swap space partition.

12. You must select which partitions to format. It is recommended that you format all of the partitions. Press the spacebar to check mark each box next to the partition indicated. Tab to the OK button and press the Enter key to continue.

13. The next dialog box will present you with possible packages you can install. Scroll down the list, selecting the ones you want by check marking the box next to each package. If you want to install everything, scroll down to the Everything selection and check mark the box. Tab to the OK button and press Enter to continue.

14. A dialog box will appear telling you that a complete log of the installation will be in /tmp/install.log. Select OK and press Enter. The system will begin formatting your partitions and copying over the files for the packages you selected.

15. After the files have been copied, the last stage in the install process will begin. Autoprobe will begin to find and configure your hardware, beginning with the mouse. Click OK to proceed.

16. In this step, you can either select to go with the mouse found by autoprobe (recommended) by selecting OK, or select a specific mouse type from the list.

17. You will be asked whether to configure LAN (not dial-up) networking for your system. Select Yes and press Enter. The install program will come back with the type of network card it found in your system, or you will have to scroll down the selection list and select the card that matches your card.

18. You need to configure the TCP/IP settings. Either select a static IP address or, if you have a BOOTP or DHCP server on your network, select either one of the two.

19. After TCP/IP information has been specified, select the time zone you are in and select OK. You will be asked what services should start once Linux has come up. Select or deselect each service accordingly.

20. You will be asked whether or not to configure a printer. Selecting Yes will bring up a dialog box where you will need to specify the location of the printer. Your choices are Local, Remote lpd, SMB/Windows 95/NT, or NetWare. Select Local if a printer is attached to the workstation. The other three options are for network printers. If a printer is communicating using lpd, select Remote lpd; otherwise, select SMB Windows 95/NT for Lan manager print servers. The last option enables you to connect to NetWare-based print servers.

Select No if you do not want to configure a printer at this point. You can always add, remove, or change printer information after Red Hat is up and running.

21. At this point you need to specify a password for root. The root user is equivalent to Administrator on Windows 2000 Professional workstations. Type in a password and tab over to reconfirm the password. Select OK and press Enter to proceed.

22. The next screen allows for additional authentication configuration. Selecting NIS will require you to specify the NIS domain and server. You can select to enable/disable shadow passwords and/or MD5 password. It is recommend that you select at least shadow password or MD5 passwords, if not both. Select OK to continue.

23. You will be asked if you want to create a boot disk. Select YES and press Enter. Insert a blank floppy disk when asked to and press Enter to create the startup disk. Using the boot disk, you can boot into Linux without concerning yourself with loading the LILO bootloader. We discussed earlier in the chapter the side effects of using the LILO bootloader and how it can disrupt use of other operating systems in your machine. If you are concerned about other operating systems on your machine, definitely create the boot disk and use it to load Linux.

24. If you want to boot from the hard drive, you must select where the bootloader should be installed. Select MBR if you have no other operating systems loaded; otherwise, select First Sector of Boot Partition. Select OK to continue.

25. In the next screen, you can specify special options that may need to be passed. You can enter those options at this point. If you are not sure, leave it blank select OK to continue.

26. autoprobe will detect any video cards you have installed. Press Enter to continue. The necessary files for the X Window software are copied over to the local machine. You will have to select the type of monitor you have connected to the machine. If you do not find yours listed, select Custom and fill in the specifications for your model.

27. Xconfigurator will probe your video card for possible modes at which it can display graphics. If it responds back successfully with settings, select Use Default to go with those settings or select Let Me Choose.

28. In the next screen, select OK to test the X Server. If a problem is found that prevents the X Server from starting, go back and respecify the values for your monitor or video card, and then try launching the Server.

29. After the X Server has successfully launched, you will be presented with an onscreen message. If you see it clearly, click Yes; otherwise, it will timeout and ask you to respecify the values for your monitor and video card.

30. At this point, you can specify to start X Windows when Linux first boots or not.

The installation is complete. The machine will reboot, Linux will be loaded, and a command prompt will appear, or X Windows will launch.

The Linux Shell

Those of you coming with a UNIX background will recognize the word shell. For those of you coming from the Windows world of operating systems, shell may not mean too much to you other than it being something you find on a beach.

The Linux shell is the interface you find yourself in when executing commands from the command prompt. The *shell* is responsible for accepting those commands and then executing them. Essentially, the shell does what COMMAND.COM did for you under MS-DOS. In the case of Linux and UNIX, however, you can choose between several different shells, which also means you may have several different commands to remember to execute the same task. The Red Hat distribution of Linux provides several shells that you can choose to work under. These include: sh, bash, tcsh, pdksh, csh, ash, and mc.

Choosing a Shell

Whichever shell you choose to run under is based on your own personnel preference. You may find one shell more powerful than the other, or you may have used the C shell (csh) because of previous UNIX experience. Either way, switching between the shells or choosing to start your Linux session using the shell of your choice can easily be done. To find the current shell you are using, type the following:

```
# echo $SHELL
```

The response will be the name of the shell you are currently using. You may not recognize the name when it is shown; for example, the Bourne shell is represented by the characters bsh. To switch between shells within a Linux session, type the name of the shell at the command prompt. For example, if I want to switch to the C shell, I must type

```
# csh
```

This will place me in a C shell.

If you want your Linux sessions to start with a particular shell, you must execute a command that will edit the /etc/passwd file. The /etc/passwd file stores information for each user, including username, password, group ID, and what shell he or she logs in to.

> **Note**
>
> Never edit the /etc/passwd file directly. If you do you, can cause some major damage to your user ID or your entire user base.

The following command will change the shell setting to the C shell for the user jsmith:

```
# usermode -s /bin/csh jsmith
```

You can view the /etc/passwd file from any text editor in Linux. One such editor is vi. However, as mentioned earlier, editing the /etc/passwd file inadvertently can cause users problems when trying to log in. To avoid the risk of damaging this file, you can use the more command. From the /etc/ directory, type the following:

```
more passwd
```

You can now view the /etc/passwd file without risking damaging the passwd file.

You will now see the /etc/passwd file onscreen. Each record or line of the /etc/passwd file represents a user. You can tell which shell each user is placed in when they log in by the last field of the record. For example, if the last field is /bin/csh, it will place the user in to a C shell.

I cover the /etc/passwd file and its fields in more detail in the "Sys Admin" section of this chapter.

Fundamental Linux Commands

Whether you are operating under the X Window system or booting right into Linux command prompt, you will need to familiarize yourself with a few essential commands. Understanding what these commands can do for you will not only save you time in the long run, but they also help to illustrate the flexibility of the Linux operating system.

In actual fact, you will find many Linux/UNIX veterans who will only work with the operating system using a simple terminal session and commands such as those discussed next. They feel inept when working around a Graphical User Interface (GUI) such as X Window. I have seen some users launch the X Window session but then open up a terminal session and begin to execute commands. My feeling is that whatever makes the job easier for you and whatever you are comfortable with is fine.

Table 25.1 shows some of the most commonly used Linux commands.

> **Note**
>
> To execute these commands, you must be in a terminal session under X Window, or at a Linux command prompt.

TABLE 25.1 Common Linux Commands

Command	Description	Example
ls	Lists the files in a directory.	From the /home directory, type **ls** and you will be presented with a list of files and directories.
grep	Used to search for a specified pattern in one or more files.	Type **grep linux myfile.** This command will find all occurrences of the word linux in the file named myfile.
cat	Takes any characters from standard input and echoes them to standard output.	Type **cat myfile**. This will echo the contents of the file named myfile.
man	Opens the online manuals to find information on a specific command	Type **man cat**. Displays the online manual for the cat command. See Figure 25.2 for an example.
crontab	Use the crontab command to add, remove, or edit commands and their scheduled launch time.	Type **crontab -1** to view commands scheduled to launch under the current user's ID.
passwd	Used to change the password for the user currently logged in.	Type **passwd**. You will be prompted for your new password.
su context.	Allows you to switch user	If logged in as root, Type **su - someuser**. This will log you in as the user called someuser.
mkdir	Allows you to create a directory in the current location.	Typing **mkdir mydirectory** creates the directory named mydirectory in your current location.

This was just a sample of commands you can execute under Linux. To truly understand the depth of commands available to you, reference any book on Linux or UNIX.

FIGURE 25.2

In this example, I have opened the man page for the ls *command.*

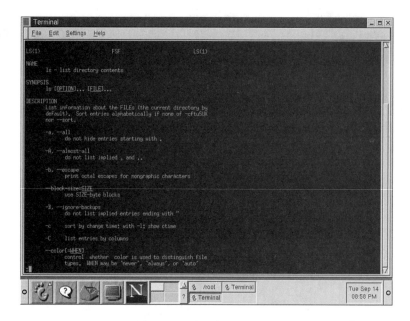

> **Note**
>
> Not all commands are common between the various platforms or flavors of UNIX out there. For example, HPUX, HP's flavor of UNIX, has the FBackup command as a built-in backup utility. Solaris, Sun's version of UNIX, has no FBackup command utility. If you are an Administrator of UNIX expecting to find commands under Linux that are familiar to you, there is a chance that may not be the case.

Processes and the Need to Kill Them

We just reviewed some general commands with which all Linux users and Administrators should be familiar. We now take a look at a command that, if not used correctly, can cause havoc with your Linux workstation or if put to good use can help to get you out of a tight jam.

Whenever you launch an application or a command under Linux, a request to create a process is sent. Launching a single application can, in turn, create several processes to be created and running in the background. Each one of these processes is assigned a process ID. Under Linux, you have the ability to *kill* or end individual processes. This is all possible as long as you have the rights to do so.

This ability to kill a process from the command line can be extremely useful if you are dealing with a runaway process. For example, an application running on your Linux workstation may be "hung," locking up resources such as memory. Issuing the `kill` command will not only end the process launched by the application, it will also help retain that memory.

In the next example, we will view all of the processes running on the Linux machine:

From the command prompt, type

```
# ps -ef
```

A list of processes currently running on the machine will be listed. The second column from the left indicates the process ID.

In the next example, we will kill a process running on the machine.

From the command prompt, type (see Figure 25.3 for an example)

```
# kill PID
```

PID is the process ID for the process you want to kill.

FIGURE 25.3

In this example, I have all of the currently running processes listed. Using the `kill` *command, I end the process with the ID* 889.

The `kill` command can be a real time saver; however, you must understand that killing an application abruptly can cause damage to the application and data on the machine.

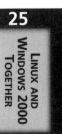

The X Window System

When you installed Red Hat Linux, you had the choice of installing XFree86. Not knowing what XFree86 was, you may have chosen not to install it. Now you find yourself operating Linux with no mouse or icon to click. Where is the graphical user interface (GUI) you are so used to when running Microsoft Windows? Well that's what XFree86 is. By choosing to install XFree86, you would have installed the X Window System. The X Window System in short is the GUI for Linux. If you did install it, this part of the chapter will go over the basics of the X Window System. However, if you did not install initially, you can always go back and use Red Hat installation packages to install XFree86 (we will review the steps in the "Installing XFree86" section).

The X Window System is known by a few different names: X, X11, X version 11, or X Window System. In this chapter, we will refer to it as X or X Window System. X was first developed at the Massachusetts Institute of Technology (MIT). Even though X provides Linux with a GUI, it is more than that. X was developed with the goal of providing networking graphics. Rather than having the local machine generate the graphics needed for X Window applications, you have a server that the client is able to connect to and run windows-based applications. You may be wondering how we expect to run X on our Linux workstation if there is no server. Well, you can still run XFree86 without needing a server because Linux can be configured to be both the client and server. You may not be taking advantage of X and its ability to lower the processing needs of the client, but, with today's hardware, you may not notice the difference.

Using the X Window System, you can gain access to a slew of powerful applications, such as Corel's WordPerfect.

The X Client/Server System

The X Window System is a client/server system. Linux enables you to run both client and server on the same workstation. It is not required that you do that. Obviously, if you have an X Server on your network, you should make use of it. The term *client/server* may not be new to your vocabulary. You see it used all the time when discussing windows and windows-based applications running on servers. In the case of Linux and the X Window System, the client provides the programs and resources to run the application in the client/server model. The server portion of the client/server model is responsible for displaying the application. The advantage to the client/server model is that applications that are processor-intense will not tax the client's processor but, instead, the server's. This frees up the user of the client machine to do other tasks. In the case where you have both client and server on the same Linux box, you will not see this performance advantage.

Installing XFree86

XFree86 can be installed during the installation of Red Hat or later. To install XFree86 after the initial installation of Red Hat, type the following command at the command line:

```
# su -c "rpm -i /mnt/cdrom/RedHat/RPMS/XFree86*rpm
```

This command will install XFree86 using the Red Hat package manager. In this case, the install files are located on a CD-ROM. If you are not installing from a CD-ROM, simply change the path to the location where the package files are located. After the installation is complete, switch to your /usr directory. There you will find a series of directories named X11R6. If you find these directories, it's a good indication that this portion of the installation completed successfully. You may have the necessary files to run the X Window System. However, before you attempt that, you need to configure your XFree86 system.

Configuring XFree86

The installation of XFree86 is one step in the process of getting the X Window System running on your Linux machine. The next step is running the configuration program for XFree86. The XFree86 system relies on several configuration files to work correctly. These configuration files tell XFree86 about the hardware on your machine, including what type of mouse you have, the type of monitor connected to your machine, and your video card capabilities. Rather than you editing each one of these files, there is a configuration program you can run through that will edit those configuration files for you. To launch the configuration program, type the following and then perform the following steps:

```
# su -c Xconfigurator
```

1. You will be presented with a welcome screen, tab to the OK button and press your Enter key (see Figure 25.4).

2. Xconfigurator probes your video card and comes back with what it found. Again, select OK and press Enter to continue.

3. Next you will be asked what type of monitor you have. Scroll down the list to select your monitor's model type (see Figure 25.5). After you have selected your monitor, tab to the OK button and press Enter. If you do not see the one you are using, select Custom and select OK.

FIGURE 25.4

The welcome screen to Xconfiguartor.

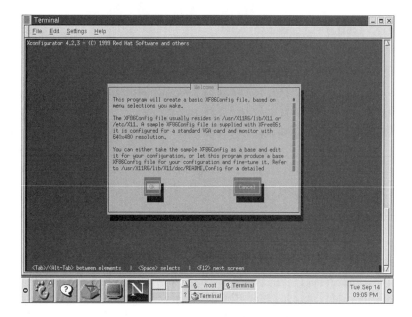

FIGURE 25.5

The choice of monitors you are presented with during configuration.

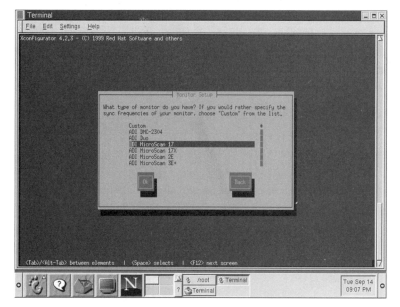

Note

You will need to know the resolution capabilities and frequency settings of your monitor. Usually you can find these settings on the back of the monitor or in the monitor's documentation. You must use caution when selecting these settings. Choosing settings that your monitor is not capable of displaying could cause permanent damage to your monitor.

4. `Xconfigurator` will now run the X server to probe the video card. The probe will let `Xconfigurator` determine the capabilities of the video card. Press Enter to continue.

5. After the video card has been probed, you will be given a choice to use the settings or change them. If you want to select different settings, such as color depths or resolution, select Let Me Choose (see Figure 25.6), otherwise press the Enter key to go with the default settings.

FIGURE 25.6

I have chosen to customize my settings to 800×600×8.

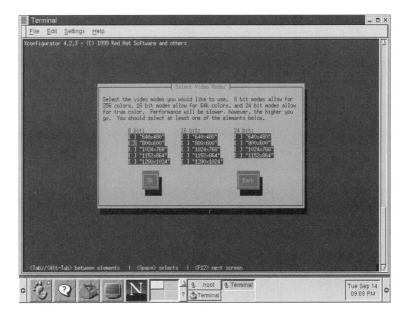

6. The last step involves `Xconfiguartor` running a final test of the X server. It is strongly recommended that you do not skip this test. Press the Enter key to begin the test. After the test is complete, you should see a dialog box asking if you can

see the screen correctly. Select Yes or No. The screen may not be visible at all; in this case, you will not be able to click anything. The test will automatically time out if no response is given, and you will have to re-run Xconfigurator.

If you have installed XFree86 and have either changed the hardware on your machine or simply want to change a setting, you can run the XF86Setup application. The XF86Setup application is a GUI application that lets you set up XFree86.

Starting the X Window System

To start the X Window system type the following command at the command prompt:

```
# startx
```

There are several options you can specify with the startx command. For example

```
# startx -- -bpp 16
```

will launch the X Window system using thousands of colors.

The Windows Manager

There are many aspects and features of Linux that make it so popular with its user base. One of these is the freedom of choice. Linux comes with several Windows managers from which to choose. This means you can choose what your desktop will look like. You can control the "look and feel" of the toolbars and menu bars or simply change what the login window looks like. Under Windows 2000 Professional, you can change desktop settings; however, you are limited to the desktop themes provided by the operating system. In the case of Linux Window managers, they not only differ in the look and feel but also with the applications they have to offer.

We will briefly cover two of the many Windows managers that come with Red Hat—GNOME and KDE.

GNOME or GNU Network Object Model Environment has been developed under the open source policy. This means that there are several developers who are behind its creation and future. GNOME consists of software libraries and X11 clients used to support an X11 desktop environment. GNOME, like any good Windows manager, provides the user with an application framework, File Manager, Windows-based applications, and a desktop panel. Some of the applications you will find specific to GNOME include gnomecard, Ghex, gEdit, and Gnumeric spreadsheet (see Figures 25.7 and 25.8).

FIGURE 25.7

Taking my mind off work through a game of Same Gnome.

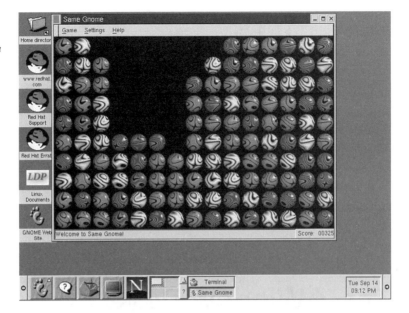

FIGURE 25.8

Getting work done using Gnumeric.

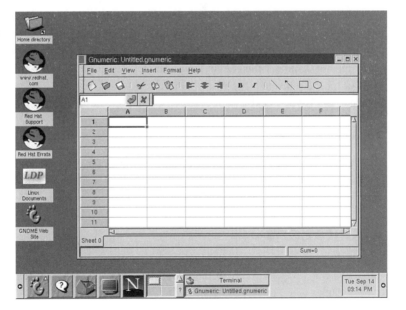

25

LINUX AND WINDOWS 2000 TOGETHER

The K Desktop Environment (KDE) is one of the newest windows managers for X11. KDE includes features such as drag-and-drop, desktop trash can for safe file deletion, pop-up menus, and built-in help. To get the latest information on KDE, browse over to the official Web site at www.kde.org.

Here you will find not only information on the desktop environment, but also software still in development. One of these is KOffice, a suite of productivity software for KDE. KOffice includes KWord, KIllustrator, KPresenter, KFormula, KDiagramm, KImage, and KSpread. As of this writing, KOffice is still in development. However, you can still download it and see what its all about—just be ready for bugs with the product.

With a choice of window managers out there for Linux, you will never be tied down to the same desktop. In the corporate world, this may be a nightmare scenario where you may have one set of users clawing for one particular window manager, while another set is asking for a different window manager. But if you are a home user and enjoy some variety in your life, you can appreciate the choice you have.

The X Window Desktop

For those of you with a Microsoft Windows background, the X Window System is more than likely your cup of tea. You will find that many of the methods of getting things done under Windows 95, 98, NT, or Windows 2000 Professional are similar to how you accomplish tasks under the X Window System. Obviously, there are differences in where icons or tools are located. It gets even more confusing, depending on which Windows Manager you have loaded.

The Taskbar

The Taskbar is located at the bottom of the screen. When you first launch the X Window Desktop, you will find some commonly used applications installed in the taskbar for you. You can add or remove these applications as needed.

Applications

To gain access to applications and tools, click the left-most icon on the taskbar. From there, you can navigate to any of the folders to launch applications, administration tools, or even games (see Figure 25.9).

FIGURE 25.9
You can launch applications or any of the many tools available to you by selecting it from its folder or the menu bar.

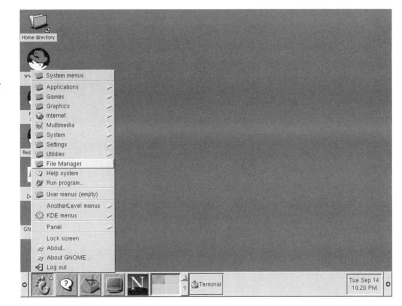

Sys Admin

Linux can be deployed as workstation or server. This chapter is focused on deploying Linux as a workstation on your network. Under Windows 2000 Professional, you are able to create users and assign specific security rights to the user. You have the same flexibility under Linux. Windows 2000 Professional has a single user management tool. With Linux, you have the ability to manage groups and users through the command line, graphical administration tools, or by editing user files through a text editor.

The passwd File

Linux stores all user information in the passwd file that resides in the /etc directory. If you view the passwd file, you will see something similar to the following:

```
user1::1001:101:usercomment:/home/user1:/bin/bash
```

The passwd file consists of

username : *password* : *user ID* : *group ID* : *comment* : *home directory* : *login*
↪*command*

When you add users to Linux manually or through some X Window System configuration tool, the passwd file is updated accordingly.

25

LINUX AND
WINDOWS 2000
TOGETHER

Only the root user should have read/write access to the passwd file; others only need read permissions.

> **Note**
>
> One of the most common ways UNIX systems are hacked into is through the passwd file. After the hacker has compromised the passwd file, he or she has free rein of the system. He or she can create or delete users as wanted.

Adding Users

How you add a user to Linux depends on in which mode you are operating. If you are logged in as root at a terminal prompt, you can add a user to the system using the adduser command. If you are logged in and running a X Window session, Red Hat Linux has some easy-to-use GUI tools available to accomplish the same task you would at the terminal prompt.

No matter what mode you use to add the user, whether through a terminal session or an X Window session, there are a few essential things you need to jot down before doing so.

Each user must have the following:

- *A distinct username*—Each user needs to be assigned a unique username. Linux also allows the use of some special characters, such as underscores and periods, to make up the username.

- *A distinct user ID number*—The Linux operating system requires that each user be assigned a unique user ID number (UID). Processes and files all have UIDs associated with them. So before killing a process, you can check as to the user context it may be running under before you do so.

- *You must choose or the user chooses a password for themselves*—Passwords can be made up of characters or numbers. It is recommended that you assign users an alphanumeric username because its harder for someone to hack into the system when he or she has to guess a mixed password.

- *Assign them a group ID*—The group ID you assign to a user designates the group to which he or she belongs. A user can only be assigned a single group ID.

- *Comments*—The kind of information you put in the comments field can range from a user's real name to his or her telephone extension. Certain applications can also use the comments field to further identify users.

- *A unique home directory*—The user's home directory is the main directory the user is first directed to when he or she logs in. The home directory also stores the profile information for that user. The profile file controls the shell the user will be placed into when he or she logs in.

Manually Adding a User

To manually add a user to Linux, you must execute the `adduser` command. In the following example, we will add the user `JSmith` to the system:

```
# adduser JSmith
```

If you view the `passwd` file, you will notice that user `JSmith` has been added and fields in the `passwd` file, such as home directory and user ID, are filled in.

The `adduser` command will create the home directory for the user and set appropriate permissions. It will also copy files from the `/etc/skel` directory to the home directory.

The last step is to set the password for the user. You can do this using the `passwd` command. To do this, log in as `root` and type **`passwd <username>`** where ***username*** is the user for whom you are setting the password.

Adding a User with Tools

Depending on the windows managers you have loaded, you may have more than one Administration application. Which one you use will be a matter of preference. To add a user using the GNMOME LinuxConf tool, perform the following steps:

1. Click the left mouse button on the left-most icon (the one that looks like a footprint) in the taskbar. Navigate to the System folder and select `LinuxConf`.

2. If this is the first time you are launching `LinuxConf`, you will be presented with a welcome screen, click Quit to close the screen. The main screen for `LinuxConf` will appear.

3. Scroll down until you find the configuration options under the Normal category. From there, select User accounts. When User accounts is selected, the right side of the screen will list the current users on the machine (see Figure 25.10).

25

LINUX AND
WINDOWS 2000
TOGETHER

FIGURE 25.10

The list of current users created on the machine.

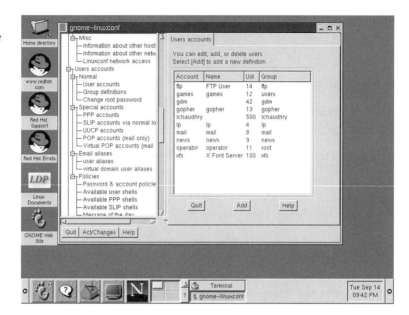

4. To add a user, click the Add button. Fill in the fields and click Accept.

5. The next screen will ask you to type in the password you want to assign the user. Click Accept when done entering the password.

6. When you're ready to quit LinuxConf, select Act/Changes so that any configuration change you made will be updated to the system.

There is a user management tool available under the KDE windows manager. To launch the User Manager tool, perform the following steps:

1. Click your left mouse button on the left-most icon on the taskbar and select KDE menus. From there, select the System folder and then User Management tool.

2. The User Management tool will launch (see Figure 25.11).

3. Click the Add button located on the toolbar.

The remaining steps to adding the user are straightforward.

Adding a Group

To add a group from the command prompt, you must edit the /etc/group file. Similar to the passwd file, the group file consists of records and fields. The fields are

group name : password : group ID : users

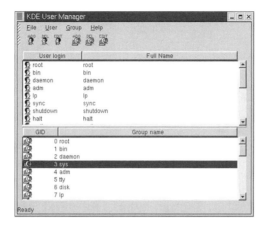

FIGURE 25.11

The user management tool under KDE.

You can add the group by adding a record to the file with the appropriate fields filled in. For example,

```
accounting:x:234:user1
```

adds the `accounting` group to the system with a group ID of `234`. The only user currently in the group is `user1`.

You may find managing groups easier through the graphical administration tools we discussed in the "Add User" section. Both tools allow you to add or remove groups through the management tools. Using `LinuxConf`, simply choose Group Definitions under the Normal configuration section. To add a group using the User Management under KDE, select Add from the Group menu.

Removing Users

When removing users, you need not completely remove the user; you can disable the account. Disabling the account will let you reactivate the account without having to recreate it. You disable the account by removing the capability to log in. To do this, place a `*` in the second field of the `/etc/passwd` file. For example,

```
Jsmith:*:282:292:James Smith:/home/jsmith:/bin/bash
```

Another more abrupt step would be to remove the user's entry from the `/etc/passwd` file. In this case, you would have to recreate the user from scratch. If you do remove the user from the `/etc/passwd` file, you can assign permissions to his or her home directory to another user. Removing the user's files from the system should be the last step you take to remove any trace of the user from the system. You need to be aware that once you remove the files, the only way you can retrieve them is by restoring from a backup.

Again, you have the graphical administration tools available for your use. If you are not the type that likes typing out commands at the command prompt, launch the user management tools.

Online Resources for the Linux Crowd

Just type in the word `Linux` in your favorite search engine, and you're guaranteed to see a number of Web pages listed with information regarding Linux. The following is a list of just a few of the Web sites that offer information regarding Linux, files, and applications:

- `www.linux.org`   This particular site has information on Linux from its history to present events that are helping to shape the future of the operating system.
- `www.kde.org`   Find information on the KDE windows manager. You can also download the latest libraries for the window manger.
- `www.redhat.com`   Red Hat office's Web site.
- `www.gnome.org`   Find information on the GNOME windows manager. You can also download the latest libraries for the window manger, and find applications submitted by others for use by you for free!
- `www.geocities.com/SiliconValley/Way/8400/index1.html`   Download applications and games for the Linux operating system.
- `www.caldera.com`   A company offering an alternative to the Red Hat distribution of Linux.

Shutting Down Linux

No matter what operating system you may use, following proper shutdown procedures is essential for maintenance and the well being of that system. Windows users: Go through the motions of clicking Start/Shutdown and then wait for the operating system to give the OK so you can turn the system off. Even under DOS, it is recommended that you exit any application you may have open and then shut down the PC.

Linux is no different. In actual fact, you will find that Linux is much more flexible with the shutdown options it has to offer the user. This can become extremely useful, especially if people are connecting to your Linux box to share files and applications. You want to ensure the processes are correctly shut down; otherwise, your users could loose data or corruption could occur with the application not being shut down correctly.

No matter what the role of Linux is, workstation or server, as the Administrator to the Linux workstation, you have the ability to execute shutdown commands from the terminal session or the X Window System.

Shutting Down Linux from the Terminal

The command to shutdown Linux from the terminal session is `shutdown`. Like most Linux commands, there are several options you can execute along with the command.

The `shutdown` command and its options are

```
shutdown [ -krhfnc] [ -t secs] time [warning message]
```

Command	Explanation
-k	Do not shutdown only warn
-r	Reboot after shutdown
-h	Halt after shutdown
-f	Initiates a faster reboot by skipping file system check (`fsck`)
-F	Causes a `fsck` upon reboot
-n	Skips the `init` process, initiates a faster shutdown
-c	Cancels the shutdown request
-t	The time interval you specify in seconds

The following is an example of shutting down Linux immediately:

```
# shutdown -h now
```

The following command will shut down the system with a 10 second "wait" before executing the actual `kill` command.

```
# shutdown -t 10
```

Shutting Down Linux under the X Window System

When working under the X Window System, simply exiting the system will not shut down Linux. To properly shut down your Linux system while still in the X Window System, execute the following command from a terminal window:

```
# linuxconf shutdown
```

25

LINUX AND WINDOWS 2000 TOGETHER

The linuxconf command will present you with a dialog box. You can specify a time delay (equivalent to the -t option from the shutdown command) and an optional message to broadcast to any users connected to the system.

For more information on the shutdown command, view the man page for the command by typing **man shutdown**.

Exchanging Information Between Linux and Windows 2000

So you have a Linux workstation installed in your environment and now you want to copy files back and forth between Linux and your Windows 2000 machines. There are a few methods available to you. In this part of the chapter, I will discuss two methods using tools that come with Linux.

FTP

The File Transfer Protocol (FTP) is a common method of transferring files between unlike systems. You do it all the time when you download a file from an FTP server on the Internet. You may not know what type of FTP server you are downloading the file from, UNIX or Windows. It just works, and that's all you care about.

Your Linux workstation has the ability to act as an FTP server. You can FTP directly to the workstation and copy files back and forth as you normally would with any FTP server. When you connect to the FTP server, you will have to log in as a valid user. Whichever user you choose to log in as, you will be restricted to what directories or files you have access to by the rights given to you under Linux. If logged in as root, you will have access to the entire directory tree.

Of course, the reverse is possible also. You can connect to a Windows 2000 FTP server on your network from the Linux box to copy files up and down from a Windows 2000 Professional workstation or Windows 2000 server. In either case, you must have an FTP server service running on the machine.

SMB

Using SMB, you can mount shared directories created on your Windows machines. These shared directories can exist on Windows for Workgroups, 0S/2-Lan Manager, Windows 95,98, NT, or Windows 2000 machines. Your windows machines must be running TCP/IP.

There are other methods available to transfer files between Windows and Linux workstations. You can configure the NFS daemon that will allow you to mount your Linux volumes so they can be shared out to other machines on your network. To connect to these shares, you will need to load a third-party NFS client tool on your Windows machines.

Summary

In this chapter, we covered the major points of the Linux operating system. Understandably, covering an entire operating system in a single chapter is not doing it justice. The objective of this chapter was to relate its history, key differences between it and Windows 2000 Professional, and provide a general overview of Linux as an operating system for your desktop.

Linux is establishing itself as a viable choice as a desktop operating system. It's being introduced into the corporate world as an alternative operating system. But there are drawbacks to Linux that are hindering it from really penetrating the industry. Such things as loose standards, a smaller amount of available applications, and multiple flavors of the same operating system are preventing it from becoming an option for corporate users.

However, Linux is still being considered a major threat to Microsoft and its Windows line of desktop and server operating systems. How much of a real threat will Linux develop into for Microsoft is yet to be seen because we are still in the beginning stages of Linux versus Microsoft.

With regard to running Linux in your environment, there are issues with which you must deal, such as determining what's the best Linux distribution for your environment. However, there are issues that are out of your hands, such as Microsoft's unwillingness to support Linux. This is a major roadblock for true interoperability between Linux and Windows 2000. For example, there is no Windows 2000/Active Directory client for Linux, therefore users of Linux workstations or servers are unable to log in to Windows 2000 machines. We cannot blame Microsoft for this lack of cooperation, neither can we applaude them. Therefore, if you find yourself having to introduce Linux in your environment, or you want to try an alternative operating system, the role Linux plays in your environment may be limited to a Web server, router, firewall, or DNS server. For a free operating system, that's not bad.

25

LINUX AND WINDOWS 2000 TOGETHER

Administering Windows 2000 Professional

PART VI

Disaster Recovery

CHAPTER 26

Computers are mechanical devices. They will fail. Even if they were faultless devices, they depend on electricity and the environment to exist. Although you can eliminate most power problems with a UPS (uninterruptible power supply) scheme of some sort, even these can have their limits. Any of the events in the following list can do a lot more than ruin your day:

- Fires
- Floods
- Sabotage (the leading cause of problems in local area networks)
- A new virus that your anti-virus software fails to detect
- Theft of the computer or its data storage subsystem
- Catastrophic drive failure
- Lightning strike

That's just a partial list of things that can hit your system.

If you are unprepared for a disk crash, it can be catastrophic—particularly if you are a professional user who is vulnerable to financial damage when a system is down.

The external threats, such as viruses and hackers, make for good stories, but user error is easily the single most common cause for the deletion, loss, or modification of critical files. Of all the non–user-based problems, inconsistent power is the single greatest maker of lost data.

> **Note**
>
> Most virus "attacks" stem from user sabotage, either intentional or unintentional.

All these threats to the security of your precious data can be overcome by implementing a regular and carefully followed schedule for backing up your system.

> **Tip**
>
> If your data is really important to you, simply making backups isn't sufficient. If your home or office burns down and your backup tapes are in the building, you might have a bit of a problem recovering data from melted tapes. Maintain a copy of your data offsite. For small installations, simply renting a safe deposit box might be adequate for the purpose. Larger installations might warrant investigating data archiving services that can provide fireproof vaults for storing offsite copies of their backups. In many cases, you can buy a good

safe/strongbox for a reasonable amount of money. Here in the U.S., I just bought a UL certified safe for less than $2,000 that protects against office class fires and is strong enough to stand an explosion. It has a capacity of 50 cubic feet or almost 2 cubic meters. We use it to store vital business documents and, of course, our backup tapes.

There are also companies that will rent out storage or computer (virtual) space.

Even if you have the time and skill to reload your operating system and all your application software from scratch, loss of your documents, spreadsheets, email, and other personal data can be extremely painful—and completely unnecessary.

DOS and Microsoft Windows class operating systems prior to 2000 did a poor job of addressing the issue of backups. The base operating system had no direct support for tape devices, so many people routinely backed up their files onto disks. Windows 95 did support some floppy–interface-based QIC tape drives that were barely sufficient for that operating system's needs. Later, Windows 98 added some more serious (such as SCSI) backup devices.

Backing up to disk is a slow and cumbersome process that few people are willing to undertake regularly, even for small volumes. The problem is exacerbated by the ever-growing size of hard drives and the size of software applications. The type of system typical for Windows 2000 is clearly impractical for floppy disk backup due to its size. It is now common for a desktop system to be configured with more than 20GB of disk space. Fortunately, the 2000 backup facilities provide an excellent solution to the problem.

The `ntbackup.exe` program supplied with Windows 2000 is designed to address the higher capacities of modern computer systems. The 2000 backup philosophy has turned 180 degrees away from the older DOS and Windows 3.1 models. Unlike the Windows NT backup routine, which backed up only to tape devices, Windows 2000's backup will use various backup schemes, including backing up to diskette. However most people use tapes for removable backup storage. Tapes have the following advantages over other currently available storage media:

- *Low media costs*—Tapes provide by far the lowest cost per megabyte of the existing storage media. It is possible to buy 4- or 8-millimeter DAT tapes for under $10 each. DAT tape drives can be costly compared to QIC ones, however. Drives start at about $400 and range upward to several thousand dollars.
- *High capacity*—The capacity of tape drives varies widely with the technology, but even extremely low-cost cartridge drives can store several hundreds of megabytes. A 4- or 8-millimeter DAT or QIC tape drive can provide capacities of 2 to 8 or more gigabytes, with media costs sometimes falling below $10 per cartridge.

That translates to storage at a cost of $1.50 to $5.00 per gigabyte. More exotic technologies, such as SCSI-attached Digital Linear Tapes, have capacities into the tens of gigabytes. There are currently no other removable (or fixed) media devices that can provide that kind of capacity.

- *Speed*—Although the speed of a tape drive is dependent on the underlying technology, relatively inexpensive drives are capable of streaming at fairly high data rates. Furthermore, the high capacity of tape drives means that media changes need not occur frequently. This also means that backups can occur quickly and efficiently without human intervention. It is possible to configure a backup system that works completely automatically, operating at some off hour. This saves the most important resource of all—your time.

- *Concurrency*—The backup program supplied with Windows 2000 Professional will work in the background, allowing normal use of the workstation. The only restriction is that backup won't work on open files.

Tape isn't perfect. It does have some disadvantages:

- *Linear*—Tape is a linear storage medium. The files are stored logically in a long line on the tape. Restoration of a file or a few files can take a long time, because the software searches the entire tape for the file or files to restore. Most optical and all hard drives are random access, allowing much faster access to individual files.

- *One purpose*—Tape drives work only as backup devices. You can't open files on a tape from Windows 2000 Professional. Other storage choices, such as spare hard drives or optical devices, can double as logical devices on your system.

- *Maintenance-intensive*—Tape drives need cleaning, fall out of alignment, and wear out. Hard drives and optical devices are much more robust.

- *The tapes*—The tapes themselves are somewhat more fragile and less long-lived than some other technologies, especially optical.

- *Speed*—DAT, modern SCSI QIC, and DLT tapes are speed demons compared to the older QIC drives or disks, but they are sluggards compared to hard drives or most modern optical devices.

Supported Tape Technologies

The following paragraphs contain a brief overview of available tape technologies supported by Windows 2000. Tape interface methods, media formats, and compatibility issues are discussed.

Tape Drive Interface Methods

Tape drives typically interface to PC systems via one of the following methods:

- Dedicated interface cards are sometimes used to connect tape drives. This was particularly true with some older cartridge tape units. Dedicated interfaces are decreasing in popularity, so it might be difficult to obtain drivers for these types of units.

- Many of the most popular low-end tape drives attach to the system floppy disk controller. Some tape drives of this type can also be driven by dedicated "accelerator" interfaces. Capacities and media formats vary for floppy–controller-based drives. Very inexpensive drives are available with capacities in the 800MB (compressed) range. These very cheap systems are almost useless on a modern computer. Higher-end drives of this type can hold up to about 6MB on a single compressed tape.

- Some tape drives can now be connected via IDE disk interfaces. Again, these tend to be very reasonably priced drives with good speed and capacity.

- Many "external" or "portable" tape units attach to the system via a parallel printer port or a SCSI converter to that port. These drives have the advantage of easy portability, so they can be easily moved from one system to another. They are also compatible with laptop and notebook computers without the need for a docking bay or PCMCIA slot. External tape units that attach to the parallel port are usually QIC drives, although a few 4mm DAT units are available with parallel interfaces. You should be very careful to ensure that any external tape drive you are considering is actually supported by Windows 2000. The tape drive vendor might provide 2000 drivers for externally connected tape units. The speed of these units is, at best, slow. Be careful here. Backing up 10 or 12 gigabytes of data at 1MB a minute is impractical.

- Most of the higher-end tape drives on the market today use SCSI interfaces, which can attach a mixture of tape, disk, and CD-ROM devices to a single SCSI adapter. SCSI tape drives typically have much higher transfer rates than do floppy–disk-based or parallel–port-attached tape units. Some SCSI-attached units can be equipped with a magazine-fed auto-loader unit capable of holding hundreds of gigabytes or even terabytes of tape storage.

Tape Media Formats

A wide variety of tape media is available. When choosing a tape subsystem, it is important to make sure that the selected device meets your requirements for reliability, capacity, and performance. Media cost is also important—particularly if you won't be able to reuse media on a regular basis. This typically happens when you have to provide long-term archival storage of your backups. The most popular tape formats are shown in Table 26.1.

TABLE 26.1 Popular Tape Formats

Type	Capacity	Comments
DLT	40GB (compressed)	Digital Linear Tapes are among the highest capacity, fastest, and most reliable tape drives on the market. They are normally available with SCSI interfaces. DLT tapes are excellent backup devices, but both the drives and the media are expensive. Media can also be difficult to find.
4mm DAT	16GB	Very reliable, fast, low media cost, small form factor. Usually requires a SCSI interface. The drives are relatively expensive when compared to TRAVAN or QIC type drives, but lower media costs can make up for that over time. You can connect multiple SCSI tape drives to a single SCSI adapter.
8mm	7GB	Very inexpensive media. Slower and less reliable than 4mm DAT with higher soft error rates. Usually available as SCSI devices, these drives are losing popularity due to newer tape technologies. Therefore, if you don't already have one, you might not want one. The advantages of SCSI apply.
TRAVAN/QIC	6000MB	Very low drive cost. Media costs are 3 to 4 times that of 4mm or 8mm tapes, but if you don't need a lot of media, the low drive cost makes the higher media cost worthwhile. These drives are available with SCSI, floppy, or parallel-port interfaces.

Installing a Tape Device

Installing a tape device under Windows 2000 is extremely simple. If installing and then starting the system doesn't cause the device to be detected, invoke the Add/Remove Hardware applet of the Control Panel. If SCSI, the system will almost always detect the drive on startup. When the new tape drive is detected, the system will attempt to load the driver so have the vendor supplied driver CD-ROM or diskette handy if your device isn't natively supported with a driver from the 2000 distribution CD-ROM.

After your tape device is installed, you can begin using `ntbackup`, included with Windows 2000 Professional. You invoke Backup by clicking Start, Programs,

Accessories, System Tools and then choosing Backup from the menu. Alternatively you can choose Start, Run, and enter **ntbackup** in the resulting dialog box.

Upon launch, the display looks something like that shown in Figure 26.1.

FIGURE 26.1

The initial tab display for the Backup program found in System Tools.

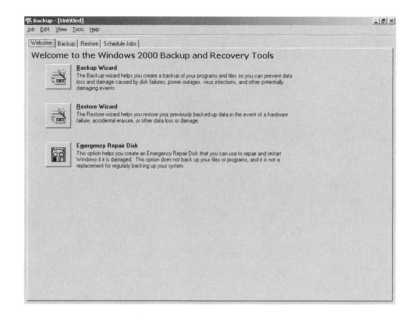

> **Note**
>
> Previous NT-based operating system located Backup under Administrative Tools. Microsoft has moved this utility from the new MMC to the Start menu.

Note that the display in Figure 26.1 has three buttons, each of which will launch a wizard to walk you through an operation. You can use the backup utility manually by choosing either the Backup or Restore tab. As with Explorer, the tree window is on the right and the details window is on the left.

The general user interface of ntbackup is modeled somewhat after the Explorer supplied with Windows 2000. Figure 26.2 shows the Backup tab that illustrates this well.

In simple terms, you select an item or items from one of the windows and then you choose an appropriate operation. In Figure 26.2, for example, you can see that the check box for drive C: has been selected.

The specifics of backing up the system are covered at length in the "Backing Up Files, Folders, and Drives" section of this chapter. You can also do standard tape maintenance.

FIGURE 26.2

Here the system is ready to backup drive C:.

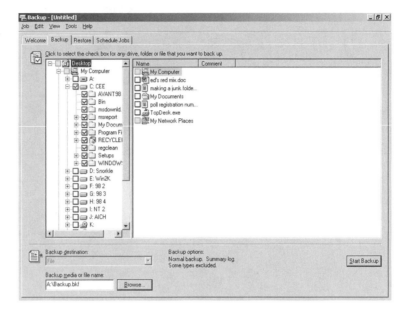

- The Erase Tape option does exactly what its name implies. This option is necessary before using some types of tapes, or if you want to ensure that sensitive material is removed from a tape. To erase a tape, click the Restore tab, choose the tape, and then choose the menu options Tools, Media Tools, and then Erase.

- Certain tape formats can get slack spots in the tape. This causes the tape to move at an inconsistent speed, which can result in tape errors. QIC cartridges are known to exhibit this behavior.

- You can format a tape by choosing the Restore tab, right clicking the tape, and then choosing Format from the context menu.

Backing Up Files, Folders, and Drives

You can back up to a removable media, another volume, or disk on your local computer or any place you have permission to on a network.

By far, the easiest way to back up is to run the wizard. This steps you though the backup procedure. If you prefer to fly manually, you can. Just navigate to the Backup tab, choose the files and folders you want to back up, choose where to place the backup (media or file located wherever you have permission to create a file), and then choose the Start Backup button.

Figure 26.3 shows the manually created backup set to go to a 4mm DAT tape system. You can see that the tape system is chosen in the Backup destination tab in the lower-left corner of the screen. Figure 26.4 shows the dialog box resulting from clicking the Start Backup button.

FIGURE 26.3

If you want to bypass the wizard, you can select files or folders to backup manually using this window.

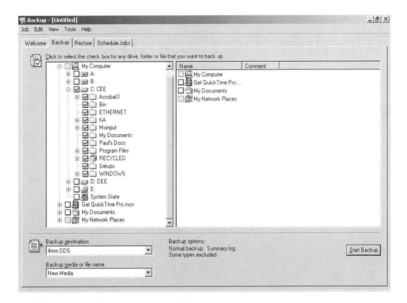

> **Tip**
>
> Selecting the check box of a drive letter doesn't necessarily select all the files contained in the drive or volume. This is because Backup normally skips over any file that you don't have permission to access. Make sure that you are logged in with the correct permissions. Then, after highlighting a drive letter, click Check in the Select menu. That way, you will select all the files on the drive.

FIGURE 26.4

Ready to start the backup to a 4mm tape.

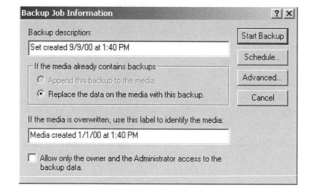

Running the Backup

As you can see from Figure 26.4, you'll have several options for your backup. You can launch the backup right off or schedule for a future time or date. You can also schedule through the Schedule tab in Backup. The Advanced button will reveal the dialog box shown in Figure 26.5.

FIGURE 26.5

The Advanced button is one place to select the type of backup you're making.

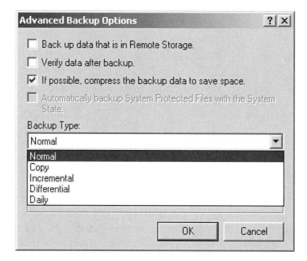

I've pulled down the combo box for the Advanced dialog box to show you the types of backups possible using this facility. The next section will describe in detail the differences between these backup types.

> **Warning**
>
> Be careful when you are backing up to a tape that already contains backup sets. Backup, by default, selects the Replace button. If the Replace option button is selected when the backup begins, all data on the tape will be lost. If you want to keep the existing data, select the Append option button. Backup will try to append the current data to the end of the tape.

The Verify After Backup option causes the Backup program to verify the tape contents against the original files. Selecting this option helps to ensure the integrity of your backups but slows the backup process considerably.

Backing Up the Registry

Select the System State option if you want to backup all your Windows 2000 Registry data (and other system data too). Backup must take special actions when backing up the Registry because many of the files comprising the Registry are open all the time. These open files would normally be skipped. Note that you can't back up the Registry information of a network resource. That one limitation is the reason that ntbackup can't be used as a general-purpose backup solution for your entire network.

You can set the Restrict Access to Owner or Administrator option if you want to make sure that only an authorized person can read the tape. Note that the Restrict Access option is available in the example shown in Figure 26.4. Unlike previous versions of Windows NT (or 2000), you can securely back up from FAT and FAT32 volumes, not just NTFS.

Finally, if your tape device supports hardware compression, you can choose to make a compressed backup. This often greatly increases the capacity of the tape, but compressed backups are inherently less portable and sometimes less reliable than uncompressed backups. Use caution when selecting compression, particularly if you intend to use the tape on more than one computer. This tape device, an Archive Python, lacks hardware compression, so the option is not enabled.

When running, Backup shows a dialog box of its progress. Figure 26.6 shows one such dialog box. Here I'm backing up one folder and its subfolders from a workstation to a server running Windows 2000 Server. The dialog boxes for Professional and Server look the same.

FIGURE 26.6

This is the backup progress dialog box.

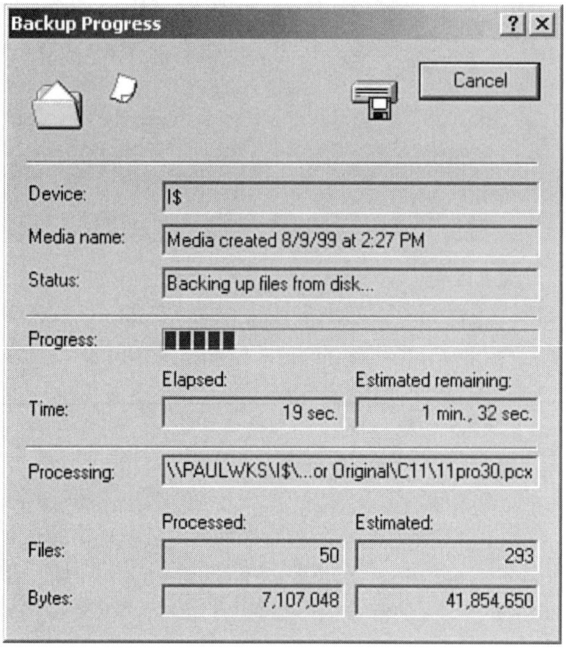

Types of Backups

Pay particular attention to the Backup Type selector. Windows 2000 Backup supports five distinct types of backups, and the contents of your tape can vary dramatically, depending on which type you select.

To understand the types of backups, it is necessary to realize that Windows 2000 maintains a special flag for each and every file on the system. This flag (called the *archive bit*) can be used to mark files as they are backed up. The flag is set if the file is later modified in any way.

Windows 2000 uses the archive bit as a way of keeping track of which files have changed since the last backup. That way, it is possible to back up only the modified data. Although that might not seem particularly important if you have a 4GB tape drive and a 3GB disk, it can be extremely important if you have many gigabytes of disk space online.

The five types of backup supported by Windows 2000 are as follows:

- The *normal backup* copies all the selected files to tape, regardless of the state of the archive bit. As the files are copied, their archive bits are cleared. Normal backups are also referred to as *full* backups.

- *Copy backups,* like normal backups, copy all the selected files to tape. Unlike normal backups, however, the archive bits of the selected files are not modified.

- *Incremental backups* look at each file in the selected file set and copy only those with archive bits set. This allows you to make a quick backup of only those files that have been modified since the last full or incremental backup. The archive bits are cleared as the files are copied to tape. Windows 2000 Professional sets the archive bit the next time the file is modified.

- The *differential backup* is a variation on the incremental backup. Differential backups copy only the files that have marked archive bits, but they do not change the files as they are copied. This is similar to a *copy* backup, but it only affects files with the archive bit set.

- Finally, you can use a *daily backup*. The daily backup copies only the files from the selected file set that have been modified that same day. This can be useful for grabbing a quick copy of your most recent work for transport to a home system.

You should make full backups of your system at regular intervals. One common strategy is to make a full backup once each week. You can then make incremental backups on a daily basis (as described in third item of the preceding list). The full backup ensures that you have a snapshot of your system in some known state. The incremental backups give you a way of quickly picking up the changed components of your system.

If your system usage doesn't justify backups this frequently, you can adjust the backup intervals to be more appropriate for your usage patterns. Remember, though, that restoring your system will require you to restore the most recent full backup and then apply incremental restores for each incremental backup that has occurred since the full backup. It's important to make sure that the full backups occur frequently enough to make this process reasonable.

Differential backups and copy backups are useful when you want to create an image of your system without modifying it. You can sometimes use this technique to replicate a set of directories and files. In most cases, you won't routinely use copy or differential backups.

Father, Son, Grandfather Backups

The *father, son, grandfather backup scheme* is a highly effective and well-used one. It requires a total of 10 tapes and saves files on a 12-week rotation. This means that any file should be available for as long as three months. If you don't notice a file is missing after that length of time, you likely don't need it all that much.

Here's how to do this routine. Take 10 new tapes and label them as follows:

1. Monday
2. Tuesday
3. Wednesday

4. Thursday

5. Friday A

6. Friday B

7. Friday C

8. Month A

9. Month B

10. Month C

Start this routine on Friday by following these steps:

1. Backup normal onto the Friday A tape.

2. On Monday, backup incremental to the Monday tape. Repeat this on Tuesday, Wednesday, and Thursday using the respectively labeled tapes.

3. On Friday, do a normal backup to the Friday B tape.

4. Repeat step 2 for the rest of the week.

5. On Friday, repeat step 3 using the Friday C tape.

6. Repeat step 4.

7. On Friday, perform step 5 using the Month A tape.

8 Repeat the cycle again but use the Month B tape when you get to step 7.

9. Repeat cycle again, but use the Month C tape when you get to step 7.

Consider storing the Friday or the Month tape(s) off premises. (If you are undergoing an EEOC audit, name the backup scheme mother, daughter, and granny.)

Logging Backup Results

The Tools, Options, Backup log (tab) dialog box is used to set the log options for your backup. It is generally a good idea to log your backups—especially if, like most people, you don't plan to sit and watch the entire backup run. Select the level of detail using the radio buttons at the bottom of the dialog box. If you choose, you can also enter a pathname for the log file in the Log File entry box.

Figure 26.7 shows the Backup Log dialog box.

FIGURE 26.7

There are three options for logging backup events. It's a good idea to choose to log because this will tell you what happened during the process.

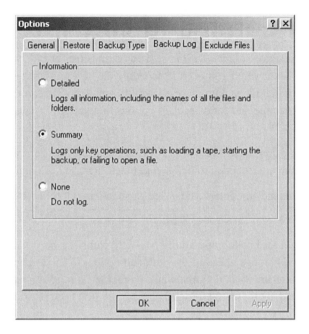

Restoring

If you're lucky, you won't need the Restore tab of Backup. If and when you do need to restore files, the operation of ntbackup is much the same as the operation described earlier for making backups.

The restore process is essentially the opposite of the backup one. You'll need to locate the backup set, either network, local, or removable storage. Choose the place you want to restore to (usually the original location) in a combo box that's analogous to the Backup destination combo box. Click Start Restore and hope for the best.

Restore Logging Options

Set any logging options using the Log Information area of the Restore Information dialog box. You can select the log detail level and pathname, just as you could when creating the backup set.

Clicking OK causes the restore to actually begin. A Restore Status dialog box appears, indicating the currently active operation. The dialog box also displays statistics concerning the number of files and bytes that have been restored. You can stop the restore operation by clicking the Abort button of the Restore Status dialog box.

Using a Command-Line Interface

There are times when you might want to use a command-line interface to run your backups. This can occur when you need to schedule the backup to run automatically, when you want to initiate a backup on one machine remotely from another system, or when you have some repeated set of backup options that you run frequently enough to justify using a script.

ntbackup provides a command-line interface for such cases. Most of the command-line options for ntbackup are intended to be used in batch files, so they require no user input.

The ntbackup command-line interface is used as shown in the following:

```
ntbackup [systemstate] [.bks name] path parameters
```

The *path* is required for backup operations. Multiple paths can be specified. The systemstate option belongs ahead of the path and options. The .bks name is the name of the backup set filename—an optional way to direct backup as to what files to back up. You create such a file using the GUI interface.

Available *parameters* are shown in Table 26.2.

TABLE 26.2   The ntbackup Parameters and Options

Parameters	*Explanation*
/A	Sets append mode. The backup sets will be appended to the end of the tape. If this option is not set, the existing contents of the tape will be overwritten.
/N "Name"	Media name.
/M {}	Backup type.
/F "Name"	Filename when backing up to file.
/DS or /IS "server name"	Backs up the directory or information stored respectively for Exchange.
/V	Causes all operations to be verified.
/R	Restricts access to saved information to Administrators or to the actual owners of the saved files.
/RS (yes¦no)	Backs up the removable storage database.
/D "Description"	Enables you to enter a textual description of the backup. Use the quotation marks if the description text contains any spaces.
systemstate	Backs up system files, including Registry.
/HC:{on/off}	/hc:on turns hardware compression on. /hc:off turns compression off. Compression sometimes greatly increases tape capacity, but it can slow the backup down or make the tape less portable.

Parameters	Explanation
/T {option}	The tape name.
/L f,s,n	The log file type (full, summary, none).
/J "name"	The job name.
/G "name"	The GUID name. Do not use with the /p switch.
/P "name"	Pool name.

Any or all of the listed options can be specified. As an example, a full backup of the
F: drive could be made on a compressed archive by using the following command:

```
ntbackup backup F:\ /d "F: Full Backup" /hc:on
```

Scheduling Automatic Backups

The command-line interface to ntbackup makes it relatively simple to automate the
process of backing up your system. You can use the 2000 AT command to schedule tasks
to be run at fixed times. If you place the ntbackup commands that you want to use into a
script file, you can cause the script to be run during some off-hour by using the AT command. In this way, you can get an automated backup every night at the same time.
Consider the following simple batch script:

```
REM backit.cmd - An automated backup script
@echo off
ntbackup backup d:\ /j "2KUnleashed" /a /t "CLI BU" /m copy
REM Map network drive
net use x: \\server1\d$
REM Now back it up
ntbackup backup x: /j "Server1 D: Backup" /hc:on /m incremental /a
net use x: /d
```

The preceding script runs a copy backup of drive C: on the local system. It then connects
the administrative share name \\server1\d$ to drive X: and runs an incremental backup
of the remote drive. Finally, it disconnects the share from the local system.

Place the preceding commands into a file called backit.cmd and then run the following
command:

```
at 01:00 /every:m,t,w,th,f,s,su backit.cmd
```

Every morning at 1 a.m., an incremental backup of drive C: and \\server1\d$ will be
run. You can expand the script by adding additional paths to the ntbackup command. You
can also put conditional logic into the script to cause the script to perform different
actions on the basis of environment variables or the output of other programs.

> **Note**
>
> The AT command uses the Windows 2000 Scheduler service to run commands. For your backup to run correctly, you must be logged on to your workstation as an Administrator or a member of a group, such as the Backup Operators group, that has appropriate permission. The AT service must also be running.

Third-Party Backup Software

Windows 2000 Backup is almost a complete backup solution. Its primary flaw lies in its inability to back up the Registry information of remote systems. A number of quality backup programs are available from third-party software vendors to address that inability. Three of the most popular are Backup Exec from Veritas Software, Networker from Legato Systems, and Cheyenne Software's ARCserve. Each has its own set of strengths and weaknesses, but any of these applications is an excellent choice for backing up networked 2000 systems.

Emergency Repair Disk

Windows 2000 Professional has a repair system built into its boot process. This system can be kicked into gear if you can't boot Windows 2000 from the Last Known Good control set. The most common reasons you might not be able to start from Last Known Good are as follows:

- Missing or corrupted system files
- Missing or corrupted Registry files
- Partition boot sector corruption

Working in conjunction with the distribution CD-ROM, an emergency repair disk (ERD) can fix these and similar problems; thus, returning you to the state you were at before the problem occurred.

In many cases, either system corruption or missing files stem from a problem with a disk subsystem. Fixing the Windows 2000 Professional installation without addressing the underlying problem will only result in a temporary restoration of function.

> **Note**
>
> After a repair, your first act should be a full backup including system state, if your backup is at all out of date.

The Setup program for Windows 2000 Professional will create an initial ERD if you let it. As soon as you install applications, change Windows 2000's optional components, or add new profiles, this disk becomes obsolete. The ERD can only restore the system as it was when the ERD was made. Think of it as a snapshot of your system. You need to update the ERD regularly—at least every time you make a major change to your system that would be inconvenient to lose.

The program that makes an ERD is the Emergency Repair Disk (ERD) option in the `ntbackup` program (Start, Programs, Accessories, System Tools, Backup). Figure 26.8 shows the start of the ERD wizard.

FIGURE 26.8

The Emergency Repair Disk utility can update or create a new ERD.

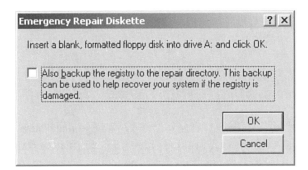

Disks are cheap, but the information contained on an ERD can be as valuable as the time you save using it rather than having to restore your Windows 2000 setup from scratch. Consider making duplicate copies of the ERD. Making an ERD takes only seconds— they are seconds well spent. You should make one each time your system changes in any significant way (such as adding a new application).

> **Note**
>
> The Save System State in backup isn't the same as the ERD. A backup using `ntbackup` requires Windows 2000 running to restore, which is obviously a catch 22 if you have a system that won't start. An ERD will give you a good shot at restoring your non-booting system, while Save System State usually will not.

Using the ERD

To use the ERD when you can't boot from your hard disk or when you can't get Windows 2000 Professional to launch, boot the computer with the Windows 2000 setup disk in the boot floppy drive. Insert setup disk number 2 when it's time to do so. Choose the Repair option (press R) when you're presented with that option. This will launch the repair sequence.

You'll get a text-based option screen that gives you the following options:

- Inspecting the Registry
- Inspecting the boot environment
- Checking and verifying the Windows 2000 system files
- Inspecting the boot sector of the boot disk (Intel computers, NVRAM on Alpha)

Choose the options you feel you need to perform and then continue with the inspection.

The option to inspect the Registry is the most complex. It will inspect the following sections by option:

- System
- Default user profile
- Security
- New user profile
- Software

The verification of system files uses a checksum routine to make sure all the needed system files exist and are in good working order. This information resides in the Setup.log file on the ERD. Figure 26.9 shows a section of a Setup.log from an ERD.

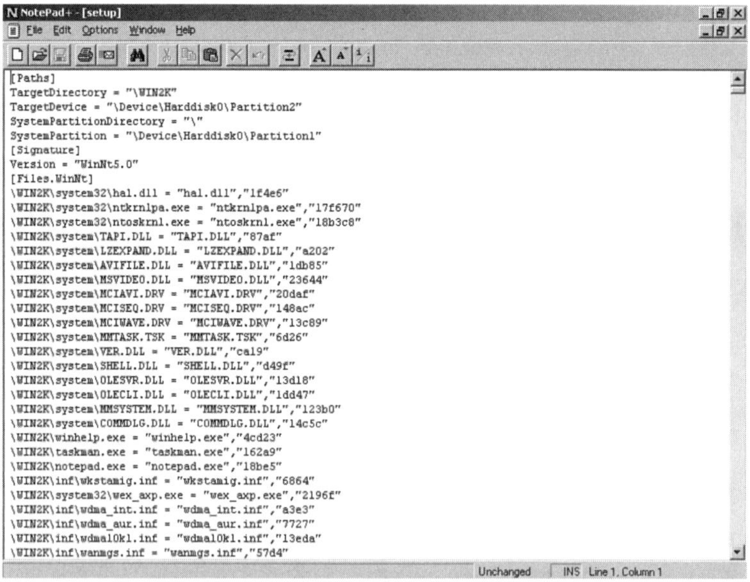

FIGURE 26.9

The Setup.log file from an ERD contains the checksum information needed by Windows 2000 to verify the existence and integrity of its system files.

The inspect boot sector option of the repair facility will verify the integrity of the Partition Boot Sector and will replace a bad or missing NTLDR. This facility only works for the first hard disk.

Restoring the Registry

There are four ways to restore the Registry or parts of it:

- For FAT systems, boot to MS-DOS and copy the Registry to a floppy or set of floppies using a disk-spanning routine such as PKZip. Restore the Registry or parts of it by reversing the process.
- If you have possession of Reg.exe from the Resource Kit, use it to back up the Registry. This utility can restore keys selectively.
- Use the ERD and Windows 2000 setup.
- Use Saved System State from Backup.

The Backup (ntbackup) will only restore the system files if you backed up having checked the System State check box.

Re-creating the Master Boot Record

You can re-create or replace the master boot record (MBR) by using fdisk. To do this, boot from a floppy formatted with MS-DOS. You'll need the fdisk.exe file that runs with the version of MS-DOS from which you boot. The DOS version must be 5 or later for this switch to work. Perform the following steps:

1. Boot using an MS-DOS floppy.
2. Enter **fdisk /mbr** at the A: prompt.

This will replace the MBR without affecting the partition table. Don't use this if you're using either of the following:

- A third-party disk manager, such as Disk Manager from Ontrack Systems or Partition Magic from Power Quest (in some configurations)
- A multiple boot or some other utility that writes information between the partition table and the MBR

If nothing else works and you have the skills, you can copy the partition table and MBR from a good installation to your corrupted disk. The Windows 2000 Professional Resource Kit contains a utility, DiskProbe, that maps the structure of a disk. Using this utility, you can edit, copy, or save disk boot information.

Summary

The single most catastrophic mistake made by both novice and advanced computer users is the simple failure to make routine backups. It's a dull, unexciting task for which many users rarely find time. Avoid that pitfall. A little forethought can make backups an automatic and painless process that can save you endless hours of frustration or financial hardship. Windows 2000's integrated backup facilities are easy to use and robust for standalone workstations, so there's no real need to defer the task. Take time today (if you haven't already done so) to plan a backup strategy. Start by immediately making a full backup of your entire system. If you ever need it, you'll realize that it was time well spent.

Also, make sure to regularly update your ERD. There's nothing like the feeling of confidence brought on by having a full backup and a current ERD. On the other hand, there's nothing like the empty feeling you get if you have neither and one day your system fails to start.

Event Viewer

27

CHAPTER

The Event Viewer

To see the Event Viewer, a supplied component of the Microsoft Management Console (MMC), open the Administrative Tools folder in Control Panel and then double-click the Event Viewer entry.

In Windows 2000 Professional, an *event* occurs whenever anything significant happens that either 2000 or a running application feels you should know about.

The definition of *significant* is left up to the developers. Thus, the events you are notified about can vary enormously—from fundamental system errors, such as a network card not working or a fault-tolerant disk failure, to much less significant events, such as a service starting or a print job completing. Security events vary, depending on your needs, from meaningless to extremely important.

When a software component detects an event to be reported, it uses the ReportEvent API to pass details about the event to Windows 2000. The Event Log service then posts these details to one of three event logs:

- *System log*—This log contains details about events that occur within the operating system, such as a driver failure.

- *Security log*—Security-related Audit events—such as when someone attempts to log on without the proper password—are stored in this log.

- *Application log*—This log contains details about events detected by applications running on your system. For example, a database application might record the failure to read a record.

All users can access the system and application logs, whereas only users with administrator rights can see the security log.

The Event Log service is responsible for writing event details to the event logs, and it is one of the standard services that are started each time you load Windows 2000 Professional.

> **Tip**
>
> When the Event Log service starts, it reports this to the System Event log. The event logged is event 6005, which can be very useful in troubleshooting. By looking for this event, you can determine when the system last rebooted and thus see all the events that have occurred since then. These events also show you how often Windows 2000 Professional has been rebooted.

To view the information that has been logged, you use the Event Viewer application. Event Viewer is automatically installed when you load Windows 2000 Professional.

Event Viewer enables you to perform the following tasks:

- See a summary of the events that have occurred
- See the details logged for each event
- Save event logs away for future analysis and view saved logs
- View the local event log and view event logs on remote systems (subject to security)

The Event Viewer is a powerful aid to troubleshooting as a first resort whenever a problem occurs on your system. Let's look at how you can use Event Viewer to diagnose problems in Windows 2000 Professional. The Event Viewer is very straightforward to use, but getting the most out of it takes practice because there is no overall consistency in what is logged when events occur.

The start of the Event Viewer service is an event itself. Figure 27.1 shows this event highlighted in the Viewer. To see this event on your machine, open the Event Viewer in the MMC, choose the System Log entry in the left pane, and finally scroll the right window until you see the event numbered 6005 for the last date your machine was booted.

FIGURE 27.1

A good way to start using the Event Viewer is to view the event viewer service launch itself.

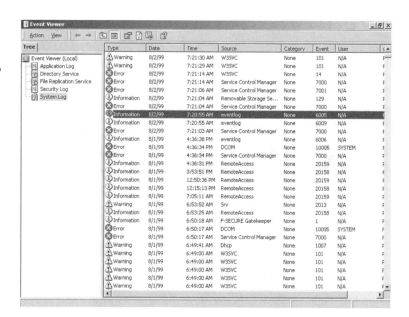

Suppose that a driver fails to start when you boot Windows 2000 Professional. If this happens, you receive a message box after you start up.

This message box tells you that something has gone wrong in the startup and that the Service Control Manager was not able to properly start one or more drivers. This message box, by itself, offers no indication as to what has happened; it only tells you that there has been a problem. If you've just changed or added a driver, this box alone might tell you what's wrong. However, often this is just the first hint that there's a problem. To determine what went wrong, you need to run the Event Viewer.

The bar above the events has seven columns:

- Type
- Date
- Time
- Source
- Category
- Event
- User
- Computer

Event Viewer to the Rescue

With the Event Viewer application, you examine and manage the three event logs. When you install Windows 2000 Professional, the installation process installs the Event Viewer application as `%SystemRoot%\system32\eventvwr.exe` and sets up a component in the Microsoft Management Console (MMC) accessed through the Administrative Tools in the Control Panel.

> **Note**
>
> Windows 2000 Professional disables security logging by default. If you want this service, you must explicitly start it.

Running this component brings up the window shown in Figure 27.1. Figure 27.2 shows the Event Detail message box that is displayed when the event highlighted in Figure 27.1 is doubled-clicked.

FIGURE 27.2

The detail view of an event.

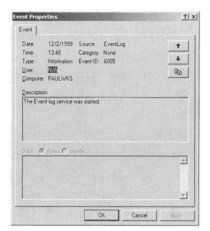

If you look at the event log, you can see that there are a number of error events (the ones with the red × sign to the left). Looking back chronologically, you can see the first event (since the last reboot). Selecting that event and pressing the Enter key (or double-clicking the event) brings up the Event Detail dialog box, shown in Figure 27.2, which provides all the details that were logged. The event—the start of a service shown in Figure 27.2— isn't too informative. Figure 27.3 is the detail view of an error event number 7000 (failure to start a service). Note that the diagnosis of not being able to find the path is quite explicit, allowing you as System Administrator to easily fix the problem.

FIGURE 27.3

The Event Detail tab in the Event on Local Computer Properties dialog box shows the greatest detail about the event in question, but sometimes it doesn't contain enough information for a full diagnostic.

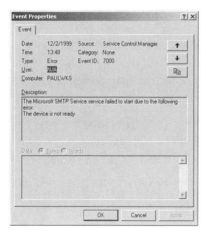

Because of its size of the screen shot, I've copied the text of the 7000 error below.

```
The Microsoft SMTP Service service failed to start due to the following error:
The system cannot find the path specified.
```

From this tab, you can see that the system could not locate the file needed to launch the service. Remember that a path is the path to a file. This is the Event Viewer equivalent to "Bad Command or Filename" error message so familiar to MS-DOS users.

The type of event will give you a good indication of whether you should worry about the event or let it slide.

In other instances, the detail message actually doesn't give you useful information on a malfunctioning device. In this case, all you need to do is make sure the missing file exists to fix the problem. Sometimes this is usually easier said than done.

> **Note**
>
> In the Event Detail dialog box shown in Figure 27.3, the Service Control Manager is reporting that the service has failed to start and that it is not functioning. There could be an obvious reason and, thus, an obvious solution. However, the event details logged might not be all that helpful. Still, it's better than nothing.

The Event Viewer Application

The Event Viewer application is an important troubleshooting tool and is also very useful administering networks of Windows 2000 systems. By examining the event log, you can solve the problems that occur, and, more importantly, you can identify and correct problems before they become more serious.

As you saw in Figure 27.1, the Event Viewer application has two bars, a menu bar and a toolbar, usually arranged side by side. These bars contain two and seven entries, respectively:

- *Action*—Actions to take with the events—entries duplicated on the toolbar.
- *View*—This option helps you to view the logs and find events within the logs.
- *Previous/Next*—Move to the next or previous entry in the Tree.
- *Up one level*—Move up a level in the Event Viewer. This isn't too useful and is probably included for consistency with the user interface.
- *Show/Hide Console Tree*—Show or hide the left pane of the Event Viewer (Tree).

- *Properties*—Show properties of selected event or log. Quite useful. Curiously, double-clicking an event will bring up its properties, but double-clicking a log won't, so this option is mostly used for viewing or editing properties of logs.

- *Refresh*—Requery the system and relog.

- *Export list*—Export to standard US or Unicode text- or comma-delimited files. Useful for archiving and/or importing into a database management system for analysis.

- *Help*—This option provides standard Help facilities.

The remainder of this chapter covers these features and how to use them best.

What Information Is Logged?

Each event log entry contains parameters that are passed by the application to the ReportEvent API call. These are as follows:

- *Source*—This is the name of the software component that is reporting the event. The Source is either an application name or a component of a larger application.

- *Event Identifier (or just Event)*—This identifies the specific event and can be used by the support staff to aid in determining the cause of the error. Event identifiers are unique to each Source.

- *Type*—Windows 2000 has five event types: Information, Warning, Error, Success Audit, and Failure Audit. Any event must be of only one of these event types.

- *Category*—To assist in organizing events (and to help users in reviewing the event log), a Source can define different categories. Although categories are not used much in the system or application logs, the security system uses several categories, including Logon/Logoff, File System Access, Privileged Actions, and Change in Security Policy.

- *User*—Who was logged on at the time of the event?

- *Computer*—The console where the event occurred.

Note

You can change the size and location of columns in the Viewer by the familiar click-and-drag method standard to all Microsoft operating systems and most Windows applications, Microsoft and non-Microsoft.

> **Note**
>
> When you view events in Event Viewer, the time and date shown will be the time on the local computer. To enable you to correlate events that occur on different systems, it is important to have a consistent time on all machines on a network. Use the NET TIME command, possibly as part of a logon script, to synchronize the clocks on all systems. Although the synchronized time might still be wrong, at least it's wrong over the entire network.

When viewing events with Event Viewer, the summary view (which you saw in Figure 27.1) shows Date, Time, Source, Category, Event, User, and Computer. To see the description and any included data, you need to look at the Event Detail (see Figures 27.2 and 27.3).

As noted earlier, each event is categorized into one of five basic event types:

- *Information*—Information events are ones that are infrequent but successful. For example, the start of the Event Viewer is a useful event to note because it is usually the first event to occur when you boot the system. Information events are noted with a blue exclamation point inside a white circle. Information events are seen in the system and application logs.

- *Warning*—Warning events can reflect problems in the making. These are events that indicate a problem that is not yet serious—for example, the browser being unable to retrieve a list of domains from the browse master. This should usually resolve itself, but if it continues, the Administrator might want to investigate and resolve this. Warning events are noted with a black exclamation point inside a yellow triangle. Warning events are seen in the system and application logs.

- *Error*—Error events are events that usually represent a problem the user should be aware of, because these events usually indicate a loss of functionality. In the example in Figure 27.1, a network card failed to start; therefore, there will be no network functionality until the underlying cause is determined and rectified. Error events are noted by a white X inside a red circle. Error events are seen in the system and application logs.

- *Success audit*—A success audit indicates that a successful audit event has occurred, such as a successful logon. Success audit events are seen only in the security log.

- *Failure audit*—A failure audit indicates that an unsuccessful audit event has occurred, such as a failed logon. Failure audit events are seen only in the security log.

System and Application Logs

The System Event log contains events detected by the Windows 2000 Professional operating system. The application log is used mainly to log events detected by applications running on your system. If possible, you should look at the logs on a regular basis. This enables you to spot problems before they become serious.

The following are some events you are likely to see in the event log:

- *Event log startup*—Each time the system restarts, the Event Log service logs an information event. This tells you when the system restarted.
- *Driver startup failures*—If a driver fails to start, an error event is logged by the Service Control Manager to list the driver that failed. This can include error codes that can be very helpful to technical support staff but are not of much use to end users.
- *Device driver errors*—If a device driver encounters an error in operation, details of this error are written away to the system log. If a particular device is constantly logging errors, you should try to determine the source of the error. In such cases, the details logged in the system log might not be too help much in determining the error's cause.
- *Browser events*—The browser services tend to log a lot of events. Although these can usually be ignored, if multiple systems are constantly forcing browser elections, some reconfiguration of the network's browsing might be in order.
- *Service startup*—Some services, such as the SMNP service, log successful startups in the event log. You can usually ignore these events. However, if they don't occur when they should, their absence might be worth investigating.
- *Directory replication*—If your system is an import server, the Directory Replication service logs events in the system log. The details logged, in this case, are cryptic at best.
- *Printer events*—Whenever a new printer is added to your system or an existing printer driver is updated, Print Manager logs the event.

Security Log

The Security Event log is used to report security-related events. These events can indicate attempted or successful breaches of your system's security.

27

EVENT VIEWER

> **Note**
>
> To view all three event logs, you must be a member of the Administrator's local group. Without membership in this group, you can only view the System and Application logs.

Unlike the System and Application logs, you determine which events are to be included in the Security log. This is done by setting the audit policy and selecting events to audit.

Before you can get any security-related events recorded, you must first set the audit policy in the Microsoft Management Console's Local Security Policy.

Open the Administrative Tools folder in Control Panel (or Explorer) and then launch the Local Security Policy entry. You'll see an item called Local Policies, open that and under it you'll see Audit Policies. Figure 27.4 shows this section of the MMC. You can also set audit policies for volumes and directories using the Properties dialog box for those objects in MMC/Computer Management/Storage/Disk Management.

> **Note**
>
> You can only activate audit policy for volumes formatted as NTFS.

FIGURE 27.4

The Audit Policy section of the MMC.

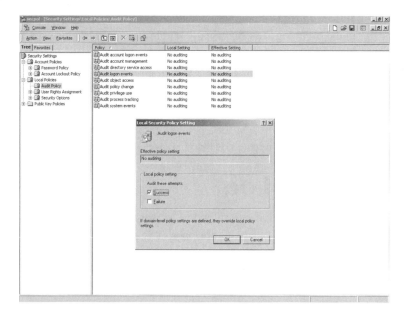

Before any security events can be logged, you must select which event (success or failure) to audit in the Local Security Policies Settings dialog box. To see this dialog box, right click any Policy in the MMC and choose Properties.

After you have set this option, you can select the specific security events to log and click OK to accept these options. There are three main places where you can set up audit events to be logged in the security log:

- General security events are set up in Security section of the MMC (as you saw in Figure 27.4).
- Registry-related security events are set up in the Registry Editor `regedt32.exe`. To set auditing, open the editor, choose Security from the menu, and then click the Advanced button. You cannot set auditing using the common registry editor, `regedit.exe`.
- File-related events are set up by using the file or directory Properties dialog box. Click the Security tab and then click the Advanced button where you'll see an Audit tab. You can set audit policy for a single file if you choose.

General security events are selected in the Audit tab of any Security/Advanced button.

Selecting these events causes all occurrences of the event to be logged. Some events, such as the Use of User Rights or Process Tracking, can log a large amount of data and might not be very useful (unless you are developing and debugging an operating system component). The large amount of data logged also will slow down your system.

Using the Windows 2000 Registry Editor (`regedt32.exe`), you can log access to the System Registry by a user or group of users. Using the Audit item from the Security menu in `regedt32.exe`, you bring up the Auditing Entry dialog box, shown in Figure 27.5.

FIGURE 27.5

You can set audit events from the Registry Editor, `regedt32.exe`.

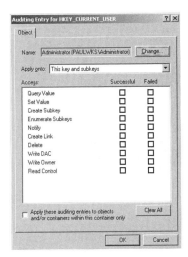

Unlike general events, you must select which users and/or groups should be audited with Registry audit events. You do this by clicking the Add button and selecting the users and groups. Then you can select which audit events should be logged.

> **Note**
>
> You won't see the dialog box in Figure 27.5 until you've added at least one user or group to the Auditing dialog box. It isn't logically sound to set a general audit policy. You set it for a group (or user). Since initially there are no users or groups in the Audit dialog box, you must add at least one to be able to set the audit-specific policies shown in Figure 27.5.

Audit events can be set up on any key or keys in the Registry. If you select Replace Permissions on Existing Subkeys, you can replicate the auditing to all subkeys. Setting the auditing this way can take a lot of time, and if you set up very much auditing, you can generate many audit events. There also can be a significant performance impact of having to log the data.

You can also log accesses by a user or group of users to any file or folder in your system. You set auditing by first right-clicking the folder or file to be audited and bringing up the Properties dialog box for the object. From the Properties dialog box, select the Security tab, which is shown in Figure 27.6.

FIGURE 27.6

The NTFS Properties Security area has three tab: Permissions, Auditing, and Owner. These tabs allow fine-tuning of security features on a file-by-file basis, if you choose that detail level. Access this dialog box by clicking the Advanced button in the Security tab on an NTFS volume.

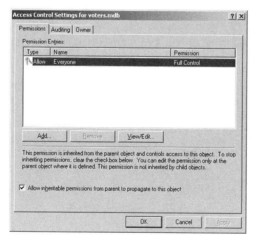

Figure 27.7 shows the Add dialog box where you can add a group or user to audit for a particular file or folder. Figure 27.8 shows the specific audit areas you can set (or unset) for that user or group. Note that 2000 can audit quite a variety of events if you so choose.

FIGURE 27.7

Here is where you add a user or group to audit for a particular file or group of files (folder).

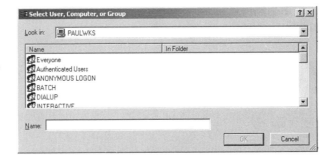

FIGURE 27.8

You have a wide variety of audit events you can monitor on a file by file basis.

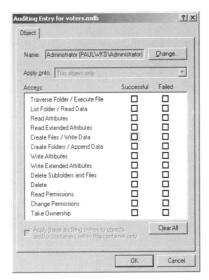

In the dialog box shown in Figure 27.7, you must first select the users whose activities should be audited. Then you select which types of activities you want to audit.

> **Warning**
>
> By default, the setting of any Auditing for a folder replaces all existing audit events on all files in the chosen folder. If you have spent time setting up different levels of auditing on different files within a folder, clicking OK when viewing in the Folder dialog box overwrites all the audit events. This might not be what you want.

Viewing Logs Locally

When you start Event Viewer, it opens your local event log and displays whatever log was last being displayed (or the System log, the first time you run the application). Depending on what logging you have chosen and how long it has been since you cleared the event logs, you might find that the event logs are rather big. The View menu in Event Viewer has some options to assist you in finding events in the logs.

By default, all events logged are displayed, and there can be a lot of data. Using the Filter Events item from the View menu brings up the Filter dialog box, shown in Figure 27.9. From here, you can reduce the amount of data to wade through.

FIGURE 27.9

You can filter the events shown in the Event Viewer to focus on particular events.

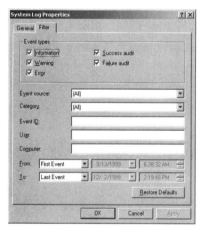

Using this dialog box, you can select events that occurred between two times, as well as select which events to view. By selecting a specific source or user, you can see just the events generated by the related software component or by a specific user.

There are many Filter options available:

- *View From*—After a time or date
- *View To*—Up to and including a date or time
- *Information*—The Information type event only
- *Warning*—The Warning type event only
- *Error*—The Error type event only
- *Success Audit*—The Success Audit type event only
- *Failure Audit*—The Failure Audit type event only
- *Source*—The application, system component, or other object capable of being a source for an event
- *Category*—Usually only for the security log; filters by the category of the event, such as logons
- *User*—The user name of the logged-on user during the event
- *Computer*—The specific machine where the event occurred
- *Event ID*—Shows only events bearing a particular ID number

By default, Event Viewer displays the newest events at the top of the log and the oldest events at the bottom. You can change this order by selecting the Oldest First (or Newest First) option from the View menu. If you have Save Settings on Exit checked from the Options menu, whatever sort options you set will persist.

> **Note**
>
> Clicking the column heads will sort the event log by that column first in ascending then descending order. This will temporarily override the settings in the View, Filter dialog box.

The Find item in the View menu can be used to find specific events. Selecting this option brings up the Find dialog box, which is shown in Figure 27.10. Here you can see I've searched for any SMTPSVC event and started the Find applet. It found such an event (see the highlight in the Event Log at the bottom of the screen).

FIGURE 27.10

*You can use View,
Find menu
command to
locate particular
events.*

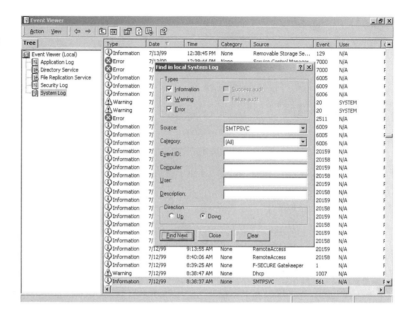

Using the Find dialog box, you select which items you are interested in seeing. Clicking the Find Next button finds the next occurrence of the event. If you are searching a large event log, click the Find Next key to find the next occurrence. For some mysterious reason, the F3 Find Next hot key is disabled in this particular Find dialog box.

If you are looking at a running system's log and events occur, you might not see them. To refresh the log, you can use the Refresh button on the toolbar. The F5 key is a shortcut to this function.

Viewing Event Logs Remotely

As a Windows 2000 Professional user, you will probably view only the logs on your computer system. In corporate networks, however, it might be useful to view remote event logs. Technical support staff, for example, might need to do this to diagnose problems remotely. Drop down the Console menu (Start, Run, MMC /a) and then choose Add/Remove Snap-in (see Figure 27.11). Choose Add. Add the computer you want to add or, if the Wizard appears, follow it to add the new computer (assuming you have the permissions).

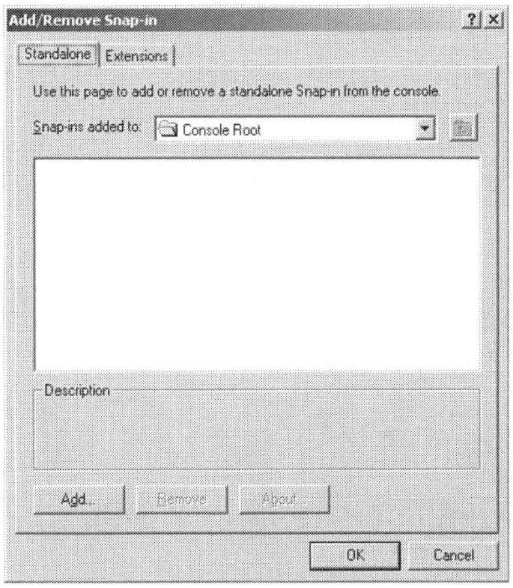

FIGURE 27.11

Add a remote computer through the standard MMC add snap-in facility.

> **Note**
>
> Before you can view a remote system's event logs, you must be able to log on to that system over the network. If you do not have those rights or you are not logged on as a user known to the remote system (with the right password), you get an error dialog box (Access is Denied).

After you select the remote system and get past the security, you can view the Security logs on a remote system. Use the Log menu to choose which log to view and the View options to filter the log or find specific events.

Viewing the event logs on a remote system is as easy as viewing the logs on your own system.

If you are accessing a network via a slow connection (such as a modem), you might want to select the Low Speed Connection option. When this is selected, Windows 2000 will not enumerate all the computers on the network into the Select Computer dialog box. This can save you time if you're using a large network from a dial-up modem connection.

Managing the Event Logs

The event log can get to be rather large, and, on most systems, the vast bulk of the information logged is of little use.

To clear the Event Log, use the Clear All Events item from the Action menu. This clears the event log currently being viewed. Because the log might contain useful information, Windows 2000 offers you the opportunity to save the log before it clears the log. Because clearing the event log is an irrevocable event, Windows 2000 also asks for further confirmation before actually clearing the log.

To keep the event logs from getting too large, you can use the Properties setting from the Action menu to set a maximum size for each log. Selecting the Log Settings item from the Log menu brings up the Event Log Settings dialog box shown in Figure 27.12.

FIGURE 27.12

The Event Log Properties dialog box is the place where you set how long the archive exists and its size.

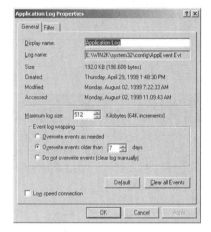

From this dialog box, you can select the maximum size of each of the three event logs. You can also use this dialog box to tell Windows 2000 what to do when the log fills up. You have three choices:

- Overwrite events as required.
- Overwrite events over a certain number of days. (The range is from 1 to 365 days.)
- Do not overwrite events.

If you choose not to overwrite events, you need to manually clear the log to get new events logged. Most sites do not need to set this option.

There is also a low speed connections option. You would choose this option is if you connect to a remote computer by a slow connection such as dial up. Don't use this if you connect through any LAN or at LAN-like speed.

Saving and Restoring Logs

Because of the importance of the event logs, you can choose to save them either when they get full or on a regular basis, rather than just clearing them, as discussed in the previous section.

To save a log, first select it from the left pane. Next, select the Save Log File As item from the Action menu. This brings up the Save As common dialog box, where you supply the filename.

> **Note**
>
> Event log filtering has no effect on the log entries saved. Saving a log saves all entries, regardless of any filtering.

You have three choices of how to save the log, depending on whether you choose the Save Log File As entry or the Export List entry in the Action menu:

- *Event log format*—This allows the saved log to be viewed by the Event Viewer application. This is the only option in the Save Log File As entry.
- *Text*—This saves the file as a simple text file. This is an option in the Export List entry. You have a Unicode option here.
- —Similar to Text, this format puts a comma between each field in the saved log. This is an option in the Export List entry. You have a Unicode option here.

> **Note**
>
> The Export List entry will save in both Unicode and standard US formats.

Saving the log as comma-delimited text enables you to consolidate the saved log into a spreadsheet or database. Most spreadsheet or database programs support importing data from comma-delimited files.

> **Note**
>
> If you are going to import a saved event log into a spreadsheet or database, note that some description fields will contain commas. This might require extra work to ensure that all description fields are properly handled.

If you save an event log as an event log, you can later view the log using Event Viewer. If you use the New entry from the Action menu, you can open a saved event log and view it. A saved log can be filtered or searched in the same way as a live log.

> **Note**
>
> More mysteries here: there is no Open entry in the Action menu for saved Event Logs. You must choose Action, New, Log View. Choose the Saved Log entry and then locate (browse for) the saved log. No, I don't know why.

Figure 27.13 shows an event log exported to a comma-delimited file and then imported into Microsoft Access. The conversion was handled automatically by Access.

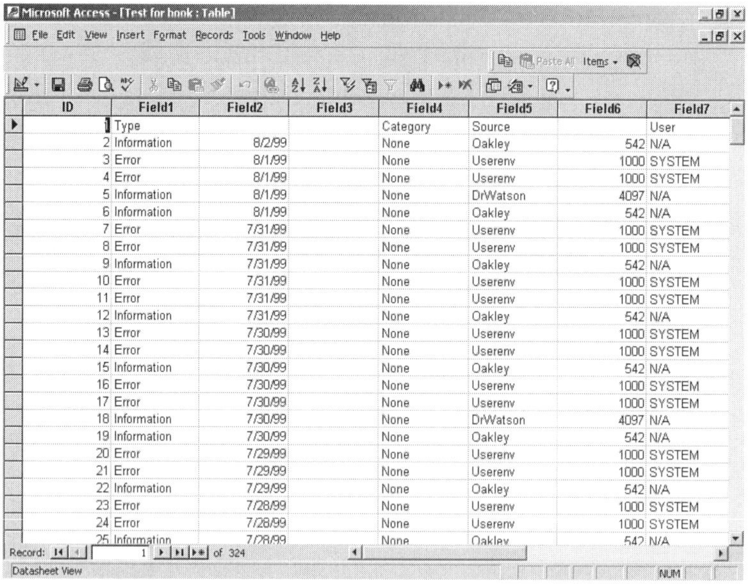

FIGURE 27.13

Microsoft Access can easily create a table containing the event log using its Import facility.

The same table queried by Access can yield statistical information, such as the number of each type of event. In Figure 27.14, I asked Access to filter for Information events and count the occurrences.

FIGURE 27.14

A Totals query in Access (or a similar facility in Excel) can give you an analysis of your event log.

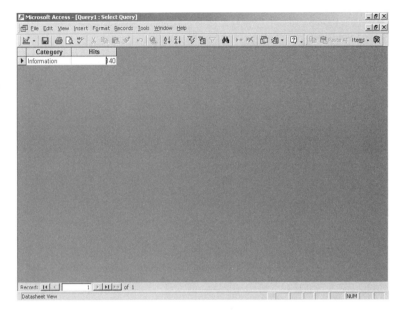

Summary

The Event Viewer application is a great place to start most troubleshooting sessions or to look for security violations. It is easy to use and can be very handy. Perhaps the biggest drawback is the quality of the messages that get posted—but this is not the Event Viewer's fault. All in all, this is a key application with which any power user must be familiar and comfortable.

Performance Monitor

The Performance Monitor

The Performance Monitor utility included with Windows 2000 is an extremely powerful and useful utility, and it is often overlooked or underused. Performance Monitor first and foremost provides a mechanism to monitor system performance on your or other networked computers in a general manner. It also provides the capability of isolating specific system components and monitoring them in minute detail to determine the root of a problem or cause of a bottleneck.

> **Note**
>
> The Windows 2000 Performance Monitor is similar to the monitor in Windows NT 4. One difference, however, is that the Windows 2000 Performance Monitor is now available as an MMC snap-in, as well as a separate menu entry in Administrative Tools.

Launching the Performance Monitor

You can start the Performance Monitor either interactively or through Administrative Tools. To launch interactively, use the menu commands Start, Run, Perfmon, or enter

```
Perfmon
```

from a CLI (command) session.

There is also a Performance entry within the Control Panel, Administrative Tools folder that, when opened, will launch the Performance Monitor.

Uses of the Performance Monitor

Using the Performance Monitor, you can perform the following tasks:

- View or change performance charts.
- Export data from Performance Monitor charts, logs, alerts, or reports to external programs such as Microsoft Access or Microsoft Excel.
- Set system alerts to either log those alerts or sound an alarm.
- Set a trigger to run a task based on system status.
- Create and append system logs for the local or other networked systems.
- View data from one or more computers.
- Save various settings or save the current global settings and then recall them as needed.

Performance Monitor has four separate components: Chart, Alert, Log, and Report. Each component monitors the performance of the specified components, but handles the data in a different manner. The following describes each of these components:

- *Chart*—The Chart utility charts the specified components at user-configurable intervals and presents the data in the form of either a graph or a histogram (bar chart).

- *Alert*—The Alert utility enables the user to specify components to monitor. The Alert utility can be configured to send an alert and/or execute a program if the counter on a specified component goes over or under a defined threshold.

- *Log*—The Log utility writes counter data to a file for components at specified intervals.

- *Report*—The Report utility generates a report based on the statistics of the specified counters.

Counters, Instances, and Objects

The Performance Monitor uses the terms objects, instances, and counters to identify its processes. An *object* is a system resource. Examples of objects are physical disks, processors, and memory. Some objects have instances that are duplicates. For example, a computer with two Pentium Pro processors has two instances of the object Processor.

A computer with only one processor has only one *instance* of that object. If a computer has four physical disks, it has that many instances of the object Physical Disk.

Counters are the statistical aspect of an object, a measurement unit as defined for a given component. For example, percentage of processor time is a statistic. It's expressed as %Processor Time in the Counter List Box of the Add to Chart dialog box shown in Figure 28.1. To open the Add Counter windows, click the toolbar button with the plus sign icon.

Only Windows 2000 native (32-bit) programs appear in the Performance Monitor. Non-compliant programs, such as Windows 16 (Win16) and programs that run in a Virtual DOS Machine (NTVDM), appear as a VDM rather than with their executable names. An exception to this rule is if they run in their own memory space, and, even then, they have their own NTVDM for each of their instances.

FIGURE 28.1

To add objects and counters to a graph, choose the computer, the object, and then the counter specific to that object. This screen shows the computer \\PAULWKS, object Processor, and counter %Processor Time.

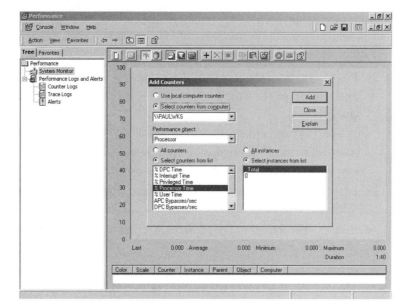

Charting

The most common use of Performance Monitor, in my experience, has been to determine the cause of poor system performance. Unfortunately for most system administrators, the time it takes to monitor system performance cannot be justified until a problem arises. If this is the case and a bottleneck exists in the system, or if the system just seems to be running poorly, the charting utility in Performance Monitor is the tool to use.

The charting utility charts the value of specified system components at any interval from 0 to 2,000,000 seconds, as defined by the user. This can give a good indication (in realtime) of where the bottleneck exists. Typically, system slowness will be in one of four areas: disk I/O, processor resources, memory resources, or the network component (if installed).

To monitor a given component, Performance Monitor uses counters. Most Windows 2000 components have counters that can be monitored, although some must be installed manually. (To monitor TCP/IP performance, for instance, the SNMP feature of TCP/IP must be installed.)

To begin monitoring, you must specify the object you want to monitor, the specific counters you want to monitor for that object (see Figure 28.1), and, if applicable, an instance of the selected object. To add objects and counters to a graph, click the Add to Chart option from the toolbar (plus sign icon). Each object counter can be customized in color, scale, line width, and style through the Add to Chart dialog box.

Typically, a good starting point for determining the area of the system causing the bottleneck is to use a general configuration, such as Total Processor Time, Memory Page Faults, Memory Bytes Available, and Paging File Usage. You'll need to scroll through the Objects combo box to find Memory objects.

If you have any questions about what a particular counter does, click the Explain button. This will expand the dialog box to include a brief explanation of each counter. Figure 28.2 shows the Performance Monitor in operation after adding the counter shown in Figure 28.1.

FIGURE 28.2

This is the Performance Monitor in operation after adding the counter shown in Figure 28.1.

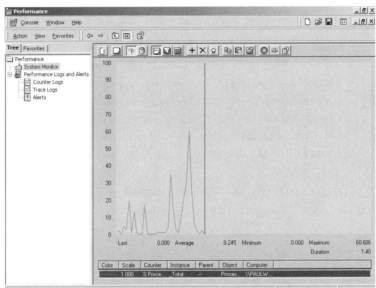

After you determine, usually through trial and error, which system component is the cause of the bottleneck, you can customize your monitoring to drill down to the details of that subsystem and determine how to relieve the bottleneck. This does not always require a hardware upgrade; sometimes it is as simple as reconfiguring a system component, changing the paging file size, or tuning the working environment.

Other options are available for customizing the chart that are also available for the Alert, Log, and Report functions. To see these options, choose View, Customize from the menu bar. Most of the operational aspects of the Performance Monitor are available from the toolbar right above the chart window.

28

PERFORMANCE MONITOR

The following list describes each option:

- *New Counter Set*—Removes all active counters and also clears the display.
- *Clear Display*—Clears (resets) the display, but does not remove the counters.
- *View Current Activity*—Displays the chart of the current counters (toggle with View Log Files).
- *View Log Files*—Displays saved log files (toggle with View Current Activity).
- *View Chart*—Displays view as a line chart.
- *View Histogram*—Displays view as histogram (bar chart).
- *View Report*—Displays view in report format (aggregates).
- *Add*—Adds a counter.
- *Delete*—Deletes a counter.
- *Highlight*—Highlights the selected counter. To use this extremely handy facility, click the counter you want to highlight in the window below the chart window. Click Highlight and Performance Monitor will highlight the selected counter. This is extremely valuable when many counters are going at the same time, and you want to rotate through them.
- *Copy Properties*—Copies properties to clipboard in HTML format. Use this to copy counter properties from one instance of Performance to another.
- *Paste Properties*—Pastes copied properties (see Copy Properties).
- *Properties*—Opens the Properties dialog box (a tabbed box) for a set of counters or consoles.
- *Freeze display*—Freezes chart area from clearing and from accepting any more updates. Very handy for studying the relationships between counters at your leisure.
- *Update data*—Forces update to chart during a freeze. This is analogous to single stepping in a debugger.
- *Help*—Launches Performance Monitor's help system.

Alerts

For those times when you are not actively trying to pinpoint a system performance problem, you can do other things to monitor ongoing system performance. Performance Monitor can alert you to potential bottlenecks before they become critical, giving you time to respond appropriately.

A useful utility for this purpose is the Alert feature of Performance Monitor. Using this feature, you can specify object counters in the same way you did previously with the

Chart. For each object counter you want to monitor, you specify a threshold value for which an alert will be generated if that threshold is crossed.

When a threshold value is exceeded (or falls below the value), a record is written to the Alerts window in Performance Monitor (see Figure 28.3). Optionally, a program can be configured to run, an alert can be configured to be sent across the network to a specified individual or computer, or the occurrence can be written to the Windows 2000 Event Viewer Application Log.

FIGURE 28.3

The Alerts window in Performance Monitor shows when monitored system events exceed your set limits.

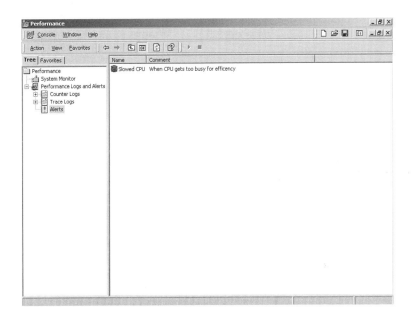

In the example shown in Figure 28.3, the Performance Monitor has been asked to create an alert if the processor works more than 20%. This isn't obvious in this screen shot because the details of the Alert aren't displayed. Instead, Windows 2000 only shows a user-defined description. In the next section, you'll see how to set an Alert and how to examine/edit existing ones.

The Alert utility provides a good method for monitoring system performance over long time periods while under normal usage, providing a clear picture of how the system holds up under real-world usage over a period of time.

This can be helpful for situations such as monitoring a system throughout the course of a typical workday to determine when and why a specified object is pushed beyond its limits.

28

PERFORMANCE MONITOR

How to Set an Alert

Start the Performance Monitor. Locate the Performance Logs and Alerts entry in the left pane of the application. Double click this entry to open the tree and reveal the Alerts entry. Your screen should resemble the left pane of Figure 28.3. Click the word Alerts to highlight it.

Right-click in the right pane of the Monitor to reveal the context menu. Choose the first entry, New Alert Settings. Give your new Alert a name and then click OK. I've given this Alert the name Disk Overload, as you can see in the screen shown in Figure 28.4 (look in the Title bar). After clicking OK, Windows will bring up the Disk Overloads dialog box.

FIGURE 28.4

This tabbed dialog box is all you need to set up an Alert system for any Windows 2000 computer.

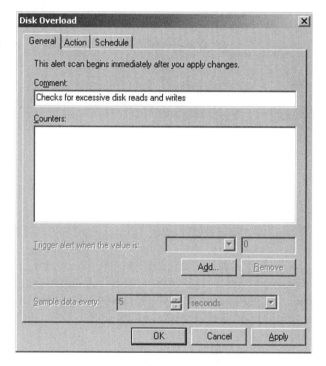

The key to an Alert is on the Action tab (see Figure 28.5). First set the objects, counters, and values on the General tab. Then set what to do when the conditions (values) are met on the Action tab. This figure shows the Action tab with a counter set on the General tab. You can set more than one counter for an Alert. For example, you can set an Alert to trigger when a CPU is busy more than a specified percentage of time or when the disk queue meets certain criteria.

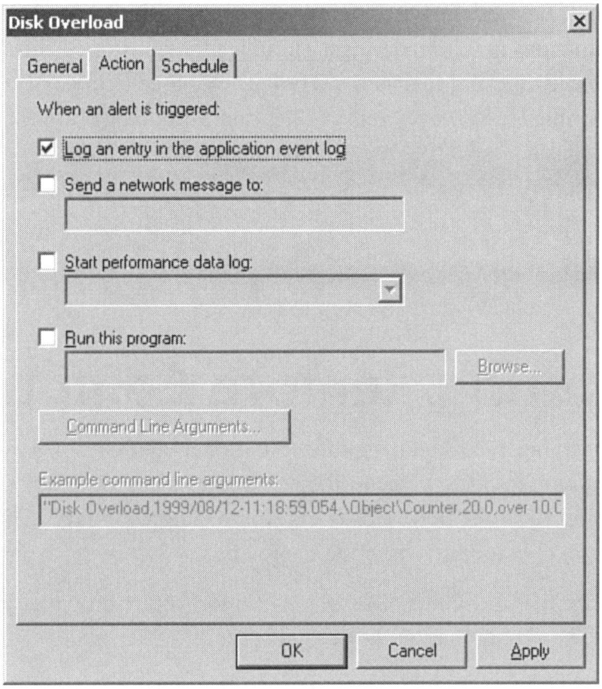

FIGURE 28.5

Here is the other part of an Alert— the action or actions to take.

Tip

I personally tend to prefer writing Alert events to the Event log where I can view or export them later. I generally dislike being notified in realtime because I find that disruptive.

You can also tell the Alert to run a program with optional parameters when a condition is met.

The real trick in setting an Alert is to set the value to something meaningful. This is an art form to a great extent. For example, you might want to set an Alert for a low threshold value (like CPU usage over a meager 60 percent), log it to the Event log, see how a computer performs, and then experiment with moving the threshold and load up until you learn where the real threshold for performance is. Your setting probably will not be 60 percent; this was just used as an example. You'll need to experiment with your system and applications to know which setting is best for your case.

I use my CPU cycles very heavily when I do graphical applications, such as rendering full frame animations or 3D renderings. These applications often cause my CPU to work 100 percent of the time and lengthen the processor queue to the extent that I see degraded performance. However, most of the time I'm doing nothing more than standard office applications and my CPU spends most of its time snoozing. For those times, I'd be better off monitoring disk queue lengths (I do a lot of database work) instead of CPU anything.

The Schedule tab of the Disk Overloads dialog box will allow you to use Scheduler to automatically or manually start and stop the Alert monitor.

Monitoring Remote Computers

You can monitor the objects on computers other than your console (workstation) at the same time you monitor local objects. To add another computer's objects to the Add to Chart dialog box, click the Select Counters from Computer button. Then select the computer you want to monitor from the combo box.

If you only want to use counters for the workstation you're on, you can simplify things by clicking the top option button, Local Computer.

Once you've located the network computer whose objects you want to monitor, add those objects, instances, and counters just as you would for a local computer.

Trace and Counter Logging

The logging utility in Performance Monitor is best used as a tool to gather system performance data over an extended period of time to export to another application for analysis. A log is a file containing, in this case, Performance Monitor information. A Counter log writes at specific intervals (similar to a chart counter). A Trace log writes only when certain events occur (such as an Alert).

Adding objects to the log is fairly similar to setting a counter or an Alert. The following is the general procedure for adding objects to the log:

1. Open up Performance Logs and Alerts by double clicking it to expand the tree (if necessary).
2. Click the log type you want to create or edit. All such logs will appear in the right pane.
3. Right click anywhere away from an object in the right pane.
4. Choose New Log Settings from the context menu and fill in the blanks.

As mentioned earlier, this utility is designed to monitor performance data over an extended period of time. It is recommended that the log interval not be set at less than 15-second intervals, because the log file grows extremely fast and quickly becomes difficult to effectively parse and analyze.

When the log period is complete, the log file can be exported to a text-format, comma-delimited file for use in other applications, such as Microsoft Access, or it can be imported into the Performance Monitor chart utility for interpretation.

Figure 28.6 shows the creation of a new log.

FIGURE 28.6

You add counters (but not values) to a counter log and then specify the log file in the Log File tab.

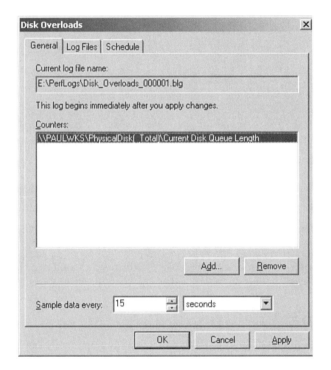

Figure 28.7 shows a counter log for total disk queue. Note that it is in the form of a report because this is a snapshot of your system at a particular interval. In this case, I asked the log to record the total disk queue for disk 0 (first physical disk) every eight seconds. Note how the queue varies up from zero (0). Many folks, including myself, find such a log file much more usable than the ever-moving chart counters.

28

PERFORMANCE
MONITOR

FIGURE 28.7

Here a disk queue counter log file reports a varying load situation.

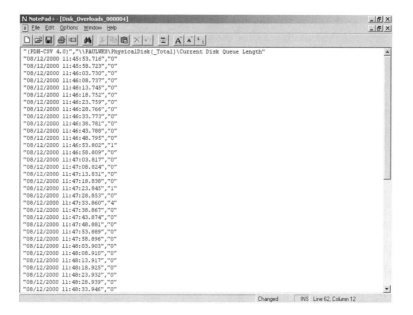

Reporting

The report view window in Performance Monitor is a very straightforward view of selected objects and counters. The selected counters and statistics are displayed in a report format similar to a spreadsheet report, providing a quick view of current activity and performance.

Figure 28.8 shows the report window of the Performance Monitor gathering information about three objects and one each of their counters.

Additional Features

You can save pretty much any setting using names and optionally putting them in Favorite Places. Favorite Places used here doesn't make a whole lot of sense as this is a transplant from a browser's use of Favorite Places on the World Wide Web. My guess is that Microsoft used this for consistency in its new Web orientation rather than logical thought process.

Remember, almost everything in Performance Monitor has properties. Right-click any right pane object and you'll be presented with the familiar context menu with a Properties entry. These dialog boxes are all the common tabbed variety, even though some only have a single tab. These dialog boxes, many of which are redundant, have self-explanatory entries for fine-tuning the Performance Monitor to your needs.

FIGURE **28.8**

The report data window is a simple display showing, in this case, three counters and their momentary values.

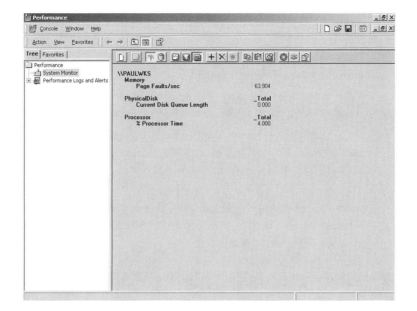

Weighty Counters

Chapter 7, "Tuning Windows 2000 Performance," provides some counter settings to watch, so you may want to cross reference this list with the list there. Here are the most important counters and their thresholds. *Thresholds* are values that impede performance when exceeded. Note that these are just general and rough guidelines to setting counters. Your most sensitive counters and their threshold values will vary with your specific applications and setup.

Take two examples as illustrations of how you must use your common sense in deciding how to monitor. First, let's take applications: A typical office computer can use a higher amount of CPU cycles before adversely affecting its performance than a graphical workstation. Second, consider hardware. A minimal Windows 2000 Professional workstation with 64MB RAM will be in dire straits when its available physical RAM drops below 20 percent. A similarly used workstation with 1GB of RAM won't be. In fact, in that example, the latter machine is in better shape with 20 percent available RAM than the first machine before it boots up.

Common sense is the rule that you must first use. That said, the following are some rules of thumb:

- Total Processor Time (load) should not exceed 80 percent for more than a few peaks.

28

PERFORMANCE
MONITOR

- Total Processor Queue Length shouldn't exceed 3 for more than a few milliseconds at a time.

- Percentage of Disk Time should not exceed 40 percent. Even 40 percent will noticeably slow down the system.

- Committed Bytes (memory) should not exceed or not greatly exceed Physical RAM except in short peaks. You can see a quick view of this in Task Manager.

- Pages/sec (memory)—the fewer of these the better. This is a disk read to resolve a hard page fault. Once they exceed 10, your system is being hit significantly. If they go up to 25 with any regularity, run, don't walk, to upgrade your physical RAM.

- Total Interrupts/sec—the fewer the better, but there is little you can do to alter this other than unloading unneeded services. And really, you don't load unneeded services anyway, do you? Anyway, if they exceed about a dozen a second, your system is being degraded.

> **Note**
>
> Performance Monitor Help has several other suggestions for counters and counter combinations to tune performance.

Summary

As you have seen here, Performance Monitor is a unique, extensive application that can provide invaluable information about system performance and ways to improve it. This tool should be well understood and utilized by any Windows 2000 system administrator or person responsible for supporting Windows 2000. It can save time and headaches if it is understood and utilized on a regular basis.

Task Manager

CHAPTER

29

How often have you posed the following questions: "How well is my computer perform-ing?" "Should I upgrade the spec of it?" Up until Windows 2000 (or previous Windows NT technology systems), it was always difficult to back up your decision with facts. Sure, you could always use the Performance Monitor. The Performance Monitor itself is a powerful tool that encompasses performance measurements based on a wide range of criteria. The Performance Monitor can build a performance trend on your workstation or on any other 2000 servers or workstations simultaneously. The downside to the Performance Monitor, however, is that it requires setup, careful definition of your moni-toring criteria, and time to build a trend on which you would base a final decision. On the other hand, the Task Manager concentrates on monitoring your applications and processes.

> **Note**
>
> Chapter 28, "Performance Monitor," covers the Performance Monitor in detail.

The Task Manager allows you to view the applications and processes that are running on your system and also lets you see what impact they have on your workstation. The Task Manager is ideally suited for quick checks on your system and provides only basic coun-ters. You should use the Task Manager as a precursor to the Performance Monitor. Armed with the Task Manager, you can rectify the obvious problems without having to go through the rigors of the Performance Monitor. Tougher, more obscure problems that you cannot pinpoint with the Task Manager, have to be weeded out by the Performance Manager. The Task Manager cannot monitor other workstations or servers, nor can it store data for later review.

Starting the Task Manager

You do not have to install the Task Manager because it comes preinstalled by default. There are a number of different ways to access the Task Manager:

- You can press a combination of the Ctrl+Shift+Esc keys.
- You can right-click the Taskbar at the base of your screen and select Task Manager from the menu (see Figure 29.1).
- You can press a combination of the Ctrl+Alt+Del keys to activate the Windows 2000 Security dialog box. Click the Task Manager from the resulting dialog box.
- You can simply type **taskmgr** from the Start, Run menu selection (see Figure 29.2).

FIGURE 29.1

The Taskbar context menu has an entry for the Task Manager.

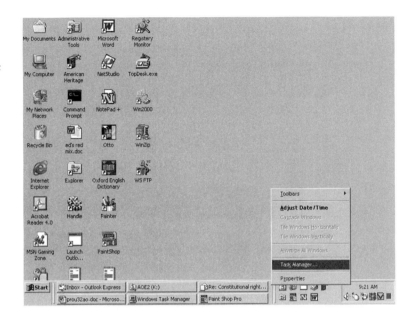

FIGURE 29.2

Accessing the Task Manager from the Run option.

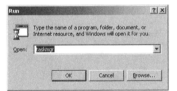

Applications

After you start the Task Manager, you are presented with the Windows 2000 Task Manager dialog box. The Task Manager is divided into three tabs: Applications, Processes, and Performance (see Figure 29.3).

The Applications tab lists the applications currently running on the workstation. The list has two columns: Task, which lists the applications, and Status, which reflects the status of the application.

You will notice three buttons located at the base of the Applications tab:

- The End Task button allows you to terminate the application that is currently selected in the Task list. This is similar to the `kill` command in UNIX.

- The Switch To button allows you to switch to the application that is currently selected.

29

TASK MANAGER

FIGURE 29.3

The Windows Task Manager with the Applications tab selected.

• The New Task button allows you to launch a new application. When clicked, the New Task button launches the Create New Task dialog box (see Figure 29.4). You can browse to the application you want using the Browse button.

FIGURE 29.4

The Create New Task dialog box.

> **Note**
>
> The select list within the Create New Task dialog box is the same history list of tasks that have been run from the Start, Run dialog box.

Right-clicking any of the running applications from the Applications tab will bring up a context menu, as shown in Figure 29.5.

This menu includes the following options:

• *Switch To*—This option allows you to switch to the selected application and make it the active application. The Task Manager minimizes to make way for the active application. You can also execute a switch-to operation by double-clicking an application from the list.

• *Bring to Front*—This brings the currently selected application to the foreground. It differs from the Switch To option in that the Bring to Front option does not make the application the active application because the Task Manager remains maximized and active.

FIGURE 29.5

The context menu of an application within the Applications tab of the Task Manager.

- *Minimize*—This option minimizes the currently selected application.
- *Maximize*—This options maximizes the currently selected application.
- *Cascade (only active when more than one task is selected)*—Arrays the selected tasks in a cascaded fashion.
- *Tile Horizontally (only active when more than one task is selected)*—Fills the screen with the selected tasks arrayed horizontally.
- *Tile Vertically (only active when more than one task is selected)*—Fills the screen with the selected tasks arrayed vertically.
- *End Task*—This button allows you to terminate the currently selected application.
- *Go To Process*—This option allows you to switch to the Processes tab with the selected application's process highlighted. The Processes tab is explained further in the "Processes" section later in this chapter.

The entries for Cascade, Tile Vertically, and Tile Horizontally, are active only if you highlight more than one application. For example, if you want to Tile Horizontally only two of a dozen running applications, highlight them both (Ctrl+Click) or a series of contiguous applications (Shift+Click) and then right click any highlighted file(s) and choose Tile Horizontally. Figure 29.6 shows the results of tiling two applications.

29

TASK MANAGER

Note

The display in Figure 29.6 looks confused when printed in the book. It is a combination of a Word 2000 document and Outlook Express 2000. It is clear and usable on a computer, even if it looks like a jumble here.

FIGURE 29.6

You can choose to tile or cascade a subset of the running applications.

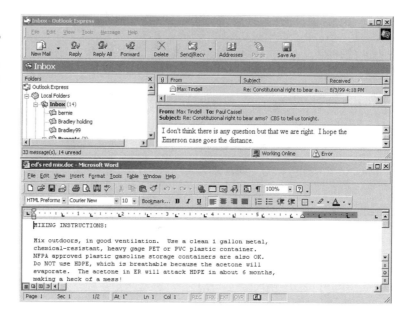

Right-clicking any area other than an application brings up a menu with the following options (see Figure 29.7):

FIGURE 29.7

The context menu of the application area.

- *New Task (Run)*—This option launches a new application using the same Create New Task dialog box described previously. The Create New Task dialog box can also be invoked by selecting New Task from the File menu.

- *Large Icons*—This option configures the associated application icons to be large. The applications are arranged one after another with large icons.

- *Small Icons*—This option configures the associated application icons to be small. The applications are arranged one after another with small icons.

- *Details*—The Details option is the default view that arranges the applications in a list with the two columns: Tasks and Status.

All the column widths can be resized as follows:

1. Simply move the mouse pointer over the split in the column headers until its shape changes (see Figure 29.8).

2. Hold down the left mouse button and drag the column split left or right to suit your needs.

FIGURE 29.8

Resizing the Task Manager columns.

Double-clicking the tab border outside the tabbed area will enable or disable the status and menu bars and the tab headers. Disabling these window elements will produce a nice compact view of the Applications tab (see Figure 29.9). Doubling-clicking the display border will restore the original view.

The Options menu at the top of the Task Manager allows you to set the following preferences:

- *Always On Top*—This option will keep the Task Manager on top—that is, the Task Manager will always be visible, even though it is not the active application.

- *Minimize On Use*—This option sets the Task Manager to minimize when you switch to another application.

- *Hide When Minimized*—This option removes Task Manager from the Taskbar. You can restore Task Manager by double-clicking it on the Tray (see Figure 29.10). As you can see from this figure, the Task Manager icon in the Tray also displays the CPU Usage when you bring the mouse pointer over it.

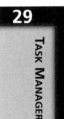

FIGURE 29.9

Disabling the status bar, menu bar, and tab header.

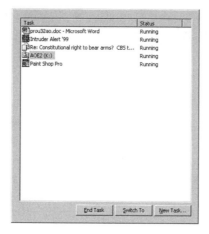

FIGURE 29.10

The Task Manager icon in the Tray.

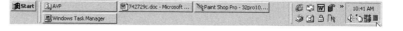

The View menu has the following preference settings:

- *Refresh Now*—This option forces Task Manager to refresh its display.

- *Update Speed*—This option allows you to set the rate at which Task Manager will refresh its data. The sample rates are Normal (default) High, Low, and Paused. Paused stops the sample for the Task Manager.

- *Large Icons, Small Icons, Details*—These options allow you to choose how the applications appear within the list. Each of these options was explained previously.

The Windows menu allows you to set the following options:

- *Tile Horizontally*—This option allows you to tile the running applications horizontally.

- *Tile Vertically*—This option allows you to tile the running applications vertically.

- *Cascade*—This option allows you to arrange the running application in a cascade of windows that looks somewhat similar to a spread out deck of cards.

- *Minimize*—This option allows you to minimize the currently selected application.

- *Maximize*—This option allows you to maximize the currently selected application.

- *Bring To Front*—This option brings the currently selected option to the front.

Processes

Selecting the Processes tab brings up a list of processes (see Figure 29.11).

FIGURE 29.11

The Processes tab.

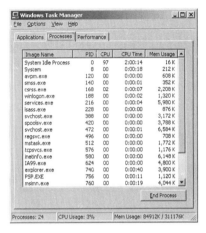

The Processes tab window can display up to 23 columns of data. By default, there are five columns displayed when you first select the Processes tab. Each of these columns is associated with a Performance Monitor Process Counter. The following is a list of the column headers and their associated Performance Monitor Process Counters; the first five are displayed by default:

- *Image Name*—The name of the process. This corresponds to the process name in the instance box of the Performance Monitor.

- *PID (Process Identifier)*—A numerical value given to the process while it is running. This corresponds to the Performance Monitor Process Counter, ID Process.

- *CPU Usage*—The percentage of time the process used the processor since the last update was taken. This corresponds to the Performance Monitor Process Counter, %Processor Time.

- *CPU Time*—The processor time the process has used since starting.

- *Memory Usage*—The amount of main memory used by the process in kilobytes. This also corresponds to the Performance Monitor Process Counter, Working set.

- *Memory Usage Delta*—The change in memory since the last update. This can also reflect negative values.

- *Peak Memory Usage*—The maximum amount of memory used since the Task Manager started.

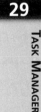

29

TASK MANAGER

- *Page Faults*—The number of page faults attributed to this process since it started. A page fault occurs when a process requires data not in its current working set. A *soft page fault* is when a process needs to go outside of its working set to RAM memory. A *hard page fault* is when the data is outside of the working set and RAM and requires a disk read. Combining a Page Fault monitor with an I/O read monitor will give you an idea of how many hard faults your system is enduring. A system normally can tolerate many soft Page Faults, but hard ones slow things down quite a bit.

- *User Objects*—Number of Windows Manager (internal objects like windows) active for the process.

- *I/O Reads*—Number of non-console reads recorded for the process. A *non-console read* is input from outside of the user-operated part of the computer.

- *I/O Read Bytes*—Amount in bytes of non-console reads.

- *Page Faults Delta*—The change in the number of page faults since the last update.

- *Virtual Memory Size*—What amount of the pagefile this process occupies. This also corresponds to the Performance Monitor Process Counter, Page File Bytes.

- *Paged Pool*—The amount of the paged pool occupied by the process. This also corresponds to the Performance Monitor Process Counter, Pool Paged Bytes. A *paged pool* is data that is queued up for writing to disk in the paging file. That is, it is the first data to be committed from physical to virtual memory when the system needs to free up some physical memory.

- *Nonpaged Pool*—The amount of nonpaged pool occupied by the process. This also corresponds to the Performance Monitor Process Counter, Pool Nonpaged Bytes.

- *Base Priority*—The priority of the process's threads. This also corresponds to the Performance Monitor Process Counter, Priority Base.

- *Handle Count*—The number of object handles in the process's object table. This also corresponds to the Performance Monitor Process Counter, Handle Count.

- *Thread Count*—The number of threads running under the process. This also corresponds to the Performance Monitor Process Counter, Thread Count.

- *GDI Objects*—Number of objects for graphical output devices active.

- *I/O Writes*—Input or output writes operations for a process.

- *I/O Write Bytes*—Amount in bytes of input or output operations for a process.

- *I/O Other*—Non-console miscellaneous input or output operations, such as network I/O for a process.

- *I/O Other Bytes*—Amount in bytes of non-console miscellaneous input or output operations, such as network I/O for a process.

The End Process button at the base of the Processes tab allows you to terminate the currently selected process. Different options appear under the menu headings when the Processes tab is selected.

Under the Options menu there is an extra option called Show 16-Bit Tasks. When checked, this menu option displays 16-bit processes in addition to the standard 32-bit ones on the Process list.

Under the View menu, the final three options (Large Icons, Small Icons, and Detail) are replaced by Select Columns. This option allows you to choose which columns appear in the list. I mentioned previously that, by default, five columns appear on the process list. Under Select Columns, you can enable any of the fourteen columns to appear. When you choose this option, you are presented with the Select Columns dialog box shown in Figure 29.12. The column headers are included by simply checking their associated check box.

FIGURE 29.12

The Select Columns dialog box.

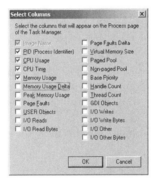

Clicking any of the column headers from the Processes tab will sort the list in ascending or descending order. If you right-click a process from the process list, you can do the following:

- *End Process*—Terminate the selected process.
- *End Process Tree*—This ends the selected process and all related processes.
- *Debug*—Debug the selected process (enabled only if you have a debugger installed).
- *Set Priority*—Choose the priority under which the selected process's threads will run. This change is not permanent, however. The process threads will have the same priority, as set by the application code, the next time they run. There are four different priority levels to choose from: High, Medium, Low, and Realtime.

Again, as with the Applications tab, if you double-click the border of the tab, the status bar, menu bar, and tab header disappear.

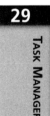

29

TASK MANAGER

Performance

The last tab on the Task Manager is the Performance tab. The Performance tab gives you an at-a-glance estimate of your workstation's performance (see Figure 29.13).

FIGURE 29.13

The Performance tab.

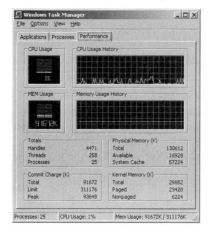

There are eight frames on the Performance tab:

- *CPU Usage*—This is a graphical indicator that illustrates the CPU usage.
- *CPU Usage History*—Again a graphical indicator, this illustrates the CPU usage over time.
- *MEM Usage*—This frame graphically illustrates the memory usage of the workstation.
- *Memory Usage History*—This frame graphically records the memory usage over time.
- *Totals*—This frame keeps a running total on the number of handles, threads, and processes.
- *Physical Memory (K)*—This frame records the total, file cache, and available memory on the workstation.
- *Commit Charge (K)*—This frame records details on the Commit memory. Commit memory is memory allocated to programs and/or the system. Detail figures include total, limit, and peak values.
- *Kernel Memory (K)*—This frame records memory allocated to the operating system. Details include total, paged, and nonpaged.

Double-clicking anywhere on the Performance tab will maximize the CPU Usage and CPU Usage History (see Figure 29.14). Double-clicking the border of the view you see in Figure 29.14 will restore the original view (toggle).

FIGURE 29.14

Double-clicking will maximize the graphic frames.

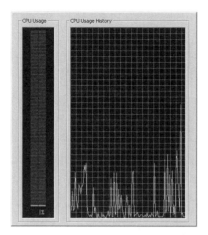

Again, as with the two previous tabs, there are extra options in the menus pertaining to the Performance tab. Under the View menu, there are two entries—CPU History and Show Kernel Times—that appear at the base of the menu when the Performance tab is selected. CPU History applies to multiprocessor machines and allows you to get a disparate graph for each CPU. Show Kernel Times, when selected, adds a graph line representing the memory usage by the kernel.

As you select each of the tabs, the Status Bar remains constant at the base of the Task Manager. The Status Bar displays the number of processes, the CPU Usage, and the Memory Usage counters.

Summary

In this chapter, you got a detailed look at the Task Manager and saw how you could use it to help evaluate your computer's performance. The Task Manager requires no setup or configuration and is installed by default on your workstation.

The Task Manager is an excellent alternative to the Performance Monitor because it's much simpler and easier to use. It allows you to monitor applications and processes and determine possible system bottlenecks. Through the Task Manager, you can launch, switch between, and close applications and processes. You also can monitor the impact an application or process has on your workstation.

Perhaps the most common use of the Task Manager is to kill applications in an error condition, such as those that stop responding to the system due to an internal fault. This is likely due to most people not knowing how much information the Task Manager can display.

Windows 2000 Diagnostics

Windows 2000 System Information is a modern version of the old MSD.exe utility that has been given a revamped look and a great deal of enhancement. Windows 2000 System Information, as the name suggests, is a tool used to aid with the diagnostics of your workstation. In its current version, Windows 2000 diagnostics is a useful and powerful tool that can help you troubleshoot many Windows 2000 system problems.

Accessing Windows 2000 System Information

To start the Windows 2000 System Information (diagnostics), choose Administrative Tools in the Control Panel, double-click the Computer Management entry, and then click the System Information entry (see Figure 30.1).

FIGURE 30.1

Accessing Windows 2000 System Information through the Computer Management MMC.

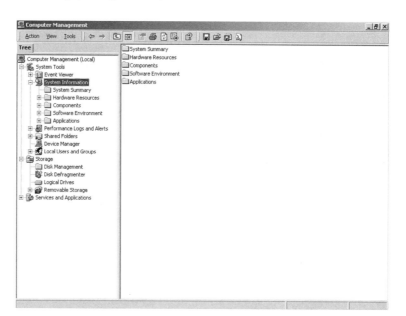

Alternatively, you can type `winmsd.exe` from the Run option (see Figure 30.2). This will bring up the MMC with only one snap-in loaded—System Information. If you prefer this view, you can create a shortcut to it.

You can run the Windows 2000 System Information for a local computer or any networked computer for which you have permissions. Figure 30.3 shows a dialog box allowing you to specify which computer to use for System Information. To get this dialog box, right click System Summary (in the left pane) and choose Properties from the context menu.

FIGURE 30.2

Accessing Windows 2000 System Information through the Run option.

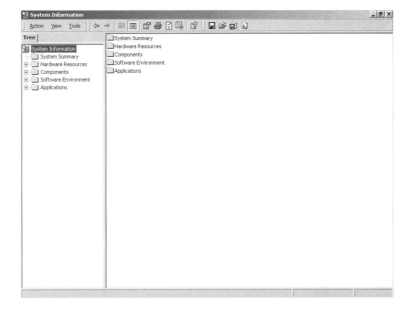

FIGURE 30.3

If you have permission, you can view system information for any networked computer.

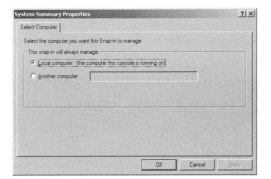

Using System Information

In theory, you won't ever need System Information. The purpose of this program when it was in its MS-DOS MSD.EXE days was to analyze system conflicts or versioning problems. A conflict comes about when two or more objects (usually hardware) try to use the same resource in such a way as to interfere with each another. Only one can win the struggle, which either leaves the other one non-functional or causes the entire system to malfunction.

The resource problem stems from the initial design of IBM-style PCs (Wintel machines). The added function of multimedia and the various hardware extensions weren't

30

WINDOWS 2000 DIAGNOSTICS

envisioned by the designers who saw these machines as small utility boxes to handle inconsequential tasks, while the real computing was done by mainframes.

Today this small box is the mainstay of corporate computing, but it still carries the heritage of its origins. Most peripherals and internal resources require both an interrupt request number and some address space. There are only a few of these available even when a computer comes from the factory, so adding hardware can be a bothersome task to say the least. In Windows NT4, it could be impossible to find the resources needed.

Windows 95, to some extent, and now Windows 2000 and later Windows 98 solved this through a dual initiative of hardware and software. Plug and Play (PnP) mediates compliant hardware (and tries with non-compliant hardware as well), while the relatively new schemes, such as IEEE1394 (FireWire) and Universal Serial Bus (USB), add to Small Computer System Interface (SCSI) to solve the limited resource problem.

In the vast majority of cases, system problems stem from the following:

- Using dated legacy hardware that insists on using a resource demanded by other resources
- Defective hardware
- Defective PnP firmware that won't properly mediate PnP devices
- An extremely poorly written program that "gets away" from Windows 2000

Now, here is the rub. While System Information is much improved over the System Diagnostics in Windows NT 4 and vastly ahead of the old MSD.EXE, it really won't do much, if anything, for those four conditions. The following are the solutions, respectively:

- Get new hardware or remove the hardware with which the recalcitrant hardware insists on interfering.
- Replace.
- Update the firmware if possible. If not, replace the mainboard or learn to live with it—making sure you don't buy from that vendor again.
- Don't run that program or run nothing but that program to avoid data loss from other programs. This is another item that in theory can't occur, but it does.

System Information can yield interesting application information for compliant programs, but again it's really information that you'd garner anyway when running the programs. In the end, System Information is a dweeb's delight—I personally enjoy browsing through it—but its time has passed.

I'll take you through a few areas of the System Information that aren't obvious by inspection.

Organization

System Information is organized in the familiar pane presentation with summary folders in the left pane and details in the right. By default you'll see five folders on the left. They are

- *System Summary*—An overall view of what your computer holds and versioning information.
- *Hardware Resources*—Here is the nub of the old diagnostics, showing your hardware devices and the resources they use.
- *Components*—This is Microsoft's definition of your computer's input/output capacities.
- *Software Environment*—This shows items such as running applications and services, driver information, and other non-hardware or firmware information. Some of the Task Manager's information duplicates here for easy access.
- *Internet Explorer[version]*—Information about your built-in browser including file locations, add-ins, security, and options.
- *Applications*—Installation and related information for compliant programs.

Advanced Items

By default, System Information will open in a basic view. You can change to Advanced view (more detail in some areas) using the View menu. You can also customize the display of System Information using View, Customize.

System Summary

The System Summary information is for the most part, either obvious or duplicated elsewhere, such as in the Task Manager or, if you set the right counters, Performance Monitor. It does contain several unique and vital pieces of information such as the version of the CPU, its speed, and the version of the main firmware (BIOS). The latter is important when you hit PnP snags because you can assist your vendor in finding out what's up by telling him what firmware you're using that causes the problem. Most vendors expect some problems down the line and have the ability to upgrade your firmware to something that has a different set of problems.

From time to time, problems arise in the actual CPU, such as the famous floating point error in the original Pentium that caused such a fuss many years ago. The versioning information in this display will tell you if you have a copy of a problem processor.

30

WINDOWS 2000
DIAGNOSTICS

Hardware Resources

Arguably this is dweeb heaven. It was the main reason for having a diagnostic of this sort back before PnP became the norm for PC hardware. The areas of interest, even in a well-running system, are the Forced Hardware and Conflicts folders. There should be no conflicts showing, even though there are conflicts in every system.

The older diagnostics from Windows NT 4 had a more comprehensive Advanced view showing all items including system reserved IRQs. I suppose this caused some sort of grief to uninformed users because this is out now. If you look at the IRQ listing in Figure 30.4, you'll get the impression that this system is ripe for adding devices with IRQ numbers such as 2, 7, 8 and 13. Not so. These are really in use, but in use by what System Information believes are system facilities, and it refuses to show you this.

FIGURE 30.4

Free IRQs? You'd be right to think so based on this display, but they are really in use.

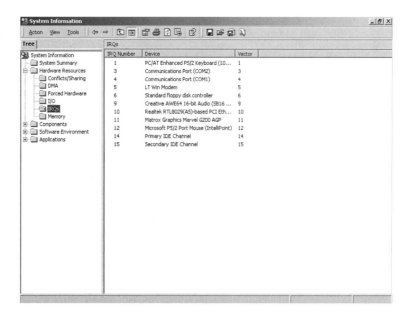

In many cases, you can force a device to a used IRQ without any ill effects. IRQ 7, the traditional place for printers, is a place that usually can do without an IRQ, so you can move this device off this area using Device Manager (see the section titled "Device Manger" later in this chapter) and then re-use it.

You do need to know what you're about before trying any of these IRQ or other resource tricks because a mistake can make your system unbootable or unstable. I, for example, use my art pad on the same IRQ as my modem (neither is PnP, but they're mine), but I know that they can't be used together. If I try to use the art pad when the modem is in use, the modem will fail to run (art pad wins!) until I do a cold reset.

The Forced Hardware section shows any non-PnP devices currently sitting on resources they won't give up. Forcing hardware is a desperate move, and I can't recommend it given the expensive nature of replacement hardware (for the most part) and the cost of your time to fix your or a user's machine when this causes some hard conflict.

The I/O area shows addresses for installed hardware. Vendors often call these *port addresses*. They are in hexadecimal (Base16) notation with A, B, C, D, E, F, representing Base10 10, 11, 12, 13, 14, 15, respectively. Here is a good place to look for a free address space if you are about to force a hardware assignment. Remember that most hardware needing some address space also needs an IRQ, which isn't nearly as easy to find.

The Memory folder shows the use of memory in the reserved system space above the traditional TPA (DOS memory). Now that DOS and real mode are things of the past, this display isn't too useful. It once was vital when we had to figure out how to address additional hardware in the 384KB above TPA. Those days are gone, and I'm glad too.

Components

There are a few areas here that are informative and many areas where, in Advanced view, you'll really get a lot of pointless detail. It's interesting to view the information on something that you think of as simple, such as a serial port, to see just how complex a modern computer is. Figure 30.5 shows such a display.

FIGURE 30.5

There is a surprising load of Advanced information on the humble serial port.

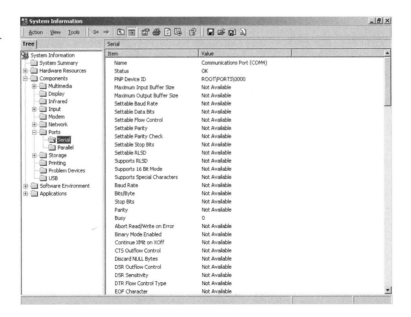

Some support personnel might find a nib of worthwhile information here, but, for the most part, it's just details. Try toggling the view from View, Basic to View, Advanced with a serial port to get an eyeful.

I find the most useful area of Components is under Multimedia, Codecs, and then the folder with the `codec` (coder/decoder) class you're interested in. A codec is a middleware-type layer that translates multimedia files to and from their compressed state. If you're having trouble playing a multimedia file and know the name of the codec you should have or the vendor, check here to make sure it exists. There are codecs for both audio and video multimedia files.

Storage sounds useful, but is composed mostly of details having dubious value. A much more useful display of your storage is under Disk Management. You can also do something to change things in Disk Management where you can't in the Display Only System Information.

> **Note**
>
> You can launch other areas of diagnostics (like the DirectX Diagnostics tool) from the Tools, Window menu.

The Problem Devices area shows I/O devices that Windows 2000 Professional thinks have problems. Figure 30.6 shows this display for one computer.

FIGURE 30.6

Here Windows 2000 shows I/O devices it thinks have problems, including those with problems Windows 2000 created.

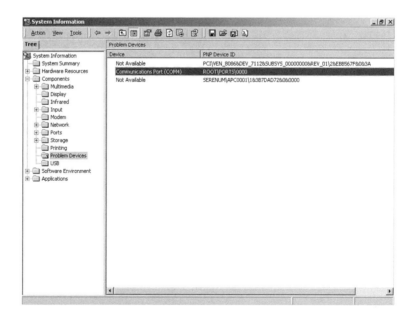

The chuckle here is that Windows 2000 has created this problem itself by some oddity of PnP. In this case, PnP generated a phantom communications port, called it COM4, and then found it wasn't working well. This is one of those areas where it makes no sense to worry about this phantom because there are no functional problems in any I/O aspect of this computer. The other two areas are vague PnP "ghosts in the machine"-type conflicts. Likewise, they cause no problems so are best forgotten.

> **Tip**
>
> The best thing to do with a fully functional machine is to leave it alone, even if conflicts or other mysteries appear in System Information. If you feel the need to fiddle, fiddle away, but I warned you...

Software Environment

This section has two classes of information—that which is duplicated elsewhere and (at last!) some really worthwhile, unique and useful stuff. The Services, Running Tasks, Jobs, and so forth are duplicates of information available elsewhere, but conveniently grouped together here for easy reference.

The Programs Group folder is an unpromising name for a very useful display showing the items from Start, Programs available to various users. Figure 30.7 shows this display for one computer. Note that some program groups are available to a single user. I've highlighted one such group (the older Resource Kit) in the figure.

FIGURE 30.7

Here you can see at a glance what program groups are available to user groups.

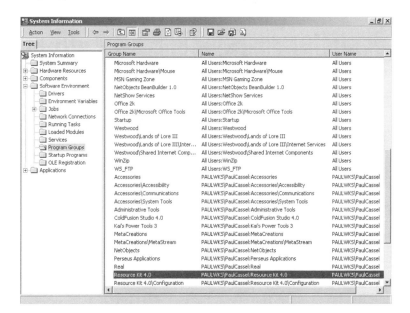

30

WINDOWS 2000 DIAGNOSTICS

The Startup Programs display shows all programs that automatically start up for the logged on user. Most folks think that the only programs that start up automatically exist in the folder Start, Programs, Startup, but that's not the case. Note in the display in Figure 30.8 that there are five items automatically starting up while there are only two (one active) items in the Startup group, as you can see from Figure 30.9.

FIGURE 30.8

Five programs start up for All Users.

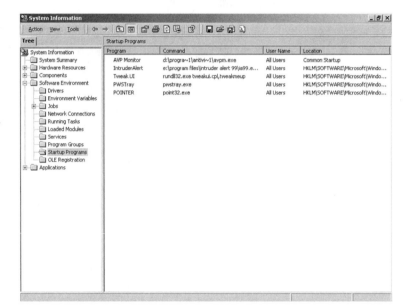

FIGURE 30.9

However, there are only two items in Startup folder, and only one of these is active.

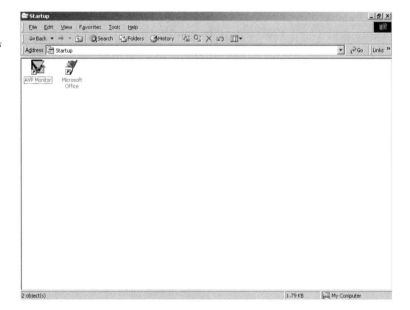

Take a close look at the Location column of the Startup Programs display in Figure 30.8. Note that only the AVP Monitor (an anti-virus program) starts from Common Startup, which is the Startup folder. The rest reside in the Registry.

If you want to manually disable these programs from starting up, delving about in the Startup folder won't help you a bit. You must go into the Registry to dig them out. If you have a need to do so (for example if they won't uninstall and give an error message), use the Find facility in your Registry editor (such as `regedit`) to dig them out. Figure 30.10 shows the Registry with the TweakUI entry shown in the foreground while the Run key is in the background. If you look carefully, you'll see that the entry in Figure 30.8 and 30.10 (`tweakmeup`) are the same.

FIGURE 30.10

Finding this somewhat hidden startup program is easy after using the information in Figure 30.8.

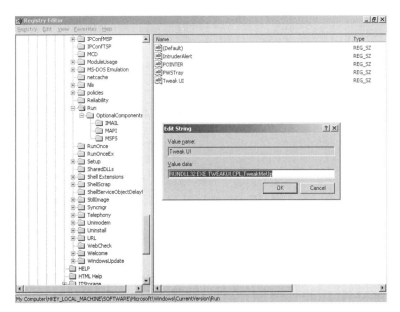

I want to make a note of the Loaded Modules section. Windows adheres to the Windows Open System Architecture (WOSA), meaning that the system is composed of a basic system extended by modules often in the form of a special executable file called a dynamic link library. These libraries are public, so the library that contains the common dialog boxes (like Open, Save As and so forth) is available to all programs. This saves each program from loading its own objects, thus saving memory.

However, sometimes these modules cause problems when a program expects one to contain something it doesn't or something appears at an unexpected address. Tracking down where the module is or what has called it can be difficult, but this section of System Information will help because it shows all loaded modules and the program that loaded them.

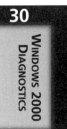

30

WINDOWS 2000 DIAGNOSTICS

Another tool, not part of Windows 2000 but available for free from
www.sysinternals.com, is called HandleEx. The information is similar, but I find the
organization more useful for much of what I do. I don't want to get into a contest as to
which is better because you can have both for the same cost (nothing), and I do use both
for diagnosing module problems. Figure 30.11 shows HandleEx in action.

FIGURE 30.11
*HandleEx gives a
useful display of
loaded programs
and modules orga-
nized differently
from System
Information. Be
safe—use them
both.*

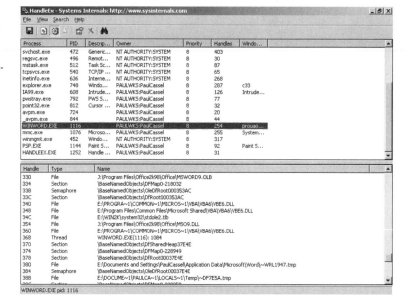

Applications

The Applications section is, to me, another dweeb area of questionable value for individuals and even dubious for Administrators. Take a look inside a few of the folders if you
have any conforming applications (such as Microsoft Office 2000), and you'll see a
wealth of information that is initially quite exciting. However, exactly what use the information is or why it is here is questionable. For example, there is a folder listing all
hyperlinks in any open Word 2000 documents. Interesting, isn't it? Yet what real use is it
and why is it here instead of someplace inside of Word itself?

> **Note**
>
> You can launch the system diagnostic from some applications, such as recent
> Microsoft Office suites. If you have such applications, the system information
> launch is usually under the Help menu in the About dialog box.

Some of the folders, such as Settings, are taken right from Options or other dialog boxes in Word. Now this might be of interest to some Administrator who is in the business of enforcing certain company rules (you must use this Style in Word!) but not of too much, if any, interest for other individuals.

Figure 30.12 shows the Styles folder for Word 2000 on a typical computer.

FIGURE 30.12

Applications has folders of interest, but of limited use for individuals, although Administrators might make some use of them.

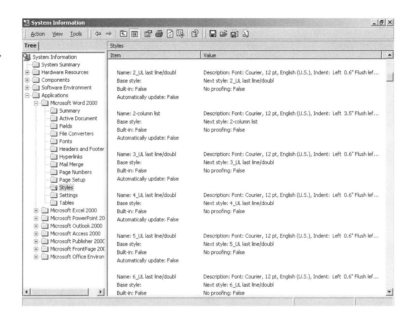

The only advantage I can see to using Applications in System Information is that you can see a lot of information about your applications collected in a single place.

> **Note**
>
> System Information needs an application installed and running to show up in Applications. If you want to view a non-running application that appears in the folder, you'll get an error message. Launch the application and then press F5 to refresh the view, and the application will load in Applications.

Device Manager

Our old friend Device Manager (DM), which first appeared in Windows 95, remains a useful tool in Windows 2000. To see the DM, launch the System applet in the Control Panel and then choose the Device Manager button on the Hardware tab. Figure 30.13

shows this applet for the same system as the System Information screens. Note that the problem with serial port COM4: is reflected in this tool too.

FIGURE 30.13

The Device Manager has some additional information to System Information.

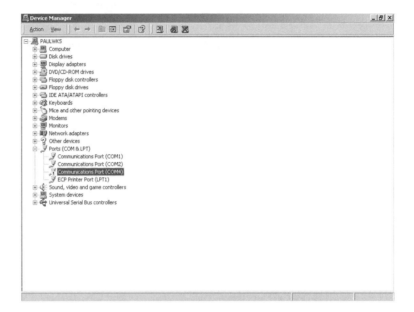

Double clicking any device shown in Device Manager brings up a Properties dialog box replete with detailed information. Figure 30.14 shows this dialog box for the defective port. Note the combo box that's pulled down in the screen. This enables you to disable this device for subsequent boots. Unless PnP reinstates this port, this should remove it from the defective hardware reports. While this port isn't causing any trouble, knowing you can turn on and off problematic hardware is a very useful piece of information. The place to do this is in Device Manager.

FIGURE 30.14

When it doubt, leave it out.

You can also uninstall this port from the DM toolbar or disable it there too. Uninstalling this port won't work on this system because PnP "finds" and installs it the same way at boot up. However, disabling it did solve the problem, slight as it was.

You can also scan (activate PnP) for new hardware from Device Manager. Hot swap hardware is supposed to be detected when plugged in, and all hardware is supposed to be initiated at boot up, but inevitably something won't be. You can run the Add/Remove Hardware applet from the Control Panel or run the scan from here if you need to manually invoke it.

Altering Drivers and Resources

Device Manager (DM) will allow you to alter the driver or the automatic (or forced) resource allocations of devices. That is, it'll do this in theory. Sometimes for no apparent reason, Windows 2000 Professional will refuse to apply the changes you want. Assume that in these cases there is a good reason, even if 2000 remains mute on the topic.

The Properties dialog box is where you can make such adjustments in DM. To open this dialog box, double-click the device (hardware component) you want to view the properties for or right-click and choose Properties from the context menu.

You'll be presented with a tabbed dialog box with the number of tabs varying depending on the type of device. All tabs bear interesting and worthwhile information. The General tab has a Troubleshooter button that will invoke a relevant section of Help to step you through the possible remedies.

The Driver and Resource tabs (if available) will allow you to manually update the drivers or set resources (such as memory address space and IRQ, respectively). Figure 30.15 shows a manual configuration dialog box. I got this dialog box by choosing the Set Configuration Manually button for a device that wasn't working properly (due to a conflict I created for demonstration purposes).

FIGURE 30.15

Windows 2000 will allow you a shot at manually changing the resources for an ill-running component.

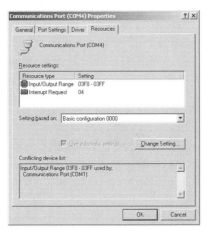

Windows 2000 is somewhat zealous in preventing you from manually configuring a device in such a way that it will interfere with another existing device. I've tried to accomplish this (a dubious accomplishment for sure) but haven't succeeded yet. I don't want to say that this is impossible, however.

The moral of this micro-rant is to always use care when adjusting resources manually.

System Properties

There is another area that belongs in this discussion, and that's the System Properties applet. To get to this, launch the System applet in the Control Panel, and then click the Advanced tab. Click the Performance button to see places to balance your system for different applications. The critical adjustment available to you is where to locate your paging file. When making this adjustment, there is a tendency for people to try to make the file too small to recover disk space. This is penny wise and pound foolish. If you are running out of disk space, get more disk, don't make Windows 2000 do with less than it needs in virtual memory.

> **Tip**
>
> Locating the paging file on a physically different disk than where Windows 2000 system is will significantly speed up the operating system because it can access system and paging file data at the same time. The trick won't work by installing the paging file on a different volume of the same physical disk. It must be a physically different disk. Ideally, the paging file will exist on a disk dedicated to this, but that's almost never the case with Windows 2000 Professional and only sometimes with Server.

While you're on the Advanced tab, visit the other two buttons. While the default settings for both are usually fine, it's a good idea to know what's there (like what to do in case of boot failure) for those times when you need it. The information is in Help, but people tend to be in a frantic mood when they need this data, so it's a good idea to see it for yourself now when you have a cool mind.

Summary

System Information, the extension of the old MSD, has grown into a sophisticated tool for diagnosing system conflicts now that we no longer need it. While some areas are of interest, most of them have a high "golly gee" dweeb factor (I love this tool) but are of little use. Still, there are areas to display conflicts and other misbehaviors. In truth, most of the computer malfunctions you'll hit will be beyond the ability of System Information to tell you about or mediate. Yet there is no harm in getting in there to whet your techie attitude.

Terminal Services and Client (Licenses Management)

Description of Terminal Services

For the first time, Windows 2000 offers interface with Terminal Services as a standard feature on the operating system.

Terminal Services has its roots back in the early days of the Information Revolution, before personal computers, point-and-click interfaces, and laptops. To use a computer, people had to share time on computer mainframes, which were very large and extremely expensive. To save money and enable as many people as possible to use the computer, programmers wrote software that let users access the computer from remote terminals for simple applications. Each terminal used only a part of the computing time and the computing power on the mainframe. Everyone got more access.

Terminal Services works on the same basic idea: to allow a simpler machine to run the programs that usually require a more complex and powerful machine.

> **Note**
>
> Terminal Services is not a part of the Windows 2000 Professional Operating System. You still have to buy the Server Version of Windows 2000 to have a complete package. But this chapter will guide you through the steps to make Terminal Services work with your Professional Operating System.

Fat and Thin Clients

Today, personal computers are powerful enough to run applications that would have strained some of the largest mainframes of past times. But a standalone PC—sometimes called a Fat Client—requires storage space (a hard drive), a processor, and enough RAM to run the programs, increasing the cost of each unit.

Terminal Services allows a computer server to host other computers so they can run some Windows applications at a lower cost than a standalone PC.

The computer that signs into Terminal Services may not be much more than just the windows-and-menus desktop on the screen (sometimes called a Graphical User Interface, or GUI). These computers, sometimes called Thin Clients, don't need the RAM or storage space or the fast processor of a standalone PC.

Using Terminal Services, Thin Clients—much simpler, lower-memory computers—can sign into the server running Windows 2000 and still run Windows 2000 applications.

Almost any machine you choose as your Thin Client will work. You can pull out your old 286, 386, or 486 machines—or hit the local garage sales to find one—and still run high-performance software on them. After you load the client software, you will be able to use Terminal Services to run the Windows 2000 Professional desktop. It's like an instant upgrade, without the hardware costs.

There are other advantages to using Thin Clients and a central server. Rather than spending a lot of time and money trying to upgrade and fix Thin Clients that don't work, you can simply take them away and cheaply replace them. When used the right way, the Terminal Service client could be just like a phone that you could plug in anywhere to access the services on the network.

Terminal Services in Windows 2000 Server can be used to run both 16- and 32-bit applications on a Windows 2000 Professional desktop. In the case where you don't need the desktop, you can have Terminal Services run just one application. Remote access to applications is also available through Terminal Services. If your clients are dialing in over slower connections, or if the applications you're running are especially large, Terminal Services can help increase accessibility. With Terminal Services, the client machine is only sent the application display, which requires less memory and bandwidth than the data.

Uses for Terminal Services

Terminal Services can be used in several situations:

- Client desktops do not have enough hardware or memory to run Windows 2000.
- Clients need to access a central application.
- Clients need to access large or complicated applications over low bandwidth or slow connections.
- Clients only need to use one or a few applications, not the entire desktop.

With Windows 2000 Professional requiring even more hardware and memory than previous versions of Windows, Terminal Services will be a useful tool for the people who don't have the resources or the desire to completely upgrade their entire computer networks. Terminal Services also gives IS Administrators a much easier way to give a standard desktop to end users without the problems of giving everyone in the organization a "Fat Client."

Before You Begin

Before Installing Terminal Services, you should keep in mind these important facts:

- *Enable Terminal Services on a standalone server*—Don't have another of your domain controllers offer *Terminal Services*. This will only slow down all of your thin clients.

- *Install Terminal Services on a server with an NTFS partition*—This will give you more choices when you're assigning security levels to directories accessed by the users of the terminals. Your ability to keep unauthorized users out of network directories depends on the type of file systems you've established on your network drives.

- *Any application you want to access with Terminal Services should be installed after you've installed Terminal Services*—This enables you to install all of those applications in the \Win2000 directory instead of a user's home directory.

What Do You Want?

Before you begin, you should also ask yourself the questions in the following sections to figure out what you can expect from Terminal Services.

What Kind of Hardware Do I Need?

Configuring your server with the right hardware is extremely important when installing Terminal Services. Determine what your server will be used for, and find out what kind of equipment you need to carry out those goals. You should check your server against the specifications in your Windows product documentation to make sure your hardware will have the memory and speed necessary to run Terminal Services.

What Applications Will Be Accessed on Terminal Services?

The load you place on your server is determined by the programs you want your clients to run using Terminal Services. Simpler programs, like data entry or word processing, aren't a real challenge to either the client's processor or the server. However, complex applications that move a lot of data—especially those that access large databases and run complex queries—can slow down not only the local processor and memory, but also eat up a lot of network bandwidth.

How Many Users Will Access Terminal Services? What Do They Require?

The amount of memory and how many processors you may need depends on how many users your network has and what type of users they are. Microsoft says there are three basic types of users:

- *Task-Based Users*—Users who normally run a single program, like data entry or simple word processing.

- *Typical Users*— Typical users might multitask by running more than one program at once. But the applications usually aren't too taxing, such as the Microsoft Office applications.

- *Advanced Users*—These are the most demanding users. The applications they access with Terminal Services take up a lot of processor time and memory. An advanced user might run complex queries on a SQL Server.

The amount of RAM and the type of processors required on your server will depend on what your users do and how many of them will access the Terminal Services at once. As each user connects to the Terminal Services, he or she will take up a slice of the processor and will need enough RAM to run his or her application. A good standard measurement is to allow between 12MB–24MB per user. If the application is data-heavy or your user load increases, consider installing a dual processor.

The following are three examples to help you decide what level of hardware and memory you want to use for your server.

Example 1: For Task-Based Users

Yourcompany needs to transfer your old sales figures from paper to electronic format. You have configured a SQL server and created a Visual Basic application for the actual data entry. A group of temps will enter the data using some old 486 machines you have set up with the Terminal Services client. The Terminal Services itself is not much more than a desktop workstation with 256MB RAM and a single Pentium Pro 200MHZ processor. Under this hardware configuration, your clients could get at least 12MB RAM each.

Example Two: For Typical Users

Several of your salespeople need to access and maintain their accounts from the road. To access the server and have it run efficiently, you will have to increase the RAM to at least 24MB per user. You also should have at least two processors in the machine. With at least 328MB RAM and dual Pentium Pro 200 Processors, you should be able to run the application to connect your sales force.

Example Three: Advanced Users

You want to audit and report on several different sales accounts now that they are in your database. You've hired more experienced computer temps to run queries on the database for the reports. Because the database in this case is local to the Terminal Services, the amount of RAM and processors should be much greater than it was in the first scenario, because the server will have to perform the tasks on the database as well as access the data and deliver it to the clients. In this case, at least 512MB RAM and 4 Pentium Pro 300MHZ processors should be installed.

These are very broad examples. As the saying goes, your mileage may vary. Make sure you set up your system specifically to meet the needs of your network architecture, the demands you plan to place on it, and the performance you expect from the applications the clients access.

Later, you can use Terminal Services management features (discussed later in this chapter) to evaluate the load your server is handling, and make adjustments.

Installing Server Side

This is where you install the Terminal Services program on the computer server or the computer you want to use as the server. If you did not choose to install Terminal Services when you set up Windows 2000 on your computer, don't worry. You can still do it without too much trouble.

1. Log in to your Windows 2000 Server as Administrator.
2. On the Start button, click Settings.
3. Select Control Panel, and double-click the Add/Remove Programs icon.
4. Select Add/Remove Windows Components (see Figure 31.1).

FIGURE 31.1

The Add/Remove Programs window—from here you can Add/Remove Windows 2000 Server components.

5. Click the Add/Remove Components button. The Windows Components Wizard starts (see Figure 31.2). Click Next to continue.

FIGURE 31.2

The Windows Components Wizard screen. Scroll down to Terminal Services to install on your server.

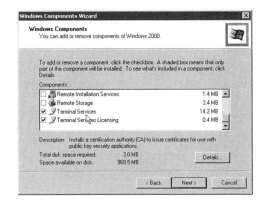

6. Choose Terminal Services and Terminal Services Licensing from the Components Selection list.

7. Click Next to continue. The next screen will list applications that might not work properly if you install Terminal Services. Take note of the warning and click Next if you still want to install the program. Setup begins copying files automatically.

8. Insert the Windows 2000 Server CD-ROM when prompted.

9. Click Finish to complete the installation.

You have now installed Terminal Services for the server.

Installing the Client Component

To install the client component, all you really have to do is load the client software. This can be placed in the ROM (Read Only Memory) of your Thin Client machines. You can install any of the following Windows systems: Windows 3.X, Windows 95, Windows 98, Windows NT, or Windows 2000 client software.

The Terminal Services Client can be run on both Intel and Alpha-based machines. (For Alpha-based machines, UNIX, and Macintosh machines to run the client, you will need a third-party add-on available from Citrix Systems.) Otherwise, Windows 2000 Server comes with the client for Windows 3.11 WFW, 95, 98, NT 3.51, NT 4.0, and Windows 2000.

The first step in setting up the client is to make sure network Server are functioning correctly. If you can get the network card running under the operating system of choice and see the server on the network, you are halfway there.

The second step is to actually install the client software.

1. First you need to create the client install disk. From the Terminal Services, login as Administrator.

2. From Start, go to Programs, Administrative Tools, Terminal Services Client Creator. The Create Installation Disks screen will appear.

3. From the Create Installation Disks screen (see Figure 31.3), select the correct client for your operating system. For Windows 95, for example, select the 32-bit client.

FIGURE 31.3

From the Create Installation Disks screen, you can choose the operating system for which the client disks should be created.

4. Insert a formatted disk and click OK. (You can also choose to have the disk formatted by the Client Creator.) You may be prompted to provide an additional formatted disk.

5. Click OK when the disk is created.

6. Next insert the disk into your client workstation. In the RUN command space, type:

`a:\setup.exe`

The Terminal Services Client Setup will launch (see Figure 31.4).

FIGURE 31.4

The Terminal Services Client Setup screen.

7. Click Continue. You're prompted to fill in your name and organization. Do so and click Continue.

8. The License Agreement screen will appear. Click I Agree.

9. Click the Continue button to continue the installation.

   Click the button to continue the installation. You can also change the default path where the software is to be installed.

10. The program will ask you if you want to create the same initial setup for all users. Click Yes. The program will then prompt you for the other disk for the installation. Click Continue to create the program group.

11. Click OK to complete the installation.

12. From Programs group, you can select the Terminal Services Client folder and launch the Terminal Services Client. You can create a session to a Terminal Services on your network.

13. Type in the name or IP address of the server to which you want to connect, or select it from the Available Servers drop-down list.

14. After you have entered the server information, you can then select

    - *Screen area*—Choose 640×480 or 800×600.

    - *Compression*—If you are dialed in or have a slow network connection, choose Low-speed Compression.

    - *Bitmaps*—If you want to cache some of the graphics, which will help with screen updates, you can select to cache bitmaps to disk.

Application Installation and Setup

This is where you will log into Windows 2000 Server under a Terminal Client session, running on a Windows 95 desktop (see Figure 31.5).

FIGURE 31.5

A terminal client session in progress.

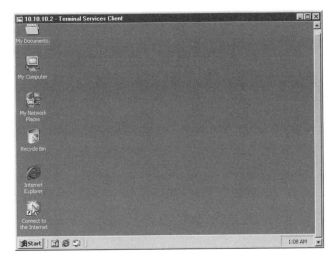

One simple method used to start up terminal sessions is to create them using the Client Connection Manager.

1. From the Terminal Services Client program group, select the Client Connection Manager and launch.

2. Choose New Connection from the File menu in the Client Connection Manager. The Client Connection Manager Wizard will start (see Figure 31.6).

FIGURE 31.6

Use the Client Connection Manager Wizard to easily create terminal Server client sessions.

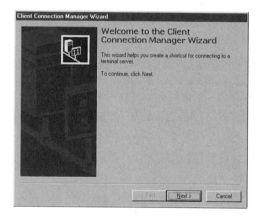

3. Click Next. The Wizard will guide you through the following steps.

4. Type in a name that will help you remember the connection you are establishing and specify the IP address or Server name for the Terminal Services. If you don't remember or don't know the IP address or server name, click Browse to find an available Terminal Services on your network.

5. In the next screen, you can specify login information. If you do not want to enter your username/password/domain every time you start the terminal service session, you can select the Log On Automatically with This Information check box.

Warning

It's not a good idea to create a terminal session and save username and password information on the computer. Storing the information where an unauthorized person can get to it increases the risk of someone breaking into your network. A person could launch one of these sessions and then have full access to the network under that username. This kind of security breach can lead to a lot of problems, all of which are time-consuming and expensive to fix. Set a policy and make sure your users follow it when using this feature.

6. The next screen is meant for fine-tuning your session. Choose the screen area you want to use for the terminal session.

7. Click Next. If you know that you are running over a slow link such as dial-in, you can select that here.

8. You can also choose to save frequently used images to your disk. That will avoid sending the same graphics over the network connection with each session, much like the images an Internet browser caches to save time. After you've determined what you prefer for this session, click Next.

9. At this point you can specify a program to launch. For example, you can select FreeCell. In the prompt for the program name and file path, type in the location of FreeCell on the server.

10. Click Next. The new connection you just created will have the default icon. You can change the icon and the Program Group where it will be located to make it easier to remember if you want.

11. Click Next to continue and Finish to complete the process.

You should now be able to play a game of FreeCell on your client machine.

Managing Users and User Sessions

After setting up Terminal Services, you're in charge of what happens with it. As the Administrator, it's up to you to know who is running terminal service sessions on your server.

But just keeping track of your users isn't enough. You also need to manage what types of sessions the user can run. You have to have a control and security policy. If you don't, users could access almost anything in the server. Clients might accidentally corrupt important data; hackers could gain access to your network; employees might open confidential or sensitive files, such as payroll records. By instituting a good management and control policy, you can avoid troubles like these.

Managing Users

This is where you will select the levels of access and security you want to give your users. Depending on a user's experience and status, you can decide what level of computing power he needs, and what level he can handle.

1. From the Terminal Services itself, launch the Computer Management application.

2. Select System Tools and expand the Local Users and Groups icon.

3. Select the Users folder. On the right pane, you will see the users defined on this server. (If you are running a Domain or Active Directory, you would want to edit the user object in those directory services.)

4. Select to edit the user's properties by double clicking them.

5. Select the Terminal Services Profile tab. You will see settings for that user's terminal services (see Figure 31.7). By default all users are given logon rights to the terminal service. Change the settings according to the user's needs and the applications required to meet them. It's a good idea to give users only as much access as they need. There's no reason a temp should have access to your payroll data.

FIGURE 31.7

Selecting the Terminal Services Profile tab shows the Terminal Services settings for that user.

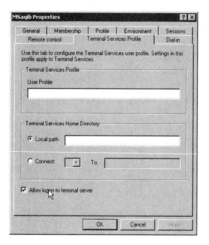

If you want to distinguish which profile a client uses when he or she logs in via Terminal Service session, you can specify that profile in the User Profile path. This is useful for those times when you want to control the user's desktop if he or she is logged in via Terminal Service session, and you don't want the user to be able to launch certain applications locally at the server, such as the command prompt.

Whichever directory you specify for the Home Directory is where application settings will be saved just for that user. You can specify a local drive path or network path.

Managing Sessions

Through the Terminal Services Manager, you can disconnect a user or send a message to the user, and you can also view detailed information: the login time, idle time and processes detail (what applications were accessed, and so on). The next sections discuss a few of the common tasks enabled by Terminal Services.

To access these tools, you'll need to go to the Terminal Services manager. From there, you can begin setting the limits on your clients from your central server.

1. Select Terminal Services Manager.
2. When you launch the Terminal Services Manager, it will list the available terminal servers on your network that you can manage.

> **Note**
>
> To search for terminal servers on other domains, right-click the icon representing All Listed Servers.

3. Choose Find Servers in All Domains, and a list of servers in other domains appears.
4. Select the server you want to manage by double-clicking.

View Terminal Services Information

After you've chosen a server, you can view User, Sessions, Processes, and Information regarding the Terminal Services.

Select the server from the server list. The detail pane on the right gives you several options:

- *Users*—Select the Users tab to view users logged in.
- *Sessions*—The Sessions tab will present you with the current sessions running on the server.
- *Processes*—Click the Processes tab to see information about the processes running on the server. You can also view which user is using what process and the process ID.
- *Information*—The Information option will give you additional information regarding the terminal server, such as service packs and/or hot fixes installed.

Send a Message to a User Connected to the Terminal Services

At any time, you might need to send a message to any of the users connected to the Terminal Services. For example, if you need to reboot the system, you can warn users so that they can save their information before the server goes down.

1. From the server list, expand the server and select any of the active user sessions.

2. From the Actions menu, click Send Message.

3. Type in your message's title and the actual message in the space provided and click OK. The message will immediately be sent to the specified user.

You Can Disconnect a User from Terminal Services Manager

Occasionally, you'll need to free up a connection for another client. For example, someone might leave his or her terminal connected when he or she leaves for lunch. Using Terminal Services, you can disconnect users from the terminal server.

1. From the server list, expand the server and select any of the active user sessions.

2. Right-click the session and select Disconnect.

Booting into a Client

Not all your clients are going to have the same familiarity with Windows and other applications. Very often, they can get into jams that will require your help to fix. If a client needs help or you want to monitor his or her activity even more closely, Terminal Services gives you the option of taking remote control.

1. From the server list, expand the server and select an active user session.

2. Right-click the session and select Remote Control.

View Real-Time Statistics of a User Connection

The speed of connections between the clients and the server can be affected by many factors. However, if your clients are complaining about the time it takes to use the network, even when your hardware is fully capable of handling the load, you can check the packet information for each session from the central server.

1. From the server list, expand the server and select an active user session.

2. Right-click the session and select Status. You will then be able to view packet information for that client. Problems with network activity will show up as Frame errors or Timeout errors (see Figure 31.8).

Terminal Services and Client (Licenses Management)

CHAPTER 31

827

31

TERMINAL
SERVICES AND
CLIENT

FIGURE 31.8

From the Terminal Services Manager, you can monitor and manage the terminal services established on the terminal server.

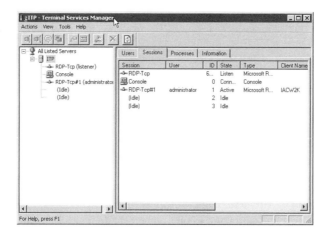

Terminal Services Licensing

Each Terminal Services client that will connect to the terminal must have a license. License information is stored locally. When a connection is attempted, the license service running on the terminal server will check for a valid license.

There must be at least one Terminal Services Licensing server on your network. From there, you can add or remove client licenses.

1. From the Programs, Administrative Tools folder select Terminal Services Licensing.
2. All Terminal Servicess available will be displayed. Select any of them.
3. From the File menu, choose License Register.
4. Add or remove licenses at this point (see Figure 31.9).

> **Note**
>
> You will notice the ability to add a Windows 2000 Server Internet Connector license. This particular license is meant for those organizations that will have users connect to the Terminal Services via the Internet. You can have up to 200 users connected anonymously to the server at a single time.

As with any licensing feature or licensing issue, you should check with Microsoft for the latest information.

FIGURE **31.9**

Adding Windows 2000 Terminal Services Client Access Licenses by using the Terminal Services Licensing tool.

Summary

Terminal Services enables even older machines to access Windows 2000 applications. This can be useful in situations ranging from simple networking applications for a small business to Administrators looking to upgrade their client services without expensive retooling of dated equipment. It can also provide ease of management and access to data about network use. Terminal Services expands Windows' reach throughout the network.

Appendixes

IN THIS PART

Glossary

Access Control List (ACL) A list of permit and deny conditions to a resource.

ActiveX A version of the technology described by Microsoft's Component Object Model (COM), usually found on the Internet or intranets

Administrator The account used to administer Windows 2000 computers, domains, and workgroups.

Applet A Windows 2000 dynamic link library (DLL) or, lately, Java routines.

AppleTalk protocol A protocol that allows Apple computers to use resources shared from an Windows 2000 system.

Asymmetrical Digital Subscriber Line Usually abbreviated to ADSL. A high speed data grade connection protocol that runs over standard copper wire telephone lines enabling high speed throughput for Internet or extranet connections.

Auditing The ability to record events and user actions while they are logged on to a Windows 2000 computer.

Authentication Validation of a user through a username/password combination.

Baud   *See bps.*

Binding   The process of establishing communication between network protocols and a network interface card.

BIOS   Basic Input/Output System. Firmware (non-volatile) programs contained on mainboard chips that contain fundamental startup instructions and configuration for a personal computer.

Boot partition   A volume that contains the Windows 2000 operating system and its support files.

bps (bits per second)   A measurement of the speed with which a device can transfer data. Roughly equivalent to and can be used interchangeably with baud.

Browser Service   A Windows 2000 service that displays a list of currently running Windows 2000 systems, domains, workgroups, file and print shares, and other shared resources on a network.

Cache   A store of information containing the most recent or most frequently accessed data.

CHAP (Challenge Handshake Authentication Protocol)   A routine to create secure encryption connections using MD5, which is a standard hashing algorithm.

Client Service for NetWare (CSNW)   A service that allows Windows 2000 connectivity to NetWare resources.

Component Object Model (COM)   A standard that defines interfaces between objects.

CSLIP (Compressed SLIP)   *See SLIP.*

Default gateway   A router or computer that possesses routing capabilities and can direct traffic to its intended destination within or outside of the local network.

Device driver   A piece of software that allows a piece of hardware to communicate with Windows 2000.

Dial-Up networking (DUN)   The client version of Remote Access Service, allowing the client to connect to a network remotely over a phone line.

Domain   A collection of Windows 2000 systems defined to share a single security database.

Domain Controller   There is multi-master capability in Windows 2000. A Windows 2000 server can be a domain controller that performs login and active directory functions, a member server, or a stand-alone server.

A

Domain Name Service (DNS)   A service that has the capability of resolving an IP address, given an IP name, or vice versa.

Dynamic data exchange (DDE)   The ability to exchange data between two or more applications.

Dynamic Host Configuration Protocol (DHCP)   A Windows 2000 service that allows a client to lease an IP address from an IP pool that is maintained by a DHCP server.

Dynamic link library (DLL)   A file that contains routines and functions that are loaded when needed.

Encryption   The process of protecting data by changing its content so that it is decipherable only with a special key.

Extranet   A TCP/IP network functioning like the Internet but using private connection media such as satellite or leased lines.

File Allocation Table or FAT   The predecessor file and disk system to NTFS. Used for MS-DOS and Windows versions technically previous to Windows 2000, FAT lacks NTFS's security and data integrity features. It also has less capacity and efficiency. Windows 2000 recognizes both the early FAT16 and later FAT32 systems.

File replication   The ability to replicate files and directories between two or more Windows 2000 machines.

File sharing   The ability to share files and directories over the network.

File Transfer Protocol (FTP)   A protocol to transfer files between remote machines.

Group   A collection of users. Permissions granted at group level are inherited by its members.

Guest   A built-in account that is used by casual users connecting to the Windows 2000 network.

Hardware Compatibility List (HCL)   A list of devices Microsoft has tested and which are fully supported by Windows 2000. Devices not on the HCL might work perfectly, but haven't been tested.

Host   A device on a TCP/IP network identified by an IP address. Can also mean any large system with ad hoc clients, such as public servers such as America Online.

Hypertext Markup Language (HTML)   A language used to create hypertext documents used for publishing on the World Wide Web. HTML is a subset of the more complex Standard General Markup Language (SGML).

Hypertext Transfer Protocol (HTTP)   An IP protocol used to transfer HTML data from a Web site to a user's desktop browser. The protocol for the World Wide Web (WWW).

Internet   A network made up of a number of public networks.

Internet Service Provider (ISP)   An enterprise or business, local or of wider scope, that people hire to provide access to Internet services.

Internetwork Packet Exchange/Sequenced Packet Exchange (IPX/SPX)   A transport protocol used in a Novell NetWare network.

Interprocess communication (IPC)   The capability of two or more processes to communicate, independent of whether they reside on the same machine.

Integrated Services Digital Network (ISDN)   A digital communication service that has found popularity in providing WAN connectivity.

Interrupt Request (IRQ)   A hardware signal used by a device to gain the attention of the processor.

Intranets   A private version of the Internet found primarily within corporations and businesses.

IP address   A unique 4-octet number with each section separated by a dot, used to identify nodes on an IP network. Example: 127.0.0.1.

Java   A programming language developed by Sun Microsystems, designed for use in applet and agent applications. The supposed advantage was cross-platform applicability when a specific "virtual engine" or execution program was installed on a local client. The same Java program or applet could then work on Windows, UNIX, and the Macintosh. Java programming uses a style familiar to C++ programmers, making it somewhat easier to learn for those people than a language with an entirely new structure.

LMHOSTS file   Used to resolve NetBIOS names to IP addresses.

Local Area Network (LAN)   A collection of interconnected computers dispersed over a relatively small area, usually within a building.

Local Security Authority (LSA)   The main component within the Windows 2000 security model. It is used to generate access tokens, maintain the system security and audit policies, and log audit alerts.

Media Access Control (MAC)   The network layer that deals with network access and collision detection.

Modem   An electronic device that converts binary data to analog tones and voltages that are suitable for transmission over standard dial-up or leased-line telephone lines. Modem is an acronym for MOdulator/DEModulator.

MS-CHAP   Microsoft implementation of Challenge Handshake Authentication Protocol, used to secure an encrypted connection between a RAS server and client. See CHAP.

Multi-homed   A machine that has more than one network interface card attached to separate physical networks.

Network Basic Input/Output System (NetBIOS)   An IBM-developed standard software interface to a network adapter.

Network Basic Input/Output System Extended User Interface (NetBEUI)   A non-routable broadcast LAN protocol (an extension of NetBIOS).

Network Interface card (NIC)   An expansion card used to connect a computer to a network.

Novell Directory Service (NDS)   Novell's method of distributing resource information to LAN clients.

Novell NetWare   A network operating system that is implemented by Novell and utilizes the IPX/SPX protocol.

NTFS   A file system specifically designed for Windows 2000.

OLE   A Microsoft implementation of data transfer and sharing between applications.

Packet Assemblers/disassemblers (PAD)   A connectivity device to an X.25 network.

Paging File   A file used to store data temporarily swapped out from RAM.

Password Authentication Protocol (PAP)   An authentication protocol that uses clear text passwords.

Ping   A command-line utility used to verify connectivity within an IP network.

Plug-and-play   An industry standard that allows an operating system to identify and configure newly added hardware.

Point to Point protocol (PPP)   A standard framing and authentication protocol that is used mostly within Microsoft's RAS but also in other protocols, such as IPX/SFX and Appletalk.

Point to Point Tunneling protocol (PPTP)   The ability to tunnel network protocols within a PPP connection. This can be used to create secure virtual private networks (VPNs).

Port   A location used to pass data in and out of a computing device.

Portable Operating System Interface (POSIX)   A standard that defines a set of operating system services.

Process   An executable program, a set of virtual memory addresses, and one or more threads. When a program runs, it is called a process.

Process Identifier (PID)   A unique number assigned to a running process.

Protocol   A set of rules and conventions used to transfer information over a network.

Proxy   A machine that accepts incoming calls and validates them against an access list. A proxy operates at a service level.

Registry   A database containing system configuration information stored in a hierarchical fashion.

Remote Access Service (RAS)   A Windows 2000 service that allows remote users to connect to a Windows 2000 network via a telephone connection.

Remote Procedure Call   Interprocess communication between processes residing on different machines.

Router   A piece of equipment that links networks. Routers find the best paths to destinations on the network and direct traffic via these best paths.

Routing Information Protocol (RIP)   The exchange of routing information between routers to build up a knowledge of the network. This information allows routers to decide on a best path.

Small Computer System Interface (SCSI)   A standard high-speed parallel interface for connecting computers to peripheral devices such as hard drives and printers.

Security Account Manager (SAM)   A database containing account information, such as passwords, account names, and policies.

Security ID (SID)   A unique identifier to identify a user to a security system.

Services   A process designed to execute specific system functions. Because services are RPC-based, they can be invoked remotely.

Simple Mail Transfer Protocol (SMTP)   A TCP/IP suite of protocols that covers the transfer of electronic mail.

Simple Network Management Protocol   A protocol used to monitor the state of a host on a TCP/IP network. Hosts can be monitored remotely via SNMP.

SLIP (Serial Line Internet Protocol)   An old communication standard. It is still incorporated within RAS to ensure interoperability with third-party remote access software.

Subnetmask   A 32-bit value that divides an IP address into a network ID and host ID.

TCP/IP   A suite of networking protocols that provide connectivity across interconnected networks.

Uniform Resource Locator (URL)   A pointer to a unique resource on the Internet.

Universal Naming Convention name (UNC)   The full name of a shared resource on a Windows 2000 network—for example, `\\servername\sharename`.

Uninterruptible Power Supply (UPS)   A battery-operated source of power that automatically supports your computer if your main electricity supply fails.

User Accounts   A way of associating attributes to a user when logged in to a Windows 2000 domain or computer. These attributes include username, password, group membership, and so on.

User Datagram Protocol (UDP)   A complementary protocol to TCP that offers a connectionless datagram service that does not guarantee delivery or sequencing.

Users and Passwords   A Windows 2000 tool used to maintain users, groups, and security policies within Windows 2000.

User Rights   A set of actions users can execute within a Windows 2000 computer or domain.

Virtual Memory   A space on your hard drive used to hold data swapped out of memory temporarily.

Virtual Private Network (VPN)   The ability to connect private LANs via a public network, such as the Internet.

Wide Area Network (WAN)   A network connected over a large global area.

Windows Internet Naming Service (WINS)   Microsoft's name resolution service for NetBIOS names.

Workgroup   A collection of computers grouped together for viewing purposes. Computers within a workgroup all have their own separate SAM databases.

WWW (World Wide Web)   An information service in the Internet whose content contains hypertext, graphics, and multimedia.

X.25   A packet-switching network.

Command-Line Reference

APPENDIX B

Starting the Command-Line Interface

You can start the command-line interface for Windows 2000 Professional by clicking Start, Run, and then entering `CMD` (case-insensitive) in the Run dialog box. `CMD` is the Windows 2000 command processor similar in function to `COMMAND.COM` used in DOS, Windows 95, and Windows 98. To make a shortcut for the CLI on your desktop, start Windows Explorer, locate the `CMD.EXE` file in `\[%systemroot%]\System32` and right-click it. Drag it to the desktop and release the right mouse button, choosing the Make Shortcut option when offered. Windows 2000 will, by default, place the MS-DOS icon for this shortcut. As with any shortcuts, you can change the icon or the title to one of your choosing.

Creating a shortcut gives you an easy way to modify the appearance of your command-line interface. Figure B.1 shows the Options tab in the Properties sheet for such a shortcut.

The Buffers option button shown in Figure B.1 is where you can set how many commands the interface stores—similar to DOS's `Doskey` command. It has nothing to do with the Buffers statement used in `CONFIG.SYS` for DOS or earlier Windows.

FIGURE B.1

Buffers sets how many commands to hold in memory.

Note that this tab gives you the choice of running your CLI either in a window or in a full screen. The Colors tab is where you can set a color and font set for your interface. There's nothing stopping you from creating several shortcuts for the CLI, each with its own set of properties.

If you've used other command-line interfaces, such as those in MS-DOS or UNIX, starting the CLI will put you in a comfortable place, as shown in Figure B.2.

FIGURE B.2

Here is the comfort zone for users of command line interfaces.

From this screen, entering commands is as simple as entering the command followed by its parameters, or switches, and pressing the Enter key.

Getting Help on Commands

Most commands respond to the *Command* /? convention used in Microsoft's other operating systems. Alternatively, you can see a list of some commands by entering **Help** after launching the CLI. The Help command, shown in Figure B.3, will bring up only a summary sheet for the most commonly used commands. If you want to see a complete listing of the commands along with some help text, choose Start, Help, and select MS-DOS Commands from the Reference section of the Contents tab or search on the word **commands**.

FIGURE B.3

The general Help screen from the command line.

The help system supplied by Microsoft isn't as complete as the written documentation provided in some of the company's older operating systems. Especially missing are usage examples for some of the trickier commands that can yield unexpected results or a lot of frustration. With that in mind, let's move on to the commands.

The Commands, Their Syntax, and Usage Examples

The following section lists the most often used commands exclusive to the CLI. They are classified by use. Some of these commands can and should be used within the CONFIG.NT or AUTOEXEC.NT files—both located in \[%systemroot%]\System32. These files, similar to the DOS and Windows CONFIG.SYS and AUTOEXEC.BAT, respectively, control some environmental variables for command sessions within Windows 2000 Professional. You can alter the contents of these files using any text editor such as EDIT or Notepad.

Many of the following commands will be familiar to those who have used DOS or Windows in the past. The reason for their inclusion is their unfamiliarity to those coming to Windows 2000 Professional from other operating systems such as UNIX, VMS, or MVS.

Unless noted, all commands and parameters are case-insensitive.

File and Disk Commands

People use these commands either because they're faster than the Graphical User Interface (GUI or Explorer) or because they offer function that the GUI fails to offer. I suppose too, that some folks coming from the command line MS-DOS or UNIX worlds, have learned command line computing and just prefer it.

Even if you're a GUI enthusiast, take a look at these commands to see if any will make your life simpler or easier. For example, I find using the Assoc command to be generally faster and easier than using Explorer. Few folks, even experienced Windows 2000 Administrators, seem to know that this and other handy command-line commands even exist.

append

Allows programs to open data files in remote directories as if they were in the current directory.

Syntax:

```
append [;] [[drive:]path[;...]] [/x:{on ¦ off}][/path:{
on ¦ off}] [/e]
```

/x tells the operating system to first search the current directory and then to extend its search to other specified directories; /e stores the append path in the environment.

Usage Examples:

```
Append /x /e
Append c:\newpath
```

These two commands will instruct the application to first search the current directory for data and then `c:\newpath`. The `\e` switch tells the operating system to store the `newpath` information in the environment.

Assoc

Associates a file extension with an application. This command also displays and deletes associations.

Syntax:

```
Assoc [.ext[=[application]]]
```

Usage Examples:

To show file extensions and their associations, enter

```
Assoc
```

To delete an association, enter

```
Assoc .ext =
```

where the `.ext` is the three-letter extension.

To add an association, enter

```
Assoc .ext =application
```

where the `.ext` is the three-letter extension and `application` is the name of the application.

> **Note**
>
> Another handy, although non-command line, way to associate a file extension with a program (executable) is to Shift+right-click a file in Explorer, choose Open With from the context menu, and then either choose from the pre-defined offerings (which will differ depending on the installed programs) or from the Choose Program open option.

B

Attrib

Sets certain attribute bits for a file.

Syntax:

Attrib [+r¦-r] [+a¦-a] [+s¦-s] [+h¦-h] [path\file] /s

The parameters *r*, *a*, *s*, and *h* represent the bits for read-only, archive, system, and hidden, respectively. The /s switch tells the operating system to process similarly all files in downstream subdirectories.

Usage Example:

Attrib -r -h \mypath\myfile

will remove the read-only and hidden attributes from myfile located in mypath.

CD and Chdir

Changes the working directory. These commands are interchangeable in all ways.

Syntax:

CD or Chdir [\] path

Usage Examples:

CD \

changes to the root directory.

CD..

moves up one entry in the tree.

CD \mypath

changes the working directory to mypath.

Chkdsk

Checks a disk and a file for errors. Similar to Chkdsk in DOS or Windows. Used mostly during console recovery after a system malfunction.

> **Note**
>
> Later versions of DOS and Windows have a similar utility, Scandisk. This utility is not part of Windows 2000 Professional.

Syntax:

Chkdsk [*path*] [/f] [/v] [/r]

where

/f tries to fix the problem(s) found.

/v verbose mode. Echoes filenames to the screen.

/r tries to recover lost information from bad sectors. Chkdsk must have exclusive access to the volume for this switch.

Usage Example:

Chkdsk c:\ /v /f

Checks the volume c: in verbose mode and tries to fix problems encountered.

Comp

Compares the contents of two files or two sets of files.

Syntax:

Comp [*files1*] [*files2*] [/d] [/a] [/l] [/n=number] [/c]

where

files1 and *files2* are the file sets for comparison.

/d yields a decimal display.

/a yields an alpha display.

/l shows the line numbers for differences rather than offset.

/n forces the line-by-line comparison for n lines, even in different length files.

/c removes case sensitivity.

Usage Example:

Comp \path1\myfiles \path2\myfiles /l

This command will compare the files in \path1\myfiles with those in \path2\myfiles and show the line numbers of any discrepancies.

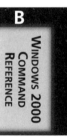

Compact

Applies, removes, or displays file compaction for NTFS systems. `Compact` can use standard wildcards.

Syntax:

`Compact [/c] [/u] [/s] [/i] [/f] [/a] [/q]` *filename(s)*

where

/c compacts the file(s).

/u removes compaction from file(s).

/s processes subdirectories.

/i ignores errors.

/f forces compaction on files, even those already compressed.

/a displays files with hidden or system attributes (properties). Not shown by default.

/q quiet mode (little echoed to screen).

Usage Examples:

`Compact`

Shows the compaction state of the current directory. Figure B.4 shows this command run without parameters.

FIGURE B.4

The Compact *command without switches.*

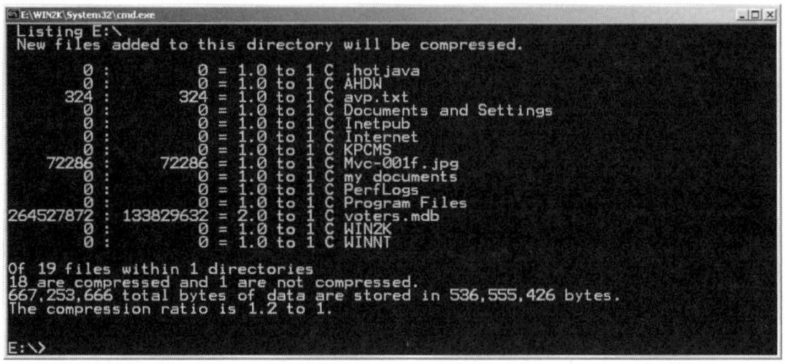

```
E:\WIN2K\System32\cmd.exe                                          _|□|x|
Listing E:\
New files added to this directory will be compressed.
        0 :        0 = 1.0 to 1 C .hotjava
        0 :        0 = 1.0 to 1 C AHDW
      324 :      324 = 1.0 to 1 C avp.txt
        0 :        0 = 1.0 to 1 C Documents and Settings
        0 :        0 = 1.0 to 1 C Inetpub
        0 :        0 = 1.0 to 1 C Internet
        0 :        0 = 1.0 to 1 C KPCMS
    72286 :    72286 = 1.0 to 1 C Mvc-001f.jpg
        0 :        0 = 1.0 to 1 C my documents
        0 :        0 = 1.0 to 1 C PerfLogs
        0 :        0 = 1.0 to 1 C Program Files
264527872 : 133829632 = 2.0 to 1 C voters.mdb
        0 :        0 = 1.0 to 1 C WIN2K
        0 :        0 = 1.0 to 1 C WINNT

Of 19 files within 1 directories
18 are compressed and 1 are not compressed.
667,253,666 total bytes of data are stored in 536,555,426 bytes.
The compression ratio is 1.2 to 1.

E:\>
```

`Compact g:\bitmaps /s`

Will compact the `bitmaps` directory and all its subdirectories on the `g:` drive.

Convert

Alters FAT volumes to NTFS ones. When run, Convert will need to absolutely control (lock) the disk volume slated for conversion. If it cannot, it will offer to do the conversion on next boot-up.

Syntax:

Convert [*volume*:] /fs:ntfs [/v] [/nametable:myfile]

where

> *volume* is the volume (drive) to be converted.
>
> /fs:ntfs means to convert to the file system NTFS. This is an obvious switch now. Microsoft might have some future plans for more types of switches.
>
> /v signifies verbose mode.
>
> /nametable:myfile creates a name table using the filename you specify. Use this if you encounter conversion problems due to having bizarre FAT filenames.

Usage Example:

Convert d: /fs:ntfs /v

Will convert drive d: from FAT to NTFS echoing messages to the console.

Copy

Copies files from one addressable device to another. Copy can use standard wildcards.

Syntax:

Copy [*source*][*destination*] /a /b /v /z /n

where

> [*source*] is the location of the files to be copied.
>
> [*destination*] is the target location of the files.
>
> /a copies ASCII files that have a ^Z character as their end of file marker.
>
> /b copies binary files which can include the ^Z character as part of their data.
>
> /v attempts to verify the copy operation.
>
> /z copies across networks.
>
> /n forces the 8.3 DOS file-naming convention.
>
> /y suppresses over writing warning dialog boxes.
>
> /-y prompts for overwrite permissions (overwriting means copying a file with the same name into the same location (folder).

Usage Example:

```
Copy c:\myfile a:\yourfile /v
```

Copies `myfile` in the root of `c:` to the root of `a:` giving it the name, `yourfile`, and then attempts to verify the write.

Del and Erase

Two commands doing exactly the same thing. These commands delete the directory entries for a file or files. They can accept the usual wildcards.

Syntax:

```
Del (or erase) myfile
```

Usage Example:

```
Del myfile
```

Deletes the file `myfile` from the current directory.

Dir

Gives a directory listing for the current or specified directory.

Syntax:

```
Dir [path][filename] [/p] [/w] [/d] [/a: (attributes) /o: (sortorder)
➥[/t: (time) [/s] [/b] [/l  [/x] [/n]
```

where

> `/p` pauses the display.
>
> `/w` shows a wide display without details.
>
> `/d` sorts wide display (in columns).
>
> `/a:` shows files having attributes hidden, system, directory, archive, or read-only by using the first letter of their attribute with the switch. Also accepts - for the inverse of the attribute.
>
> `/o:` sorts order, name, extension, date, size, grouped by directory first by using the first letter of the order with the switch.
>
> `/t:` is the time field using the following first letters of the field, creation, access (last), written to (last).
>
> `/s` shows or searches subdirectories also.
>
> `/b` shows a bare display without headers or footers.
>
> `/l` means lowercase unsorted.

/x shows 8.3 equivalent filenames also (`mylong~1.exe` for `mylongfile.exe`).

/n shows a long listing with filenames on right.

Usage Examples:

`Dir`

A listing of the current directory.

`Dir /s /x`

A listing of the current directory, its subdirectories, and the 8.3 equivalent filenames for the files shown.

`Dir /a:h`

A listing of the hidden files.

Diskcomp

Compares the contents of two disks.

Syntax:

`Diskcomp [driveA] [driveB]`

where `driveA` and `driveB` are two disk drives. You can use one floppy disk drive with `Diskcomp` by specifying the same drive on both parameters.

Usage Example:

`Diskcomp a: a:`

Will compare a disk in drive `a:` and then prompt you for the next disk to insert.

Diskcopy

Duplicates disks.

Syntax:

`Diskcopy [driveA] [driveB] /v`

where /v tries to verify writes.

Usage Example:

`Diskcopy a: a:`

Will copy the disk in drive a: and then prompt you for a target disk to use for a duplicate.

> **Note**
>
> You will need to use a disk that can be formatted the same as the one to be copied. Diskcopy requires identical capacity disks or it aborts the copy process. Diskcopy will overwrite any data on the target (copied to) diskette.

Expand

Expands cabinet (.cab) files or compressed files (.ex_) by non-destructive extraction. Cabinet files are files Microsoft uses to distribute many of its programs and operating systems. Compressed files with the .ex_ suffix are also widely used. Common expanders, such as those that work for .zip or .arc files, won't work with .cab files or .ex_ files.

Syntax:

```
Expand [-r] cabfile [target]
```

where -r renames the file.

Usage Example:

```
Expand cab1.cab
```

This command will expand the contents of the cab1.cab file to the current directory.

If you have an .ex_ file,

```
Expand f:\user32.ex_ c:\winnt\system32\user32.exe
```

will expand the contents of the user32.ex_ file to the user32.exe file located in the c:\winnt\system32\ directory.

FC

Compares two individual files and displays content discrepancies.

Syntax:

```
Fc [/a] [/b] [/c] [/l] [/lbx] [/n] [/t] [/u] [/w] [file1] [file2]
```

where

/a is an abbreviated display of discrepancies.

/b is the binary compare (ASCII is the default for files not having a binary extension).

/c means case-insensitive.

/l is the ASCII compare for files having a binary extension (such as .exe).

/lbx buffer size (the x part) for how many discrepancies Fc should tolerate before exiting.

/n shows line numbers during ASCII compare.

/t skips expanding tabs to spaces.

/u unicode compare.

/w skips consecutive whitespaces.

Usage Example:

```
Fc myfile1 myfile2 /b
```

This command compares and reports differences in the files myfile1 and myfile2 using a binary compare.

Files

Used like DOS and Windows to tell how many files a session can have open at the same time. Use in CONFIG.NT.

Syntax

```
Files = [number of files]
```

Usage Example:

```
Files = 99
```

Findstr

This is a superior version of the older Find command, also included in Windows 2000 Professional.

Syntax:

```
Findstr [/b] [/e] [/l] [/c:mystring] [/r] [/s] [/i] [/x] [/v] [/n] [/m]
```

where

/b finds pattern at start of line.

/e finds pattern at end of line.

/l uses literal find pattern.

/c:mystring is the string to search for.

/r (default) searches for non-literal strings.

/s also searches subdirectories.

/i is insensitive for case.

/x exact matching lines only.

/v opposite of /x—shows non-matching lines only.

/n prints line numbers.

/m shows matching files only.

Usage Examples:

```
Findstr "A string"myfile.txt
```

Finds the string "A" and string "string" in the myfile.txt file.

```
Findstr /c:"A String"myfile.txt /i
```

Finds the string "A String" (case-insensitive) in the myfile.txt file.

Format

Formats disks. Usage is the same as DOS or Windows with extensions noted below.

Syntax:

```
Format drive1: [/fs:file system choice] [/a:unitsize]
```

where

/fs is FAT or NTFS.

/a is unit size for NTFS volumes.

Usage Example:

```
Format e:/fs:ntfs /a:1024
```

Format drive e: as NTFS with a unit (similar to old cluster size in practice) size of 1,024 bytes.

MD and Mkdir

Usage is the same as in DOS or Windows.

Move

Usage is the same as Copy in default mode but deletes source file.

Print

The print spooler from DOS and Windows. Usage is the same.

Syntax:

```
Print /D:device [[drive:][path]filename]]
```

Usage Example:

```
Print myfile
```

Prints a file (usually text) to the default printer or another device specified by the /D: switch.

RD and Remdir

Identical expressions of the same command. Usage is the same as in DOS or Windows. This removes or deletes empty directories.

Syntax:

```
RD (or Rmdir) [/s]
```

where /s means delete subdirectories also.

Usage Example:

```
RD mydirectory
```

Removes the directory from the directory listing.

Ren and Rename

Renames files and directories. Usage is the same as later DOS and Windows.

Syntax:

```
REN (or Rename) [existingfile] [newfilename]
```

Usage Example:

```
Ren mine yours
```

Renames the directory (or file) mine as yours.

Xcopy

This is similar to the DOS or Windows XCOPY utility. It is an extended version of the internal COPY command. The chief differences are its additional switches and its capability to copy directory structures intact.

Syntax (with its more commonly used switches):

```
Xcopy source [target] [/c] [/v] [/q] [/f] [/l] [/d:] [/u] [/s] [/e] [/t] [/r]
➥[/h] [/n] [/exclude:myfile.txt]
```

where

> /c copies despite apparent errors.
>
> /v attempts verification of copy.
>
> /q quiet mode (suppresses messages).
>
> /f displays full source and destination filenames while copying.
>
> /l lists filenames during copying process.
>
> /d: with date after colon, copies only files with dates on or after specified date.
>
> /u copies only files from source that already exist on target (update).
>
> /s copies subdirectories. If used with the /e copies empty directories.
>
> /t copies the directory structure (tree), not the files. It will include empty directories if used with the /e switch.
>
> /r copies over read-only files.
>
> /h copies files with the system or hidden attribute bits set.
>
> /n copies using the 8.3 (or MS-DOS) naming convention.
>
> /exclude:myfile.txt excludes files listed in the text file myfile from being copied.

Usage Examples:

```
Xcopy c:\mypath d: /s
```

Copies the files in c:\mypath and its subdirectories to an identical directory structure on d:.

```
Xcopy r:\mypath\my long file a: /n
```

Copies a file with a long filename to the a: drive and excludes the long filename, instead using the 8.3 (MS-DOS) naming convention.

The Net Commands

Many of the Windows 2000 Professional CLI network commands start with the word Net followed by the command itself. These commands, where practical, can be run from batch files. When run from either batch files or interactively, these commands will accept the /y and /n switches for a Yes or No response to the command's query without user intervention. The /y and /n switches are especially useful for batch file operations.

Keep in mind that many Net commands have their analogs in the graphical user interface (GUI). Many Administrators prefer to use the CLI version of a command because they are usually faster than navigating through the Start menu system or even locating the shortcut icon located in a handy program group on the desktop. What you choose is up to you. In some cases, the CLI method for running a command is superior to the GUI because you can call it from batch files, optionally running them using the AT command.

Following are the most commonly used Net commands along with the most often used switches, their syntax, and usage examples.

NBTStat

Displays the status of a network running NetBIOS over TCP/IP. Note that following UNIX standards (the origin of TCP/IP), the following switches below are case-sensitive and use a dash (-) not a slash (/).

Syntax:

NBTStat [-a namedcomputer] [-A IP] [-R] [-r] [-S] [-s]

where

-a is the computer's name, such as tirilee

-A is the IP, such as 100.101.100.100

-R reloads the LMHosts file.

-r lists WINS name resolution. Requires WINS configuration to use.

-S attempts to list all clients and servers by IP.

-s same as -S but attempts to list all by computer name using the LMHosts file.

Usage Example:

NBTStat -A 100.101.100.100

Shows status for a computer with the IP 100.101.100.100.

Net Accounts

A CLI version of the utility available in the GUI User Manager. Most Administrators prefer the GUI version for administering accounts, but use the CLI version for a quick look at account status because it's faster when lending interactive support over, say, the telephone. This command is also useful for forcing user logoff.

Syntax (for the most often used parameters):

Net Accounts [/forcelogoff:{timetologoff}]

where

/forcelogoff takes the timetologoff and forces the user(s) off at that time.

When run without parameters, Net Accounts shows the current settings for user profiles.

> **Note**
>
> You must start this service before the command will work. You can start this service either through the Services GUI in Control Panel or the CLI Net Start.

Usage Example:

Net Accounts

Shows the status of the user profile in effect.

Net Config

Shows a list of devices you can configure and allows modification of these devices. This command controls either the server or workstation side of Windows 2000.

Syntax (of the most commonly used parameters):

Net Config server [/*autodisconnect:time*] [/*hidden:*]

or

Net Config workstation [/*charcount:*] [/*chartime:*] [/*charwait:*]

where

/*autodisconnect:time* is the time in minutes to automatically disconnect from an inactive client.

/*hidden:* is used with yes or no to hide the server from the list of servers. Does not affect permissions of the server.

/charcount: in bytes, the buffer Windows 2000 has for a communications device or port.

/chartime: in milliseconds. Same as /charcount, but in milliseconds.

/charwait: time in seconds Windows 2000 will wait on a communications device.

Usage Example:

```
Net Config Professional /hidden:yes
```

Run from the console, this hides the server from the list of available servers without affecting the permissions of the server.

Net Continue, Pause, Start, Stop

Continues, pauses, starts, and stops services, respectively. This is the CLI version of the Services applet available in Control Panel.

Syntax:

```
Net [continue] [pause] [start] [stop] service
```

where

service is the service you want to continue, pause, start, or stop.

Usage Examples:

```
Net stop alerter
```

Stops the alerter service.

```
Net start alerter
```

Starts the alerter service.

Net File

Displays a list of shared files and any file locks.

Syntax:

```
Net File [/close]
```

where

/close will close a file, releasing any file locks.

Run without parameters, Net File will list open shared files.

Usage Example:

```
Net File
```

Displays a list of open files.

Net Helpmsg

Displays help on an error message number.

Syntax:

```
Net Helpmsg messagenumber
```

Usage Example:

```
Net Helpmsg 2000
```

Tells you that error number 2000 means you have an invalid pixel format.

Net Print

Displays or manipulates a list of pending print jobs in queue. Similar to the Printers GUI applet in Control Panel; however, much faster if you have a CLI window open.

Syntax (most commonly used):

```
Net Print \\computername\printername [/delete] [/hold] [/release][/pause]
```

where

> *computername* is the name of the computer hosting the shared printer.
>
> *printername* is the name the printer is shared under.
>
> /delete purges print jobs.
>
> /hold pauses print jobs.
>
> /release restarts paused print jobs.

Usage Example:

```
Net Print \\tirilee\rainbow
```

Shows a list of pending print jobs for the printer rainbow hosted on the server tirilee.

Net Session

When entered from the local console, gives information about computers located on the server.

Syntax:

```
Net Session \\anycomputername /delete
```

where

`/delete` ends the session with `\\anycomputername`.

> **Note**
>
> `Net Session` given without parameters gives information about the local computer.

Usage Example:

```
Net Session \\barbara /delete
```

Ends the session connection with the computer named `barbara`.

NetStat

Shows statistics for connections on a TCP/IP network only. This command requires the TCP/IP protocol to be installed and running. Note that like `NBTStat`, this command uses the UNIX-like dash (`-`) rather than the more common slash (`/`), and the parameters aren't case-sensitive.

Syntax:

```
NetStat [-a] [-e] [-n] [-s] [-p] [-r] [time]
```

where

> `-a` displays listening ports.
>
> `-e` displays Ethernet statistics.
>
> `-n` provides a numeric display of ports rather than the default names.
>
> `-s` displays per protocol. Can be combined with `-e` for comprehensive information.
>
> `-p` is used with a protocol (such as TCP) to display only that protocol.
>
> `-r` displays routing information.
>
> `[time]` is the time in seconds to update the display. If omitted, it displays the instantaneous information.

B

Usage Example:

```
NetStat  -p tcp
```

Displays status of TCP protocol connection.

```
NetStat  -e -s
```

Displays very comprehensive Ethernet status.

Net Statistics

Displays statistics for the local computer.

Syntax:

```
Net Statistics [server] [workstation]
```

Usage Example:

```
Net Statistics server
```

Displays relevant statistics.

Net Time

Determines and can synchronize computer clocks.

Syntax:

```
Net Time \\anycomputername /set /domain
```

where

>/set sets the time on the local computer to that of the queried one.

>/domain sets the time to a domain.

Usage Examples:

```
Net Time \\tirilee
```

Displays the time on the computer named `tirilee`.

```
Net Time \\tirilee /set
```

Sets the time on the local machine to the same time as `tirilee`.

> **Note**
>
> Administrators often use this command within batch files triggered by the AT command to synchronize the clocks of all computers on a network or domain.

Net Use

Allows or disallows the use of a shared resource. This command also displays status information for shared resources.

Syntax (of the more often used parameters):

```
Net Use  [\\computername\sharename] [password or *][/persistent:]
```

where

> *computername**sharename* is the computer and the share name of the device to use.
>
> *password* or *, where *password* is the actual password for the shared device. If you use the * (asterisk) in the place of the password, Windows 2000 will prompt the user for the password.
>
> */persistent:*, when used with yes or no, will control whether the use persists from session to session.

> **Note**
>
> When used without parameters, Net Use will display shared resources on the local computer.

Usage Example:

```
Net Use \\tirilee\lily
```

Uses the shared resource lily on the computer tirilee.

The TCP/IP Commands

Windows 2000 Professional comes with several utilities commonly used in TCP/IP networks. Given the new visual tools for internetworking, few people use these CLI commands anymore, but in some cases they work well enough that they will be worthwhile tools for inclusion in your toolbox. The following are four of the most commonly used TCP/IP commands. You must have TCP/IP installed to have these commands, and the protocol must be functioning for them to work.

Ftp

A utility to transfer files (usually a binary file), using the File Transfer Protocol, to or from a computer running the Ftp daemon. As is common with the TCP/IP origin utility, Ftp uses the dash (-) rather than the slash (/) for switches. Note that the usual

```
ftp /?
```

for help will not work with Ftp because the Ftp utility will interpret the /? as a computer name and deliver an error message.

Syntax (for the most often used switches):

```
ftp [-i] [-d] [-g] [-s:myfile.txt] [daemoncomputer]
```

where

> -i stops interactive mode, which prompts you in cases of multiple file transfers.
>
> -d enables debug mode (echoing all messages).
>
> -g disables wildcard use on local files (globbing in Ftp talk).
>
> -s: is used with a text file to script a series of Ftp commands. A batch file substitute.

Usage Example:

```
ftp -d mack.rt66.com
```

Connects to a remote host running the daemon. When running the Ftp utility, your prompt will indicate this to avoid the problem of trying to execute commands remotely when you think you're local only. After you connect to the site, you navigate similarly when you're on a local computer using the command command, Dir, CD, and even MD or RD if you have permissions. When you find the file you want to transfer, use the Get command to transfer the file from the host to you, or use Put to transfer the file from you to the host. Windows 2000 Help system has a complete listing of the 14 online Ftp commands.

When you install the TCP/IP protocol on Windows 2000 Professional, you also get a shorthand version of Ftp called Tftp. This is less flexible, but also easier to use.

Ipconfig

Displays information about IPs, adapters, and Dynamic Host Configuration Protocol (DHCP). It's especially useful for the latter purposes.

Syntax:

Ipconfig [/all OR /renew [adapter] OR /release [adapter]]

where

> /all shows a complete listing.
>
> /renew renews DHCP information for a specified adapter.
>
> /release releases or disables DHCP for a local computer.

Usage Example:

Ipconfig /all

Displays complete information about a local computer.

Note

When run without parameters, Ipconfig displays a short information screen.

B

WINDOWS 2000
COMMAND
REFERENCE

Ping

A very useful command that's unfamiliar to those new to TCP/IP. `Ping` tries to echo a signal from a remote computer. This tests whether the remote computer (Internet or intranet) is responding. As with other utilities stemming from TCP/IP, `Ping` takes the dash (`-`) switch rather than the slash (`/`). Like `Ftp` and `Telnet`, `Ping /?` won't work because `Ping` will interpret the `/?` as a computer name.

Syntax (for the most commonly used switches):

```
ping [-t] [-n #] [-r #] [-w time] computers to ping
```

where

> `-t` pings until told to stop with a `^c`.
>
> `-n #` pings # times.
>
> `-r #` echoes the route up to # times. # can be from 1 to 9.
>
> `-w time` milliseconds to time out.
>
> `computers to ping` are the IPs or the names of the computers to `ping`.

Usage Examples:

```
Ping -n 2 192.100.221.000
```

Pings the computer with an IP of `192.100.221.000` twice.

```
Ping tirilee.techtryx.com
```

Pings the computer named `tirilee.techtryx.com` once.

Telnet

This utility isn't included in the online help system. Instead, Windows 2000 Professional treats it like its own program, complete with an included help system. It enables you to become a remote console on a host computer. What you can do with such a remote console depends on your permissions. As with `Ftp` and `Ping`, `Telnet /?` won't work.

Syntax:

```
Telnet computer or IP
```

where

`computer or IP` is the computer name or the IP for the computer to which you want to be connected.

Commands to Control the CLI

The following are the most often used commands to control the CLI environment.

Exit

Exits or quits a CMD instance. This command takes no parameters. It works identically to the Exit command from DOS or Windows.

Path

Same usage as in DOS or Windows. Can be used in AUTOEXEC.NT.

Syntax:

Path [*newpath*][*existingpath*]

where

%path% represents the existing path.

Usage Example:

Path = d:\windows2k;%path%

Appends the path d:\windows2k to the existing path.

Popd and Pushd

Similar in usage to identically named utilities in DOS and Windows. The names come from programmers' use of the LIFO stack where program items are pushed (stored) then popped (returned). The concept comes from a stack of spring loaded dishes in a cafeteria. Pushd stores a path, Popd restores the path.

Syntax:

Popd

Pushd [path]

Popd restores a path stored (pushed) with Pushd, so it takes no parameters.

Usage Example:

Pushd mypath

Stores the path mypath. Now change directories and do some action.

Popd

Restores you to your former mypath.

B

WINDOWS 2000
COMMAND
REFERENCE

Prompt

Alters the CLI prompt.

Syntax (of some of the more often used of many switches):

Prompt [$t] [$d] [$g] [$p] [text]

where

$t is the time.

$d is the date.

$g is the greater-than sign (>).

$p is the path (default).

text is the text you want to display.

Usage Examples:

Prompt $t $p

Shows the system time and then the path as a command-line prompt.

Prompt

Returns to the default prompt.

Subst

Substitutes an addressable device letter for a path. Similar to the Subst in later DOS or Windows.

Syntax:

Subst [Drive1] [path] /d

where /d deletes the substituted drive.

Usage Examples:

Subst g: c:\mypath\mypath1

Substitutes a "false" drive g: for the path c:\mypath\mypath1. When you enter g: on the command line or look for it in Explorer, the files contained will be those in c:\mypath\mypath1.

Subst g: /d

Eliminates the substitution.

> **Note**
>
> Use caution with the following commands on a Subst- created drive:
> Diskcomp, Format, Chkdsk, Restore, Label, Recover

Title

Changes the title of the CLI window.

Syntax:

Title *text*

where *text* is the text you want to show in the CLI window.

Usage Example:

Title Windows 2000 Rules

Displays the text Windows 2000 Rules as a title for the CLI window.

Batch Files

Windows 2000 Professional can use batch files just like DOS or Windows. A batch file is a text file containing a series of commands that execute in order unless the program control is altered by a GOTO command. Batch files under Windows 2000 Professional can take the command line replaceable parameters %1 through %9. The following are the most often used commands used in batch files, along with a concise usage example.

Call

Calls another batch file. Then after execution, returns control to the calling batch file.

Usage Example:

Call mynew.cmd

Calls the batch file mynew.cmd from within another batch file and then returns control to the calling file.

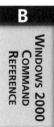

Echo

Echoes a line to the screen. By default, all batch file commands are echoed to the screen.

Usage Example:

```
Echo off
```

Ends echoing of batch file commands to the screen.

```
Echo my line
```

Echoes `my line` to the screen after the `Echo off` command.

For

Applies a command to a set of files in a list. Uses the replaceable parameter `%f` to avoid confusion with the `%1` through `%9` used as replaceable parameters in batch file command lines.

Usage Example:

```
For %f in (*.~mp) do del %f
```

Deletes files having the ~mp extension.

Goto

Branches to a label in a batch file. A label in a batch file is a line ending in a colon (`:`).

Usage Example:

```
If exist r:\myfile goto quit
...
...
quit:
```

Will jump to the line below the last line shown if the file, `myfile`, at the root of drive `r:` exists.

If

Tests a condition. If used with the `Not` switch, tests for the inverse of a condition. Often used with the `Goto` command to change program flow within the batch file.

Usage Example:

```
If not exist myfile Goto quit
```

Tests for the existence of the file, `myfile`, and if it doesn't exist, branches to the batch file label `quit`.

Rem

Remark. Tells the batch file not to process this line.

Usage Example:

```
Rem Now test for existence of file and branch if it doesn't exist
```

This line isn't evaluated, displayed, or executed by the batch file. Its only use is to inform. If you want to display a line or lines, use the `Echo` command.

Setlocal and Endlocal

Must be used in combination with each `Setlocal` having an `Endlocal`. Environmental settings run after `Setlocal` expires upon the `Endlocal` statement.

Usage Example:

```
...
Setlocal
(set some environment variable here)
Endlocal
```

Environmental variable set here expires.

Shift

Rotates the replaceable parameters in a batch file. Given the following command line:

```
Mybatch file1 file2
```

the `Shift` command will replace the variable `file1` with the variable `file2` when encountered by the batch file processor. So with that command line in mind, the batch file

```
...
Goto FirstRun
Shift:
Shift
FirstRun:
Copy %1 a: goto shift
...
```

will jump to the label `FirstRun:`, copy `file1`, jump to the label `Shift:`, and copy `file2`.

Symbols Used in the CLI

Following are some symbols used to control the CLI. Some of these symbols will be familiar to DOS, Windows, or UNIX users. Window 2000 Professional expands on the older DOS and Windows symbol set. Symbols don't have parameters. Each is shown with a short explanation and a usage example.

<

Redirects input to a program or utility.

Usage Example:

```
Sort < myoutput.out
```

Sorts the file myoutput.out using the Sort utility.

>>

Appends output. Also 1>>.

Usage Example:

```
Dir c:\*.* >> mylist.txt
```

Adds the output of Dir c:*.* to the end of the file mylist.txt.

>

Redirects output. Also 1>.

Usage Example:

```
Dir c:\*.* > prn
```

Directs the output of Dir c:*.* to the default printer.

¦ (Piping)

Pipes the output of a command to another program, often the More utility.

Usage Example:

```
Type myfile.txt ¦ More
```

Pipes the output of Type myfile.txt More, which will pause the display at each screen.

¦ ¦

A non-strict OR symbol. Used in batch files. Will execute the command to the left of the ¦ ¦ only, unless there is an error executing it. In that case, it will also execute the command to the right of ¦ ¦.

Usage Example:

```
Error.exe ¦¦ Good.exe
```

Will try to execute `Error.exe`. Upon finding an error, it will execute `Good.exe`. If `Error.exe` doesn't error, `Good.exe` will be ignored.

2>>

Redirection of error display. Useful for making log files.

Usage Example:

```
Mycommand 2>> error.log
```

Will redirect the error output of `Mycommand` to the file `error.log`.

, (comma)

Separates command-line parameters. Also use ; (semicolon) for the same purposes.

Usage Example:

```
Mycommand 1,2
```

Will feed the parameters 1 and 2 sequentially to `Mycommand`.

^ (literal)

Accepts the next symbol as a literal.

Usage Example:

```
Mycommand ^>
```

Passes the > character as a literal parameter rather than a command-line symbol to `Mycommand`.

&

Used to separate commands on a command line.

Usage Example:

```
Dir c: & Dir d:
```

Will execute first Dir c: and then Dir d:.

&&

The AND symbol twice. Will execute the command to the left only if the command to the right succeeds.

Usage Example:

Dir c: && Dir d:

Will execute Dir c: only if Dir d: completes successfully.

( )

Groups commands together.

Command1 (Command2 && Command3)

Will execute Command1 first, then Command2, and Command3 only if Command2 succeeds.

The AT Command

The AT command is so useful and so frequently used that it deserves its own section. In a nutshell, the AT command will execute a command or run a batch file at a given time of day. You need to have Administrator rights to run AT. Also, Windows 2000 Professional will not start the AT service by default. You must start it using the Net Start command or by using the Service applet in Control Panel. Because AT can start batch files, its use is only limited by imagination.

Syntax:

AT [*anyconnectedcomputer*] *time* [/interactive] [/*every:*] [/*next:*]
➥*command* [[*id*] [/delete [/yes]]

where

> *anyconnectedcomputer* is a computer where the command is to run.
>
> *time* is the time to run the command or batch file.
>
> /interactive means to run the called command or batch file interactively (involving human responses).
>
> /*every:* runs on specified days of the week (M,T,W,Th,F,S,Su) or days of the month (1-31). If the parameter after /*every:* is omitted, AT will assume the current day.
>
> /*next:* runs on the next day or date. If the parameter after /*next:* is omitted, AT will assume you mean the next occurrence of the current day of the week.
>
> *command* is the command or batch file you want AT to run.
>
> *id* is a job ID assigned sequentially by AT.

/delete removes the specified job ID from the queue. If no ID is specified, AT will remove all pending jobs from the local computer.

/yes runs the command or batch file, supplying a yes to all system queries rather than allowing the system to prompt for a yes or no.

Usage Examples:

```
AT \\tirilee 18:00 /every:Th,S archive.exe
```

Runs the command archive.exe every Thursday and Saturday at 6:00 p.m. on the computer named tirilee. As with all Windows 2000 commands, you don't need the extension .exe as part of the command-line argument.

```
AT
```

Displays pending job information and job IDs.

```
AT 23:59 Net Time \\tirilee /set
```

Synchronizes the local system time with the computer tirilee at 11:59 p.m. today.

```
AT \\tirilee
```

Displays a list of jobs slated to run on the computer named tirilee.

```
AT 18:00 /every:1,10,20,30 back.cmd
```

Runs the batch file back.cmd every 1st, 10th, 20th, and 30th day of the month at 6:00 p.m. As with all Windows 2000 commands, you don't need the extension .cmd as part of the command-line argument.

```
AT 18:00 /next: back.cmd
```

Runs back.cmd at 6:00 p.m. on the next occurrence of day of the week in which the command was entered.

Note

Windows 2000 Professional stores all AT sequences in the Registry. To preserve your AT settings, create a Registry backup or a new emergency rescue disk (ERD) or both after setting up a series of AT commands.

B

WINDOWS 2000 COMMAND REFERENCE

Deleted Commands

These commands, available in some versions of MS-DOS, aren't part of Windows 2000 Professional. There are some alternatives to these commands shown when applicable:

Assign

Backup

Choice

CTTY

Dblspace

Defrag (use third-party utilities)

Deltree (use RD /s)

Diskperf

Dosshell (replaced by Explorer)

Drvspace (replaced by Compact)

Fasthelp (use Help)

Fdisk (use the Disk Administrator)

Interlnk

Intersrv

Join (NTFS makes this pointless)

Keyb (Keyboard.sys is no more)

Mirror (use NTBackup and an ERD)

MSAV (use third-party anti-virus programs)

MSBackup (use NTBackup)

MSD (use Windows 2000 System Information in the MMC. This is the successor to MSD)

Nlsfunc

Numlock

Power (Windows 2000 Professional supports APM automatically if detected)

Ramdisk (and the earlier Vdisk)

Scandisk

Smartdrv (2000 Professional does its own caching)

Sys (2000 system will not fit on a floppy)

Undelete (use third-party utilities or the Recycle Bin)

Unformat

Vsafe

The following utilities and routines aren't in Windows 2000 Professional due to its inability to support multiple DOS configurations:

```
Include

Menucolor

Menudefault

Menuitem

Submenu
```

The following commands aren't applicable to Windows 2000 Professional due to its memory management, as opposed to DOS or Windows:

```
Memmaker
```
```
EMM386
```
MSCDEX (real mode drivers don't work under any Windows 2000)

Rump Commands

The following commands will not generate an error in Windows 2000 Professional but aren't a part of it either. Their inclusion is apparently to provide backward compatibility with old batch files:

```
Break

Buffers

Driveparm

Lastdrive

Share

Verify
```

Antiques in Windows 2000 Professional

The following commands and utilities are holdovers from DOS or Windows, but still function under Windows 2000 Professional. Their actual value is questionable, however. I've included some comments for the more commonly used ones.

```
Country
```
```
Command (use CMD)
```
Debug (Watch out! This one can still get you into gobs of trouble very quickly. Wiley Administrators will remove this from all users' computers.)

Edlin (Old soldiers never die in Windows-land. Well, most UNIX versions still have SED and celebrate VI.)

Exe2bin

Graphics

Mem (Might be a relic, but also can be quite useful especially when run with /d or /p switches)

Setver (Might be useful for some ancient MS-DOS programs. You use by loading setver.exe in the config.*xxx* file specific to that older program.)

Summary

This appendix has listed the most commonly used commands for the command-line interface (CLI) of Windows 2000 Professional. The rare commands, including those used in command-line OS/2 and retained in Windows 2000 Professional for compatibility, have been passed over to allow for sufficient room for the ones used more often.

This is a case of one size not fitting all, however. If your situation uses OS/2 character-based applications or the old IPX protocol still found lingering on in NetWare, there are commands included in Windows 2000 Professional that haven't been mentioned here. Instead, this appendix concentrates on commands a 2000 Professional Administrator will use most often with or without the TCP/IP layer.

The final part of the appendix discussed commands either deleted or made obsolete in the migration from DOS or Windows to Windows 2000. Some of these commands remain unchanged in function, but have lost their purpose (or vitality) as Windows 2000 takes over from previous Microsoft operating systems.

INDEX

CD-ROM Installation

Windows 95/NT/2000 Installation Instructions

1. Insert the CD-ROM disc into your CD-ROM drive.
2. From the Windows 95/NT/2000 desktop, double-click on the My Computer icon. Some features may be accessible by right-clicking on the CD icon from your My Computer menu.
3. Double-click on the icon representing your CD-ROM drive.
4. Double-click on the icon titled START.EXE to run the CD-ROM interface.

Note

If Windows 95/NT/2000 is installed on your computer, and you have the AutoPlay feature enabled, the START.EXE program starts automatically whenever you insert the disc into your CD-ROM drive.